ENHANCED ACT® PREP

2026 Edition

The Staff of The Princeton Review

PrincetonReview.com

Penguin
Random
House

The Princeton Review
110 E. 42nd Street, 7th Floor
New York, NY 10017
Email: editorialsupport@review.com
princetonreview.com
penguinrandomhouse.com

Published in the United States by Penguin Random House LLC, New York.

ISBN: 979-8-217-22381-7
eBook ISBN: 979-8-217-22382-4
ISSN: 3068-7799

The Princeton Review Publishing Team
Rob Franek, Editor-in-Chief
David Soto, Senior Director, Data Operations
Stephen Koch, Senior Manager, Data Operations
Deborah Weber, Director of Production
Jason Ullmeyer, Production Design Manager
Jennifer Chapman, Senior Production Artist
Selena Coppock, Director of Editorial
Aaron Riccio, Director, Editorial Admissions Content
Orion McBean, Senior Editor
Meave Shelton, Senior Editor
Laura Rose, Editor
Isabelle Appleton, Editorial Assistant

Penguin Random House Publishing Team
Tom Russell, VP, Publisher
Alison Stoltzfus, Senior Director, Publishing
Emily Hoffman, Managing Editor
Mary Ellen Owens, Assistant Director of Production
Suzanne Lee, Senior Designer
Eugenia Lo, Publishing Assistant

For customer service, please contact **editorialsupport@review.com**, and be sure to include:

- full title of the book
- ISBN
- page number

Editor: Orion McBean
Production Editors: Liz Dacey and Sarah Litt
Production Artist: Jason Ullmeyer

Printed in the United States of America.

10 9 8 7 6 5 4 3 2 1

2026 Edition

EU Contact:
Penguin Random House Ireland
32 Nassau Street, Dublin D02 YH68
https://eu-contact.penguin.ie

Acknowledgments

The completion of this book would not have been possible without the help and dedication of several individuals.

Special thanks to Kenneth Brenner, Cat Healey, Sara Kuperstein, Amy Minster, and Scott O'Neal for their expert review of, and contributions to, this edition. Thanks also to Aleksei Alferiev, Kevin Baldwin, Emily Baumbach, Nicole Cosme, Stacey Cowap, Lori DesRochers, Elizabeth Evangelista, Anne Goldberg-Baldwin, Brad Kelly, Kevin Keogh, Jomil London, Dave MacKenzie, Sionainn Marcoux, Gabby Peterson, Sara Soriano, Jess Thomas, Cynthia Ward, and Jimmy Williams for their contributions to past editions. Additional thanks to Jason Ullmeyer, Liz Dacey, and Sarah Litt for their work on the production of this book.

Special thanks to Adam Robinson, who conceived of and perfected the Joe Bloggs approach to standardized tests and many other successful techniques used by The Princeton Review.

Contents

Get More (Free) Content
at **PrincetonReview.com/prep**

As easy as 1·2·3

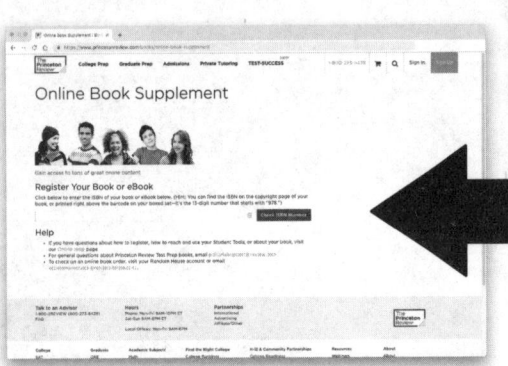

1 Go to PrincetonReview.com/prep or scan the **QR code** and enter the following ISBN for your book: **9798217223817**

2 Answer a few simple questions to set up an exclusive Princeton Review account. *(If you already have one, you can just log in.)*

3 Enjoy access to your **FREE** content!

Once you've registered, you can...

- Access two more full-length practice tests

- Find any late-breaking information released about the ACT

- Read our special "College Admissions Insider" and get valuable advice about the college application process, including tips for writing a great essay and where to apply for financial aid

- Check to see if there have been any corrections or updates to this edition

- Sort colleges by whatever you're looking for (such as Best Theater or Dorm), learn more about your top choices, and see how they all rank according to *The Best 391 Colleges*

Need to report a potential **content** issue?

Contact **EditorialSupport@review.com** and include:

- full title of the book
- ISBN
- page number

Need to report a **technical** issue?

Contact **TPRStudentTech@review.com** and provide:

- your full name
- email address used to register the book
- full book title and ISBN
- Operating system (Mac/PC) and browser (Chrome, Firefox, Safari, etc.)

Look For These Icons Throughout The Book

 PROVEN TECHNIQUES

 APPLIED STRATEGIES

 STUDY BREAK

 OTHER REFERENCES

 ONLINE ARTICLES

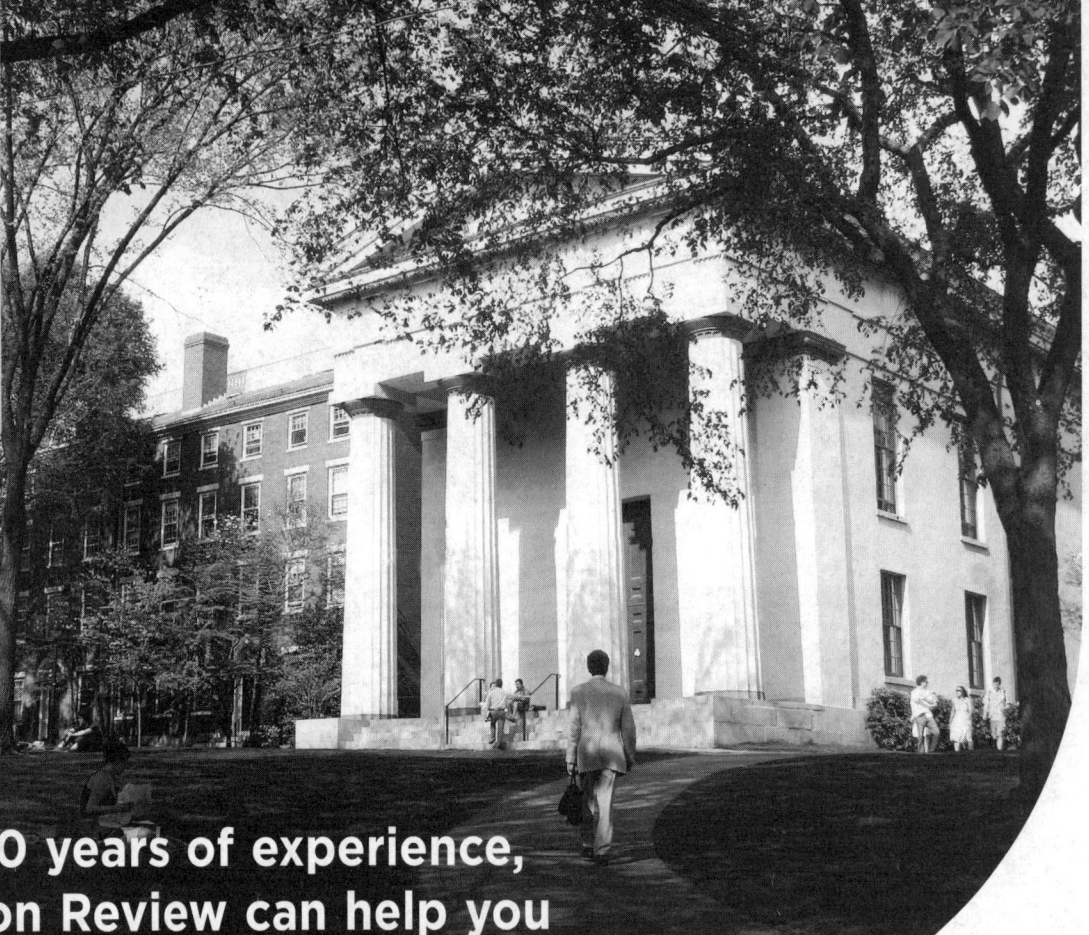

Part I
Orientation

Chapter 1
Introduction to the ACT

So you're taking the ACT. What will you need to do first? This chapter presents an overview of the current ACT as a whole and discusses registration requirements, when to take the test, how to have your scores reported to colleges (or how not to), and the ways in which colleges use your scores.

THE ACT

Welcome to *Enhanced ACT Prep, 2026 Edition*. The ACT is a standardized test used for college admissions. But you probably already knew that. In this book, we'll tell you all the things you didn't know about the ACT, in order to show you how to crack the test and get your best score.

In the United States, most students take the ACT exam on Saturday mornings. Non-Saturday testing is available but only for students who live in remote areas or who can't test on Saturdays for religious reasons. Furthermore, many states and school districts offer the ACT during the school day as part of mandated testing. Saturday test-takers can choose between the Paper ACT and the Online ACT when they register for the test. These options are also available for school-day testing, but the school or district, not the individual student, determines the format of the test.

Outside the United States, all students take the ACT Online Test; the Paper ACT is only available to students with accommodations that require a non-computer-based test. Because the test centers that ACT uses outside the United States often have limited seats available, most test dates are two separate days (often Saturday and Sunday) to accommodate more test-takers.

Where Does the ACT Come From?

The ACT is written by a nonprofit organization that used to call itself American College Testing but now just calls itself ACT. The company has been producing the ACT since it introduced the test in 1959 as an alternative to the College Board's SAT. ACT also writes ACT Aspire and PreACT, which are tests you may have taken earlier in your academic career. In addition, the organization provides a broad range of services to educational agencies and business institutions.

What Does the ACT Test?

The nice people who write the ACT—we'll refer to them as "ACT" from now on—describe the test as an assessment of college readiness, "a curriculum- and standards-based educational and career planning tool that assesses students' academic readiness for college."

We at The Princeton Review have always been skeptical when any standardized test makes broad claims of what it can measure. In our opinion, a standardized test is just a measure of how well you take that test. Granted, ACT has spent an extraordinary amount of time analyzing data and providing the results of their research to various educational institutions and agencies. In fact, ACT has contributed to the development of the Common Core Standards Initiative, an educational reform that aligns diverse state curricula into national uniform standards.

With all due respect to ACT and the various state and federal agencies working on the Common Core, we still think the ACT is just a measure of how well you take the ACT. Many factors other than mastery of the "curriculum-based" content determine your performance on a standardized test. That's why we'll teach you both the content you need as well as crucial test-taking strategies.

What's on the ACT?

The Enhanced ACT consists of three multiple-choice, timed tests: English, Math, and Reading, always given in that order. The ACT with Science includes an optional multiple-choice Science test after the Reading test. Additionally, students can choose to take the ACT with Writing, which includes an optional essay that is given after the last multiple-choice test. (ACT calls them tests, but we may also use the term "sections" in this book to avoid confusion.) In Parts II–V, we'll thoroughly review the content and strategies you need for each test.

The ACT has Changed!

In July 2024, ACT announced that the test was evolving into the *Enhanced ACT*, having fewer questions overall, featuring shorter passages on English and Reading, and making the Science section optional for students. These changes went into effect for national online test-takers in spring 2025 and paper test-takes in September 2025. The changes will apply to school-day testing in spring 2026. All of the strategy, practice, and tests in this book reflect these changes to prepare you for the Enhanced exam.

1. English Test (35 minutes—50 questions)

On the Enhanced ACT, you will be given six or seven essays total with some words or phrases underlined. The essays will be situated on the left side of the page or screen, while on the right side of the page or screen you will be asked whether each underlined portion is correct as written or whether one of the three alternatives listed would be better. The English test is a test of grammar, punctuation, sentence structure, and rhetorical skills. Throughout each essay, commonly known as a passage, there will also be questions about overall organization and style or perhaps about how the writing could be revised or strengthened.

2. Math Test (50 minutes—45 questions)

The questions in the Enhanced Math test are in a rough order of difficulty. Easier questions *tend* to be in the first third of the test, whereas harder questions tend to be toward the end. Most of the content is what ACT calls "Preparing for Higher Mathematics," which includes high school-level concepts in areas such as functions, geometry, and statistics. The remainder of the questions are "Integrating Essential Skills," which are questions that combine various math concepts. Finally, at least 20 percent of the questions in those two categories will be "Modeling" questions, which is ACT's term for word problems.

> **Unscored Questions**
> The ACT exam has some unscored questions within each section. These won't be marked in any way, so you won't know which questions don't count toward your score. There are 10 such questions in English, 4 in Math, 9 in Reading, and 6 in Science.

3. Reading Test (40 minutes—36 questions)

In the Enhanced version of this test, there will be four reading passages of about 800 words each—the average length of a magazine article but maybe not as entertaining to read. There is always one literary narrative (or prose fiction) passage followed by three passages that are usually all labeled as "Informational": one social science passage, one humanities passage, and one natural science passage. The four passages are always in that order. One of these passages will consist of a dual passage in which the *total* length of the two passages will still be about 800 words. Each passage will be followed by 9 questions.

4. Optional Science Test (40 minutes—40 questions)

The optional Science test will typically have seven passages. One passage will require analyzing disagreements among two to five scientists. The rest will typically provide scientific information in graphs, charts, tables, and research summaries. Notably, ACT Science requires actual scientific knowledge for only a handful of questions. Most questions require reading skills and common sense.

5. Optional Writing Test (40 minutes)

The ACT Plus Writing includes an additional fifth section that requires you to consider a socially relevant prompt and three perspectives on that prompt and write a single essay in response. The essay is scored by two graders. Each grader will assign four scores of 1–6 that are then added and averaged for a total score of 2–12. This score will NOT factor into your composite score.

> Our website, PrincetonReview.com, is a great resource for information on thousands of schools!

At this moment, it is unclear how many college will require the optional Science test for admissions or for acceptance into certain programs, and very few schools require the Writing test. We recommend that you research your goal schools to determine whether you should take the ACT, the ACT with Science, the ACT with Writing, or the ACT with Science and Writing.

How Is the ACT Scored?

Scores for each of the four multiple-choice tests are reported on a scale of 1 to 36 (36 being the highest score possible). The scores for the English, Math, and Reading sections are averaged to yield your composite score, which is the score colleges and universities use to help determine admission. The optional Science section, while scored on the same scale of 1 to 36 as the other multiple-choice sections, does not count toward your composite. If you take that section, you will get a separate Science score.

An average ending in .66 is rounded up, whereas an average ending in .33 is rounded down. Next to each score is a percentile ranking, which refers to how you performed on the test relative to other people who took it at the same time. For instance, a percentile ranking of 87 indicates that you scored higher than 87 percent of the people who took the test, and the other 13 percent scored equal to or higher than you.

ACT may also give two cross-test scores called "STEM" (Science, Technology, Engineering, Mathematics) and "ELA" (English, Language Arts). Your STEM score is simply an average of your Math and Science scores, so you will only get this cross-test score if you take the Science section. Your ELA score is taken from your English, Reading, and Writing scores. (If you don't take the Writing test, you won't receive an ELA score.) Neither score has any influence on your composite, nor, frankly, as far as we can tell, on your chances at admission to college.

On your score report, ACT also indicates if you met their "College Readiness Benchmark Scores": 18 in English, 22 in Math, 22 in Reading, and 23 in Science. ACT maintains that these benchmarks can predict college "success," defined as a "50 percent or higher probability of earning a B or higher in the corresponding college course or courses." These scores and their meaning have been determined by ACT's own research and data, not by any studies done by colleges and universities themselves.

When Should You Take the ACT?

If you haven't already, go to <u>ACT.org</u> and create your free ACT Web Account. You can register for tests, view your scores, and request score reports for colleges through this account. You can also view the specific test dates and centers for the upcoming academic year.

The ACT is given seven times a year: September, October, December, February, April, June, and July. The July administration is not available in New York.

Many states also offer an additional ACT as part of their state testing. Check with your high school to see if and when your state offers a special ACT. Your school will register you automatically for a state ACT. You must register yourself for all other administrations.

Traditionally, most students wait until the spring of their junior year to take the ACT. Many high schools still recommend the spring of the junior year because the content of the Math test includes topics some curricula do not cover before then. However, these topics appear in only a handful of questions, and many juniors take their first ACT in the fall or winter.

We recommend that you consider your own schedule when picking your test dates. Do you play a fall sport and carry a heavier load of extracurricular activities in the fall? Is winter a quiet time in between semesters? Do you act in the spring musical and plan to take several AP Exams? Have you been dreaming of attending Big State University since you were a toddler and already plan to apply for early decision? Let the answers to these questions determine your test dates. But we recommend taking your first test after you've done some prep and feel comfortable that you've learned enough in school to achieve your goal score. For most students, this is sometime in junior year (grade 11).

How Many Times Should You Take the ACT?

For security reasons, ACT will not let you take the exam more than 12 times in your lifetime. But we certainly hope no one is dismayed by this restriction. There are certainly better things to do with your time on a Saturday morning, and we don't believe any college will accept "taking the ACT" as an extracurricular activity!

The Princeton Review recommends that you plan to take the ACT two to three times. If you achieve your goal score in your first administration, great. Take the money and run. On the other hand, if, after three tests, you have reason and motivation to take the ACT again, do it. On your first day of college, you will neither remember nor care how many times you had to take the ACT.

In fact, at many colleges, the median number of times admitted students took the ACT (or SAT) is 3. In other words, it's perfectly fine (and normal!) to retake the ACT.

Looking for more help on the ACT? Scan the QR code below for information on self-paced courses, live courses, and tutoring!

Does ACT "Super Score"?

When a student has more than one ACT score, ACT "superscores" the results. What's a super-score? A superscore takes the best results in each section over any number of test dates to create a new composite score. In other words, if you did better on Reading in February but better on English and Math in April, ACT will take your February Reading score and average it with your April English and Math scores to create a new, higher superscore. As soon as you take your second ACT test, your superscore will be calculated and posted in your ACT account. If you took the Science section when it was still a required part of the exam, that score won't be factored into your super-score, nor will your superscore composite be affected if you take the optional Science section now.

In addition, many schools (and the Common Application) will ask you to list the score and test date of your English, Math, Reading, and Science (if that score is required for your application) and then calculate a superscore based on these scores, separate from ACT. Therefore, if you worry that some scores will rise as others fall when you take the ACT again, the superscore will reflect your best results.

However, not every college will accept ACT superscores. Therefore, The Princeton Review strongly recommends that you research each school you're applying to. While ACT will send the results only from the test dates you request or ACT's generated superscore, you should decide which and how many dates to send based on your scores and the school's guidelines about superscoring. Moreover, some schools require that you submit all test scores from every administration, and you should abide by any such requirements.

WHAT IS THE ACT ONLINE TEST?

The ACT Online Test is the ACT that you take on a computer, rather than with pencil and paper. Despite the name, you can't take the ACT from the comfort of your own home; rather, you'll have to go to a testing center (possibly your high school) and take the test on the center's computer or on your own personal or school-managed computer that you bring with you.

The Enhanced ACT Online Test has the same overall structure, timing, and number of questions as the Paper ACT. The scoring, score range, and scoring method are also the same. If the ACT Online Test is basically the same as the Paper ACT, who would take the ACT Online Test?

WHO TAKES THE ACT ONLINE TEST?

ACT has been offering versions of the ACT on the computer since about 2016. The first group of students to take the ACT on the computer were students taking the test at school. Schools and school districts decided whether to give the test on the computer.

To expand ACT Online Test options in the United States, select national testing sites began offering students a choice of the ACT Online test or the paper-and-pencil version in early 2024. ACT stated that they will continue to expand online testing availability to students.

ACT ONLINE TEST FEATURES

So, then, besides the obvious "it's on the computer," what are the differences between taking the ACT on the computer and taking it on paper? Let's start with what you can't do on the ACT Online Test. You can't "write" on the screen in a freehand way. You're limited in how you're able to mark the answer choices, and each question appears on its own screen (so you can't see multiple questions at one glance). You will also be given scratch paper or a small "whiteboard" and dry erase pen with which to make notes and do work.

The ACT Online Test will have some useful features and some you may never use. You can flag questions to come back to them later, eliminate answers on the screen, or even hide the answers until you are ready for them. You will also be able to highlight the text, magnify it, or cover part of the screen to focus on one relevant window. If you are registered for a Princeton Review course or tutorial, you will also have access to more ACT Online Tests on our website, PrincetonReview.com.

To see official ACT Online sample questions, scan the QR code below:

HOW TO PREPARE FOR THE ACT ONLINE TEST

If you are going to take the ACT Online Test, you should incorporate some computer-based practice into your prep plan. When you register this book, you will find resources that provide more information about taking the Online ACT. You also can take some of the associated tests online. We recommend that you do those sections toward the end of your preparation (and close to your test date) to give you an opportunity to practice what you've learned on a platform similar to the one you'll be using on the day of the test.

If you are planning to take the ACT online, you should practice as if you're doing all your work on the computer, even when you're working in a physical book. Use a highlighter, but don't use the highlighter on any figures (as the ACT Online Test won't let you do so). Use your pencil to eliminate answer choices and have a separate sheet of paper to do any work you need to do, instead of writing on the question itself.

Also, remember that our approaches work. Don't get misled by ACT's instructions on the day of the test—their way of approaching the test won't give you the best results!

Remember!
Your goal is to get the best possible score on the ACT. ACT's goal is to assign a number to you that (supposedly) means something to colleges. Focus on your goal!

How Do You Register for the ACT?

The fastest way to register is online, through your ACT Web Account. You can also obtain a registration packet at your high school guidance office, online at act.org/content/act/en/products-and-services/the-act/registration.html, or by writing or calling ACT at the address and phone number below.

When you register, you can see if there are any options near you for the ACT Online Test if you prefer that option to taking the paper-and-pencil test. If you want to switch back to the paper version after registering for the Online Test, you may do so up until the late registration date.

ACT Student Services Contact Information
PO Box 414
Iowa City, IA 52243-0414
By phone: 319-337-1270
By text: 202-988-4996

Bookmark ACT.org. You will start at this portal to view test dates, fees, and registration deadlines. You can also research the requirements and processes to apply for extended time or other accommodations. You will also start at ACT.org to access your account to register, view your scores, and order score reports.

When you register, you can see if there are any options near you for the ACT Online Test if you prefer that option over taking the Paper ACT. If you want to switch back to the paper version after registering for the Online Test, you may do so up until the late registration date.

Fees

Check ACT.org for the latest information about fees. If you register for the optional Science or Writing sections, you will have to pay an additional fee for each optional section. You can choose four schools to send a score report to at no additional charge when registering, but there are fees for sending reports to more schools or after you register. ACT does offer a fee waiver program that, as of August 2025, includes up to two ACT tests including add-on fees for science and writing, free access to online practice material, free ACT My Answer Key (see sidebar), and unlimited score reports. It also allows you to apply for a fee waiver for college application fees.

Test Security Changes

As part of the registration process, you have to upload or mail a photograph that will be printed on your admissions ticket. On test day, you have to take the ticket and acceptable photo identification with you.

Standby testing is available, but you must register in advance, usually before the prior Monday. Check ACT.org for more information.

HOW TO PREPARE FOR THE ACT

The Princeton Review materials and test-taking techniques contained in this book should give you all the information you need to improve your score on the ACT. For more practice materials, The Princeton Review also publishes *815+ Enhanced ACT Practice Questions*, which includes full tests and drills. This book has been written to match the format of the Enhanced ACT, so it's a great supplement to this book because the questions are realistic, and the book provides helpful explanations for all of the questions--in line with the strategies you'll learn in this book.

ACT also publishes an Official *ACT Prep Guide* with four Enhanced practice tests, but it's worth noting that you can find one of these four for free, in both the paper and online formats, on the ACT website. These official materials are helpful for getting familiar with the test and gauging your current scores, but they don't contain the most helpful explanations. This is where our materials come in to help!

Do I Need to Prepare If I Have Good Grades?

Let's take the hypothetical case of Sid. Sid is valedictorian of his class, editor of the school paper, and the only teenager ever to win the Nobel Prize. To support his widowed mother, he sold more magazine subscriptions and gift wrap than any other person in recorded history. He speaks eight languages in addition to being able to communicate with dolphins and wolves. He has recommendations from Malala Yousafzai *and* Oprah Winfrey. So if Sid had a bad day when he took the ACT (the plane bringing him back from his Medal of Freedom award presentation was late), we are pretty sure that he is going to be just fine anyway. But Sid wants to ensure that when his colleges look at his ACT score, they see the same high-caliber student they see when they look at the rest of his application, so he carefully reviews the types of questions asked and learns some useful test-taking strategies.

I Have Low Grades in School. Is There Any Hope?

Let's take the case of Tom. Tom didn't do particularly well in high school. In fact, he has been on academic probation since kindergarten. He has caused four of his teachers to give up teaching as a profession, and he prides himself on his perfect homework record: he's never done any, not ever. But if Tom aces his ACT, a college might decide that he is actually a misunderstood genius and give him a full scholarship. Tom decides to learn as much as he can about the ACT.

Most of us, of course, fall between these two extremes. So is it important to prepare for the ACT?

Want to know which colleges are best for you? Scan the QR code below to check out our College Search engine at PrincetonReview.com for information on more than 1,000 schools.

If you were to look in the information bulletin of any of the colleges in which you are interested, we can pretty much guarantee that somewhere you would find the following paragraph:

> Many factors go into a college's acceptance of a student. Test scores are *only one* of these factors. Grades in high school, extracurricular activities, essays, and recommendations are also important and may, in some cases, outweigh test scores.

> (2026, University of Anywhere Bulletin)

Truer words were never written. In our opinion, just about *every* other element in your application "package" is more important than your test scores. The Princeton Review (among other organizations) has been telling colleges for years that scores on the ACT or the SAT are pretty incomplete measures of a student's overall academic abilities. Some colleges have stopped looking at test scores entirely, and others are downplaying their importance.

What About Test-Optional?

Part of the way colleges have downplayed the importance of standardized testing is by implementing "test-optional" policies. While the COVID-19 pandemic accelerated the adoption of such policies, there was already a movement toward doing so prior to 2020. At most schools with test-optional policies, your application will be considered whether or not you submit ACT (or SAT) scores. If you submit scores, they will be considered in the admissions decision.

So, if the tests are optional at a lot of schools, why should you bother? Well, for one, many schools have reported that applicants who submit ACT or SAT scores have higher acceptance rates. (However, this doesn't mean that submitting test scores increases your chances—the sorts of students who submit scores are not doing so randomly.) Furthermore, even at schools that are test optional (or even test blind—schools that don't consider test scores whatsoever in admissions), some scholarships or programs may still require the ACT (or SAT).

So Why Should You Spend Any Time Preparing for the ACT?

Out of all the elements in your application "package," your ACT score is the easiest to change. The grades you've received up to now are written in stone. You aren't going to become captain of the soccer team or editor of the school paper overnight. Your essays will be only as good as you can write them, and recommendations are only as good as your teachers' memories of you.

On the contrary, in a few weeks, you can substantially change your score on the ACT (and the way colleges look at your applications). The test does not pretend to measure analytic ability or intelligence. It measures your knowledge of specific skills such as grammar, algebra, and reading comprehension. Mostly, it measures how good you are at taking this test.

THE ACT VS. THE SAT

You may have to take the ACT anyway, but all schools that will consider the ACT in some way will also accept the SAT. In order to determine which test may be better for you to take, invest the time to take a full-length, timed practice test for each to (1) see how you score on each test and (2) assess how you *feel* during each test. The time spent on this exercise will be incredibly beneficial for your test preparation planning. You can take these tests as part of your free Student Tools at PrincetonReview.com. Once you've decided which test is the better fit for you, you can then use that initial score as a baseline for planning your preparation to hit the target score for your dream college.

Need a Study Plan?
Go to your Student Tools to download our study plans tailored specifically for 4, 8, or 12 weeks of available prep time!

What Exactly Are the Differences?

Understanding the pressures of the ACT and Digital SAT can help you decide which test may be better for you. Consider English and Reading on the ACT and Reading and Writing on the SAT. On the ACT, English and Reading are separate sections. English has 50 questions in 35 minutes (42 seconds per question) and Reading has 36 questions in 40 minutes (nearly 67 seconds per question). The Digital SAT has two modules of combined Reading and Writing questions. Each module has 27 questions in 32 minutes (about 1 minute 11 seconds per question). However, ACT questions tend to be more direct, whereas SAT questions often require closer reading and more steps to answer. In general, students who prefer more straightforward but faster-paced questions lean toward the ACT, whereas those who appreciate a bit more time with each question, even if those questions themselves require a bit more effort, gravitate toward the Digital SAT. Our advice: take a practice test of each and see which one you prefer.

Additionally, the Digital SAT, which is only available as an online test and not on paper (unless the student has an accommodation to test in the paper modality), is what is known as an adaptive test. The first module of each area of the Digital SAT (Reading and Writing or Math) is a mix of easy, medium, and difficult questions. A test-taker who performs well on the first module will have a second module that has more difficult questions, whereas a test-taker who does not perform as well will have a second module that is easier on average. There are many reasons why College Board has decided to make the test adaptive. When ACT shortened the exam, it was not made adaptive. Therefore, one reason to take ACT over the SAT is that there is less pressure to do well early on in the test than there is to get a good score on the first module in each section of the SAT.

In terms of subject matter, though, the Digital SAT and ACT are more similar than different. The ACT does have an optional Science section, but that section is largely about reading charts and graphs. The Digital SAT includes charts and graphs in both the Reading and Writing section and the Math section.

Only the ACT has an optional essay (the Writing test). As stated above, very few colleges require or recommend the Writing test, so do your research to determine whether you need to take this section. Note that you cannot retake just the ACT Writing (you'll have to retake the entire test), so it's vitally important to determine whether you need to do this section *before* you register.

More great titles by The Princeton Review
Check out a variety of college admissions books like *The Best 391 Colleges* and more. Scan the QR code below to purchase.

To find out whether the schools in which you are interested require the ACT Science section or essay, consult their admissions webpages.

While the tests are fairly similar, some students end up scoring substantially higher on one test than the other. As mentioned above, we recommend taking a practice test of each to see whether you score higher on one than the other.

ADDITIONAL RESOURCES

In addition to the material in this book, we offer a number of other resources to aid you during your ACT preparation.

Register your book at PrincetonReview.com to gain access to your Student Tools, the companion website to this book. There, you will find more ACT practice tests, additional bubble sheets, and useful articles on the college application process.

WHAT IS THE PRINCETON REVIEW?

The Princeton Review is the world's leading test-preparation and educational services company. We run courses and offer web-based instruction at PrincetonReview.com. Our test-taking techniques and review strategies are unique and powerful. We developed them after studying all the real ACTs we could get our hands on. For more information about our programs and services, feel free to call us at **800-2REVIEW**.

HOW TO BEGIN

After this chapter, you will find Practice Test 1, along with a diagnostic answer key and explanations. This will act as your "diagnostic" test. We recommend that you take this test before going any further in order to realistically determine:

- your starting score right now
- which question types you're ready for and which you might need to practice
- which content topics you are familiar with and which you will want to carefully review

Once you have nailed down your strengths and weaknesses based on this exam, you can focus your test preparation, build a study plan, and be efficient with your time. Use the following steps to make the most of this first "diagnostic" test.

1. **Take a practice test.**
   To "diagnose" your strengths and weaknesses, take Practice Test 1 starting on page 17 of this book. Be sure to do so in one sitting, following the instructions that appear with each section of the test.

2. **Score your test online.**
   Once you register your book, you can enter the answers to your practice tests in your online tools. When you do so, you will receive a score report that details your performance on a variety of question types. You will also receive an approximate score, though the scale for the ACT does change a bit from test to test.

3. **Take stock and make a plan.**
   With the insights you'll gain from your score report, decide where to start with the content of this book. You may choose to use some parts of this book over others, or you may work through the entire book. The ways in which you use this book will depend on your needs and how much time you have. The answer key for Practice Test 1, starting on page 78, will help you determine which sections of this book you will need to work on. For the questions you answered incorrectly, make sure you review those topics by carefully studying the specific page references on the answer key.

> Note that while the tests in this book use choices A–D for odd numbered questions and F–J for even numbered questions as per print versions of the real ACT, the choices for all questions in the online scoring will be written as A–D to mimic the ACT Online Test. Therefore, you will enter (F) as (A), (G) as (B), etc.

Now let's look at how to make this determination.

When you enter your practice test answers online, you will receive a score report that starts with your Composite score, followed by a breakdown of the scores for each section of the test. Below that will be a breakdown of the questions by test section, with a tab for each one. Each question will be represented by a box with a mark to indicate if it was Correct, Incorrect, or Blank. Clicking on the box for a question brings up the explanation for it, which is also found in this book. Additionally, you can see the question category listed as "Concept Tested."

To see a section breakdown by concept, you can click the "View by Category" button. Use this view to determine the following:

- question types you are good at, to make sure you can find and correctly answer questions in these categories every time
- question types that have several questions in them but that you struggled with a bit, so you can work to improve your accuracy on these important questions
- question types that were either very difficult for you or had only 1 or 2 questions in them; practice these question types only after you're comfortable with the others

After you determine these things for English, you can do the same for Math, Reading, and Science (if you took it) by clicking on the respective tabs for each. There is also a guide at the bottom of the score report that indicates your Areas of Strength and Areas of Focus. Though this may point you to some areas to work on, make sure to verify that a given topic is worth the time it would take to master. For example, if there was only one Math question about matrices and you got it wrong, that may show up in the Areas of Focus. However, because each test has only 1 matrix question at most, studying matrices is likely not the best use of your time.

After you have mastered a few key concepts and strategies, take another practice test and analyze it the same way to see where you've improved and where you have more work to do. Continue alternating working through the chapters of this book and taking practice tests until you feel fully prepared to conquer the ACT.

A FINAL THOUGHT BEFORE YOU BEGIN

The ACT does not measure intelligence, nor does it predict your ultimate success or failure as a human being. No matter how high or how low you score on this test initially, and no matter how much you may increase your score through preparation, you should *never* consider the score you receive on this or any other test a final judgment of your abilities.

Chapter 2
Practice Exam 1

*Make sure to download a bubble sheet for this test via your online Student Tools.

ENGLISH TEST

35 Minutes—50 Questions

DIRECTIONS: In the passages that follow, certain words and phrases are underlined and numbered. In the right-hand column, you will find alternatives for the underlined part. You are to choose the best answer to each question. If you think the original version is best, choose "**No Change.**"

You will also find questions about a section of the passage or about the passage as a whole. These questions do not refer to an underlined portion of the passage, but rather are identified by a number or numbers in a box.

For each question, choose the alternative you consider best, and fill in the corresponding oval on your answer document. Read each passage through once before you begin to answer the questions that accompany it. For many of the questions, you must read several sentences beyond the question to determine the answer. Be sure that you have read far enough ahead each time you choose an alternative.

PASSAGE I

The Record

The moment I had been anticipating finally came on a seemingly routine Monday. I arrived home to find a flat package; left by the delivery man casually leaning against the front door. I immediately recognized my uncle's sloppy handwriting.

1. Which choice makes the sentence most grammatically acceptable?

  A No Change
  B. package, left by the delivery man
  C. package; left by the delivery man,
  D. package, left by the delivery man,

I quickly ushered the box inside, and my heart skipping a beat (or two). I knew what the box contained but still felt as anxious as a child on Christmas morning. Could this *really* be the old vinyl record?

2. Which choice makes the sentence most grammatically acceptable?

  F. No Change
  G. inside,
  H. inside and
  J. inside, when

My hands trembled as I opened the box, of which I was thrilled to see that it did indeed contain the record I had been seeking for years. To an outsider, this dusty disc with its faded hand-written label would seem inconsequential.

3. Which choice makes the sentence most grammatically acceptable?

  A. No Change
  B. box that
  C. box, and
  D. box

GO ON TO THE NEXT PAGE.

To others, on the other hand, it was worth something far greater.
—————————————————————————————————————
                                    4
The record was a compilation from the greatest musician I had

ever known—my grandfather.

Several years before he married my grandmother, Papa will
                                                         —————
                                                           5
make his living as a folk singer in a
—————
  5

band. Performing in music halls and local festivals. He recorded
——————————
     6
a single album before giving up his professional music career to

pursue business. This record was all that remained of his life's

passion

—in fact, there had been only one surviving copy since Papa's
————————
    7
death ten years earlier. It took many years of

begging and pleading to convince my uncle to pass the record
——————————————————
         8
down to me.

   I brought out my old record player from the attic and gently

placed the disc on the turntable. As soft, twanging notes filled

the room, I was transported to my grandfather's cabin, located at
                                                    —————————————
                                                          9
the foot of the mountains. My cousins and I would gather around
————————————————————
         9
the campfire every night, and Papa would play familiar tunes on

his guitar.

4. Given that all the choices are true, which one would most effectively illustrate the difference between outsiders' perception of the record and its actual significance to the writer's family?

   F. No Change
   G. In fact, the recording was not heard by many people outside my family.
   H. To my family, however, it was a precious heirloom.
   J. The disc would have been in better condition had my uncle stored it in a sleeve.

5. Which choice makes the sentence most grammatically acceptable?

   A. No Change
   B. would have made
   C. would have been making
   D. had made

6. Which choice makes the sentence or sentences most grammatically acceptable?

   F. No Change
   G. band; performing
   H. band, which he had performed
   J. band, performing

7. Which transition phrase is most logical in context?

   A. No Change
   B. even so,
   C. in addition,
   D. for example,

8. Which choice is least redundant in context?

   F. No Change
   G. begging
   H. pleadingly begging
   J. begging the plea

9. At this point in the essay, the writer wants to suggest the significance of his grandfather's cabin to the writer's upbringing. Given that all the choices are true, which one would best accomplish this goal?

   A. No Change
   B. where I had spent many childhood summers.
   C. which I still remembered well.
   D. a family property for many generations.

GO ON TO THE NEXT PAGE.

When the record started playing one of my favorite songs, I struggled to hold back tears. It was a bittersweet reminder of the man I loved and missed, Papa's gentle voice on the record, however, assured me that he was still with me, in spirit and in song.
$\underline{}$
10

10. Which choice makes the sentence or sentences most grammatically acceptable?

F. **No Change**
G. missed for
H. missed.
J. missed

PASSAGE II

Road Trips Back Home

During my junior year of college, it became a ritual for a group of us to "discover" a new suburb every month. We had come to college in this major city to escape what we thought were our boring lives in our various places of origin, but after a time, we realized that it would be impossible for us to turn our backs on our old lives completely.
11

11. Which choice makes the sentence most grammatically acceptable?

A. **No Change**
B. lives,
C. live's
D. lives'

I grew up in Pennsylvania, many parts of which look like the ones we drove to.
12

12

12. Given that all the choices are true, which one best supports the point that the narrator and his friends all shared a common background?

F. **No Change**
G. Many suburbs have become as populous as the cities they surround.
H. The first major migration of families from the city to the suburbs occurred in the late 1940s and early 1950s.
J. Our hometowns were all over the map, but they all shared a palpable likeness.

The first stop was typically some old diner, which reminded each of us of one from our various hometowns. There we'd usually sit, chat with the restaurant's owners drink a cup of
13
coffee, and figure out which new and exciting place we'd be driving to next.

13. Which choice makes the sentence most grammatically acceptable?

A. **No Change**
B. owners;
C. owners'
D. owners,

GO ON TO THE NEXT PAGE.

Even now that I live in a different city, I'll still sneak out to those kinds of places once in a while and just drive <u>around the</u> town. I guess, in a way, many of those memories are like the flickering diner signs we could see from the highway;

most people would never notice an old sign, but to those of us <u>who cherish it in our hearts,</u> we all harbored a great hope that it would still be flickering the same every time we came back.

14. Which choice is clearest and most precise in context?

   F. No Change
   G. among
   H. adjoining
   J. atop

15. Which choice is least redundant in context?

   A. No Change
   B. have a great fondness for it,
   C. have strong feelings of adoration for it,
   D. cherish it,

PASSAGE III

The Palio of Siena

Siena is an old, picturesque city located in the hills of Tuscany. <u>Since its inhabitants live modern lives, many historical</u> markers from as far back as medieval Italy still remain throughout the city.

[17] Another remnant from Siena's rich history that still plays a very prominent role today is the tradition of *Il Palio*.

Il Palio di Siena is a <u>biannual horse race that is held twice</u> a year, once in July and once in August. A field of ten bareback horses races three laps around a dangerously steep track circling the city's central plaza,

16. Which choice is clearest and most precise in context?

   F. No Change
   G. When
   H. As if
   J. Although

17. Which of the following true statements, if added here, would best serve as a transition between the preceding sentence and the next sentence?

   A. Like most Italian cities, Siena is very serious about soccer, a modern sport codified in England in the 1800s.
   B. Cobblestone streets and Gothic architecture are blended with modern sidewalk cafes and trendy designer stores.
   C. The city of Siena is certainly a mixture of ancient and contemporary practices.
   D. Siena is a major cultural center that offers numerous examples of art and architecture by Renaissance masters.

18. Which choice is least redundant in context?

   F. No Change
   G. biannual race that is held two times a year,
   H. horse race that is held twice a year,
   J. biannual horse race, held

GO ON TO THE NEXT PAGE.

the *Piazza del Campo*, each with two dreaded right-angle turns.
<u>19</u>

Even though *Il Palio* <u>lasted</u> only about 90 seconds, its
<u>20</u>
importance in Siena goes far beyond the race itself.

The brief race is a spectacular culmination of an entire way
of life in Siena. Every citizen belongs to a city district known as
a *contrada*, each with its own color and arms, such as the *Aquila*
(the eagle) or *Bruco* (the caterpillar). A *contrada* is the source of
so much local patriotism that every important <u>event; from</u>
<u>21</u>
baptisms to food festivals, is celebrated only within one's own
contrada and with fellow members,

<u>who</u> become more like family.
<u>22</u>

Members are fiercely committed to their *contrada* and
voluntarily tax themselves to invest in a good horse and jockey,
which can cost as much as 250,000 euros, for the biannual race.
This is, <u>however,</u> a small price to pay to achieve victory at *Il*
<u>23</u>
Palio. Seeing the colors and arms of their *contrada* in the
winner's circle is a glorious event. Old men weep openly out of
sheer joy, and elated adults and children

<u>parade. Throughout</u> the city with their newly won silk banner,
<u>24</u>
also called the *palio*.

19. Assuming that a period will always be placed at the end of the sentence, the best placement for the underlined phrase would be:

   A. where it is now.
   B. after the word *races* (setting the phrase off with commas).
   C. after the word *laps* (setting the phrase off with commas).
   D. after the word *plaza* (setting the phrase off with commas).

20. Which choice makes the sentence most grammatically acceptable?

   F. **No Change**
   G. will last
   H. lasts
   J. had lasted

21. Which choice makes the sentence most grammatically acceptable?

   A. **No Change**
   B. event, from
   C. event: from
   D. event—from

22. Which choice makes the sentence most grammatically acceptable?

   F. **No Change**
   G. for whose
   H. whose
   J. whom

23. Which transition word or phrase is most logical in context?

   A. **No Change**
   B. moreover,
   C. for instance,
   D. therefore,

24. Which choice makes the sentence or sentences most grammatically acceptable?

   F. **No Change**
   G. parade; throughout
   H. parade throughout
   J. parade throughout,

GO ON TO THE NEXT PAGE.

After the actual race day, the *Palio* festivities continue for a minimum of two weeks. Visitors from around the world travel to Siena during the <u>summer; not</u> only to witness the exciting race but also to attend the after-parties thrown by the locals. While the *Palio* is not as important to outsiders as it is to the Sienese, the race and the festivities that follow are a spectacular experience.

25. Which choice makes the sentence or sentences most grammatically acceptable?

   A. **No Change**
   B. summer. Not
   C. summer, not,
   D. summer, not

PASSAGE IV

Sherwood Anderson the Pioneer

When Sherwood Anderson's masterpiece *Winesburg, Ohio* was published in 1919, Anderson was pushed to the forefront of <u>it</u> in American literature. The book, something between a short story collection and a novel,

26. Which choice is clearest and most precise in context?

   F. **No Change**
   G. this
   H. a new movement
   J. a thing

<u>helping</u> to inaugurate an age of a truly homespun American Modernism.

27. Which choice makes the sentence most grammatically acceptable?

   A. **No Change**
   B. which helped
   C. helped
   D. was helped

Sherwood Anderson would be seen by a new generation of American writers as the first author to take a real step <u>until</u> creating a type of literature that was in tune with something previously only associated with Europe. Anderson was able to fuse his sense of the passing of the Industrial Age in America with a type of uniquely American expression that sought to replace previous literary conventions with more local expressions of fragmentation and alienation.

28. Which choice is clearest and most precise in context?

   F. **No Change**
   G. at
   H. toward
   J. **Delete** the underlined portion.

With *Winesburg, Ohio*, Anderson <u>forced</u> a younger group of writers, among whose ranks were John Steinbeck and William Faulkner, to embrace their American experiences and to express them in ways distinct from those being expressed by European writers or American expatriates.

29. Which choice is clearest and most precise in context?

   A. **No Change**
   B. forbade
   C. inspired
   D. approached

GO ON TO THE NEXT PAGE.

Anderson was among the first to explore the troubled relationship between the city and the rural town, utilize the direct style to which we so often apply the name "American," and examine the idea that deeply intellectual concerns can be relevant to everyday people as much as they can to regular folks. Even today, Anderson's initial treatment of these themes remains an important starting point for anyone interested in American culture.

30. Which choice best completes the contrast set up earlier in the sentence?

F. **No Change**
G. academics.
H. any given group of people.
J. average Americans.

PASSAGE V

Jackie Robinson: More than a Ballplayer

When baseball resumes in America every spring, one April day is always reserved to honor Jackie Robinson, the man who broke the color barrier of America's national pastime. While his accomplishments on the baseball field were numerous and impressive, his civil rights activism was according to his widow Rachel Robinson, equally important and often overlooked

31. Which choice makes the sentence most grammatically acceptable?

A. **No Change**
B. was, according,
C. was, according
D. was—according

without being noticed. The tenacious and spirited way

32. Which choice is least redundant in context?

F. **No Change**
G. while not being noticed.
H. as no one notices.
J. **Delete** the underlined portion and end the sentence with a period.

for the Brooklyn Dodgers Jackie Robinson played baseball was a reflection of his focus on civil rights.

33. The best placement for the underlined portion would be:

A. where it is now.
B. after the word *baseball*.
C. after the word *focus*.
D. after the word *rights*.

GO ON TO THE NEXT PAGE.

From the outset of the "Great Experiment" of having African-Americans in baseball; he knew that his performance on the field would be a determining factor in sports segregation. Robinson gradually converted jeers and harassment into cheers and acceptance. Robinson became a highly respected figure by continually succeeding on and off the field, all the while displaying stoic restraint in the face of initial prejudice. 35

[1] The vast amount of energy Robinson expended avoiding a myriad of potential pitfalls could have caused an ordinary man to wilt; for example, Robinson instinctively and relentlessly increased his efforts for positive civil rights changes, both in his sport and in the African-American community at large. [2] While many athletes today use their prestige to garner endorsements and live as celebrities, Robinson constantly utilized his to stimulate civil rights advancements. [3] He often used his baseball travels as opportunities to speak publicly to Black Americans in U.S. cities about ending segregation and vigilantly defending their rights. [4] Post-baseball, Robinson became an entrepreneur, but his focus did not stray as he found time to write impassioned letters and telegrams to various U.S. presidents during the Civil Rights Movement.

[5] He had the status to demand that they too remain firmly focused on civil rights measures. 38

34. Which choice makes the sentence or sentences most grammatically acceptable?

- **F.** No Change
- **G.** baseball, and he
- **H.** baseball. He
- **J.** baseball, he

35. If the writer were to delete this paragraph from the essay, which of the following would be lost?

- **A.** A scientific explanation of the "Great Experiment"
- **B.** A description of the way Robinson influenced society's outlook on segregation in baseball
- **C.** A passionate plea to end prejudice around the world
- **D.** A comment on why the Brooklyn Dodgers were the best team in baseball

36. Which transition word or phrase is most logical in context?

- **F.** No Change
- **G.** as a result,
- **H.** rather,
- **J.** therefore,

37. Which choice makes the sentence most grammatically acceptable?

- **A.** No Change
- **B.** entrepreneur,
- **C.** entrepreneur
- **D.** entrepreneur; and

38. If the writer were to divide the preceding paragraph into two shorter paragraphs in order to differentiate between Robinson's civil rights activism during and after his baseball career, the new paragraph should begin with:

- **F.** Sentence 2.
- **G.** Sentence 3.
- **H.** Sentence 4.
- **J.** Sentence 5.

GO ON TO THE NEXT PAGE.

Though Jackie Robinson's baseball exploits may be most widely known than his tireless efforts in the Civil Rights
<u>Movement</u>, his astonishing courage on the baseball field was
₃₉
itself a resounding stance against segregation and inequality. His numerous detractors consistently found that not only was Robinson undeterred, but he was excelling in his efforts. As a result, the spark of positive change was ignited. Robinson turned that spark for civil rights into a torch and carried it his entire life.

39. Which choice makes the sentence most grammatically acceptable?

A. **No Change**
B. very widely
C. more widely
D. widelier

Question 40 asks about the preceding passage as a whole.

40. Suppose the writer's primary purpose had been to describe the path Jackie Robinson took to become a professional baseball player. Would this essay accomplish that purpose?

F. Yes, because it describes Robinson's childhood and what led him to play baseball professionally.
G. Yes, because it identifies which baseball team he played on as a professional.
H. No, because it suggests that Robinson was not primarily known for his baseball career.
J. No, because it focuses on Robinson's contributions to civil rights during and after his baseball career.

PASSAGE VI

Women at Work

World War II offered numerous employment opportunities for women in the United States. As the men headed to the war front, the work force <u>retracted and diminished on the home front,</u>
₄₁
and women began to take over responsibilities traditionally assigned to men. These responsibilities included work previously deemed inappropriate for women.

The government realized that participation in the war <u>but</u>
₄₂
required the use of all national resources. American industrial facilities were turned into war production factories, and the government targeted the female population as an essential source of labor. Women worked in factories and shipyards as riveters, welders, and machinists. Making everything from uniforms to munitions to airplanes, they directly contributed to the war effort.

41. Which choice is least redundant in context?

A. **No Change**
B. retracted diminishingly
C. diminished
D. retracted to a reduced level

42. Which choice makes the sentence most grammatically acceptable?

F. **No Change**
G. and it
H. although it
J. **Delete** the underlined portion.

GO ON TO THE NEXT PAGE.

The number of women in the workforce increased from 12 million in 1940 to 18 million in 1944. By 1945, 36% of laborers were women.

The increased presence of women in wartime workforces were not limited to factories and shipyards.

[45] Thousands moved to Washington D.C. to fill government jobs exclusively held by men before the war. Some women engaged in farm labor, and others joined the military as field nurses. The shortage of men also led to openings in other non-traditional

fields, such as day-care. Since many players had been drafted into the armed services, Major League Baseball parks around the country were on the verge of collapse when a group of Midwestern businessmen devised a brilliant solution to the player shortage.

The All-American Girls Professional Baseball League was created in 1943 and offered a blend of baseball and softball considered suitable for female players. Founder Philip K. Wrigley and League president Ken Sells promoted the new league with advertising campaigns that emphasized the beauty of female athletes. Photographs displayed women players with bright smiles on their faces and baseball mitts in their hands. Their silk shorts, fashionable knee-high socks, red lipstick, and flowing hair directly contrasted with the competitive, masculine

43. Which choice is least redundant in context?

A. **No Change**
B. workforce, for example in factories and shipyards,
C. workforce, such as factories and shipyards,
D. factories, shipyards, and other areas of the workforce

44. Which choice makes the sentence most grammatically acceptable?

F. **No Change**
G. are
H. was
J. have been

45. At this point, the writer is considering adding the following true statement:

> The marriage rate increased significantly during the war, as did the rate of babies born to unmarried women.

Should the writer add this sentence here?

A. No, because it does not echo the style and tone that have already been established in the essay.
B. No, because it is not relevant to the essay's focus on the changing labor roles of women during World War II.
C. Yes, because it contributes to the essay's focus on women's roles in the home during World War II.
D. Yes, because it provides a contrast between women in the home and women in the workplace.

46. Given that all the choices are true, which one provides the most logical transition to the information presented in the rest of the essay?

F. **No Change**
G. the most notable of which was baseball.
H. which many women had to give up after the war.
J. shaking American society to the core.

47. Given that all the choices are true, which one most effectively aids the writer's purpose of helping readers visualize the appearance of the players in the photographs?

A. **No Change**
B. at the plate during a live game.
C. clearly focused on playing well.
D. showing close camaraderie.

GO ON TO THE NEXT PAGE.

nature of the game. 48 These photographs are indicative of the delicate balance between feminine appeal and masculine labor that was expected of all women throughout World War II.

Although its' success lasted only a decade, the All-American
49
Girls Professional Baseball League's role in expanding opportunities for women during World War II and thereafter is everlasting.

48. If the writer were to delete the words *silk*, *fashionable*, and *red* from the preceding sentence, it would primarily lose:

F. details that have already been presented in the vivid imagery of the previous sentence.
G. a digression from the focus of this paragraph on the athletic talent of the players.
H. a description of what was written in the captions accompanying the photographs.
J. details that highlight the femininity of the players in contrast to the masculinity of the game.

49. Which choice makes the sentence most grammatically acceptable?

A. **No Change**
B. it's
C. their
D. its

> Question 50 asks about the preceding passage as a whole.

50. Suppose the writer's goal was to write an essay that would illustrate the range of non-traditional activities women pursued during wartime. Does this essay achieve that goal?

F. Yes, because it explains the impact of the All-American Girls Professional Baseball League on public perception of women.
G. Yes, because it gives several examples of women performing jobs during World War II that were typically filled by men.
H. No, because the type of work focused on in the passage was only performed by women during World War II and not during any other wartime.
J. No, because it explains that women's importance in the workforce, especially in baseball, lasted only several years.

END OF TEST 1

STOP! DO NOT TURN THE PAGE UNTIL TOLD TO DO SO.

THIS PAGE INTENTIONALLY LEFT BLANK

MATHEMATICS TEST
50 Minutes—45 Questions

DIRECTIONS: Solve each problem, choose the correct answer, and then fill in the corresponding oval on your answer document.

Do not linger over problems that take too much time. Solve as many as you can; then return to the others in the time you have left for this test.

You are permitted to use a calculator on this test. You may use your calculator for any problems you choose, but some of the problems may best be done without using a calculator.

Note: Unless otherwise stated, all of the following should be assumed:

1. Illustrative figures are **not** necessarily drawn to scale.
2. Geometric figures lie in a plane.
3. The word "line" indicates a straight line.
4. The word "average" indicates arithmetic mean.

DO YOUR FIGURING HERE.

1. $|8 - 5| - |5 - 8| = ?$

   A. −5
   B. −3
   C. 0
   D. 6

2. A science tutor charges $60 an hour to help students with biology homework. She also charges a flat fee of $40 to cover her transportation costs. How many hours of tutoring are included in a session that costs $220?

   F. $2\frac{1}{5}$

   G. 3

   H. $3\frac{2}{3}$

   J. 4

3. Train A averages 16 miles per hour, and Train B averages 24 miles per hour. At these rates, how many more hours does it take Train A than Train B to go 1,152 miles?

   A. 20
   B. 24
   C. 40
   D. 48

GO ON TO THE NEXT PAGE.

4. Six equilateral triangles form the figure shown. If the perimeter of each individual triangle is 15 inches, what is the perimeter of *ABCDEF* in inches?

DO YOUR FIGURING HERE.

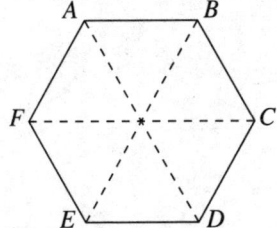

F. 30

G. 60

H. $54\sqrt{3}$

J. 90

5. The expression $(5x + 2)(x - 3)$ is equivalent to:

A. $5x^2 + 13x - 6$
B. $5x^2 - 13x - 6$
C. $5x^2 - 4x + 5$
D. $5x^2 - 6$

6. If 35% of a given number is 14, then what is 20% of the number?

F. 2.8
G. 4.9
H. 7.7
J. 8.0

7. The 7 consecutive integers represented by $x - 2$, $x - 1$, x, $x + 1$, $x + 2$, $x + 3$, and $x + 4$ add up to 511. What is the value of x?

A. 72
B. 73
C. 74
D. 75

GO ON TO THE NEXT PAGE.

8. In the standard (x,y) coordinate plane, point B with coordinates of $(5,6)$ is the midpoint of line $\overline{AC}$, and point A has coordinates at $(9,4)$. What are the coordinates of C?

   F. (13,2)
   G. (7,5)
   H. (1,8)
   J. (14,10)

9. Isosceles trapezoid $ABCD$, with equal sides $\overline{AB}$ and $\overline{CD}$, has vertices A (3,0), B (6,6), and D (15,0). These vertices are graphed as shown in the standard (x,y) coordinate plane. What are the coordinates of one possible vertex C?

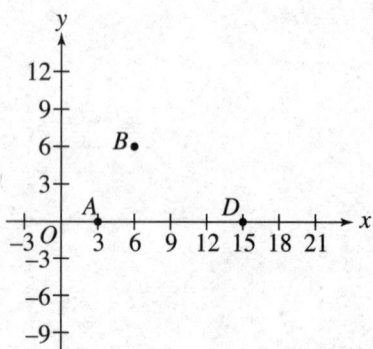

   A. (11,7)
   B. (13,6)
   C. (12,6)
   D. (13,5)

10. The town of Ashville has three bus stations (A, B, and C) that offer round-trip fares to its business district at both peak and off-peak rates. The matrices show the average weekly sales for each station at each rate and the costs for both rates. In an average week, what are the combined peak and off-peak sales for Ashville's three bus stations?

	Peak	Off-peak
A	180	60
B	200	120
C	150	70

	Cost
Peak	$3
Off-peak	$2

   F. $780
   G. $1,950
   H. $2,090
   J. $2,340

GO ON TO THE NEXT PAGE.

11. The triangle shown has exterior angles *a*, *b*, and *c*. What is the sum of those angles?

DO YOUR FIGURING HERE.

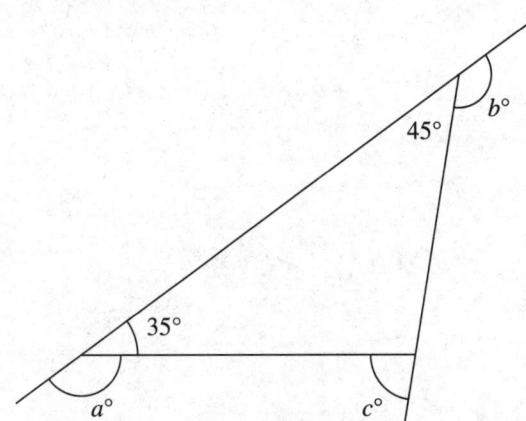

- **A.** 360°
- **B.** 315°
- **C.** 225°
- **D.** 180°

12. In rectangle *ABCD* shown, *E* is the midpoint of $\overline{BC}$, and *F* is the midpoint of $\overline{AD}$. Which of the following is the ratio of the area of quadrilateral *AECF* to the area of the entire rectangle?

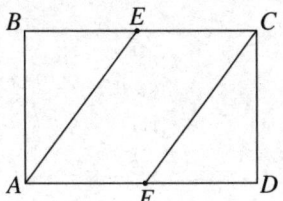

- **F.** 1:1
- **G.** 1:2
- **H.** 1:3
- **J.** 1:4

13. In the standard (*x*,*y*) coordinate plane, what is the slope of the line parallel to the line $y = \frac{1}{2}x - 3$?

- **A.** −2

- **B.** $-\frac{1}{2}$

- **C.** $\frac{1}{2}$

- **D.** 2

GO ON TO THE NEXT PAGE.

DO YOUR FIGURING HERE.

14. Aru watches a movie that is 120 minutes long in 2 sittings. The ratio of the 2 sitting times is 3:5. What is the length, in minutes, of the longer sitting?

   F. 15
   G. 45
   H. 60
   J. 75

15. Which of the following could be a value of x if $11 < x < 12$?

   A. $\sqrt{23}$

   B. $\sqrt{121}$

   C. $\sqrt{140}$

   D. $\sqrt{529}$

16. What values of x are solutions in the equation $x^2 + 4x = 12$?

   F. 0 and 4
   G. −2 and 6
   H. −4 and 0
   J. −6 and 2

17. For all $xy \neq 0$, and when both x and y are greater than 1, the expression $\dfrac{x^4 y^2}{x^2 y^4}$ equals which of the following?

   A. $-\dfrac{x^2}{y^2}$

   B. 1

   C. $\dfrac{x^2}{y^2}$

   D. $\dfrac{y^2}{x^2}$

GO ON TO THE NEXT PAGE.

18. The variable cost to produce a box of paper is $4.75. The fixed cost for the paper production machinery is $1,600.00 each day. Which of the following expressions correctly models the cost of producing *b* boxes of paper each day?

F. $1,600b + 4.75$
G. $1,600b - 4.75$
H. $1,600 + 4.75b$
J. $1,600b$

DO YOUR FIGURING HERE.

19. In the figure shown, where $\triangle ABC \sim \triangle XYZ$, lengths are given in inches and the perimeter of $\triangle ABC$ is 576 inches. What is the length, in inches, of $\overline{AC}$?

(Note: The symbol $\sim$ means "is similar to.")

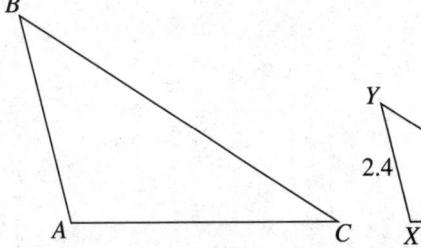

A. $126\frac{2}{5}$

B. 144

C. $168\frac{1}{5}$

D. 192

20. Given that $\dfrac{\sqrt{11}}{x} \times \dfrac{6}{\sqrt{11}} = \dfrac{3\sqrt{11}}{11}$, what is the value of *x*?

F. $\sqrt{11}$

G. $2\sqrt{11}$

H. 11

J. 121

GO ON TO THE NEXT PAGE.

21. Steve is going to buy an ice cream sundae. He first must choose 1 of 3 possible ice cream flavors. Next, he must choose 1 of 2 types of syrup. Finally, he must choose 1 of 6 kinds of candy toppings. Given these conditions, how many different kinds of sundaes could Steve possibly order?

A. 162
B. 36
C. 18
D. 9

22. The width of a rectangular cardboard box is half its length and twice its height. If the box is 12 cm long, what is the volume of the box in cubic centimeters?

F. 72
G. 216
H. 1,296
J. 1,728

23. At the end of each month, a credit card company uses the formula $D = B(1 + r) + 10m^2$ to calculate debt owed, where D is the cardholder's total debt; B is the amount charged to the card; r is the rate of interest; and m is the number of payments the cardholder has previously missed. If Daniel has charged \$2,155 to his credit card with a 13% interest rate and has missed 2 payments, which value is closest to Daniel's total credit card debt?

A. \$2,195
B. \$2,435
C. \$2,455
D. \$2,475

GO ON TO THE NEXT PAGE.

DO YOUR FIGURING HERE.

24. The figure shows a cone with dimensions given in centimeters. What is the total surface area of this cone in square centimeters? (Note: The total surface area of a cone is given by the expression $\pi r^2 + \pi rs$, where r is the radius and s is the slant height.)

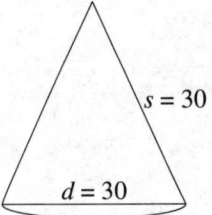

$s = 30$

$d = 30$

F. 225π
G. 465π
H. 675π
J. $18{,}000\pi$

25. Given the functions f and g are defined as $f(a) = 3a - 4$ and $g(a) = 2a^2 + 1$, what is the value of $f(g(a))$?

A. $6a^2 - 1$
B. $6a^2 - 3$
C. $2a^2 + 3a - 3$
D. $18a^2 - 48a + 33$

26. The table shows the results of a recent poll in which 262 high school students were asked to rank a recent movie on a scale from 1 to 5 stars. To the nearest hundredth, what was the average star-rating given to this movie?

Stars given	Number of students who gave this rating
1	51
2	18
3	82
4	49
5	62

F.   0.31
G.   2.02
H.   3.06
J.   3.20

GO ON TO THE NEXT PAGE.

27. Which of the following expressions is equivalent to the inequality $6x - 8 > 8x + 14$?

A. $x < -11$
B. $x > -11$
C. $x < -3$
D. $x > -3$

28. As shown in the standard (x,y) coordinate plane, A (2,4) lies on the circle with center L (10,–2) and radius 10 coordinate units. What are the coordinates of the image of A after the circle is rotated 90° counterclockwise (↺) about the center of the circle?

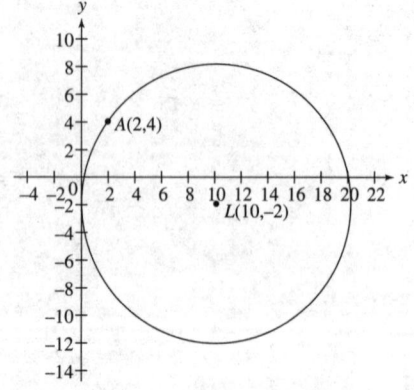

F. $(-2,10)$
G. $(2,-8)$
H. $(0,-2)$
J. $(4,-10)$

GO ON TO THE NEXT PAGE.

29. The length of the hypotenuse of the right triangle shown is 16, and the length of one of its legs is 12. What is the cosine of angle θ?

DO YOUR FIGURING HERE.

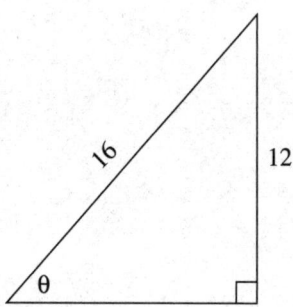

A. $\dfrac{\sqrt{112}}{16}$

B. $\dfrac{\sqrt{112}}{12}$

C. $\dfrac{12}{16}$

D. $\dfrac{16}{12}$

30. If the average number of carbon dioxide molecules per cubic inch in a container is 3×10^4 and there are 6×10^8 molecules of carbon dioxide in the container, what is the volume of the container in cubic inches?

F. 5×10^{-5}
G. 2×10^2
H. 2×10^4
J. 18×10^{12}

GO ON TO THE NEXT PAGE.

31. The figure shows the screen of an automobile navigation map. Point A represents the car's starting point, point B represents the driver's intended destination, and point C, the center of the circle, is the car's current position. Currently, point A is 15 miles from point C and 250° clockwise from due north, and point B is 20 miles from point C and 30° clockwise from due north. Which of the following represents the shortest distance (a straight line) between the car's starting point and the driver's desired destination?

(Note: For any $\triangle ABC$ in which side a is opposite $\angle A$, side b is opposite $\angle B$, and side c is opposite $\angle C$, the Law of Cosines applies: $c^2 = a^2 + b^2 - 2ab \cos\angle C$.)

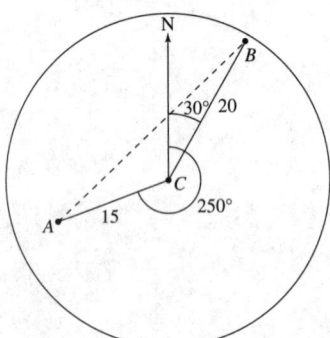

A. $\sqrt{15^2 + 20^2 - 2(15)(20)\cos 30°}$

B. $\sqrt{15^2 + 20^2 - 2(15)(20)\cos 140°}$

C. $\sqrt{15^2 + 20^2 - 2(15)(20)\cos 220°}$

D. $\sqrt{15^2 + 20^2 - 2(15)(20)\cos 280°}$

32. What real number is halfway between $\dfrac{1}{4}$ and $\dfrac{1}{6}$?

F. $\dfrac{1}{5}$

G. $\dfrac{1}{2}$

H. $\dfrac{5}{24}$

J. $\dfrac{7}{24}$

GO ON TO THE NEXT PAGE.

33. In isosceles triangle $\triangle ACE$, shown, B and D are the midpoints of congruent sides $\overline{AC}$ and $\overline{CE}$, respectively. $\angle ABE$ measures 95°, and $\angle DAE$ measures 35°. What is the measure of $\angle DEB$?

DO YOUR FIGURING HERE.

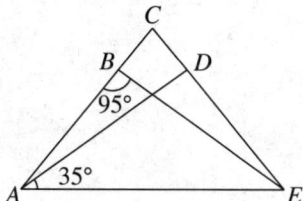

A. 50°
B. 25°
C. 15°
D. 10°

34. A small square table and an L-shaped table fit together with no space between them to create a large square table. The area of the large square table is 108 square feet and is nine times the area of the small square table. What is x, the edge of the L-shaped table labeled in the figure shown in square feet?

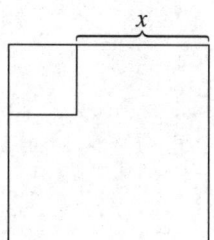

F. $2\sqrt{3}$

G. 4

H. $4\sqrt{3}$

J. $4\sqrt{6}$

35. Which of the following is **not** an irrational number?

A. $\sqrt{\pi}$

B. $\sqrt{5}$

C. $\sqrt{\dfrac{7}{49}}$

D. $\sqrt{\dfrac{81}{25}}$

GO ON TO THE NEXT PAGE.

36. If $x < 0$ and $y < 0$, then $|x + y|$ is equivalent to which of the following?

   F. $x + y$

   G. $-(x + y)$

   H. $|x - y|$

   J. $\sqrt{x^2 + y^2}$

37. Jane wants to bring her bowling average up to an 85 with her performance on her next game. So far she has bowled 5 out of 7 equally weighted games, and she has an average score of 83. What must her score on her next game be in order to reach her goal?

   A.   85
   B.   90
   C.   93
   D.   95

38. In the real numbers, what is the solution of the equation

$$9^{x-4} = 27^{3x+2}?$$

   F. -2

   G. -3

   H. $-\dfrac{7}{2}$

   J. -4

GO ON TO THE NEXT PAGE.

DO YOUR FIGURING HERE.

39. The graph of the trigonometric function $f(x) = 2 \sin \frac{1}{2}x$ is shown in the standard (x,y) coordinate plane. Which of the following is true of this function?

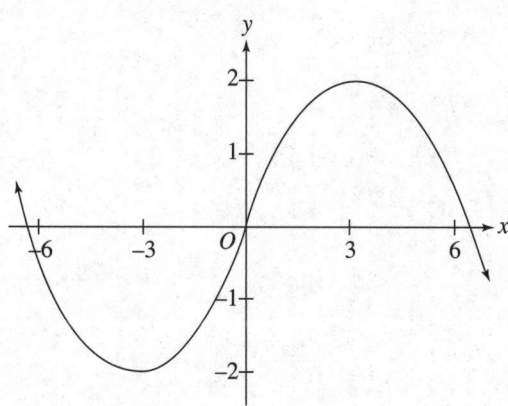

A. $f(x)$ is undefined at $x = 0$.
B. $f(x)$ is even (that is, $f(x) = f(-x)$ for all x).
C. $f(x)$ is odd (that is, $f(-x) = -f(x)$ for all x).
D. $f(x)$ falls entirely within the domain $-6 \leq x \leq 6$.

40. In the figure shown, side $\overline{MN}$ of isosceles triangle $\triangle NLM$ lies on the line $y + \frac{2}{3}x = 2$ in the standard (x,y) coordinate plane, and side $\overline{NL}$ is parallel to the x-axis. What is the slope of $\overline{LM}$?

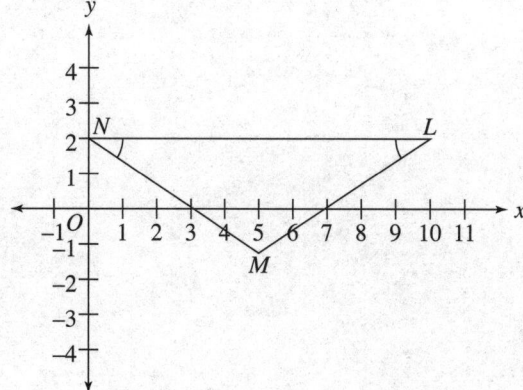

F. $\dfrac{3}{2}$

G. $\dfrac{2}{3}$

H. $-\dfrac{2}{3}$

J. $-\dfrac{3}{2}$

GO ON TO THE NEXT PAGE.

DO YOUR FIGURING HERE.

41. In the figure shown, $0 < y < x$. One of the angle measures in the triangle is $\sin^{-1}\left(\dfrac{x}{\sqrt{x^2+y^2}}\right)$. What is $\tan\left[\sin^{-1}\left(\dfrac{x}{\sqrt{x^2+y^2}}\right)\right]$?

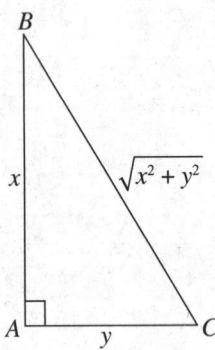

A. $\dfrac{x}{y}$

B. $\dfrac{y}{x}$

C. $\dfrac{x}{\sqrt{x^2+y^2}}$

D. $\dfrac{y}{\sqrt{x^2+y^2}}$

42. Which of the following is an equation of the circle shown?

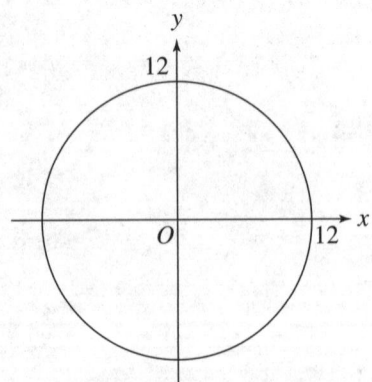

F. $(x-y)^2 = 12$
G. $(x+y)^2 = 12^2$
H. $x^2 + y^2 = 12$
J. $x^2 + y^2 = 12^2$

GO ON TO THE NEXT PAGE.

43. The graphs of the equations $y = -(x) + 1$ and $y = -(x + 1)^2 + 4$ are shown in the standard (x,y) coordinate plane. What real values of x satisfy the following inequality: $-(x + 1)^2 + 4 > -(x) + 1$?

DO YOUR FIGURING HERE.

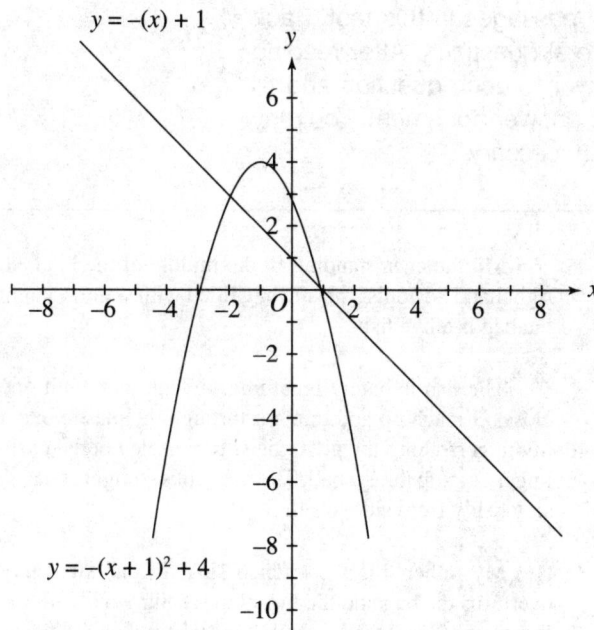

A. $x < -3$ and $x > 1$
B. $x < -2$ and $x > 1$
C. $-3 < x < 1$
D. $-2 < x < 1$

44. For any positive two-digit integer x with tens digit t, units digit u, and $t \neq u$, y is the two-digit integer formed when the digits of x are reversed. What is the greatest possible value of $(y - x)$ when t is less than u?

F. $u - t$
G. $ut - tu$
H. $t^2 - 10tu + u^2$
J. $9|u - t|$

45. The sum, S, of an arithmetic sequence with the first term x_1 is given by $S = n\left(\dfrac{x_1 + x_n}{2}\right)$, where n is the number of terms in the sequence. The sum of 5 consecutive terms in a given arithmetic sequence is 145, and x_5 is 48. What is the sixth term of this sequence?

A. 57.5
B. 77
C. 154.5
D. 174

END OF TEST 2

STOP! DO NOT TURN THE PAGE UNTIL TOLD TO DO SO.
DO NOT RETURN TO THE PREVIOUS TEST.

READING TEST

40 Minutes—36 Questions

DIRECTIONS: There are several passages in this test. Each passage is accompanied by several questions. After reading a passage, choose the best answer to each question and fill in the corresponding oval on your answer document. You may refer to the passages as often as necessary.

Passage I

LITERARY NARRATIVE: This passage is adapted from the short story "Simple Recipes" by Madeleine Thien (© 2001 by Madeleine Thien). Publisher: Little, Brown.

There is a simple recipe for making rice. My father taught it to me when I was a child. Back then, I used to sit up on the kitchen counter watching him, how he sifted the grains in his hands, sure and quick, removing pieces of dirt or sand, tiny
5 imperfections. He swirled his hands through the water and it turned cloudy. When he scrubbed the grains clean, the sound was as big as a field of insects. Over and over, my father rinsed the rice, drained the water, then filled the pot again.

The instructions are simple. Once the washing is done, you
10 measure the water this way—by resting the tip of your index finger on the surface of the rice. The water should reach the bend of your first knuckle.

My father did not need instructions or measuring cups. He closed his eyes and felt for the waterline. Sometimes I still
15 dream of my father, his bare feet flat against the floor, standing in the middle of the kitchen. He wears old buttoned shirts and faded sweatpants drawn at the waist. Surrounded by the gloss of the kitchen counters, the sharp angles of the stove, the fridge, the shiny sink, he looks out of place. This memory of him is so
20 strong, sometimes it stuns me, the detail with which I can see it.

Every night before dinner, my father would perform this ritual—rinsing and draining, then setting the pot in the cooker. When I was older, he passed this task on to me but I never did it with the same care. I went through the motions, splashing the
25 water around, jabbing my finger down to measure the water level. Some nights the rice was a mushy gruel. I worried that I could not do so simple a task right. "Sorry," I would say to the table, my voice soft and embarrassed. In answer, my father would keep eating, pushing the rice into his mouth as if he never expected
30 anything different, as if he noticed no difference between what he did so well and I so poorly. He would eat every last mouthful, his chopsticks walking quickly across the plate. Then he would rise, whistling, and clear the table, every motion so clean and sure, I would be convinced by him that all was well in the world.

35 My father is standing in the middle of the kitchen. In his right hand he holds a plastic bag filled with water. Caught inside the bag is a live fish.

The fish is barely breathing, though its mouth opens and closes. I reach up and touch it through the plastic bag, trailing
40 my fingers along the gills, the soft, muscled body, pushing my finger overtop the eyeball. The fish looks straight at me, flopping sluggishly from side to side.

My father fills the kitchen sink. In one swift motion he overturns the bag and the fish comes sailing out with the water.
45 It curls and jumps. We watch it closely, me on my tiptoes, chin propped up on the counter. The fish is the length of my arm from wrist to elbow. It floats in place, brushing up against the sides of the sink.

I keep watch over the fish while my father begins the
50 preparations for dinner. The fish folds its body, trying to turn or swim, the water nudging overtop. Though I ripple tiny circles around it with my fingers, the fish stays still, bobbing side to side in the cold water.

For many hours at a time, it was just the two of us. While
55 my mother worked and my older brother played outside, my father and I sat on the couch, flipping channels. He loved cooking shows. We watched *Wok with Yan*, my father passing judgement on Yan's methods. I was enthralled when Yan transformed orange peels into swans. My father sniffed. "I can do that," he said. "You
60 don't have to be a genius to do that." He placed a sprig of green onion in water and showed me how it bloomed like a flower. "I know many tricks like this," he said. "Much more than Yan."

Still, my father made careful notes when Yan demonstrated Peking Duck. He chuckled heartily at Yan's punning. "Take a wok
65 on the wild side!" Yan said, pointing his spatula at the camera.

"Ha ha!" my father laughed, his shoulders shaking. "*Wok on the wild side!*"

In the mornings, my father took me to school. At three o'clock, when we came home again, I would rattle off everything

GO ON TO THE NEXT PAGE.

70 I learned that day. "The brachiosaurus," I informed him, "eats only soft vegetables."

My father nodded. "That is like me. Let me see your forehead." We stopped and faced each other in the road. "You have a high forehead," he said, leaning down to take a closer look. 75 "All smart people do."

I walked proudly, stretching my legs to match his steps. I was overjoyed when my feet kept time with his, right, then left, then right, and we walked like a single unit.

1. Based on the passage, it could be assumed that the narrator learned to make rice by:

A. carefully following the complicated process her father taught her.
B. studiously watching cooking shows with her father.
C. following her father's steps in a half-hearted way that led to unsatisfying results.
D. reading about the process in books her father left her.

2. In the context of the passage, which of the following statements most strongly foreshadows the joy and connection the narrator feels in the last paragraph?

F. "There is a simple recipe for making rice" (line 1).
G. "When I was older, he passed this task on to me but I never did it with the same care" (lines 23–24).
H. "Then he would rise, whistling, and clear the table, every motion so clean and sure, I would be convinced by him that all was well in the world" (lines 32–34).
J. "My father sniffed. 'I can do that,' he said. "You don't have to be a genius to do that" (lines 59–60).

3. The passage suggests that in walking to match her father, the daughter:

A. folded her body, trying to turn away.
B. found joy in copying his movements.
C. felt inferior to her father in every way.
D. did not find Yan's puns as amusing as her father did.

4. Which of the following is true of the fish after the father has put it into the sink?

I. It does not respond to the narrator touching the water.
II. It is as long as the narrator's arm from wrist to elbow.
III. It looks straight at the narrator while flopping sluggishly.
IV. It brushes against the sides of the sink.

F. III and IV only
G. I, II, and IV only
H. II, III, and IV only
J. I and II only

5. Which of the following best paraphrases the narrator's comments in lines 5–7?

A. The rice her father made was better prepared than that of Chef Yan.
B. She viewed the many rice kernels as so many individual insects.
C. She was concerned that her father's repetitive actions signaled a mental disorder.
D. Her father was very thorough in preparing the rice for cooking.

6. As it is used in line 39, the word *trailing* most nearly means:

F. pursuing.
G. tracing.
H. losing.
J. hanging.

7. The narrator suggests that her father ate her rice out of:

A. pleasure; it was nearly as good as one of his own meals.
B. obligation; it was important never to waste any food.
C. consideration; he wanted his daughter to have the feeling that all was well.
D. embarrassment; otherwise, he would have to admit her incompetence.

8. Based on the passage, it's most logical to conclude that the fish is:

F. ill and dying.
G. restless and fearful.
H. confined and sluggish.
J. alert and watchful.

9. According to the passage, the father regarded *Wok with Yan* as:

A. providing some information worthy of his attention.
B. irrelevant to an accomplished chef like himself.
C. the primary source of his own cooking methods.
D. the funniest cooking show on television.

GO ON TO THE NEXT PAGE.

Passage II

INFORMATIONAL: Passage A is adapted from "Fertilizer History" by Gary Hergert, Rex Nielsen, and Jim Margheim (©2015 by University of Nebraska—Lincoln). Passage B is adapted from "Fertilizers, a Boon to Agriculture, Pose Growing Threat to U.S. Waterways" by Tatiana Schlossberg (©2017 by The New York Times Company).

Passage A by G. Hergert, R. Nielsen, and J. Margheim

For thousands of years after agriculture came into existence, manure was the main source of fertilizer. But sometime in the 18th century, it became common knowledge that ground-up bones provided crop nutrients. It wasn't until the 19th century
5 that ground-breaking research, done by several innovative scientists, finally ushered in the modern era of soil chemistry and plant nutrition. One of the most prominent of these chemists was Justus von Liebig (1803–1873), a German chemist who did pioneering research in organic and biological chemistry.

10 Ammonia and nitric acid, basic components of many chemical fertilizers, could be manufactured by the early 20th century, but until the middle of the century, use of chemical fertilizer was limited.

However, this would all change.

15 With the start of World War II, there was a tremendous increase in nitrogen production, mainly because nitrogen is a principal ingredient in explosives. After World War II, the need to manufacture war munitions was replaced with the need to restore food supplies in Europe and the United States.

20 The development of high-tech equipment has led to "precision" and "best-management" farming practices, which have resulted in the ability to apply various fertilizer types to a given crop in site-specific amounts. Technological advances in various fields of study, including crop genetics and breeding, plant and
25 soil testing, and the development of techniques to monitor the movement of nutrients and water within the soil profile have allowed today's farmers to use fertilizers more effectively and efficiently, in addition to being better stewards of the land and environment.

30 Manure is still an important source of plant nutrients; however, during the last 75 years, its use has been surpassed by the large-scale production and use of chemical fertilizers. In the mid- to late 1940s, about 2 million tons of chemical fertilizers were used per year. By 1960, over 7 million tons were used each
35 year and by 2014 over 20 million tons were used.

There is still much to learn about the complex interactions involving fertilizer use in differing soil and plant ecosystems; however, we have made historical progress since the first use of manure—progress that has been foundational to feeding our
40 nation and providing food and hope to other parts of the world.

Passage B by Tatiana Schlossberg

Nitrogen-based fertilizers, which came into wide use after World War II, helped prompt the agricultural revolution that has allowed the Earth to feed its seven billion people.

But that revolution came at a cost: artificial fertilizers, often
45 applied in amounts beyond what crops need to grow, are carried in runoff from farmland into streams, lakes and the ocean. New research suggests that climate change will substantially increase this form of pollution, leading to more damaging algae blooms and dead zones in American coastal waters.

50 A study published Thursday in *Science* concludes that eutrophication, excessive nutrient enrichment, is likely to increase in the continental United States as a result of the changes in precipitation patterns brought by climate change. Heavier rains caused by warmer temperatures will cause more agricultural
55 runoff, sluicing more nutrients into rivers, lakes and oceans.

The authors found that future climate change-driven increases in rainfall in the United States could boost nitrogen runoff by as much as 20 percent by the end of the century.

"When we think about climate change, we are used to think-
60 ing about water quantity—drought, flooding, extreme rainfall and things along those lines," said Anna Michalak, a professor of global ecology at the Carnegie Institution for Science in Stanford, Calif., and one of the authors of the study. "Climate change is just as tightly linked to issues related to water quality, and it's
65 not enough for the water to just be there, it has to be sustainable."

Excess nitrogen from the fertilizers can cause eutrophication in the ocean, which can lead to harmful algae blooms or hypoxia—reduced levels of oxygen that create conditions in which organisms can't survive....

GO ON TO THE NEXT PAGE.

10. In Passage A, the primary purpose of the details about the "ground-breaking research" (line 5) is to:

    F. show that few fertilizers were successful until the development of chemical fertilizers.

    G. demonstrate how manure replaced ground-up bones as the main source of fertilizer in the 18th century.

    H. connect prominent scientists to their contributions to the agricultural industry.

    J. provide details that show how knowledge of effective fertilizers grew over time.

11. According to Passage A, one reason for the development of chemical fertilizers was that:

    A. the United States needed a practical use for nitrogen left-over from the war.

    B. wartime industry created a way to mass-produce the components necessary for the fertilizer.

    C. soldiers coming home from the war were able to return to their jobs as chemists.

    D. farming practices provided crucial technologies which allowed nitrogen production to expand dramatically.

12. In the context of Passage A, the authors use the description of technological advances and techniques (lines 23–29) most nearly to:

    F. critique farmers for their reliance on technology.

    G. present factors that improved the application of chemical fertilizers.

    H. list the strategies that farmers rely on to increase their harvests.

    J. explain different technologies that are used to monitor water usage on a farm.

13. It can reasonably be inferred from Passage B that a major factor in the reshaping of global agriculture was:

    A. an increase in the use of chemical fertilizers.

    B. a revolutionary fertilizing technique that maximized crop yields.

    C. the discovery of a farming method that encouraged crop growth while avoiding ecological consequences.

    D. a focus on lessening the impacts of the agricultural industry on climate change.

14. In the context of Passage B, the statement "But that revolution came at a cost" (line 44) most nearly refers to the way that chemical fertilizers:

    F. place financial burdens on those who commit to using them.

    G. increase the amount of money required to feed 7 billion people.

    H. have environmental disadvantages in addition to economic advantages.

    J. are less effective in coastal regions than in plains regions.

15. Passage B most nearly suggests that, compared to concerns about water quantity, concerns about water quality are:

    A. equally connected to effects of climate change.

    B. less important for those in urban areas than for those in rural areas.

    C. more important on a global scale.

    D. more heavily focused on saltwater bodies.

16. Both passages suggest that the agricultural industry has been significantly impacted by types of fertilizer that were:

    F. impractical.

    G. artificially manufactured.

    H. naturally produced.

    J. ammonia-based.

17. Which of the following statements best compares the ways the authors of Passage A and Passage B use details about the effects of incorporating nitrogen-based fertilizers into agriculture?

    A. Passage A looks to the fertilizer as a source of hope for the future, while Passage B considers it a source of concern.

    B. Passage A uses the fertilizer as one example in a discussion of farming advances, while Passage B focuses exclusively on the fertilizer.

    C. Passage A considers the effects of the fertilizer on land, while Passage B considers the effects of the fertilizer on aquatic life.

    D. Both passages discuss the effects of the increased fertilizer use on the environment.

18. To support their claims about the impact of increasing use of nitrogen-based fertilizers, the authors of both passages:

    F. define key terms related to ecology.

    G. quote experts in a related field.

    H. provide statistics to support a point.

    J. outline a specific timeline of development.

GO ON TO THE NEXT PAGE.

Passage III

INFORMATIONAL: This passage is adapted from the article "And where are the lilacs?" by Andrew Motion (©2004 by *The Guardian*).

Pablo Neruda couldn't hold a tune. "My ear," he admitted, "could never recognise any but the most obvious melodies, and even then, only with difficulty." This is remarkable: Neruda's cadences are crucial to his writing. No one reading his poems
5 in their original Spanish would want to separate their sense from their sound. Even translated into English, their meaning is inseparable from their melody.

Adam Feinstein's new biography is fuelled by an infectious enthusiasm for Neruda's poems, but it also has an admirable
10 patience with his life's dizzying details. It's difficult to think of a 20th-century poet who did more than Neruda. He wrote a huge number of books, he travelled like a man possessed, he loved and lost many women, he collected a host of famous friends. Some of these things are grist to the biographer's mill:
15 Feinstein's account is crammed with adventure stories, narrow scrapes, passionate encounters. Others are harder to deal with: globe-trottings have to be logged but risk becoming a list of place-names. By pacing the story so as to give pre-eminence to the writing and the adventuring, while recording the duller
20 passages more briefly, Feinstein creates his own sympathetic music. His book turns Neruda's life into an opera—a blend of aria and recitative.

Sensibly, he relies a good deal on Neruda's own *Memoirs*. These are packed with marvellous details that give colour to the
25 story, as well as providing a way of understanding how Neruda's fascination with real things gives shape to even his most vatic poems. At a parting with a grief-stricken girlfriend, for instance: "She kissed my arms, my suit, in a kind of ritual, and suddenly slipped down to my shoes, before I could stop her. When she
30 stood up again, the chalk polish of my white shoes was smeared like flour all over her face."

Feinstein is too thorough to accept the *Memoirs* at face value, wonderful as they are. He understands that an author's reminiscences are a way of creating disguises as well as revealing
35 secrets, and regularly checks them against available evidence, amplifying the many complicated or contentious issues hushed up by Neruda himself. Feinstein acknowledges, from the first, that Neruda grew up among secrets and was therefore likely to enjoy them later.

40 Leaving his hometown for the relatively cosmopolitan Santiago, Neruda's interests expanded to accommodate social as well as family matters, and to create a more suggestive style. He relied on French symbolist poetry to stretch his imagination, combining his own fidelity to facts with surrealist touches and
45 impressionistic overviews. The result was a fusion previously unseen in Chilean poetry—or poetry anywhere—and his success was meteoric. But his exploded imagination needed a larger canvas, and the cultural and economic conditions of Chile both compelled and exasperated him.

50 Consular activity served as his means of escape. By 1927 he was in Rangoon, then moved on through France, Japan, China, Ceylon and Java (where he met his first wife, Maria), before returning home in 1932. By this time his Spanish was apparently "quite odd...very much influenced by his solitude," and his
55 sense of himself much altered. But these were not changes which threatened his audience: they added authority to his originality.

They didn't, however, do much for his political conscience, which began to develop during his posting to Spain in the early 1930s, when he fell in love with Delia del Carril. Delia per-
60 suaded him to become a communist—a process which meant that he inflicted a great deal of pain on his first wife and their sickly daughter, while producing poems that exalted the suffering masses. It confronts Feinstein with the classic biographer's dilemma—how to respect the work while dealing with a con-
65 tradictory private life—and he copes with it by presenting the facts rather than wagging his finger, and by foregrounding the writing. As the scenery changes from France to Chile again, we see Neruda the romantic lyricist turning into Neruda the "truth-teller and exposer of the world's injustices."

70 Neruda spent the late 30s and early 40s travelling round South America, converting his experience of other people's suffering into poems, standing as a senator, and defending the new emphasis of his work. Given the political climate, it was bound to end in trouble—or rather, trouble and adventure. In
75 1949 Neruda made a daring escape from Chile over the Andes into Buenos Aires, then soon set off again, speaking for the oppressed everywhere while neglecting Delia in favour of Matilde, who eventually became his third wife.

These paradoxes bring their own difficulties—but their
80 tensions are intensified by fault-lines in Neruda's politics. Feinstein lets his readers draw their own conclusions about the moral muddle of Neruda's life, shining the same clear light on his politics that he turns on his private life (even Matilde was betrayed, when Neruda had a late fling with her niece). This is
85 as well. The faults and weaknesses are plain to see, but so is the undimmed exuberance and generosity of the work, which feeds hungrily off the life and yet stands as a thing apart.

GO ON TO THE NEXT PAGE.

19. The primary function of the first paragraph is to:

   A. clarify misunderstandings about what made Neruda so talented as a Spanish singer and musician.

   B. outline how Neruda wrote his poems.

   C. tell a story from Neruda's youth.

   D. contrast a statement of Neruda's with a characteristic of his poetry.

20. Based on the passage, which of the following best describes the passage author's opinion of Neruda's poetry?

   F. He prefers Neruda's *Memoirs* to Neruda's poetry.

   G. He considers Neruda's poetry to be original.

   H. He thinks Neruda's poetry is too heavily based on his own life.

   J. He believes that Neruda's poetry shows faults and weaknesses.

21. The "melody" mentioned in lines 6–7 most nearly refers to:

   A. the aria for Neruda's opera that was discovered by Adam Feinstein.

   B. the effect Neruda's word choice and pacing has on a reader's understanding of his poems.

   C. the connection between Neruda's life and his poetry discussed by the passage author.

   D. the many adventures, narrow scrapes, and passionate encounters Neruda had during his life.

22. The passage most strongly suggests that a reader might appreciate Feinstein's treatment of the "dizzying details" (lines 9–10) of Neruda's life because Feinstein:

   F. is critical of Neruda's many travels and adventures.

   G. concentrates on explaining Neruda's writing process rather than focusing on his life.

   H. never elaborates on why Neruda was a globe-trotter and prolific writer.

   J. keeps dull passages brief to ensure the reader does not lose interest.

23. As it is used in line 17, the word *logged* most nearly means:

   A. cut.

   B. completed.

   C. recorded.

   D. harvested.

24. According to the passage, Neruda's reminiscences as related in his autobiography:

   F. amplified contentious issues.

   G. should be studied as literature.

   H. create disguises and reveal secrets.

   J. were a guide for Feinstein's writing style.

25. The passage indicates that Feinstein addresses Neruda's conversion to communism by:

   A. avoiding the topic of politics as much as possible.

   B. contradicting Neruda's own account of that time period.

   C. respecting Neruda's first wife and sickly daughter to ensure the biography does not cause pain.

   D. recording information truthfully without passing judgment on it.

26. According to Feinstein, Neruda's Spanish became "quite odd" (line 54) during his:

   F. travels to Rangoon and other countries.

   G. studies of French symbolist poetry.

   H. escape from consular activity.

   J. marriage to Delia del Carril.

27. As it is used in line 86 the word *work* refers to Neruda's:

   A. poetry.

   B. biography.

   C. travels.

   D. marriage.

GO ON TO THE NEXT PAGE.

Passage IV

INFORMATIONAL: This passage is adapted from the essay "The Higgs at Last" by Michael Riordan, Guido Tonelli, and Sau Lan Wu (©2013 by Scientific American).

The Higgs boson is the cornerstone of the Standard Model, an interwoven set of theories that constitute modern particle physics. This particle's existence had been suggested in 1964 by Peter W. Higgs of the University of Edinburgh as the result of a subtle
5 mechanism—independently conceived by François Englert and Robert Brout in Brussels plus three theorists in London—that endows elementary particles with mass. The Higgs boson is the physical manifestation of an ethereal fluid (called the Higgs field) that permeates every corner of the cosmos and imbues particles
10 with distinctive masses.

Although theorists asserted that the Higgs boson—or something like it—must exist, they could not predict what its mass might be. For this and other reasons, researchers had few clues about where to look for it. An early candidate, weighing
15 in at less than nine times the proton mass, turned up in 1984 at a refurbished, low-energy electron-positron collider in Hamburg, Germany. Yet the evidence withered away after further study.

Most theorists agreed that the Higgs mass should be 10 to 100 times higher. If so, discovering it would require a much larger
20 and more energetic particle collider than even the Fermi National Laboratory's Tevatron, a collider completed in 1983. That same year CERN began building the billion-dollar Large Electron Positron (LEP) collider, boring a 27-kilometer circular tunnel that crossed the French-Swiss border four times near Geneva.
25 Although LEP had other goals, the Higgs boson was high on its target list. Discoveries and precision measurements made at LEP and the Tevatron soon implied that the Higgs boson should be no more than 200 GeV, which put it potentially within reach of these colliders. (GeV is the standard unit of mass and energy in
30 particle physics, about equal to a proton mass.) In over a decade of searching, however, physicists found no lasting evidence for Higgs-like data bumps.

During the final LEP runs in the summer of 2000, physicists decided to push the collision energy beyond what the machine was
35 designed to handle. That is when hints of a Higgs boson began appearing. After a heated debate, CERN's then-director Luciano Maiani decided to shut LEP down and begin its planned conversion into the LHC, a machine designed to find the Higgs boson.

The LHC is the most spectacular collection of advanced
40 technology ever assembled. Built inside the original LEP tunnel, it uses little left from that collider. Its principal components include more than 1,200 superconducting dipole magnets—shiny, 15-meter-long cylinders worth nearly $1 million each. Probably the most sophisticated components ever mass-produced, by firms
45 in France, Germany and Italy, they harbor twin beam tubes that are flanked by niobium-titanium magnet coils bathed in liquid helium at 1.9 kelvins, or −271 degrees Celsius. Inside, twin proton

beams circulate in both directions at energies up to 7 TeV and velocities approaching light speed.

50   Although the LHC is a giant collider feeding multiple experiments, only the two largest ones—ATLAS and CMS—had been tasked with finding the Higgs boson. The ATLAS and CMS experiments couldn't observe a Higgs boson directly—it would decay into other particles far too quickly. They looked
55 for evidence that it was created inside. Depending on the Higgs boson's mass, it could decay into lighter particles in a variety of ways. In 2011, attention began to focus on its rare decays into two photons and four charged leptons, because these signals would stand out starkly against tremendous backgrounds of data. By
60 May 2012, the LHC was producing data 15 times faster than the Tevatron had ever achieved.

On June 15, 2012, CMS physicists began gathering to hear the preliminary reports. Signals from their data were occurring again in the same vicinity—near 125 GeV—that had
65 so tantalized researchers six months earlier. Scientists realized almost immediately that if they were to combine the new data with the 2011 results, chances were good that CMS could claim a Higgs discovery. Similar revelations occurred in the ATLAS experiment. At the thrilling moment of recognition, one ATLAS
70 group of about a dozen physicists erupted in loud clapping and cries of joy, which echoed down the hallway. CMS and ATLAS independently concluded that the chances that the apparition was a fluke, due to random fluctuations, were less than one in three million. It had to be real.

75   These results were shared at a public joint seminar at CERN on July 4, 2012. When the camera panned to Dr. Higgs, he could be seen pulling out a handkerchief to wipe his eyes.

Few physicists doubt that a heavy new particle has turned up at CERN, but there is still debate about its exact nature—since
80 July 2012, attention has focused on whether the new particle is indeed "the" Higgs boson predicted by the Standard Model. The particle opens up a fabulous new laboratory for further experimentation. Are its properties exactly as predicted? The apparent discrepancies in the early data could be random fluctuations that
85 disappear in months to come. Or perhaps they are offering subtle hints of intriguing new physics.

28. The overall organization of the passage is best described as a:

    F. chronological account of scientists determining the correct mass of various elementary particles.

    G. step-by-step explanation of how the Large Hadron Collider was constructed.

    H. series of important events leading to the discovery of the Higgs boson.

    J. collection of stories describing how the Standard Model of physics evolved over time.

GO ON TO THE NEXT PAGE.

29. The main function of the first paragraph is to:

- **A.** list the information discovered about the Higgs boson by research scientists in Hamburg.
- **B.** demonstrate what led scientists to build larger and more energetic particle colliders.
- **C.** summarize contributions made by theorists in London.
- **D.** explain the origin and importance of the Higgs boson theory.

30. Based on the passage, one similarity between the two particle colliders described in lines 18–32 is that:

- **F.** neither provided lasting evidence that definitively proved the existence of the Higgs boson.
- **G.** both cost upwards of one billion dollars to build.
- **H.** construction for both particle accelerators was completed in the same year.
- **J.** both had the size and energy that enabled them to discover the Higgs boson.

31. The main idea of the last paragraph is that:

- **A.** the properties of the new particle were predicted by the Standard Model only recently and leave physicists' results in doubt.
- **B.** recent research by physicists makes earlier data gathered by scientists look faulty by comparison.
- **C.** few doubt a new heavy particle has been discovered and additional research should explain its properties.
- **D.** the heavy particle discovered weighs far more than originally predicted by scientists.

32. According to the passage, scientists in Brussels and London:

- **F.** suggested in 1964 that the Higgs boson exists.
- **G.** developed an interwoven set of theories for particle physics.
- **H.** discovered the cornerstone of the Standard Model.
- **J.** independently conceived of a subtle mechanism that endows elementary particles with mass.

33. Based on the passage, to make the particle collider functional, French, Italian, and German firms designed the dipole magnets to be capable of:

- **A.** utilizing the principal components from the LEP accelerator and fitting in the original tunnel.
- **B.** accelerating protons to velocities approaching light speed and having the protons circulate in two directions.
- **C.** floating in the air when filled with liquid helium and achieving energies up to 7 TeV.
- **D.** costing under one million dollars each and fitting into a fifteen-meter-long cylinder.

34. The passage suggests that compared to work at the LHC, work at the Tevatron was:

- **F.** less rapid.
- **G.** less reliable.
- **H.** more expensive.
- **J.** more insightful.

35. It can reasonably be inferred from the passage that the author includes the description of the scientists' reactions to data gained from the ATLAS and CMS experiments (lines 69–71) primarily to:

- **A.** illustrate how pleased the researchers were to meet Peter Higgs when he visited CERN.
- **B.** describe their reaction to data gained from the Tevatron experiments.
- **C.** suggest that the physicists' celebration may have disrupted other scientists in the building.
- **D.** highlight the magnitude of their discovery by showing their emotional reaction to the results.

36. As it is used in line 78, the phrase *turned up* most nearly means:

- **F.** been amplified.
- **G.** been discovered.
- **H.** arrived on site.
- **J.** grown in height.

END OF TEST 3

STOP! DO NOT TURN THE PAGE UNTIL TOLD TO DO SO.

DO NOT RETURN TO A PREVIOUS TEST.

SCIENCE TEST

40 Minutes–40 Questions

DIRECTIONS: There are several passages in this test. Each passage is accompanied by several questions. After reading a passage, choose the best answer to each question and fill in the corresponding oval on your answer document. You may refer to the passages as often as necessary.

You are **not** permitted to use a calculator on this test.

Passage I

As substrate is added to an enzyme, *enzyme velocity,* or the rate at which an enzyme can change substrate into products, varies with initial substrate concentration, temperature, and time since the reaction began. Table 1 shows, for each of 4 enzymes (A, B, C, and D), the enzyme velocity 10 seconds after addition of substrate for different substrate concentrations and temperatures.

Table 1				
Enzyme	Initial substrate concentration	Enzyme velocity (mmol/s) at a substrate temperature of:		
		20°C	30°C	60°C
A	5 mM	9.1	6.5	4.6
	10 mM	13.2	8.9	6.4
	15 mM	17.6	11.4	7.5
B	5 mM	13.1	7.3	4.9
	10 mM	20.3	10.9	6.9
	15 mM	25.5	13.8	8.6
C	5 mM	20.7	14.3	10.6
	10 mM	30.3	20.8	13.1
	15 mM	35.2	23.1	14.9
D	5 mM	50.2	23.5	14.6
	10 mM	57.6	28.3	18.6
	15 mM	63.3	30.7	19.9

Figure 1 shows how each enzyme's velocity changes over time with an initial substrate concentration of 12 mM at a temperature of 40°C.

Figure 1

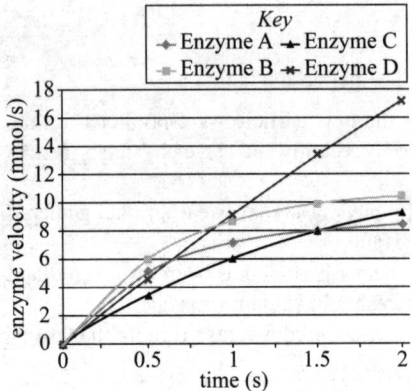

GO ON TO THE NEXT PAGE.

1. According to Table 1, which of the following graphs accurately depicts the velocities of Enzymes A, B, C, and D after 10 seconds at an initial substrate concentration of 5 mM and a temperature of 60°C?

A.

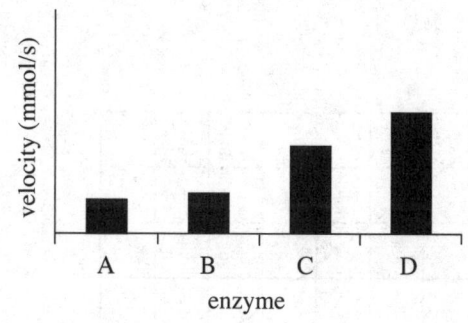

B.

C.

D.

2. Based on Table 1, the enzyme velocity of Enzyme B after 10 seconds in a solution with a substrate concentration of 10 mM at a temperature of 35°C would most likely be:

F.   less than 7 mmol/s.
G.   between 7 and 11 mmol/s.
H.   between 11 and 20 mmol/s.
J.   greater than 20 mmol/s.

3. According to Figure 1, which of the following correctly orders the enzymes according to their enzyme velocities from highest to lowest after 1 second at a substrate concentration of 12 mM and a temperature of 40°C?

A.   Enzyme A, Enzyme B, Enzyme C, Enzyme D
B.   Enzyme A, Enzyme C, Enzyme D, Enzyme B
C.   Enzyme D, Enzyme A, Enzyme B, Enzyme C
D.   Enzyme D, Enzyme B, Enzyme A, Enzyme C

4. Based on Table 1, the enzyme velocity for Enzyme C in a solution with an 8 mM substrate concentration at 60°C after 10 seconds would likely be approximately:

F.   12.0 mmol/s.
G.   13.5 mmol/s.
H.   14.5 mmol/s.
J.   16.0 mmol/s.

5. According to Figure 1, which enzyme takes the *shortest* amount of time to reach an enzyme velocity of 6 mmol/s in a solution with a substrate concentration of 12 mM at a temperature of 40°C?

A.   Enzyme A
B.   Enzyme B
C.   Enzyme C
D.   Enzyme D

GO ON TO THE NEXT PAGE.

Passage II

Ozone (O_3) is an inorganic gas found primarily in the stratosphere of Earth's atmosphere. Stratospheric ozone is formed naturally when UV (*ultraviolet*) light breaks apart an oxygen molecule to form two highly reactive oxygen atoms. The oxygen atoms each then collide with another oxygen molecule to form ozone. Though ozone makes up a very small percentage of the gas in the stratosphere, it is the primary absorber of the sun's UV-B rays, allowing only a small percentage of these harmful rays to reach Earth's surface. Ozone also absorbs light in the infrared spectrum, as does carbon dioxide (CO_2).

A researcher performed three studies on the behavior of ozone and CO_2.

Study 1

The researcher modeled the transmittance of both O_3 and CO_2 at their average concentrations in the atmosphere at various wavelengths in the UV spectrum from 0.25–0.35 microns (μm) and in the infrared spectrum from 2.5–11 μm. The *transmittance* of a gas is the percent of incoming solar radiation that is transmitted through that gas toward Earth's surface. The model is shown below in Figure 1.

Figure 1

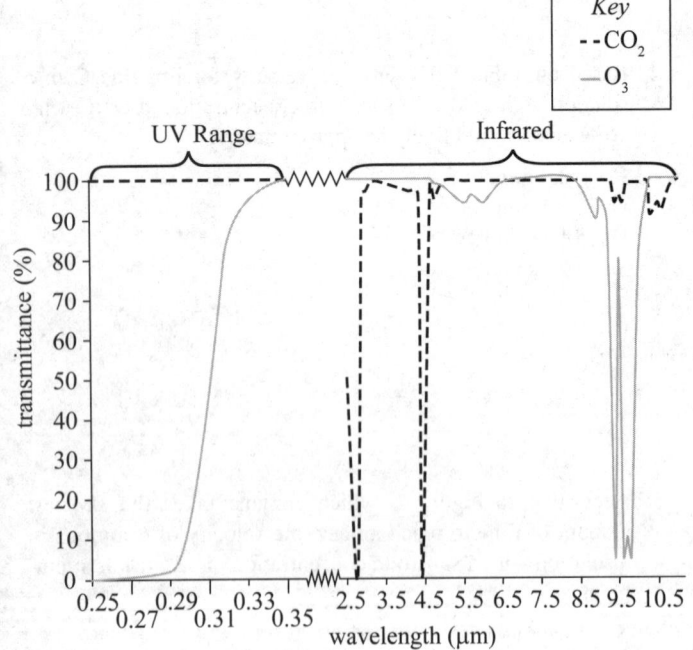

Study 2

Ozone levels vary throughout the stratosphere by both location and season. The researcher modeled the transmittance through the stratosphere at five different concentrations of ozone, in milligrams per cubic meter (mg/m^3), at a wavelength of 0.31 microns (see Figure 2).

Figure 2

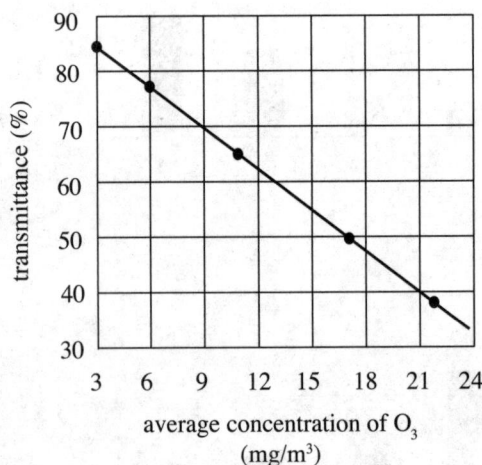

Study 3

The researcher also estimated the average stratospheric ozone concentration, in mg/m^3, at five different locations (Locations 1–5) on a particular day. The concentrations were estimated at standard temperature and pressure. The results are shown in Table 1.

Table 1	
Location	Concentration (mg/m^3)
1	10
2	6
3	21
4	14
5	9

GO ON TO THE NEXT PAGE.

6. Based on the data in Figure 2, the transmittance at 0.31 microns at a concentration of 18 mg/m^3 would most likely be:

   F. less than 45%.
   G. between 45 and 50%.
   H. between 50 and 55%.
   J. greater than 55%.

7. In Study 2, as the concentration of ozone increased from 3 to 24 mg/m^3, the transmittance at 0.31 microns:

   A. increased only.
   B. decreased only.
   C. increased and then decreased.
   D. decreased and then increased.

8. Based on the model in Study 2, which of the locations in Study 3 likely has the greatest transmittance at 0.31 microns?

   F. Location 1
   G. Location 2
   H. Location 3
   J. Location 5

9. According to the passage, which of the following pairs of equations represents the production of ozone in the stratosphere?

   A. $O_2 + UV \text{ light} = 2\,O$
      $2\,O + 2\,O_2 = 2\,O_3$

   B. $2\,O + UV \text{ light} = O_3$
      $O_3 + 3\,O_2 = 3\,O_3$

   C. $O_2 + UV \text{ light} = 2\,O$
      $O_3 + O = 2\,O_2$

   D. $O_2 + O = O_3$
      $O_3 + UV \text{ light} = 3\,O$

10. The researcher plans to repeat Study 2, but this time he wants to study the effects on transmittance of different CO_2 concentrations instead of O_3 concentrations. Based on Figure 1, should he measure the transmittance at 4.3 microns or at 9.5 microns?

    F. At 4.3 microns; the transmittance of CO_2 is lower at this wavelength than it is at 9.5 microns.
    G. At 4.3 microns; the transmittance of CO_2 is higher at this wavelength than it is at 9.5 microns.
    H. At 9.5 microns; the transmittance of CO_2 is lower at this wavelength than it is at 4.3 microns.
    J. At 9.5 microns; the transmittance of CO_2 is higher at this wavelength than it is at 4.3 microns.

11. Based on Table 1, assuming that the atmospheric gases are uniformly mixed in the stratosphere, what would be the approximate mass of O_3, in *grams*, in 100 cubic meters of stratospheric air at Location 3 on the date of the study?

    A. 0.21
    B. 2.1
    C. 210
    D. 2,100

GO ON TO THE NEXT PAGE.

Passage III

Ocean depth affects both temperature and dissolved oxygen levels. In Figure 1, the values of temperature, *t*, in degrees Celsius, and dissolved oxygen, *D.O.*, in milligrams per liter (mg/L), are graphed versus depth, *d*, in meters below the ocean's surface. Five distinct ocean zones are also identified in Figure 1.

Figure 1

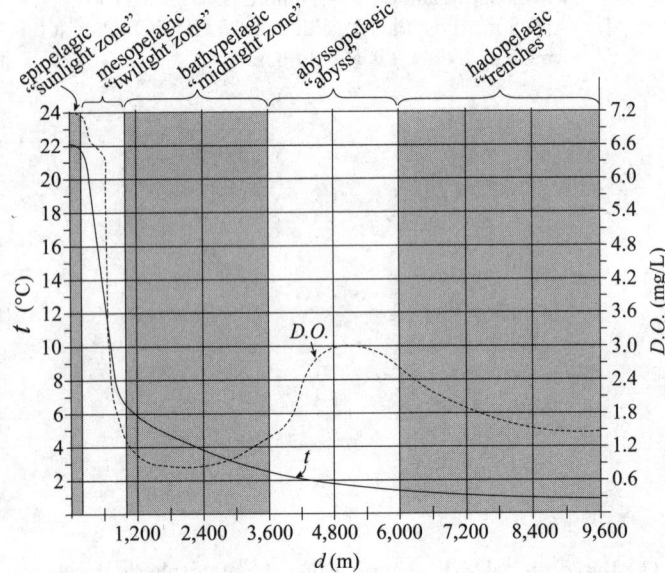

Approximately 98% of marine life is located in the epipelagic, mesopelagic, and bathypelagic zones. Figure 2 shows the percent of marine life that is located between sea level and a given depth within these three zones. For example, 20% of all marine life is located between sea level and a depth of 50 meters.

Figure 2

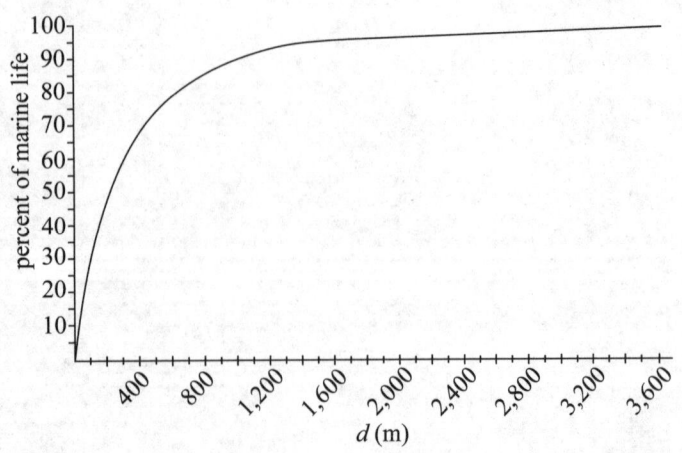

12. The range of a zone refers to the difference in depth between the top and the bottom of that zone. According to Figure 1, which two zones have similar ranges?

   F. Epipelagic and mesopelagic
   G. Mesopelagic and bathypelagic
   H. Mesopelagic and abyssopelagic
   J. Bathypelagic and abyssopelagic

13. Figure 2 indicates that approximately 35% of marine life lives between *d* = 0 m and:

   A. *d* = 50 m.
   B. *d* = 100 m.
   C. *d* = 300 m.
   D. *d* = 500 m.

14. Based on Figure 1, the dissolved oxygen levels at *d* = 10,000 m would most likely be:

   F. less than 0.3 mg/L.
   G. between 0.3 and 0.9 mg/L.
   H. between 0.9 and 1.2 mg/L.
   J. between 1.2 and 1.5 mg/L.

15. Depths below 1,000 meters are considered *aphotic* because no sunlight penetrates that deep. Based on Figure 2, the aphotic zones account for approximately what percentage of marine life?

   A. 2%
   B. 10%
   C. 90%
   D. 98%

16. Colder ocean water is denser than warmer ocean water. A scientist compares the masses of two 1-liter samples of water: one collected at *d* = 1,000 m and one collected at *d* = 3,600 m. Based on Figure 1, which of the samples of water, if either, would have a lower mass?

   F. The sample at *d* = 3,600 m has a lower mass because the water temperature is lower and the density is higher.
   G. The sample at *d* = 1,000 m has a lower mass because the water temperature is higher and the density is lower.
   H. Both samples have the same mass because the density is the same for both samples.
   J. Both samples have the same mass because the volume is the same for both samples.

GO ON TO THE NEXT PAGE.

THIS PAGE IS INTENTIONALLY LEFT BLANK.

GO ON TO THE NEXT PAGE.

Passage IV

Fibromyalgia is a central nervous system disorder characterized by chronic widespread pain and a heightened pain response. Four students each propose a theory of what causes fibromyalgia.

Student 1

Fibromyalgia is caused only by an abnormal immune response to an infection or injury. When the body detects damaged tissue, white blood cells release chemicals called cytokines that direct blood flow to the damaged cells and cause inflammation. The inflammation aggravates the nerves and makes the infected area more sensitive to pain. Usually the increased sensitivity goes away after the inflammation subsides, but sometimes the inflammation causes irreparable physical damage to the nerve cells. Fibromyalgia is the result of the damaged nerve cells disrupting the normal functioning of the central nervous system.

Student 2

Fibromyalgia is caused only by the overproduction of excitatory neurotransmitters. Neurons transmit pain signals by firing chemicals called neurotransmitters that bind to pain receptors on another neuron. The most prevalent of these neurotransmitters is glutamate. When the nerve cells chronically overproduce glutamate, the pain receptors adapt by physically changing shape to more readily absorb the signals. This change makes neurons more sensitive to pain, which results in fibromyalgia. Injury and illness can cause nerve damage to specific neurons, but they do not create the widespread pain of fibromyalgia.

Student 3

Fibromyalgia is caused only by abnormal estrogen or thyroid hormone levels. These hormones affect the production of serotonin and norepinephrine, two inhibitory neurotransmitters that suppress pain transmission through the central nervous system. When levels of these inhibitory neurotransmitters are low, the body is unable to suppress pain transmission, and fibromyalgia is the result. While it is true that some people do overproduce glutamate, sufficient levels of serotonin and norepinephrine neutralize the excess glutamate before it interacts with any pain receptors.

Student 4

Fibromyalgia results only from a diet low in L-tryptophan, an essential amino acid necessary for the production of serotonin. Serotonin helps the brain interpret pain signals. When serotonin levels drop due to inadequate L-tryptophan intake, the brain is unable to properly interpret various pain signals, causing fibromyalgia. Nerve damage from injury only creates localized pain. Excess glutamate is harmless because it is not absorbed by the pain receptors. Estrogen and thyroid hormone imbalances do not limit the production of serotonin.

17. Which of the students theorized that fibromyalgia is triggered by neurons that are in some way physically altered?

   A. Student 1 only
   B. Student 4 only
   C. Students 1 and 2 only
   D. Students 2 and 3 only

18. A researcher discovers that female fibromyalgia patients report a higher incidence of pain during pregnancy and menopause when estrogen levels are rapidly changing. This discovery best supports which student's theory?

   F. Student 1
   G. Student 2
   H. Student 3
   J. Student 4

19. Based on the information provided by Student 4, people consume L-tryptophan through foods containing which of the following?

   A. Carbohydrates
   B. Protein
   C. Saturated fat
   D. Unsaturated fat

20. Which of the students theorized that fibromyalgia is the result of low levels of certain neurotransmitters?

   F. Students 1 and 2 only
   G. Student 3 only
   H. Students 2 and 3 only
   J. Students 3 and 4 only

GO ON TO THE NEXT PAGE.

21. Which of the following research findings, if true, best supports Student 4's theory?

A. Patients with fibromyalgia have higher levels of thyroid hormone than patients that do not have fibromyalgia.

B. Patients with fibromyalgia have lower levels of thyroid hormone than patients that do not have fibromyalgia.

C. The prevalence of fibromyalgia is higher than average among people that consume diets low in L-tryptophan.

D. The prevalence of fibromyalgia is lower than average among people who consume diets low in L-tryptophan.

22. Prescription C is a powerful anti-inflammatory medication often prescribed to patients recovering from serious injury. A study examined the incidence of fibromyalgia following serious injury and found that the likelihood of developing fibromyalgia was the same among patients treated with Prescription C and patients that were not treated with any anti-inflammatory medications. These study results *weaken* the viewpoint(s) provided by which student(s)?

F. Student 1 only

G. Students 1 and 2 only

H. Student 3 only

J. Students 2 and 3 only

GO ON TO THE NEXT PAGE.

Passage V

Sufficient nitrogen levels in soil are necessary for crops to grow. Often, fertilizers rich in ammonium (NH_4^+) are applied to fields to increase crop yields, and nitrogen-fixing bacteria convert the applied ammonium into nitrate (NO_3) in a process known as *nitrification*. Nitrate is susceptible to loss through leaching before crops are able to use it, so nitrogen inhibitors are often used to prevent the conversion of ammonium into nitrate. Three studies examined the rates of nitrification in several regions using different nitrogen inhibitors: N-1, N-2, and N-3.

Soil samples of 3 cubic meters were collected from five different biomes (grassland, desert, tropical forest, coniferous forest, and deciduous forest). The samples were immediately placed in a sealed container in a cooler kept at a constant 20°C before they were transported to the same greenhouse. Each sample was thoroughly mixed, tested for the ammonium levels, and then divided evenly into three 1-cubic-meter plots in the same greenhouse. The plots had a mesh bottom to allow for drainage of the soils. The plots were each irrigated once with 2 L of water and then maintained at 20°C with constant humidity for one week before the fertilizer and nitrogen inhibitors were applied.

Study 1

The following procedures were performed for one plot from each biome. A 50 g sample of crystallized N-1 was added to 5 L of liquid fertilizer and the mixture was stirred until there were no remaining solids suspended in the mixture. The mixture was then sprayed uniformly along the top of each soil plot. For the next 8 weeks, the plots were watered once weekly with 2 L of water and the greenhouse remained at 20°C with constant humidity. After 8 weeks, the soil was analyzed to determine the percentage of the applied ammonium that was converted to nitrate over the 8-week period. The results are shown in Figure 1.

Figure 1

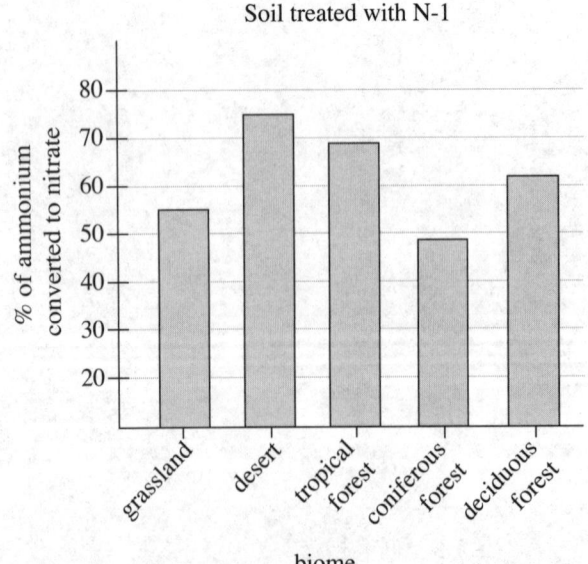

Soil treated with N-1

Study 2

Study 1 was repeated with a 50 g sample of crystallized N-2 substituted for the crystallized N-1 (see Figure 2).

Figure 2

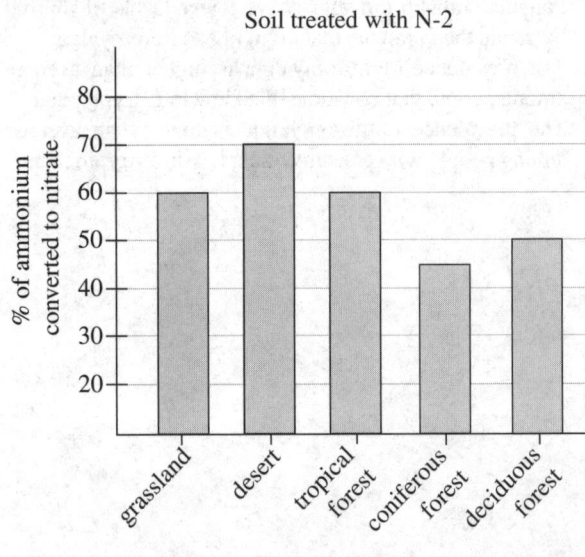

Soil treated with N-2

Study 3

Study 1 was repeated with a 50 g sample of crystallized N-3 substituted for the crystallized N-1 (see Figure 3).

Figure 3

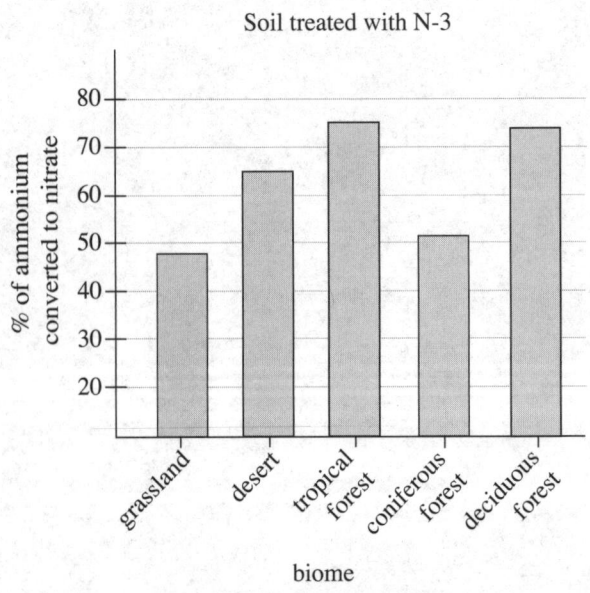

Soil treated with N-3

GO ON TO THE NEXT PAGE.

23. According to the results of the studies, the soil from which of the five biomes had the lowest percentage of ammonium converted to nitrate after treatment with N-1, N-2, and N-3, respectively?

 A. N-1: coniferous forest
    N-2: coniferous forest
    N-3: grassland

 B. N-1: coniferous forest
    N-2: deciduous forest
    N-3: grassland

 C. N-1: desert
    N-2: desert
    N-3: tropical forest

 D. N-1: tropical forest
    N-2: desert
    N-3: deciduous forest

24. According to the results of Study 2, the percent of ammonium converted to nitrate in the soils treated with N-2, averaged across all 5 biomes, was closest to which of the following?

 F. 40%
 G. 50%
 H. 60%
 J. 70%

25. Do the results of Studies 1 and 3 support the statement "A greater percentage of applied ammonium was converted to nitrate in the tropical forest soil treated with N-3 than the same soil treated with N-1"?

 A. No; 63% of the applied ammonium was converted to nitrate in N-1, whereas only 47% was converted to nitrate in N-3.

 B. No; 75% of the applied ammonium was converted to nitrate in N-1, whereas only 68% was converted to nitrate in N-3.

 C. Yes; 63% of the applied ammonium was converted to nitrate in N-3, whereas only 47% was converted to nitrate in N-1.

 D. Yes; 75% of the applied ammonium was converted to nitrate in N-3, whereas only 68% was converted to nitrate in N-1.

26. Which of the following correctly identifies the independent (experimental) variable across the three studies?

 F. Biome
 G. Concentration of ammonia
 H. Type of nitrogen inhibitor
 J. Concentration of nitrate

27. Is the mixture of N-1 and liquid fertilizer a solution when it is applied to the soil?

 A. Yes, because the N-1 dissolved in the liquid fertilizer.
 B. Yes, because the N-1 was suspended in the liquid fertilizer.
 C. No, because the N-1 dissolved in the liquid fertilizer.
 D. No, because the N-1 was suspended in the liquid fertilizer.

28. In soil, nitrogen-fixing bacteria are inactive in temperatures below 12°C. Which of the following steps was incorporated in the experimental design to ensure that the bacteria in all five soils were active?

 F. The soil samples were all gathered when the outside temperature was 20°C.
 G. The soil samples were tested for nitrate levels before the fertilizer was applied.
 H. The soil samples were transported and maintained at 20°C throughout the study.
 J. The soil samples were tested for ammonium levels before the fertilizer was applied.

GO ON TO THE NEXT PAGE.

Passage VI

Yeast cells exhibit *bipolar growth*: they grow in length from both tips in a straight-rod shape. However, the presence of an external electrical field can affect the growth patterns of yeast cells. Two researchers created a genetically modified strain of the fission yeast *Schizosaccharomyces pombe* (*S. pombe*). The genetically modified (GMO) strain was deficient in one of the proteins used to regulate the intracellular pH.

The researchers conducted two experiments to examine how an electric field affects the growth of both the non-GMO yeast cells (*S. pombe – N*) and the GMO yeast cells (*S. pombe – GM*).

Experiment 1

The researchers put a sugar-based agar into four square petri dishes (designated A, B, C, and D). Three *S. pombe* cells were placed into each of the dishes. The yeast placed in Dishes A and B were all *S. pombe – N* cells, and the yeast placed in Dishes C and D were all *S. pombe – GM*. A battery was used to generate a current through Dishes B and D. Figure 1 shows the growth of the cells in all four petri dishes and the direction of the electric fields (where present). The shaded portion of the cell represents the original shape of the cell when it was placed in the dish, while the dotted lines indicate the size and shape of the cell after 3 days at a constant temperature of 20°C. The nucleus is also shown for each cell.

Figure 1

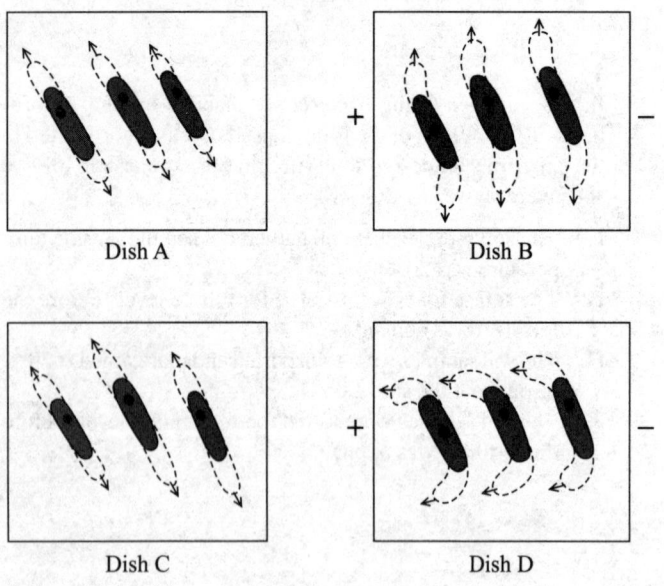

Dish A   Dish B

Dish C   Dish D

Experiment 2

A sugar-based agar was placed into four new petri dishes (designated W, X, Y, and Z). Three *S. pombe* cells were placed into each dish: *S. pombe – N* cells in Dishes W and X, and *S. pombe – GM* cells in Dishes Y and Z. A battery was used to generate a current through all four dishes. After 3 days at a constant temperature of 20°, the researchers measured the length, *L*, from tip to tip of each yeast cell along the axis parallel to the orientation of the cell body as shown for one particular yeast cell in Figure 2.

Figure 2

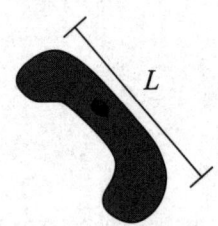

Dishes W and Y were moved to a room with a constant temperature of 15°C while Dishes X and Z were moved to a second room with a constant temperature of 30°C. The researchers measured each cell's length every 12 hours for the following three days. The results of the average cell lengths in each dish are shown in Figure 3.

Figure 3

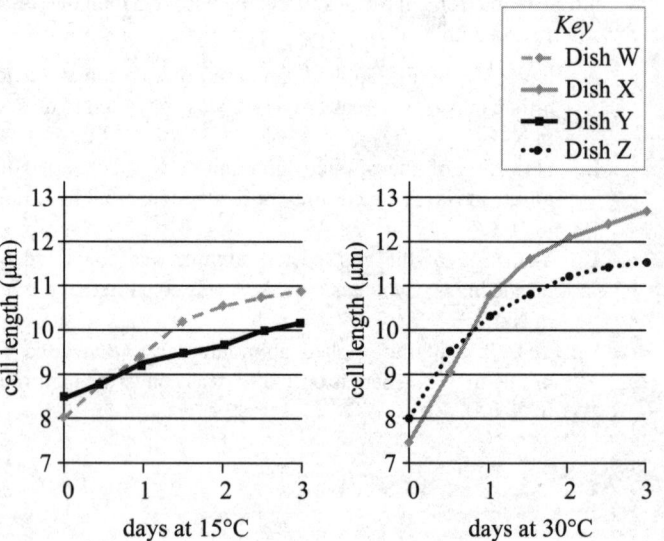

GO ON TO THE NEXT PAGE.

29. The cell shown in Figure 2 is oriented exactly how it appeared in its dish. Which of the following diagrams most likely represents the petri dish from which this cell is found?

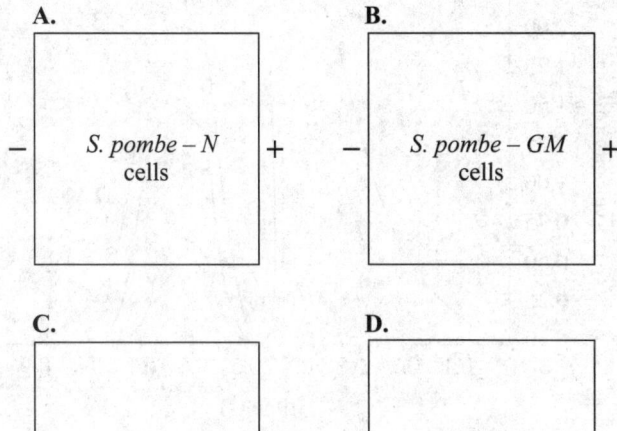

A.
− | S. pombe – N cells | +

B.
− | S. pombe – GM cells | +

C.
+ | S. pombe – N cells | −

D.
+ | S. pombe – GM cells | −

30. Before Dish X was moved to a higher temperature room, the cells in Dish X likely exhibited growth most similar to the cells in which of the dishes in Experiment 1?

F. Dish A
G. Dish B
H. Dish C
J. Dish D

31. The anode of the petri dishes in Experiment 2 is the positively charged electrode, and the cathode is the negatively charged electrode. Did the yeast cells in Dish Y likely grow toward the anode or toward the cathode?

A. Cathode; the *S. pombe – N* cells in Dish B grew toward the negatively charged electrode.
B. Cathode; the *S. pombe – GM* cells in Dish D grew toward the negatively charged electrode.
C. Anode; the *S. pombe – N* cells in Dish B grew toward the positively charged electrode.
D. Anode; the *S. pombe – GM* cells in Dish D grew toward the positively charged electrode.

32. Based on the information shown in Figure 1, is *S. pombe* a eukaryotic or prokaryotic cell?

F. Prokaryotic; each cell has a nucleus.
G. Prokaryotic; each cell does not have a nucleus.
H. Eukaryotic; each cell has a nucleus.
J. Eukaryotic; each cell does not have a nucleus.

33. In Experiment 2, how many times was the length of each cell measured?

A. 2
B. 3
C. 5
D. 7

34. If researchers wanted to examine the effects of different temperatures on the growth of *S. pombe – GM* cells, which two dishes should they compare?

F. Dish W and Dish X
G. Dish W and Dish Y
H. Dish Y and Dish X
J. Dish Y and Dish Z

GO ON TO THE NEXT PAGE.

Passage VI

An experiment is set up to look at the physics of bouncing a ball, as shown in Figure 1.

Figure 1

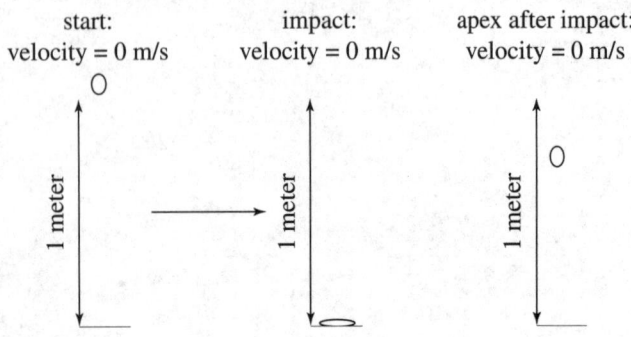

start:
velocity = 0 m/s

impact:
velocity = 0 m/s

apex after impact:
velocity = 0 m/s

When the ball is dropped, its initial velocity is 0 m/s. Velocity will increase until impact with the ground, at which point the ball's velocity immediately drops to 0 m/s again. After impact, velocity almost immediately increases to maximum post-impact velocity, and then begins to fall again as gravity works against it, slowing it down. The ball's velocity returns to 0 m/s when the ball is at its *apex*, or highest vertical point, post impact.

When a ball bounces, it deforms and becomes flatter. This is called *elasticity*. The more elasticity a material has, the better it is able to act like a spring and absorb force by being compressed, then use this force to "spring" back into the air. Post-impact velocity and the amount of time between velocity of 0 m/s at impact and velocity of 0 m/s at post-impact apex are affected by elasticity. Figure 2 shows the velocity of a ball versus time for balls with various elasticities and weights dropped from 1 meter height. Because gravity causes all objects to fall at the same speed regardless of weight, pre-impact velocities are identical for all balls.

Figure 2

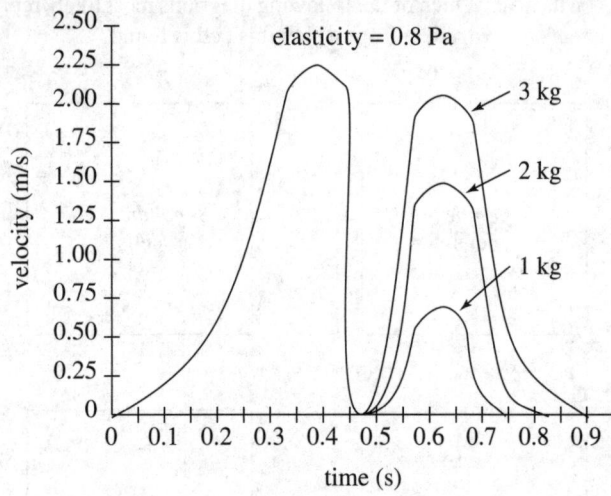

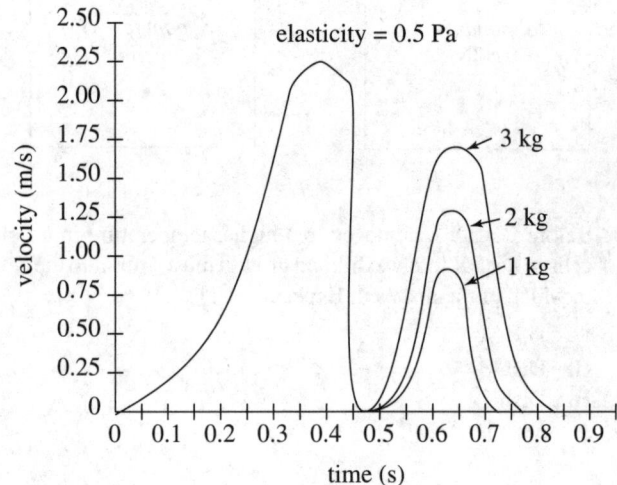

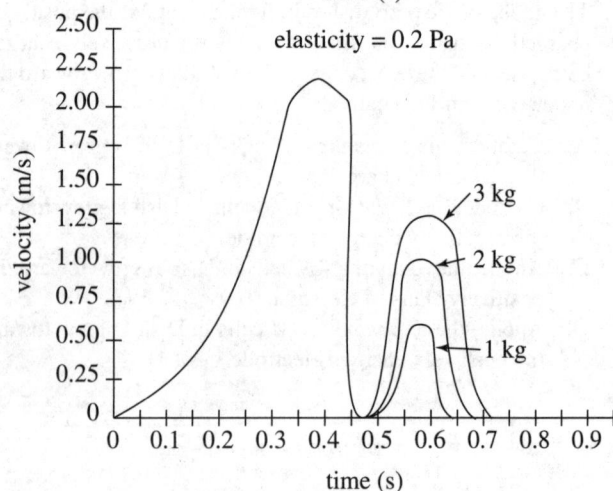

GO ON TO THE NEXT PAGE.

35. The ball with an elasticity of 0.8 Pa and a weight of 3 kg is dropped from a height of 1.5 meters. Based on the information in the passage and Figure 2, the maximum velocity of the ball after impact would be:

    A. less than 1.5 m/s.
    B. between 1.5 and 2 m/s.
    C. approximately equal to 2 m/s.
    D. greater than 2 m/s.

36. Based on the data in Figure 2, the maximum post-impact velocity of a ball will be smallest if the elasticity of the ball is:

    F. less than 0.5 Pa.
    G. between 0.5 and 1 Pa.
    H. between 1 and 1.5 Pa.
    J. greater than 1.5 Pa.

37. Based on the information in Figure 2, a ball being dropped from 1 meter height with an elasticity of 0.2 Pa and a weight of 0.5 kg would have a maximum post-impact velocity of:

    A. less than 0.50 m/s.
    B. 0.75 m/s.
    C. 1.0 m/s.
    D. greater than 1.25 m/s.

38. Consider a ball as it completes one bounce, from drop to post-impact apex. If this ball has a weight of 2 kg and an elasticity of 0.50 Pa, based on the data in Figure 2, how many times does the ball have a velocity of 1.00 m/s?

    F. One time
    G. Two times
    H. Three times
    J. Four times

39. Based on the data in Figure 2, how does the velocity of a ball change as it goes from drop to apex?

    A. Drop to impact: increases only
        Impact to apex: increases only
    B. Drop to impact: decreases only
        Impact to apex: increases then decreases
    C. Drop to impact: increases then decreases
        Impact to apex: increases then decreases
    D. Drop to impact: decreases then increases
        Impact to apex: increases only

40. A ball will deform permanently and not spring back off the ground if the velocity with which it hits the ground exceeds the ball's *elastic limit*. Based on the data in Figure 2, if a ball is dropped from one meter and has a weight of 3 kg, an elasticity of 0.8 Pa, and an elastic limit of 2.75 m/s, will the ball deform permanently?

    F. Yes, because the velocity with which the ball hits the ground is less than its elastic limit.
    G. Yes, because the velocity with which the ball hits the ground is greater than its elastic limit.
    H. No, because the velocity with which the ball hits the ground is less than its elastic limit.
    J. No, because the velocity with which the ball hits the ground is greater than its elastic limit.

END OF TEST 4
STOP! DO NOT RETURN TO ANY OTHER TEST.

DIRECTIONS

This is a test of your writing skills. You will have forty (40) minutes to write an essay. Before you begin planning and writing your essay, read the writing prompt carefully to understand exactly what you are being asked to do. Your essay will be evaluated on the evidence it provides of your ability to express judgments by taking a position on the issue in the writing prompt; to maintain a focus on the topic throughout your essay; to develop a position by using logical reasoning and by supporting your ideas; to organize ideas in a logical way; and to use language clearly and effectively according to the conventions of standard written English.

You may use the unlined pages in this test booklet to plan your essay. These pages will not be scored. *You must write your essay on the lined pages in the answer folder.* Your writing on those lined pages will be scored. You may not need all the lined pages, but to ensure you have enough room to finish, do NOT skip lines. You may write corrections or additions neatly between the lines of your essay, but do NOT write in the margins of the lined pages. *Illegible essays cannot be scored, so you must write (or print) clearly.*

If you finish before time is called, you may review your work. Lay your pencil down immediately when time is called.

DO NOT OPEN THIS BOOK UNTIL YOU ARE TOLD TO DO SO.

ACT Assessment Writing Test Prompt

Globalization

Improved travel and communication networks have the potential to transform the world population into a single, global society. We can now travel across the globe in a matter of hours. The internet enables us to spread ideas and share cultural norms instantly. Many of the products we use every day are produced on the other side of the world. Globalization can be seen as beneficial, but is generally thought of as a more complicated issue. Given the accelerating pace of globalization, what are the implications it could have for humanity?

Read and carefully consider these perspectives. Each suggests a particular way of thinking about the question above.

Perspective One	Perspective Two	Perspective Three
As the development of a single world culture becomes a real possibility, we risk losing the diversity that makes life interesting. As people become more similar, the unique elements that identify various cultures will be lost in a global melting pot.	The ability to cheaply ship goods across the planet makes necessities and luxuries more affordable to all. Increased product affordability leads to an increase in the quality of life for millions of people globally.	Globalization brings greater interaction between countries, which could lead to more conflict. The more we interact with other cultures, the more our differences and disagreements will be emphasized. It would be better for cultures to be more isolated from one another in order to exist harmoniously.

Essay Task

Write a unified, coherent essay in which you address the question of the implications of increased globalization. In your essay, be sure to:

- clearly state your own perspective and analyze the relationship between your perspective and at least one other perspective
- develop and support your ideas with reasoning and examples
- organize your ideas clearly and logically
- communicate your ideas effectively in standard written English

Your perspective may be in full agreement with any of those given, in partial agreement, or completely different.

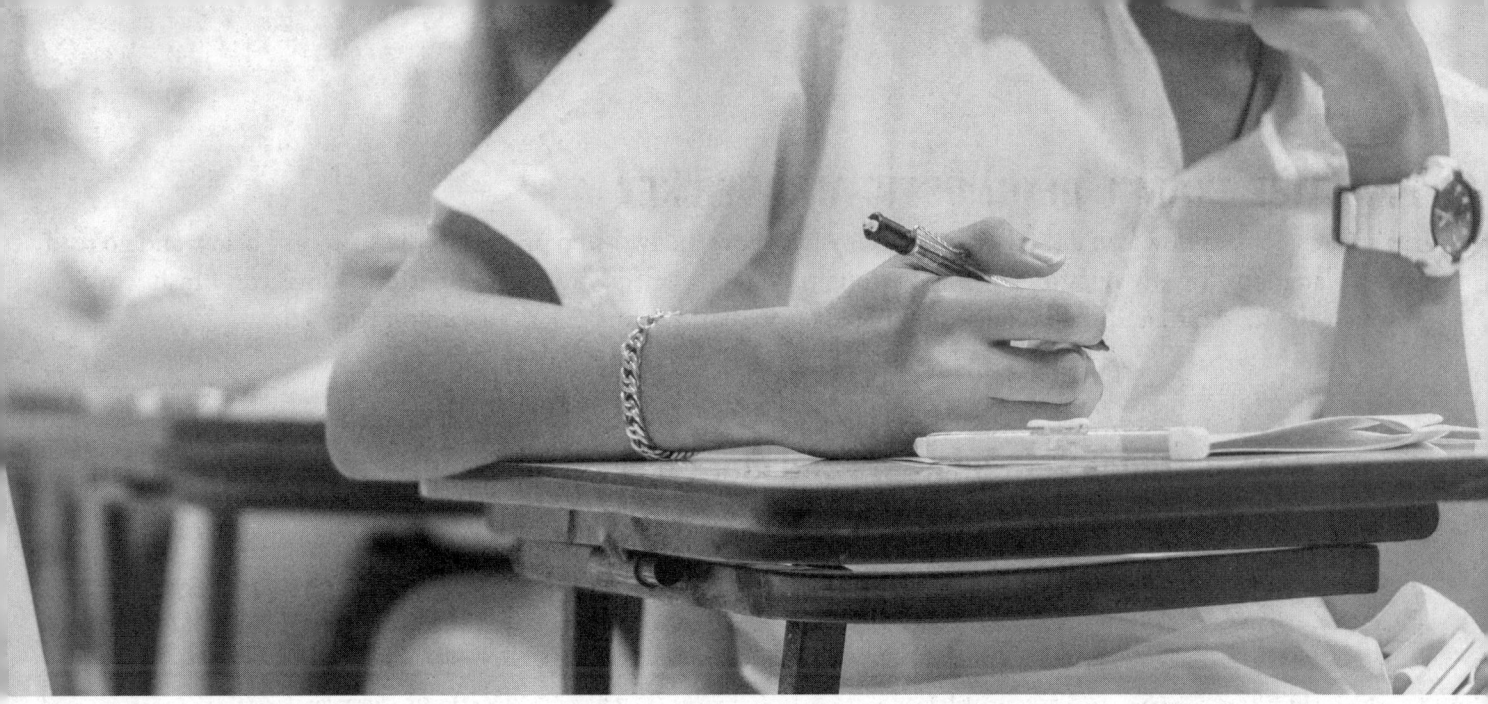

Chapter 3
Practice Exam 1: Diagnostic Answer Key and Explanations

*Note on scoring: please refer to the Scoring Conversion Worksheet and Score Conversion Chart on pages 76 and 77.

To grade your essay, see the Essay Checklist and an example of a top scoring essay online on your Student Tools.

PRACTICE EXAM 1: DIAGNOSTIC ANSWER KEY

Let's take a look at how you did on Practice Exam 1. Follow the two-step process in the scorecard below and go read the explanations for any questions you got wrong or you struggled with but got correct. Once you finish working through the scorecard and the explanations, move on to scoring your practice exam on page 76.

STEP 1 ≫ Check your answers and mark any correct answers with a ✔ in the appropriate column.

Q #	Ans.	✔	Chap. #	Section	Q #	Ans.	✔	Chap. #	Section
				English Test					
1*	D		8	Unnecessary Info	26	H		9	Precision
2*	G		7	*entire chapter	27	C		7*	*entire chapter
3*	C		8	STOP Punctuation	28	H		10	Vocabulary
4*	H		11	Purpose	29	C		10	Vocabulary
5*	D		9	Tense	30	G		11	Purpose
6*	J		8	Unnecessary Info	31	C		8	Unnecessary Info
7*	A		11	Transitions	32	J		10	Redundancy
8*	G		10	Redundancy	33	B		12	Order
9*	B		11	Purpose	34	J		8	GO Punctuation
10*	H		8	STOP Punctuation	35	B		12*	*entire chapter
11	A		9	Nouns	36	H		11	Transitions
12	J		11	Purpose	37	A		8	STOP Punctuation
13	D		8	Lists	38	H		12	*entire chapter
14	F		10	Vocabulary	39	C		9	Idioms
15	D		10	Redundancy	40	J		12	Grading the Passage
16	J		10	Vocabulary	41	C		10	Redundancy
17*	B		12	*entire chapter	42*	J		7	*entire chapter
18	J		10	Redundancy	43	A		10	Redundancy
19	C		12	Order	44	H		9	Subject-Verb Agreement
20	H		9	Tense	43*	B		12	*entire chapter
21	B		8	Unnecessary Info	46*	G		12	*entire chapter
22	F		9	Pronouns	47	A		11	Purpose
23	A		11	Transitions	48*	J		12	*entire chapter
24	H		8	GO Punctuation	49	D		9	Pronouns
25	D		8	GO Punctuation	50	G		12	Grading the Passage

Q #	Ans.	✔	Chap. #	Section	Q #	Ans.	✔	Chap. #	Section
				Math					
1	C		14	Absolute Value	24	H		16	Plane Geometry Formulas
2	G		15	Plugging In the Answers	25	A		15	Plugging In
3	B		17	Averages	26	J		17	Charts and Graphs
4	F		16	Overlapping Shapes	27	A		13	Word Problems
5	B		14	Quadratics	28	J		18	Graphing Inequalities on Number Lines
6	J		17	Percentages	29	A		18	Circles, Ellipses, and Parabolas
7	A		15	Plugging In the Answers	30	H		14	Scientific Notation
8*	H		18	Graphic Guesstimation	31*	B		19	The Law(s) of sine and cosine
9	C		18	Graphing in Two Dimensions	32	H		14	Real Numbers and Their Imaginary Friends
10	H		20	Matrices	33	C		16	Triangles
11	A		16	Triangles	34	H		16	Overlapping Shapes
12	G		16	Geometry BFFs: POE and Ballparking	35	D		14	Rational Numbers and Their Irrational Friends
13	C		18	The Slope Formula	36	G		14	Absolute Value
14	J		15	Plugging In the Answers	37	D		17	Averages
15	C		14	Roots	38	F		14	Exponents
16	J		14	Roots, Solutions, and x-intercepts	39	C		19	Advanced Trigonometry
17	C		14	Exponents	40*	G		18	The Slope-Intercept Form of a Line
18	H		13	Word Problems	41	A		19	SOHCAHTOA
19*	D		16	Similar Triangles	42	J		18	Circles, Ellipses, and Parabolas
20	G		15	Plugging In the Answers	43	D		18	Inequalities in the xy-plane
21	B		17	Ordering	44	J		15	Plugging In
22	G		16	Plane Geometry Formulas	45	A		17	Arithmetic and Geometric Sequences
23	D		17	Percentages					

Reading									
Q #	Ans.	✔	Chap. #	Section	Q #	Ans.	✔	Chap. #	Section
1*	C		22	Information	19	D		23	Analysis
2*	H		22	Information	20	G		22	Information
3*	B		22	Information	21	B		22	Information
4*	G		22	Information	22	J		22	Information
5*	D		22	Information	23	C		23	Vocabulary in Context
6*	G		23	Vocabulary in Context	24	H		22	Information
7*	C		22	Information	25	D		22	Information
8*	H		22	Information	26	F		22	Information
9*	A		22	Information	27	A		23	Vocabulary in Context
10	J		22	Rhetoric	28	H		22	Rhetoric
11	B		22	Information	29	D		22	Rhetoric
12	G		22	Rhetoric	30	F		22	Rhetoric
13	A		22	Information	31	C		22	Information
14	H		22	Information	32	J		22	Information
15	A		23	Analysis	33	B		22	Information
16	G		23	Analysis	34	F		23	Analysis
17	A		23	Analysis	35	D		22	Rhetoric
18	H		23	*Analysis*	36	G		23	*Vocabulary in Context*

Q #	Ans.	✔	Chap. #	Section	Q #	Ans.	✔	Chap. #	Section
\multicolumn{10}{Science}									
1	A		26	Tables	21	C		27	One Side at a Time
2	G		25	Trends on the Science Test	22	F		27	Compare and Contrast
3	D		26	Graphs	23	A		26	Graphs
4	F		25	Trends on the Science Test	24	H		26	Graphs
5	B		26	Graphs	25	D		26	Graphs
6	G		26	Graphs	26	H		25	How to Solve a Problem
7	B		26	Graphs	27	A		26	Outside Knowledge
8	G		26	Work the Answers	28	H		26	Read If and Only When You Need To
9	A		26	Read If and Only When You Need To	29	D		26	The 3-Step Approach and Later Passages
10	F		26	Graphs	30	G		26	Read If and Only When You Need To
11	B		25	Trends on the Science Test	31	D		26	Read If and Only When You Need To
12	J		26	Graphs	32	H		26	Outside Knowledge
13	B		26	Graphs	33	D		26	Read If and Only When You Need To
14	J		25	Trends on the Science Test	34	J		26	Read If and Only When You Need To
15	B		26	Graphs	35	D		26	Read If and Only When You Need To
16	G		26	Outside Knowledge	36	F		26	Graphs
17	C		27	Compare and Contrast	37	A		26	Graphs
18	H		27	Compare and Contrast	38	J		26	Graphs
19	B		27	One Side at a Time	39	C		26	Graphs
20	J		27	Compare and Contrast	40	H		26	Graphs

STEP 2 » To determine your score, follow the instructions below.

Step A

Determine the number of correct, scored questions in each section. On the Enhanced ACT, some "unscored" items are embedded in each section and will not count toward your score. For Test 1, these questions are marked with an asterisk on the previous chart, but here is a recap.

English questions 1 through 10
Math questions 8, 19, 31, 40
Reading questions 1 through 9
Science questions 6 through 11

Excluding any correct answers you got on the above unscored questions, count the number of remaining correct answers for each section and record the number in the space provided for your raw score on the Score Conversion Worksheet below.

Step B

Using the Score Conversion Chart on the next page, convert your raw scores on each section to scaled scores.

Score Conversion Worksheet		
Section	**Raw Score**	**Scaled Score**
English	_____ /40	_____
Math	_____ /41	_____
Reading	_____ /27	_____
Science	_____ /34	_____

The optional Science section is not part of the composite score, but if you take that section, your Science score will be reported separately.

To compute your ACT composite score, add the scaled scores for English, Math, and Reading, then divide the total by 3.

Sum of English, Math, and Reading: _____

Divided by 3: _____

This is your ACT composite score.

Step C

To grade your essay, see the Essay Checklist and an example of a top-scoring essay online on your Student Tools.

SCORING YOUR PRACTICE EXAM

SCORE CONVERSION CHART

Scaled Score	Raw Scores				Scaled Score
	Test 1 English	Test 2 Math	Test 3 Reading	Test 4 Science	
36	40	40-41	27	34	36
35	38-39	39	26	33	35
34	37	38	25	32	34
33	—	36-37	—	31	33
32	36	35	24	—	32
31	—	34	—	30	31
30	35	33	23	29	30
29	34	32	—	28	29
28	33	31	22	27	28
27	32	29-30	—	26	27
26	31	28	21	24-25	26
25	30	26-27	20	23	25
24	29	25	19	21-22	24
23	27-28	24	18	19-20	23
22	26	23	17	18	22
21	25	22	16	17	21
20	23-24	21	—	16	20
19	22	20	15	15	19
18	21	18-19	14	13-14	18
17	20	16-17	13	12	17
16	19	13-15	12	11	16
15	17-18	11-12	11	10	15
14	16	8-10	10	—	14
13	14-15	6-7	9	9	13
12	13	5	8	8	12
11	11-12	4	7	6-7	11
10	8-10	—	6	5	10
9	7	3	5	4	9
8	6	—	4	—	8
7	5	2	—	3	7
6	4	—	3	—	6
5	3	1	—	2	5
4	2	—	2	—	4
3	—	—	1	1	3
2	1	—	—	—	2
1	0	0	0	0	—

ACT TEST 1 ENGLISH ANSWERS AND EXPLANATIONS

1. **D** The question asks about grammar, so look at the answers to see what's changing. Punctuation is changing in the answer choices, so look to see whether any punctuation is needed. The phrase in the second part of the sentence, *left by the delivery man casually leaning against the front screen door,* is not an independent clause. A semicolon can only come between two independent clauses, so eliminate (A) and (C). The difference between (B) and (D) is the comma after *man*. The comma is necessary because the phrase *left by the delivery man* is unnecessary information that could be removed from the sentence without changing its main meaning. The phrase *casually leaning against the front door* logically refers to the *package* and not the *man*, so this phrase isn't part of the unnecessary information. Eliminate (B). The correct answer is (D).

2. **G** The question asks about grammar, so look at the answers to see what's changing. Commas and connecting words are changing in the answer choices, so consider whether each option produces a complete sentence. The phrase in the second part of the sentence, *my heart skipping a beat (or two),* is not an independent clause. A comma followed by *and* can only come between two independent clauses, so eliminate (F). Adding the word *and* or *when* does not produce a complete sentence, so eliminate (H) and (J). The correct answer is (G).

3. **C** The question asks about grammar, so look at the answers to see what's changing. Commas and connecting words are changing in the answer choices, so consider whether each option produces a complete sentence. The first part of the sentence, *My hands trembled as I opened the box,* is an independent clause. The second part of the sentence (after the transition), *I was thrilled to see that it did indeed contain the record I had been seeking for years,* is also an independent clause. Two independent clauses must be separated by some type of punctuation, so eliminate (D). Since the second part of the sentence already contains the pronoun *it* that refers to *the box,* it is not necessary to add *that* or *which;* eliminate (A) and (B). Choice (C) correctly links the two independent clauses with a comma followed by the coordinating conjunction *and.* The correct answer is (C).

4. **H** The question is asking for the answer that would *most effectively illustrate the difference between outsiders' perception of the record and its actual significance to the writer's family,* so eliminate any answers that don't fulfill this goal. Choice (F) contrasts *others* with *an outsider,* but it doesn't specifically refer to the *writer's family,* so eliminate (F). Choice (G) doesn't mention the record's *significance to the writer's family,* so eliminate (G). The way in which the record was stored is not relevant to the purpose stated in the question, so eliminate (J). Only (H) addresses the *significance* of the record *to the writer's family,* by calling it a *precious heirloom,* and uses the contrast word *however* to compare it to the information about *an outsider* in the preceding sentence. The correct answer is (H).

5. **D** The question asks about grammar, so look at the answers to see what's changing. Verbs are changing in the answer choices, so identify the subject: *Papa.* All four answers agree with this subject, so consider tense. The sentence is referring to something that happened before *he married my grandmother,* so past tense is needed. Eliminate (A) because it's in future tense. Eliminate (B) and (C) because the

text is referring to something that did happen, not something that *would have* happened. Choice (D) is in the correct tense to refer to something that happened before another past event (marrying the grandmother). The correct answer is (D).

6. **J**   The question asks about grammar, so look at the answers to see what's changing. Punctuation and connecting words are changing in the answer choices, so look for a complete sentence. The phrase in the second part of the sentence, *performing in music halls and local festivals,* is not an independent clause. Both periods and semicolons can only be used between two independent clauses, so eliminate (F) and (G). Adding *which* to the sentence makes it sound as if Papa "had performed the band" instead of the "band performing." Eliminate (H). The correct answer is (J).

7. **A**   The question is asking for a *logical* transition, so identify the relationships between the ideas. The first part of the sentence says that the record was all that remained, and the second part of the sentence says there had only been one surviving copy. These ideas agree, so eliminate (B) because it's an opposite-direction transition. Consider the remaining options. Eliminate (C) because this part of the sentence is reiterating the same point, not adding a new point. Eliminate (D) because this part of the sentence isn't an example of the first part. Choice (A) works because in fact serves to emphasize the point that was just made. The correct answer is (A).

8. **G**   The question is asking for the *least redundant* answer, so eliminate answers that are overly wordy or repeat information given earlier. Eliminate (F), (H), and (J) because "beg" and "plead" are synonyms and thus don't both need to be used. Keep (G) because it doesn't have any unnecessary words. The correct answer is (G).

9. **B**   The question is asking for the answer that suggests *the significance of his grandfather's cabin to the writer's upbringing,* so eliminate any answers that don't fulfill this goal. The location of the cabin is not relevant to its *significance* to the writer, so eliminate (A). Neither how well the writer *remembered* the cabin nor how many *generations* it had been in the family is relevant to *the writer's upbringing,* so eliminate (C) and (D). Choice (B) refers to the writer's *childhood,* which is consistent with the idea of *upbringing* in the question. The correct answer is (B).

10. **H**   The question asks about grammar, so look at the answers to see what's changing. Punctuation and connecting words are changing in the answer choices, so look for a complete sentence. The sentence as written contains two independent clauses: *It was a bittersweet reminder of the man I loved and missed* and *Papa's gentle voice on the record…assured me that he was still with me, both in spirit and in song.* Placing either a comma by itself or no punctuation at all between two independent clauses can't work, so eliminate (F) and (J). A coordinating conjunction such as *for* cannot connect two independent clauses unless there is a comma before it, so eliminate (G). Choice (H) correctly uses a period to separate the two independent clauses. The correct answer is (H).

11. **A**   The question asks about grammar, so look at the answers to see what's changing. Apostrophes and commas are changing in the answer choices, so consider whether there is a need for an apostrophe or a comma. A noun with an apostrophe shows possession; since nothing belongs to *lives,* no apostrophe

is needed. Eliminate (C) and (D). There is no reason to include a comma after *lives,* so eliminate (B). The correct answer is (A).

12. **J** The question is asking for the answer that indicates that *the narrator and his friends all shared a common background,* so eliminate any answers that don't fulfill this goal. Eliminate (F) because it discusses only the narrator, not the friends. Eliminate (G) and (H) because they discuss neither the narrator nor his friends. Choice (J) uses the word *our* to refer to the narrator and his friends, and it indicates that their hometowns *shared* something. The correct answer is (J).

13. **D** The question asks about grammar, so look at the answers to see what's changing. Punctuation is changing in the answer choices, so consider whether there is a need for any punctuation. A noun with an apostrophe shows possession; since nothing belongs to *owners,* no apostrophe is needed. Eliminate (C). The phrase *drink a cup of coffee, and figure out which new and exciting place we'd be driving to next* is not an independent clause. A semicolon can only come between two independent clauses, so eliminate (B). The phrase *chat with the restaurant's owners* is one item in a list of activities that the narrator and his friends would engage in. A comma is necessary to separate the items in the list of three or more items, so eliminate (A). The correct answer is (D).

14. **F** The question is asking for the *clearest and most precise* answer, so use Process of Elimination. Choice (F) seems to work, so keep it. Eliminate (G) because *among* is used for a group of several people or things, which isn't appropriate for the use of *the town* here. Eliminate (H) because *adjoining* means "connected to" and it isn't logical for one to drive "connected to the town." Eliminate (J) because it isn't correct to say that one would drive on top of a town. The correct answer is (F).

15. **D** The question is asking for the *least redundant* answer, so eliminate answers that are overly wordy or repeat information given earlier. Start with the shortest answer, (D); it doesn't have any errors, so keep it. Comparatively, (A) is overly wordy because something that is cherished is implied to be in one's heart. Eliminate (A). Choices (B) and (C) provide the same type of information as (D) but use more words, so eliminate them for being less concise. The correct answer is (D).

16. **J** The question is asking for the *clearest and most precise* answer, so use Process of Elimination. The answers contain transition words, so consider the relationship between the ideas. The first part of the sentence mentions *modern lives,* and the second part of the sentence says that *historical markers… remain.* These ideas contrast, so eliminate (F) because it's a same-direction transition. Eliminate (G) because it also doesn't imply a contrast. Choice (H) implies that the fact that people live modern lives is hypothetical, but this isn't consistent with the ideas in the sentence, so eliminate (H). Choice (J) offers a contrast, so it's consistent with the relationship between the two halves of the sentence. The correct answer is (J).

17. **B** The question is asking for the answer that *would best serve as a transition between the preceding sentence and the next sentence,* so identify the content of the two sentences. The preceding sentence mentions the inhabitants' *modern lives* as well as the *historical markers* that *remain throughout the city.* The next sentence refers to *Another remnant from Siena's rich history,* so the new sentence should introduce a

remnant from *history*. Although (A) refers to soccer's history in *England*, there is no evidence that it has any history in Siena, so eliminate (A). Choice (B) gives the specific examples of *Cobblestone streets and Gothic architecture,* which are historical remnants, and its mention of *modern* things ties back to the preceding sentence. Keep (B). Choice (C) reiterates the idea from the preceding sentence but doesn't connect to the following sentence's mention of *Another remnant*, so eliminate (C). Choice (D) indirectly mentions history but does not explicitly say that these works are from *Siena's rich history*. Eliminate (D). The correct answer is (B).

18. **J** The question is asking for the *least redundant* answer, so eliminate answers that are overly wordy or repeat information given earlier. Choice (F) is redundant because *biannual* means the same thing as *held twice a year*, so eliminate it. Choice (G) makes the same error, so eliminate it. Comparing the remaining options, (J) is more concise, so eliminate (H). The correct answer is (J).

19. **C** The question is asking for the *best placement* for the underlined portion, so try the phrase in each spot and eliminate any that don't offer a logical meaning. The underlined phrase is a descriptive phrase beginning with the word *each*, so it must come after something that there are multiple of. Eliminate (A) and (D) because there is only one plaza being discussed. The word *races* functions as a verb in the sentence, not as a noun, so the underlined portion cannot describe *races*. Eliminate (B). The underlined portion can be used to describe *laps* since it is a plural noun. In addition, it's logical that each lap of the race could contain two turns. The correct answer is (C).

20. **H** The question asks about grammar, so look at the answers to see what's changing. Verbs are changing in the answer choices, so identify the subject: *Il Palio*. All four answers agree with this subject, so consider tense. The entire paragraph is in present tense, containing verbs such as *is, races*, and *goes*. The underlined verb should also be in present tense. Eliminate (F) and (J) because they're in past tense. Eliminate (G) because it's in future tense. Choice (H) is in present tense. The correct answer is (H).

21. **B** The question asks about grammar, so look at the answers to see what's changing. Punctuation is changing in the answer choices, so consider whether any punctuation is needed. The main meaning of the sentence is *A contrada is the source of so much local patriotism that every important event is celebrated only within one's own contrada…*, and the phrase *from baptisms to food festivals* is unnecessary information that is separated from the rest of the sentence with a comma after the phrase. Because this phrase has a comma after, it also needs a comma before. Eliminate (A), (C), and (D). The correct answer is (B).

22. **F** The question asks about grammar, so look at the answers to see what's changing. Pronouns are changing in the answer choices, so identify who or what the pronoun refers to and use Process of Elimination. The pronoun is part of a phrase that refers back to *fellow members*. The members are not stated to be possessing anything here, so eliminate (G) and (H) because they use the possessive pronoun *whose*. In this case, the subject pronoun *who* is needed, rather than the object pronoun *whom*, since the pronoun is the subject of the verb *become* within the phrase. Eliminate (J). The correct answer is (F).

23. **A** The question is asking for a *logical* transition, so identify the relationships between the ideas. The preceding sentence identifies the high cost of 250,000 euros. This sentence says it's a small price to pay. These ideas contrast, so eliminate (B), (C), and (D) because they are all same-direction transitions. The correct answer is (A).

24. **H** The question asks about grammar, so look at the answers to see what's changing. Punctuation is changing in the answer choices, so consider whether any punctuation is needed. The sentence contains an independent clause (*Old men weep openly out of sheer joy*) followed by a comma and a coordinating conjunction. Thus, the part after *and* must also be an independent clause. The subject of this independent clause is *elated adults and children* and the verb is *parade*. While it could be correct to simply say that the people *parade* and end the sentence, the sentence after the period (*Throughout the city with their…banner…*) is not an independent clause, so it can't be its own sentence. Eliminate (F). A semicolon functions like a period, so eliminate (G). Thus, the sentence is saying that *elated adults and children parade throughout the city*. There is no reason to put a comma after *throughout*, so eliminate (J). The correct answer is (H).

25. **D** The question asks about grammar, so look at the answers to see what's changing. Punctuation is changing in the answer choices, so consider whether any punctuation is needed. The phrase at the end of the sentence, *not only to witness the exciting race but also to attend the after-parties…*, is not an independent clause. Both periods and semicolons can only be used between two independent clauses, so eliminate (A) and (B). Both options have a comma after *summer*, but there is no reason to put a second comma after *not*; eliminate (C). The correct answer is (D).

26. **H** The question is asking for the *clearest and most precise* answer, so use Process of Elimination. Choice (F), *it*, doesn't specify what Anderson was at *the forefront of*, so eliminate (F). Choices (G) and (J) also don't provide something specific, so eliminate them. Choice (H) offers something specific, and it's not redundant because the information has not been stated anywhere else in the sentence. The correct answer is (H).

27. **C** The question asks about grammar, so look at the answers to see what's changing. The form of the verb is changing in the answer choices, so identify what form is needed in order to produce a complete sentence. The subject of the sentence is *The book*, but there is no main verb to accompany this subject. Thus, the answer needs to be in "main verb" form in order to produce a complete sentence. Eliminate (A) because an *-ing* verb can't be the main verb in a sentence. Next, eliminate (B) because adding *which* creates a new clause, still leaving the main point of the sentence without a main verb. Comparing (C) and (D), they are both main verbs, but their meanings differ. In (C), the book *helped* with a literary movement. In (D), the book *was helped* with a movement. Choice (C) is more logical, as the paragraph is discussing the impact of the book itself within the literary community. Eliminate (D). The correct answer is (C).

28. **H** The question is asking for the *clearest and most precise* answer, so use Process of Elimination. The word *until* in this context doesn't provide a clear meaning, so eliminate (F). The phrase "take a… step at" is not correct, so eliminate (G). Choice (H) says "take a…step toward," which does provide

a clear meaning, so keep (H). With (J), the final part of the sentence, *creating a type of literature…,* would become a phrase describing Anderson taking *a real step.* If this were the case, there would need to be a comma between *step* and *creating,* so eliminate (J). The correct answer is (H).

29. **C** The question is asking for the *clearest and most precise* answer, so use Process of Elimination. Choice (A) could be supported, so keep it for now. Eliminate (B) because no other context supports the idea of Anderson forbidding anyone to do anything, and the rest of the passage is referring to how Anderson's work influenced other people to follow the movement his book was part of. Keep (C) because it's consistent with the idea of Anderson's influence on others. Eliminate (D) because, compared to (C), it's more logical that his book inspired other writers than that it somehow *approached* them. Likewise, eliminate (A) because the context can support that Anderson's book *inspired* other writers but doesn't go so far as to suggest he somehow *forced* them to do something. The correct answer is (C).

30. **G** The question is asking for the answer that would *complete the contrast set up earlier in the sentence,* so identify the contrast and eliminate any answers that don't fulfill this goal. The earlier part of the sentence says that Anderson's ideas *can be relevant to everyday people as much as they can to* some other group. Thus, the answer should contrast with *everyday people.* Eliminate (F) because this is a synonym for *everyday people* and thus not a contrast. Keep (G) because *academics* are people who might be more likely to find *deeply intellectual concerns* relevant, in contrast to *everyday people,* who might not expect such *concerns* to be relevant to them. Eliminate (H) and (J) because they are also synonyms for *everyday people.* The correct answer is (G).

31. **C** The question asks about grammar, so look at the answers to see what's changing. Punctuation before and after *according* is changing in the answer choices, so determine whether any punctuation is needed. The main meaning of the sentence is *…his civil rights activism was equally important and overlooked.* The phrase *according to his widow Rachel Robinson* is an unnecessary phrase with a comma after it, so it needs another comma before it. Eliminate (A) and (D) because they each lack a comma before the phrase. Choice (B) puts a second comma after *according,* but there is no reason to put a comma in this spot. Eliminate (B). The correct answer is (C).

32. **J** The question is asking for the *least redundant* answer, so eliminate answers that are overly wordy or repeat information given earlier. The sentence says *often overlooked,* so *without being noticed* is redundant. Eliminate (F). Choices (G) and (H) are also redundant with *often overlooked,* so eliminate them. No additional phrase is needed here, so the correct answer is (J).

33. **B** The question is asking for the *best placement* for the underlined portion, so try the phrase in each spot and eliminate any that don't offer a logical meaning. Choice (A) doesn't provide a clear meaning, so eliminate it. Keep (B) because *played baseball for the Brooklyn Dodgers* does provide a clear meaning. Eliminate (C) because the focus *on civil rights* is not *for the Brooklyn Dodgers.* Eliminate (D) because, although it's possible Robinson's focus was on rights for the team members, there is no other information in the passage to suggest this. It's more logical to say that he *played baseball* for this team. The correct answer is (B).

34. **J** The question asks about grammar, so look at the answers to see what's changing. Punctuation is changing in the answer choices, so look for independent clauses. The first part of the sentence, *From the outset of the "Great Experiment" of having African-Americans in baseball*, is not an independent clause. Eliminate (F), (G), and (H) because all of the types of punctuation in these answer choices can only connect two independent clauses. The correct answer is (J).

35. **B** The question is asking what *would be lost* if the paragraph were deleted, so consider the main idea of the paragraph. The paragraph is about Robinson's *focus on civil rights* and how his *performance on the field* made him a *highly respected figure*. Eliminate (A) because this paragraph merely mentions the *"Great Experiment"* and doesn't offer any *scientific explanation*. Keep (B) because it's consistent with the focus of the paragraph. Eliminate (C) because, while Robinson was *passionate* about ending prejudice, the author is not offering a *plea* to the audience. Eliminate (D) because the paragraph doesn't state that the Dodgers were the *best team*. The correct answer is (B).

36. **H** The question is asking for a *logical* transition, so identify the relationships between the ideas. The first part of the sentence says that an ordinary man would have wilted, and the second part of the sentence states that Robinson increased his efforts, so he didn't wilt. These ideas disagree, so eliminate (F), (G), and (J), which are all same-direction transitions. The correct answer is (H).

37. **A** The question asks about grammar, so look at the answers to see what's changing. Punctuation is changing in the answer choices, so look for independent clauses. The first part of the sentence, *Post-baseball, Robinson became an entrepreneur*, is an independent clause. The second part of the sentence, *his focus did not stray as he found time to write…letters and telegrams…*, is also an independent clause. Keep (A) because a comma with a coordinating conjunction such as *but* can connect two independent clauses. Eliminate (B) and (C) because neither a comma by itself nor a lack of punctuation can connect two independent clauses. Choice (D) contains a semicolon, which can connect two independent clauses, but adding *and* to the second half of the sentence would make that part of the sentence not an independent clause, and therefore the semicolon wouldn't work. Eliminate (D). The correct answer is (A).

38. **H** The question is asking where the paragraph should be divided *in order to differentiate between Robinson's civil rights activism during and after his baseball career*. Look at the paragraph to identify where it shifts from one topic to the other. The first three sentences discuss what Robinson did as an athlete. Sentence 4 begins with *Post-baseball*, so this sentence shifts into the second topic stated in the question. Thus, the new paragraph should begin with Sentence 4. The correct answer is (H).

39. **C** The question asks about grammar, so look at the answers to see what's changing. The wording is changing, so identify what word or phrase is most acceptable in the context of the sentence. The sentence says *than his tireless efforts*, so the underlined portion needs to be a comparative word or phrase. Eliminate (A) and (B) because *most widely* and *very widely* do not work with *than*. Keep (C) because *more widely…than* is a correct phrasing. Eliminate (D) because *widelier* is not a real word. The correct answer is (C).

40. **J** The question is asking whether the writer accomplished the goal of describing *the path Jackie Robinson took to become a professional baseball player*, so consider the overall focus of the essay. The essay begins with Robinson's significance and efforts as a baseball player, and it never discusses Robinson's life prior to playing baseball. Therefore, it does not fulfill the stated goal. Eliminate (F) and (G). Next, eliminate (H) because the essay states that Robinson is known for his *baseball career* and that his civil rights focus is *overlooked*, so the statement in (H) is not true. Choice (J) accurately summarizes the focus of the essay. The correct answer is (J).

41. **C** The question is asking for the *least redundant* answer, so eliminate answers that are overly wordy or repeat information given earlier. Choice (A) is redundant because "retract" and "diminish" both mean "to decrease." Eliminate (A). Choice (B) makes the same error, so eliminate it. Keep (C) because it uses only one of the two words. Eliminate (D) because *to a reduced level* is redundant with *retracted*. The correct answer is (C).

42. **J** The question asks about grammar, so look at the answers to see what's changing. Words connecting parts of the sentence are changing in the answer choices, so eliminate any option that doesn't produce a complete sentence. The subject of the phrase beginning with *that* is *participation in the war*. The rest of the sentence needs to state what *participation in the war* did: it *required the use of all national resources*. Thus, *but*, *and*, and *although it* should all not be used here because they make an incomplete sentence. The correct answer is (J).

43. **A** The question is asking for the *least redundant* answer, so eliminate answers that are overly wordy or repeat information given earlier. Keep (A) because it is the shortest option. Choices (B), (C), and (D) offer *factories* and *shipyards* as examples of workplaces, but the previous sentence already states that these are places women worked. Thus, the additional information isn't needed. Eliminate (B), (C), and (D). The correct answer is (A).

44. **H** The question asks about grammar, so look at the answers to see what's changing. Verbs are changing in the answer choices, so identify the subject: *presence*. This word is singular, so eliminate (F), (G), and (J), which are all plural. Only (H) is singular. The correct answer is (H).

45. **B** The question is asking whether a new statement should be added. Consider the content of the new sentence and that of the surrounding text. The new sentence is about *marriage rate* and *rate of babies born*. The sentences before and after are about *women in wartime workforces* and the different places they worked. Thus, the new sentence is not consistent with the rest of the paragraph and shouldn't be added. Eliminate (C) and (D). Next, eliminate (A) because the new sentence is not inconsistent with the *style and tone* of the passage. Keep (B) because it accurately states the focus of the paragraph and the essay as a whole. The correct answer is (B).

46. **G** The question is asking which option *provides the most logical transition to the information presented in the rest of the essay*, so read the rest of the essay to determine its focus. That next sentence mentions a *solution* to the lack of men playing baseball, and the last paragraph is all about the *All-American Girls Professional Baseball League*, so the correct answer should relate to these ideas. Eliminate (F) because

daycare isn't relevant. Keep (G) because *baseball* is the topic of the rest of the passage. Eliminate (H) and (J) because, while they may be true, they don't fulfill the goal of transitioning to the rest of the essay. The correct answer is (G).

47.   **A**   The question is asking which option *most effectively aids the writer's purpose of helping readers visualize the appearance of the players in the photographs*, so eliminate any answer that doesn't fulfill this goal. Keep (A) because the players' *smiles* and *baseball mitts in their hands* offer a visual of what the photographs look like. Eliminate (B) because the location of the photo clearly doesn't help one visualize the *players*. Eliminate (C) and (D) because they don't offer information on the *appearance* of the players. The correct answer is (A).

48.   **J**   The question is asking what the paragraph would *lose* if certain words were deleted, so try reading the sentence with and without the words to see what the difference is. Without these descriptions, the sentence would describe the players as wearing *shorts* and *knee-high socks*, which would be normal attire for athletes. The descriptive words highlight a difference in what the female players wore compared to what might be typical in a male sport. Eliminate (F) because these details have not *already been presented* in the previous sentence. Eliminate (G) because the paragraph isn't focused on the players' *athletic talent*. Eliminate (H) because the text doesn't mention any *captions*. Keep (J) because these descriptions do emphasize the players' feminine appearance. The correct answer is (J).

49.   **D**   The question asks about grammar, so look at the answers to see what's changing. Pronouns are changing in the answer choices, so identify the word the pronoun refers back to: *the All-American Girls Professional Baseball League*. This *League* is singular, so eliminate (C), which is plural. Next, consider spelling. Choice (A), *its'*, is not a word, so eliminate (A). Choice (B), *it's*, means "it is," which is not correct in this context. Eliminate (B). Choice (D) is the possessive form of "it," which is appropriate here because the sentence refers to the *success* of the league. The correct answer is (D).

50.   **G**   The question is asking whether the writer accomplished the goal of illustrating *the range of nontraditional activities women pursued during wartime*, so consider the overall focus of the essay. The essay mentions a number of *employment opportunities for women* in World War II, including *factories*, *shipyards*, *government jobs*, *farm labor*, and *baseball*. Thus, the essay does fulfill this goal. Eliminate (H) and (J). Next, eliminate (F) because this answer doesn't relate to the *range of nontraditional activities*. Keep (G) because it is consistent with the goal stated in the question and with the essay's focus. The correct answer is (G).

ACT TEST 1 MATH ANSWERS AND EXPLANATIONS

1. **C** The question asks for the difference between two absolute value expressions. Treat absolute value bars like parentheses and evaluate what's inside the absolute value bars first: $|8 - 5| - |5 - 8| = |3| - |-3| = 3 - 3 = 0$. Remember that absolute value is a measure of distance, so the result is always nonnegative. The correct answer is (C).

2. **G** The question asks for the number of hours of tutoring that come with a session costing $220. First, subtract the flat fee from the total cost to determine how much the tutor charged exclusively for tutoring: $220 – $40 = $180. Divide this amount by the cost per hour, $60, to get $180 ÷ $60 = 3 hours of tutoring. Choice (F) incorrectly uses $40 + $60 = $100 as the hourly rate. Choice (H) divides $220 by $60 without subtracting the flat fee. Choice (J) calculates the session with a $60 flat fee and $40 hourly rate. The correct answer is (G).

3. **B** The question asks for a comparison between the times it takes the two trains to travel 1,152 miles. The time it takes Train A can be found by dividing the number of miles it goes by the speed, $\frac{1,152}{16} = 72$. Follow the same steps for Train B to find that it takes $\frac{1,152}{24} = 48$ hours. To find out how many more hours it takes Train A to travel than Train B, subtract the two values: $72 - 48 = 24$ hours. Choice (A) is the result of averaging the miles per hour values, and (C) is the result of adding them. Choice (D) is the time Train B takes, not the difference. The correct answer is (B).

4. **F** The question asks for the perimeter of the figure. Use the information given about the triangles to get the sides of the hexagon. Since the triangles are equilateral and each one's perimeter is 15, each side is 5. Figure *ABCDEF* has six sides, so its perimeter is 6(5) = 30. Choice (H) finds the area of the figure rather than its perimeter. Choice (J) treats the sides of each triangle, rather than the perimeter of each triangle, as 15. Choice (G) includes the dotted interior lines in calculating the perimeter. The correct answer is (F).

5. **B** The question asks for the expression that is equivalent to the given one. Because there are two binomials being multiplied in the question, use the FOIL method (First, Outer, Inner, Last). Multiply and combine like terms to get $(5x + 2)(x - 3) = 5x^2 - 15x + 2x - 6 = 5x^2 - 13x - 6$. The correct answer is (B).

6. **J** The question asks for the value of 20% of the given number. Use the words in the problem to create an equation: *percent* means "divide by 100," *of* means "multiply," *is* means "equals," and *what* means "use a variable." The first equation is $\frac{35}{100}x = 14$ and $x = 40$. The second equation is $y = \frac{20}{100}(40) = 8$. Choice (F) is 20% of 14. Choice (G) is 35% of 14. Choice (H) is (20% + 35%) of 14. The correct answer is (J).

7. **A** The question asks for the value of x in the given situation. The list of integers adds up to $7x + 7$. This sum is equal to 511, so $7x + 7 = 511$. Subtract 7 from both sides to get $7x = 504$; then divide both sides by 7 to get $x = 72$. Choice (B) divides 511 by 7 without first subtracting 7, and (C) mistakenly adds 7 to the sum. Choice (D) is an incorrect estimate. The correct answer is (A).

8. **H** The question asks for the coordinates of point C. A sketch can help with ballparking the point's location. Draw the coordinate plane, and then plot and label the points given. Point B is the midpoint of $\overline{AC}$, so point C must be near $x = 0$ and above $y = 6$. The only choice near $(0,6)$ is (H). To check if this produces the correct midpoint, use the midpoint formula, $\left(\dfrac{x_1 + x_2}{2}, \dfrac{y_1 + y_2}{2} \right)$. This becomes $\left(\dfrac{1+9}{2}, \dfrac{8+4}{2} \right) = (5,6)$, which is the correct midpoint. Choice (F) incorrectly takes C as the midpoint. The other answers do not use the midpoint formula correctly. The correct answer is (H).

9. **C** The question asks for the coordinates of a possible vertex C. Because the trapezoid is isosceles, its two vertical halves are mirror images of each other. To get from A to B requires adding 3 to the x-value and 6 to the y-value of A, so to get from D to C, instead subtract 3 from the x-value and add 6 to the y-value of D. The correct answer is (C).

10. **H** The question asks for the combined peak and off-peak sales for the three bus stations in Asheville. To find the total average sales at each bus station, multiply the values of each column of the first matrix by the relevant row in the second matrix. This becomes $180(3) + 200(3) + 150(3) + 60(2) + 120(2) + 70(2) = 2{,}090$. Choice (F) finds the number of tickets sold, and (G) multiplies that total by \$2.50, the average of the two fare rates. Choice (J) finds the total if all of the fares were bought at the peak \$3 price. The correct answer is (H).

11. **A** The question asks for the sum of the measurements of the angles labeled a, b, and c. These angles are opposite the interior angles of the triangle, so use the fact that there are $180°$ in a line. Since $a° + 35° = 180°$, $a = 145$. Since $b° + 45° = 180°$, $b = 135$. To find the measure of c, get the third angle of the triangle. There are $180°$ in a triangle, so the third angle is $180° - 35° - 45° = 100°$. Therefore, $c = 180° - 100°$, which equals 80, and the sum of a, b, and c is $145 + 135 + 80 = 360°$. The correct answer is (A).

12. **G** The question asks for the ratio of part of the figure to the area of the entire rectangle. Because E and F are both midpoints, draw a line between them and divide the rectangle into 4 equal parts. Quadrilateral $AECF$ contains 2 of these 4 parts, and this ratio can be reduced to 1:2. Choice (J) shows the ratio using $\triangle ABE$ instead of quadrilateral $AECF$, while (F) shows the ratio of the quadrilateral to the other half of the rectangle. Choice (H) assumes the 3 parts in the original diagram are equal. The correct answer is (G).

13. **C** The question asks for the slope of a line parallel to the given line. Parallel lines have the same slope. In the slope-intercept form, $y = mx + b$, the slope of the line is $m = \frac{1}{2}$. Choice (A) is the slope of the line perpendicular to the given line. Choices (B) and (D) are the opposite and reciprocal, respectively, of the correct slope. The correct answer is (C).

14. **J** The question asks for the length of time, in minutes, that the longer sitting lasted. Try using the answer choices, starting with (G) to help eliminate answers if it is too big or too small. If the longer sitting was 45 minutes, the shorter one was 120 – 45 = 75 minutes. This doesn't make any sense, so eliminate (F) and (G). A much longer time is needed, so try (J). If the longer sitting was 75 minutes, the shorter one was 120 – 75 = 45 minutes. The ratio of 45:75 can be reduced by a factor of 15 to 3:5. This matches the question. Choice (F) is the shorter sitting time, and (G) is the factor by which the ratio can be reduced. Choice (H) would result in two equal sitting times of 60 minutes each. The correct answer is (J).

15. **C** The question asks for a possible value of x in the given inequality. Use a calculator to find the exact values of the square roots given in the answers, starting with the middle choice. In (C), $\sqrt{140} \approx 11.83$. This satisfies the inequality in the question. Choice (B) is 11 exactly; the question asks for something greater. Choice (A) adds the numbers from the problem and takes the square root without answering what is asked for, and (D) = 23, the sum of the numbers in the problem. The correct answer is (C).

16. **J** The question asks for the solutions for x in the given equation. First, bring the 12 to the left side of the equation, so the whole equation is equal to 0 (i.e., $x^2 + 4x - 12 = 0$). Factor the equation by thinking of what two numbers when multiplied together = –12 and when added together = 4: 6 and –2 satisfy those conditions. Make the equation $(x + 6)(x - 2) = 0$, and then set $(x + 6) = 0$ and $(x - 2) = 0$ and solve for x in both cases. x is either –6 or 2. Another approach would be to try the numbers from the answer choices and see which ones satisfy the equation. The correct answer is (J).

17. **C** The question asks for the expression that is equivalent to the given one. When dividing variables with exponents, subtract the exponents of common terms. To visualize what's happening, write out the expression as $\frac{x \cdot x \cdot x \cdot x \cdot y \cdot y}{x \cdot x \cdot y \cdot y \cdot y \cdot y}$. Cancel like terms in the numerator and denominator to get $\frac{x \cdot x}{y \cdot y}$, or $\frac{x^2}{y^2}$. Choice (A) negates the value of the entire expression, and (D) flips the numerator and denominator. Choice (B) incorrectly assumes $x^2 = y^2$. The correct answer is (C).

18. **H** The question asks for the expression that best represents the given situation. Translate the information in the question into an algebraic expression. The fixed cost each day of the company is $1,600 and the variable cost is the additional cost each day of producing each box. The equation then would be the fixed cost plus the variable cost, which is $1,600 + 4.75b$, or (H). Choices (F) and (J) switch the fixed and variable costs. Choice (G) is the difference between the variable costs and the fixed cost instead of adding them to form the total cost. The correct answer is (H).

19. **D** The question asks for the length of $\overline{AC}$, the base of the larger of two similar triangles. The sides of similar triangles are proportional in length. To find how many times larger the larger triangle's perimeter is than the smaller triangle's perimeter (which is 2.4 + 4 + 3.2 = 9.6), divide the two known perimeters to get $\frac{576"}{9.6"}$ = 60 times larger. $\overline{AC}$ will also be 60 times larger than $\overline{XZ}$, so $\overline{AC}$ = 3.2" × 60 = 192". The correct answer is (D).

20. **G** The question asks for the value of x in the given equation. Multiply the fractions on the left so that $\frac{6\sqrt{11}}{x\sqrt{11}} = \frac{3\sqrt{11}}{11}$. Cross-multiply to get $66\sqrt{11} = 33x$, which simplifies to $x = 2\sqrt{11}$. Another approach would be to substitute the answer choices in for x to see which works in the equation. Choice (F) is half the value needed, and (H) is its square. Choice (J) is 11^2. The correct answer is (G).

21. **B** The question asks for the number of different kinds of sundaes that Steve could order. For each of the 3 possible ice cream flavors, there are 2 possible types of syrup, so multiply 3 × 2. For each of those 6 possible orders, there are 6 possible kinds of candy toppings, so multiply 6 × 6 = 36 total possibilities. The correct answer is (B).

22. **G** The question asks for the volume of the box. The formula for the volume of a rectangular solid is $V = lwh$, so find those dimensions. The width of the box is half its length, so if its length is 12 cm, its width is 6 cm. The width is also twice the box's height, so the height is 3 cm. To find the volume, multiply all three dimensions to get V = 12(6)(3) = 216. Choice (H) incorrectly calculates the sides as 6, 12, and 24, and (J) incorrectly calculates the sides as 12, 24, and 48. Choice (F) neglects to multiply by the depth. The correct answer is (G).

23. **D** The question asks for the total value of Daniel's credit card debt. Based on the question, B = \$2,155, r = 13 percent, or 0.13, and m = 2. Substitute these values into the equation to get $D = 2,155(1 + 0.13) + 10(2)^2$. This becomes D = 2,155(1.13) + 40 = 2,435.15 + 40 = \$2,475.15. Choice (A) forgets to calculate the interest rate. Choice (B) forgets to add the 10(2)^2, while (C) adds only 20. The correct answer is (D).

24. **H** The question asks for the total surface area of the cone. The equation for surface area is given as the expression $\pi r^2 + \pi rs$, where r is the radius and s is the slant height. The radius in the figure is half of the diameter, which is given as 30, so r = 15. The slant height is 30. Plug these values into the equation to get $(15)^2\pi + (15)(30)\pi$, which equals $225\pi + 450\pi = 675\pi$. Choice (G) is the result of forgetting to square the radius. Choice (J) uses the diameter instead of the radius in the equation. Choice (F) results from evaluating only half of the expression. The correct answer is (H).

25. **A** The question asks for the value of $f(g(a))$ for the given functions f and g. To solve a composite function, work inside out starting with the value of $g(a)$, and then take the function f of $g(a)$. $g(a)$ is given as $2a^2 + 1$, so $f(g(a)) = f(2a^2 + 1)$. Substitute $2a^2 + 1$ for a in the $f(a)$ equation to get

$f(2a^2 + 1) = 3(2a^2 + 1) - 4$. Distribute the 3 within the parentheses to get $6a^2 + 3 - 4$, which simplifies to $6a^2 - 1$. The correct answer is (A).

26. **J** The question asks for the average star-rating given to the movie based on the table. The average of a list of numbers is the total divided by the number of things, which in this case is the total number of stars divided by the number of students surveyed. This becomes $\dfrac{1(51) + 2(18) + 3(82) + 4(49) + 5(62)}{262} \approx 3.20$. If time is running low at this point in the test, cross out answer choices that are too large or too small to be the average and take a reasonable guess. Choice (F) is less than the lowest star rating, so it cannot be correct. Choices (G) and (H) each drop one of the components of the numerator when calculating. The correct answer is (J).

27. **A** The question asks for the simplified inequality that is equivalent to the given one. To do this, isolate x by first subtracting $6x$ from both sides of the inequality to get $-8 > 2x + 14$. Subtract 14 from both sides to get $-22 > 2x$, and then divide both sides by 2. The inequality becomes $-11 > x$ or $x < -11$. The correct answer is (A).

28. **J** The question asks for the coordinates of point A after the circle is rotated. Since the circle is rotated counterclockwise, the point should be in Quadrant IV with a positive x-value and negative y-value, eliminating (F). With a 90° rotation, the line formed by the new point A and center L will be perpendicular to the existing $\overline{AL}$. Find the slope of $\overline{AL}$ by counting the rise over the run from A to $L = \dfrac{6}{-8}$. The perpendicular slope will be the negative reciprocal $\dfrac{8}{6}$, so move 8 units down and 6 units left from the center of the circle: $(10 - 6, -2 - 8) = (4, -10)$. The correct answer is (J).

29. **A** The question asks for the cosine of the angle labeled as θ on the triangle. According to SOHCAHTOA, $\cos\theta = \dfrac{adjacent}{hypotenuse}$. For angle θ, the *adjacent* is not given, but the *hypotenuse* is 16. Since the denominator of the cosine proportion is the *hypotenuse,* and must be 16, eliminate (B) and (D). Of the two remaining answers, (A) is more likely to be correct because it does not use the *opposite* side of 12. To find the actual length of the side *adjacent* to θ, use the Pythagorean Theorem ($a^2 + b^2 = c^2$) to see that it is $\sqrt{112}$. The correct answer is (A).

30. **H** The question asks for the volume of the container based on the number of molecules inside. To find the volume of the container, set up the equation $\dfrac{6 \times 10^8 \text{ molecules}}{x \text{ cubic inches}} = \dfrac{3 \times 10^4 \text{ molecules}}{\text{cubic inch}}$. Multiply both sides by x, and then divide both sides by 3×10^4 to get $x = \dfrac{6 \times 10^8}{3 \times 10^4}$. Remember to subtract the exponents when dividing quantities with like bases, so $x = 2 \times 10^4$. Choice (F) is $\dfrac{3 \times 10^4}{6 \times 10^8}$. Choice (G) is the result of dividing the exponents. Choice (J) is the result of multiplying the numbers in the problem. The correct answer is (H).

31. **B** The question asks for the shortest distance between the starting point of the car and the driver's desired destination. According to the question, this is the distance from point A to point B. To use the Law of Cosines, the measure of $\angle ACB$ must be determined to find the length of AB. There are $360°$ in a circle, so $\angle ACN = 360 - 250 = 110$. $\angle ACB = \angle ACN + \angle BCN = 110 + 30 = 140°$. The only difference in the answer choices is the angle used, so there is no need to worry about how to set up the rest of the Law of Cosines. The correct answer is (B).

32. **H** The question asks for the real number that is halfway between $\dfrac{1}{4}$ and $\dfrac{1}{6}$. The number halfway between $\dfrac{1}{4}$ and $\dfrac{1}{6}$ can be found by averaging the two numbers. This results in $\dfrac{\frac{1}{4} + \frac{1}{6}}{2} = \dfrac{5}{24}$, which is a real number. Choice (F) is between the two values, but it is not halfway. Choices (G) and (J) are greater than both fractions. The correct answer is (H).

33. **C** The question asks for the measure of $\angle DEB$ on the figure. Use the information given to try to find the angles in $\triangle ADE$. $\triangle ADE$ and $\triangle EBA$ are congruent because they have congruent sides: both triangles share $\overline{AE}$; $\overline{BA}$ and $\overline{DE}$ are each half the length of congruent sides; and diagonals $\overline{DA}$ and $\overline{BE}$ are equal. Therefore, $\angle EBA = \angle EDA = 95°$, and $\angle DAE = \angle BEA = 35°$. There are $180°$ in a triangle, so $\angle AED = 180 - 35 - 95 = 50°$. $\angle AED$ also equals $\angle AEB + \angle DEB$, so $50 = 35 + \angle DEB$, and $\angle DEB = 15°$. The correct answer is (C).

34. **H** The question asks for the value of x on the diagram. The measure of x is the side of the large square table minus the side of the small square table. Since $A = s^2$, $\sqrt{A} = s$. The side of the large square table is $\sqrt{108} = \sqrt{36 \times 3} = 6\sqrt{3}$. The area of the small square table is $\dfrac{108}{9} = 12$, so its side is $\sqrt{12} = \sqrt{4 \times 3} = 2\sqrt{3}$. Therefore, $x = 6\sqrt{3} - 2\sqrt{3} = 4\sqrt{3}$. Choice (F) gives the side of the small square table instead of x. Choice (G) subtracts terms with a common radical incorrectly. Choice

(J) subtracts the two areas and then takes the square root of the result, instead of first taking the square root of each area and then subtracting the results. The correct answer is (H).

35. **D** The question asks for the number that is **not** irrational. A rational number is one which can be expressed as a fraction. Only (D) can be reduced to integer values in the numerator and denominator: $\sqrt{\dfrac{81}{25}} = \dfrac{\sqrt{81}}{\sqrt{25}} = \dfrac{9}{5}$. The correct answer is (D).

36. **G** The question asks for the expression that is equivalent to the given inequality. Pick a value for both x and y. If $x = -5$ and $y = -3$, the absolute value expression becomes $|-5 + (-3)| = |-8| = 8$. Check the answer choices to see which one also equals 8 for these values of x and y. Choice (F) is $-5 - 3 = -8$. Eliminate (F). Choice (G) is $-(-5 - 3) = -(-8) = 8$. Keep (G), but check the rest of the answers just in case. Choice (H) is $|-5 - (-3)| = |-5 + 3| = |-2| = 2$, and (J) is $\sqrt{(-5)^2 + (-3)^2} = \sqrt{25 + 9} = \sqrt{34}$. The correct answer is (G).

37. **D** The question asks for the score Jane must get on her next game to reach her goal average. To determine this, figure out how many total points she will need and how many she has already earned. To find the total points she needs on the six games, multiply her desired average by the number of games: $85 \times 6 = 510$. To find the number of points she has already gotten, multiply her average on the first 5 games by the number of games, which is $5 \times 83 = 415$. The difference between these numbers is the score she must get in order to get an average of 85 on the 6 games. This means that the score she needs is $510 - 415 = 95$, which is (D). Choice (B) is the score she would have to get in the next two games for an average of 85. Choice (A) can be eliminated—Jane wants her average to go up, so she needs a higher score on the next game. The correct answer is (D).

38. **F** The question asks for the solution to the given equation. Since $9 = 3^2$ and $27 = 3^3$, make $9^{x-4} = 27^{3x+2}$ into $3^{2(x-4)} = 3^{3(3x+2)}$. The equation now reads: "3 to some power = 3 to some power." Therefore, the exponents are equal: $2(x - 4) = 3(3x + 2)$. Distribute the 2 and the 3 to get $2x - 8 = 9x + 6$. Subtract $9x$ and add 8 to each side of the equation to get $-7x = 14$. Divide both sides by -7 to get $x = -2$. The correct answer is (F).

39. **C** The question asks for a true statement about the given sine function based on the graph. Go through the answers and use Process of Elimination. Choice (A) says that the function is undefined at $x = 0$, but the graph clearly goes through the origin. Therefore, (A) is false. To test (B), try some values from the function, which appears to contain the points $(3, 2)$ and $(-3, -2)$. The value of $f(x)$ is the y-coordinate of the point, so these points reveal that $f(3) \neq f(-3)$. Eliminate (B). These same points do show, however, that $f(-3) = -f(3) = -2$. This means that the function is odd. Choice (D) is incorrect because the arrows at the ends of the sine wave indicate that it continues past the domain $-6 \leq x \leq 6$ shown here. The correct answer is (C).

40. **G** The question asks for the slope of $\overline{LM}$ on the figure. This line has a positive slope, so eliminate (H) and (J) right away. Because $\overline{NL}$ is parallel to the x-axis and $\triangle NLM$ is isosceles, the slope of $\overline{LM}$ is the negative of the slope of $\overline{MN}$. Find the slope of $\overline{MN}$ by rewriting the equation $y + \frac{2}{3}x = 2$ as $y = -\frac{2}{3}x + 2$, where the slope m is $-\frac{2}{3}$. The slope of $\overline{LM}$, therefore, is $\frac{2}{3}$. The correct answer is (G).

41. **A** The question asks for the tangent of $\sin^{-1}$ of $\frac{x}{\sqrt{x^2 + y^2}}$ based on the figure. The notation $\sin^{-1}\left(\frac{x}{\sqrt{x^2 + y^2}}\right)$ means find the angle that has a sine value of $\frac{x}{\sqrt{x^2 + y^2}}$. Recall that the sine of an angle is $\frac{\text{opposite}}{\text{hypotenuse}}$. The side marked x is opposite $\angle ACB$, so that's the angle in question. Now, use SOHCAHTOA to find that $\tan(\angle ACB) = \frac{\text{opposite}}{\text{adjacent}} = \frac{x}{y}$. The correct answer is (A).

42. **J** The question asks for the equation of the circle shown in the figure. The standard equation of a circle is $(x - h)^2 + (y - k)^2 = r^2$, where (h,k) is the center and r is the radius. In this circle, $r = 12$, so the equation must be equal to 12^2. Eliminate (F) and (H). When the center is at the origin, the equation becomes $(x - 0)^2 + (y - 0)^2 = r^2$ or just $x^2 + y^2 = r^2$. The correct answer is (J).

43. **D** The question asks for the values of x that satisfy the given inequality. Look at the graph of the two equations. Find the x-values where the y-value of the equation $y = -(x + 1)^2 + 4$ is greater than the y-value of the equation $y = (-x + 1)$. According to the figure, the parabola has a higher y-value than the line between the x-values -2 and 1. The correct answer is (D).

44. **J** The question asks for the greatest possible value of an expression under certain conditions. Test numbers to answer this question. To make the value of $y - x$ as large as possible, make y a large two-digit number and x a small two-digit number. If $t = 1$ and $u = 9$, then $x = 19$ and $y = 91$. Therefore, $y - x = 91 - 19 = 72$. That is the largest possible value given the restrictions, so these values of t and u can be used to test out the answers. The value of (F) is $9 - 1 = 8$, which is not 72. Eliminate (F). Choice (G) is $(9)(1) - (1)(9) = 9 - 9 = 0$. Eliminate (G). Choice (H) is $1^2 - 10(1)(9) + 9^2 = 1 - 90 + 81 = -8$, so (H) can be eliminated. Choice (J) is $9|9 - 1| = 9|8| = 72$, which matches the maximum value. The correct answer is (J).

45. **A** The question asks for the sixth term in an arithmetic sequence. To determine the sixth term, first find the common difference between consecutive terms in the sequence. Use the given formula to solve for x_1: $145 = 5\left(\frac{x_1 + 48}{2}\right)$, so $x_1 = 10$. The common difference in an arithmetic sequence is basically

the slope of a straight line: $difference = \dfrac{x_n - x_1}{n - 1} = \dfrac{48 - 10}{5 - 1} = 9.5$. The sixth term, therefore, is 48 + 9.5 = 57.5. Choices (B) and (D) use averages, rather than a common difference. Choice (C) incorrectly adds the difference to the sum, rather than x_5. The correct answer is (A).

ACT TEST 1 READING ANSWERS AND EXPLANATIONS

1. **C** This Information question asks about the way in which the *narrator learned to make rice*. Because this is a general question, it should be done after the specific questions. Look for the Golden Thread (more on this in Chapter 23). Lines 1–14 describe the father's method of making rice without giving any specific measurements, and lines 21–22 state, *Every night before dinner, my father would perform this ritual—rinsing and draining, then setting the pot in the cooker.* In lines 23–26, the narrator states *I never did it with the same care. I went through the motions, splashing the water around, jabbing my finger down to measure the water level. Some nights the rice was a mushy gruel.* Therefore, the narrator learned to make rice by watching her father but didn't apply the same care to making rice as he did. Eliminate answers that don't match this answer from the passage. Choice (A) indicates that the author *carefully* followed the method her father taught her, which contradicts the passage. Eliminate (A). Choice (B) mentions *watching cooking shows*, which is discussed starting in line 55. These lines, however, are not related to the method of making rice, so eliminate (B). Keep (C) because it matches the answer from the passage. Choice (D) refers to *books* the author's father left to her, but this is not mentioned in the passage. Eliminate (D). The correct answer is (C).

2. **H** This Information question asks for the statement that *foreshadows the joy and connection the narrator feels* at the end of the passage. Read the last paragraph; then read the line references given in the answer choices. The last sentence of the passage says, *I was overjoyed when my feet kept time with his, right, then left, then right, and we walked like a single unit*; the narrator is describing walking with her father, so the answer should include a connection between the narrator and her father. Eliminate answers that don't match this answer from the passage. The statement in (F) does not include joy or connection to the narrator's father, so eliminate (F). Although the statement in (G) mentions the narrator's father, it doesn't indicate joy or connection, so eliminate (G). The statement in (H) is about the narrator's father, and the phrase *I was convinced by him that all was well in the world* indicates a connection between the narrator and her father, so keep (H). The statement in (J) mentions the narrator's father, but it doesn't indicate joy or connection, so eliminate (J). The correct answer is (H).

3. **B** This Information question asks what the passage suggests about the narrator *walking with her father*. Look for the lead word *walking* to find the window. Lines 76–78 state *I was overjoyed when my feet kept time with his, right, then left, then right, and we walked like a single unit.* Eliminate answers that don't match this answer from the passage. There is no mention of the narrator folding her body (that reference is about the *fish* described in line 50), so eliminate (A). Keep (B) because it matches the answer from the passage. There is no evidence that the narrator felt *inferior*, so eliminate (C). *Yan's puns* are not mentioned in connection with the narrator and her father walking together, so eliminate (D). The correct answer is (B).

4. **G**   This Information question asks which of the statements are *true of the fish after the father has put it into the sink*. Look for the lead word *fish* to find the window. Lines 51–52 state, *Though I ripple tiny circles around it with my fingers, the fish stays still*, so the statement in I is true. Eliminate (F) and (H), which do not include I. Both (G) and (J) include II, and neither includes III, so check the statement in IV. Lines 47–48 state that the fish is *brushing up against the sides of the sink*, so IV is true. Eliminate (J). The correct answer is (G).

5. **D**   This Information question asks for the best paraphrase of the statement in lines 5–7. Read a window around the given line reference. The passage states, *He swirled his hands through the water and it turned cloudy. When he scrubbed the grains clean, the sound was as big as a field of insects.* The sentences are describing the sights and sounds of the father cleaning the rice. Eliminate answers that don't match this answer from the passage. There is no comparison with *Chef Yan* in these lines, so eliminate (A). The sound of the rice, not the *rice* itself, is compared to *insects*, so eliminate (B). There is no evidence that the narrator worried her father had a *mental disorder*, so eliminate (C). Keep (D) because it matches the answer from the passage. The correct answer is (D).

6. **G**   This Vocabulary in Context question asks what *trailing* most nearly means as it is used in line 39. Go back to the text, find the word *trailing*, and cross it out. Carefully read the surrounding text to determine another word or phrase that would fit in the blank based on the context. Lines 39–41 state that the narrator is *trailing my fingers along the gills, the soft, muscled body, pushing my finger overtop the eyeball.* Therefore, *trailing* could be replaced with "touching." Eliminate answers that don't match this answer from the passage. *Pursuing* means "following," which doesn't match "touching," so eliminate (F). *Tracing* matches "touching," so keep (G). *Losing* doesn't match "touching," so eliminate (H). *Hanging* doesn't match "touching," so eliminate (J). The correct answer is (G).

7. **C**   This Information question asks why the narrator's *father ate her rice*. The question is Hard to Find, so work the question later and use the previous questions to help find the window. Lines 28–34 state, *my father would keep eating, pushing the rice into his mouth as if he never expected anything different, as if he noticed no difference between what he did so well and I so poorly…. Then he would rise, whistling, and clear the table, every motion so clean and sure, I would be convinced by him that all was well in the world.* Eliminate answers that don't match this answer from the passage. Eliminate (A) because it contradicts the passage. There is no mention of wasting food, so eliminate (B). Keep (C) because it matches the answer from the passage. There is no evidence that her father is embarrassed, so eliminate (D). The correct answer is (C).

8. **H**   This Information question asks what would be *logical to conclude* about the *fish*. Look for the lead word *fish* to find the window for the question. Lines 35–53 describe the fish; eliminate answers that don't match the passage. Although the passage says that the fish is *barely breathing*, it doesn't say that the fish is *ill and dying*, so eliminate (F). According to the passage, the *fish floats in place and stays still*, which suggests it is not *restless*, so eliminate (G). Lines 36–37 say, *Caught inside the bag is a live fish*, and lines 41–42 describe the fish as *flopping sluggishly from side to side*. These lines support the description of the fish as *confined and sluggish*, so keep (H). Although the fish watches the narrator, it does not react when she swirls water around it, suggesting that it is not *alert*, so eliminate (J). The correct answer is (H).

9. **A** This Information question asks how the father regarded *Wok with Yan*. Use the lead words *Wok with Yan* to find the window for the question. In lines 57–60, the narrator says that her father was *passing judgement on Yan's methods*, saying, *"You don't have to be a genius to do that."* However, lines 63–64 state that he also *made careful notes when Yan demonstrated Peking Duck*. Therefore, her father gets some information from the show and disregards what he doesn't find useful. Eliminate answers that don't match this answer from the passage. Since the father took notes on some recipes, keep (A). Not everything in the show was *irrelevant* to the father, so eliminate (B). There is no mention of the show being *the primary source of his own cooking methods*, so eliminate (C). Although he laughs at Yan's puns, there is no evidence that he thinks it's the *funniest cooking show*, so eliminate (D). The correct answer is (A).

10. **J** This Rhetoric question asks for *the primary purpose of the details about the "ground-breaking research"* in Passage A. Read a window around the given line reference. The first paragraph provides a timeline of advancements in *fertilizer*. Lines 5–7 state that the *ground-breaking research, done by several innovative scientists, finally ushered in the modern era of soil chemistry and plant nutrition.* Eliminate answers that don't match this answer from the passage. Eliminate (F) because the author doesn't say that previous fertilizers were unsuccessful. Choice (G) contradicts the passage: *manure* use came before the use of *bones*, so eliminate (G). Eliminate (H) because the passage connects only one scientist, *Justus von Liebig*, to his *contribution*. Keep (J) because it matches the answer from the passage. The correct answer is (J).

11. **B** This Information question asks for *one reason for the development of chemical fertilizers based on Passage A*. There is not a good lead word in this question, so work the question later and use the previous questions to help find the window. Lines 12–17 state that *use of chemical fertilizer was limited until World War II when there was a tremendous increase in nitrogen production, mainly because nitrogen is a principal ingredient in explosives*. Eliminate answers that don't match this answer from the passage. Eliminate (A) because the passage does not state that there was nitrogen *leftover from the war*. Keep (B) because the *wartime industry* did make it possible to *mass-produce* nitrogen, which was used in *fertilizer*. Eliminate (C) because the author never mentions *soldiers* working as *chemists*. Eliminate (D) because the passage states that *nitrogen production* increased due to the wartime production of explosives, not due to *farming practices*. The correct answer is (B).

12. **G** This Rhetoric question asks why *the authors use the description of technological advances and techniques* in Passage A. Read a window around the given line reference. Lines 23–29 state, *Technological advances... have allowed today's farmers to use fertilizers more effectively and efficiently, in addition to being better stewards of the land and environment.* Eliminate answers that don't match this answer from the passage. The author does not criticize *farmers* for using *technology*, so eliminate (F). Keep (G) because it matches the answer from the passage. Eliminate (H) because, although there is a *list of strategies*, the author's purpose is not to make a list. Instead, the author provides the description of technological advances and techniques, including the list of strategies, to support the point that technology led to the farmers' efficient use of fertilizer. Eliminate (J) because, although monitoring the *movement of...water within the soil profile* is mentioned, there is no mention of water *usage*. Choice (J) also does not include the author's point about the increasing efficiency of fertilizer use. The correct answer is (G).

13.   **A**   This Information question asks for *a major factor in the reshaping of global agriculture* according to Passage B. There is not a good lead word in this question, so work the question later and use the previous questions to help find the window. The first paragraph of Passage B states, *Nitrogen-based fertilizers…helped prompt the agricultural revolution that has allowed Earth to feed its seven billion people.* Eliminate answers that don't match this answer from the passage. Keep (A) because it matches the answer from the passage. Eliminate (B) because the passage discusses the use of a new type of fertilizer, not a new fertilizing *technique*. Eliminate (C) because it contradicts the main point of Passage B, which focuses on the *ecological consequences* of fertilizers. Eliminate (D) because, while the passage does discuss *the impacts of the agricultural industry on climate change*, it doesn't discuss any efforts aimed at lessening those impacts. The correct answer is (A).

14.   **H**   This Information question asks what effect of *chemical fertilizers* the statement *"But that revolution came at a cost"* refers to in Passage B. Read a window around the given line reference. Lines 44–49 state that fertilizers *are carried in runoff from farmland into streams, lakes and the ocean* and may lead to *damaging algae blooms and dead zones in American coastal waters.* Therefore, the *cost* mentioned in the statement must be environmental. Eliminate answers that don't match this answer from the passage. Eliminate (F) because the consequences are environmental, not *financial*. Similarly, eliminate (G) because the *cost* is environmental; it is not related to *money*. Keep (H) because it mentions environmental disadvantages, which matches the answer from the passage. Eliminate (J) because the passage doesn't compare *coastal regions to plains regions.* The correct answer is (H).

15.   **A**   This Analysis question asks for a comparison between *concerns about water quantity and concerns about water quality.* Look for the lead words *water quality* and *water quantity* to find the window for the question. Lines 59–65 state that *we are used to thinking about water quantity* but that *[c]limate change is just as tightly linked to issues related to water quality.* Therefore, *water quantity* and *water quality* are both important. Eliminate answers that don't match this answer from the passage. Keep (A) because it matches the answer from the passage. Eliminate (B) because no comparison between *urban* and *rural areas* is made in this passage. Eliminate (C) because it contradicts the answer from the passage. Eliminate (D) because the passage doesn't suggest that one set of concerns is specific to *saltwater bodies.* The correct answer is (A).

16.   **G**   This Analysis question asks what *types of fertilizer* have *impacted the agricultural industry*, according to both passages. Because this question asks about both passages, it should be done after the questions that ask about each passage individually. Consider the Golden Thread of both passages (see Chapter 23 for more on this term). Passage A describes the rise and influence of *chemical fertilizers.* Passage B focuses on the impact of *artificial fertilizers.* Eliminate answers that don't match this answer from the passage. Eliminate (F) because Passage A takes a positive view of fertilizer: lines 39–40 indicate that the development of chemical fertilizer *has been foundational to feeding our nation and providing food and hope to other parts of the world.* Keep (G) because the *chemical* and *artificial* fertilizers discussed in both passages are *manufactured.* Eliminate (H) because the fertilizers that impacted the agricultural industry are manufactured, not *naturally produced.* Eliminate (J) because Passage B doesn't mention *ammonia.* The correct answer is (G).

17. **A** This Analysis question asks how each passage uses *details about the effects of incorporating nitrogen-based fertilizers into agriculture*. Because this question asks about both passages, it should be done after the questions that ask about each passage individually. The author of Passage A focuses on the positive effects of nitrogen-based (*chemical*) fertilizers: the last sentence states that the development of chemical fertilizer *has been foundational to feeding our nation and providing food and hope to other parts of the world*. The author of Passage B focuses on the negative effects of nitrogen-based fertilizer: lines 41–44 indicate that the use of *[n]itrogen-based fertilizers...comes with a cost*, and the rest of the passage describes the harmful environmental effects of these *nitrogen-based fertilizers*. Eliminate answers that don't match this answer from the passage. Keep (A) because it matches the answer from the passage. Eliminate (B) because Passage A focuses specifically on *chemical fertilizers*, not *farming advances* as a whole. Eliminate (C) because Passage A doesn't mention the effects of fertilizers *on land*. Eliminate (D) because only Passage B discusses environmental effects. The correct answer is (A).

18. **H** This Analysis question asks how both authors *support their claims*. Because this question asks about both passages, it should be done after the questions that ask about each passage individually. Eliminate any answer choices that misrepresent either passage. Eliminate (F) because only Passage B defines any *key terms related to ecology* (lines 50–51). Eliminate (G) because only Passage B quotes *experts in a related field* (lines 59–65). Both passages *provide statistics* (Passage A in lines 32–35 and Passage B in lines 56–58), so keep (H). Eliminate (J) because only Passage A includes a *specific timeline* (lines 1–9). The correct answer is (H).

19. **D** This Information question asks for the *primary function of the first paragraph*. Read the first paragraph as the window. The paragraph starts by stating that *Pablo Neruda couldn't hold a tune*, and then in lines 3–4 says, *This is remarkable: Neruda's cadences are crucial to his writing*. The first paragraph presents a contradiction between Neruda's musical ability and the musicality of his poetry. Eliminate answers that don't match this answer from the passage. Eliminate (A) because Neruda wasn't a talented *musician*. Eliminate (B) because there is no information in the first paragraph about how Neruda *wrote his poems*. Eliminate (C) because there is no *story from Neruda's youth*. Keep (D) because it matches the answer from the passage. The correct answer is (D).

20. **G** This information question asks what *best describes the passage author's opinion of Neruda's poetry*. The question is Hard to Find, so work the question later and use the previous questions to help find the window. Eliminate (F) because the author doesn't express a preference for *Neruda's* Memoirs. Keep (G) because lines 45–46 say, *The result was a fusion previously unseen in Chilean poetry—or poetry anywhere*, which indicates that the author finds Neruda's poetry *original*. Eliminate (H) because, although the passage does say that Neruda's poetry *feeds hungrily off the life,* it does not say that it relies *too heavily* on Neruda's life. Eliminate (J) because in the passage, the phrase *faults and weaknesses* refers to Neruda's himself, not to his poetry. The correct answer is (G).

21. **B** This Information question asks what the word *melody* refers to. Read a window around the given line reference. Lines 3–7 say, *Neruda's cadences are crucial to his writing. No one reading his poems in their original Spanish would want to separate their sense from their sound and that their meaning is inseparable from their melody.* Eliminate answers that don't match this answer from the passage. Eliminate (A)

because it takes words in the passage out of context: the author says figuratively that Feinstein's *book turns Neruda's life into an opera—a blend of aria and recitative*. There is no mention of Neruda writing a literal *opera*. Keep (B) because *word choice and pacing* matches *cadence*, and the *effect...on a reader's understanding of his poems* matches *their meaning is inseparable from their melody*. Eliminate (C) because the word *melody* is not part of the author's discussion of *Neruda's life*. Similarly, eliminate (D) because the word *melody* refers to Neruda's poetry, not to his life experiences. The correct answer is (B).

22.   **J**   This Information question asks what *a reader might appreciate* about *Feinstein's treatment of the "dizzying details"* of *Neruda's life*. Read a window around the given line reference. Lines 18–21 say, *By pacing the story so as to give pre-eminence to the writing and the adventuring, while recording the duller passages more briefly, Feinstein creates his own sympathetic music*. Eliminate answers that don't match this answer from the passage. Eliminate (F) because the passage does not suggest that Feinstein is critical of *Neruda's travels*. Eliminate (G) because *Feinstein's account is crammed with adventure stories, narrow scrapes, passionate encounters* (lines 15–16), not with information about Neruda's *writing process*. Eliminate (H) because the passage does not say that Feinstein *never elaborates* about Neruda's motivations. Keep (J) because it matches the answer from the passage. The correct answer is (J).

23.   **C**   This Vocabulary in Context question asks what the word *logged* most nearly means as it is used in line 17. Go back to the text, find the word *logged*, and cross it out. Carefully read the surrounding text to determine another word or phrase that would fit in the blank based on the context. Lines 16–18 say, *globe-trottings have to be logged but risk becoming a list of place-names*. Therefore, *logged* could be replaced with "noted." Eliminate answers that don't match this answer from the passage. *Cut* does not match "noted," so eliminate (A). *Completed* does not match "noted," so eliminate (B). *Recorded* matches "noted," so keep (C). *Harvested* does not match "noted," so eliminate (D). Note that (A), (B), and (D) are each based on other meanings of the word *logged* that do not match the way the word is used in this context. The correct answer is (C).

24.   **H**   This Information question asks how *Neruda's reminiscences are related in his autobiography*. Look for the lead word *reminiscences* to find the window for the question. Lines 33–35 say, *He understands that an author's reminiscences are a way of creating disguises as well as revealing secrets*. Eliminate answers that don't match this answer from the passage. Eliminate (F) because the contentious *issues* were *hushed up by Neruda*. Eliminate (G) because there is no indication that Neruda's recollections *should be studied as literature*. Keep (H) because it matches the answer from the passage. Eliminate (J) because, although the passage states that Feinstein relied on *Neruda's* Memoirs, it does not say that they guided his *writing style*. The correct answer is (H).

25.   **D**   This Information question asks how *Feinstein addresses Neruda's conversion to communism*. Look for the lead word *communism* to find the window for the question. Lines 59–60 say, *Delia persuaded him to become a communist*, and lines 65–67 state that Feinstein *copes with it by presenting the facts rather than wagging his finger, and by foregrounding the writing*. Eliminate answers that don't match this answer from the passage. Eliminate (A) because Feinstein does include the topic of *politics*. Eliminate (B) because the passage describes Neruda's *life* as *contradictory*; it does not state that Feinstein contradicted Neruda's account of that time. Eliminate (C) because the *pain* suffered by Neruda's

wife and sickly daughter is discussed in reference to Neruda's actions, not Feinstein's writing. Keep (D) because it matches the answer from the passage. The correct answer is (D).

26. **F** This Information question asks when *Neruda's Spanish became "quite odd."* Read a window around the given line reference. Lines 50–53 say, *By 1927 he was in Rangoon, then moved on through France, Japan, China, Ceylon and Java...before returning home in 1932. By this time, his Spanish was apparently "quite odd."* Eliminate answers that don't match this answer from the passage. Keep (F) because it matches the answer from the passage. Eliminate (G) because *French symbolist poetry* is mentioned in a different part of the passage and not in relation to *Neruda's Spanish*. Eliminate (H) because line 50 states, *Consular activity served as his means of escape*; it does not say that he escaped *from consular activity*. Eliminate (J) because the passage indicates that Neruda's *marriage to Delia del Carril* happened after his Spanish became odd. The correct answer is (F).

27. **A** This Vocabulary in Context question asks what the word *work* most nearly means as it is used in line 86. Go back to the text, find the word *work*, and cross it out. Carefully read the surrounding text to determine another word or phrase that would fit in the blank based on the context. Lines 85–87 say, *The faults and weaknesses are plain to see, but so is the undimmed exuberance and generosity of the work, which feeds hungrily off the life and yet stands as a thing apart*. The phrase *faults and weaknesses* refers to the *moral muddle* of Neruda's life. Therefore, the author is contrasting Neruda's life with his writing, so the word *work* refers to Neruda's poetry. Eliminate answers that don't match this answer from the passage. Keep (A) because it matches the answer from the passage. Eliminate (B) because *biography* refers to Feinstein's biography of Neruda, rather than to Neruda's poetry. Eliminate (C) and (D) because *travels* and *marriage* refer to aspects of Neruda's life, rather than his writing. The correct answer is (A).

28. **H** This Rhetoric question asks for *the overall organization of the passage*. Because this is a general question, it should be done after the specific questions. The passage proceeds chronologically, starting with 1964 in the first paragraph and leading to 2012 at the end of the passage. It describes the events leading up to and the eventual discovery of the *Higgs boson*. Eliminate answers that don't match this answer from the passage. The passage is *chronological*, but the focus isn't finding the *mass of various elementary particles*, so eliminate (F). Choice (G) includes some words from the passage, but the focus of the passage is not the *construction* of the *Large Hadron Collider*, so eliminate (G). The *events leading to the discovery of the Higgs boson* is a close match, so keep (H). There's no *collection of stories* or discussion of how the *Standard Model of physics evolved*, so eliminate (J). The correct answer is (H).

29. **D** This Rhetoric question asks for *the main function of the first paragraph*. Read the first paragraph as the window. The first paragraph states that a scientist suggested that the *Higgs boson* existed *in 1964* and explains briefly what the Higgs boson is, calling it the *cornerstone of the Standard Model*. Eliminate answers that don't match this answer from the passage. Eliminate (A) because it answers the wrong question: discoveries made in *Hamburg* are mentioned in the second, not first, paragraph. Eliminate (B) because the first paragraph doesn't talk about scientists building *particle colliders*. The paragraph is focused on the *Higgs boson*, not the *theorists*, so eliminate (C). The focus is the *Higgs boson* and its *importance*, so keep (D). The correct answer is (D).

30. **F** This Rhetoric question asks for a *similarity between the two particle colliders described in lines* 18–32. Read a window around the given line reference. The paragraph states that the *Tevatron and Large Electron Positron* colliders both provided *precision measurements* that *implied that the Higgs boson should be no more than 200 GeV*. But according to the last sentence, the scientists *found no lasting evidence*. Eliminate answers that don't match this answer from the passage. Keep (F), which matches the answer from the passage. Eliminate (G) because the cost of the Tevatron is not discussed. Eliminate (H) because the Tevatron was completed in 1983, but the LEP only began to be built that year. Eliminate (J) because it contradicts the last sentence of the paragraph. The correct answer is (F).

31. **C** This Information question asks for the *main idea of the last paragraph*. Read the last paragraph as the window. The first sentence of the last paragraph states, *Few physicists doubt that a heavy new particle* has been discovered, but *there is still debate about its exact nature*. Eliminate answers that don't match this answer from the passage. Eliminate (A) because the paragraph doesn't say the particle's properties were predicted *only recently*. In fact, earlier the passage states that the Higgs boson was predicted decades ago. Eliminate (B) because the paragraph doesn't mention *recent research*. Choice (C) matches the answer from the passage, so keep it. Eliminate (D) because the paragraph doesn't say that the particle weighs *more than originally predicted*. The correct answer is (C).

32. **J** This Information question asks for information about *scientists in Brussels and London*. Look for the lead words *Brussels* and *London* to find the window for the question. Lines 3–7 indicate that two scientists from Brussels and three theorists in London both *independently conceived* of the *subtle mechanism* that *endows elementary particles with mass*. Eliminate answers that don't match this answer from the passage. Choice (F) answers the wrong question: it was *Peter W. Higgs*, not the *scientists in Brussels and London*, who suggested the particle's existence, so eliminate (F). Eliminate (G) because it describes the *Standard Model*, which isn't credited to these scientists. The *cornerstone of the Standard Model* is the Higgs boson, and that isn't what these scientists discovered, so eliminate (H). Choice (J) matches the answer from the passage, so keep it. The correct answer is (J).

33. **B** This Information question asks what the *dipole magnets* were *capable of*. Look for the lead words *dipole magnets* to find the window for the question. Lines 41–49 state that inside the *dipole magnets, twin proton beams circulate in both directions…approaching light speed*. Eliminate answers that don't match this answer from the passage. Eliminate (A) because it contradicts the passage, which says that there was *little left* from the LEP collider. Keep (B) because it matches the answer from the passage. Eliminate (C) because the passage doesn't indicate that the dipole magnets float *in the air*, and it is the *proton beams* that circulate at *energies up to 7 TeV*, not the *dipole magnets*. Eliminate (D) because the dipole magnets are cylinders; they don't *fit into* cylinders. The correct answer is (B).

34. **F** This Analysis question asks how *work at the Tevatron* compares with *work at the LHC*. Look for the lead words *Tevatron* and *LHC* to find the window for the question. Lines 59–61 state that *the LHC was producing data 15 times faster than the Tevatron had ever achieved*, so the correct answer will address the speed of the work. Eliminate answers that don't match this answer from the passage. Keep (F) because it matches the answer from the passage. Eliminate (G), (H), and (J) because they do not relate to speed. The correct answer is (F).

35. **D** This Rhetoric question asks why the author includes the *scientists' reactions* in lines 69–71. Read a window around the given line reference. Lines 65–69 indicate that the scientists realized *chances were good* that they *could claim a Higgs discovery*. Lines 69–71 state that *a dozen physicists erupted in loud clapping and cries of joy*, which demonstrates how excited they were by the discovery. Eliminate answers that don't match this answer from the passage. Eliminate (A) because they were not excited *to meet Peter Higgs*. Eliminate (B) because it was the *LHC*, not the *Tevatron*, that produced the exciting results. Eliminate (C) because the passage doesn't say that the cheers *disrupted* anyone. The scientists were excited about the *magnitude of their discovery*, so keep (D). The correct answer is (D).

36. **G** This Vocabulary in Context question asks what the phrase *turned up* means in line 78. Go back to the text, find the phrase *turned up*, and cross it out. Carefully read the surrounding text to determine another phrase that would fit in the blank based on the context. Lines 78–79 state, *Few physicists doubt that a heavy new particle has turned up at CERN*. Therefore, *turned up* could be replaced with "been identified." The phrase *been amplified* does not match "been identified," so eliminate (F). *Been discovered* matches "been identified," so keep (G). *Arrived on site* and *grown in height* do not match "been identified," so eliminate (H) and (J). Note that (F), (H), and (J) are trap answers based on alternative meanings of *turned up* that do not fit the given context. The correct answer is (G).

ACT TEST 1 SCIENCE ANSWERS AND EXPLANATIONS

1. **A** The question asks which graph best represents the enzyme velocities of Enzymes A, B, C, and D in solutions with *an initial substrate concentration of 5 mM* at *60°C* after *10 seconds,* based on Table 1. According to the description above Table 1, 10 seconds is a constant for all measurements in Table 1. Look at Table 1 and find the enzyme velocity of each enzyme at 60°C with an initial substrate concentration of 5 mM. Under these conditions, Enzymes A, B, C, and D have velocities of 4.6, 4.9, 10.6, and 14.6 mmol/s, respectively, so Enzyme A has the smallest enzyme velocity. Eliminate (B), (C), and (D) because these graphs do not show Enzyme A as having the smallest enzyme velocity. The correct answer is (A).

2. **G** The question asks for the most likely enzyme velocity if Enzyme B solution had *a substrate concentration of 10 mM* at *35°C,* based on Table 1. Look for the data for Enzyme B at an initial substrate concentration of 10 mM. The enzyme velocity is listed for substrate temperatures of 20°C, 30°C, and 60°C. The enzyme velocity decreases with higher temperatures. Thus, the enzyme velocity at 35°C will fall between the values for 30°C and 60°C. At 30°C the enzyme velocity is 10.9 mmol/s, and at 60°C the enzyme velocity is 6.9 mmol/s. Therefore, the enzyme velocity at 35°C will be between 10.9 mmol/s and 6.9 mmol/s. The correct answer is (G).

3. **D** The question asks for the enzyme velocities from *highest to lowest* after 1 second with a *substrate concentration of 12 mM* at 40°C, based on Figure 1. The description for Figure 1 states that the graph shows the change in enzyme velocity over time at a substrate concentration of 12 mM and

a temperature of 40°C. Find 1 second on the horizontal axis and draw a vertical line from 1 second on the *x*-axis to the enzyme velocity curves for all four enzymes. Enzyme D has the highest enzyme velocity at 1 second, so eliminate (A) and (B). Enzyme B has the second highest enzyme velocity, so eliminate (C). The correct answer is (D).

4. **F** The question asks for the enzyme velocity for Enzyme C *after 10 seconds* at an *8 mM substrate concentration at 60°C,* based on Table 1. According to the description above Table 1, 10 seconds is a constant for all measurements in Table 1. Look for the data for Enzyme C at 60°C. The enzyme velocity is listed for initial substrate concentrations of 5 mM, 10 mM, and 15 mM. The enzyme velocity increases with higher substrate concentrations. Thus, the enzyme velocity at an 8 mM substrate concentration will fall between the values for 5 mM and 10 mM. At 5 mM the enzyme velocity is 10.6 mmol/s, and at 10 mM the enzyme velocity is 13.1 mmol/s. Therefore, the enzyme velocity will be between 10.6 mmol/s and 13.1 mmol/s. The only value between 10.6 mmol/s and 13/1 mmol/s is 12.0 mmol/s in (F). The correct answer is (F).

5. **B** The question asks for the enzyme that *takes the shortest amount of time to reach an enzyme velocity of 6 mmol/s*, given that the substrate concentration is 12 mM and the temperature is 40°C, according to Figure 1. The description for Figure 1 states that the graph shows the change in enzyme velocity over time at a substrate concentration of 12 mM and a temperature of 40°C. Find the enzyme velocity of 6 mmol/s on the vertical axis. Draw a horizontal line from 6 mmol/s on the *y*-axis. The first enzyme to reach an enzyme velocity of 6 mmol/s is Enzyme B at 0.5 seconds. The correct answer is (B).

6. **G** The question asks for *the transmittance at 0.31 microns at a concentration of 18 mg/m^3*, based on Figure 2. According to the description for Study 2, Figure 2 shows the transmittance at 0.31 microns at various average concentrations of O_3. Look at Figure 2 for the transmittance at a concentration of 18 mg/m^3. At 18 mg/m^3, the transmittance is approximately 48%, which is between 45 and 50%. The correct answer is (G).

7. **B** The question asks how *the transmittance at 0.31 microns varied* as *the concentration of ozone increased from 3 to 24 mg/m^3*, based on Study 2. According to the description for Study 2, Figure 2 shows the transmittance at 0.31 microns at various average concentrations of O_3. Use Figure 2 and look for the relationship between transmittance and average concentration of O_3. Figure 2 shows an inverse relationship between concentration and transmittance. As the concentration increased, the transmittance decreased. The correct answer is (B).

8. **G** The question asks which of the five locations has the *greatest transmittance at 0.31 microns,* according to Studies 2 and 3. According to the description for Study 2, Figure 2 shows the transmittance at 0.31 microns at various average concentrations of O_3. Study 3 shows the *average stratospheric ozone concentration,* and the results of Study 3 are shown in Table 1. Use Figure 2 and look for the relationship between transmittance and average concentration of O_3. Figure 2 shows an inverse relationship between concentration and transmittance. As the concentration increased, the transmittance decreased. The question asks for the *greatest transmittance,* so this would be found at the

location with the lowest concentration. Table 3 indicates that the lowest concentration is at Location 2. The correct answer is (G).

9. **A** The question asks which equations represent *the production of ozone in the stratosphere,* based on the passage. Use the information in the first paragraph to determine the equations. The passage states that *ozone is formed naturally when UV light breaks apart an oxygen molecule to form two highly reactive oxygen atoms.* Eliminate (B) and (D) because ozone (O_3) is not involved in same reaction as UV light. The passage then states that *oxygen atoms collide with another oxygen molecule to form ozone.* This means that the oxygen atoms (O) and the oxygen molecules (O_2) should be on one side of the equation and ozone (O_3) should be alone on the other side of the equation. Eliminate (C) since ozone (O_3) should be the only product. The correct answer is (A).

10. **F** The question asks, based on Figure 1, whether the researcher should measure the transmittance at *4.3 microns or at 9.5 microns,* given that the researcher wants to repeat Study 2 to study the effects on transmittance of different CO_2 *concentrations instead of O_3 concentrations.* Look at Figure 1 and determine the CO_2 transmittance at 4.3 microns and 9.5 microns. The CO_2 transmittance is approximately 0% at 4.3 microns and approximately 95% at 9.5 microns. Eliminate (G) and (H) because these incorrectly state that the transmittance is lower at 9.5 microns. Now, consider the original wavelength used in Study 2. The transmittance of O_3 varied from approximately 0% to 100% between 0.27 and 0.35 microns, and the researchers used a wavelength in the middle of this range. Similarly, a wavelength of 4.3 microns is in the middle of a range of wavelengths where the transmittance of CO_2 varies from approximately 0% to 100%. The correct answer is (F).

11. **B** The question asks for the mass of O_3, in *grams,* in 100 cubic meters of stratospheric air at Location 3, based on Table 1. Look at Table 1 and find the concentration of O_3 at Location 3. Table 1 shows that Location 3 has a concentration of 21 mg/m^3. Therefore, 100 cubic meters would contain 21 $mg/m^3 \times 100\ m^3 = 2{,}100$ mg of O_3 per 100 cubic meters of stratospheric air. Be careful! The question asks for *grams,* not milligrams, so eliminate (D). Since 1 g = 1,000 mg, a volume of 2,100 mg would be equal to 2.1 g. The correct answer is (B).

12. **J** The question asks, according to Figure 1, *which two zones have similar ranges.* The question states that the *range refers to the difference in depth between the top and bottom of that zone.* The horizontal axis in Figure 1 shows the depth, so the width of each zone along the horizontal axis would correspond to the range. Use POE. The epipelagic zone is very narrow, indicating a much smaller range than any of the other zones. Eliminate (F). The mesopelagic zone is larger than the epipelagic zone, but still much smaller than any others, so it is not close in range to any other zone. Eliminate (G) and (H) because both include mesopelagic. Only bathypelagic and abyssopelagic have approximately the same width for their zones in Figure 1. The correct answer is (J).

13. **B** The question asks, according to Figure 2, for which value of *d* does *approximately 35% of marine life [live] between 0 m and d.* Figure 2 shows the percent of marine life between sea level (0 m) and a given value of *d.* Find 35% on the vertical axis of Figure 2 and draw a horizontal line over until you reach the curve and then down to the horizontal axis. It's hard to tell exactly what the depth is

at 35%, but it is definitely less than 200 m, so eliminate (C) and (D) because they are too large. In the description preceding Figure 2, the passage states that *20% of all marine life is located between sea level and a depth of 50 m.* Eliminate (A) since 20% is not 35%. The depth must be somewhere between 50 m and 200 m. The correct answer is (B).

14. **J**   The question asks, based on Figure 1, what the dissolved oxygen level is at $d = 10,000$ m. In Figure 1, there are two vertical axes, and two curves, t and D.O. To answer this question, use the D.O. curve and make sure to use the vertical axis on the right-hand side of the graph. At $d = 9,600$ m, the D.O. is between 1.2 and 1.5 mg/L. The curve is increasing very slightly at 9,600 m, so eliminate (F), (G), and (H), which would all indicate a substantial decrease between 9,600 m and 10,000 m. Since the rate of increase is so small, the values will stay between 1.2 and 1.5 mg/L at 10,000 m. The correct answer is (J).

15. **B**   The question asks for the approximate *percentage of marine life* that *the aphotic zones account for.* The question defines *the aphotic zones* as *depths below 1,000 m.* Figure 2 shows *the percent of marine life located between sea level and a given depth.* Find 1,000 m on the horizontal axis and draw a straight line up until the curve and then over to the vertical axis. Approximately 90% of marine life is located between sea level and 1,000 m. The question asked for the percentage of marine life *below* 1,000 m, so there is 10% of marine life remaining at a depth below 1,000 m. The correct answer is (B).

16. **G**   The question asks, based on Figure 1, *which of the samples of water, if either, would have a lower mass.* The two samples are both *1-liter samples of water collected,* and one was *collected at* d = *1,000 m* and the other was *collected at* d = *3,600 m.* Refer to Figure 1. Notice that the temperature, represented by the solid line, is decreasing as the depth increases. Therefore, the water gets colder as the depth increases. The question states that *colder ocean water is denser than warmer ocean water,* so the water at 1,000 m is less dense than the colder water at 3,600 m. Eliminate (H) because the density of the two samples is not the same. To choose between the remaining answers, outside knowledge is necessary: density is equal to mass divided by volume. Since both of these samples have the same volume, the less dense sample, which is the sample from 1,000 m, must have the smaller mass. The correct answer is (G).

17. **C**   The question asks *which of the students theorized that fibromyalgia is triggered by neurons that are in some way physically altered.* Student 1 states that fibromyalgia results after *irreparable physical damage to nerve cells,* so the answer must include Student 1. Eliminate (B) and (D) because they do not include Student 1. Student 2 states that when there is a chronic excess of glutamate, the pain receptors on neurons *adapt by physically changing shape* and this change *results in fibromyalgia.* Therefore, Student 2 also believes that fibromyalgia is triggered by physically altered neurons. The correct answer is (C).

18. **H**   The question asks which student's theory is best supported by evidence that *female fibromyalgia patients report a higher incidence of pain during pregnancy and menopause when estrogen levels are rapidly changing.* Student 3 states that *fibromyalgia is caused only by abnormal estrogen or thyroid hormone levels.* None of the other students believe that estrogen contributes to fibromyalgia. The correct answer is (H).

19. **B** The question asks which types of foods provide L-tryptophan, based on Student 4's description. Find L-tryptophan in Student 4's description. Student 4 states that L-tryptophan is *an essential amino acid*. Outside knowledge is necessary here: amino acids are the building blocks of proteins. The correct answer is (B).

20. **J** The question asks *which of the students theorized that fibromyalgia is the result of low levels of certain neurotransmitters*. Use POE. Student 3 is in three of the answers, so check Student 3's explanation for mention of neurotransmitters. Student 3 states that serotonin and norepinephrine are *two inhibitory neurotransmitters* and that fibromyalgia results *when the levels of these inhibitory neurotransmitters are low*. Therefore, the answer must include Student 3. Eliminate (F) because it does not include Student 3. Student 2 states that *fibromyalgia is caused by the overproduction of neurotransmitters*. Overproduction is the opposite of low levels, so Student 2 cannot be in the correct answer. Eliminate (H). Now, determine if the answer needs to include Student 4 or not. Student 4 says that fibromyalgia is caused *when serotonin levels drop*. Serotonin was previously defined as an *inhibitory neurotransmitter* in Student 3's description, so Student 4 also believes that fibromyalgia is the result of *low levels of neurotransmitters*. The correct answer is (J).

21. **C** The question asks which of the findings, if true, *best supports Student 4's theory*. Student 4 states that *Fibromyalgia results only from a diet low in L-tryptophan*. This would mean that diets low in L-tryptophan would be associated with a higher number of cases of fibromyalgia. Eliminate (D), which states that *the prevalence of fibromyalgia is* lower *than average* for people who consume diets low in L-tryptophan. Keep (C) as it states the prevalence is higher. Choices (A) and (B) deal with levels of thyroid hormone. Student 4 states that *estrogen and thyroid hormone imbalances do not limit the production of serotonin*. Eliminate (A) and (B). The correct answer is (C).

22. **F** The question asks which of the students' viewpoints would be weakened by the results of a study involving Prescription *C, a powerful anti-inflammatory medication often prescribed to patients recovering from serious injury*. Since the question states that *the likelihood of developing fibromyalgia was the same among patients treated with Prescription C and patients that were not treated with any anti-inflammatory medications*, viewpoints attributing fibromyalgia to inflammation would be weakened by these results. Scan the viewpoints to see which ones mention inflammation or injury. Student 3 does not mention inflammation or injury, so eliminate (H) and (J). Student 2 mentions injury, but says that injury and illness *do not create the widespread pain of fibromyalgia*. Eliminate (G). Student 1 states that fibromyalgia results when *inflammation causes irreparable physical damage to the nerve cells*. The correct answer is (F).

23. **A** The question asks which soil samples had *the lowest percentage of ammonium converted to nitrate after treatment with N-1, N-2, and N-3*, according to the results of the studies. Figure 1 shows the results soil samples treated with N-1, Figure 2 shows the results of soil samples treated with N-2, and Figure 3 shows the results of soil samples treated with N-3. Start by looking at Figure 1 to determine which biome sample had the lowest percent of ammonium converted to nitrate for N-1. Figure 1 shows that the coniferous forest had the smallest percent of ammonium converted to nitrate in soil treated with

N-1. Eliminate (C) and (D). Figure 2 shows that the coniferous forest had the lowest percentage of ammonium converted to nitrate for N-2. Eliminate (B). The correct answer is (A).

24. **H** The question asks for the approximate *percent of ammonium converted to nitrate in the soils treated with N-2, averaged across all 5 biomes*, according to the results of Study 2. The results of Study 2 are shown in Figure 2, so look at Figure 2. In Figure 2, the highest percentage of ammonium converted to nitrate is 70% and the lowest percentage is 45%. Eliminate (F) since the average cannot be less than the smallest value. Eliminate (J) because the average must be smaller than the greatest value. Since the majority of the values are 60% or greater and only one value is less than 50% (45% for the coniferous forest), the average must be closer to 60% than 50%. Eliminate (G). The correct answer is (H).

25. **D** The question asks whether *a greater percentage of ammonium was converted to nitrate in the tropical forest soil treated with N-3 than the same soil treated with N-1,* based on Studies 1 and 3. Figure 1 shows the soil samples treated with N-1, and Figure 3 shows the soil samples treated with N-3. Start by looking at Figure 1 to determine percent of ammonium converted to nitrate in the tropical forest soil treated with N-1. According to Figure 1, tropical forest soil treated with N-1 had approximately 68% of the ammonium converted to nitrate. Eliminate (A), (B), and (C) because these answers do not identify 68% as the value for the soil sample treated with N-1. The correct answer is (D).

26. **H** The question asks for the *independent (experimental) variable across the 3 studies.* This question requires outside knowledge. An *independent variable* is also known as a manipulated variable because it is the variable that is manipulated by the experimenter in order to measure the effect on the dependent variable. Since the question asks for the independent variable *across the 3 studies,* consider which variable is different among the three studies. The same five biomes were used for each study, so eliminate (F). The concentration of ammonia and the concentration of nitrate are both dependent variables, so eliminate (G) and (J). Each of these studies uses a different nitrogen inhibitor, so the experimental variable is the type of nitrogen inhibitor. The correct answer is (H).

27. **A** The question asks whether *the mixture of N-1 and liquid fertilizer is a solution.* Use POE. Notice that two answers say N-1 was dissolved in the fertilizer, while the other two say that N-1 was suspended. Study 1 uses N-1, so look in the description of Study 1 for reference to *dissolved* or *suspended.* The description of Study 1 states that the *mixture was stirred until there were no remaining solids suspended in the mixture.* Therefore, the N-1 was not suspended; eliminate (B) and (D). To choose between (A) and (C), outside knowledge is needed. In chemistry, a solution is a homogenous mixture in which all solids are dissolved in the mixture. Since the N-1 was stirred until there were no remaining solids, the mixture is a solution. The correct answer is (A).

28. **H** The question asks which *step was incorporated in the experimental design to ensure that the bacteria in all five soils were active.* Since the question states that *nitrogen-fixing bacteria are inactive in temperatures below 12°C,* the correct answer must relate to the temperature of the soil. Eliminate (G) and (J), which do not relate to soil temperature. Look at the introduction and study description for information regarding soil temperature. The passage states that the soil samples were *maintained*

at 20°C for one week before the studies began and *remained at 20°C* during the studies. The passage never specifies the outside temperature at the time of collection, so eliminate (F). The correct answer is (H).

29. **D** The question asks which diagram most likely represents the petri dish where the cell in Figure 2 would be found, given that *the cell shown in Figure 2 is oriented exactly how it appeared in its dish*. Look at Figure 1 and determine which cells are most similar in shape to the cell in Figure 2. The cell in Figure 2 most resembles the cells in Dish D in Experiment 1. Eliminate (A) and (B) because the direction of the electric field is reversed from that in Dish D. According to the description for Experiment 1, *the yeast placed in Dishes C and D were all* S. pombe – GM. The correct answer is (D).

30. **G** The question asks which dish of cells in Experiment 1 had the most similar growth to the cells in Dish X *before Dish X was moved to a higher temperature room*. Look at the description of Experiment 2. The passage states that Dish X contained *S. pombe – N* cells, so eliminate (H) and (J) which both contained *S. pombe – GM* cells. The passage also states that *a battery was used to generate a current through all four dishes*. Since Dish A in Experiment 1 did not have an electric field, eliminate (F). The correct answer is (G).

31. **D** The question asks whether *the yeast cells in Dish Y likely grew toward the anode or toward the cathode*, according to Experiment 2. The question also states that *the anode of the petri dish is the positively charged electrode, and the cathode is the negatively charged electrode*. Look at the description of Experiment 2. The passage states that Dish Y contained *S. pombe – GM* cells. The passage also states that *a battery was used to generate a current through all four dishes*. Since the yeast cells in Dish Y were *S. pombe – GM* in the presence of an electric field, the cells in Dish Y would exhibit growth similar to Dish D, which also contained *S. pombe – GM* in the presence of an electric field. Eliminate (A) and (C) because these answers refer to Dish B, rather than Dish D. According to Figure 1, the yeast cells in Dish D grew toward the positively charged electrode, so this is the anode. The correct answer is (D).

32. **H** The question asks whether *S. pombe* is *a eukaryotic or prokaryotic cell*, based on Figure 1. Look at the description of Experiment 1. The description of Experiment 1 states that *the nucleus is shown for each cell*. Eliminate (G) and (J). To choose between the remaining choices, outside knowledge is necessary. Eukaryotic cells have a nucleus, while prokaryotic cells do not. The correct answer is (H).

33. **D** The question asks *how many times* the length of each cell was measured in Experiment 2. The results of Experiment 2 are shown in Figure 3, so look at Figure 3. Figure 3 shows a data point for each time data was collected during Experiment 2. Each dish has 7 data points, so each cell was measured 7 times. The correct answer is (D).

34. **J** The question asks which two dishes researchers should compare if they want to *examine the effects of different temperatures on the growth of* S. pombe – GM *cells*. In Experiment 1, the dishes were held *at a constant temperature of 20°C*, and in Experiment 2, the temperature was varied, so look at the description for Experiment 2. Dishes Y and Z contained *S. pombe – GM*, and Dishes W and X

contained *S. pombe – N* cells. Since the researchers want to examine *the growth of* S. pombe – GM *cells,* eliminate (F), (G), and (H), which refer to Dishes W and/or X. The correct answer is (J).

35. **D** The question asks about the maximum velocity after impact for a ball with an elasticity of 0.8 Pa and a weight of 3 kg dropped from a height of 1.5 meters. The top graph of Figure 2 shows a ball with this elasticity and weight dropped from 1 meter. According to Figure 2, the maximum velocity after impact for the 3 kg ball is approximately 2.0 m/s. A ball dropped from a height of 1.5 meters instead of 1 meter would have a faster velocity prior to impact, and therefore, would have a faster post-impact velocity than the one shown in Figure 2. The correct answer is (D).

36. **F** The question asks which elasticity would cause a ball to have the smallest *maximum post-impact velocity,* according to Figure 2. Look at Figure 2. The graphs display the velocity of a ball over time after it has been dropped. The curve begins at 0 seconds and 0 m/s, just before the ball is dropped. Each ball increases in velocity until it hits the ground at around 0.45 seconds. The *maximum post-impact velocity* is shown in each graph as the second peak. The *maximum post-impact velocity* of the 3 kg ball in the first graph with *elasticity = 0.8 Pa* is about 2.05. The *maximum post-impact velocity* of the 3 kg ball in the second graph with *elasticity = 0.5 Pa* is about 1.75. The *maximum post-impact velocity* of the 3 kg ball in the third graph with *elasticity = 0.2 Pa* is about 1.30, which is the smallest. Therefore, the lower the elasticity, the smaller the *maximum post-impact velocity.* Choice (F) has the lowest value for elasticity. The correct answer is (F).

37. **A** The question asks for the *maximum post-impact velocity* of *a ball being dropped from 1 meter height with an elasticity of 0.2 Pa and a weight of 0.5 kg,* based on the information in Figure 2. Look for similar conditions in Figure 2. The third graph displays information regarding a ball with 0.2 elasticity. Look at the curve representing a 1 kg ball. Its *maximum post-impact velocity* is 0.50. As weight decreases, so does *maximum post-impact velocity,* so the *maximum post-impact velocity* of a ball that weighs 0.5 kg should be less than that of the 1 kg ball. Eliminate (B), (C), and (D) because they are greater than 0.5 kg. The correct answer is (A).

38. **J** The question asks how many times a ball, with a weight of 2 kg and an elasticity of 0.50 Pa, had a velocity of 1.00 m/s, according to the data in Figure 2. Look for similar conditions in Figure 2. The second graph shows data regarding a ball with an elasticity of 0.50. Locate 1.00 m/s on the *y*-axis and draw a straight line to the other side of the graph. The curve representing the velocity of the 2 kg ball intersects the line drawn four times, which means the 2 kg ball had a velocity of 1.00 m/s four times. The correct answer is (J).

39. **C** The question asks *how the velocity of a ball change[s] as it goes from drop to apex,* according to Figure 2. Look at Figure 2. The curve representing the velocity of the ball begins at 0 m/s, when the ball is at rest, just before it is dropped. The ball then increases in velocity until just before it hits the ground. There is a rapid decrease to 0 m/s at the moment when the ball hits the ground. Eliminate (A) because it says the velocity increases only from drop to impact. Eliminate (B) because it says the velocity decreases only from drop to impact. Keep (C) because it correctly states that, from drop to

impact, the velocity increases and then decreases. Eliminate (D) because it states the opposite. The correct answer is (C).

40. **H** The question asks whether, according to Figure 2, a ball will deform permanently if it has *a weight of 3 kg, an elasticity of 0.8 Pa, and an elastic limit of 2.75 m/s,* given that *a ball will deform permanently...if the velocity with which it hits the ground exceeds the ball's elastic limit.* Look for similar conditions in Figure 2. The first graph displays data regarding a ball with an elasticity of 0.8 Pa. The ball begins at rest and increases in velocity until it impacts the ground at just before 0.45 seconds; the velocity just before it hits the ground is 2.25 m/s. This is less than the *elastic limit of 2.75 m/s,* so the ball will not *deform permanently.* Eliminate (F) and (G) because they state that it will deform permanently. Keep (H) and eliminate (J) because *the velocity with which the ball hits the ground is less than its elastic limit.* The correct answer is (H).

Chapter 4
ACT Strategy

You will raise your ACT score by working smarter, not harder, and a smart test-taker is a strategic test-taker. You will target specific content to review, you will apply an effective and efficient approach, and you will employ common sense.

Each test on the ACT demands a specific approach, and even the most universal strategies vary in their applications. In Parts II–V, we'll discuss these strategies in greater detail customized to English, Math, Reading, Science, and Writing.

THE BASIC APPROACH

The ACT is different from the tests you take in school, so you need to approach it differently. The Princeton Review's strategies are not arbitrary. To be effective, ACT strategies have to be based on the ACT and not on any other test.

You need to know how the ACT is scored and how it's constructed.

Scoring

When students and schools talk about ACT scores, they typically mean the composite score, a range of 1–36. The composite is an average of the three core multiple-choice tests, each scored on the same 1–36 scale. Neither the Writing test score nor the combined English plus Writing score affects the composite. Similarly, the optional Science section will not be used to calculate the composite.

The scaled score in each section is based on the number of questions you get right in that section, with an important catch. Prior to April 2025, ACT gave an unscored 5th section to students who opted to skip the Writing portion. Now the unscored questions are included in each scored section. These aren't marked in any way, so you won't know which ones they are.

The Composite

When you look at your score online, the biggest number on the page is always the composite. While admissions offices will certainly see the individual scores of all five tests if you take them, most schools and programs will use the composite to evaluate your application, and that's why in the end it's the one that matters most.

The composite is an average. Add the scores for the English, Math, and Reading, and divide the total by three. Do you add one test twice? Um, no. Do you omit one of the tests in the total? Er, no again. The three tests are weighted equally to calculate the composite. But do you need to bring up all three equally to raise your composite? Do you need to be a superstar in all three tests? Should you focus more on your weakest tests than your strongest tests? No, no, and absolutely not. The best way to improve your composite is to shore up your weaknesses but exploit your strengths as much as possible.

> To lift the composite score as high as possible,
> maximize the scores of your strongest tests.

You don't need to be a rock star on all three tests. Identify one or two tests, and focus on raising those scores as much as you can to raise your composite score. Work on your weakest scores to keep them from pulling you down. Are you strongest in English and Math, or maybe in Math and Reading? Then work to raise those scores as high as you can. You shouldn't ignore your weaknesses, but recognize that the work you put in on your strengths will yield greater dividends. Think of it this way: if you had only one hour to devote to practice the week before the ACT, you would put that hour toward your best subjects.

Structure

Let's quickly review the current structure of the ACT. The five tests are always given in the same order.

English	Math	Reading	Science (Optional)	Writing (Optional)
35 minutes	50 minutes	40 minutes	40 minutes	40 minutes
50 questions	45 questions	36 questions	40 questions	1 essay

Enemy #1: Time

How much time do you have per question on the Math and Reading tests? You have just under 67 seconds, and that's generous compared with the time given per question on the English and Science tests. But how often do you take a test in school with about a minute per question? If you do at all, it's maybe on a multiple-choice quiz but probably not on a major exam or final. Time is your enemy on the ACT, and you have to use it wisely and be aware of how that time pressure can bring out your worst instincts as a test-taker.

> English has 50 questions in 35 minutes (42 seconds per question) and Reading has 36 questions in 40 minutes (nearly 67 seconds per question).

Enemy #2: Yourself

Many people struggle with test anxiety in school and on standardized tests. But there is something particularly evil about tests like the ACT and SAT. The skills you've been rewarded for throughout your academic career can easily work against you on the ACT. You've been taught since birth to follow directions, go in order, and finish everything. But that approach won't necessarily earn you your highest ACT score.

On the other hand, treating the ACT as a scary, alien beast can leave your brain blank and useless and can incite irrational, self-defeating behavior. When you pick up a No. 2 pencil or sit in front of the computer, you may tend to leave your common sense at the door. Test nerves and anxieties can make you misread a question, commit a careless error, see something that isn't there, blind you to what *is* there, talk you into a bad answer, and worst of all, convince you to spend good time on "bad" questions.

There is good news. You can—and will—crack the ACT. You will learn how to approach it differently from how you would a test in school, and you won't let the test crack you.

ACT STRATEGIES

Personal Order of Difficulty (POOD)

If time is going to run out, would you rather it run out on the hardest questions or the easiest? Of course, you want it to run out on the questions you are less likely to get right.

You can easily fall into the trap of spending too much time on the hardest questions and either never getting to or rushing through the easiest. You shouldn't work in the order ACT provides just because the test is in that order. Instead, find your own Personal Order of Difficulty (POOD).

Make smart decisions quickly for good reasons as you move through each test.

The Best Way to Bubble In

If you're taking the Paper ACT, work a page at a time, circling your answers right on the booklet. Transfer a page's worth of answers to the answer document at one time. It's better to stay focused on working questions rather than disrupt your concentration to find where you left off on the answer document. You'll be more accurate at both tasks. Do not wait to the end, however, to transfer all the answers of that test to your answer document. Go one page at a time on English and Math, a passage at a time on Reading (and Science if taking it). In the last few minutes, though, bubble the answer after working each question. In the very last minute or two, bubble in an answer to any questions you didn't have time to work.

Letter of the Day (LOTD)

Just because you don't *work* a question doesn't mean you don't *answer* it. There is no penalty for wrong answers on the ACT, so you should never leave any blanks on your answer document. When you guess on Never questions, pick your favorite letter or, on the Paper ACT, two-letter combo of answers and stick with it. For example, always choose A/F or C/H. If you're consistent, you're more likely to pick up more points.

Now

Does a question look okay? Do you know how to do it? Do it *Now*.

Later

Will this question take a long time to work? Leave it and come back to it *Later*. Circle the question number or flag the question on the computer for easy reference to return.

Never

Test-taker, know thyself. Know the topics that are your worst, and learn the signs that flash danger. Don't waste time on questions you should *Never* do. Instead, use more time to answer the Now and Later questions accurately.

Pacing

The ACT may be designed for you to run out of time, but you shouldn't rush through it as fast as possible. All you'll do is make careless errors on easy questions you should get right and spend way too much time on difficult ones you're unlikely to get right. Let your POOD help determine your pacing. Go slowly enough to answer correctly all the Now questions but quickly enough to get to the number of Later questions you need to reach your goal score.

Process of Elimination (POE)

Multiple-choice tests offer one great advantage: they provide the correct answer right there on the page. Of course, they hide the correct answer amid 3 incorrect answers. It's often easier to spot the wrong answers than it is to identify the right ones, particularly when you apply a smart Process of Elimination (POE).

POE works differently for each test on the ACT, but it's a powerful strategy for all of them. For some question types, you'll always use POE rather than wasting time trying to figure out the answer on your own. For other questions, you'll use POE when you're stuck. ACT hides the correct answer behind wrong ones, but when you eliminate just one or two wrong answers, the correct answer can become more obvious, sometimes jumping right off the page or screen.

For an example of how powerful POE can be, consider the following question:

> *What is the capital of Cyprus?*

Now, the ACT would never ask a question such as this (unless it was with a Reading passage that included the answer). In the real world, you'd probably reach for your phone to search for the answer. On the ACT, that's not an option. Fortunately, the ACT is a multiple-choice test, which means POE is a great tool:

What is the capital of Cyprus?

A. London
B. Tokyo
C New Cyprusburg
D. Nicosia

> ### Use Your Pencil...
> If you take the Paper ACT, you own the test booklet, and you should write where and when it helps you. Use your pencil to literally cross off wrong answers on the page.

Even if you had no idea, LOTD would give you a 25% chance of getting this version of the question correct. But POE increases that further: London is the capital of the United Kingdom, so (A) is wrong, and Tokyo is the capital of Japan, so (B) is wrong. At this point, you have a 50% chance, and you might feel that (C) is a trap (it is!), leading you to (D), Nicosia, as the correct answer.

POOD, Pacing, and POE all work together to help you spend your time where it does the most good: on the questions you can and should get right.

> ### ...or Use Your Tools
> When you take the test on a computer, you can't write on the computer screen, but you can eliminate answers using the Answer Eliminator tool. Additionally, use the highlighter tool in the passage, question, and answer choices, and use the whiteboard or scratch paper for any work you need to do.

Be Ruthless

The worst mistake a test-taker can make is to throw good time at "bad" questions. You read a question but don't understand it, so you read it again. And again. If you stare at it really hard, you know you're going to just *see* the answer. And you can't move on, because really, after spending all that time it would be a waste not to keep at it, right?

Wrong. You can't let one tough question drag you down, and you can't let your worst instincts tempt you into self-defeating behavior. Instead, the best way to improve your ACT score is to follow our advice.

- Use the techniques and strategies in the lessons to work efficiently and accurately through all your Now and Later questions.
- Know your Never questions, and use your LOTD.
- Know when to move on. Use POE, and guess from what's left.

In Parts II–V, you'll learn how POOD, Pacing, and POE work on each test.

Chapter 5
Taking the ACT

Preparing yourself both mentally and physically to take the ACT is important. This chapter helps you learn exactly what you're in for so you can plan ahead and be as comfortable as possible on test day. We talk about not only what to do but also what *not* to do.

PREPARING FOR THE ACT

The best way to prepare for any test is to find out exactly what is going to be on it. This book provides you with just that information. In the following chapters, you will find a comprehensive review of all the question types on the ACT, complete information on all the subjects covered by the ACT, and some powerful test-taking strategies developed specifically for the ACT.

To take full advantage of the review and techniques, you should practice on the tests in this book as well as on real ACT questions. We've already told you how to obtain copies of real ACT exams. Taking full practice exams allows you to chart your progress (with accurate scores for each test), gives you confidence in our techniques, and develops your stamina.

The Night Before the Test

Unless you are the kind of person who remains calm only by staying up all night to do last-minute studying, we recommend that you take the evening off. Go to a movie or read a good book (besides this one), and make sure you get to bed at a normal hour. No final, frantically memorized math formula or grammatical rule is going to make or break your score. A positive mental attitude comes from treating yourself decently. If you've prepared over the last several weeks or months, then you're ready.

If you haven't really prepared, there will be other opportunities to take the test, so get some rest and do the best you can. Remember, colleges will see only the score you choose to let them see. No *single* ACT is going to be crucial. We don't think night-before-the-test cramming is very effective. For example, we would not recommend that you try going through this book in one night.

Don't Leave Home Without 'Em

Here are some items you'll want to have on test day.

- Admissions ticket
- Photo ID or letter of identification
- Plenty of sharpened No. 2 pencils (if you're taking the Paper ACT)
- A watch
- An acceptable calculator with new or charged batteries

On the Day of the Test

It's important that you eat a real breakfast, even if you normally don't. We find that about two-thirds of the way through the test, people who didn't eat something beforehand suddenly lose their will to go on. Equally importantly, take a snack to the test center. You will get a break during which food is allowed. Some people spend the break out in the hallways comparing answers and getting upset when their answers don't match. Ignore the people around you, and eat your snack. Why assume they know any more than you do?

Warming Up

While you're having breakfast, get your mind going by doing a couple of questions from an ACT test on which you've already worked. You don't want to use the first test on the real exam to warm up. And please don't try a hard question you've never done before. If you miss it, your confidence will be diminished, and that's not something you want on the day of the test.

At the test center, you'll be asked to show some form of picture ID or provide a note from your school—on school stationery—describing what you look like. You'll also need to take a calculator (a must for the Paper ACT but also nice to have for the Online ACT). Check ACTStudent.org/faq to see if your calculator model is permitted. If you haven't changed the batteries recently (or ever), you should do that before the test or take a back-up calculator. If your calculator requires charging, charge it a day or two before. Finally, if you're taking the Paper ACT, you'll need to take No. 2 pencils and an eraser. You'll also want to take a reliable watch—not the beeping kind (or the smart kind)—because the time remaining is not always announced during the test sections.

When you get into the actual room in which you'll be taking the exam, make sure you're comfortable. Is there enough light? Is your desk sturdy? If you're taking the ACT Online Test, do the mouse and keyboard work? Don't be afraid to speak up; after all, you're going to be spending three and a half hours at that desk if you take all 5 sections. And it's not a bad idea to go to the bathroom *before* you get to the room. It's a long haul to that first break.

While your college search may be the furthest thing from your mind on test day, don't forget that your Student Tools is a great resource for informative articles and advice on financial aid, the application process, letters of recommendation, and much more!

ZEN AND THE ART OF TEST TAKING

Once the exam begins, tune out the rest of the world. That girl with the annoying cough in the next row? You don't hear her. That guy who is fidgeting in the seat ahead of you? You don't see him. It's just you and the exam. Everything else should be a blur.

As soon as one section ends, erase it completely from your mind. It no longer exists. The only thing that matters is the one you are taking right now. Even if you are upset about a particular section, try to forget about it. If you are busy thinking about the last section, you cannot focus on the one on which you are currently working, and that's a sure-fire way to make costly mistakes. Most people aren't very good at assessing how they performed on a given section of the exam, especially while they're still taking it, so don't waste your time and energy trying.

Some Things to Remember

- Make sure you know where the test center is located and where you need to go once you are there.
- Show up early; you can't show up right when the test is scheduled to begin and expect to get in.
- Lay out everything you need, including your calculator, admission ticket, and photo identification, the night before the test. The last thing you want to do on the morning of the test is run around looking for a calculator. Also, it's important to take your own watch if you're taking the Paper ACT because there's no requirement for the room you're in to have a working clock.
- Take a snack and a bottle of water just in case you get hungry. There's nothing worse than testing on an empty stomach.

Keep Your Answers to Yourself

Please don't let anyone cheat off you. Test companies have developed sophisticated anti-cheating measures that go way beyond having a proctor walk around the room. We know of one test company that gets seating charts of each testing room. Its computers analyze the results of people sitting in the immediate vicinity for correlations of wrong answer choices. Innocent and guilty are invited to take the exam over again, and their scores from the first exam are invalidated.

Using the Index Tool
On the ACT Online Test, the Index Tool helps you move through the questions. Use this tool to make sure you've answered every question before time runs out. We recommend doing so at the 5-minute warning.

Beware of Misbubbling Your Answer Sheet

Probably the most painful kind of mistake you can make on the Paper ACT is to bubble in choice (A) with your pencil when you really mean choice (B), or to have your answers one question number off (perhaps because you skipped one question on the test but forgot to skip it on the answer sheet). Aargh! The proctor isn't allowed to let you change your answers after a section is over, so it is critical that you either catch yourself before a test section ends or—even better—that you don't make a mistake in the first place.

We suggest to our students that they write down their answers in their test booklets. This way, whenever you finish a page of questions in the test booklet, you can transfer all your answers from that page in a group. We find that this method minimizes the possibility of misbubbling, and it also saves time. Of course, as you get near the end of a test, you should go back to bubbling question by question. And you should do your practice tests with an answer sheet. It's important to make the practice tests as close to the real test as possible, including seemingly simple tasks such as bubbling in your answers!

Write Now
Feel free to write all over your test booklet. Don't do computations in your head. Put them in the booklet; you paid for it. Go nuts!

If you get back your ACT scores and they seem completely out of line, you can ask the ACT examiners to look over your answer sheet for what are called "gridding errors." If you want to, you can even be there while they look. If it is clear that there has been an error, ACT will change your score. An example of a gridding error would be a test in which, if you moved all the responses over by one, they would suddenly all be correct.

Should I Ever Cancel My Scores?

We recommend against canceling your scores, even if you feel you've done poorly. You should register for the test without sending scores to any schools and possibly not even to your high school. This way, the score you receive won't go anywhere unless you send it on later. There is no need to panic and cancel your score without knowing what it is if no one will ever see it. You never know—perhaps you did better than you think. Furthermore, if you've taken the ACT two or more times (something we heartily recommend), you can choose which score you want colleges to see or send a superscore when you request reports from ACT.

If you do decide to cancel your scores, you need to go to ACT's website to request a cancellation form. You may also be able to request this form by calling ACT at 319-337-1270.

Part II
How to Crack the ACT English Test

Chapter 6
Introduction to the ACT English Test

The English test is not a grammar test. It's also not a test of how well you write. In fact, it tests your editing skills: your ability to fix errors in grammar and punctuation and to improve the organization and style of five different passages. In this chapter, you'll learn the basic strategy of how to crack the passages and review the grammar you need to know.

WHAT'S ON THE ENGLISH TEST

Before we dive into the details of the content and strategy, let's review what the English test looks like. Remember, the tests on the ACT are always given in the same order, and English is always first. The English test includes six or seven prose passages on topics ranging from historical essays to personal narratives. Each passage is accompanied by either 5 or 10 questions for a total of 50 questions that you must answer in 35 minutes. Portions of each passage are underlined, and you must decide if these are correct as written or if one of the other answers would fix or improve the selection. Other questions will ask you to add, cut, or reorder text, while still others will ask you to evaluate the passage as a whole. Either one 10-question passage or two 5-question passages will not count toward your score, but you won't know which passages these are.

> On the previous version of the ACT English Test, some questions only had answer choices—no actual question. On the enhanced test, all English questions have a question stem.

> If you take the Online ACT, the underlined portions of the passage will also be highlighted. Where you see boxed question numbers within the passage in this book and on the Paper ACT, the Online ACT will show an asterisk that will be highlighted when you click onto the corresponding question.

WRITING

While the idea of English grammar makes most of us think of persnickety, picky rules long since outdated, English is actually a dynamic, adaptive language. We add new vocabulary all the time, and we let common usage influence and change many rules. Pick up a handful of style books, and you'll find very few rules that everyone agrees upon. This is actually good news for studying for the ACT: you're unlikely to see questions testing the most obscure or most disputed rules. However, few of us follow ALL of even the most basic, universally accepted rules when we speak, much less when we email, text, or Snapchat.

LEARN WHAT'S ACTUALLY TESTED

ACT test-writers will never make you name a particular error. But with 50 questions, they can certainly test a lot of different rules—and yes, that's leaving out the obscure and debated rules. You would drive yourself crazy if you tried to learn, just for the ACT, all of the grammar you never knew in the first place. You're much better off with a common-sense approach. We'll teach you the rules that show up most often, and we'll show you how to crack the questions that test them. The other good news is that over half of the questions don't test grammar or punctuation rules at all. Instead, you'll be tested on the consistency of ideas within a sentence, paragraph, or passage.

HOW TO CRACK THE ENGLISH TEST

The Passages

As always on the ACT, time is your enemy. With only 35 minutes to review six or seven passages and answer 50 questions, you can't read a passage in its entirety and then go back to do the questions (even though the ACT instructs you to do so!). For each passage, work the questions as you make your way through the passage. Read from the beginning until you get to the end of a sentence with an underlined selection, work that question, and then resume reading until the next underlined portion or boxed number and the next question.

The Questions

Not all questions are created equal. In fact, ACT divides the questions on the English test into three categories: Production of Writing, Knowledge of Language, and Conventions of Standard English. These designations will mean very little to you when you're taking the test. All questions are worth the same number of points, after all, and you'll crack most of the questions the same way, regardless of what ACT calls them. Many of the Production of Writing questions, however, are on organization and style, and some take longer to answer than other questions. Since the passages and questions don't follow any order of difficulty, all that matters is that you identify your *Now*, *Later*, and *Never* questions and make sure you finish. (And remember, any Later questions should be done before moving on to the next passage. Most questions will be Now or Never.) The best way to make sure you finish with as many correct answers as possible is to use our 4-step Basic Approach. We'll go through the steps with one type of question and then with another.

Step 1: Identify the Question Type

Although ACT breaks the English questions into three categories, we think you'll find it easier and more helpful to identify questions within just two categories: Grammar questions and Content questions. Let's take a look at the first of these types.

Nigerian <u>author Chimamanda Ngozi Adichie,</u>
                                              [1]
is highly acclaimed for her novels, short stories,

and essays.

1. Which choice makes the sentence most grammatically acceptable?
   A. **No Change**
   B. author, Chimamanda Ngozi Adichie
   C. author Chimamanda Ngozi Adichie
   D. author, Chimamanda Ngozi Adichie,

This is an example of what we call a **Grammar question**. How do you know? Because the question asks for the *most grammatically acceptable* answer. All Grammar questions will ask this same question. This category includes all of the questions that test you on punctuation and grammar rules.

The "grammatically acceptable" question lets you know that you're dealing with a question on grammar or punctuation, but it's not very specific. You won't know whether the question is testing you on commas, verbs, or any other specific topic until you look at the answer choices. Notice what is the same and what changes within the four answer choices (including the underlined **No Change** option).

Step 2 for Grammar Questions: Look at the Answers to See What's Changing

As we just noted, we can't tell what is actually being tested on a Grammar question until we look at the answers. In this case, the original underlined portion and the other three options all contain commas in varying places or no punctuation at all. Right away, this lets us know that the topic is punctuation, and specifically commas. We don't need to think about verbs or semicolons or any other topic that isn't being tested in this question. We may even be able to be more specific and note that the commas are moving around the phrase *Chimamanda Ngozi Adichie*, so the question is testing whether this phrase needs to be separated from the rest of the sentence with commas.

Step 3: Read and Mark Up the Text as Needed

Now, we are going to follow the same step regardless of the question type, but let's see how it works on this Grammar question. We need to read the full sentence and consider whether there is any reason to use a comma before the author's name and/or after the author's name. In this case, there isn't any reason to use a comma before, since the word *author* is a title for Adichie. No punctuation should be used between a title and a person's name (don't worry—we will go over these rules later on in this book). There also isn't a reason to use a comma after Adichie's name, and if it were the case that a comma had been used after her name but not before, the sentence would have a single punctuation mark in between a subject and its verb, which is never allowed.

Step 4: Use Process of Elimination

We've recognized that there is no reason to use a comma either before or after Adichie's name, so we can eliminate all the answers with commas: (A), (B), and (D). This means we're left with (C) and can pick that option and move on.

Now, let's see the steps for Content questions.

Step 1: Identify the Question Type

After Adichie won a MacArthur Genius
Grant in 2008, she will publish a book of short
stories called *The Thing Around Your Neck*. In
March 2017, a panel chose Adichie's book
Americanah as its selection for a citywide book
club. Among a generation of new writers,
Adichie has <u>emerged as one of the freshest, most</u>
<u>original voices.</u>
₂

2. Which choice is least redundant in context?

   F. **No Change**
   G. emerged and come out as
   H. started to become considered
   J. begun to emerge and be called

Unlike the last question, this one is a **Content question**. You can tell because it doesn't ask about the *most grammatically acceptable* answer. It's as simple as that. Any question asking for something other than a grammatically acceptable answer is going to be categorized as Content. These questions will always ask you for something specific, whether it is about redundancy, tone, where a sentence should go within a paragraph, whether a new sentence should be added, or anything else.

Step 2 for Content Questions: Underline/Highlight What the Question is Asking For

Here, we don't need to start by looking at the answers because the question itself is going to let us know what's being tested. In this case, we're looking for the *least redundant answer*, so you should underline or highlight that phrase (depending on whether you are taking the test on paper or on a computer).

Step 3: Read and Mark Up the Text as Needed

For this question, we still need to read the whole sentence, and we may find it helpful to read (or reread) the sentence before the one with the underlined portion. That's because questions on redundancy can include answers that are redundant because they repeat information from the previous sentence(s). If you only read the sentence with the blank, you may not realize when an answer choice is actually redundant. It also makes a lot of sense on redundancy questions to start with the shortest option and compare it to the longer ones to see whether any additional words are needed.

Step 4: Use Process of Elimination

In question 2, we can identify that the short option, (F), seems to work, but we need to check the other options to see if there is any reason to use the additional words. Choice (G) is redundant because "emerge" and "come out" mean the same thing, so we can eliminate it. Choice (H) is also redundant because "start" and "become" are synonyms, so it can be eliminated. Choice (J) doesn't have any synonyms but uses a lot more words than (F) without contributing to the sentence's meaning in any way, so we can eliminate that one too. Thus, our answer is (F).

ADDITIONAL WORDS OF WISDOM FOR THE ENGLISH TEST

Don't Fix What Isn't Broken

As you saw in question 2, the "no change" option is a legitimate answer choice, and it's correct about 25% of the time that it appears. Sometimes students assume that keeping the sentence as it is written couldn't possibly be correct—after all, why would ACT bother to put the question on the test if the sentence didn't have something wrong with it? Well, that's where it pays off to prepare for the test. Treat (A) the same as any other answer choice. You should neither dismiss it as an answer nor favor it.

Don't Always Trust Your Ear

If you've taken the ACT or a practice test already, you probably found yourself answering a good portion of the questions based on how the sentence sounds with each answer choice. That should have gotten you some number of the questions right, but it's safe to assume you also missed some, or you wouldn't be reading this chapter. How we speak isn't always the same as how things are written—think about words like *its* and *it's*, which sound the same when spoken but have different written meanings. Moreover, we now encounter far more "incorrect" text than we ever used to, thanks to social media and text messaging. Of course, it's fine to speak or write "incorrectly" on a normal basis. But when you're taking a test on the English language, you have to know the actual rules.

On the ACT, an answer that looks or sounds bad can actually be correct. Likewise, an answer that sounds perfectly fine and normal can have an error. It's okay to use your ear as a tool, but you'll need to learn (or re-learn) some punctuation and grammar rules in order to do well on this section. Not every ACT English question tests you on a specific rule, but many do, and learning those rules can really help you boost your score. Of course, we'll teach you all the rules you need to know in this book.

Use the Context

As we noted on question 2, you may need to read more than just the sentence with the underlined portion in order to answer a question. For most Grammar questions, you'll only need the one sentence. The majority of Content questions, on the other hand, will require you to read at least one sentence before the underlined portion. In some cases, you'll need to consider the focus of the whole paragraph or even the entire passage. For these reasons, you should always read in between the questions. Don't just go from underlined portion to underlined portion. You'll end up wasting time having to go back when you encounter a question that does require that context, and you'll risk making a mistake by not realizing what was said in the non-underlined portion. And as we noted earlier, it's okay to skip questions and come back to them. For instance, if a question asks for a sentence to introduce a paragraph, you'll need to read the rest of the paragraph (and may want to do any other questions in that paragraph) before coming back to the question about the introductory sentence once you understand the focus of the paragraph.

Don't Forget What the Question is Asking

As we just saw, Step 2 for Content questions is to underline or highlight the task in the question. This step is super important because it can be easy to ignore the question and go straight to the answer choices—especially because that's exactly what we do for Grammar questions. But for Content questions, it's all about what answer choice fulfills what the question is actually asking. On these questions, it's usually the case that all four answers are grammatically correct, so you won't need to think about following rules or being concise, unless the question asks you to do so. It's easy to go wrong on these questions and pick the answer that you personally like best, based on how it sounds, how interesting it is, or whether you believe the information in the answer choice is true. However, none of this will help you get the correct answer. You must focus on what the question is actually asking and eliminate any answer that doesn't fulfill that goal.

Focus on Process of Elimination

There are many correct ways to say the same thing. So, you might read a sentence with an underlined portion, spot an error, and come up with your own idea of how to fix it. The problem with that is that the ACT writers may not have chosen to fix the sentence in exactly the same way you wanted to. If you go to the answers and look for your revision, you could actually pick a trap answer because the answer that made the change you wanted could have some other mistake in it. Instead, don't try to fix the error yourself. If you know the original is wrong, eliminate it, and then continue to use Process of Elimination with the remaining options, considering what is actually on the page or screen and not how you might like to rewrite the sentence. Many ACT English questions test multiple topics, so several aspects of the underlined portion may be changed in the correct answer!

Pace Yourself Properly

The English questions don't follow an order of difficulty. That is, you'll see some questions that are easier and some that are harder, but they're all mixed up within the passages. What's more, it doesn't really matter whether ACT thinks the questions are easy or hard. The difficulty will vary for every student depending on what the individual student finds easy or hard. For you, this means that your goal is to get to the end of the section. If you run out of time for the last passage, you're likely passing up some easy questions that you could have gotten right. Use your practice tests to gauge your ability to finish the section within the time limit. If you find yourself having trouble doing so, consider skipping some of the harder or more time-consuming questions as you go. It's not too hard to spot the time-consuming ones—they usually look a lot longer than the faster ones. By skipping a few of these, you might boost the odds of getting to all the questions and ultimately getting more correct answers. Of course, if you decide to skip any questions, be sure to put a random guess rather than leave the question blank.

CONCLUSION

The flow chart below offers a visual description of the process we described in this lesson. Follow these simple steps throughout the English section, and you're likely to see an improvement in your score just from that.

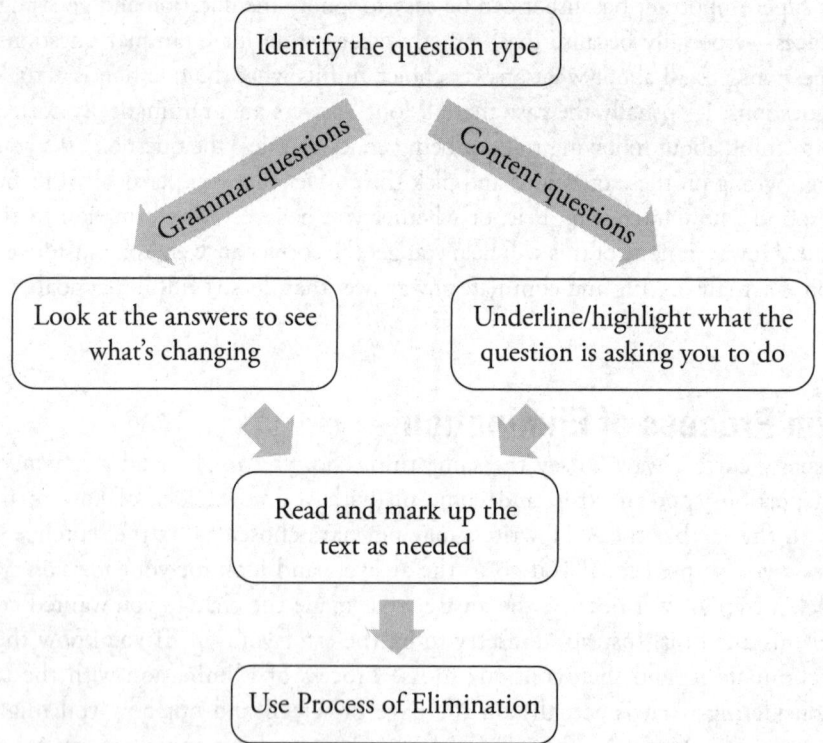

Another important way to improve your score is to learn the punctuation and grammar rules that are regularly tested. While Content questions can often be answered with nothing more than an understanding of what the question is asking and what the text is saying, Grammar questions do require outside knowledge in the form of specific rules pertaining to how sentences are structured. Take a look at the grammar review on the next few pages to see a preview of the types of rules that will be covered in some of the chapters that follow.

GRAMMAR REVIEW

This is not an exhaustive review of English grammar. It is an overview of the most common rules tested on the English test. We focus on the rules that show up the most AND that we know you can easily identify. In the next several chapters, we'll teach you how to crack those questions on the ACT. For now, we'll introduce you to the terms and rules you need to know.

Verbs

What's wrong with the following sentences?

1. Ryan play soccer.
2. Mary and Allison practices every day.
3. Next week, the team traveled to play its bitter rival.
4. Shivani has became the star of the team.

Your ear may have caught some, or all, of the verb errors in these sentences. But as we discussed, your ear will only go so far because we're all used to hearing, and saying, things that may not follow the rules of proper grammar. You don't always need to know why a sentence is wrong to get the right answer, but the more you know why, the more you can count on getting that question right the next time it appears and every time after that. Know the likely errors for verbs.

Subject-Verb Agreement

First, know your terms. A *subject* is the performer of an action. A *verb* is an action, feeling, or state of being. Verbs have to be consistent with their subjects. Singular subjects take the singular forms of verbs, and plural subjects take plural forms of verbs.

> ### The Rule
> Your ear can alert you to many, if not most, subject-verb agreement errors. **As a general rule, singular verbs end with *s* and plural verbs do not.**

*Ryan **plays** soccer.*

*Mary and Allison **practice** every day.*

Verb Tense

The tense of the verb changes with the time of the event. On the ACT, verb tense is tested far less frequently than subject-verb agreement is.

Simple Tenses

ACT tests your ability to choose from among the three simple tenses.

Past: *Last year, the team **finished** in last place.*

Present: *This year, the team **plays** a demanding schedule.*

Future: *Next week, the team **will travel** to play its bitter rival.*

Perfect Tenses

The perfect tenses provide additional ways to place an event in time. On the ACT, the perfect tenses appear less often than do the simple tenses.

Past perfect: *Before I went to the performance with Kelly, I **had** never **appreciated** ballet.*

Use the past perfect to make clear the chronology of two events completed at a definite time in the past, one before the other.

Present perfect: *I **have lived** in Chicago for ten years. I **have read** all the* Harry Potter *books.*

Use the present perfect to describe an event that began in the past and continues into the present, or to describe an event that was completed at some indefinite time before the present.

Future perfect: *Jim **will have left** by the time I arrive.*

Use the future perfect to describe an event that will be completed at a definite later time.

Irregular Verbs

ACT occasionally tests the correct past *participles* of irregular verbs. Participle refers to the form the verb takes when it's paired with the helping verb *to have* to form a perfect tense. For regular verbs, the simple past tense and the past participle are the same.

*I **called** you last night. I **have called** you several times today.*

For irregular verbs, the two are different.

*Shivani **became** the star of the team,* or *Shivani **has become** the star of the team.*

Here is a list of some common irregular verbs.

Infinitive	Simple Past	Past Participle
become	became	become
begin	began	begun
blow	blew	blown
break	broke	broken
bring	brought	brought
choose	chose	chosen
come	came	come
drink	drank	drunk
drive	drove	driven
eat	ate	eaten
fall	fell	fallen
fly	flew	flown
forbid	forbade	forbidden
forget	forgot	forgotten
forgive	forgave	forgiven
freeze	froze	frozen
get	got	gotten
give	gave	given
go	went	gone
grow	grew	grown

Infinitive	Simple Past	Past Participle
hide	hid	hidden
know	knew	known
lay	laid	laid
lead	led	led
lie	lay	lain
ride	rode	ridden
ring	rang	rung
rise	rose	risen
run	ran	run
see	saw	seen
shake	shook	shaken
sing	sang	sung
speak	spoke	spoken
spring	sprang	sprung
steal	stole	stolen
swim	swam	swum
take	took	taken
teach	taught	taught
tear	tore	torn
throw	threw	thrown
wear	wore	worn
write	wrote	written

Pronouns

What's wrong with the following sentences?

1. The team nominated their goalie as the most valuable player.
2. My friends and me took the train downtown.
3. Her and I worked on the group project together.
4. The crowd pushed Cesar and I onto the stage.

Pronoun Agreement

First, know your terms. *Pronouns* take the place of nouns. Pronouns have to be consistent with the nouns they replace in number and in gender.

	Female	Male	Things
Singular	she, her, hers	he, him, his	it, its
Plural	they, them, their	they, them, their	they, them, their

*The team nominated **its** goalie as the valuable player.*

Worth Noting
The ACT is written with a focus on prescriptive grammar rules and therefore uses they/them as plural pronouns only. The Princeton Review recognizes that they/them pronouns may also be used as singular pronouns outside of standardized tests.

Pronoun Case

Pronouns also need to be consistent with the function they perform in a sentence. There are three different cases of pronouns: *subject*, *object*, and *possessive*.

	1st person	2nd person	3rd person
Subject	I, we	you	she, he, it, they, who
Object	me, us	you	her, him, it, them, whom
Possessive	my, mine, our, ours	your, yours	her, hers, his, its, their, theirs, whose

*My friends and **I** took the train downtown.*

***She** and I worked on the group project together.*

*The crowd pushed Cesar and **me** onto the stage.*

Modifying Words and Phrases

What's wrong with these sentences?

1. No one took her warnings serious.
2. Blizzard is a charmingly energetically puppy.
3. Farid is more busy than Wesley is.
4. Lara was the beautifulest girl at the prom.
5. Singing with great intensity, I listened to the famous opera star.
6 Ethanol is commonly mixed with gasoline (typically made from corn).

> ### Modifying Phrases
>
> In addition to adjectives and adverbs, entire phrases can be used as modifiers. In order to be clear, all modifiers must be next to what they are modifying.
>
> *I listened to the famous opera star **sing with great intensity**.*
>
> *Ethanol **(typically made from corn)** is commonly mixed with gasoline.*

Adjectives and Adverbs

Adjectives modify nouns. *Adverbs* modify everything else, including verbs, adjectives, and other adverbs. Most adverbs are formed by adding *-ly* to the end of an adjective.

*No one took her warnings **seriously**.*

*Blizzard is a charmingly **energetic** puppy.*

Comparisons and Superlatives

For most adjectives, an *-er* at the end makes a comparison, and an *-est* makes a superlative. But some adjectives need instead the word *more* for a comparison and the word *most* for a superlative.

*Farid is **busier** than Wesley is.*

*Lara was the **most beautiful** girl at the prom.*

In the following chapters, we'll show you how these rules appear on the ACT and how to crack those questions. We'll also discuss some of the more difficult and challenging concepts that you may face.

Summary

- Follow the Basic Approach:
    1. Identify the question type (Grammar or Content)
    2. For Grammar questions, look at the answers to see what's changing. For Content questions, underline or highlight what the question is asking for.
    3. Read and mark up the text as needed
    4. Use Process of Elimination

- Grammar questions ask for the *most grammatically acceptable* answer. Anything else is classified as a Content question.

- The **No change** option is a legitimate answer choice, so don't be afraid to pick it.

- Right answers can "sound bad," and wrong answers can "sound good." Learn the rules instead of following your ear.

- Read in between questions, as the context will be needed.

- Pay close attention to what the question is asking, and always use Process of Elimination.

- If you aren't likely to get to all 50 questions, try skipping and guessing on the more time-consuming (that is, longer) questions as you go.

Chapter 7
Sentence Basics

A key topic on the ACT English test is sentence structure. When punctuation is changing in the answers, it may be more obvious that the structure of the sentence is being tested. However, you'll also see questions that don't explicitly test punctuation but contain different combinations of words in the answers that might or might not produce a complete sentence. In this lesson, you'll learn what a complete sentence looks like, in order to tackle this type of question; after that, in the next chapter, you'll learn the punctuation rules, which build on the concepts from this lesson.

As you know from the previous chapter, questions that ask for the "most grammatically acceptable" answer, which we call Grammar questions, test you on punctuation and grammar rules. All of the questions where punctuation changes in the answer choices, and some of the ones where the words change, are testing you on the structure of a sentence. Some of the rules will probably seem very intuitive to you. Most people wouldn't have trouble recognizing that *The color of the sunset* isn't a complete sentence. But what about longer, more complex sentences? And how do you know when to use a semicolon or a colon? In this chapter, we'll look at some of the basic rules for constructing a complete sentence and see how ACT can test you on those rules. Then, in the next chapter, you'll learn specific rules for when to use (and not use) commas, semicolons, and other types of punctuation.

Let's begin with what every sentence needs: a **subject** and a **verb**. Some sentences can be as simple as that:

> *She swims.*
> *The children are laughing.*
> *I disagreed.*

A **verb** is an action word. It can also represent a state of being: words such as *is*, *are*, and *was* are verbs. A **subject** is typically a noun (like *children* above) or a pronoun (like *she* or *I*). It's important to keep in mind that a complete sentence doesn't need to answer any possible question you might have. For instance, we don't know who *she* is or what I *disagreed* with. That's okay—these are still complete sentences.

> Every complete sentence needs a **subject** and a **verb**.

On the other hand, some verbs require the sentence to have a little more in order to be complete. For instance, while *They are* does contain a subject and a verb, it isn't a complete sentence because the verb *are* requires another word after it to complete the sentence. Likewise, *He gave me* isn't a complete sentence because the verb *give* requires another word somewhere after it to indicate what was given. That being said, this concept isn't really tested on the ACT.

What is regularly tested is the form of the verb in the sentence. We know a complete sentence needs both a subject and a verb, but that verb must be in a particular form. If we were to rewrite the first example as *She swimming*, it wouldn't be a complete sentence. Likewise, *The children to laugh* wouldn't be a complete sentence. There isn't a single type of verb that can make a sentence complete, since it could be in past, present, or future tense. However, there's a simple rule about the type of verb that CANNOT produce a complete sentence:

> An *-ing* or "to" verb can't be the main verb in a sentence.

The reason we use the phrase "main verb" is that a sentence can certainly have an *-ing* or a "to" verb in it—that verb just can't be the main verb that goes along with the subject to make the sentence complete. Note that an *-ing* verb attached to a regular verb, like *are laughing* above, works just fine as a main verb. The *-ing* word on its own can't be the main verb.

Let's see some examples of how these rules can be tested on the ACT. Please note that in this chapter, as well as several others in this book, you won't have a complete understanding of the context of each question. The example questions are meant to look like they came from longer passages, and we've only given you what you need in order to answer the question. On the test, you'll be given passages with 5 or 10 questions, not single sentences by themselves.

—⊙—

Apparently, <u>experiencing</u> the quietest place
                    ¹
in the United States deep in a rainforest, on the

Olympic Peninsula in Washington State.

1. Which choice makes the sentence most grammatically acceptable?

   A. **No Change**
   B. an experience of
   C. one can experience
   D. **Delete** the underlined portion.

Here's How to Crack It

The question asks for the *most grammatically acceptable* answer, so this is a Grammar question. That tells us to look at the answers to see what's changing. In this case, there's an *-ing* verb in the original, a noun in (B), a subject and a verb in (C), and nothing at all in (D). If you see an option with a subject and a verb and one or more options without a subject or without a verb, that's a sign to consider whether you have a complete sentence with each answer choice. Start with the original. As it is, the sentence contains an *-ing* verb, which can't be the main verb in a sentence. There's also no subject accompanying the verb. (You might read the sentence with *experiencing* being the subject, but in that case, it still has no main verb, which is always needed.) So, (A) has to be eliminated. Choice (B) has a noun, *experience*, that could be the subject of the sentence, but there's no verb later on in the sentence at all, so it can't be a complete sentence. Eliminate (B). Choice (C) has a subject, *one*, and a verb, *can experience*. That makes a complete sentence! Keep (C). With (D), the subject of the sentence becomes *the quietest place*, but again, there's no verb in the sentence, so it's not complete. Thus, (D) has to be eliminated, and the answer is (C).

—⊙—

Station <u>walls</u> covered with colorful,
2

geometric tiles made of ceramic.

2. Which choice makes the sentence most grammatically acceptable?

  F. **No Change**
  G. walls are
  H. walls, which are
  J. walls being

Here's How to Crack It

The phrase *grammatically acceptable* in the question tells us it's a Grammar question, so look at the answers to see what's changing. Here, every option has a noun, *walls*, that could be the subject of the sentence, and then there are different forms for the verb that comes after it, such as a regular verb in (G) and an *-ing* verb in (J). Thus, we need to look for a complete sentence. The original isn't a complete sentence—the subject is *walls*, but the only verb in the sentence, *covered*, is used as a description here. It could say that the station walls covered something, in which case *covered* could be the main verb, but the sentence isn't structured that way. The walls are *covered with* something, so this is a description for the walls and doesn't actually provide a verb. Choice (F) must be eliminated. Choice (G) offers a main verb, *are*, to go with the subject, so keep it. Although (H) also contains *are*, it adds a comma and the word *which* in between the subject and the verb. In that case, the verb *are* wouldn't directly follow the subject—it's part of a separate phrase—and therefore the sentence still doesn't contain a main verb. Eliminate (H). Choice (J) should be easy to eliminate because of the rule that an *-ing* verb can't be the main verb in the sentence. Thus, the answer has to be (G).

For a fraction of a second, a team of

physicists, working with the Large Hadron

Collider in Geneva, <u>and was</u> able to turn lead
3

ions into gold ions, a dream of early chemists.

3. Which choice makes the sentence most grammatically acceptable?

  A. **No Change**
  B. who was
  C. was
  D. **Delete** the underlined portion.

Here's How to Crack It

The question tells us this is Grammar, so look to see what's changing in the answers. Here, three answers contain a verb, *was*, and one answer contains a subject for the verb, *who*. There's also an option, (D), that has neither a subject nor a verb. All of this tells us to look for a complete sentence. This time, the sentence already has a subject: *a team of physicists*. Then, it contains a describing phrase, *working with the Large Hadron Collider in Geneva*, that's separated by commas, so ignore this phrase as it isn't part of the main point of the sentence. Therefore, the sentence as written is saying *…a team of physicists and was able to turn lead ions into gold ions.…* This clearly doesn't work because the main verb, *was able*, is being separated from the subject with the word *and*, which creates a separate phrase. Eliminate (A). Choice (B) adds a new subject, *who*, to the verb, but the sentence already has a subject that needs a main verb, so there shouldn't be another subject here. Eliminate (B). Choice (C) says *a team of physicists…was able to turn…*, which does create a complete sentence with a subject and a main verb, so keep (C). Choice (D) lacks a main verb; remember that *to turn* can't be the main verb because it's not in the right form. Thus, the answer is (C).

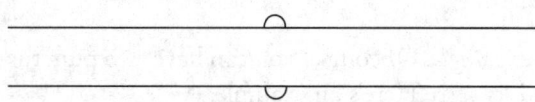

English zoologist Philip Scaleter, who in 1858 identified six zoogeographic regions, asserting that there existed a theoretical
<u>4</u>
continent between Madagascar and India that he named Lemuria.

4. Which choice makes the sentence most grammatically acceptable?

   F. **No Change**
   G. asserted
   H. he asserted
   J. to assert

Here's How to Crack It

Use the question itself to identify that this is a Grammar question, and then look at the answers to see what's changing. This should look familiar by now! One choice, (H), has a subject and a verb, while the remaining answers have verbs in different forms. So, look for a complete sentence. Like the previous question, this one already has a subject in the sentence (*Philip Scaleter*), and it's followed by a describing phrase separated by commas, so you can ignore that. Thus, the original sentence says *…Philip Scaleter…asserting that…*, which isn't a complete sentence. It has a verb, but an *-ing* verb can't be the main verb in a sentence. Thus, you can eliminate (F). Eliminate (J) as well, since a "to" verb also can't be the main verb. Next, notice that (H) has a subject and a verb, but the sentence already has a subject—Scaleter. There's no reason to add a second subject, *he*, and in fact it's incorrect to do so here, so eliminate (H). The correct answer is (G) because it provides a main verb to produce a complete sentence.

As you can see, most ACT questions include sentences that are a bit more complex than the examples we looked at in the beginning of this chapter. However, they still need to have the same basic structure that includes a subject and a main verb, even if they contain other verbs, multiple clauses, and punctuation within the sentence. This type of question is extremely common on the ACT. To identify this type of question, look for subjects and verbs changing in the answers. You will usually see one or more answers with a subject and a verb, along with other answers that have only a subject, only a verb, or neither. Many of these questions also include connecting words such as *which*, *that*, and *while* in one or more answers.

There's another simple rule that can really come in handy on the ACT:

> A single punctuation mark can never come between a subject and its verb.

The key word in this rule is *single*. Of course, you can have two punctuation marks between the subject of a sentence and its verb. Here's an example:

Sophia, my next-door neighbor, invited me to her birthday party.

Here, the subject is *Sophia* and the verb is *invited*. There's a phrase in between that describes Sophia, and it's separated with commas around it since it's not essential to the meaning of the sentence (it's the type of thing you could put in parentheses). This is totally fine. But what you can't do is put just ONE punctuation mark between the subject and the verb. Let's see an example of how this rule can be helpful on the ACT.

———————○———————

For Taylor, the <u>fear they provoke:</u> is a result
of an unfair reputation.
₅

5. Which choice makes the sentence most grammatically acceptable?

   A. **No Change**
   B. fear they provoke,
   C. fear they provoke
   D. fear, they provoke,

Here's How to Crack It

The *most grammatically acceptable* question tells us that this is a Grammar question, so look to the answers to see what's changing. In this case, it's punctuation before and after the phrase *they provoke*. Although this is different from what we saw in the last few examples, we should still look for a complete sentence, since punctuation questions also relate to complete sentences. In this case, the subject of the sentence is *the fear they provoke* (or just *the fear*) and the verb is *is*. As we just saw, you can never put a single punctuation mark between a subject and its verb, so that's a simple way to eliminate both (A) and (B). Choice (D) doesn't make this error, but it surrounds the phrase *they provoke* with punctuation. This phrase is essential to the meaning of the sentence and shouldn't be separated from the rest of the sentence with punctuation (we'll take a closer look at this later on). Thus, eliminate (D), and the correct answer is (C). No punctuation is needed here.

———————○———————

Now you have learned the basic concepts behind a complete sentence. Try the drill on the following page to practice applying the rules for yourself. In the next chapter, we'll examine the types of punctuation that can connect two complete ideas within the same sentence.

Sentence Basics Drill

This drill consists of questions on just the topics from this lesson. On the actual ACT, you'll see passages with a mix of topics. If you want to time yourself while completing this drill, allot 6 minutes.

Corals in the Arctic: Dark, Cold, and Full of Life

Coral reefs <u>having been</u> popularly associated with tropical
₁
seas, warm bodies of water that, despite their lack of nutrients, receive significant sunlight. However, deep-water coral reefs can grow in cold oceans far away from the tropics.

Marine <u>biologists, who discovered</u> deep-water coral only in
₂
recent decades due to the reefs' location far below the ocean's surface, beyond the reach of sunlight. One of the northernmost deep-water coral reefs is Norway's Røst Reef, located inside the Arctic Circle and first explored in 2002.

<u>Home to the</u> largest known colony of *Lophelia pertusa* coral,
₃
hosting populations of lobsters, marine worms, and fish.

<u>These are just some</u> of the inhabitants of this rich underwater
₄
environment.

Despite its remoteness, Røst Reef is not immune to pressures from human activity. Fishing trawlers, skimming the ocean bottom in search of their <u>catch, and they</u> have at times
₅
disturbed the delicate *Lophelia* colonies.

1. Which choice makes the sentence most grammatically acceptable?

   A. **No Change**
   B. are
   C. being
   D. that are

2. Which choice makes the sentence most grammatically acceptable?

   F. **No Change**
   G   biologists who discovered
   H. biologists, discovering
   J. biologists discovered

3. Which choice makes the sentence most grammatically acceptable?

   A. **No Change**
   B. The
   C. It is home to the
   D. Being home to the

4. Which choice makes the sentence most grammatically acceptable?

   F. **No Change**
   G   Just some
   H. Some
   J. Which are some

5. Which choice makes the sentence most grammatically acceptable?

   A. **No Change**
   B. catch that they
   C. catch, and
   D. catch,

The damaged corals then take centuries to recover due to their
<u>   </u>
₆
extremely slow growth rates. Additionally, ocean

acidification, threatening the reef, thought to be even more
<u>   </u>
₇
sensitive to increased levels of dissolved carbon dioxide than

its tropical cousins.

    To combat these challenges, the Norwegian government is

monitoring the reef's health and has passed an amendment to

its Coral Regulation of 1999. The new amendment, which bans
<u>   </u>
₈
the use of fishing equipment that touches the sea bottom within

5 kilometers of Røst Reef, with the aim of protecting this

hidden yet vulnerable ecosystem for many years to come.

6. Which choice makes the sentence most grammatically
acceptable?

   F.   **No Change**
   G   corals taking
   H.   corals, then taking
   J.   corals to take

7. Which choice makes the sentence most grammatically
acceptable?

   A.   **No Change**
   B.   acidification, which threatens
   C.   acidification threatens
   D.   acidification that threatens

8. Which choice makes the sentence most grammatically
acceptable?

   F.   **No Change**
   G   amendment bans
   H.   amendment banning
   J.   amendment that bans

SENTENCE BASICS DRILL EXPLANATIONS

1. **B**   In this Grammar question, verb forms are changing in the answer choices, so it's testing complete sentences. The subject of the sentence is *Coral reefs*, and there is no main verb. Eliminate any answer that doesn't provide a main verb to produce a complete sentence.

    - (A) and (C) are wrong because an *-ing* verb can't be the main verb in a sentence.
    - (B) is correct because it's in the right form to be a main verb.
    - (D) is wrong because *that* creates a separate phrase, leaving the subject with no main verb.

2. **J**   In this Grammar question, subjects and verbs are changing in the answer choices, so it's testing complete sentences. The subject of the sentence is *biologists*, and there is no main verb for this subject. Eliminate any answer that doesn't provide a main verb to produce a complete sentence.

    - (F) and (H) are wrong because a single punctuation mark can't come between a subject and its verb.
    - (G) is wrong because the word *who* creates a separate phrase, leaving the subject with no main verb.
    - (J) is correct because *discovered* is in the right form to be a main verb.

3. **C**   In this Grammar question, subjects and verbs are changing in the answer choices, so it's testing complete sentences. As written, the sentence has no subject or verb, so the answer needs to provide both. Eliminate any answer that doesn't provide a subject and a main verb.

    - (A), (B), and (D) are wrong because they don't provide a subject and a main verb.
    - (C) is correct because it provides a subject (*It*) and a main verb (*is*).

4. **F**   In this Grammar question, subjects and verbs are changing in the answer choices, so it's testing complete sentences. The non-underlined portion of the sentence doesn't contain a subject or a verb, so the answer must provide both. Eliminate any answer that doesn't provide a subject and a main verb.

    - (F) is correct because it provides a subject (*These*) and a main verb (*are*).
    - (G) and (H) are wrong because they don't contain a verb.
    - (J) is wrong because *Which* can't begin a sentence and needs to describe something that came before it in the same sentence.

5. **D**   In this Grammar question, punctuation and connecting words are changing in the answer choices, so it's testing complete sentences. The subject of the sentence is *trawlers*, and it's followed by a describing phrase separated by commas, which can be ignored. The underlined portion needs to provide a main verb for the subject *trawlers*, so eliminate any answer that doesn't do this.

    - (A) and (B) are wrong because the pronoun *they* shouldn't be used before the verb, since there is already a subject for this verb (*trawlers*).

- (C) is wrong because it says *Fishing trawlers...and have at times...*, moving the verb to a different phrase by putting the word *and* before it and thus making the verb *have* not accompany the subject *trawlers*.
- (D) is correct because it says *Fishing trawlers...have at times...*, offering a main verb (*have*) for the subject with no additional words in between.

6. **F** In this Grammar question, verb forms are changing in the answer choices, so it's testing complete sentences. The subject of the sentence is *corals*, and there is no main verb outside of the underlined portion. Eliminate any answer that doesn't provide a main verb to produce a complete sentence.

- (F) is correct because *take* is in the right form to be a main verb.
- (G), (H), and (J) are wrong because an *-ing* or a "to" verb can't be the main verb in a sentence.

7. **C** In this Grammar question, verb forms are changing in the answer choices, so it's testing complete sentences. The subject of the sentence is *ocean acidification*, and there is no main verb (the phrase beginning with *thought to be* is describing *the reef*). Eliminate any answer that doesn't provide a main verb to produce a complete sentence.

- (A) and (B) are wrong because a single punctuation mark can't come between a subject and its verb.
- (C) is correct because *threatens* is in the right form to be a main verb.
- (D) is wrong because putting the word *that* before *threatens* creates a separate phrase, leaving the subject with no main verb.

8. **G** In this Grammar question, verb forms are changing in the answer choices, so it's testing complete sentences. The subject of the sentence is *amendment*, and there is no main verb for this subject. Eliminate any answer that doesn't provide a main verb to produce a complete sentence.

- (F) and (J) are wrong because adding *which* or *that* before the verb creates a separate phrase, leaving the subject with no main verb.
- (G) is correct because *bans* is in the right form to be a main verb.
- (H) is wrong because an *-ing* verb can't be the main verb in a sentence.

Summary

o   A complete sentence needs a subject and a main verb.

o   That verb can't be an *-ing* verb or a "to" verb.

o   When you see answer choices that add or remove subjects and verbs, look for a complete sentence.

o   Answer choices that add or remove connecting words, such as *and*, *which*, *that*, and *who* are another clue that the question is likely testing complete sentences.

o   A single punctuation mark can never come between a subject and its verb.

Chapter 8
Punctuation Rules

The ACT English test contains a number of questions that test sentence structure and punctuation. This chapter discusses how to identify ideas as complete or incomplete and then explains how to punctuate different ideas. In addition to covering punctuation, the chapter also covers how to change ideas with the addition or removal of conjunctions or relative pronouns.

COMPLETE AND INCOMPLETE IDEAS

Many questions on the English test involve sentence structure and punctuation. The correct structure and punctuation all depend on whether the ideas are complete or incomplete. Now that we have established what a complete sentence looks like, let's see how two complete sentences, or complete ideas, can be put together in questions that test punctuation.

STOP PUNCTUATION

Imagine two trucks heading toward a busy intersection, one from the south and one from the west. If there were no traffic signals at the intersection, the two trucks would crash. Writing is just like traffic, depending on punctuation to prevent ideas from crashing into each other.

Two complete ideas are like two trucks and need the strongest punctuation to separate them. All of the punctuation in the box below can come in between only two complete ideas.

> STOP Punctuation
> Period (.) Semicolon (;) Question mark (?) Exclamation mark (!) Comma + FANBOYS

| **FANBOYS** stands for the conjunctions For, And, Nor, But, Or, Yet, So. |

Let's see how this works in a question.

After the thumping music
started. The bird began to dance.

1. Which choice makes the sentence most grammatically acceptable?

   A. **No Change**
   B. started, the bird began,
   C. started; the bird began
   D. started, the bird began

Here's How to Crack It

Begin with Step 1 of the Basic Approach and identify the question type. Based on the *grammatically acceptable* question stem, this is a Grammar question, so use the differences and similarities in the answer choices to identify the topic. Whenever a question is testing STOP punctuation, use the Vertical Line Test. On the Paper ACT, draw a vertical line where the STOP punctuation is to help you determine whether the ideas before and after the line are complete or incomplete.

After the thumping music started. | The bird began to dance.

On the Online ACT, draw a "t" on your whiteboard. In the lower-left corner, write "started." In the lower-right corner, write "The."

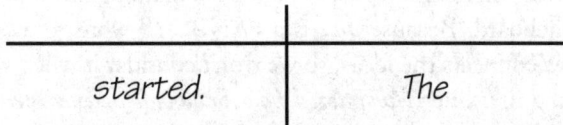

After the thumping music started is incomplete. *The bird began to dance* is complete. Mark the left side of the vertical line with an "I" and the right side with a "C." Since STOP punctuation can come in between *only* two complete ideas, go to POE. Eliminate all the answers that don't fix the error (that is, the answers that include STOP punctuation), and compare those that are left.

1. Which choice makes the sentence most grammatically acceptable?
   A. ~~No Change~~
   B. started, the bird began,
   C. ~~started; the bird began~~
   D. started, the bird began

We can use the context of the rest of the sentence to confirm that we don't need the second comma that (B) offers. Choice (D) is the correct answer.

GO PUNCTUATION

Let's go back to the traffic analogy. Imagine a road with a stop sign at every block. Those stop signs prevent accidents, but when rush hour hits, traffic backs up. Stop signs need to be used strategically, so that they don't cause more problems than they solve. Punctuation functions the same way: use it to prevent accidents, but don't slow down ideas and make the sentence longer than necessary, or just plain incomprehensible.

> GO punctuation could be either a comma or no punctuation at all, depending on the sentence. GO punctuation can link anything EXCEPT two complete ideas.

A sentence is a complete idea, regardless of how many complete and incomplete ideas it's made of, so it will always end with STOP punctuation. Within a sentence, use punctuation only to avoid an error or to make your meaning clear. Use STOP punctuation in between two complete ideas. Use a comma to slow down, but not stop, ideas. If you don't need to stop or slow down, don't use any punctuation. Keep traffic moving, and keep ideas flowing.

Here's another example.

I wondered how Snowball had learned to

dance, and asked his trainer.
‾‾‾‾‾
   2

2. Which choice makes the sentence most grammatically acceptable?
   F. **No Change**
   G. dance and
   H. dance; and
   J. dance. And

Here's How to Crack It

This is a Grammar question, so look to see that punctuation is changing in the answer choices. Use the Vertical Line Test whenever you see STOP punctuation, either in the test booklet or on your scratch paper/whiteboard. Because *and* is a FANBOYS word, draw two lines around the word *and*. The word *and* connects the ideas, so we won't consider it when we do the Vertical Line Test. The part before the first line, *I wondered how Snowball had learned to dance,* is complete. The part after the second line, *asked his trainer,* is incomplete. Remember, a comma plus *and* is STOP punctuation and can link only complete ideas. Eliminate (F) because the comma plus FANBOYS is not allowed here. Choices (H) and (J) use a semicolon or a period, but the second part of the sentence still isn't complete, so STOP punctuation can't be used. Therefore, (G) is the correct answer. In this case, GO punctuation (which here is no punctuation at all) is needed.

Commas

Commas work like blinking yellow lights: they slow down but do not stop ideas. In the real world, there is variation in when writers use commas, but when it comes to the ACT, all commas must be in the sentence for a reason. On the ACT, there are only four reasons to use a comma.

STOP

A comma by itself can't come in between two complete ideas, but it can when it's paired with what we call FANBOYS: *for, **and**, **nor**, **but**, **or**, **yet**, **so**.* A comma plus any of these is the equivalent of STOP punctuation. These words also impact direction, which might influence the correct answer.

> *The music changed suddenly, but Snowball picked up the new beat.*

Draw a vertical line on either side of *but* (either on the page or on your whiteboard) to help break the sentence into separate ideas. *The music changed suddenly* is complete. *Snowball picked up the new beat* is complete.

For the record, all conjunctions link things, but coordinating conjunctions—that is, FANBOYS—specifically come in between two ideas and are never a part of either idea.

A comma can link an incomplete idea to a complete idea, in either order.

> *After Snowball stopped dancing, the trainer gave the bird another treat.*

> *Snowball rocked out to Lady Gaga, oblivious to the growing crowd of fans.*

Check for Commas

Look out for:

- words and phrases in a series
- introductory phrases and words
- mid-sentence phrases that are not essential to the sentence

---

For the Record

Semicolons can be used to separate items in a very complicated list, but ACT almost never tests this. Exclamation points and question marks show up only occasionally.

Lists

Use a comma to separate items in a list.

> *Snowball prefers songs with a regular, funky beat.*

Regular and *funky* are both describing *beat*. If you would say *regular and funky*, then you can say *regular, funky*.

> *Snowball seems to like best the music of Backstreet Boys, Lady Gaga, and Queen.*

Whenever you have three or more items in a list, always use a comma before the *and* preceding the final item. This is a rule that not everyone agrees on, but on the ACT, always use the comma before the word *and* or the word *or* in a list of three or more things.

Unnecessary Info

Use a pair of commas around unnecessary information.

> *Further research has shown that parrots, including cockatoos, can dance in perfect sync to music.*

If information is necessary to the sentence in either meaning or structure, don't use the commas. If the meaning would be exactly the same but the additional information makes the sentence more interesting, use a pair of commas—or a pair of dashes—around the information.

Try the next questions.

Many people point to dog dancing competitions to argue that birds are not the only animals that can dance.[3]

3. Which choice makes the sentence most grammatically acceptable?

A. **No Change**
B. argue, that birds are not the only animals,
C. argue, that birds are not the only animals
D. argue that birds are not the only animals,

Here's How to Crack It

This is a Grammar question, so look to see what's changing in the answer choices. The changes in the answers identify the topic of the question: commas. Remember, there are only four reasons to use a comma on the ACT, and if you can't name the reason to use one, don't use one. If you thought the sentence was fine, leave NO CHANGE, and confirm none of the answers fixed something you missed. Think of ACT's comma rules, and determine whether any apply here. With neither STOP punctuation nor FANBOYS in play, it can't be two complete ideas or a list. If the Unnecessary Info rule is in play, (B) would mean *that birds are not the only animals* isn't necessary, but the sentence would make no sense without this phrase, so eliminate (B). The only other possible rule is GO, linking a complete idea to an incomplete idea. Neither (C) nor (D) offers a complete idea on one side of a comma, so eliminate both. The correct answer is (A), NO CHANGE.

Scientists now believe that the ability to

mimic, which only some creatures are capable,
_____
                        4

of acquiring, is necessary for an animal to keep a

synchronized beat.

4. Which choice makes the sentence most
   grammatically acceptable?

   F. **No Change**
   G. mimic, which only some creatures
           are capable
   H. mimic, which, only some creatures
           are capable
   J. mimic which only some creatures are
           capable

Here's How to Crack It

The changes in the answers identify the topic of the question: commas. By reading to the end of the sentence, you catch the comma that isn't underlined. Since the Unnecessary Info rule requires two commas, not three, check that rule first. The extra information is *which only some creatures are capable of acquiring,* and thus the correct answer is (G).

Because unnecessary information can also be separated from the rest of the sentences with a pair of dashes, it is particularly important with these questions to read all the way to the end of the sentence.

Even among those animals that can

mimic, such as nonhuman primates including
_____
      5

chimpanzees, bonobos, and orangutans—the

ability to keep a beat is rare.

5. Which choice makes the sentence most
   grammatically acceptable?

   A. **No Change**
   B. mimic such
   C. mimic, such,
   D. mimic—such

Here's How to Crack It

As always, with a Grammar question, look at the answer choices. The changes in the answers identify the topic of the question: commas and dashes. By reading to the end of the sentence, you catch the dash that isn't underlined. Since the Unnecessary Info rule can use two dashes in the place of two commas, check that rule first. The extra information is *such as nonhuman primates including chimpanzees, bonobos, and orangutans,* and thus the correct answer is (D).

HALF-STOP

Colons and single dashes are very specific pieces of punctuation, and they are very flexible. They can link a complete idea to either an incomplete idea or another complete idea. The complete idea must come first, and the second idea will be a definition, explanation, or list. Since they are always used with at least one complete idea, use the Vertical Line Test whenever they appear in and out of answer choices.

Let's see two examples.

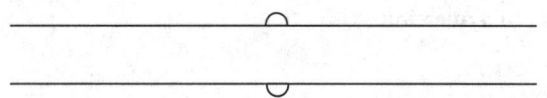

Parrots don't respond well to genres with the

least noticeable upbeat; waltzes and salsa.

6

6. Which choice makes the sentence most grammatically acceptable?

   F. **No Change**
   G. upbeat, waltzes,
   H. upbeat: waltzes,
   J. upbeat: waltzes

Here's How to Crack It

Draw the vertical line in between *upbeat* and *waltzes*. The first idea is complete, but the second is incomplete. Eliminate (F). The list isn't *upbeat, waltzes, and salsa*, so eliminate (G). The list is only two things, so the comma in (H) is unnecessary. The correct answer is (J).

A waltz is particularly difficult—it follows

7

a three-beat pattern.

7. Which choice makes the sentence most grammatically acceptable?

   A. **No Change**
   B. difficult it follows
   C. difficult, it follows
   D. difficult, it follows,

Here's How to Crack It

Draw the vertical line between *difficult* and *it*. Both are complete ideas, so eliminate (B), (C), and (D). Choice (A) is correct.

Identical Punctuation

In question 7, a period, a semicolon, or a colon could have been used. Notice, however, that none of those appeared among the answer choices. ACT won't make you evaluate those subtle differences that might make one punctuation mark better than the others when they all perform essentially identical functions. Knowing which forms of punctuation are identical is a powerful POE tool. After all, you can't have two right answers, so if two or more choices are identical, they all must be wrong.

CONJUNCTIONS AND RELATIVE PRONOUNS

Punctuation isn't the only way to link ideas. On some of the more difficult questions on sentence structure, you have to change between complete and incomplete ideas by adding or deleting conjunctions or relative pronouns.

Here are some of the more common conjunctions and relative pronouns you may see:

> ### Common Conjunctions
> although, as, because, if, since, that, until, while
>
> ### Relative Pronouns
> what, where, where, which, who, whom

For the purpose of succeeding on ACT English, knowing the difference between the two groups of words (or their correct grammatical terms) isn't important. What does matter is that conjunctions and relative pronouns (when not used in a question) make ideas incomplete.

Add a conjunction or relative pronoun to make an idea incomplete, or take one out to make the idea complete.

Let's see how this works in a question.

The videos of Snowball dancing have
$\underline{}$
8
sparked a serious area of study, researchers
admit they appreciate the sheer entertainment
value.

8. Which choice makes the sentence most grammatically acceptable?

   A. **No Change**
   B. Although the videos
   C. The videos appearing all over the internet
   D. Since the videos

Here's How to Crack It

If it sounded fine to your ear, using the answers to identify the topic will help you either spot something you missed or verify that **No Change** is correct. If conjunctions change in the answer choices, it is likely testing complete sentences. Check whether the entire sentence makes a complete idea and that all ideas within are joined correctly. There are two complete ideas in the sentence, separated only by a comma. A comma alone is GO punctuation, so eliminate (A) and (C). You need a choice with a conjunction added to the first idea, making it incomplete. Conjunctions vary by direction. The two ideas show a contrast—*serious* and *entertainment*—so (B) is correct.

English Drill 1

Try an English passage on your own. Use the Basic Approach explained in Chapter 7. This drill contains a mix of topics and is longer than the passages you'll see on the test, which will have only 5 or 10 questions. If you want to time yourself, allot 11 minutes.

Portraiture for the Common Man

Kehinde Wiley's paintings are powerfully disorienting for the way they blur the lines between new and old styles. Wiley paints large canvases that <u>watch the many</u>
₁

<u>achievement's</u> of African American men. His portrait of
₂

Ice-T, the rapper and reality-TV star, draws from a nineteenth-
₃
century portrait of Napoleon. His striking portrayal of singer

Michael Jackson <u>drawing</u> on the influence of Peter Paul
₄

Rubens. <u>Although each of Wiley's subjects is famous,</u> his
₅
portraits cannot help but make his audience see them in

new ways.

1. Which choice is clearest and most precise in context?
   A. **No Change**
   B. color
   C. celebrate
   D. speak

2. Which choice makes the sentence most grammatically acceptable?
   F. **No Change**
   G. achievements's
   H. achievements'
   J. achievements

3. Which choice makes the sentence most grammatically acceptable?
   A. **No Change**
   B. Ice-T
   C. Ice-T:
   D. Ice-T;

4. Which choice makes the sentence most grammatically acceptable?
   F. **No Change**
   G. drawn
   H. draws
   J. while drawing

5. Which choice makes the sentence most grammatically acceptable?
   A. **No Change**
   B. Often painted in large dimensions,
   C. Born in 1977 in Los Angeles,
   D. Loved and adored by art critics,

In these paintings, Wiley uses very traditional techniques. Inspired by the Dutch masters, Wiley oversees a painting workshop: the ideas are his own, but the artisan assistants in his workshop aid in the completion of the paintings. This
<u>6</u>
collaborative process allows for Wiley's vast output and allows him to impartially oversee the quality of the work. In addition,

Wiley's assistants gather the raw materials and mix the paints,
<u>7</u>
thereby making

them a classical work from start to finish. This attention to
<u>8</u>
detail and process made Wiley an art-world celebrity

in the time of life known as the early 20s. Wiley has forced art
<u>9</u>
lovers to reconsider the relationship between the old and the new. After all, paintings created by such profoundly traditional means do not usually have the faces of contemporary celebrities staring out of them.

Wiley's father was Nigerian, and Wiley did not meet him
<u>10</u>
until a trip to Africa in his early 20s. Some of his most famous
<u>10</u>
works

of Harlem portray various, anonymous men Wiley has seen on
<u>11</u>
the streets.

6. Which choice best avoids wordiness and redundancy in context?

   F. **No Change**
   G. complete
   H. end with completing
   J. complete the end of

7. Which choice makes the sentence most grammatically acceptable?

   A. **No Change**
   B. have gathered
   C. were gathering
   D. gathered

8. Which choice makes the sentence most grammatically acceptable?

   F. **No Change**
   G. it
   H. each
   J. each painting

9. Which choice best avoids wordiness and redundancy in context?

   A. **No Change**
   B. at the young age of being in his 20s.
   C. in his 20s.
   D. between the ages of 20 and 30.

10. Given that all the choices are true, which one most effectively introduces the paragraph?

   F. **No Change**
   G. Wiley grew up in South Central Los Angeles, but he made his name in Harlem.
   H. Although it was difficult financially for his mother, Wiley received the best art education money could buy.
   J. However, Wiley's focus is not exclusively on celebrities, and he is just as interested in "average" people.

11. The best placement for the underlined portion would be:

   A. where it is now.
   B. after the word *portray*.
   C. after the word *Wiley*.
   D. after the word *streets* (and before the period).

In his more recent work, Wiley brings his classic style to the
<u>12</u>
common people of Israel and the West Indies.

[13] To glorify people from oppressed cultures all over the
world,

by depicting his subjects in the types of poses and backgrounds
<u>14</u>
usually reserved for royalty. He shows that even those to whom
history pays no attention can have their own regal dignity.

Wiley's works can be seen in galleries all over the world
because the everyday appearance of those he portrays has an
<u>15</u>
almost universal appeal. Wiley may draw on the work of many
<u>15</u>
earlier artists, but his unique contribution is to show that art
need not be restricted to those who can afford to commission it,
or even those who are interested in viewing it.

12. Which choice makes the sentence most grammatically acceptable?

F. **No Change**
G. its
H. them
J. their

13. At this point, the writer is considering adding the following true statement:

> His paintings were shown in the National Portrait Gallery in Washington, D.C., in 2008.

Should the writer make this addition here?

A. Yes, because it gives another instance of Wiley's popularity.
B. Yes, because it demonstrates why Kehinde Wiley traveled abroad.
C. No, because it strays from the paragraph's focus on Wiley's body of work.
D. No, because it shifts the focus of the paragraph from the streets of Harlem to a museum in D.C.

14. Which choice makes the sentence most grammatically acceptable?

F. **No Change**
G. depicting
H. by which Wiley depicted
J. Wiley depicts

15. The writer is considering deleting the underlined portion (adjusting the punctuation as needed). Should the underlined portion be kept or deleted?

A. Kept, because it gives additional information about how Wiley chooses his subjects.
B. Kept, because it offers one idea for why Wiley's popularity is so far-reaching.
C. Deleted, because it repeats other information given in the previous paragraph.
D. Deleted, because it undermines claims made in the previous paragraph about Wiley's importance.

ENGLISH DRILL 1 ANSWERS AND EXPLANATIONS

1. **C** This Content question is asking for the *clearest and most precise* answer, so underline this phrase and use Process of Elimination, considering slight differences in the meanings and implications of the words.

   - (A) is wrong because *canvases* can't *watch* anything.
   - (B) is wrong because *canvases* can't *color* anything.
   - (C) is correct because a painted canvas can represent a celebration of a subject.
   - (D) is wrong because *canvases* can't *speak*.

2. **J** This is a Grammar question, so look to see what's changing in the answers: apostrophes on nouns. Consider whether any apostrophes are needed. The word *many* indicates that *achievements* should be plural, but the achievements aren't possessing anything. Eliminate any answer that misuses apostrophes.

   - (F), (G), and (H) are wrong because *achievements* should be plural but not possessive.
   - (J) is correct because no apostrophe is needed.

3. **A** This is a Grammar question, so look to see what's changing in the answers: punctuation after *Ice-T*. The main meaning of the sentence is *His portrait of Ice-T draws from a nineteenth-century portrait of Napoleon*. The phrase *the rapper and reality-TV star* is unnecessary to the meaning of the sentence and has a comma after it. Thus, it needs a matching comma before it. Eliminate any answer that doesn't put a comma before *the rapper and reality-TV star*.

   - (A) is correct because it uses a matching comma before the unnecessary information.
   - (B), (C), and (D) are wrong because they don't have a comma before the phrase.

4. **H** In this Grammar question, verb forms are changing in the answer choices, so it's testing complete sentences. The subject of the sentence is *His striking portrayal*, and there is no main verb for this subject. Eliminate any answer that doesn't provide a main verb to produce a complete sentence.

   - (F) and (J) are wrong because an *-ing* verb can't be the main verb in a sentence.
   - (G) is wrong because *drawn* creates a phrase that describes the portrayal and doesn't function as a main verb.
   - (H) is correct because *draws* is a main verb that produces a complete sentence.

5. **A** In this Grammar question, different phrases are changing in the answer choices. Try each option and eliminate any that is incomplete, unclear, or grammatically incorrect.

   - (A) is correct because *them* refers back to the famous *subjects*.
   - (B) is wrong because there is no word for *them* to refer back to.
   - (C) is wrong because it describes the *portraits* as having been *Born in 1977*, which isn't correct.
   - (D) is wrong because *them* would refer back to *art critics*, which isn't the intended meaning.

6. **G**   This Content question is asking for the answer that *best avoids wordiness and redundancy*, so under-line this phrase and start with the shortest option. Then, consider the other options and look for words that are redundant with this sentence or the one(s) before.

- (F) is wrong because it's overly wordy compared with (G).
- (G) is correct because it doesn't contain anything that is overly wordy or redundant.
- (H) and (J) are wrong because *end* is redundant with *completing* or *complete*.

7. **A**   This is a Grammar question, so look to see what's changing in the answers: verbs. Identify the subject of the verb, which is *Wiley's assistants*. This subject is plural, but all the answers work with a plural subject, so consider tense. The other sentences in the paragraph are all in present tense, including verbs such as *uses, oversees, complete,* and *allows*. This sentence begins with *In addition*, so it should also be in present tense. Eliminate any answer not in present tense.

- (A) is correct because it's in present tense.
- (B), (C), and (D) are wrong because they're not in present tense.

8. **J**   This is a Grammar question, so look to see what's changing in the answers: pronouns and nouns. Identify who or what each pronoun option would refer back to and consider whether a noun should be used instead.

- (F) is wrong because *them* could refer back to *assistants, raw materials,* or *paints,* so the pro-noun is unclear.
- (G) is wrong because there is nothing in the sentence for *it* to refer back to.
- (H) is wrong because *each* doesn't refer to anything specific.
- (J) is correct because it clarifies what the *classical work* is.

9. **C**   This Content question is asking for the answer that *best avoids wordiness and redundancy*, so under-line this phrase and start with the shortest option. Then, consider the other options and look for words that are redundant with this sentence or the one(s) before.

- (A), (B), and (D) are wrong because they are overly wordy compared to (C).
- (C) is correct because it doesn't contain any more words than are needed.

10. **J**   This Content question is asking for an answer that *most effectively introduces the paragraph*, so under-line this phrase. Ignore the underlined sentence and identify the subject of the rest of the paragraph. It mentions *Some of his most famous works* that involve *anonymous men* from *the streets* and recent work involving *common people*. It also describes Wiley as giving *regal dignity* to people who aren't in high esteem. Eliminate any answer inconsistent with these ideas.

- (F) is wrong because the paragraph doesn't mention anything about *Wiley's father* or *Africa*.
- (G) is wrong because the paragraph isn't about where Wiley *grew up* or lived.
- (H) is wrong because the paragraph doesn't mention Wiley's *art education*.
- (J) is correct because *"average" people* is consistent with the ideas from the paragraph.

11. **D**   This Content question is asking for the *best placement for the underlined portion*, so underline this phrase. Try the phrase in each spot to see whether it provides a clear and correct meaning.

  - (A) is wrong because *works of Harlem* doesn't provide a clear meaning.
  - (B) is wrong because *portray of Harlem* doesn't provide a clear meaning.
  - (C) is wrong because *Wiley of Harlem* isn't correct.
  - (D) is correct because *seen on the streets of Harlem* provides a clear meaning regarding where the men were found.

12. **F**   This is a Grammar question, so look to see what's changing in the answers: pronouns. Identify and underline the word the pronoun refers back to, which in this case is *Wiley*. Based on the rest of the story, Wiley should be referred to as *he*. Eliminate any answer inconsistent with this.

  - (F) is correct because the work belongs to *Wiley*, who is identified in the rest of the passage with the pronoun *he*.
  - (G) is wrong because any form of "it" can't be used to refer to people.
  - (H) and (J) are wrong because they're not consistent with the male pronouns used to refer to Wiley throughout the passage.

13. **C**   This Content question is asking whether a new sentence should be added, so underline this task. Consider the content of the sentence and that of the surrounding sentences. The paragraph is about Wiley's many works that involve ordinary people. The new sentence is about Wiley's work being shown in a gallery. Although this sentence is about Wiley's work, it's not directly connected to the focus of this paragraph. Therefore, the sentence should not be added. Eliminate any answer that is inconsistent with this.

  - (A) and (B) are wrong because the sentence shouldn't be added.
  - (C) is correct because it accurately describes the relationship between the new sentence and the rest of the paragraph.
  - (D) is wrong because *the streets of Harlem* aren't the focus of the paragraph.

14. **J**   In this Grammar question, subjects and verbs are changing in the answer choices, so it's testing complete sentences. The sentence has no subject, so the underlined portion needs to provide a subject as well as a main verb for the subject. Eliminate any answer that doesn't do this.

  - (F) and (G) are wrong because they don't include a subject.
  - (H) is wrong because adding *by which* before the subject and verb creates a new phrase that wouldn't be part of the main meaning of the sentence, thus making the sentence still not have a main subject and verb.
  - (J) is correct because it provides a subject and main verb to produce a complete sentence.

15. **B** This Content question is asking whether the words should be *kept or deleted*, so underline this phrase. Consider the content of the sentence and that of the surrounding sentences. The paragraph is about the *unique contribution* of *Wiley's works*. The phrase in question explains why Wiley's works *can be seen in galleries all over the world*. This is relevant to the point of the paragraph since it explains how his art is intended to reach ordinary people. Therefore, the phrase should be kept. Eliminate any answer that is inconsistent with this.

- (A) is wrong because the phrase doesn't indicate *how Wiley chooses his subjects*.
- (B) is correct because it's consistent with the role of the phrase.
- (C) and (D) are wrong because the phrase should be kept.

Summary

o ACT writers like to test your knowledge of whether sentences are put together and punctuated correctly.

o A complete idea can stand on its own as a complete sentence even though it may be part of a longer sentence. An incomplete idea can't stand on its own as a complete sentence and must be appropriately linked to another idea.

o STOP punctuation includes a period, a semicolon, an exclamation mark, a question mark, and a comma plus FANBOYS. STOP punctuation can come only between complete ideas.

o GO punctuation includes a comma and nothing at all. GO punctuation can link anything except two complete ideas.

o Always put a comma before *and* at the end of a list with three or more items.

o Always put a pair of commas (or a pair of dashes or parentheses) around unnecessary info.

o HALF-STOP punctuation includes a colon and a dash. For HALF-STOP punctuation, the first part of the sentence must be complete. The second part of the sentence can be either complete or incomplete.

o Conjunctions and relative pronouns not used in questions make ideas incomplete.

Chapter 9
Grammar Rules

Now that you have learned a whole bunch of punctuation rules, there are a few more rules to know that relate to what you might traditionally think of as grammar. Luckily, ACT tests these rules in a fairly narrow way, so there's not as much that you need to know. The rules we'll be going over in this chapter relate to verbs, pronouns, nouns, modifiers, and parallelism.

VERBS

In the Sentence Basics chapter, we saw that the form of a verb has to do with constructing a complete sentence. That topic is heavily tested on the ACT. There are two other verb topics that can be tested: subject-verb agreement and tense. We'll start with subject-verb agreement.

Subject-Verb Agreement

The idea behind this rule is simple and should be familiar. We say *The girl walks* and not *The girl walk*. We say *The boys walk* and not *The boys walks*. This is what is called subject-verb agreement. The verb needs to agree with the subject. In the first example, *girl* is singular, so it needs a singular verb: *walks*. In the second example, *boys* is plural, so it needs a plural verb: *walk*. (You might think that if a verb ends in *-s* it's plural, like with nouns, but as you can see, that's not the case.)

Sometimes ACT is nice and tests you on subject-verb agreement in a sentence almost as simple as these examples. Most of the time, however, the subject is a bit harder to find, which makes the question more difficult.

After several months, numerous artifacts that had remained buried for centuries were carefully exhumed, and, today, the recovered Incan serving vessels and pottery showcases the
₁
impressive craftsmanship of this ancient culture.

1. Which choice makes the sentence most grammatically acceptable?

   A. **No Change**
   B. showcase
   C. has again showcased
   D. is showcasing

Here's How to Crack It

Just as we've seen before, the question is asking for what's *most grammatically acceptable*, so look to see what's changing in the answers. In this case, verbs are changing. In the Sentence Basics chapter, we noted that if you see "to" verbs or *-ing* verbs changing in the answer choices, or if you see answers that add or remove a subject, you should look for a complete sentence. That isn't the case here, though, so we won't need to think about the structure of the sentence. Instead, we need to find the subject and determine whether the verb agrees with it. Here, the subject is *recovered Incan serving vessels and pottery*. This is a compound subject—two things connected with *and*—so it's considered plural. (You can always give yourself a simpler example—you'd say "Blue and green are my favorite colors," so the subject *Blue and green* must be plural because they go with the plural verb *are*.)

Since the subject is plural, the verb also needs to be. You should be able to tell right away that (C) and (D) are both singular, since *has* and *is* are singular verbs. Choices (A) and (B) might be a bit trickier, so try substituting with pronouns. The pronoun *it* is singular, and you would say "it showcases," not "it showcase," so *showcases* must be singular. The pronoun *they* is plural, and you would say "they showcase," not "they showcases," so *showcase* must be plural. Since our subject is plural, the verb must also be, and therefore (A) can be eliminated and the answer must be (B).

One of the most characteristic examples of these colorful paintings <u>are</u> at the San Francisco Museum of Modern Art.

2

2. Which choice makes the sentence most grammatically acceptable?

F. **No Change**
G. were located
H. resides
J. have been

Here's How to Crack It

Once again, this is a Grammar question, so look at the answers and identify what's changing. As with the last question, verbs are changing in the answers, but it's not testing complete sentences. Identify the subject. Here, it's a bit tricky. You might think the subject is *paintings* since that comes right before the verb. But, is the sentence saying that the paintings are at the museum? No, it's saying that just *One* of the paintings is at the museum. Therefore, the subject of the sentence is actually *One*. This pronoun is singular, so a singular verb is needed. From there, the rest of it should be pretty easy. Choices (F), (G), and (J) are all plural, so they must be eliminated, and the correct answer is (H).

In the Sentence Basics chapter, we mentioned the importance of identifying the subject of the verb, since that helps you to know whether you have or need a main verb. As you can see, finding the subject is just as important for subject-verb agreement. The subject normally comes before the verb, but on the ACT, there's a good chance it may not come right before the verb. You'll often see words in between the subject and the verb. Keep an eye out for prepositional phrases, which often appear there. If you're taking the test on paper, you may find it helpful to cross out any phrases that separate the subject and the verb.

Prepositions are little words that show a relationship between nouns. Some examples are *at, between, by, in, of, on, to,* and *with*. A prepositional phrase modifies—that is, describes—a noun. ACT will add prepositional phrases to distract you from the subject, so be on the lookout for them. Always look to the left of the preposition to find your subject. Try the following examples. Does the subject agree with its verb?

Only one of the dresses fit me.
A selection of fruit, cheese, and nuts were served at the party.
The argument between Pat and Ron sadden all of us.
The books on the table is due back to the library.

Cross out the prepositional phrases to find the subject and confirm the verb.

Only **one** ~~of the dresses~~ **fits** me.
A **selection** ~~of fruit, cheese, and nuts~~ **was** served at the party.
The **argument** ~~between Pat and Ron~~ **saddens** all of us.
The **books** ~~on the table~~ **are** due back to the library.

Another part of the last question that can be tricky is that the subject is a pronoun. In this case, you may not have too much trouble identifying that *One* is singular, but there are other pronouns that might seem plural but are actually singular. The following pronouns are all singular:

anybody	either	nobody
anyone	everybody	somebody
each	everyone	someone

Subject-verb agreement errors involving these pronouns will likely sound wrong, even if you thought some of these words were plural. Consider the following examples:

*Somebody **love** me.*
*Everyone **like** ice cream.*
*Each **are** beautiful.*
*Nobody **do** it better.*

Your ear probably automatically fixed these:

*Somebody **loves** me.*
*Everyone **likes** ice cream.*
*Each **is** beautiful.*
*Nobody **does** it better.*

But remember, the sentences on the ACT won't usually be this simple. When you have other words in between the pronoun and the verb, it's a lot harder to spot the error with your ear. That's why it's so important to know the subject-verb agreement rule and have a good strategy for approaching these questions.

Tense

The final verb topic is tense, and it's likely the one you're most familiar with. Students typically look at a question with verbs changing in the answer choices and assume that tense is being tested. Now that you've learned about two other verb topics, hopefully you won't jump to that conclusion. One reason we say this is that tense actually isn't tested all that frequently on the ACT. You're much more likely to see a question about sentence structure (including verb form) or about subject-verb agreement than you are to see a question on tense. So, we'll go over it here, but try to keep in mind that just because you see verbs changing in the answer choices, it doesn't mean the question is testing tense. In fact, it's probably not.

Visitors to the hut are treated to a simple
lunch made from ingredients grown on the
surrounding land. The guests <u>enjoyed</u> hearing
₃
stories from the owners of the hut.

3. Which choice makes the sentence most
grammatically acceptable?

A. **No Change**
B. would have enjoyed
C. enjoy
D. were enjoying

Here's How to Crack It

Once again, we have a Grammar question, so look at the answers to see what's changing. Here, verbs are changing, so as usual, identify the subject. The subject here is *guests*, but all four answers agree with this plural subject. So, the question must be testing tense (again, don't waste time considering tense unless you have already ruled out subject-verb agreement). Look for clues regarding tense. The preceding sentence uses the verb *are*, and this sentence is talking about the same topic—what the *Visitors* or *guests* experience. Therefore, present tense should be used. Choices (A), (B), and (D) are not in present tense, so the answer must be (C).

Nevertheless, the iguanas that had higher
body mass fasted during each daily low tide and
still <u>ate</u> at the time predicted by the local tide
₄
schedule.

4. Which choice makes the sentence most
grammatically acceptable?

F. **No Change**
G. will eat
H. eaten
J. would ate

Here's How to Crack It

Identify that this is a Grammar question, and then look to see that verbs are changing in the answer choices. The subject is *iguanas*, which is plural, but all of the answers work with a plural subject, so consider tense. Here, the verb is part of a set of two verbs that refer to what the *iguanas* did: they *fasted* and did something else. Thus, the answer must be consistent with *fasted*. Choices (G) and (J) should be easy to eliminate because they're both not in past tense and therefore don't match with *fasted*. Although (H) may not sound right, it may be helpful to understand the reason it's wrong. The verb *eaten* is in the past participle form and requires a helping verb—*has*, *have*, or *had*. It wouldn't be correct to say that *the iguanas eaten* (you would need to say "have eaten" or "had eaten"), so (H) can't work. Of course, in addition to this, it's not in the simple past tense like the other verb in the sentence, *fasted*. Therefore, (F) is the answer because *ate* is in the same tense and form as *fasted*.

As you can see from the previous question, the correct form for irregular verbs is sometimes tested. Regular verbs follow a predictable pattern.

You Don't Have to Be Perfect

The perfect tenses change the time of an event in subtle ways. Choose the present perfect to refer to something that started in the past and continues to the present. Choose the past perfect to establish an order of one event happening in the past before another.

*Present: I **study** for the ACT every day.*
*Present perfect: I **have studied** for months.*
*Simple past: I **studied** all day yesterday.*
*Past perfect: I **had studied** for the SAT before I decided to switch to the ACT.*

Irregular verbs are the problem. On pages 134–135, you can see a list of irregular verbs in their simple past and past participle forms. The *infinitive* is the form of the verb used with *to*; the simple past works on its own, without a helping verb; and the perfect tenses work with a *past participle* and a form of the helping verb *to have*. This topic isn't very commonly tested on the ACT, though, so don't worry about memorizing every single one!

*Infinitive: Jacob would like **to become** a biotech engineer.*
*Present perfect: Hannah **has become** a star swimmer.*
*Simple past: Samara **became** a voracious reader.*
*Past perfect: Jonah **had become** tired of practicing.*

One last thing to note is that it's possible to see subject-verb agreement and tense tested in the same question. Or, you could see verb form, from the Sentence Basics chapter, be tested alongside either of these topics. In most cases, these three verb topics are kept separate, so follow the basic approaches you have learned for each one, but if more than one answer remains, you may need to consider one of the other sets of rules.

Verbs Basic Approach
1. Identify and underline or highlight the subject of the verb.
2. If you see any *-ing* or "to" verb forms, consider what type of verb is needed in order to make the sentence complete. If you see some answers that are plural and some that are singular, identify whether the subject is singular or plural.
3. If there are still answers remaining, consider whether past, present, or future tense is needed.
4. Use Process of Elimination.

PRONOUNS

Pronouns take the place of nouns and make your writing more concise. On the ACT, several questions will test the correct usage of pronouns. Let's see some examples.

Unless the entire coral community is thriving, survival becomes perilous, leaving Atlantic goliath groupers particularly vulnerable to depopulation in its habitat.
<u>5</u>

5. Which choice makes the sentence most grammatically acceptable?

    A. **No Change**
    B. its'
    C. their
    D. it's

Here's How to Crack It

The question stem shows that this is a Grammar question, so look to see what's changing in the answer choices. In this case, pronouns are changing, so look for the noun that the pronoun is standing in for. In this case, it's the *Atlantic goliath groupers*. You may not know what this means, but clearly it is plural. And that's all you need! The pronoun "it" is singular, so any form of this pronoun can't agree with *groupers*. Therefore, (A), (B), and (D) can all be eliminated, and the answer is (C), which is plural.

Two of the specimens were selected to be flown to the high security lab where a specially trained contagious disease expert carefully examined it.
<u>6</u>

6. Which choice makes the sentence most grammatically acceptable?

    F. **No Change**
    G. that
    H. this
    J. them

Here's How to Crack It

Here, we have another Grammar question in which pronouns are changing in the answers. Find the word or phrase the pronoun refers back to: *Two of the specimens*. The number *Two* means that the pronoun should be plural, so we can eliminate (F), (G), and (H), which are all singular. The answer has to be (J).

Social philosopher Salvador Cordova, whose written extensively about this strange [7] phenomenon and it's effect on scientists' [7] understanding of reality, contends that quantum entanglement has not been satisfactorily explained by any current materialistic theory.

7. Which choice makes the sentence most grammatically acceptable?

   A. **No Change**
   B. whose written extensively about this strange phenomenon and its
   C. who's written extensively about this strange phenomenon and it's
   D. who's written extensively about this strange phenomenon and its

Here's How to Crack It

This is a Grammar question, so look to see what's changing in the answer choices. In this case, pronouns are changing in two places. Let's start with the first one, where we have a choice between *whose* and *who's*. The pronoun *whose* is possessive, as in "Whose book is this?", whereas *who's* means "who is" or "who has." Here, the sentence is not describing Cordova as owning anything. Instead, it means to say "who has written extensively," so *who's* should be used. Eliminate (A) and (B).

Next, consider the pronoun at the end. Similar to the pair we just looked at, the pronoun *it's* means "it is," while *its* means "belonging to it." The sentence shouldn't say "it is effect"; instead, it's referring to the effect of the *phenomenon*. Therefore, the possessive pronoun should be used. Eliminate (C). The answer is (D).

As you can see, many pronoun questions test not only whether the pronoun should be singular or plural but also whether it needs an apostrophe or not.

Whenever you see a pronoun with an apostrophe, it's (it is) a contraction, which means the apostrophe takes the place of at least one letter.

Consider the following examples.

It is important. = ***It's** important.*
They are happy to help. = ***They're** happy to help.*
Who is the leader of the group? = ***Who's** the leader of the group?*

If you see an apostrophe on a pronoun, expand it and decide whether the phrase is correct. On the other hand, possessive pronouns, such as *its*, *hers*, and *his*, don't have apostrophes, so eliminate the options with apostrophes if you recognize that a possessive pronoun is needed.

The vast majority of pronoun questions will be similar to the last three examples, but there is one more pronoun topic that is occasionally tested: pronoun case. Let's see some examples.

Slowly but surely, <u>me and him</u> began
interacting with each other more and more
comfortably, both of us seemingly remembering
why we had been so close for so many years.

8. Which choice makes the sentence most grammatically acceptable?

F. **No Change**
G. he and I
H. him and I
J. my brother and me

Here's How to Crack It

Once again, we have a Grammar question with pronouns changing in the answer choices. This time, the question is testing pronoun case, which has to do with whether the pronoun is functioning as a subject or an object in the sentence. Here, both pronouns represent the subject of the sentence, with the verb being *began*. Since the pronouns are the subject, they need to be in the subject form. With these pronouns, *he* and *I* are subject pronouns, whereas *him* and *me* are object pronouns. Therefore, (F), (H), and (J) need to be eliminated because they each contain at least one object pronoun. The answer is (G) because it uses only subject pronouns.

She eventually transformed her studio into
an eclectic gallery, with each exhibit showcasing
the colorful works of a different Mexican folk
artist <u>whom</u> had inspired Frida Kahlo, especially
her later works.

9. Which choice makes the sentence most grammatically acceptable?

A. **No Change**
B. of whom
C. who
D. being one who

Here's How to Crack It

Since this is a Grammar question, look to see what's changing in the answer choices. Like those you have seen in the last few questions, *who* and *whom* are pronouns. And like the previous question, their difference has to do with subject and object, with *who* being a subject pronoun and *whom* being an object pronoun. Here, the pronoun comes just before the verb *had inspired*. These people *inspired Frida Kahlo*, so a subject pronoun should be used, since they are the ones doing the action of inspiring, as opposed to receiving an action. Eliminate (A) and (B) because the subject pronoun *who* should be used. There is no reason to use the phrase *being one*, so eliminate (D). The correct answer is (C).

Who Versus Whom

These questions can be tough because we almost never use "whom" in everyday speech or writing. It's not that "whom" is more formal, but for whatever reason people tend to use "who" in a lot of cases where "whom" should technically be used. There's nothing wrong with that, but it makes it really difficult to take a grammar test, since your ear won't help that much—you're not used to hearing "whom" used.

The rule is actually pretty simple. Most people don't find it hard to know when to use "they" and when to use "them." Well, "who" and "whom" work exactly the same way. So, if you would say "They will help you," then you can say "Who will help you?" If you would say "You helped them," then you can say "Whom did you help?" or "…whom you helped." As you can see, the words move around a bit when a sentence includes the pronoun "whom." But it's still the same set of rules. So, if you're asked to choose between the two on the ACT, try to determine whether you would use "they" or "them" in the sentence, and use "who" and "whom" accordingly. It's also worth noting that "who" is going to be the correct answer most of the time—if you have to guess. Don't assume that the answer is "whom" just because the ACT is a hard test!

In short, pronoun questions can test several different topics. No matter what, always underline or highlight the word that the pronoun refers back to and consider whether it's singular or plural. Then, eliminate remaining answers that are incorrectly punctuated with or without apostrophes or are in the wrong case.

NOUNS

Nouns aren't tested frequently on the ACT, but you may see one or two questions on this topic. Questions on nouns will typically test you on whether a noun should be singular or plural and/or whether or not it should be possessive. Let's see some examples.

Artist Titus Kaphar originally thought the

conversations with his father would be

interesting as a documentarys subject.
<u>10</u>

10. Which choice makes the sentence most grammatically acceptable?

F. **No Change**
G. documentaries'
H. documentaries
J. documentary's

Here's How to Crack It

Since this is a Grammar question, look to see what's changing in the answers. In this case, nouns and apostrophes are changing, so we need to determine whether the noun should be singular or plural and whether or not it should be possessive. The word *a* appears before the underlined portion, so *documentary* should be singular. This actually eliminates (F), (G), and (H) because they are all plural (the original is also a misspelling). That being said, another reason

(J) is correct is that it's possessive. The phrase here is referring to the *subject* of the documentary, so a possessive pronoun is needed.

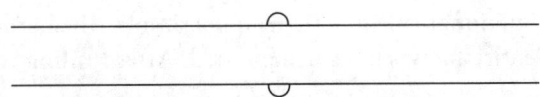

Displayed at London's Natural History Museum in 2024, a photograph shows a pair of guanacos standing on a hill as pumas crouch
₁₁
among the shrubs.

11. Which choice makes the sentence most grammatically acceptable?

  A. **No Change**
  B. hill's as puma crouch
  C. a hill as puma crouches
  D. hills as puma's crouches

Here's How to Crack It

This is a Grammar question, so identify what's changing in the answer choices. Here, two nouns change (*a hill* vs. *hill's* vs. *hills* and *pumas* vs. *puma* vs. *puma's*) as well as a verb (*crouch* vs. *crouches*). When you're doing this on your own, start with whatever part is easiest for you. We'll begin with the noun and verb combination at the end of the underlined portion. Choice (A) says *pumas crouch*, which is fine, so keep it. Choice (B) says *puma crouch*, which isn't correct because *puma* is singular and would need to have the verb "crouches." Eliminate (B). Choice (C) says *puma crouches*, which is a correct combination, but the word "a" or "the" would be needed before *puma*. Eliminate (C). Choice (D) says *puma's crouches*, which isn't correct because *puma* shouldn't be possessive. Therefore, only (A) works.

Unlike with pronouns, apostrophes on nouns show possession. To show possession with singular nouns, add *'s*, and with plural nouns ending with *s*, add just the apostrophe after the *s*. For tricky plurals that do not end in *s*, add *'s*.

Consider the following examples.

The new car of Peter = Peter's new car
The room of the girls = the girls' room
The room of the men = the men's room

Although questions involving nouns aren't all that common, the rules are very simple and the questions tend to be very quick, so it's worth understanding how to use apostrophes on nouns.

MODIFIERS

Although the topics of verbs, pronouns, and nouns probably sound familiar, the term "modifiers" may be less so. This grammar rule is actually quite simple. The hardest aspect of it is being aware of the rule and identifying when it's being tested. After reading this section, you should be able to do both!

To understand modifiers, consider the following:

As a child, my father took me to the playground most days.

Wanting to prevent them from profiting from her music, new versions of Swift's earlier albums hit the shelves and the radio.

You may find the intended meanings of these sentences perfectly clear, but they both contain errors. Did you spot them? In the first sentence, *my father* is described as a *child*, which produces a silly meaning given that he couldn't be a child while taking you to the playground. In the second sentence, the *new versions* of the *albums* are described as *wanting* something, which again does not make logical sense. The problem is with the describing phrase, or **modifier**, that comes at the beginning of the sentence.

Let's see how these sentences could be fixed.

As a child, I enjoyed going to the playground with my father most days.
When I was a child, my father took me to the playground most days.

Wanting to prevent them from profiting from her music, Swift recorded new versions of her earlier albums.
After Swift resolved to prevent them from profiting from her music, new versions of her earlier albums hit the shelves and the radio.

As you can see, two common ways to fix the modifier error are to rephrase the second part of the sentence so that the person or thing the modifier is intended to describe (*I* or *Swift* here) comes right after the modifier, or to add a subject to the describing phrase so that it is no longer a modifier at all. The change will depend on what portion of the sentence is underlined. Anytime you see a describing phrase, ensure that the person or thing it should describe comes as close as possible to the modifier. You can also watch out for the order of words changing in the answer choices, which is a good clue that the question could be testing modifiers.

Considered beloved inhabitants of Florida's

waters, <u>a type of manatee is</u> facing increased
12
threats of climate change and habitat destruction.

12. Which choice makes the sentence most grammatically acceptable?

  F. **No Change**
  G. the manatee is
  H. a manatee is a type of aquatic animal that is
  J. manatees are

Here's How to Crack It

This is a Grammar question, but it may be a little tough to tell what's changing in the answer choices. That's probably the hardest part about questions testing modifiers. So, keep an eye out for describing phrases that come at the beginning of a sentence and are followed by a comma. Here, the phrase is *Considered beloved inhabitants of Florida's waters*. Underline or highlight this phrase. Whatever the *inhabitants* are needs to come directly after the comma. It may appear that all of the answer choices begin more or less the same, but there's actually a big difference. Remember, the key word here is *inhabitants*, which is plural. Choices (F), (G), and (H) all begin with a singular noun, so they can't be described as *inhabitants*. Thus, only (J) can work.

In orbit since 1972, <u>the mission of the</u>
13
<u>spacecraft to reach Venus was a failure, circling</u>
13
Earth for fifty years instead until it crashed into

the Indian Ocean.

13. Which choice makes the sentence most grammatically acceptable?

  A. **No Change**
  B. the spacecraft failed in its mission to reach Venus, circling
  C. its mission to reach Venus was failed by the spacecraft, circling around
  D. Venus was not reached by the spacecraft, circling

Here's How to Crack It

Once again, the question tells us this is a Grammar question. Here, you might notice that the beginning words in the answer choices change, which is a good clue that it could be testing modifiers. Underline the modifying phrase: *In orbit since 1972*. Whatever was *In orbit* needs to come right after the comma. Choices (A) and (C) begin with the *mission*, but a mission itself can't be *In orbit*, so these answers must be eliminated. Choice (D) begins with *Venus*, but Venus is a planet that has been in orbit far longer than *since 1972*. Choice (B), on the other hand, begins with *the spacecraft*, which is completely logical as something that was *In orbit since 1972*. Thus, (B) is the correct answer.

While most modifier questions involve a phrase at the beginning of the sentence followed by a comma, with the underlined portion coming after it, it's worth noting that a modifier can come anywhere in the sentence, including after the underlined portion. If you see the order of the words changing, there's a good chance the question is testing modifiers.

PARALLELISM

A topic that can incorporate several parts of speech from this lesson is parallelism. This rule indicates that items in a list must follow the same format or be in the same form, whether they are verbs, nouns, or anything else. Let's see some examples.

Ninson used his time in New York to search secondhand bookstores, reach out to publishers, and <u>collecting</u> books in his apartment and
₁₄
storage units.

14. Which choice makes the sentence most grammatically acceptable?

   F. **No Change**
   G. to collect
   H. collect
   J. the collection of

Here's How to Crack It

The question tells us that this is a Grammar question, so look at the answers to see what's changing. Here, the form of the verb, or noun, is changing in the answers. This could mean that the question is testing complete sentences, as we saw in the Sentence Basics chapter. Here, though, you'll notice that the question has a list in it. Therefore, it's testing the topic of parallelism. Once you spot that, it should be pretty easy. The other list items are *search secondhand bookstores* and *reach out to publishers*. Therefore, the first word in the last item needs to be consistent with *search* and *reach*. This eliminates (F), (G), and (J), so the answer must be (H).

Chinese architect Liu Jiakun's work can be viewed at Chengdu's West Village, <u>viewed at Chongqing's Sichuan Fine Arts Institute</u>, and
₁₅
Suzhou's Museum of Imperial Kiln Brick.

15. Which choice makes the sentence most grammatically acceptable?

   A. **No Change**
   B. Chongqing's Sichuan Fine Arts Institute,
   C. at Chongqing's Sichuan Fine Arts Institute,
   D. viewing at the Sichuan Fine Arts Institute in Chongqing,

Here's How to Crack It

This is a Grammar question, so identify what's changing in the answer choices. Here, they all look pretty similar, but if you notice the list in the sentence, then you'll be able to tell that this is another parallelism question. The third list item says *Suzhou's Museum of Imperial Kiln Brick*, which is just the name of a museum. So, the second list item should also only have the name of a place and not include a verb or any other types of words. This means that (A) can't work because it repeats *viewed*, which doesn't appear in the third item, (C) can't work because it repeats *at*, which isn't in the third item, and (D) can't work because *viewing at the* isn't in the third item. Therefore, (B) is the answer because it contains only the name of the institute, which is consistent with the other list items.

If you see answer choices that have a similar meaning but are in a different form, such as one involving a noun and others involving a related verb (like "invent" and "invention"), look to see if the sentence contains a list. If it does, the underlined portion needs to be in the same form as the other list items.

IDIOMS

Another topic that is occasionally tested on Grammar questions is idioms. When you hear the word "idiom," you might think of something like "raining cats and dogs," but here we are referring to ordinary phrases that native English speakers probably never think about, such as "point to" (instead of "point as" or "point for") or "lack of" (instead of "lack for" or "lack with"). Here's an example.

The essay's detailed footnotes and references

are a testament of Agarwal's incredibly thorough
$\overline{16}$
research.

16. Which choice makes the sentence most grammatically acceptable?

   F. **No Change**
   G. with
   H. to
   J. by

Here's How to Crack It

This is a Grammar question, so look to see what's changing in the answers: prepositions. These little words are part of numerous idioms in English. Here, the word that the preposition belongs to is *testament*. The correct idiom is "testament to." Therefore, (H) is correct.

As you'll see with the vocabulary questions in the next chapter, if you didn't know the phrase "testament to," you'd simply have to take your best guess and move on. These questions rarely test the same phrase twice, so don't bother trying to prepare. Do your best when you encounter them, and focus your study time on the questions that you can prepare for.

PRECISION AND FREQUENTLY CONFUSED WORDS

Have you ever had someone tell you something that was too vague to understand? For instance, they might have said something like, "I'm so glad it's over!" and you might have wondered what exactly "it" is supposed to refer to. Although shorter options are often preferred on the ACT because they can be more concise, sometimes an answer can actually be too short. Let's see an example.

Nine states currently host regulation duckpin bowling. The sport is ideal for a family because duckpin balls are smaller and lighter than them.
17

17. Which choice makes the sentence most grammatically acceptable?

- **A.** **No Change**
- **B.** then them.
- **C.** than those used in ten-pin bowling.
- **D.** then those used in ten-pin bowling.

Here's How to Crack It

Here, you might have spotted the error just from reading the sentence, but you'll still want to check the answers to see what's changing, since this has the Grammar question and thus doesn't tell you exactly what's being tested. There are two changes here. First is *then* versus *than*, and second is the pronoun *them* versus a more specific description. Let's start with the frequently confused words *then* and *than*. The word *than* is used for a comparison. Here, there is a comparison, as indicated by the comparison words *smaller* and *lighter*. So, *than* is correct. This eliminates (B) and (D). Next, consider the pronoun *them* in (A). There's no plural noun that *them* could refer back to aside from *states* in the previous sentence, which is too far away from the pronoun and wouldn't make sense in context. Therefore, (A) doesn't work. Choice (C) specifies exactly what the *duckpin balls* are being compared with, so it's the correct answer.

If the question involves changes in punctuation or grammar in addition to more and less precise words, you'll see the standard *most grammatically acceptable* question. However, it's also possible to see a question that only tests the topic of precision, in which case the question will likely ask for the answer that is *clearest and most precise in context*, which will give you a much bigger clue as to what you are looking for.

Speaking of frequently confused words, although a variety can be tested, there are a few sets of frequently confused words that ACT tests more regularly:

Affect vs. Effect

Affect—(verb) to cause to happen or change

*The rain did not **affect** my weekend plans.*

Effect—(noun) the result of something

*The rain did not have any **effect** on my weekend plans.*

Cite vs. Site vs. Sight

Cite—to point to or show as a source

*Opponents of the bill **cite** an increase in pollution as a potential downside.*

Site—the location of something

*This lot is the future **site** of a new school.*

Sight—related to seeing

*At the **sight** of the bus approaching, I began to run.*

Lay vs. Lie vs. Laid

Lay—to place or put down

*Please **lay** the papers on the table.*

Laid—past tense of *lay*

*I **laid** the papers on the table as you asked me to.*

Lie—to recline

*I like to **lie** on the couch while I watch TV.*

Lay—past tense of *lie*

*Yesterday I **lay** on the couch while watching TV.*

Hint: In present tense, if you can replace the verb with *put*, you want *lay*. If not, it's *lie*. A few idioms to know are *lay the foundation for*, *lay the groundwork for*, and *lay claim to*.

Lead vs. Led

Lead—(rhymes with deed) to guide or be in charge of something

*Our choir teacher will **lead** us in the next song.*

Led—past tense of *lead*

*Our choir teacher **led** us in the last song.*

Hint: People get this one confused because of the word *lead*, which sounds like *led* but refers to a type of metal. When referring to leadership, *lead* is pronounced with a long -e sound. The past tense is *led*.

Than vs. Then

Than—used to make a comparison

*I have seen more episodes **than** you have.*

Then—used to refer to time

*It was **then** that I decided to major in English.*

Bonus: "Rather then" is never correct. It's *rather than*.

It's not essential to memorize these words, since there's a pretty small chance you'll see any given one on your test. However, if you're doing extremely well on every other part of the English section besides this, go ahead and learn them to help get yourself to 100% accuracy. It's also worth noting that, as in question 17, you may see this topic, along with the idioms one, tested alongside other grammar topics, such as pronouns, and you may also see individual questions that test two different sets of frequently confused words.

And that's all! One final note we'll offer is that the writers of the ACT like to test multiple rules in the same question. You may see a question that tests pronoun and noun apostrophes, subject-verb agreement and idioms, and so on. You'll also see questions that test these grammar rules alongside the punctuation rules you learned in the previous chapters. This is why Process of Elimination is so helpful on the ACT English section. With so many changes, it's hard to know in advance what the correct answer will look like. Instead of having a particular phrasing or type of punctuation in mind, use Process of Elimination with what is actually there in the answer choices, since the correct answer may not be what you're expecting.

Try the following drill to assess your knowledge of the rules from this chapter. Then, we'll move on from Grammar questions to Content questions.

Grammar Rules Drill

This drill contains questions only on topics from this lesson. Try to apply the rules and strategies you've learned. If you want to time yourself, allot 7 minutes.

A Thread Woven Through History

The ancient civilizations of Peru, such as the Inca Empire, were known for their intricate and colorful textiles woven from cotton and wool. Today, the country continues to produce textile art, and its' weavers treasure age-old traditions of
<u>1</u>
collecting, spinning, and dyeing the fibers by hand, despite the rise of industrial mass production. Notable

1. Which choice makes the sentence most grammatically acceptable?

   A. **No Change**
   B. it's weavers
   C. its weavers
   D. its weavers'

among the Indigenous weavers <u>whom</u> have sought to document
<u>2</u>
and preserve traditional methods is Nilda Callañaupa Alvarez.

2. Which choice makes the sentence most grammatically acceptable?

   F. **No Change**
   G. who
   H. which
   J. **Delete** the underlined portion.

<u>Callañaupa was born in Chinchero,</u> a mountain town not far
<u>3</u>
from the old Incan capital of Cusco. Callañaupa's early life,

3. Which choice makes the sentence most grammatically acceptable?

   A. **No Change**
   B. Chinchero was the birthplace of Callañaupa,
   C. Callañaupa grew up in Chinchero in a farming family,
   D. Chinchero was where Callañaupa was born and raised,

like <u>the life of</u> many children in Chinchero, was filled with
<u>4</u>
responsibilities, including watching the family's flock of sheep and learning weaving from her mother. The weaving designs used in the Peruvian highlands are complex and unique; for example, a sequence of indigo-dyed blue bands

4. Which choice makes the sentence most grammatically acceptable?

   F. **No Change**
   G. that belonging to
   H. them belonging to
   J. the lives of

<u>are used to distinguish</u> *llikllas*, or shoulder cloths, made in
<u>5</u>
Chinchero from those made in neighboring towns.

Callañaupa soon became fascinated with these designs and

5. Which choice makes the sentence most grammatically acceptable?

   A. **No Change**
   B. were to distinguish
   C. distinguishes
   D. have distinguished

their origins, an interest that continued into adulthood. Seeking to preserve history and to earn an independent income, <u>nearly</u>
<u>lost patterns were reproduced by Callañaupa as part of a group</u>
<u>of weavers from her hometown.</u> Today, this group of women
                    6

are the nucleus of the Center for Traditional Textiles of
                    ‾
                    7
Cusco (CTTC), a nonprofit that promotes the local weaving

community and

<u>introduced it's</u> handmade products to a global audience.
         8

The many tourists who <u>visit the area are</u> able to watch
                              9
demonstrations and participate in lessons organized by the

members of the CTTC. In addition to serving as the Center's

director, Callañaupa is an author: she wrote *Weaving in the*

Peruvian Highlands (published in 2007),

<u>another book of hers is</u> *Textile Traditions of Chinchero* (published
         10
in 2012), and *Faces of Tradition: Weaving Elders of the Andes*

(coauthored with Christine Franquemont and published in 2013).

Through these books and through presentations at conferences

throughout the world, she hopes to spread awareness of a living

art and pay homage to its ancient roots.

6. Which choice makes the sentence most grammatically acceptable?

   F. **No Change**
   G. Callañaupa organized a group of weavers from the hometown to recreate nearly lost patterns.
   H. patterns that had nearly been lost were recreated by Callañaupa and a group of weavers from the hometown.
   J. wool was woven by Callañaupa and a group of weavers from her hometown into patterns that had nearly been lost.

7. Which choice makes the sentence most grammatically acceptable?

   A. **No Change**
   B. have become
   C. exist as
   D. is

8. Which choice makes the sentence most grammatically acceptable?

   F. **No Change**
   G. introduces its
   H. introduced it's
   J. also introduces it's

9. Which choice makes the sentence most grammatically acceptable?

   A. **No Change**
   B. visit the area is
   C. visits the area is
   D. visits the area are

10. Which choice makes the sentence most grammatically acceptable?

   F. **No Change**
   G. she wrote
   H. authored
   J. **Delete** the underlined portion.

GRAMMAR RULES DRILL EXPLANATIONS

1. **C** This is a Grammar question, so look to see what's changing in the answers: pronouns and nouns with apostrophes. All of the answers involve *it*, so consider whether a possessive pronoun or a pronoun with a verb is needed. The pronoun is referring back to the *country* and the *weavers* of that country, so a possessive pronoun should be used. However, *weavers* isn't possessing anything and shouldn't have an apostrophe. Eliminate any answer that doesn't use apostrophes correctly.

   - (A) and (B) are wrong because the possessive pronoun *its* should be used here.
   - (C) is correct because it uses the possessive pronoun *its* and doesn't use an apostrophe on *weavers*.
   - (D) is wrong because *weavers* shouldn't be possessive.

2. **G** This is a Grammar question, so look to see what's changing in the answers: pronouns. Identify who or what the pronoun is referring back to: *weavers*. This pronoun is the subject of the verb *have sought*, so the subject pronoun *who* should be used and not the object pronoun *whom*. Eliminate any answer with a pronoun error.

   - (F) is wrong because the subject pronoun *who* should be used, not the object pronoun *whom*.
   - (G) is correct because the pronoun here functions as a subject.
   - (H) is wrong because *which* isn't used for people.
   - (J) is wrong because it makes the sentence incomplete.

3. **A** This is a Grammar question, so look to see what's changing in the answers: the order of the words. This could indicate a modifier in the sentence. The part of the sentence after the comma says *a mountain town…*, so the end of the underlined portion needs to end with the name of a mountain town. Eliminate any answer that doesn't end with something that could be described as *a mountain town*.

   - (A) is correct because *Chinchero* could be the name of a town, and the following sentence confirms this.
   - (B) is wrong because it ends with a person's name, not a town.
   - (C) and (D) are wrong because they don't end with something that can be described as *a mountain town*.

4. **J** This is a Grammar question, so look to see what's changing in the answers: pronouns and nouns. Try each answer and eliminate any option that is inconsistent or unclear.

   - (F) and (G) are wrong because *the life* and *that* are singular but they are referring to multiple *children* who have multiple lives, not just one collective life.
   - (H) is wrong because *them* would refer back to *life*, which isn't consistent.
   - (J) is correct because there is no pronoun agreement error and *lives* is consistent with *children*.

5. **C** This is a Grammar question, so look to see what's changing in the answers: verbs. Identify the subject of the verb, which is *a sequence*. This subject is singular, so eliminate any answer that is plural or makes another error.

- (A), (B), and (D) are wrong because they're all plural.
- (C) is correct because it's singular.

6. **G** This is a Grammar question, so look to see what's changing in the answers: the order of the words. This could indicate a modifier in the sentence. The first part of the sentence says *Seeking to preserve history and to earn an independent income*, so the part after this modifier needs to begin with someone who was *Seeking* to do something. Eliminate any answer that doesn't begin with someone who could have been *Seeking*.

- (F) and (H) are wrong because *patterns* can't seek anything.
- (G) is correct because *Callañaupa* could have been seeking to do something.
- (J) is wrong because *wool* can't seek something.

7. **D** This is a Grammar question, so look to see what's changing in the answers: verbs. Identify the subject of the verb, which is *group*. This subject is singular, so eliminate any answer that is plural or makes another error.

- (A), (B), and (C) are wrong because they're all plural.
- (D) is correct because it's singular.

8. **G** This is a Grammar question, so look to see what's changing in the answers: verbs and pronouns. The verb is part of a list of two things that CTTC does, the first one being *promotes*. Therefore, the underlined verb should be consistent with *promotes*. The pronoun refers to the *handmade products* that belong to the *local weaving community*, so a possessive pronoun should be used. Eliminate any answer with an incorrect verb or pronoun.

- (F) and (H) are wrong because *introduced* isn't consistent with *promotes*.
- (G) is correct because *introduces* is consistent with *promotes* and *its* is the correct spelling to show possession.
- (J) is wrong because *it's* means "it is," which isn't correct in this context.

9. **A** This is a Grammar question, so look to see what's changing in the answers: verbs. Identify the subject of the verb, which is *tourists*. This subject is plural, so both verbs should be plural here since they both refer back to *tourists*. Eliminate any answer with a singular verb.

- (A) is correct because *visit* and *are* are both plural.
- (B) and (C) are wrong because *is* is singular.
- (D) is wrong because *visits* is singular.

10.　**J**　This is a Grammar question, so look to see what's changing in the answers: the type of phrase. The sentence involves a list, which needs to be parallel. The other items in the list are *Weaving in the Peruvian Highlands (published in 2007)* and *Faces of Tradition: Weaving Elders of the Andes (coauthored with Christine Franquemont and published in 2013)*, so the third item should also be a book title. Eliminate any answer that's not consistent with the other list items.

- (F), (G), and (H) are wrong because they all involve a verb, but the list item should contain the title of the book without a verb in order to be consistent.
- (J) is correct because it's consistent in form with the other items in the list.

Summary

○ When verbs are changing in the answers, identify the subject. A plural subject requires a plural verb, and a singular subject requires a singular verb.

○ Only consider tense if the question is not testing complete sentences or subject-verb agreement, as tense is tested less frequently than these topics.

○ Pronouns need to agree in number (singular or plural) with the nouns they are referring back to.

○ The word "who" is a subject pronoun, like "they," while "whom" is an object pronoun, like "them."

○ Apostrophes on pronouns represent contractions. Apostrophes on nouns show possession.

○ When the order of the words changes, look for a modifier. A modifier needs to come as close as possible to the person or thing it's describing.

○ Items in a list must all be in the same form.

○ For idioms and frequently confused words, take your best guess and move on if you're not confident about the rule.

○ An answer that is unclear is grammatically incorrect; there should be no doubt as to who or what a pronoun refers to.

Chapter 10
Content Questions: Single Sentences

In this first chapter on Content questions, we'll go over how to approach a few different types of questions you're likely to see: those that mention redundancy, those that ask for the clearest and most precise option, and those that ask about the essay's tone.

Everything you saw in the previous chapters would be categorized as Grammar questions: those that have the *most grammatically acceptable* question and test some type of punctuation or grammar rule. Now, we're going to move on to Content questions. There are a few important differences compared with Grammar questions. For one thing, these questions aren't really about rules. In that sense, it may be a bit tougher to prepare for these questions. On the other hand, if you are short on prep time or struggle to remember rules, you may actually find some of these questions easier.

Another feature that can make Content questions easier is the question itself. Unlike Grammar questions, Content questions actually ask you for something. Before you ever look at the answer choices, you'll already know what the question is asking you to do. On the other hand, Content questions, even if you do find them easier in some cases, can be more time-consuming—especially the ones in the final English chapter that deal with the meaning of entire paragraphs and essays. Content questions may have longer questions and answers and may require you to read and understand more of the text, unlike Grammar questions, which typically require you to read only a single sentence and understand very little of its meaning.

Keep all of this in mind as you follow your Personal Order of Difficulty. As we mentioned earlier, it's not the best plan to skip around a lot in the English section, but you may find it strategic to skip and guess on a few of the questions that are hardest for you if you have trouble finishing the section on time.

In this chapter, we'll begin the Content questions with ones that are a bit more related to Grammar questions in that they test the wording of the answer choices and they primarily center on individual sentences. The first topic to go over is common and should be an easy question type to pick up points on: redundancy.

REDUNDANCY

These questions will ask you for the answer choice that is *least redundant in context*. In that case, we recommend starting with the shortest answer choice to see whether it works and then identifying any redundancies, or repetitive information, in the remaining answer choices that allows them to be eliminated. Let's see a few examples.

The security guards spread out apart from each other and guarded as the exhibit filled with interested patrons.
[1]

1. Which choice is least redundant in context?

  A. **No Change**
  B. spread out
  C. dispersed and guarded
  D. spread out, guarding

Here's How to Crack It

First off, notice right away what the question is asking. In this case, it's asking for the *least redundant* answer. Underline or highlight this phrase (depending on whether you are taking the test on paper or on a computer). Then, start with the shortest option, which in this case is (B). There isn't anything immediately wrong with (B), so hold on to it, but you should still check the other options to make sure there isn't something (B) might be missing. Choice (A) is redundant because there is no need to say *apart from each other* when it already says *spread out*, so (A) can be eliminated. Choices (C) and (D) both mention guarding, but the sentence is about *security guards*, so it doesn't need to be stated that they are guarding. Thus, these answers are also redundant and the correct answer is (B).

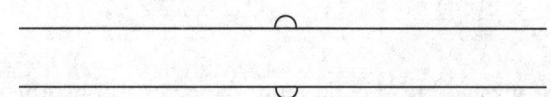

Writing many pages to assess their progress, [2]
the students take annual exams in their core
subjects, writing dozens of pages.

2. Which choice is least redundant in context?

F. **No Change**
G. To assess
H. Every year, to assess
J. Writing for exams as a way of assessing

Here's How to Crack It

Look at the question, which is a Content question since it doesn't ask about what's grammatically acceptable. Thus, you should underline what the question is asking for: the *least redundant* answer. Next, start with the shortest option, (G). This answer seems okay, so keep it in but check the other ones. In comparison, (F) is redundant because *writing dozens of pages* is already stated at the end of the sentence. Eliminate (F). Choice (H) may seem okay initially, but consider the new information, *Every year*. Is this redundant with anything that's already stated? Yes, because the sentence already uses the word *annual*. Eliminate (H). At this point, it should be pretty easy to eliminate (J) because it repeats both *exams* and *writing* from the non-underlined part of the sentence. Thus, the short option, (G), is the correct answer.

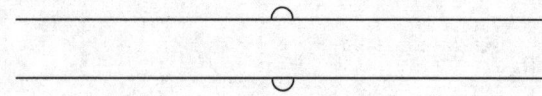

Additionally, an album released by musicians
Stacy Jones, Jamie Arentzen, Drew Parsons, and
Jason Sutter in 2004 produced two singles and
was part of a US tour. The album (it was [3]
released in 2004) was nominated for Album of [3]
the Year at the Boston Music Awards but
garnered mixed critical reviews.

3. Which choice is least redundant in context?

A. **No Change**
B. that was released by Jones, Arentzen, Parsons, and Sutter
C. that was the same one that had two singles
D. **Delete** the underlined portion.

Here's How to Crack It

Once again, identify this as a Content question and underline *least redundant* so you know what you're looking for. Then, start with the shortest option, which in this case is (D), the option to Delete. The sentence seems fine without the underlined portion, but try the other options to see whether any of that information is actually needed. Choice (A) is redundant because this information was stated in the previous sentence. The same is true for the other information in (B) and (C). All of these answers can be eliminated because they state information from the previous sentence, and the phrase *The album* already clearly refers to the album described in the previous sentence—there's no reason to specify which album it was. Thus, the option to Delete, (D), is correct.

As you can see, you'll be given a big clue on redundancy questions: the question itself will ask you for the *least redundant* answer. You may also see similar wording, such as *Which choice best avoids wordiness and redundancy in context?*. That's why it's so important to read and underline, or highlight, the task in the question. When you identify this redundancy question, you'll know not to worry about punctuation or grammar, or how much you like the sound of the sentence. You should only be thinking about eliminating answers that are redundant. This usually means the answer provides information that has been stated or is implied elsewhere in the sentence, or in the sentence or sentences prior. In some cases, especially if the question asks about *wordiness*, a wrong answer could also be overly wordy compared to a shorter answer that provides the same information in a more concise way, or it could contain information that is simply not relevant to the text.

For redundancy questions, start with the shortest answer choice. If it works, keep it in the running, but find a reason to eliminate each of the other options. You might be wondering if the shortest option is always correct on redundancy questions. That's typically the case, but in some cases an answer can be too short. An answer that is too short might affect the completeness of the sentence or might be unclear or confusing. So, don't assume that the shortest answer is correct. It probably is, so start with that answer, but make sure there is a reason to eliminate each of the other options.

PRECISION AND CLARITY

There are a few topics that are tested with a question that asks for the *clearest and most precise* answer. For these questions, regardless of the topic, you'll be asked to choose a word or phrase with a meaning that is consistent with the rest of the sentence and passage.

Vocabulary

Most of the questions with the *clearest and most precise* question actually test vocabulary. That might sound a little scary, but the good news is that most of the words you are likely to see should be at least relatively familiar. You may see words as easy as *take* and *went* or ones as challenging as *elicit* and *appraise*. You're not likely to see "advanced" words like *mollify* or *superfluous*, however. Although the ACT passages fall into different genres, they are all written in an academic but not overly formal style, so very challenging vocabulary words generally aren't used anywhere in the passages, or in the answer choices to vocabulary questions. Let's see an example.

To <u>command</u> the effects of gravity, the

4

scientists conducted the experiment on a

suborbital flight that allowed for several minutes

of floating.

4. Which choice is clearest and most precise in context?

   F. **No Change**
   G. approach
   H. control for
   J. evacuate

Here's How to Crack It

Because it's not asking about grammar, this is a Content question, so underline or highlight the phrase *clearest and most precise*. You'll notice that the answer choices are all different vocabulary words, so try each one in the sentence and eliminate any that don't provide a clear and correct meaning. The sentence implies that the scientists don't want *gravity*, since they *conducted the experiment* in a way that *allowed for several minutes of floating*. Thus, (F) doesn't work because it would suggest that they were trying to use gravity in some way. Choice (G), which says *approach the effects of gravity*, doesn't provide a clear meaning, so it too can be eliminated. Choice (H) provides a clear and correct meaning because *control for gravity* means that the scientists didn't want gravity to be part of the experiment, which is consistent with the rest of the sentence. On the other hand, *evacuate* means "leave for safety," and that isn't consistent with the rest of the sentence, so (J) is wrong. The correct answer is (H).

You may be wondering how to prepare for this type of question. Unfortunately, if you don't know one or more of the words or have trouble distinguishing between two words, you will just need to take your best guess. Since these questions typically don't test advanced words, studying high school-level vocabulary words may not necessarily help (though it can't hurt!). Of course, you'll only see a handful of these on the test. Try your best on them, but it will probably pay off more to focus your study time on the topics that you can more easily prepare for. It's also worth noting that vocabulary questions may have answer choices that are very similar to each other either in meaning (like *talk* and *speech*) or in sound (like *attribute* and *attrition*). Take your time, read carefully, and consider any slight differences in how the answer choices work within the context of the sentence. Two words with similar meanings may not both be appropriate within a given context or sentence structure.

Another type of question that gets the *clearest and most precise* question stem is one testing directional words. These are similar to the transitions questions that you'll see in the next chapter. Here's an example:

――――――――――○――――――――――

<u>Since</u> I was embarrassed by my mistake, I
⁵
knew that making mistakes was all part of the

process.

5. Which choice is clearest and most precise in context?
   A. No Change
   B. If
   C. Unless
   D. Although

Here's How to Crack It

Underline or highlight what the question is asking for: *clearest and most precise*. Here, the words that are changing in the answers are directional words, so consider the relationship between ideas in the sentence. The first part of the sentence says *I was embarrassed*, and the second part says *I knew that making mistakes was all part of the process*. These ideas conflict with each other because the first part is negative but the second part is positive. So, we want an answer that implies a change of direction. This eliminates (A) because *Since* is same-direction. *If* is used for a hypothetical, but in this context it reads like a cause-and-effect, and there's no reason to think this person's recognition of the importance of making mistakes hinges on being embarrassed. Eliminate (B). Choice (C) implies that the narrator wouldn't know the importance of making mistakes if they weren't embarrassed, which isn't logical, as one can understand that *making mistakes* can be *part of the process* even if one isn't embarrassed. Eliminate (C). Choice (D) matches the relationship between the ideas since it's an opposite-direction word.

――――――――――○――――――――――

In the next chapter, you'll see questions that explicitly test transition words and get a different question stem. For now, let's look at another type of question you can see.

TONE

This next type of question asks for the answer choice that *most effectively maintains the essay's tone*. As with any ACT English topic, it has some relationship to real-world writing skills. We all know that you need to use a different tone for an email to a college admissions office or an employer than you would when texting a friend. When it comes to the ACT, though, you won't see any passage as casual as a text to a friend, nor will you see a passage that is as formal as a legal document. Whether the passage is a personal narrative or an article about a historical figure, for example, it will still have a fairly standard tone: academic—not overly casual—but written at a simple enough level for any middle- or high schooler to understand.

Therefore, you have two tools that can be helpful on questions about tone. The first tool is the tone of the passage you are reading. In the English Intro, we advised you to always read in between the questions. This will be helpful on tone questions, as you'll want to get a sense of the tone of the passage overall. The second tool is simply being familiar with the ACT. Although you always want to understand the tone of a particular passage, there's a good chance you would be able to answer a tone question without any reference to the passage if you are just familiar with the ACT, which you will be after reading this book. Let's see an example.

Some questioned whether the image was a

legit shot of what had actually happened.
<u>   </u>
6

6. Which choice most effectively maintains the essay's tone?

   F. **No Change**
   G. realistic portrayal
   H. verifiably bona fide simulacrum
   J. for sure accurate representation

Here's How to Crack It

Underline what the question is asking for: *maintains the essay's tone*. Although we didn't give you much of the essay here, as we just mentioned, all ACT passages have a similar tone. So, eliminate any answer that is too casual, too formal, or too dramatic. Choice (F) uses slang, *legit*, so eliminate it. Keep (G) because there isn't anything immediately wrong with it. Choice (H) might seem appealing because of how "fancy" it sounds, but no matter how challenging you find the ACT English, the essays simply are not written with such a formal tone. So, eliminate (H) because it's not consistent with the ACT's tone. Choice (J) uses slang with *for sure*, so it also needs to be eliminated. Therefore, the answer must be (G), which is simple, clear, and not overly casual.

As you can see, any answer that uses slangy, casual language, such as *totally cool* or *pic*, is almost certainly going to be wrong on this type of question. Likewise, ACT may throw in answers that are either overly formal or overly dramatic, such as *indubitably portended a cessation* or *baffled the scientists to their wits' end*. The more experience you have with ACT passages, the more obviously inconsistent these types of phrases will be!

Now that you have seen a few more types of Content questions, try the drill on the next page to practice your skills.

Content Questions: Single Sentences Drill

This drill contains questions from only the topics in this lesson. On the actual test, you'll see a mix of topics within passages, unlike the individual questions given here. If you would like to time yourself, allot 3 minutes.

I realized that I had forgotten to <u>reply</u> to the email from the admissions officer.
₁

1. Which choice is least redundant in context?

   A. No Change
   B. reply with a response
   C. reply in response to
   D. send a reply back

After writing a page, I'd reread what I'd written, looking for any misspellings or punctuation errors <u>obvious to me while I</u> <u>was rereading.</u>
₂

2. Which choice is least redundant in context?

   F. No Change
   G. that I could find in rereading.
   H. that would become apparent when I reread my writing.
   J. Delete the underlined portion and end the sentence with a period.

Although some have considered them pests, the red-capped parrot has been shown to <u>institute</u> only minor damage to orchard crops.
₃

3. Which choice is clearest and most precise in context?

   A. No Change
   B. enact
   C. inflict
   D. consume

<u>Made up of pop and techno stuff,</u> the song features English lyrics that focus on unrequited love.
₄

4. Which choice most effectively maintains the essay's tone?

   F. No Change
   G. Having been subject to an infusion of both pop and techno elements,
   H. Bringing together things from pop and things from techno,
   J. Composed with pop and techno elements,

CONTENT QUESTIONS: SINGLE SENTENCES DRILL EXPLANATIONS

1. **A**   This Content question is asking for the *least redundant* answer, so underline this phrase and start with the shortest option. Then, consider the other options and look for words that are redundant with this sentence or the one(s) before.

    - (A) is correct because it doesn't contain anything *redundant*.
    - (B) and (C) are wrong because *reply* and *response* are redundant with each other.
    - (D) is wrong because a *reply* is already a response *back*, so this is redundant.

2. **J**   This Content question is asking for the *least redundant* answer, so underline this phrase and start with the shortest option. Then, consider the other options and look for words that are redundant with this sentence or the one(s) before.

    - (F), (G), and (H) are wrong because they all repeat *rereading*, which there is no reason to repeat, as the sentence is clear without it.
    - (J) is correct because no additional words are needed and the other options contain redundancies.

3. **C**   This Content question is asking for the *clearest and most precise* answer, so underline this phrase and use Process of Elimination, considering slight differences in the meanings and implications of the words.

    - (A) and (B) are wrong because *institute* and *enact* are both actions that only humans can do, such as putting into place a policy or rule.
    - (C) is correct because *inflict damage* is a clear and precise phrasing.
    - (D) is wrong because *consume damage* doesn't provide a clear meaning.

4. **J**   This Content question is asking for an answer that *most effectively maintains the essay's tone*, so underline this phrase. Although the full essay isn't provided here, eliminate answers that are inconsistent with the general tone of ACT passages.

    - (F) and (H) are wrong because *stuff* and *things* are too casual and imprecise.
    - (G) is wrong because it sounds overly technical and complex compared to (J).
    - (J) is correct because it's not overly formal or informal and is clear in meaning.

Summary

- When the question mentions redundancy, start with the shortest answer. Only choose a longer answer if the shortest option makes a grammar error or is unclear.

- When vocabulary is tested, try your best. Consider slight differences in the meanings of similar words, and use the context of the sentence. If that's not enough to pin down the answer, take your best guess and move on.

- When directional words are tested, consider whether the ideas agree or disagree and use POE accordingly.

- For tone questions, eliminate answers that use overly casual or overly fancy language.

Chapter 11
Content Questions: Transitions and Purpose

Two more Content question types you'll almost certainly see on your test are Transitions and Purpose questions. In this lesson, you'll learn how to approach Transitions questions, and you'll learn the keys to mastering Purpose questions—a deceptively simple question type.

In this chapter, we'll cover two more categories of content questions. The first one is extremely easy to spot because it always looks the same. Let's see an example.

———————————◯———————————

Those flimsy plastic shopping bags, often accumulating in drawers and bins after a single use, represent a significant source of waste in landfills and our environment. Through a simple process of cutting and knotting, however, these discarded bags can be upcycled into a surprisingly durable and versatile material known as "plarn," a portmanteau of plastic and yarn, used to create waterproof sleeping mats and even durable outdoor furniture.

1. Which transition word is most logical in context?

   A. **No Change**
   B. indeed,
   C. furthermore,
   D. therefore,

Here's How to Crack It

As always with a Content question, underline what the question is asking, in this case for the *transition word* that is *most logical*. Since this is a transitions question, we need to consider the relationship between this sentence and the one before it. The preceding sentence says that *plastic shopping bags* are *a significant source of waste*. This sentence says that they can be *upcycled into a surprisingly durable and versatile material*. These ideas disagree with each other, so an opposite-direction transition is needed. Eliminate any answer that is same direction: (B), (C), and (D). Thus, the answer must be (A), the only opposite-direction transition offered.

———————————◯———————————

Transitions questions will always ask you for the *transition word* (or *phrase*) that is *most logical in context*. Here is the basic approach for this question type:

> ### Transitions Basic Approach
> 1. Underline or highlight what the question is asking.
> 2. Read the sentence before and consider the relationship between ideas, starting with whether they agree or disagree.
> 3. Use Process of Elimination.

We mentioned before that one difference between Content questions and Grammar questions is that many Content questions require you to read more than just the one sentence. This is especially true for transitions questions. These questions are normally asking for a transition that links the sentence with the underlined portion to the sentence before it. So, you'll want to read (or reread) the previous sentence and determine whether the sentence with the underline agrees or disagrees with that idea. You may find it helpful to actually write down the word "agree" or "disagree" on your paper. Then, eliminate answers that go the wrong direction. After that, if more than one answer remains, eliminate options that aren't the right match with the specific relationship between the ideas.

Let's look at another example.

———————◯———————

Invasive fish disrupt ecosystems, leading to declines in native fish populations and disruption of the entire food chain. In addition, the silver
<u>2</u>
carp, a highly efficient invasive filter-feeder, consumes vast quantities of plankton, the base of the aquatic food web, and directly competes with native planktivorous fish species such as gizzard shad and paddlefish.

2. Which transition word or phrase is most logical in context?

F. No Change
G. Therefore,
H. For example,
J. Meanwhile,

Here's How to Crack It

Start by underlining what the question is asking for. Then, compare this sentence to the one before, ignoring the underlined transition. The sentence before says that *Invasive fish disrupt ecosystems.* This sentence mentions a specific fish, the *silver carp*, and how it *consumes vast quantities* of *the base of the aquatic food web* and *directly competes with native…species*. This is a way that invasive fish can disrupt an ecosystem, so these two sentences agree. Unfortunately, all four answers are same-direction transitions, so eliminate any that may agree but don't match the specific relationship.

While (F) may seem appealing, *In addition* should be used for an additional point. Here, the author is making the same point by use of a specific instance, so this isn't a separate, additional point. Eliminate (F). *Therefore* should be used for a conclusion, but this sentence isn't a conclusion based on the previous sentence, so eliminate (G). Choice (H) works well because this sentence is an example of a specific fish that can *disrupt ecosystems*, so keep (H). *Meanwhile* refers to two things happening at the same time, which isn't the case here. Thus, the answer is (H).

> Always ignore the underlined transition when considering the relationship between the ideas. You don't want to get fooled by a wrong answer!

Here are the most common same-direction and opposite-direction transitions on the ACT:

Common Same-Direction Transitions			
additionally	for example	besides	consequently
furthermore	in other words	likewise	moreover
similarly	therefore	thus	

Common Opposite-Direction Transitions

conversely	even so	however	in contrast
instead	nevertheless	nonetheless	on the other hand
otherwise	still		

There's one more way transitions can be tested.

We may imagine barren landscapes devoid of life in extreme environments, yet hydrothermal vents resulting from fissures in the seabed are filled with organisms thriving in conditions once thought uninhabitable. Likewise, these harsh [3] ecosystems challenge our preconceived notions, revealing life's remarkable adaptability and resilience in the face of intense heat and volcanic toxicity.

3. Which transition word or phrase, if any, is most logical in context?

A. **No Change**
B. These
C. For instance, these
D. However, these

Here's How to Crack It

This question looks very similar to the last two, but it has a key difference: the phrase *if any*. This means that there is an option to remove the transition, in this case (B). When you see this option in a transitions question, consider it carefully, as it's usually the correct answer. Either way, though, we need to follow the basic approach. The previous sentence states that *hydrothermal vents* are *filled with organisms thriving* in harsh conditions, despite what people might *imagine*. The sentence with the underline goes on to emphasize how *these harsh ecosystems challenge our preconceived notions*. Beginning with (B), the sentences do work without any transition, so keep this option in, but consider the other choices. Since the ideas agree, (D) can be eliminated right away. *Likewise* should be used to compare two different things, which isn't the case here, so (A) is out. Choice (C) should be used for an example, but this sentence isn't an example. Therefore, the answer must be (B)—no transition is needed.

Pay attention to when the question uses the phrase *if any*. Chances are, the transition word or phrase is not needed because the two sentences can flow without a transition—or because none of the three transitions provided could link them. Of course, if the option without a transition doesn't make a complete sentence, or if the sentences don't flow together without a transition, then eliminate the option without a transition.

PURPOSE

Now, let's examine a very common type of Content question: purpose questions. Although all Content questions have some type of purpose within the question itself, these questions will ask you for an answer choice that achieves a specific goal, and it might not be one that you're expecting. For instance, if you were to skip the actual question on a transitions question, you could probably still get the answer because you could infer that the test-writers wanted you to find a transition that worked in the passage. For these questions, however, if you go straight to the answers, there's a very good change you would pick a wrong answer. That's because the wrong answers for these questions will most likely use correct punctuation and grammar and may make perfect sense within the passage. You may even prefer one of the wrong answers. But, it's wrong because it doesn't fulfill the goal stated in the question. Thus, the most important thing to know about purpose questions is the importance of reading, understanding, and underlining or highlighting the goal stated in the question. Once you do that, the question should be no problem.

After that, the program director gave

a speech detailing the past year's successes.
4

4. Which choice most effectively illustrates that the ceremony was emotional for the narrator?

F. **No Change**
G. an impressively well-crafted speech.
H. a brief yet thought-provoking speech.
J. a tear-jerking speech that threatened to ruin my mascara.

Here's How to Crack It

Although underlining the question may not be all that helpful or necessary for the transitions questions we just looked at, it's incredibly important for Purpose questions. In fact, you won't be able to answer these questions at all without understanding what the question is asking. So, here, underline or highlight *illustrates that the ceremony was emotional for the narrator*. Then, just go to POE. Choices (F) and (G) very clearly don't relate to anything that is *emotional*. Choice (H) says *thought-provoking*, but thinking about something doesn't necessarily imply that you're feeling emotions. On the other hand, (J) says *tear-jerking* and *threatened to ruin my mascara*, which clearly indicates the emotional feeling the speech gave the narrator. Thus, (J) is the answer because it's the only one that fulfilled the goal in the question.

As part of her process, Hernandez flattens the
<u>   </u>
                 5
dough balls to an even thickness.

5. Which choice most specifically indicates
how Hernandez prepares her tortillas?

   A. **No Change**
   B. Using a cast iron press,
   C. For her next step,
   D. To make a meal,

Here's How to Crack It

Underline what the question is asking for: *most specifically indicates how Hernandez prepares her tortillas.* Eliminate any answer that doesn't fulfill this goal. Choices (A), (C), and (D) mention that this is a step in the process of making a meal, but there's nothing about *how* Hernandez prepares the tortillas. On the other hand, (B) offers a specific detail about *how* she does so, so it's the answer.

As you can see, you don't always even need the non-underlined part of the sentence to get the answer. These questions have nothing to do with how the sentence as a whole sounds or even whether the answer is consistent with the rest of the passage. You only need to think about how well it fulfills the goal stated in the question.

The exhibit's contents are diverse: a Roman

bust made of dry spaghetti, a pair of shoes

composed of metal bolts, <u>some type of fabric.</u>
                                    6

6. Which choice best maintains the pattern
established in the sentence's two previous examples?

   F. **No Change**
   G. a car assembled from lace.
   H. other household materials.
   J. objects of many different shapes and
sizes.

Here's How to Crack It

As always for Content questions, underline the goal stated in the question: *maintains the pattern established in the sentence's two previous examples.* Unlike the last two questions, this one does require us to get some context from the non-underlined portion. Both of the *two previous examples* mention an object (*a Roman bust* and *a pair of shoes*) and describe it as being made of something. So, the third item needs to be in that same format. Use POE. Choices (F) and (H) don't mention any object, so they can be eliminated. Choice (J) says *objects* but doesn't mention a specific example, nor does it state the composition of any additional objects. On the other hand, (G) is in the same format as the other two examples: there's a specific object and what it's made of. Therefore, (G) has to be the answer.

The PTA allotted just $500 for the five
₇
sixth-grade classes to visit three historic sites.

7. The writer wants to emphasize that $500 was a small budget for the class trip. Which placement of the underlined portion best accomplishes that goal?

   A. Where it is now
   B. After the word *PTA*
   C. After the word *for*
   D. After the word *visit*

Here's How to Crack It

Again, identify that it's a Content question and underline the goal: *emphasize that $500 was a small budget for the class trip.* The underlined portion is the word *just*, so it needs to be placed in a spot that fulfills this goal. Try each option. Where it is now, it says *just $500*. That does imply that $500 is a *small budget*, so keep (A). With (B), the sentence says *The PTA just allotted*, which implies that the action happened recently, not that $500 is a *small budget*, so eliminate (B). With (C), the sentence says *The PTA allotted $500 for just the five…classes*, which suggests that the number of classes is small, not that the *budget* is small, so (C) is out. Finally, (D) says *to visit just three historic sites*, which suggests that the number of sites is low, not the *budget*. Therefore, the answer must be (A).

As you may notice, many of these questions actually require very little reference to the rest of the sentence or the themes of the passage as a whole. That's not to say you shouldn't read the context—you always should—but you should always be focusing on eliminating answers that don't fulfill the purpose stated in the question. You may like an answer choice, it may sound good in the sentence, or you might *personally* think it's the best phrasing, but if it doesn't match with the stated purpose, that answer is wrong. Of course, you may also see questions in this category that ask you specifically to be consistent with some other part of the passage, whether it's the same sentence, the sentences before, or even the overall point of the passage. In that case, be sure to read (or reread) as much as is needed in order to fulfill that goal.

Try your skills on the topics from this chapter in the following drill.

Transitions and Purpose Drill

This drill consists of only questions in the two topics from this chapter. On the actual test, you'll see a mix of topics within passages, unlike the individual questions given here. If you would like to time yourself, allot 7 minutes.

Molokini's vibrant coral reefs and teeming marine life are breathtaking in their beauty and colors. For instance, the pockmarked surface of the caldera is desolate and gray, a silent testament to Molokini's sad history as a bombing target during World War II.

1. Which transition word or phrase is most logical in context?
   A. **No Change**
   B. In contrast,
   C. Still,
   D. Even so,

The densely packed, timber-framed buildings of 17th-century London created highly combustible conditions for fires to spread rapidly. Thus, when a blaze began in Thomas Farriner's bakery on Pudding Lane in 1666, the flames quickly engulfed a vast area of the city, starting the Great Fire of London.

2. Which transition word is most logical in context?
   F. **No Change**
   G. Instead,
   H. Nevertheless,
   J. Moreover,

Despite the hardships and injustices she faced during her family's internment during World War II, these experiences profoundly shaped Ruth Asawa's artistic vision and later explorations of form and space; in other words, the very act of creating intricate wire sculptures can be seen as a response to the confinement and displacement that she endured.

3. Which transition word or phrase is most logical in context?
   A. **No Change**
   B. generally,
   C. in fact,
   D. nonetheless,

Silicon transistors were initially expensive to manufacture due to the purity required for the silicon crystals. Nevertheless, the market for early transistorized devices was limited until manufacturing techniques improved and drove down production costs.

4. Which transition word or phrase is most logical in context?
   F. **No Chang**
   G. For instance,
   H. Even so,
   J. As a result,

The highest peak of Mount Pilatus, named *Tomlishorn*, is

quite tall.
5

5. Which choice provides the clearest and most specific information about the height of Mount Pilatus?

A. **No Change**
B. approximately 2,100 meters tall.
C. a number of meters tall.
D. above the height of several other mountains.

The exhibit incites reactions that guests describe as eye

opening, mind blowing, etc.
6

6. Which choice best maintains the descriptive pattern established in the list of reactions?

F. **No Change**
G. and jaw drops.
H. and a dropping of the jaw.
J. and jaw dropping.

After the controversial bike lanes were installed, a study by
7
the city transportation department showed an increase in the

number of daily cyclists.

7. Which choice most clearly conveys that support for the bike lanes was not unanimous?

A. **No Change**
B. city's
C. planned
D. approved

In the book, Poulton described how predators could

maintain DNA variations in their prey, a now-accepted process
8
called frequency-dependent selection.
8

8. The writer wants to emphasize that Poulton's explanation of frequency-dependent selection represented a groundbreaking theory. Which choice most effectively accomplishes this goal?

F. **No Change**
G. the first explicit statement of
H. a theory known as
J. a viewpoint he called

TRANSITIONS AND PURPOSE DRILL EXPLANATIONS

1. **B** This Content question is asking for a *logical transition word*, so underline these words and consider the relationship between this sentence and the one before. The preceding sentence refers to *vibrant coral reefs*, and this sentence refers to something *desolate and gray*. These ideas disagree, so eliminate any answer that doesn't match this relationship.

   - (A) is wrong because it's a same-direction transition.
   - (B) is correct because the two ideas are in direct contrast with each other.
   - (C) and (D) are wrong because this sentence isn't referring to something that is true in spite of the previous sentence; rather, it's a direct contrast.

2. **F** This Content question is asking for a *logical transition word*, so underline these words and consider the relationship between this sentence and the one before. The preceding sentence refers to London's *highly combustible conditions*, and this sentence describes how a *blaze began* and *quickly engulfed a vast area of the city*. These ideas agree, so eliminate any answer that doesn't match this relationship.

   - (F) is correct because it's logical that the *Great Fire* happened as a result of the *highly combustible conditions*.
   - (G) and (H) are wrong because they're opposite-direction transitions.
   - (J) is wrong because this sentence is giving a result of the conditions in the previous sentence, rather than adding a second point.

3. **C** This Content question is asking for a *logical transition word*, so underline these words and consider the relationship between this sentence and the one before. The first part of the sentence says that Asawa's *hardships profoundly shaped* her *artistic vision*, and the second part of the sentence elaborates by stating that *creating intricate wire sculptures can be seen as a response* to her experiences. These ideas agree, so eliminate any answer that doesn't match this relationship.

   - (A) is wrong because the second part of the sentence is not a restatement of the first part, since the specific type of art isn't mentioned until the second part.
   - (B) is wrong because this statement is more specific, not more general.
   - (C) is correct because *in fact* is used to emphasize and elaborate on a point.
   - (D) is wrong because it's an opposite-direction transition.

4. **J** This Content question is asking for a *logical transition word*, so underline these words and consider the relationship between this sentence and the one before. The preceding sentence states that *Silicon transistors were initially expensive to manufacture*, and this sentence says that *the market…was limited* until costs came down. These ideas agree, so eliminate any answer that doesn't match this relationship.

   - (F) and (H) are wrong because they're opposite-direction transitions.
   - (G) is wrong because this sentence isn't an example of the one before.
   - (J) is correct because it's logical that the market being *limited* was a result of the initial high costs.

5. **B** This Content question is asking for an answer that *provides the clearest and most specific information about the height of Mount Pilatus*, so underline this phrase. Read the context of the sentence and eliminate any answer that doesn't fulfill this goal.

- (A), (C), and (D) are wrong because they don't provide any *specific* information about the height.
- (B) is correct because *approximately 2,100 meters tall* is a *specific* piece of information about *height*.

6. **J** This Content question is asking for an answer that *best maintains the descriptive pattern established in the list of reactions*, so underline this phrase. The other items in the *list of reactions* are *eye opening* and *mind blowing*, so the underlined portion should be consistent with these words. Eliminate any option that isn't in the same format.

- (F), (G), and (H) are wrong because they don't follow the *pattern* of *eye opening* and *mind blowing*.
- (J) is correct because *jaw dropping* is consistent with the other list items.

7. **A** This Content question is asking for an answer that *most clearly conveys that support for the bike lanes was not unanimous*, so underline this phrase. Read the context of the sentence and eliminate any answer that doesn't fulfill this goal.

- (A) is correct because *controversial* means that people disagreed about the bike lanes, which matches with *support…was not unanimous*.
- (B), (C), and (D) are wrong because they don't imply any lack of support.

8. **G** This Content question is asking for an answer that would *emphasize that Poulton's explanation of frequency-dependent selection represented a groundbreaking theory*, so underline this phrase. Read the context of the sentence and eliminate any answer that doesn't fulfill this goal.

- (F) is wrong because the idea that the theory is now accepted does not necessarily mean that it was *groundbreaking* at the time Poulton proposed it.
- (G) is correct because *first* matches with *groundbreaking*.
- (H) and (J) are wrong because they don't provide any evidence that the theory was *groundbreaking*.

Summary

○ For transitions questions, look back at the preceding sentence and consider how it relates to the sentence with the underlined portion. Eliminate answers that don't match with this relationship.

○ It's best to ignore the underlined portion when reading the passage for transitions questions, until the POE step.

○ Purpose questions can be simple and often don't require much reading, but it's critical to identify the purpose stated in the question.

○ For Purpose questions, don't consider grammar or punctuation unless it's mentioned in the purpose, and don't consider your personal opinion of each answer. All that matters is how well it fulfills the goal stated in the question.

Chapter 12

Content Questions: Paragraph and Whole Essay

This final Content questions chapter offers strategies for approaching the wide variety of questions you may see that require you to read and understand entire paragraphs or even the essay as a whole.

Finally, we've reached the very last set of English questions to go over. The basic approach for this category will be similar to what you have seen in the other Content questions chapters. The main difference is that the questions in this chapter will always require you to understand more *content*—the main focus of a paragraph or the essay as a whole. Here are the most common tasks you will be asked to perform on these types of questions:

- Determine whether a phrase, sentence, or paragraph should be added, deleted, or revised and why
- Choose the best introduction or conclusion to a paragraph
- Choose the best transition within a paragraph or between two paragraphs
- Choose whether and/or where to divide a paragraph in two
- Determine why a phrase or sentence shouldn't be deleted or should be added
- Identify where a word, sentence, or paragraph should go
- Choose the sequence of sentences within a whole paragraph
- Decide whether or not the author fulfilled a given goal in writing the essay as a whole

In this chapter, we'll see some examples of these types of questions. Unlike those in most of the other chapters, these questions will all be part of the same passage, so consider the context from the previous questions as needed.

I remember well the day I first saw Wheezie at the animal shelter. In truth, I think Wheezie is the one who adopted me. Before taking her home, I took a class to learn how to manage my new dog's behavior. Wheezie's puppy playfulness masked the steely determination of a true French bulldog, and she stubbornly resisted all the lessons from our obedience class. [1]

1. At this point, the writer is considering adding the following true statement:

   > My nephews trained Blizzard, a black lab with a sweet disposition, very easily.

   Should the writer add this sentence here?

   A. Yes, because it explains why the author felt so insecure about her difficulties training her dog.
   B. Yes, because it provides an important detail about another breed of dog.
   C. No, because it doesn't explain how Blizzard was trained.
   D. No, because it distracts the reader from the main point of this paragraph.

Here's How to Crack It

Whenever a strategy question asks if you should add new text or delete existing text, consider the relevance of the text to the rest of the paragraph. Then, evaluate the reasons in the answer choices carefully. The reason should correctly explain the purpose of the selected text. In this case, the paragraph is focused on the narrator's dog, Wheezie, so a sentence about a different dog isn't relevant. If the paragraph were to continue with a comparison between Wheezie and Blizzard, then the sentence could work, but the paragraph ends here and the passage continues without referring to Blizzard. So, the sentence shouldn't be added. That eliminates (A) and (B). Choice (C) is true in saying that the new sentence doesn't *explain how Blizzard was trained*, but even if it did, that wouldn't be a reason to add it. Eliminate (C). Choice (D), on the other hand, accurately states that the sentence isn't relevant to the topic of the paragraph, so that's the correct answer.

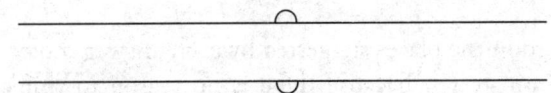

Most puppy books no longer recommend using newspapers to housebreak dogs. I bought three safety gates to block off the kitchen from the rest of the house. I also brought home a crate, baby blankets to make it cozy, a stylish collar and matching leash, several bags of food, and of course, plenty of toys.

2. Given that all choices are true, which one most effectively introduces this paragraph?

   F. **No Change**
   G. When I was growing up, my family had an Irish Setter and four cats.
   H. I made sure I had all the supplies we'd need before bringing Wheezie home.
   J. Many people prefer cats as pets.

Here's How to Crack It

Be careful! You must read the entire paragraph before answering this question. In fact, it's a good idea to skip the underlined sentence entirely. There's a good chance that this sentence doesn't introduce the topic of the paragraph, so you're better off ignoring it to see what the paragraph is actually about. The other sentences refer to the items the narrator got in preparation for the dog coming home. Once that has been established, use Process of Elimination. Choices (F), (G), and (J) don't relate to the focus of the paragraph. Choice (H), on the other hand, does—it mentions *supplies*. Thus, (H) is the correct answer.

ORDER

There are also several types of Order questions, but they all involve the correct placement of ideas. Some order questions will ask you to correctly place a modifier or additional text. Other questions will ask you to evaluate and possibly correct the order of sentences within a paragraph or the paragraphs themselves. All Order questions work best with POE. Ideas should be consistent and the meaning should be clear, but that meaning can be difficult to understand until ideas are in their proper place. Let's look at a few examples.

Once Wheezie was home, I noticed her snoring and struggling to breathe. French bulldogs can face a serious number of health
<u>3</u>
issues affecting the respiratory system, knees, and eyesight. I decided to take Wheezie to get checked out.

3. The best placement for the underlined word would be:

A. where it is now.
B. before the word *French* (revising the capitalization accordingly).
C. before the word *health*.
D. before the word *respiratory*.

Here's How to Crack It

Use POE, trying the word in the places suggested by each answer choice. Choice (A) has some support, so keep it. Eliminate (B) because there is no reason to think the dogs themselves should be described as *serious*. Choice (C) works because *serious health issues* provides a clear meaning. Choice (D) doesn't work because there's no reason to describe the *respiratory system* as *serious*, so eliminate (D). Between (A) and (C), the correct answer is (C) because it clearly indicates that the *health issues* are a *serious* concern. Although the idea that the *number of health issues* is of concern may be valid, describing that *number* as being *serious* is less clear and precise compared to the wording in (C), so (A) must be eliminated.

Order of Sentences

If there is a question on order of the sentences or placement of new text within a paragraph, all of the sentences in the paragraph will be numbered. **No Change** could be the answer to the order of the sentences, but if you're reading along and get confused by a sudden shift in the action, that's a good sign the sentences are, in fact, out of order. Do not go back and reread, but instead wait until you get to the question. Don't waste time trying to reorder all of the sentences yourself. Look for transition words that indicate an introduction, a conclusion, or a pair of sentences that should go back-to-back, and use POE.

[1] He recommended an excellent specialist to perform the surgery. [2] When the day came, I drove to the hospital, dreading the moment I'd need to leave her behind. [3] While we waited for her to be admitted, Wheezie sensed something was wrong and curled up on my lap, trembling. [4] My vet broke the bad news that Wheezie would have to have surgery to correct the problems in her nasal passage and vocal cords.

4. Which of the following sequences of sentences will make the paragraph most logical?

F. **No Change**
G. 2, 3, 1, 4
H. 4, 3, 2, 1
J. 4, 1, 2, 3

Here's How to Crack It

Use POE. The surgery isn't properly introduced until the end, which means Sentence 4 should be the introduction. Eliminate (F) and (G), and determine whether Sentence 3 or 1 should be next. Sentence 1 should come before Sentence 3 because Sentence 1 happens before the surgery and Sentence 3 is on the day of the surgery, so the answer is (J).

Order of the Paragraphs

If there is a question on the order of the paragraphs, there will be a warning at the beginning of the passage, alerting you that the paragraphs may or may not be in the correct order and identifying which question will ask about which paragraph.

Almost no one ever spots this warning. Treat these the same way you treat the order of the sentences. If you suddenly find yourself confused by an inexplicable shift in the action, check above the title to see if the warning is there. Alternatively, continue reading and working the questions and bet safely you'll encounter a question on the order of the paragraphs at the end of the passage.

AND IN THE END...

> Questions 9 and 10 ask about the passage as a whole.

Other than order of the paragraphs, two other questions routinely appear at the end and are always preceded by the announcement above.

Placement of New Info

The paragraphs will also be numbered for a question testing the placement of additional info.

---

9. The writer is considering adding the following sentence to the essay:

   > After a night spent winning the hearts of all of the attendants, Wheezie bounded out of the recovery room and into my waiting arms.

   If the author were to add this sentence, it would most logically be placed at:

   A. Point A in Paragraph 1.
   B. Point B in Paragraph 3.
   C. Point C in Paragraph 3.
   D. Point D in Paragraph 5.

Here's How to Crack It

Okay, so this is a little unfair: we didn't give you the entire passage, so you can't answer this one. However, we'll give you some tips for answering these questions when you do have a whole passage. First off, if the topic of the sentence fits more with the ideas toward the beginning or end of the passage, or in a certain paragraph, you could start with those options. If you're not sure, go straight to POE. Then look for clues in the sentence. Pronouns and phrases beginning with *this* and *such* are good clues about what must have been mentioned in the previous sentence. Look at the sentences surrounding the bracketed letter in the passage to see how the new sentence fits in.

Grading the Passage

Questions at the end that ask you to evaluate the passage are another version of a strategy question. The question identifies the purpose of the passage and asks you to determine whether the author succeeded. These are always at the end, so we waited to show you here.

10. Suppose that one of the writer's goals had been to address the role obedience classes can play in the healthy development of dogs. Would this essay fulfill that goal?

   F. Yes, because the essay implies the writer and her dog benefited from obedience classes.
   G. Yes, because the essay indicates French bulldogs are not easily trained.
   H. No, because the essay is focused on one anecdote about one dog.
   J. No, because the essay indicates the dog displayed aggressive and territorial behavior.

Here's How to Crack It

Start by underlining or highlighting the goal stated in the question: *address the role obedience classes can play in the healthy development of dogs*. Then, consider how well the essay did or did not fulfill that goal. It's important to note that there is nothing wrong with saying "no" to the question. You might think that means you're criticizing the test-writers, but you're not. The answer to these questions will be "no" at least as often as "yes." In this case, the essay does mention a training class, but there's no mention of how it helped Wheezie develop. Moreover, it doesn't give any information about dogs in general. Eliminate (F) and (G) because the essay doesn't fulfill the given goal. Choice (H) is accurate, so keep it. Eliminate (J) because the essay doesn't state this—but even if it did, that wouldn't be a reason it doesn't fulfill the goal. The correct answer is (H).

These questions should help illustrate why we advise you to read in between the questions. You should also consider the meaning of what you're reading, even when you're answering Grammar questions that don't really require you to do so. You may not always be given a question about the entire essay, but you will likely see some questions on each passage that at least relate to the content of whole paragraphs. Pay attention to the flow of ideas and overall points in each passage so that you don't have to waste time going back and rereading.

Paragraph and Whole Essay Drill

In the drill below, you will find 9 questions focusing only on Content question types from this chapter and the previous chapter. Be sure to use the strategies discussed in these lessons.

> The following paragraphs may or may not be in the most logical order. Each paragraph is numbered, and question 9 will ask you to choose where Paragraph 2 should most logically be placed.

---

[1]

The golden age of television means many things to many people. To the small band of actors, writers, and directors who would rise to <u>prominence</u> in the late '50s and early '60s,

1

without a doubt it meant the television shows such as *Playhouse 90*, on which many of them worked for the first <u>live</u> time.

2

[2]

Despite the undeniable risks of live performances—or perhaps because of them—the results rank among the greatest achievements in American entertainment. Many of the show's productions were later remade, for both television and film, including *Requiem for a Heavyweight, Judgment at Nuremberg,* and *Days of Wine and Roses.* [3] Many critics maintain none of the remakes could match the brilliance and electricity of the live performances displayed in *Playhouse 90*.

[3]

[1] Each week, a new "teleplay" was created from scratch—written, cast, rehearsed, and performed. [2] *Playhouse 90* was truly a remarkable training ground for young talents. [3] Such future luminaries as Rod Serling, Sidney Lumet, Paddy Chayefsky, Marlon Brando, and Patricia Neal worked long

1. Which of the following alternatives to the underlined word would be **least** acceptable?

    A. fame
    B. projection
    C. stardom
    D. greatness

2. The best placement for the underlined word would be:

    F. where it is now.
    G. before the word *actors*.
    H. before the word *doubt*.
    J. before the word *television*.

3. The writer is considering deleting the preceding sentence. Should the sentence be kept or deleted?

    A. Kept, because it provides context for the reference to remakes in the next sentence.
    B. Kept, because it is crucial to understanding why *Playhouse 90* was a success.
    C. Deleted, because it does not match the objective tone of the essay.
    D. Deleted, because it contains information that has already been provided in the essay.

hours memorizing their lines. [4] In some cases, when there were problems with the censors, it would have to be created

twice. 5

[4]

Due to the frantic pace, accidents happened frequently. David Niven once revealed that, during an early show, he inadvertently locked his costume in his dressing room two minutes before air time. As the announcer read the opening credits, the sound of axes splintering the door to Niven's dressing room could be heard in the background. 7

4. Which choice would most clearly indicate that the actors, writers, and directors became extremely skilled?

F. No Change
G. honing their crafts.
H. constructing the set.
J. skimming the want-ads.

5. Which sequence of sentences makes the paragraph most logical?

A. No Change
B. 1, 2, 4, 3
C. 2, 1, 4, 3
D. 2, 3, 1, 4

6. Given that all choices are true, which one most effectively introduces this paragraph?

F. No Change
G. The ratings for *Playhouse 90* were unimpressive.
H. Broadway has produced many famous actors as well.
J. *Playhouse 90* ran on CBS from 1956 to 1961.

7. The writer is considering deleting the preceding sentence. If the writer were to make this deletion, the essay would primarily lose a statement that:

A. explains the organization of the last paragraph.
B. adds a much needed touch of humor to the essay.
C. explains how one accident was resolved.
D. adds nothing, since the information is provided elsewhere in the essay.

Questions 8 and 9 ask about the preceding passage as a whole.

---

8. Suppose that one of the writer's goals had been to write a brief essay describing an influential program in television's history. Would this essay fulfill that goal?

F. Yes, because it explains that many future stars underwent valuable training working on *Playhouse 90*.
G. Yes, because it mentions that *Playhouse 90* had the greatest number of viewers in its time slot.
H. No, because it fails to mention any future stars by name.
J. No, because even though many future stars received their start on *Playhouse 90*, few ever returned to television.

9. For the sake of the logic and coherence of this essay, Paragraph 2 should be placed:

A. where it is now.
B. before Paragraph 1.
C. after Paragraph 3.
D. after Paragraph 4.

PARAGRAPH AND WHOLE ESSAY DRILL EXPLANATIONS

1. **B** This Content question is asking for an answer that *would be **least** acceptable*, so try each option and mark it with a checkmark or an X, then choose the odd one out.

   - (A), (C), and (D) are wrong because *fame*, *stardom*, and *greatness* are all synonyms for *prominence* and work in the sentence.
   - (B) is correct because *rise to projection* doesn't provide a clear meaning.

2. **J** This Content question is asking for the *best placement* for *live*, so try it in each spot and eliminate any that don't provide a clear meaning.

   - (F) is wrong because *the first live time* doesn't provide a clear meaning.
   - (G) is wrong because while it's correct to describe *actors, writers, and directors* as *live*, there's really no reason to put this word there because it's a given that these people were living when they worked on television.
   - (H) is wrong because *without a live doubt* doesn't provide a clear meaning.
   - (J) is correct because *live television* is a phrase that refers to broadcasts that aren't pre-taped.

3. **A** This Content question is asking whether the sentence should be *kept or deleted*, so underline this phrase. Consider the content of the sentence and that of the surrounding sentences. The paragraph is about how the TV show ranks *among the greatest achievements in American entertainment* and that *remakes* of it couldn't match the original. The sentence in question introduces the idea that the show was *remade* in several ways. Since the sentence after the one in question refers to *the remakes* and this sentence introduces the remakes, this sentence should be kept. Eliminate any answer that is inconsistent with this.

   - (A) is correct because it's consistent with the role of this sentence.
   - (B) is wrong because *crucial* is too strong, and this sentence doesn't in and of itself provide evidence that the show was *a success*.
   - (C) and (D) are wrong because the sentence shouldn't be deleted.

4. **G** This Content question is asking for an answer that *would most clearly indicate that the actors, writers, and directors became extremely skilled*, so underline this phrase. Read the context of the sentence and eliminate any answer that doesn't fulfill this goal.

   - (F), (H), and (J) are wrong because they don't offer any evidence that these people became better at doing anything, merely that they did something.
   - (G) is correct because *honing their craft* reveals that they improved in their skills.

5.   **D**   This Content question is asking for a logical *sequence of sentences*, so underline this phrase. Look for clues in the sentences that indicate the order they should go in. Sentence 4 says *it would have to be created twice*, so this sentence must come after a sentence that contains a word for *it* to refer back to, which is the *"teleplay"* mentioned in Sentence 1. Sentence 2 mentions *young talents*, and Sentence 3 mentions some specific people, so these two sentences should stay together. Eliminate any answer not consistent with these clues.

- (A) and (B) are wrong because Sentence 4 should come directly after Sentence 1.
- (C) is wrong because Sentences 2 and 3 should be kept together.
- (D) is correct because Sentence 4 should come after Sentence 1, and Sentences 2 and 3 should be kept together.

6.   **F**   This Content question is asking for an answer that *most effectively introduces the paragraph*, so underline this phrase. Ignore the underlined sentence and identify the subject of the rest of the paragraph. It focuses on a mistake that happened when someone *inadvertently locked his costume in his dressing room*, so eliminate any answer inconsistent with these ideas.

- (F) is correct because *accidents* is consistent with the mishap described in the paragraph.
- (G), (H), and (J) are wrong because they don't relate to the idea of something going wrong.

7.   **C**   This Content question is asking for what the paragraph *would primarily lose* if the sentence were deleted, so read the paragraph with and without the sentence to determine the difference. With the sentence, there is an explanation of what happened on the live show when a mishap occurred. Without the sentence, the paragraph doesn't state what happened when the costume was locked in the dressing room or how it affected the live show. Eliminate any answer inconsistent with this difference.

- (A) is wrong because this sentence doesn't relate to the *organization of the last paragraph*.
- (B) is wrong because although this sentence might be humorous, there's no objective reason to state that this humor is *much needed* in the passage.
- (C) is correct because it accurately describes the role of the sentence.
- (D) is wrong because the essay does not state *elsewhere* what happened as a result of the accident.

8.   **F**   This Content question is asking whether the essay describes *an influential program in television's history*, so underline this phrase and consider the overall point of the essay. The essay focuses on a show called *Playhouse 90* and describes it as one of *the greatest achievements in American entertainment* and as having *brilliance and electricity*. This matches with the program being *influential*, so the essay does accomplish the goal. Eliminate any answer that doesn't match with this.

- (F) is correct because the essay mentions *future luminaries* and how the show was *a remarkable training ground* for them.
- (G) is wrong because the essay doesn't mention the *number of viewers* compared to other shows.
- (H) and (J) are wrong because the essay does fulfill the goal.

9. **D** This Content question is asking where *Paragraph 2 should be placed*, so underline this phrase. Consider the content of Paragraph 2 and how it might relate to other paragraphs. Paragraph 2 mentions *undeniable risks of live performances*, which ties back to the accident described in Paragraph 4. Furthermore, it's more logical for Paragraph 3 to follow Paragraph 1 because Paragraph 3 describes how the show worked, and it's also logical for the passage to end with Paragraph 2 instead of Paragraph 4 because Paragraph 4 doesn't end with any type of concluding point. Therefore, Paragraph 2 should follow Paragraph 4.

- (A) is wrong because as it is now, Paragraph 2 separates the ideas in Paragraphs 1 and 3 that should be put together.
- (B) is wrong because Paragraph 2 can't begin the essay, since it doesn't provide an introduction to the topic.
- (C) is wrong because the first sentence of Paragraph 2 ties in to the topic of accidents in Paragraph 4, so it should go after Paragraph 4, not before.
- (D) is correct because this order follows a consistent flow of ideas.

Summary

o There are many types of questions that fall into this category. Always read the task carefully and underline or highlight what you're being asked.

o You will need to read and comprehend much more for these questions—often an entire paragraph or more. Reading in between the questions, therefore, is needed so that you'll have the context to answer them.

o For questions asking about introduction, conclusion, or transition sentences, ignore the underlined portion until after you have understood the focus of the paragraph and can use POE.

o For questions about the location of a word, phrase, or sentence, try each spot and use POE.

o For questions about the order of all of the sentences in a paragraph, look for a clue about a sentence that must go before or after another sentence, and use POE based on that.

o When the question asks whether the essay fulfilled a certain goal overall, *No* is a legitimate option.

Part III
How to Crack the ACT Mathematics Test

Chapter 13
Introduction to the ACT Mathematics Test

The second section of the ACT will always be the Math test. To perform your best, you'll need to become familiar with the structure and strategy of the ACT Math test. In this chapter, we discuss the types of questions you can expect to see and how you can use organizational strategy, estimation, and elimination skills to improve your Math score.

Old and New
If you took or prepared for the old version of the ACT, you had 60 minutes for 60 questions, and there were five answer choices instead of four. The math topics that are tested have not changed.

WHAT TO EXPECT ON THE MATH TEST

On the Enhanced ACT, you will have 50 minutes to answer 45 multiple-choice questions based on "topics covered in typical high school classes." For those of you who aren't sure if you went to a typical high school, these questions break down into rather precise areas of knowledge.

Preparing for Higher Math (33 questions)
- Number and Quantity (4–5 questions)
- Algebra (7–8 questions)
- Functions (7–8 questions)
- Geometry (7–8 questions)
- Statistics and Probability (5–6 questions)

Integrating Essential Skills (8 questions)

Modeling (8+ questions)
This category reflects how well a student uses modeling skills across math concepts, so these questions are also counted in one of the categories above.

If you did some quick math using the numbers above, you might have noticed that 33 Preparing for Higher Math questions + 8 Integrating Essential Skills question = 41 total questions. But wait, aren't there 45 questions on the ACT Math Test? What about the other 4? Those are what ACT calls "Field Test" questions, which means they don't count towards your score. It's impossible to tell which questions are unscored, so treat every question as if it counts.

Because ACT's categories are not the clearest, let's break this outline down further. "Preparing for Higher Math" is content that ACT believes would be included in the high school curriculum. "Number and Quantity" includes questions about irrational and complex numbers, as well as exponents, matrices, and vectors. The other categories in Preparing for Higher Math are more straightforward; you may have taken classes with those exact names!

"Integrating Essential Skills" questions are exactly what they sound like: combining your knowledge and skills in more complex questions. You will see familiar math concepts—such as percentages, proportions, surface area, 3-D visualization, rates, and unit conversions—but with multiple steps. Finally, "Modeling" is ACT's term for Word Problems; these questions will also fall under "Preparing for Higher Math" or "Integrating Essential Skills."

What Not to Expect on the Math Test

The ACT does not provide any formulas at the beginning of the Math test. Before you panic, take a second look at the chart above. Because the ACT is so specific about the types of questions it expects you to answer, preparing to tackle ACT Math takes a few simple steps.

A NOTE ON CALCULATORS

Not all standardized tests allow calculators. Fortunately, ACT does. We're not about to give you the stodgy advice that you shouldn't use a calculator—quite the opposite, in fact. A calculator can help to save a ton of time on operations that you may have forgotten how to do or that are easy to mess up. Adding fractions, multiplying decimals, doing operations with big numbers: why not use a calculator on these? The place where you have to be really careful with your calculator, though, is on the easy ones. Let's see an example.

———————◯———————

1. What is the value of $3x^2 + 5x - 7$ when $x = -1$?

    A.   −15
    B.   −9
    C.   −1
    D.   5

Here's How to Crack It

If you have your calculator handy, use it. This question is pretty straightforward, but a calculator can help to put everything together. BUT, make sure you're treating the −1 with the respect it deserves. What you enter into a calculator should look something like this:

$$3(-1)^2 + 5(-1) - 7$$

When working with negative numbers or fractions, make doubly sure that you use parentheses. If not, a lot of weird stuff can happen, and unfortunately all of the weird, wrong stuff that can happen is reflected in the wrong answer choices. If you computed this expression and found −9, (B), you got the right answer. Well done. If not, go back and try to figure out where you made your calculator mistake.

———————◯———————

Types of Calculators

Calculators are permitted throughout the Math test, and this book will discuss ways to solve calculator-friendly questions in an accurate and manageable way. If you take the computer-based version of the ACT, you can take your own calculator *and* use the built-in calculator. For the paper version, be aware that not all calculators are permitted on the ACT. We will show you how to do the calculations on a TI-80 series calculator, as this family of calculators is very popular. If you don't plan to use a TI-80 series calculator on the test, we recommend that you confirm that your calculator is acceptable for use on the test and that it can do the following:

- handle positive, negative, and fractional exponents
- use parentheses
- graph simple functions
- convert fractions to decimals and vice versa

> Use your calculator or the built-in calculator, but use it wisely. Be careful with negative numbers and fractions.

THE PRINCETON REVIEW APPROACH

Because the test is so predictable, the best way to prepare for ACT Math is with:

- a thorough review of the very specific information and question types that come up repeatedly
- an understanding of The Princeton Review's test-taking strategies and techniques

In each Math chapter in this book, you'll find a mixture of review and technique, with a sprinkling of ACT-like questions. At the end of each chapter are both a summary of the chapter and a drill designed to pinpoint your math test-taking strengths and weaknesses. In addition to working through the questions in this book, we strongly suggest you practice our techniques on some real ACT practice tests. Let's begin with some general strategies.

Order of Difficulty: Still Personal

The Math test is the only part of the ACT that is in Order of Difficulty (OOD). What this means is that the easier questions tend to be a bit earlier in the exam, and the harder questions are later. Usually, this means that question 1 is a freebie and question 45 is a doozy. None of the other tests have an OOD, unfortunately, so they are all about Personal Order of Difficulty (POOD).

Now, we all love easy questions, but hold on for a second. If you and I both get a B on a math test at school, is it necessarily because we got exactly the same questions right or wrong? Unfortunately, no. What makes for a hard question? Is it hard because it's a long word problem, or is it hard because it tests some arcane concept that your teacher went over for like five seconds?

Only the very hardest questions will be both. So even on the Math test of the ACT, you still need to use your POOD. The things you might find easy or hard won't necessarily jibe with ACT's OOD.

Additionally, the Math OOD on the Enhanced ACT might be looser than it was on earlier versions of the ACT. Don't be alarmed if a question seems easier or harder than it "should" based on the question number. What matters, after all, is how easy or hard **you** think it is.

Now, Later, Never

Hard questions take a long time. Easy ones take a short time. That's obvious, but as we've seen, the definition of an "Easy" question is a tough one to pin down. That's why you should be careful trusting ACT's Order of Difficulty on the Math test. The no-brainer approach is to open the test booklet and work questions 1 through 45 in order, but you can get a lot of extra points by out-thinking this test. You'll have a much easier time drawing your own road map for this test than letting ACT guide you.

This is why when you arrive at each question, you should first determine whether it is a Now, Later, or Never question. Do the Now questions immediately: they're the freebies—the ones you know how to do and can do quickly and accurately. Skip any questions you think might take you a bit longer or which test unfamiliar concepts—save them for Later. Make sure you get all the points you can on the questions you know you can do, no matter what the question number.

Once you've done all the Now questions, go back to all the ones you left for Later. But here you should be careful as well. For both Now and Later questions, don't rush and make careless errors. On the other hand, don't get stuck on a particular question. In a 50-minute exam, think of how much spending 5 minutes on a single question can cost you!

Finally, there's no problem with leaving a few questions behind in the Never category. The good news here is that these questions are not necessarily totally lost. Fill them in with a Letter of the Day: choose one pair of letters and bubble in all the blanks this way. For example, always bubble in A or F, B or G, etc. ACT doesn't have a guessing penalty, so there's nothing to lose, and you can even get lucky and score a few free points.

Now
Do the questions you're sure you can do quickly and accurately.

Later
If a question looks time-consuming, save it for later. Do the Nows first.

Never
Sometimes it's better to just walk away. If a question has you totally stumped, answer with your Letter of the Day and move on.

Flag Later, Not Never
On the ACT Online Test, use the Flag tool on Later questions so you can easily go back. *Don't* flag the Never questions—you don't want to waste your time looking at those questions again! In either case, put in your LOTD as you skip the question.

USE PROCESS OF ELIMINATION (POE)

Remember the major technique we introduced in Chapter 4: POE, or Process of Elimination. ACT doesn't take away points for wrong answers, so you should always guess, and POE can help you improve those chances of guessing. Don't make the mistake of thinking that POE is a strategy reserved only for English, Reading, and Science. Math has its own kind of POE, one facet of which we like to call Ballparking.

BALLPARKING

You can frequently get rid of several answer choices in an ACT Math question without doing any complicated math. Narrow down the choices by estimating your answer. We call this Ballparking. Let's look at an example.

Cross Out the Unreasonable Answers

What's the average of 100 and 200?

~~A. 500~~
B. 150
~~C. a billion~~

3. There are 600 school children in the Lakeville district. If 54 of them are high school seniors, what is the percentage of high school seniors in the Lakeville district?

   A. 0.9%
   B. 9%
   C. 11%
   D. 90%

Here's How to Crack It

Before we do any serious math on this question, let's see if we can get rid of some answer choices by Ballparking.

First, we need to estimate what percent 54 is of 600. It's pretty small, definitely way less than 50%, so we can eliminate (D) right off the bat. Now, think about easy percentages that you know—10% and 25%—and start from there. What's 10% of 600? Just move the decimal one place to the left to get it, and you'll find that 10% of 600 is 60. Therefore, if the number from the question is 54, the answer must be less than 10%. Let's get rid of (C). Now, we know that 54 is pretty close to 60, so we want something close to 10% but slightly less, and the only possible answer is (B).

It may feel like we somehow cheated the system by doing the question that way, but here's what ACT doesn't want you to know: the quick, easy way and the "real" way get you the same number of points. Not all questions will be so easily ballparkable, but if you think before you start frantically figuring, you can usually eliminate at least an answer choice or two.

WORD PROBLEMS

You've seen the breakdown of the topics that are tested on the ACT Math test. At a glance, it actually looks like the ACT should be kind of an easy test: you've definitely learned a lot of this stuff in school, some of it by the end of middle school. So what's the deal? Well, part of the deal is that ACT makes familiar stuff unfamiliar by putting it into word problems. Word problems add some confusing steps that mask the often simple concepts trapped in the questions. Trap answers, partial answers, and weird phrasing abound in word problems. Is anyone else getting the feeling that this whole exam is about reading comprehension?

Word problems look a lot of different ways and test a lot of different math concepts, but if you keep these three steps in mind, you should be able to get started on most word problems.

> When dealing with word problems on the ACT Math test:
> 1. **Know the question.** Read the whole question before calculating anything, and underline or highlight the actual question.
> 2. **Let the answers help.** Look for clues on how to solve and ways to use POE (Process of Elimination).
> 3. **Break the question into bite-sized pieces.** Calculate at each step necessary and watch out for tricky phrasing.

We'll demonstrate these steps in action on the next page.

Let's try a question.

---

7. On a table of cookies at a wedding reception, 20% of the cookies are chocolate chip, and 35% of the remaining cookies are shortbread. Of the cookies that are **not** chocolate chip or shortbread, 25% are gingersnaps and the rest are peanut butter. If there are 200 cookies on the table, how many of the cookies are peanut butter?

   A. 40
   B. 70
   C. 78
   D. 150

Here's How to Crack It

Step 1: Know the Question

There is a slightly tricky step to this one. First of all, the question doesn't tell you until near the end that there are 200 cookies on the table. Without this piece of information, the percentages don't mean much of anything. Second, the question is asking for the number of cookies that are peanut butter, and we're going to have to figure out a bunch of other things before we can figure that out.

Step 2: Let the Answers Help

There aren't any unreasonable answers in this one, though if you noticed how much we're subtracting from 200, you're probably thinking that the answer won't be 150.

Step 3: Break the Question into Bite-Sized Pieces

The starting point of this word problem actually comes near the end: there are 200 cookies on the table. Once you've got that, work the question sentence by sentence, and pay particular attention to the language of the question.

20% of the cookies are chocolate chip.

A nice easy way to start. You can translate 20% as either $\frac{20}{100}$ or 0.20 to do the math. There are 200 cookies, and 20% of 200 is 40, so 40 cookies are chocolate chip.

35% of the remaining cookies are shortbread.

This is just like the last piece, except for one HUGE exception, which comes from the word *remaining*. First, we'll need to figure out how many remaining cookies there are from the first step. There are 200 total cookies and 40 of them are chocolate chip, so there are 160 cookies remaining. Since 35% of 160 is 56, 56 cookies are shortbread.

Of the cookies that are **not** chocolate chip or shortbread, 25% are gingersnaps…

This time, the word *not* is bolded, which makes it easier to spot that there's another extra step. There were 160 cookies left after the last step, but 56 of them are short-bread, so now there are 104 cookies that are **not** chocolate chip or shortbread. Since 25% of 104 is 26, 26 of the cookies are gingersnaps.

…and the rest are peanut butter.

There were 104 cookies left over in the last step, and 26 of them are gingersnaps, which means there must be 78 cookies left that are peanut butter. Choice (C) is the correct answer, which is nice because C is for Cookie. Notice that 40 is one of the numbers you wrote down along the way, but (A) is not the correct answer. Partial answers like this are common on word problems, which is why Know the Question is such as important step.

If it seems like this took a long time to do, don't worry; they won't all take this long. Most of these steps will come naturally after a while, and you'll have a solid base with which to begin any ACT Math question in such a way that enables you to get to the answer as efficiently as possible.

> **Write it down!**
> Don't do the steps of a Math question in your head, especially on word problems. Write each step on your scratch paper/white-board or test booklet. You will increase your accuracy *and* save time by not having to redo steps.

Pacing

As you work through the following lessons, revisit your POOD. The more content you review and the more you practice, the more you may find more Now questions and fewer Never questions.

Goal Score

In the passage-based sections of the ACT, a whole passage will be unscored. In the Math section, the unscored questions are scattered throughout the section, and there are only four of them. As such, you can use the estimated Math scale on page 77 to estimate how many questions you need to do to reach your goal score. For example, 25 correct, scored answers will give you a Math score of 24. To reach this goal score, make sure to attempt 27 or 28 questions in case you make any mistakes or correctly answer any unscored questions.

Summary

○ On the ACT Math test, you have 50 minutes to attempt 45 questions. The vast majority of these questions will cover math concepts you learned in middle and high school.

○ Use your calculator (and/or the built-in calculator on the Online ACT) liberally but wisely!

○ Use your Personal Order of Difficulty to determine if a question is for Now, Later, or Never.

○ Just because the Math test is technically in order of difficulty doesn't mean you need to do it in order.

○ Never leave any blanks! Fill in the Never questions with your Letter of the Day.

○ Look to use POE, eliminating unreasonable answers.

○ Remember the Basic Approach for Word Problems.
  • **Know the question**. Read the question all the way through and underline the question.
  • **Let the answers help**. Look for clues on how to solve. Use POE and Ballparking.
  • **Break the question into bite-sized pieces**. Every question has lots of information: process each piece one at a time, calculate at each step necessary, and watch out for tricky phrasing.

Chapter 14
Fundamentals

A solid base in the fundamentals of the math tested on the ACT is essential to getting a good score. We'll see a number of strategies that will help to work around some of the more advanced concepts, but there's often no way to work around questions that test the fundamentals.

VOCABULARY

Calculators can solve a lot of problems, but vocabulary is one aspect of math with which a calculator can't help. Let's review some of the main terms.

A Note on Calculators

This chapter will deal mainly with concepts rather than operations. As mentioned in the previous chapter, we encourage you to use your calculator liberally but wisely. The operations discussed in this chapter will be those for which a calculator might be unhelpful or confusing.

Basics

Use the numbers below to answer questions 1 through 6 that follow. Check your answers against the Answer Key at the end of this chapter.

$$-81, -19, -9, -6, -\frac{1}{4}, -0.15, 0, 1.75, 2, 3, 12, 16, 81$$

1. List all the *positive numbers*. _____

2. List all the *negative integers*. _____

3. List all the *odd* integers. _____

4. List all the *even* integers. _____

5. List all the *positive*, *even* integers in *consecutive* order. _____

   _____

6. List all the numbers that are neither *positive* nor *negative*. _____

   _____

Now try these questions.

7. What is the *reciprocal* of $-\frac{1}{4}$? _____

8. What is the *opposite reciprocal* of 2? _____

9. When a number and its reciprocal are multiplied, what is the product?

   _____

10. How many times does 2 go into 15 evenly? _____

11. In question 10, how much is left over? _____

12. What is 15 divided by 2? _____

Let's try it the other way. Use the following list of terms to answer questions 13 through 18.

> Number, Integer, Positive, Negative, Even, Odd,
> Consecutive, Reciprocal, Remainder

13. Which terms describe 6? _____

14. Which terms describe $-\dfrac{1}{5}$? _____

15. Which terms describe 0? _____

16. When 14 is divided by 3, it has a _____ of 2.

17. The _____ of $-\dfrac{1}{4}$ is -4.

18. The numbers 2, 4, 6 are listed in _____ order, but the numbers 3, 1, 14 are not.

Factors and Multiples

Factors and multiples are all numbers that are divisible by other numbers. Start with examples, and the definitions will become easier.

> Example
> - The factors of 10 are 1, 2, 5, 10.
> - The first four positive multiples of 10 are 10, 20, 30, 40.

1. List the factors of 12. _____

2. List the first four multiples of 12. _____

3. List the factors of 30. _____

4. List the first four multiples of 30. _____

5. Is 12 a multiple or factor of 24? _____

6. Is 8 one of the factors of 64? _____

7. What is the greatest common factor of 27 and 45? _____

8. What is the greatest common factor of 9 and 36? _____

9. What is the least common multiple of 9 and 12? _____

10. What is the least common multiple of 24 and 48? _____

A Good Rule of Thumb
- The factors of a number are always equivalent to that number or *smaller*.
- The multiples of a number are always equivalent to that number or *larger*.
- A handy way to remember this is that **f**actors are **f**ew, and **m**ultiples are **m**any.

Prime

> A prime number is any number with only two distinct factors:
> 1 and itself.

1. What are the single-digit prime numbers? _____

2. What is the only even prime number? _____

3. Is 1 a prime number? _____

> The prime factorization of a number is the reduction of a number to
> its prime factors. Find the prime factorization of a number by
> using a factor tree. Consider this example:
>
>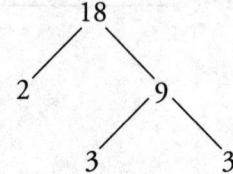
>
> The prime factorization of 18 is $2 \times 3 \times 3$ or 2×3^2.

4. What is the prime factorization of 36?

Distinct = Different
The word *distinct* is important. It means different, so don't count any number twice. For example, 24 has 4 prime factors (2, 2, 2, 3) but only 2 *distinct* prime factors (2, 3).

5. What is the sum of all the prime factors of 36? _____

6. What is the product of all the distinct prime factors of 36? _____

Absolute Value

Absolute value is a measure of the distance between a number and 0. Since distances are always positive, the absolute value of a number is also always positive. The absolute value of a number is written as $|x|$.

When solving for the value of a variable inside the absolute value bars, it is important to remember that the variable could be either positive or negative. For example, if $|x| = 2$, then $x = 2$ or $x = -2$, as both 2 and -2 are a distance of 2 from 0.

Here is a simple example:

$$|2 - 5| - |7 - 3| = |-3| - |4| = 3 - 4 = -1$$

Now here's one with a variable:

$$|4x - 5| - 1 = 6$$
$$|4x - 5| = 7$$

$$
\begin{array}{lll}
4x - 5 = 7 & \text{or} & 4x - 5 = -7 \\
4x = 12 & \text{or} & 4x = -2 \\
x = 3 & \text{or} & x = -0.5
\end{array}
$$

ADVANCED TERMS

Real Numbers and Their Imaginary Friends

ACT uses the term "real" a lot, but it's usually only there to scare you. Sometimes, though, ACT will test it directly, so it's good to have at least a sense of what the term means.

1. How much would you like to earn in your eventual job?_____

2. How much scholarship money do you want from your eventual college? _____

3. What's the temperature in the South Pole right now? (Ballpark it!)_____

4. How many slices of pizza could you eat in a single sitting? _____

Unless you have some interesting ideas about money and/or pizza, ALL of the numbers above are real. The only numbers that aren't real are imaginary—a negative number under an even root.

5. What is $\sqrt{1}$? _____

6. What is -1×-1? _____

7. What is $-1 \times -1 \times -1$? _____

8. What is $\sqrt{-1}$? _____

9. What real number could you square to get a product of -1? _____

That last question was a trick: there is no real number that you can square to get a negative product. The only way to get the square root (or any even root) of a negative number is to *imagine* it.

> $\sqrt{-1}$ is defined as the imaginary number i. All other imaginary numbers are something multiplied by i.

Rational Numbers and Their Irrational Friends

1. Write 0.5 as a fraction. _____

2. Write 3 as a fraction. _____

3. In the number 0.166$\overline{6}$, what digit is coming next? _____

4. In the number, 0.1919$\overline{19}$, what digit is coming next? _____

A *rational* number is any number that can be written as a fraction—that includes integers and repeating decimals. An *irrational* number is any number that cannot be written as a fraction because it goes on unpredictably. *Both* types of numbers are *real*.

Different calculator? No problem!

We're discussing the TI-80 series calculators in this book, but you should use the calculator that you're familiar with or the one built into the testing app if you take the Online ACT. Check out your calculator's manual or look up the calculator online to learn how to do these key operations.

Love Your Calculator for Real, but Be Rational

Your calculator can be a really handy tool for questions dealing with imaginary and irrational numbers. If you have a Texas Instruments TI-80 series calculator (such as the TI-84), the second function of the decimal is *i*. Use this function to solve the following questions.

5. $(2 + i)(2 - i) =$ _____

6. $(3 + i)^2 =$ _____

To determine if a number is rational or irrational, it can help to try to convert it into a fraction. In the MATH menu, the first item is >*Frac*. This will convert a decimal to a fraction if the number is rational. For each question below, after you have typed in the number provided, hit ENTER and then MATH>ENTER>ENTER. Give the result in the blank and identify whether it is rational or irrational.

7. $0.375 =$ _____ Rational   Irrational

8. 0.16666666666 (until the end of the screen) $=$ _____ Rational   Irrational

9. $\pi =$ _____ Rational   Irrational

10. $0.479109801431 =$ _____ Rational   Irrational

Exponents

Exponents are a shorthand way of indicating that a number is multiplied by itself. The exponent tells you how many times (for example, $5^4 = 5 \times 5 \times 5 \times 5$). Exponents are tricky when you have to combine them in some way. Here's a great way to remember all the rules.

Remember MADSPM!

- When you *multiply* two numbers with common bases, *add* the exponents.
- When you *divide* two numbers with common bases, *subtract* the exponents.
- When you raise an exponential number to a *power*, *multiply* the exponents.

Basic Rules

1. $(x^2)(x^3) =$

2. $\dfrac{x^4}{x^3} =$

3. $(x^4)^3$

4. $2x^2 \times 6x^3 =$

5. $(2x^2)^3 =$

6. $\dfrac{9x^6}{3x^2} =$

7. $\dfrac{(x^2)(x^5)}{x^4} =$

Special Rules

Follow the basic rules to see how some of these special rules are derived.

1. $\dfrac{x^4}{x^4} =$

2. $x^0 =$

3. $\dfrac{x^2}{x^5} =$

4. $x^{-3} =$

5. $x^1 =$

6. $1^{513} =$

7. $0^{619} =$

8. $(-2)^2 =$

9. $(-2)^3 =$

10. $-2^2 =$

11. $\left(\dfrac{1}{2}\right)^2 =$

12. $\left(\dfrac{2}{3}\right)^2 =$

Scientific Notation

Scientific notation is a way to concisely write very large or very small numbers.

Examples:

$$437,000,000,000,000 = 4.37 \times 10^{14}$$

$$0.000000000057 = 5.7 \times 10^{-11}$$

When representing a number with scientific notation, first move the decimal to the left or right until only a single digit from 1 to 9, inclusive, remains before the decimal. In first the example, 437 trillion, the decimal was moved to the left 14 places so that the value was 4.37. Scientific notation always uses some multiple of 10 to represent the movement of the decimal. To determine the exponent of 10, simply count the number of places the decimal moved: in the first example, 14 places to the left. If the decimal moves to the left when creating scientific notation, the exponent will be positive. If it moves to the right when creating scientific notation, the exponent will be negative, as in the second example above.

The ACT may also contain questions that ask you to convert numbers from scientific notation back to the original number. To do that, work in reverse! If the number has a positive exponent of 10, move the decimal that many places to the right to make the number greater than 1.

> On the TI-80 series calculators, you can press "MODE" and select "SCI" in the first row to get all results in scientific notation. The first number on this page would be displayed as "4.37ᴇ14."

$$3.9 \times 10^6 = 3\underline{900000}$$

If the number has a negative exponent of 10, move the decimal that many places to the left to make the number less than 1.

$$2.5 \times 10^{-4} = 0.\underline{00025}$$

The ACT will also ask you to do calculations with numbers in scientific notation. The good news is that a calculator can do a lot of the work for you. Most calculators represent scientific notation by replacing $\times$ 10 with ᴇ. What your calculator returns will probably look like this:

$$7,320,000,000 = 7.32\text{ᴇ}9$$

Type the numbers below into your calculator and hit enter or = ; write what your calculator returns.

1. $37,600,000,000 = $ _____

2. $0.00000000043 = $ _____

3. $7.1 \times 10^{-12} = $ _____

4. $520,000 = $ _____

In most calculators, the last number will come back as the same thing you typed in, 520,000. In situations like that, it's important to know how to represent scientific notation without the help of your calculator.

Now that you know how to enter numbers in scientific notation, let's see how to use a calculator to do calculations on those numbers. First, determine what the question is asking and then plug the question in exactly as you wrote it. Make sure you put parentheses around the numerator and denominator and close any parentheses your calculator opens.

But what if your calculator has trouble with scientific notation? Another option is to work the question by hand. Let's simplify:

$$\frac{6.2 \times 10^5}{3.1 \times 10^3}$$

Here's how:

6.2×10^5 is the same as $6.2 \times 10 \times 10 \times 10 \times 10 \times 10$, and $3.1 \times 10^3 = 3.1 \times 10 \times 10 \times 10$.

If a question asks you to divide numbers in scientific notation, there are some shortcuts you can take to make the question easier.

For example,

$$\frac{6.2 \times 10^5}{3.1 \times 10^3} = \frac{6.2 \times 10 \times 10 \times 10 \times 10 \times 10}{3.1 \times 10 \times 10 \times 10} = \frac{6.2 \times 10 \times 10}{3.1} \times \frac{10}{10} \times \frac{10}{10} \times \frac{10}{10}$$

And any number divided by itself is 1, so this expression simplifies to

$$\frac{6.2 \times 10 \times 10}{3.1} \times 1 \times 1 \times 1 \text{ OR } \frac{6.2 \times 10 \times 10}{3.1}$$

One way to simplify this expression further is as follows:

$$\frac{6.2}{3.1} \times \frac{10}{1} \times \frac{10}{1} = 2 \times 10 \times 10 = 200$$

This process is time consuming, and time is a luxury on the ACT. Here's quicker version of the same solution:

$$\frac{6.2 \times 10^5}{3.1 \times 10^3} = \frac{6.2}{3.1} \times \frac{10^5}{10^3} = 2 \times 10^2 = 200$$

Let's try one:

_____○_____

23. A biology experiment requires 1.59×10^9 bacteria. The laboratory can produce 5.3×10^4 bacteria every hour. How many hours will it take the laboratory to produce the bacteria needed for the experiment?

   A. 3.0×10^4
   B. 3.3×10^5
   C. 3.3×10^8
   D. 3.0×10^{13}

Here's How to Crack It

The question asks for the number of hours it will take the laboratory to produce the bacteria needed for the experiment. The experiment requires 1.59×10^9 bacteria, and the laboratory can produce 5.3×10^4 bacteria every hour. In order to determine the number of hours it will take the laboratory to produce 1.59×10^9 bacteria, we need to divide 1.59×10^9 bacteria by the number of bacteria the laboratory can produce each hour, 5.3×10^4. The expression looks like this: $\dfrac{1.59 \times 10^9}{5.3 \times 10^4}$, and it can be rewritten as $\dfrac{1.59}{5.3} \times \dfrac{10^9}{10^4}$. Divide the first fraction to get 0.3. Divide the second fraction and remember the MADSPM rules of exponents. The DS part of the acronym indicates that Dividing matching bases means to Subtract the exponents. The fraction becomes $\dfrac{10^9}{10^4} = 10^{(9-4)} = 10^5$. Put the results of the two fractions together to get 0.3×10^5. This answer isn't in scientific notation, but the answer choices are, so it needs to be converted. Scientific notation requires an integer between 1 and 10, so rewrite 0.3 as 3.0×10^{-1}. Now multiply by 10^5 to get $3.0 \times 10^{-1} \times 10^5$. The MA part of the MADSPM acronym indicates that Multiplying matching bases means to Add the exponents. The expression becomes $3.0 \times 10^{(-1+5)} = 3.0 \times 10^4$. The correct answer is (A).

_____○_____

Roots

You can add or subtract square roots only when the numbers under the square root sign are the same.

Example:

$$4\sqrt{x} + 2\sqrt{x} = 6\sqrt{x}$$

But $4\sqrt{x} + 2\sqrt{2x}$ can't be combined!

Multiplication and division are more flexible. Different values can be combined under the root as long as the root has the same degree.

Example:

$$\left(\sqrt{x}\right)\left(\sqrt{y}\right) = \sqrt{xy}$$

$$\frac{\sqrt{x}}{\sqrt{y}} = \sqrt{\frac{x}{y}}$$

1. $\sqrt{x} + \sqrt{x} =$

2. $3\sqrt{x} + 5\sqrt{x} =$

3. $x\sqrt{3} + x\sqrt{5} =$

4. $\left(\sqrt{2x}\right)\left(\sqrt{y}\right) =$

5. $\left(\sqrt{x}\right)\left(\sqrt{xy}\right) =$

If ACT asks you to simplify exponents or roots with numbers instead of variables, use your calculator if necessary, but be extra careful with parentheses!

6. $4\sqrt{12} \times 2\sqrt{3} =$

7. $\dfrac{\sqrt{72}}{\sqrt{2}} =$

8. $\left(\sqrt{529} - \sqrt{361}\right)^{\frac{1}{2}} =$

Quadratics

A quadratic equation is an equation of the second degree, which means that the highest exponent in the equation is 2. The standard form of a quadratic equation is $ax^2 + bx + c = 0$. On the ACT, you will need to know some important vocabulary associated with quadratic equations.

To give you an idea of how quadratics are sometimes calculated, let's start by multiplying two binomials. A binomial is an expression of the sum or difference of two terms, and one example is $(x + 2)$.

Given the binomials $(x + 2)$ and $(x + 1)$, let's multiply to get a quadratic expression in standard form. We do this by using FOIL, an acronym standing for First, Outer, Inner, Last.

$$(x + 2)(x + 1)$$

FIRST: multiply the first terms of each binomial:

$$(x)(x) = x^2$$

OUTER: multiply the outer terms of each binomial:

$$(x)(1) = x$$

INNER: multiply the inner terms of each binomial:

$$(2)(x) = 2x$$

LAST: multiply the last terms of each binomial:

$$(2)(1) = 2$$

Now add those terms together and combine like terms:

$$x^2 + x + 2x + 2 = x^2 + 3x + 2$$

Factoring a quadratic is the opposite of FOILing it. When you are working with a quadratic equation in standard form, $ax^2 + bx + c = 0$, determine what the FIRST terms will be by looking at the coefficient of the x^2 term. Try the equation $x^2 + 5x - 6 = 0$. For this equation, the coefficient is 1, so the FIRST term of each binomial will be x. Write:

$$(x \quad)(x \quad) = 0$$

The second terms in each binomial will add up to b and multiply to c. One way to keep the work organized is to put it into a table with the first column representing the factor pairs that equal c and the second column representing the sums of those factors. Start by determining the factors of c, and then sum those factors in the second column.

In the equation $x^2 + 5x - 6 = 0$, $c = -6$, so the chart will look like this:

	Factors of –6	Sum of factors
I.	1, –6	$1 + (-6) = -5$
II.	2, –3	$2 + (-3) = -1$
III.	–1, 6	$-1 + 6 = 5$
IV.	–2, 3	$-2 + 3 = 1$

Row III gives factors of –6 that add up to 5, the *b* value in $x^2 + 5x - 6 = 0$. This means that the second terms in the binomials will be –1 and 6. Write:

$$(x - 1)(x + 6) = 0$$

Try a few yourself!

1. $x^2 + 7x + 12 = 0$ _____

2. $x^2 - 4x + 4 = 0$ _____

3. $x^2 - 6x - 16 = 0$ _____

Roots, Solutions, and *x*-intercepts

You may be wondering why the standard form of the quadratic equation is always set equal to 0, and that's a great question. A quadratic equation is another way to represent a parabola; you may also have seen it written $y = ax^2 + bx + c$. When you graph a parabola, in some cases it will intersect the *x*-axis. By setting $y = 0$, we can find the coordinates of *x* where the parabola crosses the *x*-axis, also known as the *x*-intercepts, roots, or solutions to the quadratic equation. One of the cool things about factoring a quadratic equation into binomials comes from the rule that anything multiplied by 0 is equal to zero.

Let's explore with the equation above.

$$x^2 + 5x - 6 = (x - 1)(x + 6) = 0$$

Since we are multiplying the binomials $(x - 1)(x + 6)$ and the result is equal to 0, we know that one or both the binomials must be equal to 0.

$$x - 1 = 0 \qquad x + 6 = 0$$

Solving those binomials results in the following:

$$x = 1 \qquad x = -6$$

Therefore, the roots/solutions/*x*-intercepts of quadratic equation $x^2 + 5x - 6 = 0$ are 1 and –6.

Let's try a question.

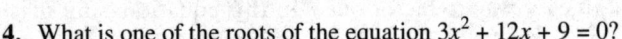

4. What is one of the roots of the equation $3x^2 + 12x + 9 = 0$?

F. –4
G. –3
H. 1
J. 3

Here's How to Crack It

Notice that the coefficient in front of the x^2 is not equal to 1. Check to see if you can factor out a constant before factoring the quadratic. In this equation, 3 can be factored out: $3(x^2 + 4x + 3) = 0$. Now factor the quadratic.

	Factors of 3	Sum of factors
I.	1, 3	$1 + 3 = 4$

There is only one option for factors of 3, and the sum is correct! Rewrite the equation using the factors: $3(x + 1)(x + 3) = 0$. Set the factors equal to 0 and solve for x, ignoring 3 for now since $3 \neq 0$.

$$(x + 1) = 0 \qquad (x + 3) = 0$$

$$x = -1 \qquad x = -3$$

While both -1 and -3 are valid roots, ACT gives only one of the roots as an option: -3, (G).

Quadratic Formula

But what happens if you have a quadratic equation that isn't so easy to factor? Well that's when the quadratic formula becomes your friend!

The quadratic formula is another way to solve for the roots, solutions, and x-intercepts of a quadratic equation in the standard form, $ax^2 + bx + c = 0$, and it looks like this:

$$x = \frac{-b \pm \sqrt{b^2 - 4ac}}{2a}$$

Let's see how it works in a question.

---

23. What are the solutions for $7x^2 - 3x + 15 = 0$?

Here's How to Crack It

First, notice that there isn't an easy way to factor out 7 in this equation, so it's faster and more accurate to use the quadratic formula to solve for the solutions. The equation is already in standard form, so we know $a = 7$, $b = -3$, and $c = 15$. Filling those numbers into the quadratic formula gives the following:

$$x = \frac{-(-3) \pm \sqrt{(-3)^2 - 4(7)(15)}}{2(7)}$$

Simplifying the equation gives:

$$x = \frac{3 \pm \sqrt{-411}}{14}$$

You may see the answer choices written in this form, or they may be separated into two solutions like this:

$$x = \frac{3 + \sqrt{-411}}{14} \qquad x = \frac{3 - \sqrt{-411}}{14}$$

Try a few yourself!

4. $4x^2 - 2x + 7 = 0$ _____

5. $x^2 - 3x - 23 = 0$ _____

Discriminant

You may be looking at the solutions to the last few equations wondering how there can be an x-intercept value that contains a negative under the square root. After all, negatives under a square root are imaginary numbers. You're absolutely correct! If you have a graphing calculator, go to the Y= screen and enter $y = 7x^2 - 3x + 15$ and hit GRAPH (you might have to zoom out to see the parabola). It should look like this:

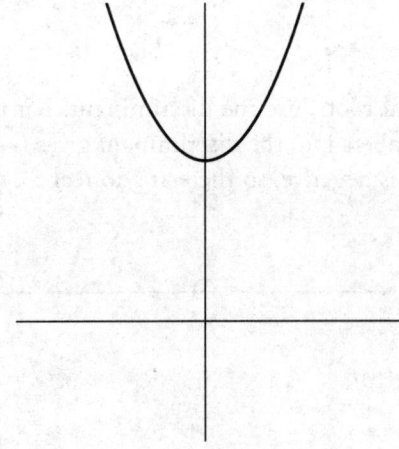

Well look at that! The parabola doesn't intersect the x-axis at all!

The portion of the quadratic formula that is under the radical, $b^2 - 4ac$, is called the discriminant, and we can use it to tell us about the number of x-intercepts a quadratic equation in standard form has without solving for the roots.

If the discriminant is:

- positive, the quadratic has 2 distinct real roots
- zero, the quadratic has 1 real root
- negative, the quadratic has 0 real roots

Find the discriminants of the following quadratic equations and the number and type of roots:

6. $5x^2 + 4x + 9 = 0$ _____   roots: _____

7. $x^2 - 13x + 12 = 0$ _____   roots: _____

Remember: the Answer Keys for the preceding drills can be found at the end of this chapter after the Summary page.

Let's use our knowledge of discriminants on this question.

---

26. How many real roots does the equation $3x^2 - 4x + 2 = 0$ have?

    F. None
    G. One
    H. Two
    J. Four

Here's How to Crack It

Since the question asks for real roots, use the discriminant. For this quadratic, $a = 3$, $b = -4$, and $c = 2$. Plugging those numbers into the discriminant gives $(-4)^2 - 4(3)(2) = 16 - 24 = -8$. The value of the discriminant is negative, so there are no real roots for this quadratic equation, and the answer is (F).

FUNDAMENTALS VOCABULARY DRILL

Write out the definitions for each of the following math terms. If possible, write them in your own words.

Absolute Value: _____

_____

Consecutive: _____

_____

Decimal: _____

_____

Difference: _____

_____

Digits: _____

_____

Discriminant: _____

_____

Distinct: _____

_____

Divisible: _____

_____

Even: _____

_____

Exponent/Power: _____

_____

Factor: _____

_____

FOIL: _____

_____

Fraction: _____

_____

Greatest Common Factor: _____

_____

Imaginary: _____

_____

Integers: _____

_____

Irrational: _____

_____

Least Common Multiple: _____

_____

Multiple: _____

_____

Negative: _____

_____

Number: _____

_____

Odd: _____

_____

Opposite: _____

_____

Order of Operations: _____

_____

Positive: _____

_____

Prime: _____

_____

Product: _____

_____

Quadratic Formula: _____

_____

Quotient: _____

_____

Real: _____

_____

Radical: _____

_____

Rational: _____

_____

Reciprocal: _____

_____

Remainder: _____

_____

Roots (solutions, _x_-intercepts): _____

_____

Scientific Notation: _____

_____

Sum: _____

_____

GLOSSARY

Absolute Value The distance from zero on the number line

Consecutive An order in which numbers are arranged in increasing order with no gaps (e.g., 6, 7, 8)

Decimal A way of expressing a fraction in which numbers are divided by ten, one hundred, one thousand, and other powers of ten

Difference The result of subtraction

Digits The integers 0 through 9

Discriminant The portion of the quadratic formula under the radical sign $b^2 - 4ac$

Distinct Different

Divisible An integer can be divided by another integer evenly, with no fraction or decimal left over

Even Divisible by 2

Exponent/Power A number that indicates the number of times to multiply a base by itself

Factor Integers that multiply together to make a given product

FOIL First, Outer, Inner, Last—a method used to multiply binomials

Fraction A way of expressing the division of numbers by stacking one over the other

Greatest Common Factor The largest factor common to two numbers

Imaginary The square (or any other even) root of a negative number

Integers All real numbers other than decimals or fractions

Irrational A number that can be expressed as a decimal but not a fraction

Least Common Multiple The smallest multiple common to two numbers

Multiple The product of an integer and another integer

Negative Less than 0

Number A count or measure, including zero, all positive and negative values, and all integers, fractions, and decimals

Odd An integer NOT divisible by 2

Opposite Two numbers that have the same magnitude but are opposite in signs. That is, two numbers with the same distance from zero on the number line, but one is positive and the other negative.

Order of Operations Parentheses, Exponents, Multiplication and Division (from left to right), Addition and Subtraction (from left to right)

Positive Greater than 0

Prime A number that has itself and 1 as its only factors (1 is not prime)

Product The result of multiplication

Quadratic Formula A formula used to solve for the roots of a quadratic equation in standard form:

$$x = \frac{-b \pm \sqrt{b^2 - 4ac}}{2a}$$

Quotient The result of division

Real Zero, all positive and negative integers, fractions, decimals, and roots

Radical Another word for the $\sqrt{}$ sign

Rational A number that can be expressed as the ratio of two other numbers, making a fraction

Reciprocal The inverse of a number—flip the numerator and denominator

Remainder The number left over when a number is not evenly divisible by another number

Roots (solutions, x-intercepts) The x-values of a quadratic equation in standard form: the x-value at which the quadratic equation crosses the x-axis

Scientific Notation A representation of a large number using fewer digits: a decimal number between 1 and 10 multiplied by 10 to a power

Sum The result of addition

Fundamentals Drill

In the drill below, you will find questions focusing only on fundamental skills. Before you start, take a few moments to go back over the review material and techniques.

8. What is the product of the distinct prime factors of 54?

    F. 3
    G. 6
    H. 11
    J. 54

10. If x is the least odd prime number and y is the least positive integer multiple of 10, what is the positive difference between x and y?

    F. 3
    G. 7
    H. 11
    J. 17

12. If $x^2 - 2x - 35 = 0$, what are the values of x?

    F. −7 and −5
    G. −7 and 5
    H. −5 and 7
    J. 5 and 7

16. For all x and y, $\left(x^{-1}y^{-3}\right)^{-2}\left(x^4y^7\right)^3 = ?$

    F. $x^{10}y^{15}$
    G. x^5y^{10}
    H. x^3y^4
    J. $x^{14}y^{27}$

17. Which of the following is an irrational number?

    A. $\dfrac{\sqrt{8}}{\sqrt{2}}$

    B. $\dfrac{\sqrt{27}}{\sqrt{3}}$

    C. $\dfrac{\sqrt{9}}{\sqrt{3}}$

    D. $\sqrt{4}$

21. Which of the following is equal to the result of squaring the expression $(i + 4)$?

(Note: $i^2 = -1$)

    A. $16i$
    B. $15 + 8i$
    C. $16 + i$
    D. $17 - 18i$

22. What is the least possible sum of three distinct prime numbers between 10 and 20?

    F. 33
    G. 39
    H. 41
    J. 45

24. $\dfrac{9.1 \times 10^{-7}}{1.3 \times 10^3} =$

    F. 7.0×10^{-10}
    G. 7.0×10^{-4}
    H. 7.8×10^{-10}
    J. 7.8×10^{-4}

28. The graph of which of the following does not intersect the x-axis?

    F. $-x^2 + 5x - 1 = 0$
    G. $x^2 + 6x - 9 = 0$
    H. $x^2 - 3x + 10 = 0$
    J. $3x^2 + 12x + 12 = 0$

FUNDAMENTALS DRILL ANSWERS AND EXPLANATIONS

8. **G**   The question asks for the product of the *distinct prime factors* of a number. *Distinct* means "different," and *prime* means "evenly divisible by only itself and 1." Start by finding the prime factors of 54 by using a factor tree. Since 54 is even, first factor out a 2 to get 2 and 27 on the first branches of the tree. Next factor 27 into 3 and 9, and then factor 9 into 3 and 3. That means that the prime factors of 54 are 2, 3, 3, 3, and the distinct prime factors of 54 are 2 and 3. *Product* means to multiply, so the product is $2 \times 3 = 6$. The correct answer is (G).

10. **G**   The question asks for the *positive difference* between the *least odd prime number* and the *least positive integer multiple of 10*. Start by determining the value of x, the least odd prime number. *Prime* means "evenly divisible by only itself and 1." The least prime number is 2, but it is even, so move to the next prime number, 3. It is odd; therefore, $x = 3$. Now determine the least positive integer multiple of 10. A *multiple* of 10 is the value when a number is multiplied by 10. Since the question asks for the least integer value, multiply 10 by the smallest positive integer, 1, to get $10 \times 1 = 10$. Therefore, $y = 10$. Finally, find the *positive difference* between 10 and 3, which is $10 - 3 = 7$. The correct answer is (G).

12. **H**   The question asks for the values of x. To find the values of x of a quadratic equation, factor. To do so, determine the factors of -35 that add to -2. These factors are -7 and 5. Therefore, the factored form of the equation is $(x - 7)(x + 5) = 0$. Set each of these factors equal to zero and solve: $x - 7 = 0$, or $x = 7$; and $x + 5 = 0$, or $x = -5$. The correct answer is (H).

16. **J**   The question asks for the solution to an expression using exponents. When dealing with questions about exponents, remember the MADSPM rules. The PM part of the acronym indicates that an exponent raised to a Power means to Multiply the exponents. Start by distributing the exponents to each of the variables in the parentheses to get $(x^{-1}y^{-3})^{-2}(x^4y^7)^3 = (x^{-1(-2)}y^{-3(-2)})(x^{4(3)}y^{7(3)}) = (x^2y^6)(x^{12}y^{21})$. Because all the variables are multiplied, the parentheses can be removed, and the matching bases can be combined. The MA part of the MADSPM acronym indicates that Multiplying matching bases means to Add the exponents; do so to get $(x^2y^6)(x^{12}y^{21}) = x^{(2+12)}y^{(6+21)} = x^{14}y^{27}$. The correct answer is (J).

17. **C**   The question asks for the answer that is an irrational number. Irrational numbers cannot be expressed as a fraction. To solve this question using a calculator, input the answer choices and use the MATH -> FRAC tool to determine whether the answer can be written as a fraction. Choice (A), $\dfrac{\sqrt{8}}{\sqrt{2}}$, is equal to 2, which is a rational number; eliminate (A). $\dfrac{\sqrt{27}}{\sqrt{3}}$ is equal to 3; eliminate (B). $\dfrac{\sqrt{9}}{\sqrt{3}}$ is approximately 1.732 and does not convert to a fraction. Therefore, because it cannot be written as a fraction, $\dfrac{\sqrt{9}}{\sqrt{3}}$ is irrational. The correct answer is (C).

21. **B**   The question asks for the *result of squaring* a complex number, which is a number with a real part and an imaginary part. Start by writing out the expression to get $(i + 4)(i + 4)$ and use FOIL— First Outer Inner Last—to expand the expression. This becomes $i^2 + 4i + 4i + 16 = i^2 + 8i + 16$. Substitute $i^2 = -1$ into the expression to get $-1 + 8i + 16$, which simplifies to $15 + 8i$. The correct answer is (B).

22. **H**   The question asks for the *least sum* of three *distinct prime numbers* between 10 and 20. *Distinct* means "different," and *prime* means "evenly divisible by only itself and 1." *Between* means that 10 and 20 are not included in the list of numbers that can be used. Since the question asks for the least sum possible, find the smallest prime allowed in the question. The smallest prime that fits the requirements is 11. Continue through the list of numbers between 10 and 20 to find the next two smallest primes: 13 and 17. To find the *sum*, add the three distinct primes to get $11 + 13 + 17 = 41$. The correct answer is (H).

24. **F**   The question asks for the equivalent of a fraction with numbers in scientific notation. If solving this on a calculator, pay special attention to the order of operations and place parentheses carefully. It may be more effective to start solving this expression by hand. Since the numerator and denominator both have multiplication, the fraction can be split into more manageable pieces to get $\frac{9.1 \times 10^{-7}}{1.3 \times 10^{3}} = \frac{9.1}{1.3} \times \frac{10^{-7}}{10^{3}}$. Use the calculator to find that $\frac{9.1}{1.3} = 7.0$. Eliminate (H) and (J). because they have 7.8 instead of 7.0. Use the DS portion of the MADSPM acronym to Subtract the exponents of like bases that are Divided to get $\frac{10^{-7}}{10^{3}} = 10^{-7-3} = 10^{-10}$. The expression becomes 7.0×10^{-10}. The correct answer is (F).

28. **H**   The question asks which graph represented by the answer choices does not intersect the x-axis. If a graphing calculator is available, graph each of the answer choices with y in place of 0 to visually determine which answer does not intersect the x-axis. If a graphing calculator is not available, remember that a quadratic with a negative discriminant has no real roots or places where the function intersects the x-axis. Use the discriminant, which is $b^2 - 4ac$ when the quadratic is in the standard form $ax^2 + bx + c = 0$, to evaluate the answers. Since all of the answers are in standard form, start by finding the discriminant for (F). In that quadratic, $a = -1$, $b = 5$, and $c = -1$, so the discriminant is $5^2 - 4(-1)(-1) = 25 - 4 = 21$. Eliminate (F) because the discriminant is not negative. Repeat the process for the remaining choices. The discriminant for the quadratic in (G) is $6^2 - 4(1)(-9) = 36 + 36 = 72$; eliminate (G). Choice (H) gives a discriminant of $(-3)^2 - 4(1)(10) = 9 - 40 = -31$. This discriminant is negative, so this quadratic has no roots and does not cross the x-axis. There can only be one correct answer, so there is no need to check (J). The correct answer is (H).

Summary

o Learn the basics for the ACT Math test before you move on to more difficult concepts. The Fundamentals are the one thing on the ACT that you can't fake!

o Know your vocabulary. The Math test requires its own Reading Comprehension.

o Know your rules for 0.
   - 0 is an even number.
   - 0 is neither positive nor negative.
   - Anything multiplied by 0 is 0.
   - 0 raised to *any* power is 0.
   - Anything raised to the 0 power is 1.

o A number's factors are always smaller than or the same as that number. A number's multiples are always larger than or the same as that number.

o A prime number has only two distinct factors: 1 and itself.
   - 1 is NOT a prime number.
   - 2 is the only even prime number. It is also the smallest prime number.

o All imaginary and complex numbers use i. All other numbers are real.

o Rational numbers can be written as a fraction. Irrational numbers cannot be written as fractions.

o Use your calculator or the built-in calculator on the Online ACT well and wisely. A calculator is particularly helpful with:
   - imaginary numbers (represented as i in algebra questions)
   - square roots that don't contain variables (and often those that do)
   - converting decimals or other expressions into fractions
   - multiplying and dividing large numbers

o When combining numbers with exponents, remember MADSPM.
   - When you *multiply* two numbers with common bases, *add* the exponents.
   - When you *divide* two numbers with common bases, *subtract* the exponents.
   - When you raise an exponential number to a *power*, *multiply* the *exponents*.

o   Scientific notation always has exactly one digit, 1–9, to the left of the decimal and includes a power of 10.

o   When working with roots:
- You can add or subtract roots only when the numbers under the sign are the same.
- You can combine different values under the same radical if you are multiplying or dividing.

o   When working with quadratics:
- When given two binomials, FOIL.
- When given a quadratic, factor.
- Roots, solutions, and x-intercepts are all terms for values of x.
- On challenging quadratics questions, use the quadratic formula, which is
$$x = \frac{-b \pm \sqrt{b^2 - 4ac}}{2a}.$$
- The discriminant ($b^2 - 4ac$) will give the number of roots to a quadratic:
  - o   If the discriminant is less than 0, there are no real roots.
  - o   If the discriminant is equal to 0, there is one distinct real root.
  - o   If the discriminant is greater than 0, there are two distinct real roots.

FUNDAMENTALS LESSON ANSWER KEY

Basics (pages 238–239)

1. 1.75, 2, 3, 12, 16, 81
2. −81, −19, −9, −6
3. −81, −19, −9, 3, 81
4. −6, 0, 2, 12, 16
5. 2, 12, 16
6. 0
7. −4
8. $-\dfrac{1}{2}$
9. 1
10. 7
11. 1
12. 7 R 1 (7 *remainder* 1)
13. Number, Integer, Positive, Even
14. Number, Negative
15. Number, Integer, Even
16. Remainder
17. Reciprocal
18. Consecutive

Factors and Multiples (page 239)

1. 1, 2, 3, 4, 6, 12
2. 12, 24, 36, 48
3. 1, 2, 3, 5, 6, 10, 15, 30
4. 30, 60, 90, 120
5. Factor
6. Yes
7. 9
8. 9
9. 36
10. 48

Prime (page 240)

1. 2, 3, 5, 7
2. 2
3. No, it does not have two *distinct* factors.
4. $2 \times 2 \times 3 \times 3$ or $2^2 \times 3^2$
5. $2 + 2 + 3 + 3 = 10$
6. $2 \times 3 = 6$

Real Numbers and Their Imaginary Friends (page 241)

5. 1
6. 1
7. −1
8. No answer, or imaginary, or i
9. None

Rational Numbers and Their Irrational Friends (page 242)

1. $\dfrac{5}{10}$, or $\dfrac{1}{2}$

2. $\dfrac{3}{1}$

3. 6
4. 1

Love Your Calculator for Real, but Be Rational (page 242)

5. 5
6. $8 + 6i$

7. $\dfrac{3}{8}$ Rational.

8. $\dfrac{1}{6}$ Rational.

9. No result. Irrational.

10. $\dfrac{479,109,801,431}{10,000,000,000,000}$ Rational.

Basic Rules (page 243)

1. x^5
2. x^1, or x
3. x^{12}
4. $12x^5$. Don't forget the coefficients!
5. $8x^6$
6. $3x^4$
7. x^3

Special Rules (pages 243)

1. x^0, or 1
2. 1

3. x^{-3}, or $\dfrac{1}{x^3}$

4. $\dfrac{1}{x^3}$

5. x
6. 1
7. 0
8. 4
9. -8
10. -4
11. $\dfrac{1}{4}$
12. $\dfrac{4}{9}$

Scientific Notation (page 244)

1. 3.76E10
2. 4.3E−10
3. 7.1E−12
4. 520,000

Roots (page 247)

1. $2\sqrt{x}$
2. $8\sqrt{x}$
3. Can't be combined!
4. $\sqrt{2xy}$
5. $\sqrt{x^2 y} = x\sqrt{y}$
6. $8\sqrt{36} = 8(6) = 48$
7. $\sqrt{36} = 6$
8. $(23 - 19)^{\frac{1}{2}} = (4)^{\frac{1}{2}} = 2$

Quadratics (pages 249, 251, and 252)

1. $(x + 3)(x + 4)$
2. $(x - 2)(x - 2)$ or $(x - 2)^2$
3. $(x + 2)(x - 8)$
4. $\dfrac{2 \pm \sqrt{-108}}{8}$ or $\dfrac{1 \pm 3\sqrt{-3}}{4}$
5. $\dfrac{3 \pm \sqrt{101}}{2}$
6. -164; no real roots
7. 121; two distinct real roots

Chapter 15
No More Algebra

Once you have a solid foundation in basic operations
and vocabulary, you are well-equipped to solve a wide
variety of questions. This chapter will look at some of
the questions that test concepts you may have seen in
Algebra classes, and it will show how to work around
some of the toughest algebra concepts.

ALGEBRA AND THE ACT

Plug-and-Chug questions are ones that look like questions that you might see in Math class. Rather than burying the math in a word problem, ACT puts the question in a more straightforward form. We've already seen some of the easier plug-and-chug algebra questions in Chapter 14. Most questions that ACT considers "algebra" questions won't be so straightforward. ACT expects you to use algebra to solve word problems as well as plug-and-chug questions. Let's see how you can make this work in your favor.

HOW I LEARNED TO STOP WORRYING AND LOVE VARIABLES

Let's look at the following question:

16. John has x red pencils, and three times as many red pencils as blue pencils. If he has four more yellow pencils than blue pencils, then in terms of x, how many yellow pencils does John have?

F. $x + 7$

G. $\dfrac{x}{6}$

H. $\dfrac{x + 12}{6}$

J. $\dfrac{x + 12}{3}$

Let's think about the bigger picture for a second here. We're all familiar with these x values from algebra class, but what we often forget is that x is substituting for some real value. Equations use x because that value is an unknown. The variable x could be 5 or 105 or 0.36491. In fact, the ACT writers are asking you to create an expression that will answer this question to find what that "certain number" is. And they want you to make it even harder on yourself by forgetting that x is a number at all.

PLUGGING IN

If you had 1 dollar and you bought 2 pieces of candy at 25 cents apiece, how much change would you have? 50 cents, of course. If you had d dollars and bought p pieces of candy at c cents apiece, how much change would you have? Um, Letter of the Day.

Numbers are a lot easier to work with than variables. Therefore, when you see variables on the ACT, you can usually make things a lot easier on yourself by using numbers instead. Whenever there are variables in the answer choices or the question, you can use Plugging In.

Use Plugging In:

- when there are variables in the answer choices
- when there are variables defined in relation to one another
- when there are non-specified numbers in relation to one another

Let's go back to question 16.

16. John has x red pencils and three times as many red pencils as blue pencils. If he has four more yellow pencils than blue pencils, then in terms of x, how many yellow pencils does John have?

F. $x + 7$

G. $\dfrac{x}{6}$

H. $\dfrac{x + 12}{6}$

J. $\dfrac{x + 12}{3}$

Here's How to Crack It

1. Know the Question. Underline or highlight "how many yellow pencils does John have?" We're not solving for x here; we need the number of yellow pencils. ACT just wants us to name the value "in terms of x."

2. Let the answers help. The answers help a lot here: each contains the variable x, which means we can plug in.

3. Break the question into bite-sized pieces. We know we can plug in. Let's take it step by step from there.

Make sure to keep your work organized when Plugging In. Always circle your target answer.

We want to make the math easy on ourselves. Let's say $x = 3$, so John has 3 red pencils. Now that we've dispensed with the variable, let's work the rest of the question.

John has 3 red pencils and *three times as many red pencils as blue pencils*. He therefore must have 1 blue pencil. He has *four more yellow pencils than blue pencils*, so he must have 5 yellow pencils.

Now we can answer the question with what is called our *target answer*. The question asks *How many yellow pencils does John have?*, to which our answer is 5. Circle this answer on your paper. Let's go to the answer choices to see which one gives us our target. Remember, $x = 3$.

F.	$(3) + 7 = 10$	Not our target answer. Cross it off.
G.	$\dfrac{(3)}{6} = \dfrac{1}{2}$	Not our target answer. Cross it off.
H.	$\dfrac{(3) + 12}{6} = \dfrac{15}{6}$	Not our target answer. Cross it off.
J.	$\dfrac{(3) + 12}{3} = 5$	

Only (J) works, so this is our correct answer. Look how easy that was, and not a bit of algebra necessary! Plugging in *any* number would have led to (J) matching the target answer. Don't believe it? Try your own number and see what happens.

Now let's try another.

---

13. For all $x \neq 3$, which of the following is equivalent to the expression $\dfrac{3x^2 - 7x - 6}{x - 3}$?

A. $3x + 2$

B. $3x - 2$

C. $3(x - 2)$

D. $3(x + 2)$

Here's How to Crack It

This looks a lot more like a standard plug-and-chug than the last question did, but remember, we can always plug in when there are variables in the answer choices. This will be a tough problem to factor, so Plugging In will probably be your best bet, even if you're an ace with quadratic equations. The only thing the problem tells us is that $x \neq 3$, so let's say $x = 2$.

$$\frac{3(2)^2 - 7(2) - 6}{(2) - 3}$$

$$\frac{3(4) - 14 - 6}{-1}$$

$$\frac{-8}{-1} = 8$$

We now know that for the value we've chosen, the value of this expression is 8. That means **8** is our target answer. Circle that number. Let's plug our *x* value into the answer choices to find the one that matches the target.

    A. $3(2) + 2 = 8$ ✔   This matches our target answer, but when you plug in, always check all 4 answers.

    B. $3(2) - 2 = 6 - 2 = 4$ Not our target answer. Cross it off.

    C. $3((2) - 2) = 3(0) = 0$ Not our target answer. Cross it off.

    D. $3((2) + 2) = 3(4) = 12$ Not our target answer. Cross it off.

Only (A) worked, and it is the correct answer. So as we can see, Plugging In works for all kinds of algebra questions. Let's review what we've done so far.

What to Do When You Plug In

1. Identify the opportunity. Can you plug in on this question?

2. Choose a good number. Make the math easy on yourself.

3. Find a target answer. Answer the question posed in the problem with your number, and circle your target answer.

4. Test all the answer choices. If two of them work, try a new number.

Let's try a tougher one.

    27. In my dear Aunt Sally's math class, there are four exams. The first three exam scores are averaged, and the resulting score is averaged with the final exam score. If *a*, *b*, and *c* are the first three exam scores, and *f* is the final exam score, which of the following gives a student's final score in the class?

        A. $\dfrac{a + b + c}{3} + f$

        B. $\dfrac{a + b + c + 3f}{6}$

        C. $\dfrac{a + b + c + f}{4}$

        D. $\dfrac{a + b + c + 3f}{4}$

Here's How to Crack It

This is a word problem, so remember the Basic Approach.

1. Know the question. Underline or highlight the actual question that is asked: *which of the following gives a student's final score in this class?*

2. Let the answers help. There are variables in each of these answer choices, which means we can plug in, so these answers will help a lot.

3. Break the question into bite-sized pieces. If you rush through this question, it's very easy to mess up. Let's go piece by piece as we did in the earlier question.

The first three exam scores are averaged.

There's no reason to give realistic exam scores here: we can pick whatever numbers we want, so let's use numbers that make the math easy. We know from this question that the first three exam scores are represented by a, b, and c, so let's say $a = 2$, $b = 3$, and $c = 4$. The average of these three numbers can be found as follows: $\dfrac{2 + 3 + 4}{3} = \dfrac{9}{3} = 3$.

The resulting score is then averaged with the final score.

The resulting score is 3, and we need to plug in some final score, f. Let's use another easy number and say $f = 5$. In averaging these two numbers together, we find $\dfrac{3 + 5}{2} = \dfrac{8}{2} = 4$. Thus, we have our target answer: a student's final score with these exam scores will be **4**. Circle that number.

Let's go to the answer choices and look for the one that matches the target. Remember, $a = 2$, $b = 3$, $c = 4$, and $f = 5$.

A. $\dfrac{2 + 3 + 4}{3} + 5 = \dfrac{9}{3} + 5 = 8$ ✗

B. $\dfrac{2 + 3 + 4 + 3(5)}{6} = \dfrac{24}{6} = 4$ ✔

C. $\dfrac{2 + 3 + 4 + 5}{4} = \dfrac{14}{4} = 3.5$ ✗

D. $\dfrac{2 + 3 + 4 + 3(5)}{4} = \dfrac{24}{4} = 6$ ✗

Choice (B) is the correct answer, and no tough algebra necessary!

Hidden Plug-Ins

Both of the above questions had variables in the answer choices, which is a dead giveaway that we can plug in. The good news is that that's not the only time. In any question in which there are hypothetical values or values relative to each other, Plugging In will work. Let's have a look at an example.

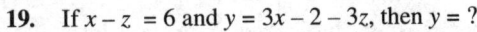

19.   If $x - z = 6$ and $y = 3x - 2 - 3z$, then $y = ?$

    A.   4
    B.   14
    C.   16
    D.   18

Here's How to Crack It

There aren't any variables in the answer choices, but notice all values in the question are defined relative to one another. Let's plug in.

Using the first equation in the question, let's make the numbers easy on ourselves and say $x = 8$ and $z = 2$. Using these values, let's find the value for the expression given in the question: $y = 3(8) - 2 - 3(2) = 24 - 2 - 6 = 16$, (C).

It may feel like we just pulled these numbers out of thin air, but try any two numbers that work in the equation $x - z = 6$, and you'll find that it always works.

PLUGGING IN THE ANSWERS

So, we've seen that Plugging In is a great strategy when there are variables in the question or the answers. How about when there aren't? Does that mean we have to go back to algebra? Of course not! On most Math questions on the ACT, there are a variety of ways to solve. Let's look at another way to simplify the math in algebra-related questions.

4.   Lilith earns $75 for each of the first 5 phone plans she sells in a week and $115 for each plan she sells beyond the first five. If Lilith earned $720 in a given week, how many phone plans did she sell?

    F.   6
    G.   7
    H.   8
    J.   9

Before we get started cracking this question, we should note a few things about it. First of all, there aren't any variables, but you probably have the feeling that you're going to have to put the $75, $115, and $720 in some sort of relationship and, oh yeah, how does the 5 fit in too? However, notice that the question is asking for a specific number, the number of phone plans Lilith sold, and the answer choices give possibilities for that specific number. All of this taken together means that we can plug in the answers (PITA).

Use Plugging In The Answers (PITA) when:

- answer choices are numbers in ascending or descending order.
- the question asks for a specific amount. Look for "what is the value," "how many," or similar wording.
- you get the urge to do algebra even when there are no variables in the question.

Let's see what this looks like.

---

4. Lilith earns $75 for each of the first 5 phone plans she sells in a week and $115 for each plan she sells beyond the first five. If Lilith earned $720 in a given week, how many phone plans did she sell?

    F. 6
    G. 7
    H. 8
    J. 9

Here's How to Crack It

1. Know the question. As we've already identified, we need to find the number of *phone plans* Lilith sold.

2. Let the answers help. Because there are only numbers in the answer choices, we'll be able to use PITA on this question.

3. Break the question into bite-sized pieces. We're going to use the answer choices to walk through each step of the question, working it in bite-sized pieces.

Because the answer choices are listed in ascending order, it will be best to start with one of the middle answer choices. That way, if it's too high or too low, we'll be able to use POE more effectively.

Therefore, if we start with 7 as the number of phone plans Lilith sold, we can find how much she earned. She made $75 for each of the first 5 plans, which is $75 × 5 = $375. For the additional 2 plans she sold, she made $115 × 2 = $230, for a total of $375 + $230 = $605. Because the question told us Lilith made $720, we know (G) is too low, which also eliminates (F).

Let's try (H). You may find it helpful to keep your work organized in columns as shown below:

# of Phone Plans	First 5 Plans	Additional Plans	Total	= $720?
F. 6				
G. 7	$75 × 5 = $375	$115 × 2 = $230	$605	✗
H. 8	$75 × 5 = $375	$115 × 3 = $345	$720	Yes! ✔
J. 9				

We haven't introduced any of our own numbers into this question, so once we find the correct answer, we can stop. The correct answer is (H).

———————◯———————

Let's try a harder one.

———————◯———————

37. In a piggy bank, there are pennies, nickels, dimes, and quarters that total $2.17 in value. If there are 3 times as many pennies as there are dimes, 1 more dime than nickels, and 2 more quarters than dimes, then how many pennies are in the piggy bank?

(Note: Pennies are worth $0.01, nickels are worth $0.05, dimes are worth $0.10, and quarters are worth $0.25.)

A. 12
B. 15
C. 18
D. 21

Here's How to Crack It

1. Know the question. *How many pennies are in the piggy bank?*

2. Let the answers help. There are no variables, but the specific question coupled with the numerical answers in ascending order gives a pretty good indication that we can use PITA.

3. Break the question into bite-sized pieces. Make sure you take your time with this question; you'll need to multiply the number of each coin by its monetary value. In other words, don't forget that 1 nickel will count for 5 cents, 1 dime will count for 10 cents, and 1 quarter will count for 25 cents. As in the previous question, let's set up some columns to keep our work organized and begin with one of the middle answer choices, (C).

Since ACT has already given us the answers, we will plug in the answers and work backward. Each of the answers listed gives a possible value for the number of pennies. Using the information in the question, we can work backward from that number of pennies to find the number of nickels, dimes, and quarters. When the values for the number of coins add up to $2.17, we know we're done.

If we begin with the assumption that there are 18 pennies, then there must be 6 dimes *(3 times as many pennies as there are dimes)*. Six dimes means 5 nickels *(1 more dime than nickels)* and 8 quarters *(2 more quarters than dimes)*.

Now multiply the number of coins by the monetary value of each to see if they total $2.17.

	Pennies ($P)	Dimes ($D)	Nickels ($N)	Quarters ($Q)	Total = $2.17?
C.	18 ($0.18)	6 ($0.60)	5 ($0.25)	8 ($2.00)	Total = $3.03

That's too high, so we can eliminate not only (C) but also (D). Cross them off, and try either (A) or (B). If the one you try works, pick it! If the one you try doesn't work, the other one must be correct.

	Pennies ($P)	Dimes ($D)	Nickels ($N)	Quarters ($Q)	Total = $2.17?
A.	12 ($0.12)	4 ($0.40)	3 ($0.15)	6 ($1.50)	Total = $2.17 ✔
B.	15 ($0.15)	5 ($0.50)	4 ($0.20)	7 ($1.75)	Total = $2.60 ✗
C.	18 ($0.18)	6 ($0.60)	5 ($0.25)	8 ($2.00)	Total = $3.03 ✗
D.	21	Eliminated through POE			

Only (A) works. No algebra necessary!

A NOTE ON PLUGGING IN AND PITA

Plugging In and PITA are not the only ways to solve these questions, and it may feel weird using these methods instead of trying to do these questions "the real way." You may have even found that you knew how to work with the variables in Plugging In questions or how to write the appropriate equations for the PITA questions. If you can do either of those things, you're already on your way to a great Math score.

But think about it this way. We've already said that ACT doesn't give any partial credit. So do you think doing it "the real way" gets you any extra points? It doesn't: on the ACT, a right answer is a right answer, no matter how you get it. "The real way" is great, but unfortunately, it's often a lot more complex and offers many more opportunities to make careless errors.

The biggest problem with doing things the real way, though, is that it essentially requires that you invent a new approach for every question. Instead, notice what we've given you here: two strategies that will work toward getting you the right answer on any number of questions. You may have heard the saying, "Give someone a fish and you've fed that person for a day, but teach someone to fish and you've fed that person for a lifetime." Now, don't worry; our delusions of grandeur are not quite so extreme, but Plugging In and PITA are useful in a similar way. Rather than giving you a detailed description of how to create formulas and work through them for these questions that won't themselves ever appear on an ACT again, we're giving you a strategy that will help you to work through any number of similar questions on future ACTs.

Try these strategies on your own in the drill that concludes this chapter.

No More Algebra Drill

2. What is the largest value of x that satisfies the equation $x^2 - 4x + 3 = 0$?

    F.   1
    G.   3
    H.   4
    J.   5

9. For all $x \neq -9$, $\dfrac{x^2 + 6x - 27}{(x + 9)} = ?$

    A. $x + 9$
    B. $x - 3$
    C. $x + 3$
    D. $2x + 3$

10. If 2 less than 3 times a certain number is the same as 4 more than the product of 5 and 3, what is the number?

    F.   7
    G.   10
    H.   11
    J.   15

14. In the equation $s = \dfrac{1}{2}at^2$, s is the displacement of an object starting at rest then moving with an acceleration of a for a time of t. Which of the following could be used to solve for t in terms of a and s?

    F. $\dfrac{2s}{a}$

    G. $\sqrt{\dfrac{a}{2s}}$

    H. $\sqrt{\dfrac{as}{2}}$

    J. $\sqrt{\dfrac{2s}{a}}$

20. If $x \neq 0$, which of the following expressions is equivalent to $\dfrac{5}{x^2} - \dfrac{3}{x}$?

    F. $\dfrac{2}{x}$

    G. $\dfrac{2}{x^2 - x}$

    H. $\dfrac{5x - 3}{x^2}$

    J. $\dfrac{5 - 3x}{x^2}$

27. What is the value of $\dfrac{b}{a}$ if the equation $\dfrac{3a + b}{a - b} = \dfrac{5}{4}$ is true?

    A. $-\dfrac{7}{2}$

    B. $-\dfrac{11}{9}$

    C. $-\dfrac{4}{5}$

    D. $-\dfrac{7}{9}$

29. A lacrosse team has a starting lineup of 10 players, and these players are to be chosen from a total roster of 22 players. In previous years, $\frac{1}{5}$ of the people invited to tryouts did not show up. Of those that did try out for the team, 25% were put on the roster. This process is illustrated in the diagram shown. If this year follows the same pattern, how many people should the lacrosse team invite to tryouts to end up with a roster of 22 players?

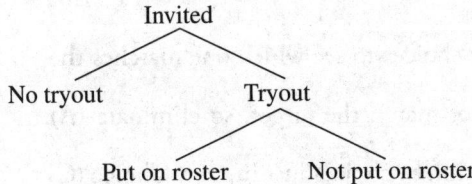

A. 88
B. 110
C. 160
D. 440

33. A certain number of books are to be given away at a promotion. If $\frac{2}{5}$ of the books are distributed in the morning and $\frac{1}{3}$ of the remaining books are distributed in the afternoon, what fraction of the books remains to be distributed the next day?

A. $\frac{1}{5}$

B. $\frac{2}{5}$

C. $\frac{5}{7}$

D. $\frac{8}{9}$

38. In the equation $a = \frac{3}{b}$, b is a positive, real number. As the value of b is increased so it becomes closer and closer to infinity, what happens to the value of a?

F. It remains constant.
G. It gets closer and closer to zero.
H. It gets closer and closer to three.
J. It gets closer and closer to infinity.

42. If x is a number greater than 0, y is a number less than 0, and $|x| < |y|$, which of the following has the least value?

F. $\left| \dfrac{x+y}{x-y} \right|$

G. $\left| \dfrac{x-y}{x+y} \right|$

H. $\left| \dfrac{x+y}{y} \right|$

J. $\left| \dfrac{x-y}{x} \right|$

NO MORE ALGEBRA DRILL ANSWERS AND EXPLANATIONS

2. **G** The question asks for the largest value of x that satisfies the provided equation. Since the question asks for a specific value and the answers contain numbers in increasing order, plug in the answers. Begin by labeling the answers as "x." Since the question asks for the largest value, start with (J). Plug 5 in for x to get $5^2 - 4(5) + 3 = 25 - 20 + 3 = 8$. This does not equal 0, so eliminate (J) and try (H) next. Plug 4 in for x to get $4^2 - 4(4) + 3 = 16 - 16 + 3 = 3$; eliminate (H) and try (G). Plug 3 in for x to get $3^2 - 4(3) + 3 = 9 - 12 + 3 = 0$. This equals 0, so 3 is the largest value of x that satisfies the equation. The correct answer is (G).

9. **B** The question asks for an equivalent form of an expression. There are variables in the answer choices, so plug in. Make $x = 2$; the expression becomes $\dfrac{2^2 + 6(2) - 27}{(2 + 9)} = \dfrac{4 + 12 - 27}{11} = \dfrac{-11}{11} = -1$. This is the target value; circle it. Now plug $x = 2$ into the answer choices to see which one matches the target value. Choice (A) becomes $2 + 9 = 11$. This does not match the target, so eliminate (A). Choice (B) becomes $2 - 3 = -1$. Keep (B), but check the remaining choices just in case. Choice (C) becomes $2 + 3 = 5$; eliminate (C). Choice (D) becomes $2(2) + 3 = 4 + 3 = 7$; eliminate (D). The correct answer is (B).

10. **F** The question asks for a certain number that satisfies a situation. Since the question is asking for a specific value and the answers contain numbers in increasing order, plug in the answers. Begin by labeling the answers as "the number" and start with the easier of the two middle numbers and try (G), 10. Since there are several steps in the question, work in bite-sized pieces. The first piece says a value is *2 less than 3 times a certain number*, so first find 3 times the number and then subtract 2. For (G), this becomes $3(10) - 2 = 30 - 2 = 28$. According to the question, that will be the same as *4 more than the product of 5 and 3*, or $5(3) + 4 = 15 + 4 = 19$. Since 28 is not equal to 19, this is not the correct number; eliminate (G). Eliminate (H) and (J) as well since the calculation needs to be equal to 19 and these will produce values larger than the one found in (G). To check (F), plug in 7 to get $3(7) - 2 = 21 - 2 = 19$. This matches the value calculated earlier; stop here. The correct answer is (F).

14. **J** The question asks for an expression for a variable in terms of two other variables. There are variables in the answers and the question is about variables in relation to each other, so plug in. Make $a = 2$ and $t = 4$, and use those numbers to solve for s. The equation becomes $s = \dfrac{1}{2}(2)(4^2) = \dfrac{1}{2}(2)(16) = 16$. The question asks for the value of t, which is 4, so this is the target value; circle it. Now plug $a = 2$ and $s = 16$ into the answer choices to see which one matches the target value. Choice (F) becomes $\dfrac{2(16)}{2} = \dfrac{32}{2} = 16$. This does not match the target, so

eliminate it. Choice (G) becomes $\sqrt{\dfrac{2}{2(16)}} = \sqrt{\dfrac{2}{32}} = \sqrt{\dfrac{1}{16}} = \dfrac{1}{4}$. Eliminate (G). Choice (H) be-

comes $\sqrt{\dfrac{2(16)}{2}} = \sqrt{\dfrac{32}{2}} = \sqrt{16} = 4$. Keep (H), but check (J) just in case. Choice (J) becomes

$\sqrt{\dfrac{2(16)}{2}} = \sqrt{\dfrac{32}{2}} = \sqrt{16} = 4$. Keep (J). Since two answers worked, plug in new numbers. Make $a = 3$

and $t = 2$. The expression becomes $s = \dfrac{1}{2}(3)(2^2) = \dfrac{1}{2}(3)(4) = 6$. Since $t = 2$, the new target is 2; circle

it. Now plug $a = 3$ and $s = 6$ into (H) and (J) again. Choice (H) becomes $\sqrt{\dfrac{(3)(6)}{2}} = \sqrt{\dfrac{18}{2}} = \sqrt{9} = 3$.

Eliminate (H). Choice (J) becomes $\sqrt{\dfrac{2(6)}{3}} = \sqrt{\dfrac{12}{3}} = \sqrt{4} = 2$. This matches the target. The correct

answer is (J).

20. **J** The question asks for an equivalent form of an expression. There are variables in the answers, so

plug in. Make $x = 2$. The expression becomes $\dfrac{5}{2^2} - \dfrac{3}{2} = \dfrac{5}{4} - \dfrac{3}{2} = \dfrac{5}{4} - \dfrac{6}{4} = -\dfrac{1}{4}$. This is the target val-

ue; circle it. Now plug $x = 2$ into the answer choices to see which one matches the target value.

Choice (F) becomes $\dfrac{2}{2} = 1$. This does not match the target, so eliminate (F). Choice (G) becomes

$\dfrac{2}{2^2 - 2} = \dfrac{2}{4-2} = \dfrac{2}{2} = 1$. Eliminate (G). Choice (H) becomes $\dfrac{5(2)-3}{2^2} = \dfrac{10-3}{4} = \dfrac{7}{4}$. Eliminate (H).

Choice (J) becomes $\dfrac{5-3(2)}{2^2} = \dfrac{5-6}{4} = -\dfrac{1}{4}$. This matches the target value. The correct answer is (J).

27. **D** The question asks for the value of an expression. The question asks for a specific value and the an-

swers contain numbers in increasing order, so plug in the answers. Begin by labeling the answers

as "$\dfrac{b}{a}$" and start with (C), $-\dfrac{4}{5}$. Make $b = -4$ and $a = 5$ and plug them into the original equation.

The equation becomes $\dfrac{3(5)+(-4)}{5-(-4)} = \dfrac{15-4}{5+4} = \dfrac{11}{9}$. This does not equal $\dfrac{5}{4}$, so eliminate (C). The

result of (C) was slightly too small, so try (D) next. Make $b = -7$ and $a = 9$ and plug them into the

original equation: $\dfrac{3(9)+(-7)}{9-(-9)} = \dfrac{27-7}{9+7} = \dfrac{20}{16} = \dfrac{5}{4}$. This matches the value given in the question, so

stop here. The correct answer is (D).

29. **B** The question asks how many people the lacrosse team needs to invite to have a roster of 22 players. Since the question is asking for a specific value and the answers contain numbers in ascending order, plug in the answers. Begin by labeling the answers as "# invited to tryouts" and start with (B), 110. Work the problem in bite-sized pieces. The question states that $\frac{1}{5}$ *of the people invited to tryouts do not show up,* so take $\frac{1}{5}$ of the 110 invited to get $\frac{1}{5}(110) = 22$. This is the number of people who do not show up. Subtract 22 from 110 to get 88, which is the number of people that did show up to try out. Of those that did show up to try out, 25% were put on the roster, so take 25% of 88 to get $\frac{25}{100}(88) = 22$. This is the number of players that are put on the roster. This matches the number given in the problem, so stop there. The correct answer is (B).

33. **B** The question asks for the fraction of books that will be given away on the second day of a promotion. Since the question is asking about fractions of a non-specified value, this is a Hidden Plug-In question. Start by plugging in a number for the number of books that will be given away. Any number of books will work, but for ease of calculations, the number of books should be divisible by both 5 and 3. Plug in 15 for the number of books, and work in bite-sized pieces to find that $\frac{2}{5}$ of the 15 books, or $\frac{2}{5}(15) = 6$ books were distributed in the morning. Then, $\frac{1}{3}$ *of the remaining books* were distributed in the afternoon. The number of remaining books is $15 - 6 = 9$, and $\frac{1}{3}(9) = 3$ books. During the day, $6 + 3 = 9$ books were distributed, leaving $15 - 9 = 6$ books to be distributed the next day. To find the fraction of books remaining to be distributed, divide 6 by 15 and simplify to get $\frac{6}{15} = \frac{2}{5}$. The correct answer is (B).

38. **G** The question asks how a variable changes in relation to another variable. This is a Hidden Plug-In question. To see how a will change as b gets closer to infinity, plug in at least 2 different values for b and eliminate answers that are incorrect. Start by plugging in a positive real number for b, such as $b = 3$, to find that $a = \frac{3}{3} = 1$. Next plug in a large number for b to see how a will change: $b = 3,000$ will make $a = \frac{3}{3,000} = \frac{1}{1,000} = 0.001$. Therefore, as b gets larger, a gets smaller. Eliminate (F). Choices (H) and (J) state that a approaches a number greater than 1, which is not true. The value of a is decreasing and smaller than 1 when $b = 3,000$. Eliminate (H) and (J). The correct answer is (G).

42.   **F**   The question asks which expression with absolute values has the least value. There are variables in

the answers, so plug in. Make $x = 2$ and $y = -3$ to match the requirements of the problem. Plug

$x = 2$ and $y = -3$ into the answers to determine which has the least value. When working with abso-

lute values, do the calculations inside the absolute value symbols as if they were parentheses, and

then take the absolute value. Choice (F) becomes $\left|\dfrac{2+(-3)}{2-(-3)}\right| = \left|\dfrac{-1}{5}\right| = \left|-\dfrac{1}{5}\right| = \dfrac{1}{5}$. Choice (G) becomes

$\left|\dfrac{2-(-3)}{2+(-3)}\right| = \left|\dfrac{5}{-1}\right| = |-5| = 5$. Eliminate (G) because (F) is smaller, so (G) cannot be the least value.

Choice (H) becomes $\left|\dfrac{2+(-3)}{-3}\right| = \left|\dfrac{-1}{-3}\right| = \left|\dfrac{1}{3}\right| = \dfrac{1}{3}$. Eliminate (H) because (F) is smaller. Choice (J)

becomes $\left|\dfrac{2-(-3)}{2}\right| = \left|\dfrac{5}{2}\right| = \dfrac{5}{2}$. Eliminate (J) because (F) is smaller. The correct answer is (F).

Summary

- o Remember the Basic Approach for Word Problems:
  - Know the question.
  - Let the answers help.
  - Break the question into bite-sized pieces.

- o Use Plugging In when there are variables in the answer choices or the question. Keep the following pointers in mind:
  - Choose numbers that make the math easy.
  - Try all the answer choices.
  - On more complex questions, keep your variables straight!

- o Plugging In Steps:
  - Identify the opportunity.
  - Choose a good number.
  - Find the target answer.
  - Test all the answer choices.

- o Use Plugging In the Answers (PITA):
  - when there are numbers in the answers
  - when the question asks for a specific amount
  - if you have the urge to write your own algebraic expression

- o Plugging In the Answers Steps:
  - Identify the opportunity.
  - Label the answer choices.
  - Start with an answer in the middle.
  - Work the problem in bite-sized pieces.
  - Eliminate answers that are too big or too small.
  - When an answer works, STOP!

Chapter 16
Plane Geometry

The ACT test-writers say that there are 7–8 geometry questions in the "Preparing for Higher Math" questions, as well as some additional geometry questions in the "Integrating Essential Skills" category. However, you may need algebra to solve some geometry questions, and other skills in this book—such as Plugging In and POE—will also work on geometry questions. What matters most is that you can identify the topics that make a question Now, Later, or Never for you, and then apply good test-taking strategies.

While there may occasionally be a more advanced formula or complex shape, the majority of the geometry questions on the ACT test the basic rules on the basic shapes. This chapter will review a cross-section of those formulas and concepts and give you a basic strategic approach to apply those rules on the ACT.

CRACKING THE GEOMETRY ON THE ACT

Plug-and-chug geometry questions can have so much information in them that they feel like word problems, so treat them like word problems. Let's review the Basic Approach to word problems. We'll then add some points specific to geometry.

STEP 1 »

Step 1: Know the Question

Read the whole question before calculating anything, and underline or highlight the actual question.

STEP 2 »

Step 2: Let the Answers Help

Look for clues on how to solve and ways to use POE (Process of Elimination).

STEP 3 »

Step 3: Break the Question into Bite-Sized Pieces

Calculate at each step necessary and watch out for tricky phrasing.

For geometry questions, Step 3 has two specific additions:

> **Step 3a:** If you're taking the ACT Online Test, copy the figure onto your whiteboard or scratch paper. If there is no figure (regardless of which ACT you are taking), draw your own. Then, write all the information given in the question on the figure.
>
> **Step 3b:** Write down any formulas you need, and fill in any information you have.

Plugging In: Not Just Algebra

Many of the strategies already covered in this book apply to Geometry questions as well. The main requirements for a Plugging In question are variables in the question or answer choices. When a Geometry question involves variables or non-specified values, think about Plugging In!

Let's look at a short, straightforward example.

---

13. A circle with center O has a radius r. What is the area of a circle with a radius three times the length of r?

    A. $3\pi r$

    B. $9\pi r$

    C. $3\pi r^2$

    D. $9\pi r^2$

Here's How to Crack It

Step 1: Know the question. You need to find the area of this new larger circle, not the larger radius.

Step 2: Let the answers help. First of all, you're looking for the area, which means the radius will have to be squared, so you can eliminate (A) and (B), which can't be right. Now, notice that each of these answer choices has a variable in it. If you're thinking Plugging In, you're thinking right.

Step 3: Break the question into bite-sized pieces. Pick an easy value for r, like $r = 2$.

Step 3a: Write all the information given in the question on the figure. There's no figure here, so draw 2 circles. Label the radius of the smaller one: $r = 2$.

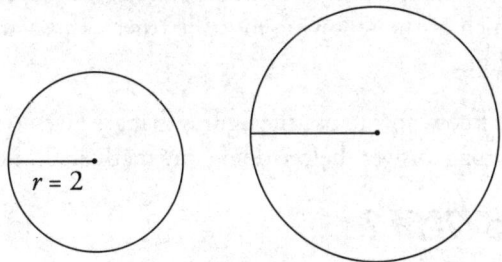

Step 3b: Write down any formulas you need and fill in any information you have. The formula for the area of a circle that you'll need is $A = \pi r^2$.

If the original radius is 2, then the larger radius, which is three times the length of r, must be 6. Label this on the figure, which now looks like this:

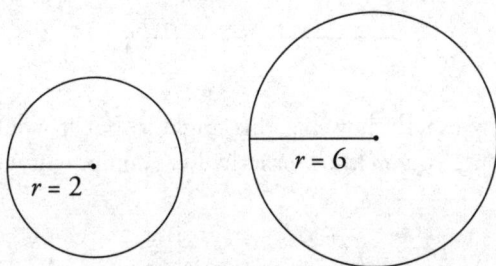

The area of the larger circle is $A = \pi(6)^2 = 36\pi$. We've got a target answer, so let's try it in the answer choices. Remember, we've already eliminated (A) and (B).

    A. ~~$3\pi r$~~
    B. ~~$9\pi r$~~
    C. $3\pi(2)^2 = 12\pi$ ✗
    D. $9\pi(2)^2 = 36\pi$ ✓

Choice (D) is the correct answer. Have another look at those answer choices and think of all the ways you could make mistakes on this question. Plugging In saves the day again by minimizing the possibility for algebra errors.

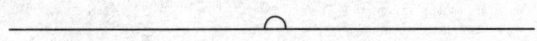

Geometry BFFs: POE and Ballparking

Step 2 of the Basic Approach is particularly important to geometry questions. In the last few chapters, we've seen how POE and Ballparking can help to narrow down the answer choices when you're confused. Before you rush to calculate, Ballparking, in particular, will help you a ton on geometry questions because most figures are drawn to scale.

To Scale or Not to Scale?

That is the question. The ACT makes a big deal in the instructions about the fact that their figures are "**not** necessarily drawn to scale." Here's the thing, though: they usually are drawn to scale or at least enough to use them in broad strokes. Use Ballparking to eliminate answers that are too big or too small rather than to determine a precise value. Questions on angles and area especially lend themselves to Ballparking. The main place to be skeptical is on those questions that ask things like, "Which of the following must be true?" Those are the ones whose figures can be purposely misleading.

In most other cases, if you know how to use the figures that are given (or how to draw your own), you can eliminate some wrong answers before doing any math at all. Let's see how this works.

How Big Is Angle *NLM* ?

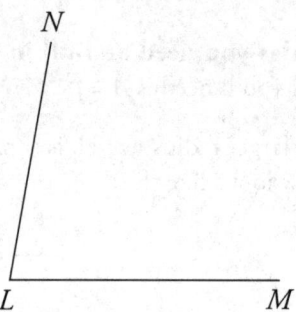

Obviously, you don't know exactly how big this angle is, but it would be easy to compare it with an angle whose measure you *do* know exactly. Let's compare it with a 90° angle.

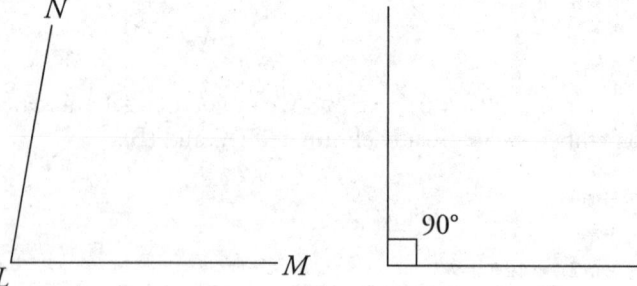

Angle *NLM* is clearly a bit less than 90°. Now look at the following question, which asks about the same angle *NLM* .

11. In the figure shown, O, N, and M are collinear. If the lengths of $\overline{ON}$ and $\overline{NL}$ are the same, the measure of angle LON is 30°, and angle LMN is 40°, what is the measure of angle NLM?

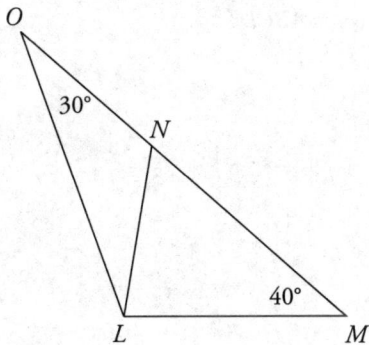

    A. 30°
    B. 80°
    C. 90°
    D. 110°

Here's How to Crack It

Start with Step 1: Know the question. Underline or highlight *what is the measure of angle NLM?* and even mark the angle on your figure. You don't want to answer for the wrong angle. Now move to Step 2, and focus on eliminating answer choices that don't make sense. You've already decided that ∠*NLM* is a little less than 90°, which means you can eliminate (C) and (D). How much less than 90°? 30° is a third of 90°. Could ∠*NLM* be that small? No way! The answer to this question must be (B).

In this case, it wasn't necessary to do any "real" geometry at all to get the question right, and it took about half the time. ACT has to give you credit for right answers no matter how you get them. What's more, if you worked this question the "real" way, you might have picked one of the other answers: as you can imagine, every answer choice gives some partial answer that you would've seen as you worked the question.

Let's Do It Again

34. In the figure shown, if $AB = 27$, $CD = 20$, and the area of triangle $ADC = 240$, what is the area of polygon $ABCD$?

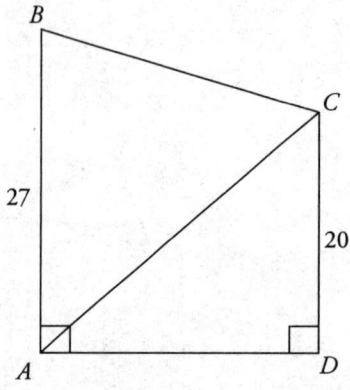

F. 480
G. 540
H. 564
J. 1,128

Here's How to Crack It

Start with Step 1: Know the question. Underline or highlight *what is the area of polygon ABCD?* This polygon is not a conventional figure, but if we had to choose one figure that the polygon resembled, we might pick a rectangle. Try drawing a line at a right angle from the line segment $\overline{AB}$ so that it touches point C, thus creating a rectangle.

It should look like the following:

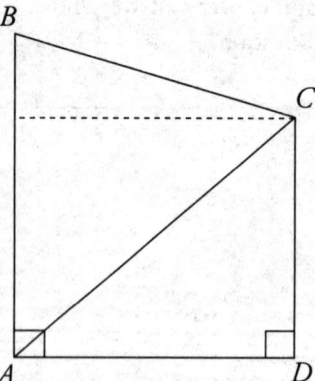

The area of polygon $ABCD$ is equal to the area of the rectangle you've just formed plus a little bit at the top. The question tells you that the area of triangle ADC is 240. What is the area of the rectangle you just created? If you said 480, you are exactly right, whether you knew the geometric rules that applied or whether you just measured it with your eyes.

So the area of the rectangle is 480. Roughly speaking, then, what should the area of the polygon be? A little more. Let's look at the answer choices. Choice (F) is equal to 480; get rid of it. Choices (G) and (H) both seem possible; they are both a little more than 480; let's hold on to them. Choice (J) seems pretty unrealistic. We want more than 480, but 1,128 is ridiculous.

What Should I Do If There Is No Figure?
Draw one! It's always easier to understand a question when you can see it in front of you. If possible, draw your figure to scale so that you can estimate the answer as well.

The answer to this question is (H). To get this final answer, you'll need to use a variety of area formulas, which we'll explore later in this chapter. For now, though, notice that your chances of guessing have increased from 25% to 50% with a little bit of quick thinking. Now what should you do? If you know how to do the question, you do it. If you don't or if you are running out of time, you guess and move on.

However, even as we move into the "real" geometry in the remainder of this chapter, don't forget:

> Always look for opportunities to Ballpark on geometry questions even if you know how to do them the "real" way.

GEOMETRY REVIEW

By using the figures ACT has so thoughtfully provided and by making your own figures when they are not provided, you can often eliminate several of the answer choices. In some cases, you'll be able to eliminate every choice but one. Of course, you will also need to know the actual geometry concepts that ACT is testing. We've divided our review into the following four topics:

- angles and lines
- triangles
- four-sided figures
- circles

ANGLES AND LINES

Here is a line.

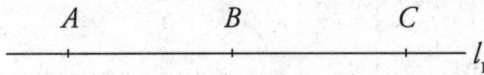

A line extends forever in both directions. This line, called l_1, has three points on it: *A*, *B*, and *C*. These three points are said to be **collinear** because they are all on the same line. The piece of the line in between points *A* and *B* is called a line **segment**. ACT will refer to it as segment *AB* or simply $\overline{AB}$. *A* and *B* are the **endpoints** of segment *AB*.

A line forms an angle of 180°. If that line is cut by another line, it divides that 180° into two angles that together add up to 180°.

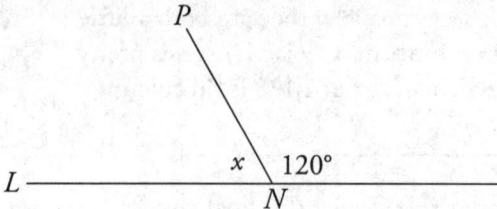

In the above figure, what is the value of *x*? If you said 60°, you are correct. To find *x*, just subtract 120° from 180°.

An angle can also be described by points on the lines that intersect to form the angle and the point of intersection itself, with the middle letter corresponding to the point of intersection. For example, in the previous figure, ∠*x* could also be described as ∠*LNP*. On the ACT, instead of writing out "angle *LNP*," they'll use math shorthand and put ∠*LNP* instead. So "angle *x*" becomes ∠*x*. Furthermore, if the ACT wants to describe the measure of angle *x*, they can use "m∠*x*." In this case, m∠*x* = 60°.

If there are 180° above a line, there are also 180° below the line, for a total of 360°.

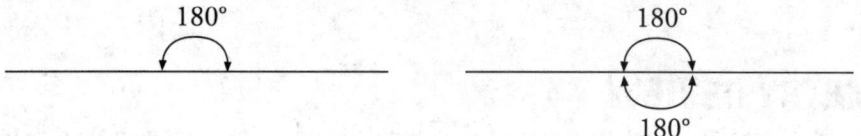

When two lines intersect, they form four angles, represented below by letters *A*, *B*, *C*, and *D*. ∠*A* and ∠*B* together form a straight line, so they add up to 180°. Angles that add up to 180° are called **supplementary** angles.

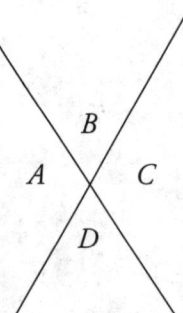

∠*A* and ∠*C* are opposite from each other and always equal each other, as are ∠*B* and ∠*D*. Angles like these are called **vertical** angles.

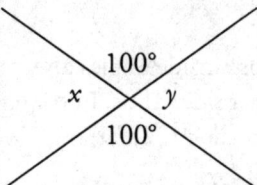

In the figure above, what is the value of $\angle x$? If you said 80°, you're right. Together with the 100° angle, x forms a straight line. What is the value of $\angle y$? If you said 80°, you're right again. These two angles are vertical and must equal each other. The four angles together add up to 360°.

When two lines meet in such a way that 90° angles are formed, the lines are called **perpendicular**. The little box at the point of intersection of two lines below indicates that they are perpendicular. It stands to reason that all four of these angles have measures of 90°. The symbol for perpendicular is ⊥.

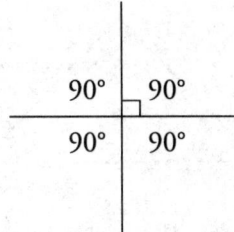

When two lines in the same plane are drawn so that they could extend into infinity without ever meeting, they are called **parallel**. In the figure below, l_1 is parallel to l_2. The symbol for parallel is | |.

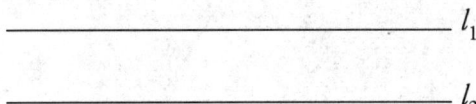

When two parallel lines are cut by a third line, eight angles are formed, but in fact, there are really only two angle measures—a big one and a little one. Look at the figure below.

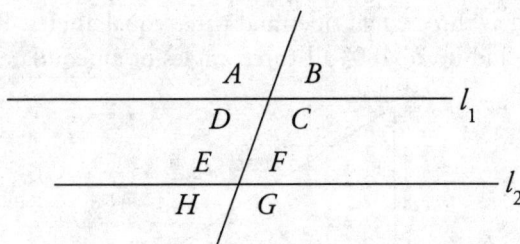

If $\angle A = 110°$, then $\angle B$ must equal 70° (together they form a straight line). $\angle D$ is vertical to $\angle B$, which means that it must also measure 70°. $\angle C$ is vertical to $\angle A$, so it must measure 110°.

The four angles $\angle E$, $\angle F$, $\angle G$, and $\angle H$ are in exactly the same proportion as the angles above. The little angles both measure 70°. The big angles both measure 110°.

TRIANGLES

A triangle is a three-sided figure whose inside angles always add up to 180°. The largest angle of a triangle is always opposite its longest side. Thus, in triangle XYZ below, XY is the longest side, followed by YZ, followed by XZ. On the ACT, "triangle XYZ" will often be written as $\triangle XYZ$.

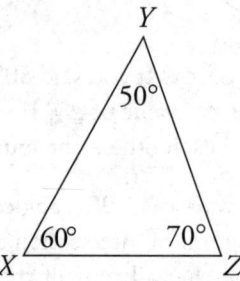

The ACT likes to ask about certain kinds of triangles in particular.

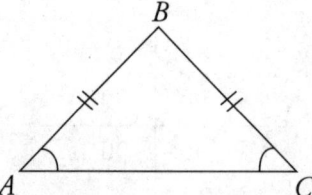

An **isosceles** triangle has two equal sides. The angles opposite those sides are also equal. In the isosceles triangle above, if $\angle A = 50°$, then so does $\angle C$. If $AB = 6$, then so does BC.

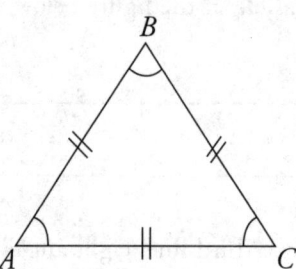

An **equilateral** triangle has three equal sides and three equal angles. Because measures of the three equal angles must add up to 180°, all three angles of an equilateral triangle always measure 60°.

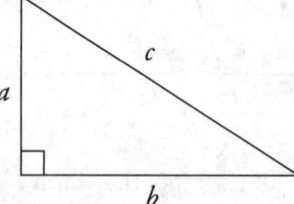

A **right triangle** has one inside angle that has measure equal to 90°. The longest side of a right triangle (the one opposite the 90° angle) is called the **hypotenuse**.

Pythagoras, a Greek mathematician, discovered that the sides of a right triangle are always in a particular proportion, which can be expressed by the formula $a^2 + b^2 = c^2$, where a and b are the shorter sides of the triangle (also called the **legs**), and c is the hypotenuse. This formula is called the **Pythagorean Theorem**.

There are certain right triangles that the test-writers at ACT find endlessly fascinating. Let's test out the Pythagorean Theorem on the first of these.

$$3^2 + 4^2 = c^2$$

$$9 + 16 = 25$$

$$c^2 = 25, \text{ so } c = 5$$

The ACT writers adore the 3-4-5 triangle and use it frequently, along with its multiples, such as the 6-8-10 triangle and the 9-12-15 triangle. Of course, you can always use the Pythagorean Theorem to figure out the third side of a right triangle, as long as you have the other two sides, but because ACT questions very often use "triples" like the ones we've just mentioned, it makes sense just to memorize them.

The ACT has three commonly used right-triangle triples.

3-4-5 (and its multiples)

5-12-13 (and its multiples)

7-24-25 (not as common as the other two)

Don't Get Snared

- Is this a 3-4-5 triangle?

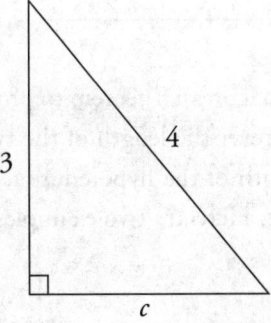

> **Pythagoras's *Other* Theorem**
> Pythagoras also developed a theory about the transmigration of souls. So far, this has not been proven, nor will it help you on this exam.

No, because the hypotenuse of a right triangle must be its *longest* side—the one opposite the 90° angle. In this case, we must use the Pythagorean Theorem to discover side c: $3^2 + c^2 = 16$, so $c = \sqrt{7}$.

- Is this a 5-12-13 triangle?

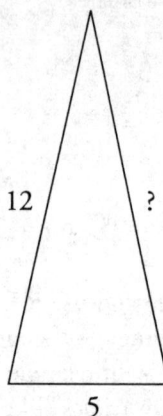

No, because the Pythagorean Theorem—and triples—apply only to *right* triangles. We can't determine definitively the third side of this triangle without knowing the specific angle measures.

The Isosceles Right Triangle (The 45-45-90 Triangle)

As fond as the ACT test-writers are of triples, they are even fonder of two other right triangles. The first is called the **isosceles right triangle**. The sides and angles of the isosceles right triangle are always in a particular proportion.

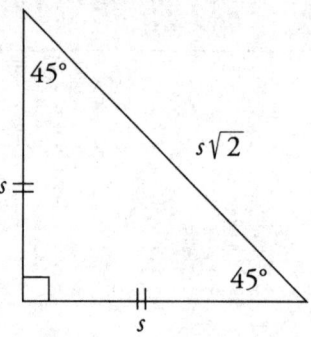

You could use the Pythagorean Theorem to prove this (or you could just take our word for it). Whatever the length of the two equal sides of the isosceles right triangle, the length of the hypotenuse is always equal to one of those side lengths times $\sqrt{2}$. Here are two examples.

Be on the Lookout . . .

for questions in which the application of the Pythagorean Theorem is not obvious. For example, every rectangle contains two right triangles. That means that if you know the length and width of the rectangle, you also know the length of the diagonal, which is the hypotenuse of both triangles created by the diagonal.

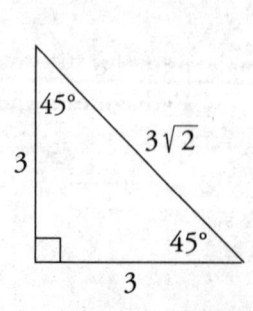

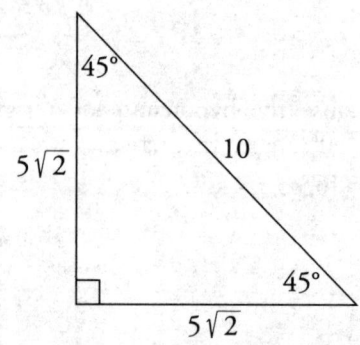

The 30-60-90 Triangle

The other right triangle tested frequently on the ACT is the **30-60-90 triangle**, which also has sides that are always in a particular proportion.

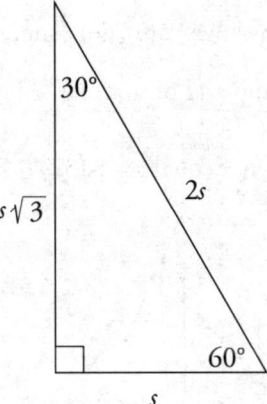

You can use the Pythagorean Theorem to prove this. Whatever the length of the short side of the 30-60-90 triangle, the hypotenuse is always twice as long. The length of the medium side is always equal to the length of the short side times $\sqrt{3}$. Here are two examples.

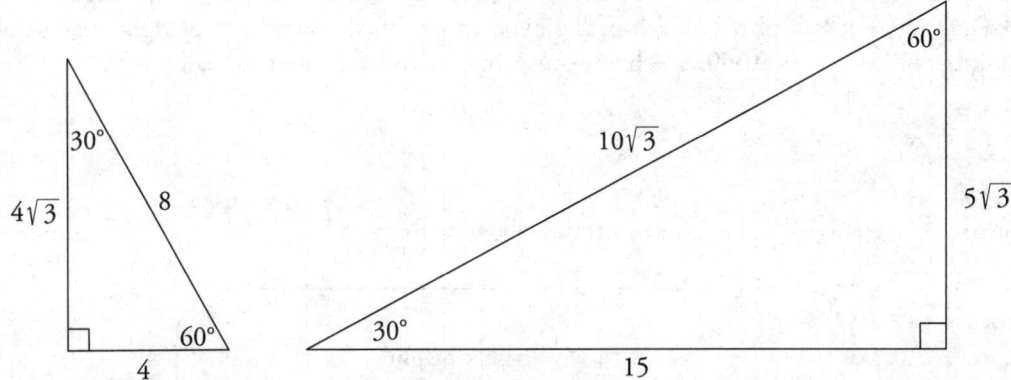

Because these triangles are tested so frequently, it makes sense to memorize the proportions rather than waste time deriving them each time they appear.

Don't Get Snared

- In the isosceles right triangle below, are the sides equal to $3\sqrt{2}$?

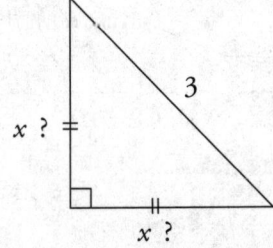

No. Remember, in an isosceles right triangle, hypotenuse = the side $\sqrt{2}$. In this case, 3 = the side $\sqrt{2}$. If we solve for the side, we get $\dfrac{3}{\sqrt{2}}$ = the side.

For arcane mathematical reasons, we are not supposed to leave a radical in the denominator, but we can multiply top and bottom by $\sqrt{2}$ to get $\dfrac{3\sqrt{2}}{2}$.

- In the right triangle below, is x equal to $4\sqrt{3}$?

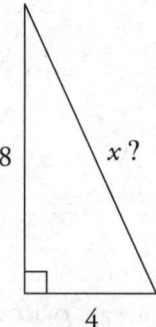

No. Even though it is one of ACT's favorites, you have to be careful not to see a 30-60-90 where none exists. In the triangle above, the length of the short side is half of the length of the *medium* side, not half of the length of the hypotenuse. This is some sort of right triangle all right, but it is not a 30-60-90. The hypotenuse, in case you're curious, is really $4\sqrt{5}$.

Area

The **area** of a triangle can be found with the following formula:

$$\text{Area} = \frac{1}{2}(\text{base} \times \text{height})$$

$$A = \frac{1}{2}bh$$

Height is measured as the perpendicular distance from the base of the triangle to its highest point.

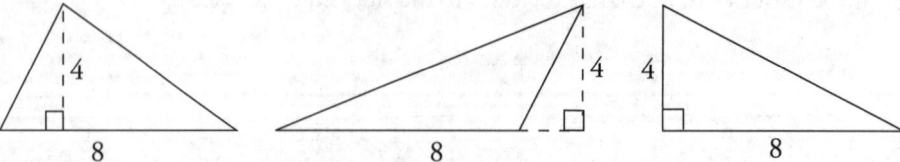

In all three of the above triangles, the area is

$$\frac{8 \times 4}{2} = 16$$

Don't Get Snared

- Sometimes the height of a triangle can be *outside* the triangle itself, as we just saw in the example above.
- In a right triangle, the height of the triangle can also be one of the sides of the triangle, as we just saw in the third example. However, be careful when finding the area of a *non-right* triangle. Simply because you know two sides of the triangle does not mean that you have the height of the triangle.

Similar Triangles

Two triangles are called similar if their angles have the same degree measures. This means their side lengths will be in proportion. For example, the two triangles below are similar.

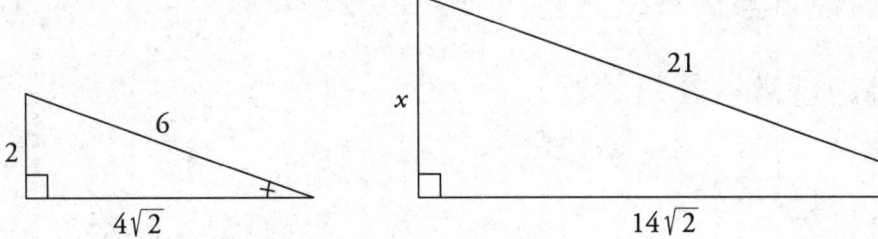

Because the side lengths of the two triangles are in the same proportion, you can find the missing side length, x, by setting up a proportion equation.

$$\begin{array}{ccc} & \text{small triangle} & \text{big triangle} \\ \dfrac{\text{short leg}}{\text{hypotenuse}} & \dfrac{2}{6} \quad = & \dfrac{x}{21} \end{array}$$

$$(6)(x) = (2)(21)$$
$$6x = 42$$
$$x = 7$$

ACT TRIANGLE QUESTIONS

In this chapter, we've pretty much given you all the basic triangle information you'll need to do the triangle questions on the ACT. The trick is that you'll have to use a lot of this information all at once. Let's have a look at a typical ACT triangle question and see how to use the Basic Approach.

29. In the figure shown, square *ABCD* is attached to △*ADE* as shown. If ∠*EAD* measures 30° and *AE* is equal to $4\sqrt{3}$, then what is the area of square *ABCD*?

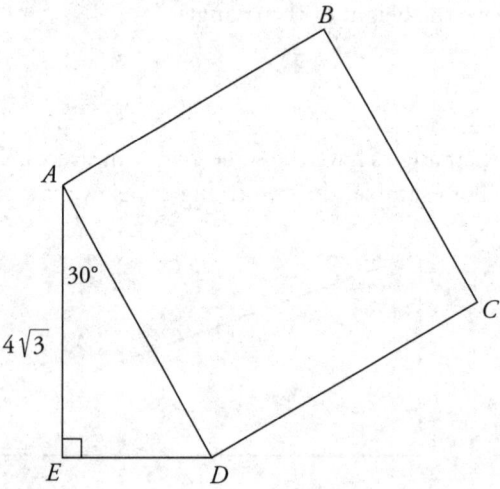

A. $8\sqrt{3}$

B. 64

C. 72

D. $64\sqrt{2}$

Here's How to Crack It

Start with Step 1: Know the question. Underline or highlight *what is the area of square ABCD?* Move to **Step 2:** Look at the answers. We don't have any values for areas of other shapes within the figure, so there is nothing to Ballpark. But note the presence of $\sqrt{2}$ and $\sqrt{3}$ in the answers. They're an additional clue, if you haven't absorbed the info given, that 30-60-90 and/or 45-45-90 triangles are in play.

The triangle in the figure is, in fact, a 30-60-90. Now move to **Step 3:** Break the question into bite-sized pieces. Because angle *A* is the smaller angle, the side opposite that angle has length 4 and the hypotenuse has length 8. Now move on to **Step 3a:** Mark your figure with these values. Now move to **Step 3b:** Write down any formulas you need. The area for a square is s^2. Because that hypotenuse is also the side of the square, the area of the square must be 8 squared, or 64. This is (B). If you forgot the ratio of the sides of a 30-60-90 triangle, go back and review it. You'll need it.

POE Pointers

If you didn't remember the ratio of the sides of a 30-60-90 triangle, could you have eliminated some answers using POE? Of course. Let's see if we can use the figure to eliminate some answer choices.

The figure tells us that $\overline{AE}$ has length $4\sqrt{3}$. A good approximation for $\sqrt{3}$ is 1.7. So $4\sqrt{3} \approx 6.8$. We can now use this to estimate the lengths of the sides of square $ABCD$. Just using your eyes, would you say that $\overline{AD}$ is longer or shorter than $\overline{AE}$? Of course it's a bit longer; it's the hypotenuse of $\triangle ADE$. You decide to write down what you think its length might be. To find the area of the square, simply square whatever value you decided the side measured. This is your answer.

Now all you have to do is see which of the answer choices still makes sense. Could the answer be (A)? $8\sqrt{3}$ equals roughly 13.6. Is this close to your answer? No way. Could the answer be (B), which is 64? Quite possibly. Could the answer be 72? It might be. Could the answer be $64\sqrt{2}$? An approximation of $\sqrt{2}$ is 1.4, so $64\sqrt{2} \approx 89.6$. This seems rather large. Thus, on this question, by using POE, we could eliminate (A) and (D).

FOUR-SIDED FIGURES

The interior angles of any four-sided figure (also known as a quadrilateral) add up to 360°. The most common four-sided figures on the ACT are the rectangle and the square, with the parallelogram and the trapezoid coming in a far distant third and fourth.

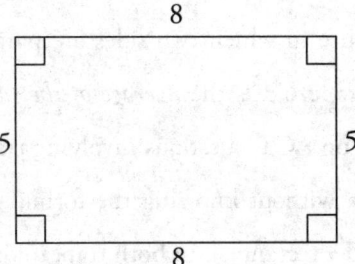

> **Your Friend the Triangle**
> Because a quadrilateral is really just two triangles, its interior angles must measure twice those of a triangle: 2(180) = 360.

A **rectangle** is a four-sided figure in which each of the four interior angles measures 90°. The area of a rectangle is *base × height*. Therefore, the area of this rectangle is 8 (*base*) × 5 (*height*) = 40. The perimeter of a rectangle is the sum of all four of its side lengths. The perimeter of that same rectangle is 8 + 8 + 5 + 5 = 26.

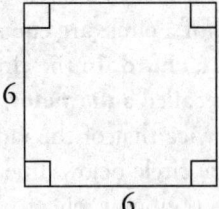

A **square** is a rectangle whose four sides are all equal in length. You can think of the area of a square, therefore, as **side squared**. The area of the square above is 6 (*base*) × 6 (*height*) = 36. The perimeter is 24, or 4*s*.

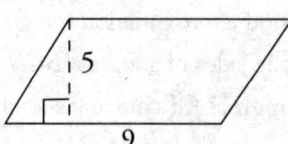 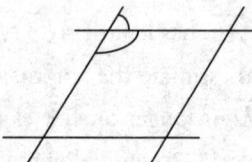

A **parallelogram** is a four-sided figure made up of two sets of parallel lines. We said earlier that when parallel lines are crossed by a third line, eight angles are formed, but in reality, there are only two angle measures—the big one and the little one. In a parallelogram, when each side is extended, 16 angles are formed, but there are still, in reality, only two angle measures.

The area of a parallelogram is also *base × height*, but because of the shape of the figure, the height of a parallelogram is not necessarily equal to one of its side lengths. Height is measured by a perpendicular line drawn from the base to the top of the figure. The area of the parallelogram above is 9 × 5 = 45.

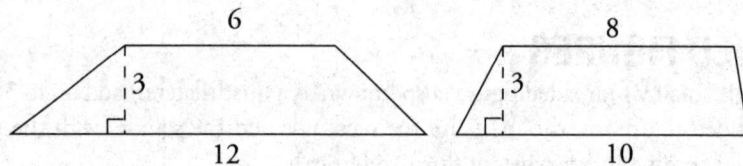

A **trapezoid** is a four-sided figure in which two sides are parallel. Both of the figures above are trapezoids. The area of a trapezoid is the *average of the two parallel sides × the height*, or $\frac{1}{2}$ (*base* 1 + *base* 2)(*height*), but on ACT questions involving trapezoids, there is almost always some easy way to find the area without knowing the formula (for example, by dividing the trapezoid into two triangles and a rectangle). In both trapezoids above, the area is 27.

CIRCLES

The ACT loves to try to confuse you with all the different terms and facts about circles. A circle has **360°**. The distance from the center of a circle to any point on the circle is called the **radius**. All radii (the plural of radius) of a circle are equal. A line from one point on the circle to another point on the circle is called a **chord**. In the circle below, *AB* is a chord. A chord that goes through the center of the circle is called a **diameter**. The diameter of a circle is the longest chord of the circle, and its length is twice that of the radius. The **circumference** of a circle is the perimeter of a circle. Finally, in the circle below, line *CD* is **tangent** to the circle. A radius drawn from the center of the circle to the point where *CD* intersects the circle will be perpendicular to *CD*.

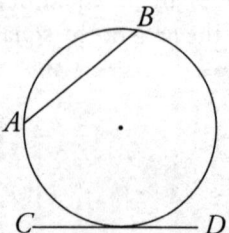

> The formula for the **area** of a circle is πr^2.
>
> The formula for the **circumference** is $2\pi r$.

In the circle below, if the radius is 4, then the area is 16π, and the circumference is 8π.

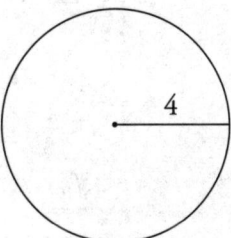

The key to circle questions on the ACT is to look for the word or phrase that tells you what to do. If you see the word *circumference*, immediately write down the formula for circumference and plug in any numbers the question has given you. By solving for whatever quantity is still unknown, you have probably already answered the question. Another tip is to find the radius. The radius is the key to many circle questions.

---

4. If the area of a circle is 16 square meters, what is its radius in meters?

F. $\dfrac{8}{\pi}$

G. 12π

H. $\dfrac{4\sqrt{\pi}}{\pi}$

J. $\dfrac{16}{\pi}$

Here's How to Crack It
Step 1: Know the question. We need to solve for the radius.

Step 2: Let the answers help. We don't have a figure, so there's nothing to Ballpark. But no figure?

Step 3a: Draw your own.

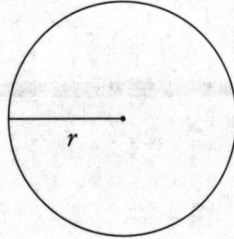

Step 3b: Write down any formulas you need and fill in the information you have. Plug the value you know into the formula for the area of a circle: $\pi r^2 = 16$. The question is asking for the radius, so you have to solve for r. If you divide both sides by π, you get

$$r^2 = \frac{16}{\pi}$$

$$r = \sqrt{\frac{16}{\pi}}$$

$$r = \frac{4}{\sqrt{\pi}}$$

$$r = \frac{4\sqrt{\pi}}{\pi}$$

The correct answer is (H).

The ACT will also test you on different parts of a circle. A portion of the circumference of the circle is called an **arc**, and a portion of the area of the circle created by two radii and an arc is called a **sector**. In the circle below, angle AOB is the **central angle** of minor arc AB ("$\overarc{AB}$") and sector AOB. Arcs are sometimes measured by the measure of the central angle, so $\overarc{AB} = 60°$.

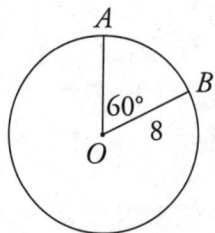

Because the radius is given in the circle above, you can also determine the length of the arc.

Arcs and sectors are proportional to the central angle of a circle.

$$\frac{\text{part}}{\text{whole}} = \frac{\text{central angle}}{360°} = \frac{\text{arc length}}{2\pi r} = \frac{\text{sector area}}{\pi r^2}$$

In the circle on the previous page, minor arc AB can be found using the proportion $\dfrac{60°}{360°} = \dfrac{x}{2\pi(8)}$, which can be simplified to $\dfrac{1}{6} = \dfrac{x}{16\pi}$. Cross-multiply to get $16\pi = 6x$. Divide both sides by 6 to determine that the arc equals $\dfrac{8}{3}\pi$. Similarly, you can find the area of sector AOB using $\dfrac{60°}{360°} = \dfrac{x}{\pi(8)^2}$, which can be simplified to $\dfrac{1}{6} = \dfrac{x}{64\pi}$. Once again, cross-multiply to get $64\pi = 6x$ and divide both sides by 6 to get $\dfrac{32}{3}\pi$.

OVERLAPPING SHAPES

Some ACT questions will include overlapping shapes or shapes within shapes. When this happens, find the link between the two shapes. It could be, for example, that the hypotenuse of the triangle is also the diameter of the circle. There will also be questions with oddly-shaped shaded regions. Don't worry: you won't need area under a curve or anything resembling calculus. Instead, find information about the normal shapes in the figure and add or subtract to get the shaded region.

Take a look at the following example.

---

14. The circle with center O is inscribed inside square $ABCD$ as shown in the figure. If a side of the square measures 8 units, what is the area of the shaded region?

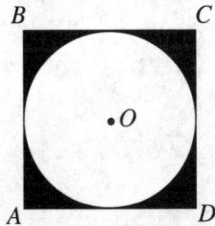

    F. $8 - 16\pi$
    G. 8π
    H. $64 - 16\pi$
    J. $64 - 8\pi$

Here's How to Crack It

Begin with Step 1, and underline or highlight *what is the area of the shaded region?* Step 2 brings us to the answers, and we see all of the answers have π in them. Since π is approximately 3, (F) would be a negative area. Eliminate this answer. If no other answer choice can be obviously eliminated via Ballparking, move to Step 3. Break the question into bite-sized pieces, but don't get hung up on "inscribed." Yes, that's an important term to know, but since we have the figure, it's irrelevant. Move to Step 3a and 3b: mark the side of the square "8," and write down the formulas for the area of a circle and square: πr^2 and s^2.

Is there a formula for the shape made by the shaded region? Nope. We just need the basic formulas for the basic shapes. $8^2 = 64$, so we at least know the shaded region is less than 64, the area of the square. At this point, we know that the answer must be 64 minus the area of the circle, so we can eliminate (G) because it does not match this format. What's the link between the square and the circle? The side length of the square equals the diameter of the circle. So if the diameter is 8, then the radius must be 4. Use that in the area formula: $4^2 \pi = 16\pi$. Subtract the area of the circle from the area of the square, and we get (H).

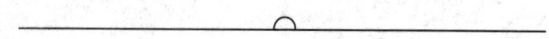

Alternatively, some questions will require you to break up shapes you don't know into shapes you do. As mentioned above, this strategy can also be used for shapes such as trapezoids to avoid unnecessary memorization of formulas, but sometimes, ACT will create strange shapes for the purpose of forcing you to break them up.

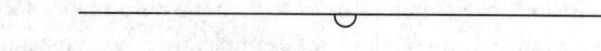

17. In the figure shown, all angles are perpendicular. What is the area of the figure in square units?

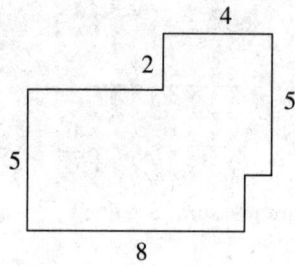

A. 40
B. 48
C. 51
D. 60

Here's How to Crack It

Begin with Step 1, and underline or highlight *What is the area of the figure in square units?* Step 2 brings us to the answers. You may notice that two of the sides are 5 and 8, and the area of a rectangle with those sides would be $5 \times 8 = 40$, but the figure is larger than that, so (A) can be eliminated. The remaining answers are all reasonable, so move on to Step 3. In this case, breaking the problem into bite-sized pieces requires breaking the shape into bite-sized pieces. One way to do so is to start by completing the rectangle that has sides of 5 and 8 and an area of 40:

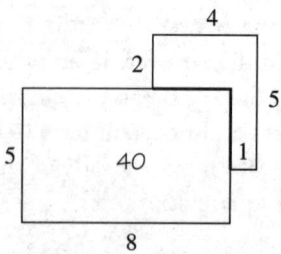

Next, extend the right-hand side of the rectangle that was just created to make two more rectangles. The rightmost rectangle has sides 5 and 1 and an area of 5. The remaining rectangle's sides are 2 and 3 (be sure to subtract the 1 from the side length of 4) for an area of 6.

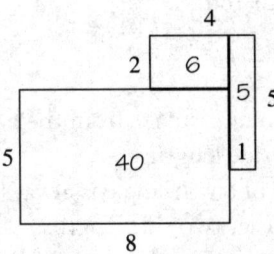

The total area is 40 + 6 + 5 = 51. The correct answer is (C).

FUN FACTS ABOUT FIGURES

Read and review the following facts you need to know about plane geometry.

Angle Facts

- There are 90° in a right angle.
- When two straight lines intersect, the angles opposite each other are equal.
- There are 180° in a straight line.
- Two lines are perpendicular when they meet at a 90° angle.
- The sign for perpendicular is ⊥.
- Bisect means to cut exactly in half.
- There are 180° in a triangle.
- There are 360° in any four-sided figure.

Parallel lines:
- Parallel lines never intersect.
- The sign for parallel is | |.
- When parallel lines are transected with another line, the angles created are all either big angles or small angles.
    - All big angles are equal.
    - All small angles are equal.
    - The sum of any big angle and any small angle is 180°.

Triangle Facts

In any triangle:
- The longest side is opposite the largest angle.
- The shortest side is opposite the smallest angle.
- All angle measures add up to 180°.
- Area = $\dfrac{1}{2}$ (base × height) = $\dfrac{1}{2}bh$
- The height is the perpendicular distance from the base to the opposite vertex.
- Perimeter is the sum of the side lengths.
- The length of the third side of any triangle is always less than the sum and greater than the difference of the other two side lengths.

In an isosceles triangle:
- Two side lengths are equal.
- The two angles opposite the equal sides also have equal measures.

In an equilateral triangle:
- All three side lengths are equal.
- All angles measure 60°.

In a right triangle:
- The side opposite the right angle is the hypotenuse.
- The two sides adjacent to the right angle are legs.
- The relationship between the lengths of the sides can be determined using the Pythagorean Theorem, $a^2 + b^2 = c^2$, where c is the hypotenuse.

Pythagorean triples:
- 3-4-5
- 5-12-13
- 7-24-25

Special right triangles:
- In an isosceles right triangle, if the legs are length s, the hypotenuse is $s\sqrt{2}$.
- In a 30-60-90 triangle, the side opposite the 30° angle is s, the side opposite the 60° angle is $s\sqrt{3}$, and the hypotenuse is $2s$.

Four-Sided Figure Facts

In a quadrilateral:
- All four angle measures add up to 360°.

In a parallelogram:
- Opposite sides are parallel and have equal length.
- Opposite angles have equal measures.
- Adjacent angles are supplementary (their measures add up to 180°).
- Area = base × height = bh
- The height is the perpendicular distance from the base to the opposite side.

In a rhombus:
- Opposite sides are parallel.
- Opposite angles have equal measures.
- Adjacent angles are supplementary (their measures add up to 180°).
- All 4 sides have equal length.

- Area = base × height = bh
- The height is the perpendicular distance from the base to the opposite side.
- The diagonals are perpendicular.

In a rectangle:
- Rectangles are special parallelograms; thus, any fact about parallelograms also applies to rectangles.
- All 4 angles measure 90°.
- Area = length × width = lw
- Perimeter = 2(length) + 2(width) = $2l + 2w$
- The diagonals have equal length.

In a square:
- Squares are special rectangles; thus, any fact about rectangles also applies to squares.
- All 4 sides have equal length.
- Area = $(\text{side})^2 = s^2$
- Perimeter = 4(side) = $4s$
- The diagonals are perpendicular and have equal lengths.

Circle Facts

Circle:
- There are 360° in a circle.

Radius (r):
- The distance from the center to any point on the edge of the circle is the radius.
- All radii in a circle are equal.

Diameter (d):
- The length of a line that connects two points on the edge of the circle, passing through the center, is the diameter.
- The diameter is the longest line in a circle.
- The diameter is twice the radius.

Chord:
- Any line segment connecting two points on the edge of a circle is a chord.
- The longest chord is the diameter.

Circumference (C):
- The distance around the outside of the circle is the circumference.
- $C = 2\pi r = \pi d$

Arc:
- An arc is a part of the circumference.
- The length of an arc is proportional to the measure of the interior angle.

Area:
- The amount of space within the boundaries of a circle is its area.
- $A = \pi r^2$

Sector:
- A sector is a part of the area formed by two radii and the outside of the circle.
- The area of a sector is proportional to the measure of the interior angle.

Line Facts

Line:

- A line has no width and extends infinitely in both directions.
- The angle formed by a line measures 180°.
- A line that contains points A and B is called $\overleftrightarrow{AB}$ (line AB).
- If a figure on the ACT looks like a straight line, and that line looks like it contains a point, it does.

Ray:

- A ray extends infinitely in one direction but has an endpoint.
- The degree measure of a ray is 180°.
- A ray with endpoint A that goes through point B is called $\overrightarrow{AB}$. Pay attention to the arrow above the points and the order in which they are given; those will determine the direction the ray is pointing!

Line Segment:

- A line segment is a part of a line and has two endpoints.
- The degree measure of a line segment is 180°.
- A line segment, which has endpoints of A and B, is written as $\overline{AB}$.

Tangents:

- Tangent means intersecting at one point. For example, a line tangent to a circle intersects exactly one point on the circumference of the circle. Two circles that touch at just one point are also tangent.
- A line tangent to a circle is always perpendicular to the radius drawn to that point of intersection.
- If $\overleftrightarrow{AB}$ intersects a circle at point T, then you would say, "$\overleftrightarrow{AB}$ is tangent to the circle at point T."

PLANE GEOMETRY FORMULAS

Here's a list of all the plane geometry formulas that could show up on the ACT. Memorize the formulas for perimeter/circumference, area, and volume for basic shapes. ACT usually provides the more advanced formulas if they are needed.

> You won't be able to take any notes into the test with you, so it's a good idea to make sure you know these formulas by heart!

Circles

- Area: $A = \pi r^2$
- Circumference: $C = 2\pi r = \pi d$

Triangles

- Area: $A = \dfrac{1}{2}bh$

- Perimeter: P = sum of the side lengths

- Pythagorean Theorem: $a^2 + b^2 = c^2$

SOHCAHTOA

- $\sin(\theta) = \dfrac{\text{opposite}}{\text{hypotenuse}}$

- $\cos(\theta) = \dfrac{\text{adjacent}}{\text{hypotenuse}}$

- $\tan(\theta) = \dfrac{\text{opposite}}{\text{adjacent}}$

- $\csc(\theta) = \dfrac{1}{\sin}$

- $\sec(\theta) = \dfrac{1}{\cos}$

- $\cot(\theta) = \dfrac{1}{\tan}$

Quadrilaterals

Parallelograms

- Area: $A = bh$
- Perimeter: P = sum of the side lengths

Rhombuses

- Area: $A = bh$
- Perimeter: P = sum of the side lengths

Trapezoids

- Area: $A = \dfrac{1}{2}h\left(b_1 + b_2\right)$
- Perimeter: P = sum of the side lengths

Rectangles

- Area: $A = lw$
- Perimeter: $P = 2l + 2w = 2(l + w)$

Squares

- Area: $A = s^2$
- Perimeter: $P = 4s$

Polygons

- Sum of angle measures in an n-sided polygon: $(n-2)180°$

- Angle measure of each angle in a regular n-sided polygon: $\dfrac{(n-2)180°}{n}$

3-D Figures

- Surface area of a rectangular solid: $S = 2(lw + lh + wh)$
- Surface area of a cube: $S = 6s^2$
- Surface area of a right circular cylinder: $S = 2\pi r^2 + 2\pi rh$
- Surface area of a sphere: $S = 4\pi r^2$
- Volume of a cube: $V = s^3$
- Volume of a rectangular solid: $V = lwh$
- Volume of a right circular cylinder: $V = \pi r^2 h$
- Volume of a sphere: $V = \dfrac{4\pi r^3}{3}$

GLOSSARY

Arc	Any part of the circumference
Bisect	To cut in half
Chord	Any line segment connecting two points on the edge of a circle
Circumscribed	Surrounded by a shape as small as possible
Collinear	Lying on the same line
Congruent	Equal in size and shape
Diagonal (of a polygon)	A line segment connecting opposite vertices
Equilateral triangle	A triangle in which all sides have equal length and each angle measures 60°
Inscribed (angle in a circle)	An angle in a circle with its vertex on the circumference
Isosceles triangle	A triangle with two equal side lengths
Parallel	Two distinct lines that do not intersect
Perpendicular	At a 90° angle
Plane	A flat surface extending in all directions
Polygon	A closed figure with three or more sides
Quadrilateral	A four-sided figure
Regular polygon	A figure with all sides equal in length and all angle measures equal
Sector	Any part of the area formed by two radii and the outside of the circle
Similar	Having equal angle measures and proportional sides
Surface area	The sum of the areas of each face of a figure
Tangent	Intersecting at one point
Vertex/Vertices	A corner point. For angles, it's where two rays meet. For figures, it's where two adjacent sides meet.

Geometry Drill

4. In △ABC shown, the measure of ∠A is equal to the measure of ∠B, and the measure of ∠C is twice the measure of ∠B. What is the measure, in degrees, of ∠A?

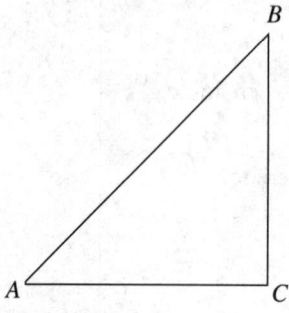

- **F.** 30
- **G.** 45
- **H.** 50
- **J.** 90

5. In the figure shown, $l_1 \parallel l_2$. Which of the labeled angles must have equal measure?

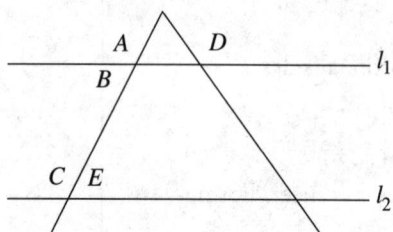

- **A.** A and C
- **B.** A and B
- **C.** D and B
- **D.** C and B

7. If the area of circle A is 16π, then what is the circumference of circle B if its radius is $\frac{1}{2}$ that of circle A?

- **A.** 2π
- **B.** 4π
- **C.** 6π
- **D.** 8π

12. In the figure shown, right triangles ABC and ACD are drawn as shown. If AB = 20, BC = 15, and AD = 7, what is CD?

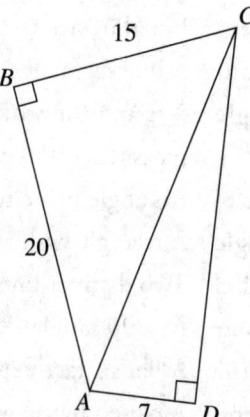

- **F.** 21
- **G.** 22
- **H.** 24
- **J.** 25

19. In the figure shown, $\overline{MO}$ is perpendicular to $\overline{LN}$, LO is equal to 4, MO is equal to ON, and LM is equal to 6. What is MN?

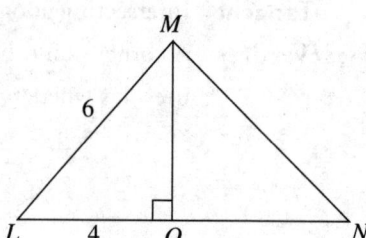

- **A.** $2\sqrt{10}$
- **B.** $3\sqrt{5}$
- **C.** $4\sqrt{5}$
- **D.** $3\sqrt{10}$

21. A rectangular box has a base measuring a by a meters and height of b meters. Which of the following represents the surface area of the box?

A. $6ab$

B. $a^2 + 2ab$

C. $2a(a + 2b)$

D. $2(a^2 + b^2)$

22. Points A and B lie on a circle with center O. If the length of minor arc AB is 2π and $\angle AOB = 45°$, what is the area of the circle?

F. 8π

G. 16π

H. 32π

J. 64π

41. In the figure shown, O is the center of the circle, $XY = OZ$, and $YZ = 4\sqrt{3}$. What is the length of minor arc YZ?

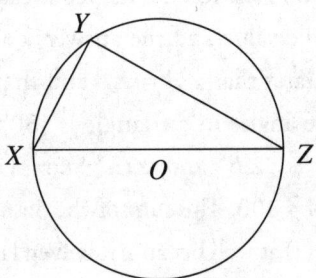

A. $\dfrac{8}{3}\pi$

B. $\dfrac{16}{3}\pi$

C. 8π

D. $4\pi\sqrt{3}$

GEOMETRY DRILL ANSWERS AND EXPLANATIONS

4. **G** The question asks for the degree measure of an angle in a given triangle. Since the question asks for a specific value and the answers contain numbers in increasing order, plug in the answers. The question states that $\angle A = \angle B$ and that $\angle C$ is equal to twice $\angle B$. Additionally, remember that the sum of the angles in a triangle is 180°. Begin by labeling the answers "$\angle A$." Create additional columns labeled "$\angle B$" and "$\angle C$." Start with (H), which indicates $\angle A = 50$. Therefore, $\angle B = 50$, and $\angle C = 2(50) = 100$. The sum of the 3 angles is $50 + 50 + 100 = 200$. This is too large; eliminate (H). Eliminate (J) as well because it is even larger. Repeating the process for (G) gives the values of $\angle A = 45$, $\angle B = 45$, and $\angle C = 2(45) = 90$. The sum of these angles is $45 + 45 + 90 = 180$. This matches the number of degrees in a triangle, so stop here. The correct answer is (G).

5. **A** The question asks which angles are equal in measure. Use the Geometry Basic Approach: start by writing all information given in the problem on the figure. Mark lines l_1 and l_2 as parallel. When parallel lines are crossed by another line, called a transversal, BIG and SMALL angles are created. The BIG angles are equal to other BIG angles, and SMALL angles are equal to other SMALL angles. However, in this figure there are 2 different transversals that cross the parallel lines, and it cannot be assumed that BIG or SMALL angles from one transversal are equal to BIG or SMALL angles formed by the other. Since D is the only angle labeled on the transversal on the right, it will not always be equal to any angle from the other transversal. Eliminate (C) for this reason. Since the answer choices are providing pairs of angles, start with (A) and eliminate any answers that are not always true. Choice (A) says A and C are equal. A and C are both angles formed by the same transversal crossing l_1 and l_2 and are both BIG angles. Therefore, they are always equal in measure. Keep (A), and check the remaining answers just in case. Choices (B) and (D) both mention a BIG angle and a SMALL angle; eliminate (B) and (D) for that reason. The correct answer is (A).

7. **B** The question asks for the circumference of a circle given the area of another circle and the relationship of their radii. Use the Geometry Basic Approach and start by drawing 2 circles, A and B, and labeling the area of circle A as 16π.

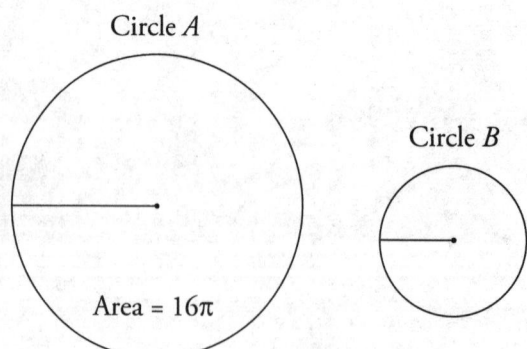

Circle A

Circle B

Area = 16π

Next, write down the formulas related to circles: area is $A = \pi r^2$, and circumference is $C = 2\pi r$. Note that the formulas have the radius in common, so start by solving for the radius of circle A. Plug in the known area to get $16\pi = \pi r^2$; then divide both sides by π to get $16 = r^2$. Take the square root of both sides to get $4 = r$ for circle A. The question states that the radius of circle B is $\frac{1}{2}$ that of the radius of circle A, so the radius of circle B is $\frac{1}{2}(4) = 2$. Label both radii on the figure, which now looks like this:

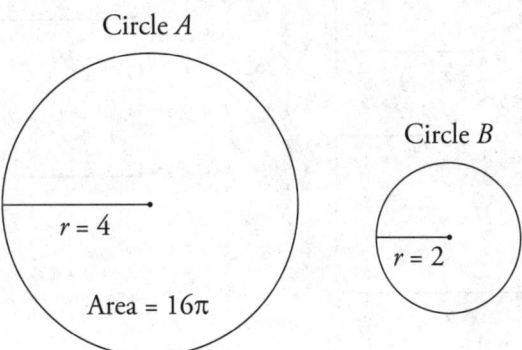

Now plug that value into the formula for the circumference to get $C = 2\pi(2) = 4\pi$ for circle B. The correct answer is (B).

12. **H** The question asks for the length of the side of a right triangle. To find side CD, the length of side AC is needed. The two triangles share side AC, and the right triangle ABC has 2 known sides, so use the Pythagorean Theorem, $a^2 + b^2 = c^2$, or Pythagorean triples, to find side AC. The Pythagorean Theorem gives $AB^2 + BC^2 = AC^2$, which becomes $20^2 + 15^2 = AC^2$, then $400 + 225 = AC^2$. This simplifies to $625 = AC^2$, so $AC = 25$. Triangle ABC is also the Pythagorean triple 3-4-5 multiplied by 5. Knowing Pythagorean triples can help solve for sides more quickly than using the Pythagorean Theorem, but using the theorem is always an option. Label side $AC = 25$ and note that there is another Pythagorean triple for triangle ACD, 7-24-25, or use the Pythagorean Theorem again to find side $CD = 24$. The correct answer is (H).

19. **A** The question asks for the length of the side of a triangle. Use the Geometry Basic Approach and write all information given in the problem on the figure. For this question, label MO equal to ON. Triangles LMO and MON share side MO. There is enough information for triangle LMO to solve for the length of side MO, which can then be used to find hypotenuse MN. Use the Pythagorean Theorem to find that the length of MO is $LO^2 + MO^2 = LM^2$, which becomes $4^2 + MO^2 = 6^2$. This simplifies to $16 + MO^2 = 36$, so $MO^2 = 20$ and $MO = \sqrt{20}$. This value for MO could be simplified, but only do so if it becomes necessary to answer the question. Since $MO = ON = \sqrt{20}$, use the Pythagorean Theorem a second time to get $ON^2 + MO^2 = MN^2$. This becomes $\left(\sqrt{20}\right)^2 + \left(\sqrt{20}\right)^2 = MN^2$, which becomes $20 + 20 = MN^2$. Therefore, $MN^2 = 40$ and $MN = \sqrt{40} = 2\sqrt{10}$. The correct answer is (A).

21.   **C**   The question asks for the surface area of a rectangular box. Use the Geometry Basic Approach and draw a figure. The surface area of a geometric figure is the sum of the areas of its faces, so draw one face with dimensions $a \times a$ and two faces with dimensions $a \times b$.

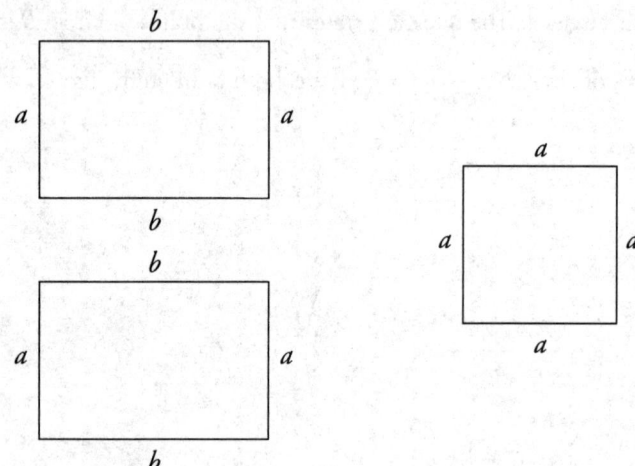

Next, write down the formula for the surface area of a rectangular solid: $S = 2(lw + lh + wh)$. Since there are variables in the answer choices, plug in values and make $a = 2$ and $b = 3$. Relabel the figure with these numbers.

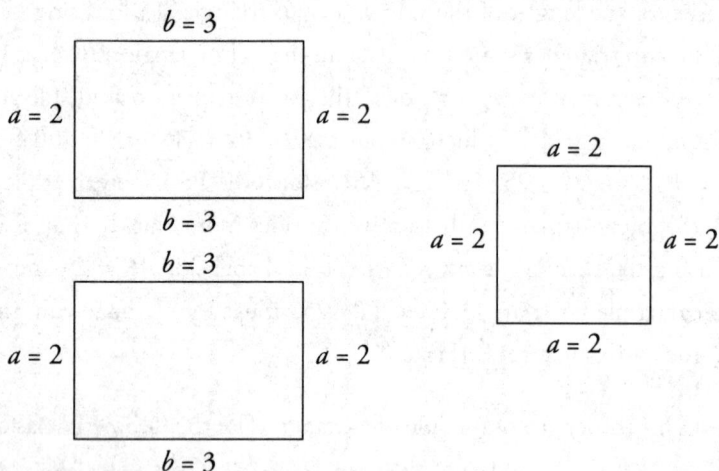

The surface area becomes $S = 2[(2)(2) + (2)(3) + (2)(3)] = 2(4 + 6 + 6) = 2(16) = 32$. This is the target value; circle it. Now plug $a = 2$ and $b = 3$ into the answer choices to see which one matches the target value. Choice (A) becomes $6(2)(3) = 36$; this does not match the target, so eliminate (A). Choice (B) becomes $(2)^2 + 2(2)(3) = 4 + 12 = 16$. Eliminate (B). Choice (C) becomes $2(2)[2 + 2(3)] = 4[2 + 6] = 4(8) = 32$. Keep (C), but check the remaining answer just in case. Choice (D) becomes $2(2^2 + 3^2) = 2(4 + 9) = 2(13) = 26$. Eliminate (D). The correct answer is (C).

22.   **J**   The question asks for the area of the circle. Use the Geometry Basic Approach and start by drawing a circle with center O and points A and B on the circle. Draw in the radii AO and BO and label the angle AOB as 45° and the arc AB as 2π. The figure should look something like this:

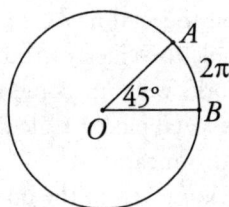

Next, write down the formula for the area of a circle: $A = \pi r^2$. The arc of a circle is related to the total circumference with the relationship $\dfrac{central\ angle}{360°} = \dfrac{arc}{2\pi r}$. Fill in the information given to get $\dfrac{45°}{360°} = \dfrac{2\pi}{2\pi r}$. Simplify both sides to get $\dfrac{1}{8} = \dfrac{1}{r}$, or $r = 8$. Plug $r = 8$ into the area formula to get $A = \pi(8)^2$, which is 64π. The correct answer is (J).

41.   **A**   The question asks for the length of minor arc YZ. Use the Geometry Basic Approach and start by drawing the figure if needed. Label $XY = OZ$ and YZ as $4\sqrt{3}$. Next, write down the relationship between the arc of a circle and the total circle: $\dfrac{central\ angle}{360°} = \dfrac{arc}{2\pi r}$. Work in bite-sized pieces to determine the central angle. All radii of a circle are the same, so $OX = OZ = XY$. Because XZ is the diameter of circle O and Y is the vertex of the triangle on the same circle, angle $Y = 90°$. The hypotenuse XZ is twice the leg XY, so the triangle is a 30-60-90 special triangle, with angle $Z = 30°$ and angle $X = 60°$. (The side length of XY having $\sqrt{3}$ is a clue that this triangle may be a 30-60-90.) In a 30-60-90 triangle, the side opposite the 60° angle is $s\sqrt{3}$, so XY is $4\sqrt{3} = s\sqrt{3}$. Divide both sides by $\sqrt{3}$ to find that $s = 4$. Label XY, OX, and OZ as 4. The radius of the circle is also 4. To find the central angle for arc YZ, draw in OY. Because OY and OZ are radii of the same circle, triangle OYZ is isosceles. Because angle Z is 30°, angle OYZ is also 30°. A triangle has 180°, so angle $YOZ = 180 - 30 - 30 = 120°$. Plug 120° as the central angle and $r = 4$ into the proportion above and solve: $\dfrac{120°}{360°} = \dfrac{x}{2\pi(4)}$, which simplifies to $\dfrac{1}{3} = \dfrac{x}{8\pi}$. Cross-multiply to get $3x = 8\pi$. Divide both sides by 3 to find that minor arc $YZ = \dfrac{8}{3}\pi$. The correct answer is (A).

Summary

- o   Use the Basic Approach.
  - **Step 1:** Know the question. Read the whole problem before calculating anything and underline (on the Paper ACT) or highlight (on the Online ACT) the actual question.
  - **Step 2:** Let the answers help. Look for clues on how to solve and ways to use Process of Elimination (POE). Ballparking works well on geometry questions on area and angles.
  - **Step 3:** Break the question into bite-sized pieces. Calculate at each step necessary and watch out for tricky phrasing. On geometry, this means:
    - o   **Step 3a:** Write all the information given in the question on the figure. If there is no figure, draw your own. On the Online ACT, redraw any figures given in the question.
    - o   **Step 3b:** Write down any formulas you need and fill in any information you have.

- Don't forget that you can plug in on geometry questions that have variables in the answer choices.

- Refer to pages 305–310 for a complete list of facts and formulas needed for ACT geometry.

Chapter 17
Word Problems

Now that you've refreshed some of the essential fundamentals and geometry topics and learned some alternatives to algebra, we will see how to integrate those concepts with your test-taking strategy. In addition, we'll see some other word problem strategies that will help you to answer questions quickly and accurately.

WORD PROBLEMS VS. PLUG-AND-CHUG QUESTIONS

We prefer a simple definition of a word problem: it has enough words to complicate working the problem (whether or not ACT thinks it's a "Modeling" question). We worked through some Geometry word problems in Chapter 16, but let's review the word problem Basic Approach again.

STEP 1 ≫

Step 1: Know the Question

Read the whole problem before calculating anything, and underline or highlight the actual question.

STEP 2 ≫

Step 2: Let the Answers Help

Look for clues on how to solve and ways to use POE.

STEP 3 ≫

Step 3: Break the Question into Bite-Sized Pieces

Calculate at each step necessary and watch out for tricky phrasing.

ARITHMETIC

When it comes to writing word problems, ACT test-writers can draw on both algebra and geometry, as we've seen. But lots of word problems, and even some plug-and-chugs, will test a variety of arithmetic concepts. The rest of this chapter will review those topics.

PERCENTAGES, PROBABILITIES, AND RATIOS: DIDN'T WE JUST DO THIS?

Percentages, probabilities, and ratios can get mighty complex in your math classes at school. Do you want the good news or the bad news? Well, the bad news is that ratios, percentages, and probabilities will all appear on the ACT Math test, but the good news is that they're all testing the same basic concept: parts to wholes.

Let's say you're taking batting practice. You are thrown 100 pitches and hit 20 of them. Ignoring the fact that you're probably not ready for major league baseball, let's put this into some math language. Once we get the basics down, we'll try some more advanced concepts.

First, what percentage of the pitches did you hit? Well, that's an easy one because we're dealing with 100. But you can always find percentages with this simple part-to-whole formula:

$$\frac{part}{whole} \times 100\%$$

Once we put the numbers in, we'll get this: $\frac{20}{100} \times 100\% = 0.2 \times 100\% = 20\%$. If you hit 20 of the 100 pitches, you hit 20% of them.

Next, what is the probability that you were to hit any given pitch? Remember, this is just a matter of parts to wholes, so we can find this probability as follows: $\frac{part}{whole} = \frac{hits}{pitches} = \frac{20}{100} = 0.2$. In other words, there's a 0.2, or $\frac{1}{5}$, probability you hit any given pitch during batting practice.

Ratios are a little different. Usually these will ask for the relationship of some part to some other part. If we're still using our batting practice statistics, we might want to know something like, what's the ratio of the pitches you hit to the pitches you missed?

Even though we're not dealing with the whole this time, we'll find the ratio the same way, but instead of $\frac{part}{whole}$, we'll use $\frac{part}{part} = \frac{hits}{misses} = \frac{20}{80} = \frac{1}{4}$. The ratio of hits to misses is $\frac{1}{4}$, or 1 to 4, or 1:4.

If it feels like we just did the same thing three times, it was supposed to. As we've seen a few times already, just because things have different names doesn't mean that they are unrelated. Let's try some questions.

Percentages

19. A restaurant offers a 10% discount to first-time customers. If a first-time customer orders a meal regularly priced at $18 and pays a delivery fee equal to 15% of the discounted meal, how much does the customer pay for the meal, not including tax or tip?

    A. $13.50
    B. $18.63
    C. $18.90
    D. $20.70

Here's How to Crack It

Step 1: Know the question. We want the price of the discounted meal plus the delivery fee.

Step 2: Let the answers help. We are reducing a number by 10% and then increasing it by 15%, so it's not likely that the final number will be much less or much greater than $18. Let's eliminate (A) and (D).

Step 3: Break the question into bite-sized pieces.

First, we'll need to figure out what the discounted price of the meal is. There are a number of ways to do this, but if you find this $\frac{part}{whole}$ method useful, you could find the discount this way:

$$10\% = discount$$

$$\frac{10}{100} = \frac{discount}{\$18}$$

$$discount = \$1.80$$

The price of the discounted meal, then, is $18 − $1.80 = $16.20. Let's find the delivery fee the same way.

$$15\% = delivery\ fee$$

$$\frac{15}{100} = \frac{delivery\ fee}{\$16.20}$$

$$delivery\ fee = \$2.43$$

The price of the discounted meal plus delivery fee, therefore, is $16.20 + $2.43 = $18.63. The correct answer is (B).

Another Way to Deal with Percents

A percentage is a fraction in which the denominator equals 100. In literal terms, the word *percent* means "divided by 100," so any time you see a percentage in an ACT question, you can punch it into your calculator quite easily. If a question asks for 40 percent of something, for instance, you can express the percentage as a fraction: $\frac{40}{100}$. Any time you are looking for a percent, you can use your calculator to find the decimal equivalent and multiply the result by 100. If four out of five dentists recommend a particular brand of toothpaste, you can quickly determine the percent of doctors who recommend it by typing (4/5) × 100 and hitting the

ENTER key. The resulting "80" just needs a percent sign tacked onto it. To properly translate all percent questions, it is helpful to have a decoding table for the various terms you'll come across.

English	Math Equivalent
percent	divide by 100
of	multiplication (×)
what	variable (*x*, *y*, *z*)
is, are, were, did, does	=
what percent	$\dfrac{x}{100}$

Percentage Shortcuts

In the last question, we could have saved a little time if we had realized that $\dfrac{1}{5} = 20$ percent. Therefore, $\dfrac{4}{5}$ would be 4×20 percent, or 80 percent. In the gray box, you'll find some fractions and decimals whose percent equivalents you should know.

Another fast way to do percents is to move the decimal place. To find 10 percent of any number, move the decimal point of that number over one place to the left.

$$10\% \text{ of } 500 = 50$$

$$10\% \text{ of } 50 = 5$$

$$10\% \text{ of } 5 = 0.5$$

To find 1 percent of a number, move the decimal point of that number over two places to the left.

$$1\% \text{ of } 500 = 5$$

$$1\% \text{ of } 50 = 0.5$$

$$1\% \text{ of } 5 = 0.05$$

> **The Big Four: Fraction/Percent Equivalents You Should Know**
>
> $$\frac{1}{5} = 0.2 = 20\%$$
>
> $$\frac{1}{4} = 0.25 = 25\%$$
>
> $$\frac{1}{3} = 0.\overline{33} = 33\frac{1}{3}\%$$
>
> $$\frac{1}{2} = 0.5 = 50\%$$

You can use a combination of these last two techniques to find even very complicated percentages by breaking them down into easy-to-find chunks.

- 20% of 500: 10% of 500 = 50, so 20% is twice 50, or 100.
- 30% of 70: 10% of 70 = 7, so 30% is three times 7, or 21.
- 32% of 400: 10% of 400 = 40, so 30% is three times 40, or 120. 1% of 400 = 4, so 2% is two times 4, or 8. Therefore, 32 percent of 400 = 120 + 8 = 128.

Let's have a look at another ACT percentage question.

9. When 15% of 40 is added to 5% of 260, the resulting number is:

   A. 19
   B. 40
   C. 95
   D. 180

Here's How to Crack It

Let's try this one using the decoding table. Although this isn't a real-world scenario, there are enough words in this question that treating it as a word problem and breaking it into bite-sized pieces is the best approach.

First, 15% of 40. Remember, % translates to divide by 100, and "of" translates to multiplication. Therefore, we can rewrite 15% of 40 as $\frac{15}{100} \times 40$. Put this expression in your calculator to find that $\frac{15}{100} \times 40 = 6$.

Now, find 5% of 260. Use the same translations to find $\frac{5}{100} \times 260 = 13$. We've done the tough part, so let's substitute what we've found back into the question: *When 6 is added to 13, the resulting number is*: Now that's a question we can handle! 6 + 13 = 19, so the answer is (A).

Now let's look at a harder one that takes several percentages in a row.

43. An elementary school class just finished its annual fundraiser that it has been running for several years. The changes in the money earned from one year to the next for the fundraiser were a 10% decrease, a 45% increase, and a 20% decrease. What was the percent increase in the class's fundraising money over the last 3 years?

    A. 4.4%
    B. 15%
    C. 85%
    D. 95.6%

Here's How to Crack It

When faced with multiple percent changes, do each percent change calculation individually. Use the answer from the previous percent change calculation as the starting value for the next calculation. The difficulty here is that you aren't given the starting number! When dealing with a percent of an unknown total, what strategy do you use? Plugging In! The easiest number to plug in for a percent question is 100. If the class made $100 the first year, then it made 10% less, or 0.10(100) = $10 less the second year. Therefore, it made $100 − $10 = $90 the second year, and 45% more, or 0.45(90) = $40.50 more the third year. It made $90 + $40.50 = $130.50 the third year, and 20% less, or 0.20(130.50) = $26.10 less the final year. The final amount was $130.50 − $26.10 = $104.40. The difference between the starting amount and the final amount was $104.40 − $100 = $4.40, so the percent difference is $4.40 ÷ $100 = 0.044 or 4.4%. The correct answer is (A). Keep a close eye out for trap answers on questions about percentages. The ACT test-writers want you to forget that percents of different values give different results. If you just took −10 + 45 − 20, you would get 15. But that isn't how percents work, and (B) is there to trick you.

Probability

7. Herbie's practice bag contains 4 blue racquetballs, 1 red racquet-ball, and 6 green racquetballs. If he chooses a ball at random, which of the following is closest to the probability that the ball will **not** be green?

   A. 0.27
   B. 0.36
   C. 0.45
   D. 0.54

Here's How to Crack It

Step 1: Know the question. Make sure you read carefully! We want the probability that the chosen ball will **not** be green.

Step 2: Let the answers help. Green balls account for slightly more than half the number of balls in the bag, so the likelihood that the ball will **not** be green should be slightly less than half. That eliminates (A) and (D). Not bad!

Step 3: Break the question into bite-sized pieces. This is a pretty straightforward $\frac{part}{whole}$ question: $\frac{part}{whole} = \frac{not\ green}{all} = \frac{5}{11}$. The only slight difficulty is that the answers are not listed as fractions, but it's nothing a calculator can't help. Find $5 ÷ 11 ≈ 0.45$, (C).

Expected Value

Sometimes the ACT will ask about the "expected value" of the results of a situation. The expected value is based on both the values and the probability that those values will occur.

To find the expected value, multiply the value of each possible outcome by the probability that outcome will occur, then add those products together.

Here's what it looks like in practice:

---

40. Lovell the Magician creates a deck of 25 cards. The deck has cards numbered 2 through 9 in the following distribution:

Number on Card	# of Cards
2	3
3	3
4	1
5	3
6	4
7	4
8	4
9	3

An audience member draws a card at random from this deck. If the random variable c represents the number on the card drawn from the deck by the audience member, what is the expected value of c?

F. 0.16
G. 5
H. 5.8
J. 6

Here's How to Crack It

The question asks for the *expected value of* c. To find this, multiply the probability of drawing each card by the number on that card, then add those values together. The table does not provide the probability of drawing each card, so that must be found before the expected value can be calculated. Because there are 25 cards in the deck, divide the number of cards with a given number by 25 to determine the probability of drawing that card:

Number on Card	# of Cards	Probability
2	3	0.12
3	3	0.12
4	1	0.04
5	3	0.12
6	4	0.16
7	4	0.16
8	4	0.16
9	3	0.12

Next, multiply the probability for each card by the number on the card:

Number on Card	# of Cards	Probability	Number × Probability
2	3	0.12	0.24
3	3	0.12	0.36
4	1	0.04	0.16
5	3	0.12	0.60
6	4	0.16	0.96
7	4	0.16	1.12
8	4	0.16	1.28
9	3	0.12	1.08

Add those values together to determine the expected value: 0.24 + 0.36 + 0.16 + 0.60 + 0.96 + 1.12 + 1.28 + 1.08 = 5.8, which is (H).

———————————————○———————————————

Finally, ACT will occasionally test that the sum of all probabilities for a given situation will equal 1. We can see that in the above question: 0.12 + 0.12 + 0.04 + 0.12 + 0.16 + 0.16 + 0.16 + 0.12 = 1. If you see a table of probabilities, check to see if ACT is giving every possibility. If the sum of the probabilities is less than 1, there are values that ACT is not giving you.

Ratios

14. If the ratio of $2x$ to $5y$ is $\dfrac{1}{20}$, what is the ratio of x to y?

    F. $\dfrac{1}{40}$

    G. $\dfrac{1}{10}$

    H. $\dfrac{1}{8}$

    J. $\dfrac{1}{4}$

Here's How to Crack It

The difficulty of this question is all in the setup. Just remember that you're comparing parts to parts, and you'll be fine.

$$\frac{2x}{5y} = \frac{1}{20}$$

To isolate $\dfrac{x}{y}$ on the left side of this equation, let's multiply both sides of the equation by $\dfrac{5}{2}$.

$$\frac{5}{2} \times \frac{2x}{5y} = \frac{1}{20} \times \frac{5}{2}$$

$$\frac{x}{y} = \frac{5}{40}$$

$\dfrac{5}{40}$ reduces to $\dfrac{1}{8}$. The answer is (H).

If you got stuck on this one, look at those answer choices: you could've used PITA!

Let's see how ACT might test ratios in a word problem.

---

17. The ratio of boys to girls at the Milwood School is 4 to 5. If there are a total of 27 children at the school, how many boys attend the Milwood School?

    A.   4
    B.   9
    C.   12
    D.   14

Here's How to Crack It

Step 1: Know the question. It's in the last line: *how many boys attend the Milwood School?*

Step 2: Let the answers help. The answers are pretty close together, and they're all less than 27, so there isn't anything to cross out yet. But watch out for trap answers: if you can do something basic like add 4 and 5 to get 9, (B) is probably a trap.

Step 3: Break the question into bite-sized pieces. The question is about ratios, so remember that a ratio is a part-to-part relationship. That means the whole is missing but can be found. The ratio of 4 boys to 5 girls means we're dealing with groups of 9 children. Out of every 9 children, 4 are boys and 5 are girls, so $\frac{4}{9}$ are boys and $\frac{5}{9}$ are girls. The question states that *there are a total of 27 children at the school*, and $\frac{4}{9}(27) = 12$. There are 12 boys at the school, and (C) is correct.

You might have noticed another way to approach this question. The question asks for a specific value and the answers contain numbers in increasing order, so you can plug in the answers! Begin by labeling the answers as "number of boys" and start with (C), 12. If there are 27 children and 12 of them are boys, then there are 27 − 12 = 15 girls. The ratio of $\frac{12 \text{ boys}}{15 \text{ girls}}$ reduces to $\frac{4 \text{ boys}}{5 \text{ girls}}$. This matches the ratio given in the problem, so stop here. That gives you two ways to find the right answer.

Playing the Averages

Arithmetic mean—the average you're most familiar with: the total of all the values divided by the number of things.

Median—the one in the middle, like the median strip on the highway (when the numbers are arranged in ascending order).

Mode—you're looking for the element that appears most. Get it? MOde, MOst.

Range—how spread out the numbers are. Subtract the smallest number from the largest number.

AVERAGES

There are only three parts to any average question. Fortunately for you, the ACT must give you two of these parts, which are all you need to find the third. For any question about averages, use the formula $T = AN$, in which T is the total, A is the average, and N is the number of things.

For example, if you want to find the average of 9, 12, and 6, you know you have 3 items with a total of 27. The formula becomes $27 = A(3)$. You can divide both sides by 3 to find that $A = 9$.

Although you probably could have done that without the formula, more difficult average questions involve multiple calculations and lend themselves particularly well to using the formula. Let's take a look at one:

The Missing Number
The ACT loves to leave out totals on average questions. You aren't done until you've found it.

25. Over 9 games, a baseball team had an average of 8 runs per game. If the average number of runs for the first 7 games was 6 runs per game and the same number of runs was scored in each of the last 2 games, how many runs did the team score during the last game?

   A.   5
   B.   15
   C.   30
   D.   46

Here's How to Crack It
Step 1: Know the question. *How many runs did the team score during the last game?*

Step 2: Let the answers help. Eliminate (A). Since the average for the first 7 is lower than all 9, the runs scored in the last two games can't be that few. Similarly, (D) is probably too big. If you don't trust your sense of numbers and you're not comfortable Ballparking here, however, leave both. It's a complicated question on a more advanced topic.

Step 3: Break the question into bite-sized pieces. Let's use Bite-Sized Pieces to plug the information from the first line of this question into our trusty average formula. We get $T = (8)(9) = 72$.

Now let's put the information from the second line into the formula. We get $T = (6)(7) = 42$.

If the number of runs scored in all 9 games added up to 72 and those of 7 of these games added up to 42, then the number of runs scored in the remaining 2 games had a total of 72 – 42, or 30. In case you are feeling smug about getting this far, the ACT writers made 30 one of the answer choices.

But of course you know that they only want the runs scored in the last game. Because the same number of runs was scored in each of the last two games, the answer is $\frac{30}{2}$ or 15, (B).

Some ACT questions will combine several statistical concepts. Mean, median, mode, and range might appear in various combinations. When that happens, start with the easiest piece to calculate, use POE, and look for ways to ballpark.

Here's an example with all four at once.

---

16. A data set consists of the numbers 19, 24, 31, 32, 39, 39, and 48. If a negative number is added to the data set, the value of which of the following measures will change the most?

   F. Mean
   G. Median
   H. Mode
   J. Range

Here's How to Crack It

The question asks which measure will change the most when one value is added to a set of numbers. Use Process of Elimination to tackle this question and start with a measurement that is easy to calculate. The mode of a list of values is the value that occurs most often. The current mode of the data set is 39, and the mode will still be 39 if a new, negative number is added. The mode changes by 39 – 39 = 0.

The median of a list of numbers is the middle number when all values are arranged in order. In lists with an even number of items, the median is the average of the middle two numbers. Since there are 7 items, the current median is the fourth value, which is 32. Adding a new number will give the list 8 items, so the median will be the average of the fourth and fifth values. The new number is negative, so it will be the new first value and the fourth and fifth values will be 31 and 32, respectively. The new median is $\frac{31 + 32}{2} = 31.5$.

The median changes by 32 – 31.5 = 0.5. This is greater than the change in the mode, so eliminate (H).

Next, check the range. The range of a list of values is the greatest value minus the least value. The current greatest value is 48, and the least value is 19. That makes the current range 48 – 19 = 29. The new value isn't specified, but it is negative. Use –1 as the new least value to see what happens. The range would become 48 – (–1) = 49. The range changes by 49 – 29 = 20. A number smaller than –1 will make the range change by even more than 20. This is greater than the 0.5 change in the median, so eliminate (G).

Next, evaluate the mean, or average. For averages, use the formula $T = AN$, in which T is the total, A is the average, and N is the number of things. In the current list, the *Total* is 19 + 24 + 31 + 32 + 39 + 39 + 48 = 232. The *Number of things* is 7, so the *Average* is $\frac{232}{7} \approx 33$. Try –1 again for the new value. The new *Total* would be 232 + (– 1) = 231, and the new *Number of things* would be 8, making the new *Average* $\frac{231}{8} \approx 29$.

The change in average is 33 – 29 = 4. This is less than the change in range of 20, but try a much smaller negative number and compare the changes to the mean and range again. Make the new number –1,000. The mean becomes $\frac{-768}{8} = -96$, for a change in mean of 33 – (–96) = 129. The range becomes 48 – (–1,000) = 1,048, for a change in range of 1,048 – 29 = 1,019. This change in range is still larger than the change in mean, so eliminate (F). The correct answer is (J).

CHARTS AND GRAPHS

Since you are allowed to have a calculator with you when you take the ACT, more and more of the test has been composed of questions on which calculators are of little or no use, such as questions based on charts and graphs. On this type of question, your math skills aren't really being tested at all; what ACT is interested in is your ability to read a simple graph (a skill you will also use if you take the Science portion of the ACT). All of the questions we have seen in this format have been very direct. If you can read a simple graph, you can always get them right. What's most important on questions like these is paying attention to the labels on the information.

Let's take a look at a graph question.

—————————————————○—————————————————

17. Between which two months was the change in total rainfall the greatest?

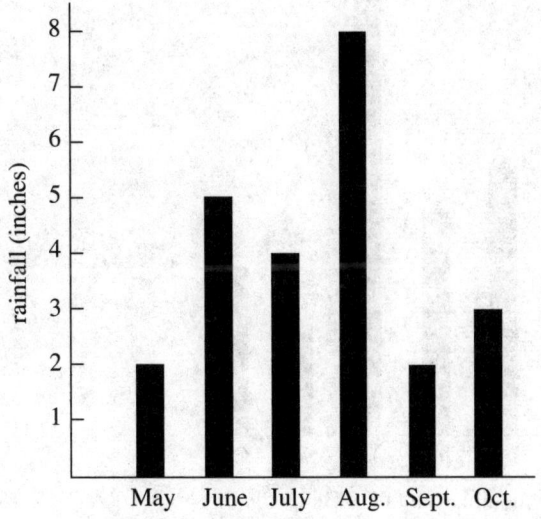

average monthly rainfall in Belleville, IL.

   A. May and June
   B. June and July
   C. July and August
   D. August and September

Here's How to Crack It

The ACT test-writers want to see if you can decipher the information presented in the graph. Before you read the question, then, you need to take a look at the graph. What is measured here? It says on the bottom: *Average monthly rainfall in Belleville, IL.* You should look at the values along the *x*-axis and *y*-axis of the graph as well. When you do, you'll see that the rain is measured in inches on the *y*-axis, and the measurements were made each month as indicated on the *x*-axis.

Now for the question. To determine which two months had the greatest change, we need to compare the change between each pair of months, discarding the smaller ones until we have only one left. The difference from May to June is about 3, and that's larger than June to July, so (B) is out. July to August is larger still, though, so (A) is out, leaving only (C) and (D). It should be pretty apparent that the August to September change is larger than the July to August change, though, so the correct answer must be (D).

—————————————————○—————————————————

Although most questions involving graphs on the Math test are this simple, you may see slightly more complicated variations. Here's another question based on the same bar graph.

18. Based on the information presented in the graph shown, what is the approximate average monthly rainfall, in inches, in Belleville, IL, for the period given?

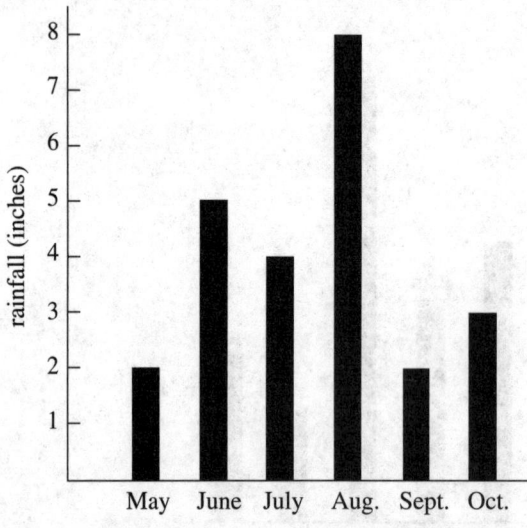

average monthly rainfall in Belleville, IL.

F. 2
G. 3
H. 4
J. 5

Here's How to Crack It

As with the last question, the first thing you want to do is examine the graph and figure out what information is being given to you and how it is being presented. Because you already did that for this graph, we'll skip that step on this one.

This question combines graph reading with average calculation, so the next thing you'll have to do is estimate the rainfall for each month. Because the question uses the word *approximate*, you don't have to worry too much about making super-exact measurements of the heights of the bar graphs. Eyeballing it and rounding to the closest value given on the left-hand side will be good enough to get you the right answer. Do that now before you read the next sentence.

To us, it looks like about 2 inches fell in May and September, and around 3 fell in October. July saw about 4, June roughly 5, and August about 8. Your estimates should be the same as ours. If they're not, go back now and figure out why not. You probably need to be a little more careful in your estimating. On the Paper ACT, you can use your answer sheet or a pencil as a guide. On the Online ACT, use your pencil or a finger (don't write on the screen!).

Now it's just a matter of calculating the average. Find the total first.

$$2 + 2 + 3 + 4 + 5 + 8 = 24$$

There are 6 months, so the formula $T = AN$ becomes $24 = A(6)$, and you just need to divide both sides by 6.

So the answer is 4, or (H).

ORDERING: CAN YOU SLOT ME IN?

Some ACT questions ask you how many different ways a number of things could be chosen or combined. The rules for ordering questions on the ACT are straightforward.

> **1.** Figure out the number of slots you need to fill.
> **2.** Fill in those slots.
> **3.** Find the product.

Seem confusing? It's not. Let's look at an example. This is what most ordering questions on the ACT will look like:

---

20. At the school cafeteria, students can choose from 3 different salads, 5 different main dishes, and 2 different desserts. If Isabel chooses one salad, one main dish, and one dessert for lunch, how many different lunches could she choose?

 F. 10
 G. 15
 H. 25
 J. 30

Here's How to Crack It

We've got three slots to fill here, one for each item: salad, main dish, dessert. And the number of possibilities for each is pretty clear. Set up the slots and take the product as your answer.

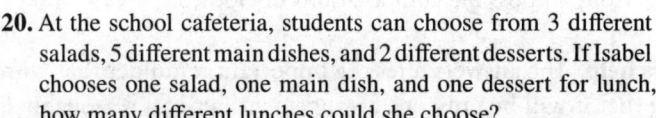

$$\underline{3} \times \underline{5} \times \underline{2} = 30$$
$$\text{Salad} \quad \text{Main} \quad \text{Dessert}$$

The correct answer here is (J).

On a more difficult question, you may run into a combination with more restricted elements. Just be sure to read the question carefully before attempting it. If the question makes your head spin, leave it and return to it later, or pick your Letter of the Day and move on.

―――――――――――○―――――――――――

Let's try one that tests a few things.

―――――――――――○―――――――――――

6. Elias has to select one shirt, one pair of pants, and one pair of shoes. If he selects at random from his 8 shirts, 4 pairs of pants, and 3 pairs of shoes, and all his shirts, pants, and shoes are different colors, what is the likelihood that he will select his red shirt, black pants, and brown shoes?

F. $\dfrac{1}{3}$

G. $\dfrac{1}{15}$

H. $\dfrac{1}{32}$

J. $\dfrac{1}{96}$

Here's How to Crack It

Step 1: Know the question. The question is asking what the probability is that he will select this one group of clothes from all possible combinations of clothes.

Step 2: Let the answers help. The answers offer the important reminder that we're looking for a probability. We know that it will be only one arrangement out of a reasonably large number of them, so we should at least get rid of (F).

Step 3: Break the question into bite-sized pieces. First, we should find the total number of possible combinations. Then, we can deal with the probability.

We have three slots to fill here, and we want to find the product of the three.

$$\underset{\text{Shirts}}{\underline{\quad 8 \quad}} \times \underset{\text{Pants}}{\underline{\quad 4 \quad}} \times \underset{\text{Shoes}}{\underline{\quad 3 \quad}} = 96 \text{ arrangements}$$

Of the 96 possible arrangements, an ensemble of red shirt, black pants, and brown shoes is only one. Therefore, we can go to our $\frac{part}{whole}$ ratio to find $\frac{part}{whole} = \frac{\text{red, black, brown}}{\text{ALL arrangements}} = \frac{1}{96}$, (J).

————————◯————————

Combinations and Permutations

Another type of ordering question on the ACT involves the terms *combinations* and *permutations*. The question might include the notation you see on your calculator: $_nC_r$ for combinations and $_nP_r$ for permutations, where n is the number of items available to choose from and r is the number of slots to fill. More often, the question will make you figure out that it's about a combination or permutation by using key words. What's important is to know the difference between combinations and permutations.

A combination is a grouping of elements in which order doesn't matter. For example, a group of 3 people—Erin, Sarah, and Alex—is the same group of 3 people if you put their names in alphabetical order: Alex, Erin, and Sarah.

> **Order in the Question**
> **Combination** = Group = Order doesn't matter
>
> **Permutation** = Arrangement = Order matters

Permutations, on the other hand, are groupings in which the order does matter. For example, if Erin plays first base, Sarah plays second base, and Alex plays third base, that's a different arrangement than if Alex plays first base, Erin plays second base, and Sarah plays third base.

Let's see what this looks like in practice.

————————◯————————

40. The verification code for a website is a four-digit number. Each digit can be anything from 1 to 9, inclusive, but the same digit cannot be used twice. The total number of possible codes can be calculated using which of the following expressions?

  F. (4)(3)(2)(1)

  G. 9(4)

  H. $\dfrac{(9)(8)(7)(6)}{(4)(3)(2)(1)}$

  J. (9)(8)(7)(6)

Here's How to Crack It

The question is asking for the number of ways to arrange four digits to form a verification code. Because code 1234 is not the same as code 4231, order matters and this is a permutation. You might know how to do this on your calculator, but let's use the method from earlier of filling in slots. The verification code has four digits, so draw four slots:

___   ___   ___   ___

The first digit can be anything from 1 through 9, so there are 9 options for the first digit. Fill that in.

9   ___   ___   ___

The question states that the same digit cannot be used twice, and one digit has already been used, so there are 8 options for the second digit. Now two digits have been used, so there are 7 options for the third digit. Keep going, and there are 6 options for the fourth digit. The slots are now filled.

9   8   7   6

Take the product as usual.

9 × 8 × 7 × 6

Because this is a permutation, stop here. If the order did not matter, the next step would be to divide by the factorial of the number of spaces, essentially dividing out the ways to arrange the four digits once they're chosen. Be wary: (H) is in this form, but order matters so we need the permutation, not the combination. The correct answer is (J).

○

Sometimes, the answer choices will use the $_nC_r$ and $_nP_r$ notation discussed above. With these questions, use Bite-Sized Pieces and POE.

○

Permutations, Combinations, and Factorials

Occasionally, the equations for $_nC_r$ and $_nP_r$ notation will appear in questions. The equations are

$$_nC_r = \frac{n!}{r!(n-r)!}$$

$$_nP_r = \frac{n!}{(n-r)!}$$

The exclamation mark represents factorial; see the next page for more about factorials.

41. A coach is choosing a starting lineup for a hockey team. The starting lineup is made up of 3 forwards, 2 defenders, and 1 goalie. If the team has 10 forwards, 6 defenders, and 2 goalies available, how many different starting lineups are possible?

A. $_{18}C_6$
B. $_{18}P_6$
C. $(_{10}C_3)(_6C_2)(_2C_1)$
D. $(_{10}P_3)(_6P_2)(_2P_1)$

Here's How to Crack It

Step 1: Know the question. The question asks for the number of possible starting lineups.

Step 2: Let the answers help. The answer choices are using $_nC_r$ and $_nP_r$ notation. We don't need to determine a numerical answer for this question; rather, we need to use Bite-Sized Pieces to eliminate answers.

Step 3: Break the question into bite-sized pieces. First, we should determine whether order matters. Consider the forwards alone. If players A, B, and C are chosen, that is the same as players B, C, and A being chosen, so order does not matter. Eliminate (B) and (D) because they use permutations, not combinations. Next, determine what the different groups are. Here, the players aren't chosen as a whole; rather, the players are chosen based on position. We must multiply the different groups together. Taking forwards again, there are 10 possible forwards, and 3 will be chosen. This makes $n = 10$ and $r = 3$, so that term should be $_{10}C_3$. Eliminate (A), as it does not include that term. The correct answer is (C).

Finally, you will encounter questions using factorials, which use the exclamation point ("!"). Factorials are calculated by multiplying the number by every positive integer less than that number. For instance, $4! = 4 \times 3 \times 2 \times 1 = 24$ and $6! = 6 \times 5 \times 4 \times 3 \times 2 \times 1 = 720$. Factorials appear in the formulas for permutations and combinations (see above for those formulas), but occasionally ACT will test factorials directly.

32. If n is an integer and $n \geq 2$, $\dfrac{n!}{n(n-2)!} =$

   F. $(n-1)!$
   G. $(n-3)!$
   H. n
   J. $n-1$

Here's How to Crack It

There is a variable in the question and answer choices, so plug in. n must be an integer greater than or equal to 2, so make $n = 4$. The expression becomes $\dfrac{4!}{4(4-2)!}$, which is $\dfrac{4!}{4(2)!}$. Either use your calculator (on the TI-80 series, factorials are found under MATH -> PRB) or expand: $\dfrac{4!}{4(2)!} = \dfrac{(4)(3)(2)(1)}{(4)(2)(1)}$, which is $\dfrac{24}{8}$ or 3. This is the target value, so circle it. Next, make $n = 4$ in each answer choice. Choice (F) becomes $(4-1)!$, which is 3! or $(3)(2)(1) = 6$. This is not 3; eliminate (F). Choice (G) becomes $(4-3)!$, which is 1! or 1; eliminate (G). 4 is not equal to 3, so eliminate (H). Check (J) to be sure: $4 - 1$ does equal 3. The correct answer is (J).

PATTERNS

A pattern as it is used on the ACT is a sequence or grouping of numbers that increases or decreases in a predictable way. There are two types of common sequences that the ACT tests. The first is an arithmetic sequence, a sequence with a constant difference between subsequent terms. The second is a geometric sequence, a sequence with a constant ratio between subsequent terms.

Arithmetic and Geometric Sequences

> **Patterns**
>
> **Arithmetic sequence**—add or subtract by the same value
>
> **Geometric sequence**—multiply or divide by the same value

Arithmetic sequence examples:

$$2, 7, 12, 17, 22\ldots$$

Each term in this sequence is found by adding 5 to the previous term.

$$19, 17, 15, 13, 11\ldots$$

Each term in this sequence is found by subtracting 2 from the previous term.

Geometric sequence examples:

$$2, 8, 32, 128, 512\ldots$$

Each term in this sequence is found by multiplying the previous term by 4.

$$1{,}380;\ -230;\ 38\frac{1}{3};\ -6\frac{7}{18}\ldots$$

Each term in this sequence is found by dividing the previous term by –6.

Let's explore a question dealing with an arithmetic sequence.

10. In January, a diner donated 300 meals to the local food bank. In February, the same diner donated 323 meals, and in March, the diner donated 346 meals. If the number of meals the diner donates each month increases by a constant amount, how many meals will the diner donate in July?

    F.   392
    G.   415
    H.   438
    J.   461

Here's How to Crack It

The question states that the number of meals donated each month increases by a constant amount. That means there is a sequence being represented in the question, and since the amount is constant, the sequence is an arithmetic sequence. Look at the number of donations in January. Comparing that to the number of meals donated in February gives you the difference, so calculate $323 - 300 = 23$ meals. Now that you know the difference between months, you can use that information to determine the number of meals donated in July. The last month the question told you about is March, which was 346 meals, so add 23 to determine how many meals were donated in April: $346 + 23 = 369$. Add another 23 for May: $369 + 23 = 392$; June: $392 + 23 = 415$; and July: $415 + 23 = 438$. The correct answer is (H).

If there was more space between the terms, such as asking for the number in July three years from now, it wouldn't make sense to do each addition individually; it is way too time consuming for the ACT. There's a shortcut you can use to make this type of calculation faster. Let's look at how to do that when asked, "What is the 89th term of an arithmetic sequence whose fifth and sixth terms are 12 and 15, respectively?"

This question is nice because the terms that were provided are right next to each other. It's very easy to find the constant difference in this arithmetic sequence: $15 - 12 = 3$.

But the next part of the process can be tricky. Finding the 89th term will be very time-consuming if you have to add $15 + 3 = 18$, $18 + 3 = 21$,…all the way up to the 89th term.

Let's make it easier by finding the number of "jumps" you take from the sixth term to the 89th term. To do so, subtract $89 - 6 = 83$. In this sequence, we would need to add 3 a total of 83 times, which is an additional $3 \times 83 = 249$ added to the sixth term of the sequence: $15 + 249 = 264$. The 89th term of the sequence is 264.

Let's try a question dealing with a geometric sequence.

41. In a geometric sequence whose second term is $\dfrac{6}{5}$ and fifth term is $\dfrac{1{,}296}{5}$, what is the first term?

    A. $-\dfrac{12}{5}$

    B. $-\dfrac{6}{5}$

    C. $\dfrac{1}{6}$

    D. $\dfrac{1}{5}$

Here's How to Crack It

This question gave us the second and fifth term of a geometric sequence. In a geometric sequence, the ratio between each term is constant, so you need to determine what that ratio is.

First, let's find the ratio between the second and fifth terms: $\dfrac{\frac{1{,}296}{5}}{\frac{6}{5}} = \dfrac{1{,}296}{6} = 216$. Now take a look at how many "jumps" there are between the second and fifth terms.

		$\dfrac{6}{5}$			$\dfrac{1{,}296}{5}$
term #	1st	2nd	3rd	4th	5th

In order to move from the second term to the fifth term, you would have multiplied each term by the ratio three times. Mathematically, if c is the ratio, the formula would be $\dfrac{6}{5} \times c \times c \times c = \dfrac{1{,}296}{5}$, which can also be written as $\dfrac{6}{5}c^3 = \dfrac{1{,}296}{5}$. You already determined that to get from the second term, $\dfrac{6}{5}$, to the fifth term, $\dfrac{1{,}296}{5}$, you need to multiply by 216, which is the same as c^3. Set $216 = c^3$ and solve to get $c = 6$. Now you know that to get from one term to the next you multiply it by 6. The question asks for the first term. You are given the second term and asked for the first, moving backward in the sequence. Therefore, you need to do the opposite of multiplication: divide the second term, $\frac{6}{5}$, by 6 to get $\frac{\frac{6}{5}}{6} = \frac{1}{5}$. The first term of the sequence is $\frac{1}{5}$, which is (D).

The above solution might seem a little complicated. What you hopefully discovered from the solution above is that when you find the ratio between non-subsequent terms in a geometric sequence and the difference between the term numbers, that is enough information to find the ratio for your geometric sequence. And don't forget to use your POOD and skip questions like this one if you are running short on time!

———————————◯———————————

Word Problems Drill

5. In the process of milling grain, 3% of the original is lost because of spillage, and another 5% of the original is lost because of mildew. If the mill starts out with 490 tons of grain, how much (in tons) remains to be sold after milling?

    A. 420.5
    B. 425
    C. 440
    D. 450.8

12. Aubrie computed the average of her six biology test scores by mistakenly adding the totals of five scores and dividing by five, giving her an average score of 88. When Aubrie realized her error, she recalculated and included the sixth test score of 82. What is the average of Aubrie's six biology tests?

    F. 85
    G. 86
    H. 87
    J. 88

13. If a 3-pound bag of flour costs 5 dollars, which of the following best approximates the cost of flour in cents per ounce?

    (Note: 1 pound = 16 ounces)

    A. 1.7
    B. 5.3
    C. 8.0
    D. 10.4

21. In the word HAWKS, how many ways is it possible to rearrange the letters if none repeat and the letter W must go last?

    A. 15
    B. 24
    C. 120
    D. 650

22. The starting team of a baseball club has 9 members who have an average of 12 home runs apiece for the season. The second-string team for the baseball club has 7 members who have an average of 8 home runs apiece for the season. What is the average number of home runs for the starting team and the second-string team combined?

    F. 8
    G. 10
    H. 10.25
    J. 14.2

34. An arcade game requires the participant to drop quarters into the machine; each quarter dropped into the machine will in turn push several quarters off the edge of a ledge, and the participant will win that many quarters. For each quarter dropped into the machine, the chance of a certain number of quarters falling off the ledge is represented in the table shown. What is the expected number of quarters a participant will win for each quarter dropped into the machine?

# of Quarters	Probability
0	0.5
1	0.3
2	0.15
3	0.03
4	0.02

    F. 0
    G. 0.15
    H. 0.77
    J. 1

37. There are 7 terms in a finite arithmetic sequence, and the first term is 11. Which of the following is true about the median and the mean of the 7 terms?

    A. The median is 11 more than the mean.
    B. The median and the mean are equal.
    C. The median is 11 less than the mean.
    D. The median is 7 less than the mean.

38. An integer from 299 through 1,000, inclusive, will be chosen randomly. What is the probability that the number chosen will have 1 as at least 1 of its digits?

    F. $\dfrac{234}{1,000}$

    G. $\dfrac{134}{702}$

    H. $\dfrac{70}{702}$

    J. $\dfrac{17}{702}$

WORD PROBLEMS DRILL ANSWERS AND EXPLANATIONS

5. **D** The question asks for the remaining amount of grain after some grain is lost. Read carefully to note that both percentages are of the original weight. Work in bite-sized pieces; start by calculating the 3% lost to spillage from the original weight of 490 tons to get $\frac{3}{100}(490) = 14.7$ tons lost. Now calculate the amount lost to mildew, 5%, of the original weight of 490 tons to get $\frac{5}{100}(490) = 24.5$ tons lost. The total amount of the original lost in the milling process is $14.7 + 24.5 = 39.2$ tons lost. Subtract that from the original weight to get $490 - 39.2 = 450.8$ tons left to sell. The correct answer is (D).

12. **H** The question asks about the average of a set of numbers and gives information about how the set relates to another set. For averages, use the formula $T = AN$, in which T is the total, A is the average, and N is the number of things. Calculate the total of the original set of 5 tests. The *Average* is 88 and the *Number of things* is 5, so the *Total* = $(88)(5) = 440$. The new set adds in the missed test score. To calculate a new total number of points, add the total number of points from the 5 tests to the points from the 6th test to get $440 + 82 = 522$. To find the new average, plug these numbers back into the $T = AN$ formula to get $522 = A(6)$. Divide both sides of the equation by 6 to get $A = \frac{522}{6} = 87$. The correct answer is (H).

13. **D** The question asks for a measurement and gives conflicting units. When dealing with different units of measure, make a proportion, being sure to match up units. The question gives the cost of a 3-pound bag of flour and states that 1 pound is 16 ounces. Set up a proportion to convert pounds to ounces: $\frac{1 \text{ pound}}{16 \text{ ounces}} = \frac{3 \text{ pounds}}{x \text{ ounces}}$. Cross-multiply to get $x = 48$ ounces. Next, convert the cost in dollars to the cost in cents. The bag of flour costs 5 dollars, and there are 100 cents in 1 dollar, so set up another proportion: $\frac{100 \text{ cents}}{1 \text{ dollar}} = \frac{y \text{ cents}}{5 \text{ dollars}}$. Cross-multiply to get $y = 500$ cents. Finally, determine the cost in cents per ounce by dividing the number of cents by the number of ounces: $\frac{500 \text{ cents}}{48 \text{ ounces}} = 10.42$ cents per ounce. The question asked which *best approximates* the cost, and the closest answer is 10.4. The correct answer is (D).

21. **B** The question asks for the number of ways that the letters in a word can be arranged and gives a restriction that "W" must come last. Start by drawing 5 lines, one for each letter of the arrangement. Now fill in the number of options on each line. The letter "W" must come last, so start by writing a 1 on the last of the 5 lines. The remaining 4 letters may go in any order but cannot be repeated. Therefore, there are 4 letter options for the first blank, 3 for the next blank, 2 for the following blank, and 1 for the 4th blank. The blanks should now look like this: __4__ __3__ __2__ __1__ __1__ . Finally, multiply all the numbers in the blanks to get the total number of ways the letters can be arranged: $4 \times 3 \times 2 \times 1 \times 1 = 24$. The correct answer is (B).

22. **H** The question asks for a combined average given the averages for two different groups. For questions like this, the average will almost certainly not be the average of the two averages. In this case, the average of 12 and 8 is 10, so (G) is a trap answer; eliminate it. For averages, use the formula $T = AN$, in which T is the total, A is the average, and N is the number of things. For the starting team, the *Number of things* is the 9 members, and the *Average* is 12 home runs. The formula becomes $T = (12)(9) = 108$ home runs scored by the starting team. The question states that the 7 members of the second-string team have an average of 8 home runs each. The formula becomes $T = (8)(7) = 56$ home runs scored by the second-string team. Add all of the home runs scored by both teams to get $108 + 56 = 164$. This is the *Total* for the two teams combined. The *Number of things* for the two teams combined is $9 + 7 = 16$ members. The formula becomes $164 = A(16)$. Divide both sides of the equation by 16 to get $A = 10.25$. The correct answer is (H).

34. **H** The question asks for the expected value of winnings for each quarter dropped into an arcade game. To calculate expected value, find the products of each value and the probability of obtaining that value; then sum the results. In this question, find the products of the number of quarters in each row and the probability of that number of quarters falling to get $(0)(0.5) + (1)(0.3) + (2)(0.15) + (3)(0.03) + (4)(0.02) = 0 + 0.3 + 0.3 + 0.09 + 0.08 = 0.77$. The correct answer is (H).

37. **B** The question asks what is true about the median and mean of a finite arithmetic sequence. Since the sequence is not provided, use the information given in the question and plug in to create a sequence that fits the requirements. The question states that the first number in the sequence is 11. An arithmetic sequence changes by a constant difference, so for this sequence plug in a change of 1, making the sequence 11, 12, 13, 14, 15, 16, 17. Now calculate the median by locating the number in the middle of the sequence, 14. To find the mean, use $T = AN$, where T is the total, A is the average, and N is the number of things. First calculate the *Total* as $T = 11 + 12 + 13 + 14 + 15 + 16 + 17 = 98$. There are 7 numbers, so that is the *Number of things*. Plug these into the equation to get $98 = A(7)$. Divide both sides by 7 to get $A = 14$. The mean and median are both 14. The correct answer is (B).

38.   **G**   The question asks for the probability that a randomly selected number will have 1 as at least one of its digits. Probability is defined as the number of outcomes that fit the requirements divided by the total number of outcomes. Start by finding the total number of outcomes. It is tempting to just subtract, but that does not include the numbers at both ends of the spectrum. To get *299 through 1,000, inclusive,* find the difference and then add 1. The total outcomes = 1,000 − 299 + 1 = 702. Choice (F) mistakenly uses 1,000 for the denominator, so eliminate it. Now find the number of integers that have at least one 1, listing them out at first to make sure none are skipped. From 299 to 399, the list is 301, 310, 311, 312, 313, 314, 315, 316, 317, 318, 319, 321, 331, 341, 351, 361, 371, 381, and 391. There are 19 numbers on the list, and there will be another 19 for 400–499, 500–599, 600–699, 700–799, 800–899, and 900–999. This means there is a total of 7 sets of 19 numbers, or 133 numbers. The final one that works is 1,000, so the probability is $\dfrac{134}{702}$. The correct answer is (G).

Summary

- When a question is wordy (whether or not it's a "Modeling" question), use the word problem Basic Approach:
  - Step 1: Know the Question
  - Step 2: Let the Answers Help
  - Step 3: Break the Question into Bite-Sized Pieces

- Percentages and probabilities are both based on a relationship of PART to WHOLE.

- Percentages can typically be found by multiplying $\dfrac{part}{whole} \times 100$.

- When dealing with percentages, remember to convert English into Math with this handy chart.

English	Math Equivalent
percent	divide by 100
of	multiplication (×)
what	variable (x, y, z)
is, are, were, did, does	=
what percent	$\dfrac{x}{100}$

- Probabilities can be found by taking the *part* (the number of things that meet some given criteria) divided by the *whole* (all possibilities, including those that don't meet the criteria).

- To find the Expected Value, multiply the value of each possible outcome by the probability that that outcome will occur, then add those products together.

- Ratios are based on a relationship of PART to PART.

- On Average questions, use the average formula $T = AN$.
  - T is the total.
  - A is the average.
  - N is the number of things.

o   Median is the *middle* number in a list of numbers arranged in ascending order.

o   Mode is the number that occurs *most* often in a list of numbers.

o   Range is the difference between the greatest value and the least value in a list of numbers.

o   On Charts and Graphs questions, read carefully and check the labels.

o   On Ordering questions:
   •   Figure out the number of slots you need to fill.
   •   Fill in those slots.
   •   Find the product.
   •   Divide if order doesn't matter.

o   Combinations are when order doesn't matter.

   •   The formula for combinations is $_nC_r = \dfrac{n!}{r!(n-r)!}$, where n is the number of options and r is the number of options chosen.

o   Permutations are when order does matter.

   •   The formula for permutations is $_nP_r = \dfrac{n!}{(n-r)!}$, where n is the number of options and r is the number of options chosen.

o   Factorials ("!") are calculated by multiplying the number by every positive integer less than that number.

o   In an arithmetic sequence, each term is determined by adding or subtracting the same value from the previous term.

o   In a geometric sequence, each term is determined by multiplying or dividing the same value from the previous term.

Chapter 18
Graphing
and Coordinate
Geometry

We've covered most of what you'll need to get a great score on the ACT Math test. This chapter will give a brief overview of Coordinate Geometry. While it's not tested as heavily as Plane Geometry, Coordinate Geometry offers many fast plug-and-chug opportunities. Though we will be discussing the basic rules and formulas you need, we will always have an eye on how we can crack some of these questions more strategically as well.

COORDINATE GEOMETRY

The major difference between coordinate geometry and plane geometry is that you need to draw a standard (*x,y*) coordinate plane for many coordinate geometry questions. We'll cover the basics of graphing and its related functions, but don't forget, you know a lot of this stuff from the earlier geometry chapter!

Graphing Inequalities on Number Lines

Here's a simple inequality:

$$3x + 5 > 11$$

Solve an inequality the same way that you solve an equality. By subtracting 5 from both sides and then dividing both sides by 3, you get the expression:

$$x > 2$$

This can be represented on a number line as shown below.

An Open Circle
On the number line, a hollow circle means that point is *not* included in the graph.

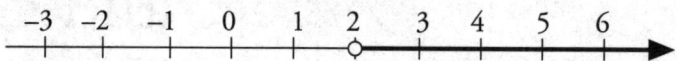

The open circle at 2 indicates that *x* can include every number greater than 2, but not 2 itself or anything less than 2.

If we had wanted to graph $x \geq 2$, the circle would have to be filled in, indicating that our graph includes 2 as well.

A Solid Dot
On the number line, a solid dot means that point is included in the graph.

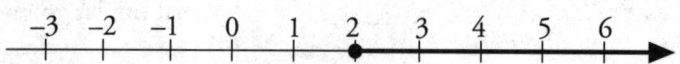

An ACT graphing question might look like this.

11. Which of the following represents the range of solutions for inequality $-5x - 7 < x + 5$?

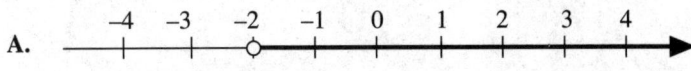

Here's How to Crack It

The ACT test-writers want you first to simplify the inequality, and then figure out which of the answer choices represents a graph of the solution set of the inequality. To simplify, isolate x on one side of the inequality.

$$
\begin{array}{r}
-5x - 7 < x + 5 \\
-x \qquad -x \\
\hline
-6x - 7 < \quad 5 \\
+7 \quad +7 \\
\hline
-6x \quad < \quad 12
\end{array}
$$

Now divide both sides by -6. Note that when you multiply or divide an inequality by a negative, the sign flips over.

$$
\frac{-6x}{-6} < \frac{12}{-6}
$$
$$
x > -2
$$

> **Flip Flop**
> When you multiply or divide an inequality by a negative, the sign flips.

Which of the choices answers the question? If you selected (A), you're right.

Graphing in Two Dimensions

More complicated graphing questions concern equations with two variables, usually designated *x* and *y*. These equations can be graphed on a Cartesian grid, which looks like this.

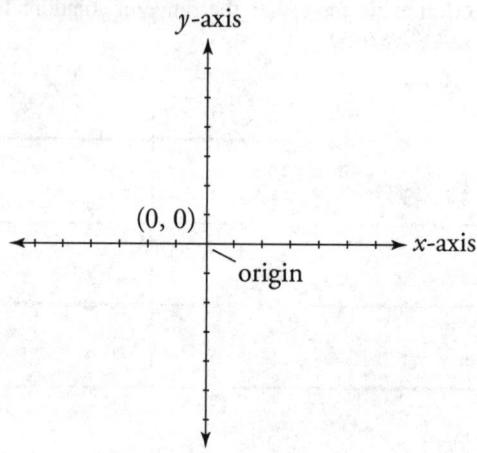

Every point (*x*,*y*) has a place on this grid. For example, the point *A* (3,4) can be found by counting over on the *x*-axis 3 places to the right of (0,0)—known as the **origin**—and then counting on the *y*-axis 4 places up from the origin, as shown below. Point *B* (5,–2) can be found by counting 5 places to the right on the *x*-axis and then down 2 places on the *y*-axis. Point *C* (–4,–1) can be found by counting 4 places to the left of the origin on the *x*-axis and then 1 place down on the *y*-axis.

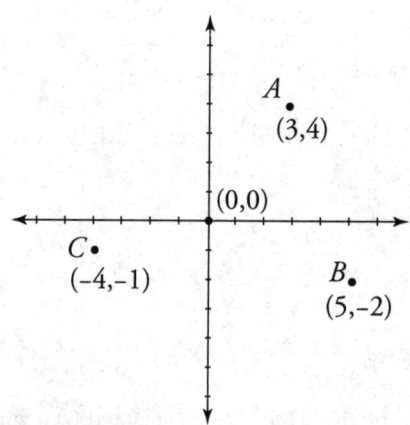

The grid is divided into four quadrants, which go counterclockwise.

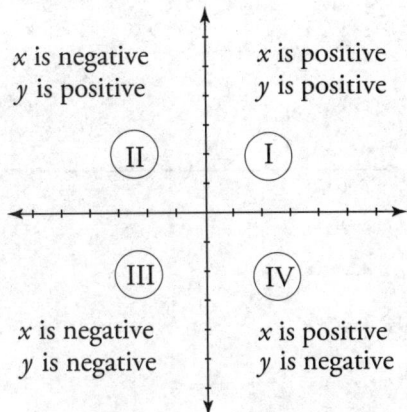

- In the first quadrant, both *x* and *y* are positive.
- In the second quadrant, *x* is negative but *y* is positive.
- In the third quadrant, both *x* and *y* are negative.
- In the fourth quadrant, *x* is positive but *y* is negative.

Note: This is when a graphing calculator (if you have one, or if you take the Online ACT that has one built in) will really get a chance to shine. Practice doing all the ACT coordinate geometry questions on the calculator you will use on test day, and you'll blow them away when you actually take the test.

Graphic Guesstimation

A few questions on the ACT might involve actual graphing, but it is more likely that you will be able to make use of graphing to *estimate* the answers to questions that the ACT test-writers think are more complicated.

---

16. Point *B* (4,3) is the midpoint of line segment *AC*. If point *A* has coordinates (0,1), then what are the coordinates of point *C*?

    F.   (−4,−1)
    G.   (4,1)
    H.   (8,5)
    J.   (8,9)

Here's How to Crack It

You may or may not remember the midpoint formula: the ACT test-writers expect you to use it to answer this question. We'll go over it in a moment, along with the other formulas you'll need to solve coordinate geometry questions. However, it is worth noting that by drawing a rough graph of this question, you can get the correct answer without the formula.

First, draw an (x,y) coordinate plane on your scratch paper.

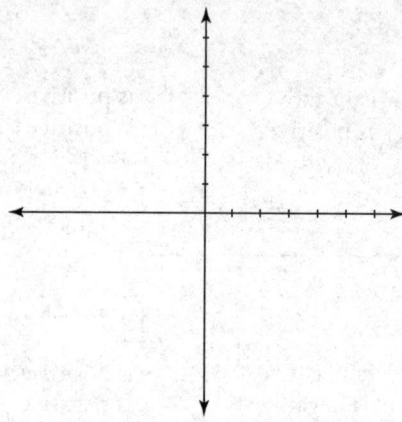

Next, plot the points *A* and *B* using the coordinates given in the question. *B* is supposed to be the midpoint of a line segment *AC*. Draw a line through the two points you've just plotted and extend it upward until *B* is the midpoint of the line segment. It should look like this:

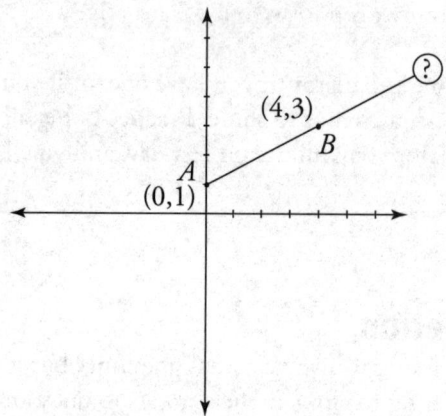

The place where you stopped drawing is the approximate location of point *C*. Now let's look at the answer choices to see if any of them are in the ballpark.

F.   (–4,–1): These coordinates are in the wrong quadrant.
G.   (4,1): This point is way below where it should be.
H.   (8,5): Definitely in the ballpark. Hold on to this answer choice.
J.   (8,9): Possible, although the *y*-coordinate seems a little high.

Which answer choice do you want to pick? If you said (H), you are right.

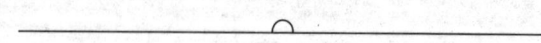

THE IMPORTANT COORDINATE GEOMETRY FORMULAS

By memorizing a few formulas, you will be able to answer virtually all of the coordinate geometry questions on this test. Remember, too, that in coordinate geometry you almost *always* have a fallback: just graph it out.

And always keep your graphing calculator handy on these types of questions. Graphing calculators are great for solving line equations and giving you graphs you can use to ballpark. Be sure you know how to solve and graph an equation for a line on the calculator you are planning to use before you take the ACT.

The following formulas are listed in order of importance.

> **x and y**
> In any equation or inequality with *x* and *y*, when graphed in the *xy*-plane, any pair of values (*x,y*) that satisfy the equation or inequality will be a point on the graph.

The Slope-Intercept Form of a Line

$$y = mx + b$$

> **To find the x-intercept**
> Set *y* equal to zero, and solve for *x*.

Using the form above, you can find two pieces of information that ACT likes to test: the **slope** and the **y-intercept**.

The **slope** is a number that tells you how sharply a line is inclining, and it is equivalent to the variable **m** in the equation above. For example, in the equation $y = 3x + 4$, the number 3 (think of it as $\frac{3}{1}$) tells us that from any point on the line, we can find another point on the line by going up 3 and over to the right 1.

In the equation $y = -\frac{4}{5}x - 7$, the slope $-\frac{4}{5}$ tells us that from any point on the line, we can find another point on the line by going up 4 and over 5 to the left.

The **y-intercept**, equivalent to the variable **b** in the equation above, is the point at which the line intercepts the y-axis. For example, in the equation $y = 3x + 4$, the line will strike the y-axis at a point 4 above the origin. In the equation $y = 2x - 7$, the line will strike the y-axis at a point 7 below the origin. A typical ACT $y = mx + b$ question might give you an equation in another form and ask you to find either the slope or the y-intercept. Simply put the equation into the form we've just shown you.

4. What is the slope of the line with the equation
$5x - y = 7x + 6$?

   F.   −6
   G. −2
   H. 2
   J.   6

Here's How to Crack It

Isolate y on the left side of the equation. Do it by hand by subtracting $5x$ from both sides.

> Sometimes, a line will be given in the standard form $Ax + By = C$. For the equation in question 6, the standard form is $2x + y = -6$. In this form, the slope is $-\dfrac{A}{B}$, and the y-intercept is $\dfrac{C}{B}$.

$$\begin{array}{rcl} 5x - y &=& 7x + 6 \\ -5x & & -5x \\ \hline -y &=& 2x + 6 \end{array}$$

We aren't quite done. The format we want is $y = mx + b$, not $-y = mx + b$. Let's multiply both sides by −1.

$$(-1)(-y) = (2x + 6)(-1)$$
$$y = -2x - 6$$

The slope of this line is −2, so the answer is (G).

Inequalities in the *xy*-plane

Inequalities can be graphed in the *xy*-plane as well as on number lines. To graph an inequality in the *xy*-plane, treat the inequality as an equation. The resulting line will be the boundary line of the inequality. If points on the line are included in the inequality, the line will be solid; if not, the line will be dotted. Next, shade the part of the *xy*-plane that would be included in the inequality.

34. Which of the following correctly graphs the solution set to the system of inequalities $y \geq \frac{1}{3}x - 3$ and $y \leq -2x + 2$?

F.

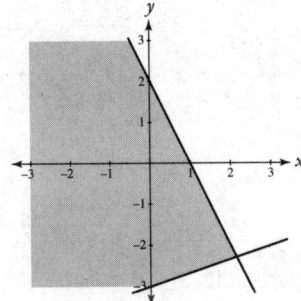

H.

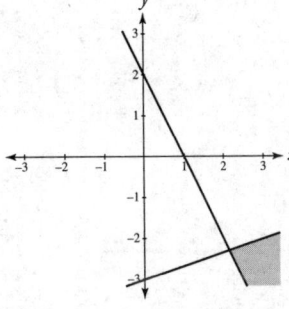

G.

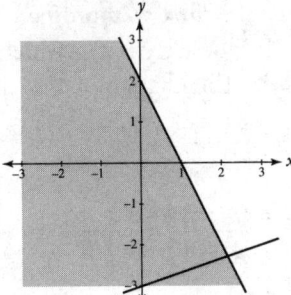

J.

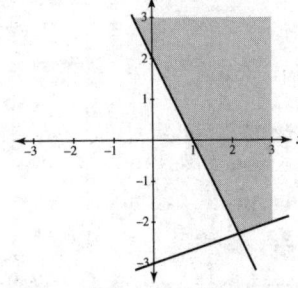

Here's How to Crack It

The line defined by the inequality $y \geq \frac{1}{3}x - 3$ is the line with a slope of $\frac{1}{3}$ and a y-intercept of -3. Because the inequality has y to the left of the greater than or equal to sign, only the area above that line should be shaded. Eliminate (G) and (H). The line defined by the inequality $y \leq -2x + 2$ is the other line. Because the inequality has y to the left of the less than or equal to sign, only the area below the line should be shaded. Eliminate (J). The correct answer is (F).

The Slope Formula

You can find the slope of a line, even if all you have are two points on that line, by using the slope formula.

$$\text{slope} = \frac{\text{change in } y}{\text{change in } x} \quad \text{or} \quad \frac{y_2 - y_1}{x_2 - x_1}$$

The Slippery Slope

A line going from bottom left to upper right has a positive slope. A line going from top left to bottom right has a negative slope.

2. What is the slope of the straight line passing through the points (–2,5) and (6,4)?

F. $-\dfrac{1}{16}$

G. $-\dfrac{1}{8}$

H. $\dfrac{1}{5}$

J. $\dfrac{4}{9}$

Parallel Tracks

If two lines have the same slope, those lines are *parallel* to one another.

If two lines have opposite reciprocal slopes, those lines are *perpendicular* to one another.

So how about if the question on this page asked for the slope of a line parallel to the one given in the question? How about perpendicular?

A *parallel* line would have a slope of $-\dfrac{1}{8}$.

A *perpendicular* line would have a slope of 8.

Here's How to Crack It

Find the change in y and put it over the change in x. The change in y is the first y-coordinate minus the second y-coordinate. (It doesn't matter which point is first and which is second.) The change in x is the first x minus the second x.

$$\frac{y_2 - y_1}{x_2 - x_1} = \frac{5 - 4}{-2 - 6} = \frac{1}{-8}$$

The correct answer is (G).

If you take a look at the formula for finding the slope, you'll see that the part on top ("change in y") is how much the line is rising (or falling, if the line points down and has a negative slope). That change in position on the y-axis is called the *rise*. The part on the bottom ("change in x") is how far along the x-axis you move and is called the *run*. So the slope of a line is sometimes referred to as "rise over run."

In the question we just did, then, the rise was 1 and the run was –8, giving us the slope $-\dfrac{1}{8}$. Same answer, different terminology.

Midpoint Formula

If you have the two endpoints of a line segment, you can find the midpoint of the segment by using the midpoint formula.

$$\left(x[m], y[m] \right) = \left(\frac{x_1 + x_2}{2}, \frac{y_1 + y_2}{2} \right)$$

It looks much more intimidating than it really is.

To find the midpoint of a line, just take the *average* of the two *x*-coordinates and the *average* of the two *y*-coordinates. For example, the midpoint of the line segment formed by the coordinates (3,4) and (9,2) is just

$$\frac{(3+9)}{2} = 6 \text{ and } \frac{(4+2)}{2} = 3$$
$$\text{or } (6,3)$$

Remember the first midpoint question we did? Here it is again.

> ### The Shortest Distance Between Two Points Is...a Calculator?
> If you want to draw a line between two points on your TI-80 series calculator, you can use the Line function. To access this, press [2nd] [PRGM] to access the [DRAW] menu. From there, select option [2:Line]. The format of the line function is Line (X1, Y1, X2, Y2); for example, if you wanted to view the line that passes through the points (−2, 5) and (6, 4), enter Line (−2,5,6,4). Hit [ENTER] to see your line.

16. Point *B* (4,3) is the midpoint of line segment *AC*. If point *A* has coordinates (0,1), then what are the coordinates of point *C*?

    F. (−4,−1)
    G. (4,1)
    H. (8,5)
    J. (8,9)

Here's How to Crack It

You'll remember that it was perfectly possible to answer this question just by drawing a quick graph of what it ought to look like. However, to find the correct answer using the midpoint formula, we first have to realize that, in this case, we already *have* the midpoint. We are asked to find one of the endpoints.

The midpoint is (4,3). This represents the average of the two endpoints. The endpoint we know about is (0,1). Let's do the *x*-coordinate first. The average of the *x*-coordinates of the two endpoints equal the *x*-coordinate of the midpoint. So $\frac{(0+?)}{2} = 4$. What is the missing *x*-coordinate? 8. Now let's do the *y*-coordinate: $\frac{(1+?)}{2} = 3$. What is the missing *y*-coordinate? 5. The answer is (H).

If you had trouble following that last explanation, just remember that you already understood this question (and got the answer) using graphing. Never be intimidated by formulas on the ACT. There is usually another way to get the answer to the question.

The Distance Formula

The distance formula exists, but it's not necessary to know it for the ACT because there are easier ways to find the distance between two points. The distance formula is just the Pythagorean Theorem rearranged, so think of the distance between two points as the hypotenuse of a right triangle. Here's an example.

---

24. What is the distance between points *A* (2,2) and *B* (5,6)?

   F.   3
   G.   4
   H.   5
   J.   6

Here's How to Crack It

Let's make a quick graph of what this ought to look like.

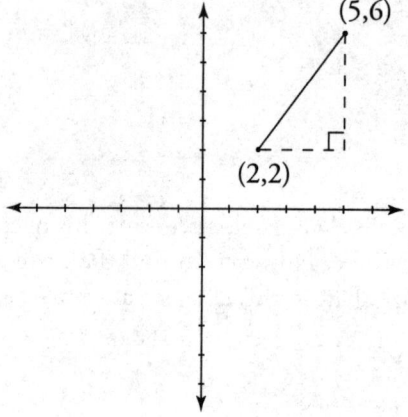

If we extend lines from the two points to form a right triangle under the line segment *AB*, we can use the Pythagorean Theorem to get the distance between the two points. What is the length of the base of the triangle? It's 3. What is the length of the height of the triangle? It's 4. So what is the length of the hypotenuse? It's 5. Of course, as usual, it is one of the triples of which ACT is so fond. The answer is (H). You could also have popped the points into your calculator and had it calculate the distance for you.

> Here's the distance formula if you must know (or know how to program into your calculator):
> $d = \sqrt{(x_2 - x_1)^2 + (y_2 - y_1)^2}$.
> Isn't the triangle method so much easier?

Circles, Ellipses, and Parabolas, Oh My!

You should probably have a *vague* idea of what the equations for these figures look like; just remember that there are very few questions concerning these figures, and when they do come up, in many cases, you can figure them out by graphing or making good guesses using POE.

The standard equation for a circle is shown below.

$$(x - h)^2 + (y - k)^2 = r^2$$

(h, k) = center of the circle

r = radius

The standard equation for an ellipse (just a squat-looking circle-like shape) is shown below.

$$\frac{(x - h)^2}{a^2} + \frac{(y - k)^2}{b^2} = 1$$

(h, k) = center of the ellipse

$2a$ = horizontal axis (width)

$2b$ = vertical axis (height)

We include the ellipse formula because it has shown up on previous exams, but if you can't remember it, don't worry. It shows up only once in a blue moon, and you never need to reproduce it from memory.

The ACT can ask you about the foci (plural of focus) of an ellipse. Every ellipse has two foci. They are defined as 2 fixed points inside the ellipse and are used to create the curve. They look like this:

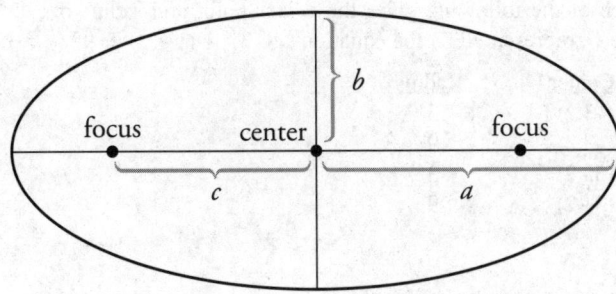

ACT could ask you to find the coordinates of the foci or ask you to determine something about the ellipse based on the location of the foci. If you know the foci are inside the ellipse and on the longest axis, you can probably use POE on at least a few answers. If you want to actually answer these questions, keep this formula in mind, and you'll have all you need.

$$c^2 = a^2 - b^2$$

a = half the length of the horizontal axis (width)

b = half the length of the vertical axis (height)

Finally, some graphing questions will ask about parabolas. As discussed in the earlier section about Quadratics, a parabola is the result of graphing a quadratic equation. Be sure to review the information about roots or solutions, factors, and how to switch between standard form and factored form. The third form of a quadratic equation is vertex form, shown below.

$$y = a(x - h)^2 + k$$

(x,y) is any point on the parabola

(h,k) is the vertex of the parabola

a shows which way the parabola opens:
upward if positive and downward if negative

Let's try some example questions using these shapes.

26. Which of the following gives the center point and radius of circle O, represented by the equation $(x - 3)^2 + (y + 2)^2 = 9$?

	Center	Radius
F.	(–3,2)	3
G.	(–3,2)	9
H.	(3,–2)	3
J.	(3,–2)	9

Here's How to Crack It

The question asks for the center of a circle given the equation of the circle in standard form. The equation of a circle is $(x - h)^2 + (y - k)^2 = r^2$, where (h, k) is the center point of the circle and r is the radius. Since the equation in the question is in standard form and is equal to 9, $r^2 = 9$. Take the square root of both sides to find that the radius is 3. Eliminate (G) and (J) because they have the wrong radius. Eliminate (F) since it assigns the wrong sign to the x- and y-coordinates for the center of the circle. The correct answer is (H).

35. A circle and an ellipse, both centered at the origin, are shown in the standard (x,y) coordinate plane. The circle has the equation $x^2 + y^2 = 100$ and intersects the ellipse at only 2 points, both on the y-axis. Which of the following represents the equation of the ellipse?

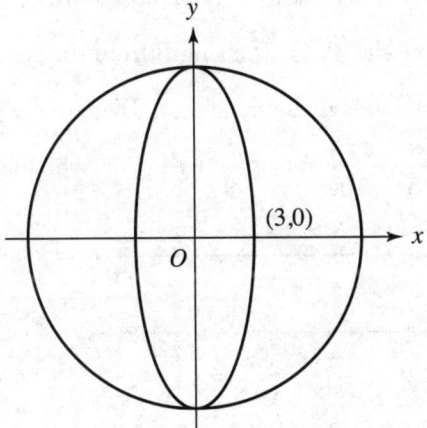

A. $\dfrac{x^2}{3} + \dfrac{y^2}{10} = 1$

B. $\dfrac{x^2}{9} + \dfrac{y^2}{100} = 1$

C. $\dfrac{x^2}{9} + \dfrac{y^2}{10} = 1$

D. $\dfrac{x^2}{3} + \dfrac{y^2}{100} = 1$

Here's How to Crack It

Your first inclination might be to reach for your graphing calculator, but unfortunately, to graph the equations given, you would have to first solve all the equations for y, which is time-consuming and leaves a lot of room for error. If you remember the equations of a circle, $(x - h)^2 + (y - k)^2 = r^2$, and an ellipse, $\dfrac{(x-h)^2}{a^2} + \dfrac{(y-k)^2}{b^2} = 1$, there is a quicker solution. The question states that both the circle and the ellipse are centered at the origin, $(0,0)$. That's great news because (h,k) is equal to $(0,0)$ for both figures, and the circle and ellipse formulas simplify to $x^2 + y^2 = r^2$ and $\dfrac{x^2}{a^2} + \dfrac{y^2}{b^2} = 1$, respectively. The question also states that the figures intersect at only two points. Those points are collinear and on a diameter of the circle. You can tell from the picture that those points are also the end points of the vertical axis of the ellipse. Since the diameter and the axis are the same, the value of b in the ellipse equation is equal to the radius of the circle. The question has given you the radius disguised in the formula for the circle: $x^2 + y^2 = 100$. Therefore, $100 = r^2$, and the radius of the circle is 10. This means that $b = 10$ as well. Plugging b into the equation of the ellipse gives $\dfrac{x^2}{a^2} + \dfrac{y^2}{10^2} = 1$ or $\dfrac{x^2}{a^2} + \dfrac{y^2}{100} = 1$. The only answer choices that contain an equation in that format are (B) and (D). Comparing these shows that the only difference is the value of a, or half of the distance of the horizontal axis of the ellipse. Luckily, ACT has given you a point on the ellipse to help. Point (0,3) is on the x-axis, 3 units from the center of the circle, (0, 0). The length from the center of the ellipse to a point on the edge along the horizontal axis is the same as a. Therefore, $a = 3$. Plugging a into the equation of the ellipse gives you $\dfrac{x^2}{3^2} + \dfrac{y^2}{100} = 1$ or $\dfrac{x^2}{9} + \dfrac{y^2}{100} = 1$, which is (B).

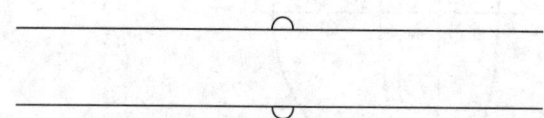

25. A parabola with equation $y = -2(x - 5)^2 + 9$ is graphed in the standard (x,y) coordinate plane. Which of the following points represents the vertex of the parabola?

A. (–5,9)
B. (–2,–9)
C. (5,–9)
D. (5,9)

Here's How to Crack It

This question is testing your knowledge of vertex form of a parabola, so work in bite-sized pieces and be careful with positives and negatives. The vertex form of a parabola is $y = a(x - h)^2 + k$, in which (h,k) is the vertex. In the given equation, $x - 5$ is in parentheses, so $x - h = x - 5$. Subtract x from both sides of the equation to get $-h = -5$, and then multiply both sides of the equation by -1 to get $h = 5$. Notice that the x-coordinate of the vertex has the *opposite* sign of what's shown in the vertex form of the equation. Since the x-coordinate of the vertex is 5, eliminate (A) and (B).

Next, find the y-coordinate of the vertex. This stands alone as k in vertex form, so it has the *same* sign. The given equation has + 9 in the same place as + k in vertex form, so $k = 9$. Eliminate (C) since it has the wrong sign for the y-coordinate. Only (D) is left, and it gets both coordinates of the vertex right, so (D) is the answer.

What about that –2 in the equation? In vertex form, the a value shows whether the parabola opens up or down and how wide or narrow it is. It has nothing to do with the vertex, so any answer with –2 is just there to distract you.

Asymptotes

Finally, you'll occasionally see questions about asymptotes. Asymptotes are lines that approach, but never intersect, a curve. Rather than memorizing all the rules about asymptotes for the very small chance that they appear on the ACT, use a graphing calculator or the provided graph to determine the answer.

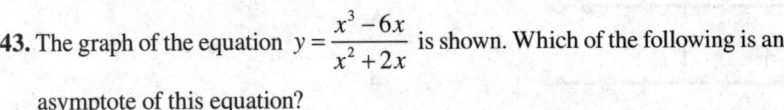

43. The graph of the equation $y = \dfrac{x^3 - 6x}{x^2 + 2x}$ is shown. Which of the following is an

asymptote of this equation?

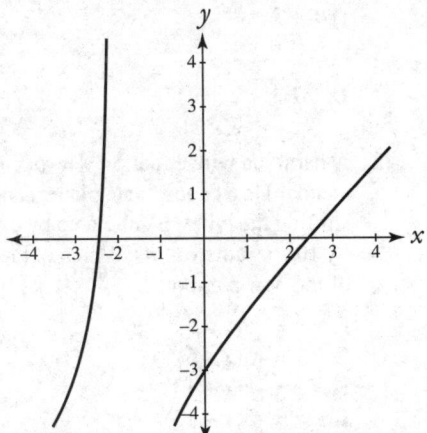

   A. $y = -2$
   B. $x = 2$
   C. $y = x - 2$
   D. $y = x + 2$

Here's How to Crack It

Asymptotes are lines that approach but do not intersect a curve. Both parts of the graph do not have horizontal asymptotes because there are no places that approach a slope of 0. Eliminate (A) because it is a horizontal asymptote. The left side of the graph approaches but never intersects $x = -2$, but not $x = 2$. Eliminate (B). On the right side of the graph, the curve goes along a line that would intersect the y-axis at -2, but (D) has a y-intercept of 2, so eliminate (D). The correct answer is (C).

Graphing and Coordinate Geometry Drill

8. Which of the following represents the solution of the inequality $-3x - 6 > 9$?

F.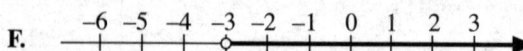

G.
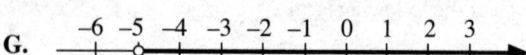

H.

J.

9. What is the midpoint of the line segment whose endpoints are represented on the coordinate plane by the points (3,5) and (–4,3)?

A. (–2,–5)

B. $(-\frac{1}{2},4)$

C. (1,8)

D. $(4,-\frac{1}{2})$

16. What is the slope of the line represented by the equation $10x + 2x = y + 6$?

F. 10
G. 12
H. 14
J. 16

18. What is the length of the line segment whose endpoints are represented on the coordinate plane by the points (–2,–1) and (1,3)?

F. 3
G. 4
H. 5
J. 7

19. What is the slope of the line that contains the points (6,4) and (13,5)?

A. $-\frac{1}{7}$

B. $\frac{1}{7}$

C. 1

D. 7

42. A parabola with equation $y = -5(x + 3)^2 - 8$ is graphed in the standard (x,y) coordinate plane. A new parabola is created by shifting the initial parabola up by 2 coordinate units and right by 10 coordinate units. Which of the following is the equation of the new parabola?

F. $y = -5(x - 7)^2 - 6$
G. $y = -5(x + 5)^2 + 2$
H. $y = -5(x + 13)^2 - 10$
J. $y = -5(x + 13)^2 - 6$

44. The ellipse shown in the standard (x,y) coordinate plane has the equation $\dfrac{x^2}{25} + \dfrac{(y-2)^2}{9} = 1$. Which of the following ordered pairs is one focus of this ellipse?

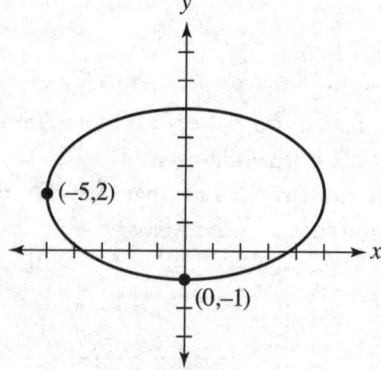

F. (–4,2)
G. (–2,1)
H. (0,2)
J. (3,5)

GRAPHING AND COORDINATE GEOMETRY DRILL ANSWERS AND EXPLANATIONS

8. **J** The question asks for the solution to an inequality. Use Process of Elimination. The equation has a > sign, which will be represented by an open circle on the number line. Eliminate (H) because it has a closed circle. Now solve the inequality by first adding 6 to both sides to get $-3x > 15$. Divide both sides by -3 and flip the sign to get $x < -5$. Eliminate (F), which has an open circle on -3 instead of on -5. The inequality includes all values *less than* -5, so eliminate (G), leaving (J) as correct. Another way to answer this question would be to plug in some numbers. In two of the answers, the value of 0 is included in the graph. If $x = 0$, the inequality becomes $-3(0) - 6 > 9$. This simplifies to $0 - 6 > 9$ or $-6 > 9$. This is not true, so eliminate (F) and (G), which both include 0. Now pick a value included in the graph in (H) but not in (J), such as $x = -4$. The inequality becomes $-3(-4) - 6 > 9$, which simplifies to $12 - 6 > 9$ or $6 > 9$. This is not true, so eliminate (H). Either way, the correct answer is (J).

9. **B** The question asks for the midpoint of a line segment given two points. The midpoint formula is $\left(\dfrac{x_1 + x_2}{2}, \dfrac{y_1 + y_2}{2}\right)$. Look at the answers to see that all of the choices have different x-coordinates, so solving for the x-coordinate of the midpoint will be enough to find the answer. The x-coordinate is $\dfrac{3 + (-4)}{2} = -\dfrac{1}{2}$. The correct answer is (B).

16. **G** The question asks for the slope of a line given the equation of the line. The slope-intercept form of a line is $y = mx + b$, where m is the slope. Manipulate the given equation into the slope-intercept form by combining like terms to get $12x = y + 6$. Then subtract 6 from both sides to get $12x - 6 = y$ or $y = 12x - 6$. The slope for this equation is 12. The correct answer is (G).

18. **H** The question asks for the length of a line given the endpoints. Use the distance formula or the triangle method to find the length of the line between the provided points. For the triangle method, sketch a coordinate plane and the points $(-2, -1)$ and $(1, 3)$. Form a right triangle with the line between the two points as the hypotenuse. The horizontal side of the triangle is length $1 - (-2) = 3$, and the vertical side is length $3 - (-1) = 4$. Use the 3-4-5 Pythagorean triple or the Pythagorean Theorem to solve for the length of the hypotenuse. Using the theorem, $a^2 + b^2 = c^2$, the result is $3^2 + 4^2 = c^2$. This becomes $9 + 16 = c^2$, which simplifies to $25 = c^2$, so $c = 5$. The correct answer is (H).

19. **B** The question asks for the slope of a line given two points. The formula for the slope of a line with points (x_1, y_1) and (x_2, y_2) is $\dfrac{y_2 - y_1}{x_2 - x_1}$. Plug the points in the question into the slope formula to get $\dfrac{5 - 4}{13 - 6} = \dfrac{1}{7}$. The correct answer is (B).

42.   **F**   The question asks for the equation of a parabola that is created by shifting the location of another parabola. Work in bite-sized pieces. Start by finding the vertex of the first parabola. Vertex form of a parabola is $y = a(x - h)^2 + k$, in which (h,k) is the vertex. In the given equation, $x + 3$ is in parentheses, so $x - h = x + 3$. Subtract x from both sides of the equation to get $-h = 3$, and then multiply both sides of the equation by -1 to get $h = -3$. The given equation has -8 in the same place as $+ k$ in vertex form, so $k = -8$. The vertex of the first parabola is $(-3,-8)$. Next, shift the parabola up by 2. Movement up or down is along the y-axis, so k should increase by 2. Add 2 to -8 to get -6. The value of k in the equation for the new parabola is -6. Eliminate (G) and (H) since they have the wrong value for k. Next, shift the parabola right by 10. Movement left or right is along the x-axis, so h should increase by 10 to move the graph to the right. Add 10 to -3 to get 7. The value of h in the equation for the new parabola is 7. Vertex form includes $(x - h)$, so the equation for the new parabola must contain $(x - 7)$. Eliminate (J) since it has the wrong value for h. The correct answer is (F).

44.   **F**   The question asks for a focus of an ellipse given its equation and a drawing. Foci are the points on the major axis of the ellipse that define the shape and size of the ellipse. Since a focus must be on the inside of an ellipse, eliminate (J) because that point is outside the ellipse. The foci are also on the longest axis, and in this ellipse that means that the foci will have a y-coordinate of 2. Eliminate (G), which does not have this y-coordinate. Foci are also not at the center point of the ellipse, so eliminate (H). The correct answer is (F).

Summary

o Inequalities can be graphed on a number line. Solve the inequality for the variable to determine the correct graph.
  - An open circle means that point is not included in the graph.
  - A solid circle means that point is included in the graph.

o If you are stuck on a coordinate geometry question, sketch a graph and draw in a few points.

o In any equation or inequality with x and y, when graphed in the xy-plane, any pair of values (x, y) that satisfy the equation or inequality will be a point on the graph.

o Many coordinate geometry questions can be solved by putting the equations into the format $y = mx + b$, where m is the slope of the line and b is the y-intercept.

o Inequalities in the xy-plane are defined by the line (or curve) created if the inequality sign was an equals sign, with a dashed line if the inequality is only less than or greater than a value but not equal to it. A portion of the xy-plane is then shaded based on the direction in which the inequality symbol points.

o The slope formula is slope $= \dfrac{change\ in\ y}{change\ in\ x}$ or $\dfrac{y_2 - y_1}{x_2 - x_1}$.

o Parallel lines have equal slopes.

o Perpendicular lines have slopes that are opposite reciprocals.

o Review the midpoint equation.

$$\left(x[m], y[m]\right) = \frac{x_1 + x_2}{2}, \frac{y_1 + y_2}{2}$$

o You can avoid using the confusing distance formula by drawing a right triangle and using the Pythagorean Theorem.

○ Review the circle equation.

$$(x - h)^2 + (y - k)^2 = r^2$$

$(h,k) =$ center of the circle

$r =$ radius

○ Every once in a while, ACT asks a question based on the equations of ellipses and parabolas. If you need a very high score, it might help to memorize these equations, but remember, these questions can frequently be done by using graphing to estimate the correct answer.

○ Asymptotes are lines that approach but never intersect a curve.

Chapter 19
Trigonometry

We've covered most of what you'll need to get a great score on the ACT Math test. This chapter will give a brief overview of one of the more advanced topics covered on the exam: trigonometry. Though we will be discussing the identities and rules you need, we will always have an eye on how we can crack some of these questions more strategically as well.

A NOTE ON ACT MATH "DIFFICULTY"

As we noted in the first Math chapter in this book, "difficulty" is kind of a weird thing on the ACT. Is a question difficult because it tests an unfamiliar concept? Or is it difficult because it tests a very familiar concept in a long word problem? We've seen that Plugging In and PITA can make some of the toughest questions pretty easy, so this part of the exam is more about POOD than ever. In this chapter, we will review trigonometry. Trigonometry is one of the more advanced topics on the ACT, and ACT wants to make you think it and the other advanced topics are very difficult. Some of these questions *are* difficult, tapping some of the most advanced topics of Algebra II. But as you will see with trigonometry, most, if not all, of these questions can be answered correctly with a smart approach. We will review the relevant concepts, but we will also keep an eye on how to use the strategies from earlier chapters.

TRIGONOMETRY

It's easy to get freaked out by the trigonometry on the ACT. But remember, there are usually only two or three questions on any given exam that deal with trig. What this means is that if you haven't learned trig before, it's not worth your time to try to do it now. If you are familiar with trig, on the other hand, here are a few topics that might come up.

Finally, as ever, remember that you don't get bonus points for doing anything the "real" way on the ACT. Always be on the lookout to use some of the great new techniques you've learned in this book.

SOHCAHTOA

There are four trig questions on any given ACT Math test, and typically two of them will ask about very basic trig concepts, covered by the acronym SOHCAHTOA. If you've had trig before, you probably know this acronym like the back of your hand. If not, here's what it means:

$$\mathbf{S}\text{ine} = \frac{\mathbf{O}\text{pposite}}{\mathbf{H}\text{ypotenuse}} \qquad \mathbf{C}\text{osine} = \frac{\mathbf{A}\text{djacent}}{\mathbf{H}\text{ypotenuse}} \qquad \mathbf{T}\text{angent} = \frac{\mathbf{O}\text{pposite}}{\mathbf{A}\text{djacent}}$$

Sine is **O**pposite over **H**ypotenuse. **C**osine is **A**djacent over **H**ypotenuse. **T**angent is **O**pposite over **A**djacent. So in the triangle on the facing page, the sine of angle θ [*theta*, a Greek letter] would be $\frac{4}{5}$. The cosine of angle θ would be $\frac{3}{5}$. The tangent of angle θ would be $\frac{4}{3}$.

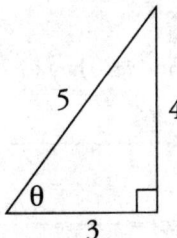

Sine, cosine, and tangent are often abbreviated as sin, cos, and tan, respectively.

The easier trig questions on this test involve the relationships between the sides of a right triangle. In the right triangle below, the trigonometric functions of the angle x can be expressed in terms of the ratios of different sides of the triangle.

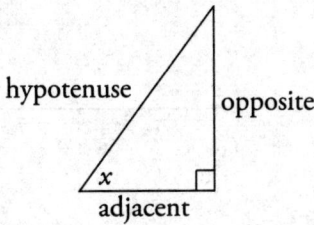

The **sine** of angle $x = \dfrac{\text{length of side opposite angle } x}{\text{length of hypotenuse}}$

The **cosine** of angle $x = \dfrac{\text{length of side adjacent angle } x}{\text{length of hypotenuse}}$

The **tangent** of angle $x = \dfrac{\text{length of side opposite angle } x}{\text{length of side adjacent angle } x}$

RECIPROCAL TRIG RATIOS

There are three more relationships to memorize. They involve the reciprocals of the previous three.

$$\text{cosecant (csc)} = \frac{1}{\text{sine}} = \frac{\text{hypotenuse}}{\text{opposite}}$$

$$\text{secant (sec)} = \frac{1}{\text{cosine}} = \frac{\text{hypotenuse}}{\text{adjacent}}$$

$$\text{cotangent (cot)} = \frac{1}{\text{tangent}} = \frac{\text{adjacent}}{\text{opposite}}$$

Let's try a few questions.

23. What is $\sin \theta$, if $\tan \theta = \frac{4}{3}$?

   A. $\frac{3}{4}$

   B. $\frac{4}{5}$

   C. $\frac{5}{4}$

   D. $\frac{5}{3}$

Helpful Trig Identities

$$\sin^2 \theta + \cos^2 \theta = 1$$

$$\frac{\sin \theta}{\cos \theta} = \tan \theta$$

Here's How to Crack It

It helps to sketch out the right triangle and fill in the information we know.

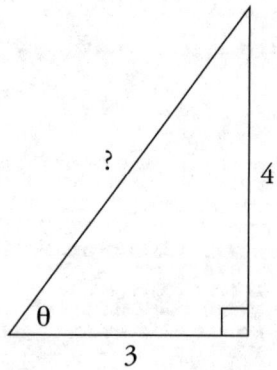

What kind of right triangle is this? That's right—a 3-4-5. Now, we need to know the sine of angle θ: opposite over hypotenuse, or $\dfrac{4}{5}$, which is (B).

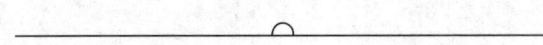

There are many, many trig identities. However, the ACT only tests two: $\sin^2 \theta + \cos^2 \theta = 1$ and $\dfrac{\sin \theta}{\cos \theta} = \tan \theta$.

32. For all θ, $\dfrac{\cos \theta}{\sin^2 \theta + \cos^2 \theta} = \ ?$

    F. $\sin \theta$
    G. $\csc \theta$
    H. $\cos \theta$
    J. $\tan \theta$

Here's How to Crack It

Because $\sin^2 \theta + \cos^2 \theta$ always equals 1, $\dfrac{\cos \theta}{1} = \cos \theta$. The answer is (H).

Because θ is a variable, it is possible to plug in for question 32 as well. When plugging in for trigonometry questions, avoid 45° (or $\dfrac{\pi}{2}$ in radians) or its multiples, because $\sin 45° = \cos 45°$. Also, when plugging in for functions such as $\sin^2 \theta$, solve for the value of the trig function first and square that result second. For example, $(\sin 60°)^2 = (0.866025404)^2 = 0.75$.

38. In a right triangle shown, sec θ is $\frac{25}{7}$. What is sin θ?

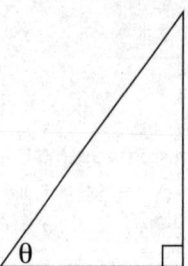

F. $\frac{3}{25}$

G. $\frac{7}{25}$

H. $\frac{24}{25}$

J. $\frac{25}{7}$

Here's How to Crack It

The secant of any angle is the reciprocal of the cosine, so the cosine of angle θ is $\frac{7}{25}$.

Are you done? No! Cross off (G) because you know it's not the answer.

You need to find sine, which is opposite over hypotenuse. Let's sketch it.

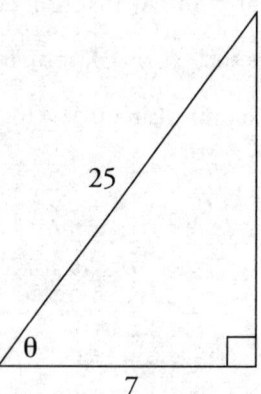

As you can see, we now have two sides of a right triangle. Can we find the third side? If you said this was one of the triples we told you about before, you are absolutely correct, although you also could have derived this by using the Pythagorean Theorem. The third side must be 24. The question asks for sin θ; sine = opposite over hypotenuse, or $\frac{24}{25}$, which is (H).

THE UNIT CIRCLE

When you see trig questions without triangles, you may need to use the *Unit Circle* instead of SOHCAHTOA. The Unit Circle is centered at (0,0) in a coordinate plane and has a radius of 1. Angle measures are measured counterclockwise from the point (1,0). A full revolution is 360°, or 2π in radian measure. You should familiarize yourself with the angle measures and coordinates in the figure below.

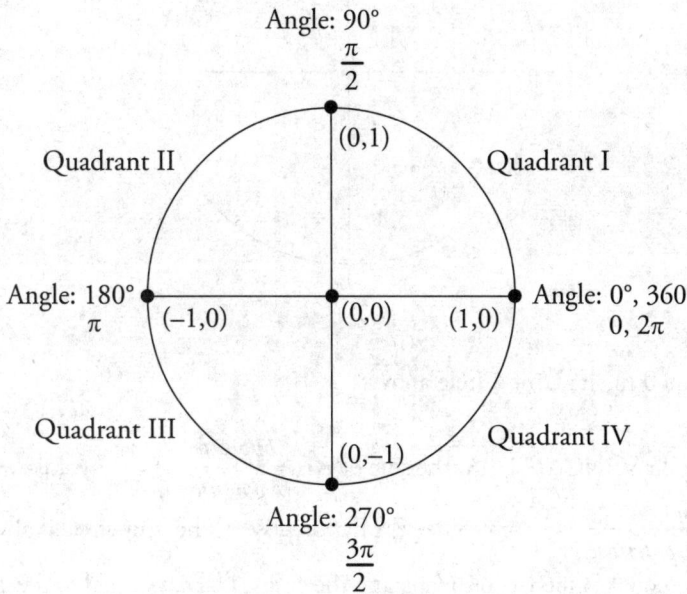

Since $360° = 2\pi$, you can convert radian measures to degrees and vice versa using any of the equations below:

$$\frac{degree\ measure}{360} = \frac{radian\ measure}{2\pi}$$

$$\text{radians} = \frac{degrees\left(\pi\right)}{180} \text{ and degrees} = \frac{radians\left(180\right)}{\pi}$$

Negative angle measures are used to indicate that the angle moves clockwise from the point (1,0) instead of counterclockwise. For example, –90° is 90° clockwise from (1,0), which is the point (0,–1). This means that 270°, $\frac{3\pi}{2}$, –90°, and $-\frac{\pi}{2}$ all have the same coordinates!

Similarly, angle measures greater than 360° or 2π merely represent more than one revolution around the circle. For example, if $\theta = 450°$ (which is $\frac{5\pi}{2}$ in radians), this represents a full revolution of 360° (or 2π) and then an additional 90°, so the coordinates would be equal to those of $\theta = 90°$ and $\theta = \frac{\pi}{2}$.

Trig in the Unit Circle

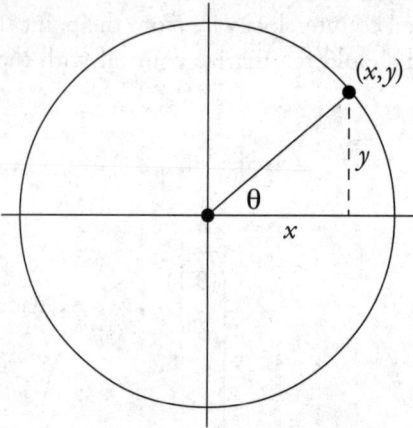

Consider the angle θ in the Unit Circle above.

Based on SOHCAHTOA, the sine of θ is $\frac{opposite}{hypotenuse} = \frac{y}{1} = y$. Likewise, the cosine of θ is $\frac{adjacent}{hypotenuse} = \frac{x}{1} = x$. Since the hypotenuse in the unit circle is always 1, the sine is always equal to the y-coordinate, and the cosine is always equal to the x-coordinate. The tangent is always $\frac{y}{x}$. You can use these ideas to determine the signs for sine, cosine, and tangent just by identifying the quadrant. Sine is positive when y is positive: Quadrants I and II only. Cosine is positive when x is positive: Quadrants I and IV only. Lastly, tangent is positive when x and y have the same sign: Quadrants I and III. Determining the signs can be a very useful tool for POE!

Let's try one.

---

35. If $\frac{5\pi}{6} \leq \theta \leq \frac{7\pi}{6}$, which of the following could be the value of cos θ?

A. $\frac{\sqrt{3}}{2}$

B. $\frac{\sqrt{2}}{2}$

C. $-\frac{\sqrt{3}}{2}$

D. $-\sqrt{3}$

Here's How to Crack It

Work this one step at a time. Start with the basics: sine and cosine are always between –1 and 1, inclusive. You can eliminate (D) since $-\sqrt{3}$ is outside of this range. Now determine the sign. $\theta = \pi$ falls on the border between Quadrant II and Quadrant III, so this range includes values from these two quadrants. Since $x < 0$ in both of these quadrants, $\cos \theta$ must be negative. Eliminate (A) and (B), and you've now successfully—and correctly!—answered the question without even needing to calculate any values. Just for clarity, though, to test (C), punch $\cos^{-1}\left(\dfrac{-\sqrt{3}}{2}\right)$ into your calculator. If your calculator is in radians mode, it will return the value of $\dfrac{5\pi}{6}$, which is clearly within the range of $\dfrac{5\pi}{6} \le \theta \le \dfrac{7\pi}{6}$. Choice (C) is correct.

Note that if your calculator is in degree mode, it will return 150°. Remember that you can convert this to radians with the formula:

$$\text{radians} = \frac{degrees\left(\pi\right)}{180} = \frac{150\pi}{180} = \frac{5\pi}{6}$$

ADVANCED TRIGONOMETRY

When graphing a trig function, such as sine, there are two important **coefficients**, A and B.

$$y = A[\sin (B\theta)]$$

The two coefficients, A and B, govern the **amplitude** of the graph (how tall it is) and the **period** of the graph (how long it takes to get through a complete cycle), respectively. If there are no coefficients, then that means $A = 1$ and $B = 1$, and the graph is the same as what you'd get when you graph it on your calculator.

- Increases in A increase the amplitude of the graph. It's a direct relationship.

That means if $A = 2$, then the amplitude is doubled. If $A = \dfrac{1}{2}$, then the amplitude is cut in half.

- Increases in B decrease the period of the graph. It's an inverse relationship.

That means if $B = 2$, then the period is cut in half, which is to say the graph completes a full cycle faster than usual. If $B = \dfrac{1}{2}$, then the period is doubled.

You can add to or subtract from the function as a whole and also to or from the variable, but neither of those actions changes the shape of the graph, only its position and starting place. For example, $y = \sin \theta + 1$ is shifted 1 unit up from $y = \sin \theta$, and $y = \sin\left(\theta + \dfrac{\pi}{2}\right)$ is shifted $\dfrac{\pi}{2}$ units to the left of $y = \sin \theta$. The ACT rarely tests this transformation of trig functions, but they do appear sometimes (usually as irrelevant, distracting details).

Here's the graph of sin x. What are the amplitude and period?

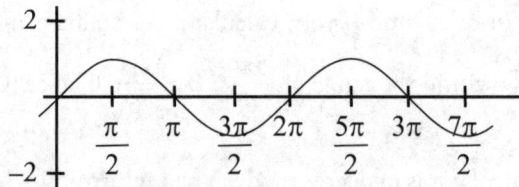

The simple function sin θ goes from –1 to 1 on the y-axis, so the amplitude is 1, while its period is 2π, which means that every 2π on the graph (as you go from side to side), the graph completes a full cycle. That's what you see in the graph above.

The graph below is also a sine function, but it's been changed. What is the function graphed here?

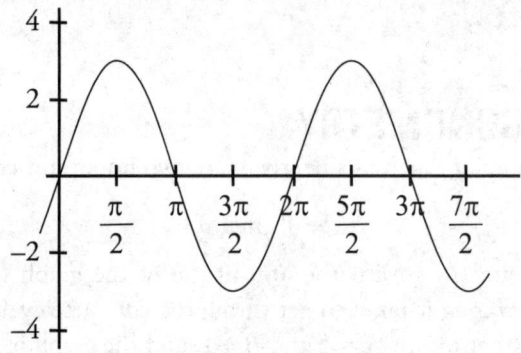

You have three things to check when looking at this graph: is it sin or cos, is the period changed, and is the amplitude changed?

- This is a sin graph because it has a value of 0 at 0; cos has a value of 1 at 0.
- It makes a complete cycle in 2π, so the period isn't changed. In other words, $B = 1$.
- The amplitude is triple what it normally is, so $A = 3$. The function graphed, therefore, is 3 sin θ.

How about here?

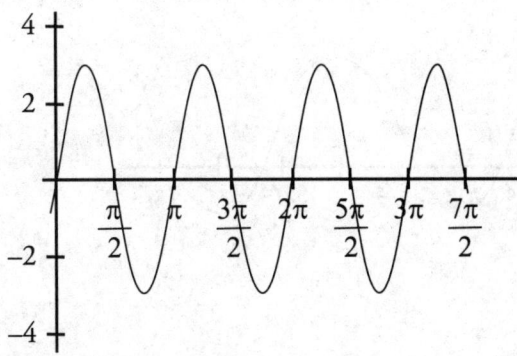

Once again, there are three things to check.

- This is a sin graph because it has a value of 0 at 0; cos has a value of 1 at 0.
- It makes a complete cycle in π, so the period has changed—it's half of what it usually is. B has an inverse effect, which means $B = 2$.
- The amplitude is triple what it normally is, so $A = 3$. The function graphed, therefore, is $3 \sin 2\theta$.

Let's try some practice questions.

37. As compared with the graph of $y = \cos x$, which of the following has the same period and three times the amplitude?

    A. $y = \cos 3x$

    B. $y = 3 \cos \frac{1}{2}x$

    C. $y = 1 + 3 \cos x$

    D. $y = 3 + \cos x$

Here's How to Crack It

Recall that the coefficient on the outside of the function changes the amplitude, and the one on the inside changes the period. Because the question states that the period isn't changed, you can eliminate (A) and (B). The amplitude is three times greater, you're told; because there's a direct relationship between A and amplitude, you want to have a 3 multiplying the outside of the function. That leaves only (C) as a possibility.

39. The graph of which of the following equations is shown?

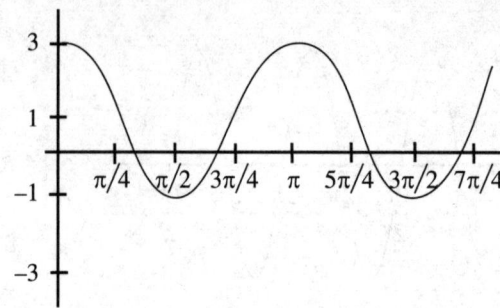

A. $2 \cos x$
B. $1 + 2 \cos x$
C. $1 + \cos 2x$
D. $1 + 2 \cos 2x$

Here's How to Crack It

At first, it looks like this graph has an amplitude of 3, but if you look closer, you'll see that though the top value is 3, the bottom value is –1, which means that the whole graph has been shifted up. Because (A) doesn't add anything to the function (which is how you move a graph up and down), it's out. The period of this graph is half of what it usually is, so $B = 2$, which eliminates (B). Because the amplitude is changed also, you can eliminate (C). The answer is (D).

Finally, you may occasionally see answer choices that include tangent as a possible answer. The graph of $y = \tan \theta$ is very different from that of sine and cosine (for instance, the graph goes to positive and negative infinity, and the default period is π rather than 2π), so ACT isn't looking for you to understand how this graph works. Rather, you need to know that tangent doesn't work the same way as sine and cosine and thus won't be the answer.

The Law(s of sine and cosine)

You may also see questions that test the law of sines or the law of cosines. Luckily, ACT almost always gives you the formulas you need. Your job is to apply the convention used with these equations: side a is opposite angle A, side b is opposite angle B, and side c is opposite side C.

39. In the figure shown, what is the value of x?

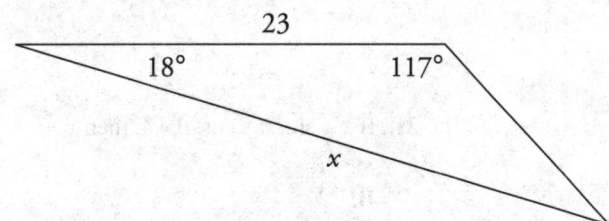

(Note: The law of sines states that $\dfrac{\sin A}{a} = \dfrac{\sin B}{b} = \dfrac{\sin C}{c}$.)

A. $23 \sin 117°$

B. $23 \sin 18°$

C. $\dfrac{23 \sin 117°}{\sin 18°}$

D. $\dfrac{23 \sin 117°}{\sin 45°}$

Here's How to Crack It

To find x, use the law of sines, which is provided in the note following the diagram. The angle

opposite x is $117°$, so make $a = x$ and $A = 117°$. The angle opposite the side with length 23 is not

given, but there are $180°$ in a triangle, so it must be $180° - 117° - 18° = 45°$. Make $b = 23$ and

$B = 45°$. Set up the proportion and solve: $\dfrac{\sin A}{a} = \dfrac{\sin B}{b}$, so $\dfrac{\sin 117°}{x} = \dfrac{\sin 45°}{23}$. Cross-multiply

to get $23 \sin 117° = x \sin 45°$. Divide both sides by $\sin 45°$ to get $\dfrac{23 \sin 117°}{\sin 45°} = x$, which is (D).

Trigonometry Drill

16. In $\triangle ABC$ shown, $\tan \theta = ?$

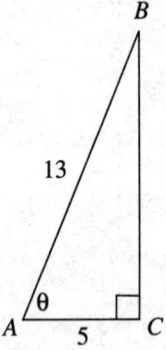

F. $\dfrac{5}{12}$

G. $\dfrac{12}{13}$

H. $\dfrac{17}{12}$

J. $\dfrac{12}{5}$

24. If the cotangent of an angle θ is 1, then the tangent of angle θ is:

F. -1

G. 0

H. 1

J. 2

31. If $x + \sin^2 \theta + \cos^2 \theta = 4$, then $x = ?$

A. 1

B. 3

C. 4

D. 5

33. If $\cos \theta = \dfrac{-7}{25}$ and $\sin \theta > 0$, then $\tan \theta = ?$

A. $\dfrac{24}{25}$

B. $\dfrac{7}{24}$

C. $-\dfrac{24}{25}$

D. $-\dfrac{24}{7}$

38. Which of the following angles has the same terminal side as $\dfrac{17\pi}{3}$?

F. $-720°$

G. $-60°$

H. $60°$

J. $720°$

TRIGONOMETRY DRILL ANSWERS AND EXPLANATIONS

16. **J** The question asks for the tangent of an angle in a right triangle. There is a trigonometric function in the question, so write SOHCAHTOA to remember the trig functions. In this figure, the labeled sides are the sides adjacent to angle θ and the hypotenuse. Since $\tan \theta = \dfrac{opposite}{adjacent}$, use the Pythagorean Theorem or Pythagorean triples to find that the opposite side, *BC*, of the triangle is 12. Now plug in the values for the sides of the triangle to find that $\tan \theta = \dfrac{12}{5}$. The correct answer is (J).

24. **H** The question asks for the tangent of an angle given the cotangent of that same angle. The tangent and the cotangent are related such that $\tan \theta = \dfrac{1}{\cot \theta}$. Substitute the value of the cotangent into the equation to get $\tan \theta = \dfrac{1}{1} = 1$. The correct answer is (H).

31. **B** The question asks for the value of a variable given an equation with trigonometric functions. The equation contains the trig identity $\sin^2 \theta + \cos^2 \theta$, which is equal to 1. Substitute 1 for the trig identity in the equation to get $x + 1 = 4$. Subtract 1 from both sides of the equation to get $x = 3$. Without knowledge of this trig identity, it is still possible to answer this question with Plugging In. Make θ = 30°. The equation becomes $x + (\sin 30°)^2 + (\cos 30°)^2 = 4$. Use a calculator to find that $\sin 30° = 0.5$ and $\cos 30° = 0.866$ when rounded. The equation becomes $x + (0.5)^2 + (0.866)^2 = 4$; then $x + 0.25 + 0.75 = 4$. This simplifies to $x + 1 = 4$, so $x = 3$. Either way, the correct answer is (B).

33. **D** The question asks for the value of a trigonometric function given other trigonometric functions, so write SOHCAHTOA to remember the trig functions. The definitions are $\cos \theta = \dfrac{adjacent}{hypotenuse}$ and $\tan \theta = \dfrac{opposite}{adjacent}$. Given $\cos \theta = \dfrac{-7}{25}$ in this question, the *adjacent* side is –7. Therefore, the tangent will have –7 in the denominator. Eliminate (A), (B), and (C), which all have incorrect denominators. The correct answer is (D).

38. **G** The question asks for the terminal side of an angle given in radians. Since the answers are in degrees, convert the radians to degrees using the ratio $\dfrac{radians(180°)}{\pi}$ to get $\dfrac{\frac{17\pi}{3}(180°)}{\pi} = \dfrac{17\pi(60°)}{\pi} = 17(60°) = 1{,}020°$. None of the answers match this value, so determine the angles that will have the same terminal side as 1,020° by adding or subtracting a full rotation, 360°, from the angle. Since all the answers are less than 1,020°, subtract 360° until the angle matches an answer, eliminating any answers that are skipped over in the process. Doing so will get 1,020° − 360° = 660°. This skips 720°, so eliminate (J). Continue the subtraction to get 660° − 360° = 300° and 300° − 360° = −60°. The correct answer is (G).

Summary

o   If you haven't had trigonometry in school, use your Letter of the Day on these trig questions. There aren't very many of them!

o   Remember SOHCAHTOA!

$$\text{sine} = \frac{\text{opposite}}{\text{hypotenuse}} \; ; \; \text{cosine} = \frac{\text{adjacent}}{\text{hypotenuse}} \; ; \; \text{tangent} = \frac{\text{opposite}}{\text{adjacent}}$$

o   For reciprocal functions, remember:

$$\csc \theta = \frac{1}{\text{sine}} \qquad \sec \theta = \frac{1}{\text{cosine}} \qquad \cot \theta = \frac{1}{\text{tangent}}$$

o   Remember the special trig identities.

$$\sin^2 \theta + \cos^2 \theta = 1 \qquad \frac{\sin \theta}{\cos \theta} = \tan \theta$$

o   Remember that in the unit circle, sin = y, cos = x, and tan = $\frac{y}{x}$.

o   When graphing sine and cosine in the xy-plane, remember $y = A[\sin (B\theta)]$.

- A is the amplitude.
- The period is $\frac{2\pi}{B}$.

o   Other transformations move the function up and down or left and right; these transformations are usually not necessary to solve the question.

o   For questions with the laws of sines or cosines, remember that side a is opposite angle A, side b is opposite angle B, and side c is opposite side C.

Chapter 20
Advanced Math

You may see logs, vectors, or matrices on your test. It's good to be familiar with these topics if you're aiming for a 30+ on the Math test, but if any of these concepts make your head spin, don't sweat it: it's unlikely that you will see more than one question in each of these topics.

LOGARITHMS

A logarithm is an alternative way to express an exponent.

> If no value is given for the base (b), then $b = 10$. For example, $\log 6 = x$ means $10^x = 6$.

$$\log_b n = x \text{ is the same as } b^x = n$$

Take a look at this question.

---

34. If $\log_x 81 = 4$, then $x = ?$

    F.   2

    G.   3

    H.   9

    J. $\dfrac{81}{4}$

Here's How to Crack It

Following the definition of logarithms, $\log_x 81 = 4$ can be rewritten as $x^4 = 81$. Take the fourth root of both sides to get $\sqrt[4]{x^4} = \sqrt[4]{81}$; this simplifies to $x = 3$, which is (G).

Trickier logarithms can look scary, but often you only need to remember the definition of logarithms.

---

43. If $\log_{(x-3)}(x^2 - 7x + 10) = 2$, then $x =$

    A. -3

    B. -1

    C.   1

    D.   3

Here's How to Crack It

Following the definition of logarithms, $\log_{(x-3)}(x^2 - 7x + 10) = 2$ can be rewritten as $(x - 3)^2 = x^2 - 7x + 10$. FOIL the left side to get $x^2 - 6x + 9 = x^2 - 7x + 10$. Subtract x^2 from both sides to get $-6x + 9 = -7x + 10$. Add $7x$ to both sides to get $x + 9 = 10$. Subtract 9 from both sides to get $x = 1$. The correct answer is (C).

MADSPM

Since logs are used to express exponents, they follow the same MADSPM rules as exponents:

> **M**ultiply $\rightarrow$ **A**dd $\log xy = \log x + \log y$
>
> **D**ivide $\rightarrow$ **S**ubtract $\log \left(\dfrac{x}{y} \right) = \log x - \log y$
>
> **P**ower $\rightarrow$ **M**ultiply $\log (x^y) = y \log x$

As with exponents, MADSPM rules apply only to logs with the same base.

Try an example question.

---

40. Whenever x and y are positive real numbers, which of the following expressions is equal to $4\log_3 x - \log_3 5y$?

F. $4\log_3 (x - 5y)$

G. $4\log_3 \left(\dfrac{x}{y^5} \right)$

H. $\log_3 (4x - 5y)$

J. $\log_3 \left(\dfrac{x^4}{5y} \right)$

Here's How to Crack It

Use Bite-Sized Pieces. Since all of the logs in the expression and answers have the same base (3), you can use the MADSPM rules. Using the Power/Multiply rule, $4\log_3 x = \log_3 x^4$. The whole expression can therefore be written as $\log_3 x^4 - \log_3 5y$. Now, use the Divide/Subtract rule: $\log_3 x^4 - \log_3 5y = \log_3 \left(\dfrac{x^4}{5y} \right)$, (J).

VECTORS

You may also come across a vector question on your test. Vectors are used to notate changes in the *x*- and *y*-values on a coordinate plane.

> Vectors are a measure of *displacement*, rather than absolute position on a coordinate plane.

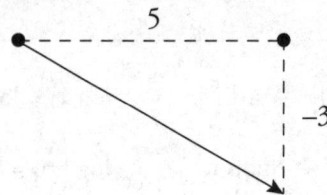

Unit Vector Notation:

i indicates the horizontal change
j indicates the vertical change

In unit vector notation, vectors are expressed as addition or subtraction of the unit vectors **i** and **j**.

Vector **v** above has the unit vector notation **v** = 5**i** – 3**j**.

To add two vectors, add the **i** to the **i** and the **j** to the **j**:

$$(5\mathbf{i} - 3\mathbf{j}) + (c\mathbf{i} + d\mathbf{j}) = (5 + c)\mathbf{i} + (-3 + d)\mathbf{j}$$

To multiply a vector by a constant, multiply both the **i** and **j** values by the constant:

$$a\mathbf{v} = a(5\mathbf{i} - 3\mathbf{j}) = 5a\mathbf{i} - 3a\mathbf{j}$$

Let's try a question:

---

34. Vectors $\overrightarrow{AB}$ and $\overrightarrow{CD}$ are shown in the standard xy-plane. What is the unit vector notation of vector $\overrightarrow{AB} + \overrightarrow{CD}$?

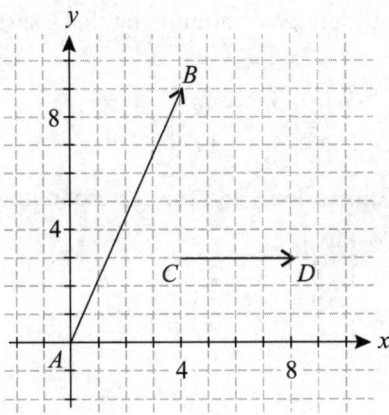

   F.   4**i** + 3**j**
   G.   4**i** + 9**j**
   H.   8**i** + 9**j**
   J.   8**i** + 12**j**

Here's How to Crack It

Unit vector notation of a vector describes the vector in terms of the changes in the x- and y-values. Vector $\overrightarrow{AB}$ starts at (0, 0) and ends at (4, 9), so it increases the x value by 4 and the y value by 9. Therefore, the unit vector notation of vector $\overrightarrow{AB}$ is 4**i** + 9**j**. Vector $\overrightarrow{CD}$ starts at (4, 3) and ends at (8, 3), so the unit vector notation is 4**i** + 0**j**. When adding or subtracting vectors, add or subtract the **i** coefficients and the **j** coefficients. $\overrightarrow{AB} + \overrightarrow{CD}$ = (4 + 4)**i** + (9 + 0)**j** = 8**i** + 9**j**, which is (H).

There is one other way you may see vectors described besides unit vector notation. Instead of using **i** and **j**, the ACT will use component form, which looks like (x, y) coordinates but with angled brackets: $\langle x, y \rangle$. For instance, in question 34 above, the answer could have been written as $\langle 8, 9 \rangle$ instead of 8**i** + 9**j**. Don't get distracted by the different ways the ACT can describe vectors; they're just different conventions for the same information.

MATRICES

An $m \times n$ matrix is an array of numbers organized in m rows and n columns.

Matrices may sound scary, but knowing a few basic rules will help you tackle many of the concepts with confidence.

To multiply a matrix by a constant, simply multiply every number by that constant:

$$a\begin{bmatrix} 3 & -2 \\ 4 & 1 \end{bmatrix} = \begin{bmatrix} 3a & -2a \\ 4a & 1a \end{bmatrix}$$

> You will not be expected to solve for the determinant of anything other than 2 x 2 matrices.

To add two matrices with the same dimensions, add the corresponding elements:

$$\begin{bmatrix} 3 & -2 \\ 4 & 1 \end{bmatrix} + \begin{bmatrix} 5 & -1 \\ -3 & 3 \end{bmatrix} = \begin{bmatrix} 3+5 & -2-1 \\ 4-3 & 1+3 \end{bmatrix} = \begin{bmatrix} 8 & -3 \\ 1 & 4 \end{bmatrix}$$

The determinant of a 2×2 matrix $\begin{bmatrix} a & b \\ c & d \end{bmatrix} = ad - bc$.

MULTIPLYING MATRICES

Multiplying two matrices is more complicated than adding them. Let your calculator do the hard work when possible, but some questions will require you to understand the concepts. Brush up on your skills if you're familiar with matrices, but if you've never worked with matrices before, then your best bet on difficult multiplication questions is to use your LOTD and keep moving.

> The product of two matrices is defined (in other words, it is possible to multiply the matrices) only when the number of columns in the first matrix is equal to the number of rows in the second. When you multiply an $m \times n$ matrix by an $n \times p$ matrix, the resulting product will be an $m \times p$ matrix.

To find the product, multiply the elements in each row of the first matrix by the elements in each column of the second and then add the products.

$$\begin{bmatrix} a & b \\ c & d \\ e & f \end{bmatrix} \times \begin{bmatrix} u & v & w \\ x & y & z \end{bmatrix} = \begin{bmatrix} au+bx & av+by & aw+bz \\ cu+dx & cv+dy & cw+dz \\ eu+fx & ev+fy & ew+fz \end{bmatrix}$$

Here's an example:

$$\begin{bmatrix} 3 & 2 \\ 1 & 5 \\ 4 & -1 \end{bmatrix} \begin{bmatrix} 6 & 7 \\ -2 & 8 \end{bmatrix} = \begin{bmatrix} 3(6)+2(-2) & 3(7)+2(8) \\ 1(6)+5(-2) & 1(7)+5(8) \\ 4(6)+-1(-2) & 4(7)+-1(8) \end{bmatrix} = \begin{bmatrix} 14 & 37 \\ -4 & 47 \\ 26 & 20 \end{bmatrix}$$

It's a little easier to remember this process when you consider that matrices can be used to represent linear equations. Consider the system of linear equations below:

$$2x + 3y = 10$$

$$6x - 5y = 13$$

This system can be represented by the following matrix equation:

$$\begin{bmatrix} 2 & 3 \\ 6 & -5 \end{bmatrix} \begin{bmatrix} x \\ y \end{bmatrix} = \begin{bmatrix} 10 \\ 13 \end{bmatrix}$$

Notice how solving the matrix equation using the matrix multiplication rule gives you $\begin{bmatrix} 2x + 3y \\ 6x - 5y \end{bmatrix} = \begin{bmatrix} 10 \\ 13 \end{bmatrix}$, which yields the two original equations $2x + 3y = 10$ and $6x - 5y = 13$.

Try this example:

35. The Wittenberg Boating Club sponsors a 2-day sailing excursion. 35 members and 15 nonmembers attend both days of the excursion. For the first day, members are charged $25 and nonmembers are charged $35. For the second day, members are charged $15 and nonmembers are charged $25. Which of the following product matrices represents the total charges each day made by the 35 members and 15 nonmembers who attended both days of the excursion?

A. $\begin{bmatrix} 35 & 15 \\ 35 & 15 \end{bmatrix} \begin{bmatrix} 25 & 15 \\ 35 & 25 \end{bmatrix}$

B. $\begin{bmatrix} 15 & 35 \end{bmatrix} \begin{bmatrix} 25 & 15 \\ 35 & 25 \end{bmatrix}$

C. $\begin{bmatrix} 35 & 15 \end{bmatrix} \begin{bmatrix} 25 & 35 \\ 15 & 25 \end{bmatrix}$

D. $\begin{bmatrix} 35 & 15 \end{bmatrix} \begin{bmatrix} 25 & 15 \\ 35 & 25 \end{bmatrix}$

Here's How to Crack It

The product matrix should multiply the number of members by the prices charged for members and the number of nonmembers by the prices charged to nonmembers, giving a total for each day. Because there should be a total for each day, there should be only two numbers in the resulting product matrix. Choice (A) multiplies a 2 × 2 by a 2 × 2. The product matrix will have the same number of rows as the first matrix (2), and the same number of columns as the second matrix (2), resulting in a 2 × 2 matrix. This matrix will have four numbers, not two, so eliminate (A). Use POE on the remaining choices. For (B), the row $\begin{bmatrix} 15 & 35 \end{bmatrix}$ would first be multiplied by the first column $\begin{bmatrix} 25 \\ 35 \end{bmatrix}$, resulting in 15 × 25 + 35 × 35. This should represent the total charges for the first day, but this multiplies the number of nonmembers (15) by the price that the members paid (25) and the number of members (35) by the price the nonmembers paid (35). This is incorrect, so eliminate (B). Choice (C) multiplies the row $\begin{bmatrix} 35 & 15 \end{bmatrix}$ by the column $\begin{bmatrix} 25 \\ 15 \end{bmatrix}$. The number of members (35) is multiplied by a price members paid the first day (25), but the number of nonmembers (15) should be multiplied by 35 not 15. This is incorrect; eliminate (C). The answer is (D).

You're in the Home Stretch!
You've tackled the Math section masterfully! Once you've completed the Advanced Math Drill, give yourself a study break. Let these lessons sink in before diving into Part IV.

Advanced Math Drill

17 If $\log_3 x = 5$, then $x = ?$

A. $\sqrt[5]{3}$

B. $\sqrt[3]{5}$

C. 125

D. 243

32. Using unit vector notation, $\mathbf{u} = -3\mathbf{i} + 2\mathbf{j}$, $\mathbf{v} = 7\mathbf{i} + 5\mathbf{j}$, and $4\mathbf{u} + (-2\mathbf{v}) + \mathbf{w} = 0$. Which of the following is $\mathbf{w}$?

F. $-26\mathbf{i} - 2\mathbf{j}$
G. $-4\mathbf{i} - 7\mathbf{j}$
H. $10\mathbf{i} + 3\mathbf{j}$
J. $26\mathbf{i} + 2\mathbf{j}$

33. What value of a satisfies the given matrix equation?

$$3\begin{bmatrix} 5 & a \\ 1 & 6 \end{bmatrix} + \begin{bmatrix} 2 & 7 \\ 3 & 4 \end{bmatrix} = \begin{bmatrix} 17 & 13 \\ 6 & 22 \end{bmatrix}$$

A. 2
B. 4
C. 6
D. 7

40. Matrices A and B are shown. Which of the following is BA?

$$A = \begin{bmatrix} 5 & -2 \\ 1 & -3 \end{bmatrix} \quad B = \begin{bmatrix} 8 & 3 \\ -1 & 7 \end{bmatrix}$$

F. $\begin{bmatrix} 43 & -25 \\ 2 & -19 \end{bmatrix}$

G. $\begin{bmatrix} 42 & 1 \\ 11 & -18 \end{bmatrix}$

H. $\begin{bmatrix} 40 & -6 \\ -1 & -21 \end{bmatrix}$

J. $\begin{bmatrix} 34 \\ -22 \end{bmatrix}$

ADVANCED MATH DRILL

17. **D** The question asks for the value of x in a logarithm. Logs are another way to write exponent equations such that $\log_b n = x$ is the same as $b^x = n$. Use this to rearrange the given log to get $3^5 = x$ and solve for x to get 243. The correct answer is (D).

32. **J** The question asks for a vector in unit vector notation given an equation with two other vectors in the same form. In unit vector notation, the horizontal displacement is given by the coefficient of **i**, and the vertical displacement is given by the coefficient of **j**. When given a multiplier in front of a vector, distribute the multiplier to both the horizontal and vertical displacement values. Thus, $4\mathbf{u} = 4(-3\mathbf{i} + 2\mathbf{j}) = -12\mathbf{i} + 8\mathbf{j}$. Similarly, $-2\mathbf{v} = -2(7\mathbf{i} + 5\mathbf{j}) = -14\mathbf{i} - 10\mathbf{j}$. Plug these results into the equation for $4\mathbf{u}$ and $-2\mathbf{v}$ to solve for **w**: $(-12\mathbf{i} + 8\mathbf{j}) + (-14\mathbf{i} - 10\mathbf{j}) + \mathbf{w} = 0$. Combine the **i** and **j** terms to get $(-12 - 14)\mathbf{i} + (8 - 10)\mathbf{j} + \mathbf{w} = 0$, or $-26\mathbf{i} - 2\mathbf{j} + \mathbf{w} = 0$. Add the **i** and **j** terms to both sides of the equation to isolate **w** and get $\mathbf{w} = 26\mathbf{i} + 2\mathbf{j}$. The correct answer is (J).

33. **A** The question asks for the value of a variable given a matrix equation. The scalar, or multiplier, of a matrix is distributed to all the values within the matrix. When matrices are added, the value in each position of the matrix will be added to the number in the same position in the corresponding matrix and be in the same position in the final matrix. This is done for all values in the matrix, but since the question asks only for the value of a, work just with the values in the upper right position of each matrix to get $3a + 7 = 13$. Solve the equation for a to get $3a = 6$, so $a = 2$. The correct answer is (A).

40. **F** The question asks for the product of two matrices. Matrices can be multiplied when the number of columns in the first matrix is equal to the number of rows in the second matrix, which is true here. The order matters, meaning BA is not the same as AB. To make this clear, rewrite the matrices in the correct order before multiplying them:

$$\begin{bmatrix} 8 & 3 \\ -1 & 7 \end{bmatrix}\begin{bmatrix} 5 & -2 \\ 1 & -3 \end{bmatrix} =$$

The product matrix will have the same number of rows as the first matrix and the same number of columns as the second matrix, which means the product of matrix B and matrix A will be a 2×2 matrix. Eliminate (J) because it has the wrong dimensions. To multiply matrix B by matrix A, multiply the numbers in the first row of matrix B by the corresponding numbers in the first column of matrix A and add the results. This becomes the upper left value in the resulting matrix. This is $[(8)(5) + (3)(1)] = [40 + 3] = 43$. Only one answer has 43 in the upper left corner, so (F) must be correct. To check, multiply the second row of matrix B by the first column of matrix A, then the first row of matrix B by the second column of matrix A, and then the second row of matrix B by the second column of matrix A. It should look like this: $\begin{bmatrix} [(8)(5)+(3)(1)] & [(8)(-2)+(3)(-3)] \\ [(-1)(5)+(7)(1)] & [(-1)(-2)+(7)(-3)] \end{bmatrix}\begin{bmatrix} 43 & -25 \\ 2 & -19 \end{bmatrix}$. The correct answer is (F).

Summary

o   A logarithm is another way to express an exponent. The equation $b^x = n$ can also be written as $\log_b n = x$.

o   Logarithms follow the same MADSPM rules as exponents.

$$\log xy = \log x + \log y$$

$$\log \frac{x}{y} = \log x - \log y$$

$$\log\left(x^y\right) = y \log x$$

o   Vectors are a measure of displacement and can be used to notate changes in the x- and y-values on a coordinate plane.

o   Vectors can be written in unit vector notation, expressed as the addition or subtraction of unit vectors **i** and **j**.

o   Vectors can also be described using component form, which is $\langle x, y \rangle$.

o   Vectors can be added or subtracted by adding or subtracting the two parts separately. Vectors can also be multiplied or divided by a constant by applying that operation to both parts of the vector.

o   Matrices are arrays of numbers arranged in rows and columns.

o   Matrices can be added or subtracted by adding or subtracting the corresponding numbers in each position. Matrices can also be multiplied or divided by a constant by applying that operation to the number in each position of the matrix.

o   The determinant of a 2 × 2 matrix $\begin{bmatrix} a & b \\ c & d \end{bmatrix}$ is $ad - bc$.

o   The product of two matrices can be found by multiplying the elements in each row of the first matrix by the elements in each column of the second matrix and then adding the products. The product will have the same number of rows as the first matrix and the same number of columns as the second matrix. If the number of rows in the first matrix does not match the number of columns in the second matrix, the product is undefined.

Part IV
How to
Crack the ACT
Reading Test

Chapter 21
Introduction to the ACT Reading Test

The ACT Reading test always comes third, after the Math test and before the Science test, if taken. Reading is a unique challenge on a timed standardized test. There are no rules and formulas to review, and the reading skills you've developed throughout your school career do not necessarily work as well on the ACT.

To maximize your score on the ACT Reading test, you need to develop reading skills specific to this test and learn how to use your time effectively.

We'll teach you how to work the passages in a personal order of difficulty that makes best use of the time allotted. We'll also teach you how to employ a strategic and efficient approach that will earn you your highest possible score.

Passage Content

Within the 4 categories, ACT selects excerpts from books and articles to create one long passage or two shorter passages. Passages chosen will change from test to test, but the topics are always chosen from the same content areas and usually follow this order:

Literary Narrative (or Prose Fiction)

The passages can be excerpts from novels or short stories, or even short stories in their entirety. While there are occasional uses of historical fiction, most passages are contemporary, emphasize diversity, and often center on family relationships.

Informational 1: Social Science

Topics are drawn from the fields of anthropology, archaeology, biography, business, economics, education, geography, history, political science, psychology, and sociology.

Informational 2: Humanities

These passages are nonfiction, but they are usually memoirs or personal essays that can read much like fiction. Topics are drawn from the fields of architecture, art, dance, ethics, film, language, literary criticism, music, philosophy, radio, television, and theater.

Informational 3: Natural Science

Topics are drawn from the fields of anatomy, astronomy, biology, botany, chemistry, ecology, geology, medicine, meteorology, microbiology, natural history, physiology, physics, technology, and zoology.

WHAT'S ON THE READING TEST

On the Reading test, you have 40 minutes to work through four passages and a total of 36 questions. One of the passages will typically be split in two, with passages by different authors or from different works. The category, or genre, of the passages usually appears in the same order: one Literary Narrative (or Prose Fiction) passage, followed by one passage based on Social Science, one based on Humanities, and one based on Natural Science, in that order. The ACT will typically call the last three passages "Informational" rather than specifying that they are Social Science, Humanities, and Natural Science. Regardless of the headings, you can expect to see passages from these categories. Occasionally, a passage in the Reading test may be accompanied by one or more tables, graphs, or other figures that contain information related to the passage. The passages are roughly the same length, 800–1,000 words, and each is usually followed by 9 questions.

The passages feature authors and topics that the ACT writers judge typical of the type of reading required in first-year college courses. And your goal, according to ACT, is to read the passages and answer questions that prove you understood both what was "directly stated" in the passage as well as what were the "implied meanings" of what was stated.

That's a pretty simple summary of the Reading test, but what is simple in theory can be more challenging in practice. In other words, the description from ACT doesn't really match the experience of trying to read 3,600 words and prove "your understanding" 36 times with a nub of a No. 2 pencil or a click of your mouse as you're dealing with the pressure of a ticking clock.

Your reading comprehension skills and the challenge of the ACT format are intertwined. In Chapter 22, we'll teach you a Basic Approach that draws upon your skills to crack the Reading test. But first, let's pull both apart for further examination.

READING SKILLS

For school, most of your reading is done with no time limits, at least theoretically. You have assignments of chapters, essays, and articles that you read, reread, highlight, and notate outside of class. You may even make flashcards. In class, group discussions and even lectures from the teacher help you grasp the significance, meaning, and context of what you have read. You may need to "show your understanding" in a quiz, test, in-class essay, or paper, but you have had time to work with the text to develop a thorough understanding.

Outside of school, serious readers take time to process what they've read and form an opinion.

As a college student, you'll be asked not only to read but also to think about what you've read and offer an opinion. Any professor will tell you that understanding takes thought, and thought usually takes time, more than 40 minutes.

When you take the ACT, you don't have the luxury of time. You can't read thoroughly, much less reread, notate, or make flashcards. There's certainly no group discussion to help elicit the meaning of each passage. So the first step in raising your score is to *stop treating the Reading test as a school assignment.* You need to read differently on the ACT, but you also need to know that a thorough, thoughtful grasp of the meaning isn't needed to answer the questions correctly.

In this section, we'll teach you how to read the passages and apply the Basic Approach to answer the questions correctly. But the next step in raising your scores is to apply your own Personal Order of Difficulty to the order of the passages.

HOW TO CRACK THE READING TEST

Order the Passages

You shouldn't work the passages in the order ACT offers *just because they're in that order.* Always choose your own order, working first the passages that are easiest for you and leaving for last the most difficult. What if natural science is the easiest for you? If you did the four passages in the order ACT offers, you could easily run out of time before even getting to the natural science passage or find yourself with so little time that you manage to answer correctly only half the number of questions you would have otherwise sailed through.

Now, Later, Never

When time is your enemy, as it is on the ACT, find and work Now the passages that are easiest for you. Leave for Later, or perhaps even Never, the passages that are the most difficult for you.

> - **Your POOD**: categories and topics you like best
> - **Paragraphs**: smaller and many are better than big and few
> - **Questions**: the more line references, the better*
> - **Answers**: short are better than long
>
> *On the Enhanced ACT Online Test, use the Index tool to view all nine questions at a glance and scan for instances of the phrase "highlighted text," which will be used in place of line references. Additionally, since it would be time-consuming to attempt to scan the answer choices for all 36 questions on the Online Test, make your decision based only on POOD, paragraph count, and instances of highlighting.

Every time you take an ACT Reading Test, for practice and for real, spend the first minute or so to pick your own order of the passages. In practice, you will likely build up a track record to determine your Personal Order of Difficulty (POOD). However, each ACT features all new passages, and certain characteristics may vary enough to affect the difficulty of a passage. Pay attention to the particulars of each test, and be willing to adapt your order for that day's test.

Let's discuss what each of these mean.

Your Personal Order of Difficulty (POOD)

The best way to determine which categories you work the best is through repeated practice tests followed by self-analysis. Regardless of where it is in your order, do you consistently do the best on social science? Do you usually prefer the literary narrative and humanities over the social science and natural science?

Before you've developed your POOD, identify your own likes and dislikes. For example, do you rarely read fiction outside of school? If so, then the literary narrative is unlikely to be a smart choice to do first. On the following pages, we've supplied brief excerpts of each category to give you an idea of what each is like.

Literary Narrative   On the literary narrative passages, facts typically matter less than do the setting, the atmosphere, and the relationships between characters. The plot and dialogue may even be secondary to the characters' thoughts and emotions, not all of which will be directly stated.

> Allen's grandmother was readying herself to leave. She was, in fact, putting the final touches on her makeup which, as always, looked to Allen as though someone had thrown it on her face with a shovel. As Mrs. Mandale placed her newly purchased
> 5 bracelet over her wrist, a look of troubled ambivalence came over her. "Perhaps this bracelet isn't right for me," she said. "I won't wear it."
>
> Waiting now for 30 minutes, Allen tried to be tolerant. "It is right for you," he said. "It matches your personality. Wear it."
> 10 The bracelet was a remarkable illustration of poor taste. Its colors were vulgar, and the structure lacked any sign of thoughtful design. The truth is, it did match his grandmother's personality. All that she did and enjoyed was tasteless and induced in Allen a quiet hopelessness.

The questions are more likely to involve identifying the implied meanings than what was directly stated.

1. Allen most likely encouraged his grandmother to wear her bracelet because he:

   A. found it colorful and approved of its appearance.
   B. found its appearance pathetic and wished his grandmother to look pretty.
   C. was impatient with his grandmother for spending time worrying about the bracelet.
   D. felt the bracelet matched his grandmother's bright personality.

If you like to read fiction for school assignments or for pleasure, you may find the literary narrative one of the easier passages. If you don't like to read fiction, you may find that passage unclear and confusing. Do the literary narrative Later, or perhaps Never.

Don't worry about the answer right now. There are explanations for the questions in this chapter on page 419, but don't review them until you get there. The point of this exercise is POOD!

Informational: Social Science   The topics of these passages should remind you of the papers you write for school. The organization will flow logically with clear topic sentences and well-chosen transitions to develop the main idea. The author may have a point of view on the subject or may simply deliver informative facts in a neutral tone.

Religion is so fundamental a part of human existence that one might easily forget to ask how it started. Yet it had to start somewhere, and there had to be a time when human beings or their apelike ancestors did not entertain notions of the super-
5 natural. Hence the historian should want to probe the origins of religious belief.

It is doubtful that morality played a part in the beginnings of religious belief. Rather, religion is traceable to a far more fundamental human and animal characteristic. Storms, floods,
10 famine, and other adversities inspired *fear* in the hearts of primitive peoples as well they should have. Curiously, humankind early took the position that it might somehow subject such catastrophes to its control. Specifically, it believed it might control them by obedience and submission and by conforming its behavior to
15 their mandates. Worship, ritual, sacrifice of life, and property became means through which early peoples sought to cajole the powers and avoid the blights and miseries the peoples dreaded. As Petronius, in Lucretius's tradition remarked, "It was fear that first made the gods."

11. According to the passage, natural disasters contributed to the development of religion by:

    A. motivating human beings to acquire some command over their environment.
    B. making human beings distinguish themselves from animals.
    C. causing human beings to sacrifice their lives and goods.
    D. providing a need for ritual and tradition.

12. The author believes that the origins of religion:

    F. are extremely easy to ascertain and understand.
    G. should not be questioned by historians because religion is fundamental to civilized life.
    H. are directly tied to apelike subhuman species.
    J. should be the subject of serious historical inquiry.

Informational: Humanities   The topics of these passages are nonfiction, but because they are memoirs or personal essays, they can feel similar to the fiction passages. The narrative may use a more organic development instead of a linear one, and the tone will be more personal and perhaps more emotional than the more objective tones found in social and natural science.

Swiping impatiently at the layer of dust that
had settled on the cardboard flaps, I opened the box.
I was expecting another stack of wrinkled school
papers and childhood drawings from no particular
5 year, but sitting on top of the haphazard stack was
a small, yellowed program and a ticket stub, held
together with a rusting paper clip that left its orange
imprint on the paper. "New York City Center presents
the Alvin Ailey City Center Dance Theater." As I
10 brushed my fingers over the words, memories that
had sat for years in a dusty backstage corner came
tumbling, polished and shining, into the limelight. I
could feel the skin on the backs of my legs sticking
to the plastic subway seats in the August swelter,
15 hear the swell of the music as the lights went down
in the midtown theater, see the beads of sweat on
the dancers' faces as they leapt and glided across
the stage.

24. The author uses the phrase "dusty backstage corner" (line 11)
most likely to emphasize that she:

F. is no longer able to recall the performance that the ticket
stub was for.
G. has not thought of the events described in the passage for
some time.
H. watched the Alvin Ailey dance company from backstage.
J. made costumes for friends from old clothing found in her attic.

Informational: Natural Science   These passages feature a lot of details and sometimes very technical descriptions. Similar to the social science passage, the natural science passage typically features a linear organization with clear topic sentences and transitions to develop the main idea. The author may or may not have an opinion on the topic.

It is further noteworthy that the terrestrial vertebrate's most
significant muscles of movement are no longer located lateral to
the vertebral column as they are in the fish but rather in ventral
and dorsal relation to it. This trend in terrestrial evolution is highly
5 significant and means that the terrestrial vertebrate's principal
movements are fore and back, not side to side. The trend is well
documented in the whale, an aquatic animal whose ancestors are
terrestrial quadrupeds. The whale, in other words, has "returned"
to the sea secondarily after an ancestral stage on the land. Un-
10 like the fish, and in accordance with its ancestry, it propels itself
by moving the tail up and down, not side to side. In a sense, the
whale moves itself by bending up and down at the waist. Indeed,
that very analogy is recalled by the mythical mermaid figure
who seems to represent a humanlike line returned to the water
15 secondarily like the whale.

The questions usually track the text pretty closely and require you to make few inferences.

31. Which of the following best represents a general trend associated with mammalian evolution?

    A. Enhancement of bodily movement from right to left and left to right

    B. Minimization of muscle groups oriented lateral to the vertebral column

    C. The development of propulsive fins from paired limbs

    D. Secondary return to the sea

Order the Passages, Redux

As you take practice Reading tests, develop a consistent order that works for you, but always be willing to mix it up when you start each test, practice or real. The passages all run roughly the same number of words (800–1,000), and each features 9 questions followed by 4 answer choices each. But the chosen topics, revealed in the blurb, and the way the passages, questions, and answers look can provide valuable clues that should make you reconsider that day's order.

Paragraphs

Which passage would you rather work, one with 8–10 medium-sized paragraphs or one with three huge paragraphs? The overall length is the same, but the size and number of the paragraphs influences how easily you can navigate the passage and retrieve answers as you work the questions.

Some fiction passages can feature too many paragraphs, with each paragraph an individual line of dialogue. Too many paragraphs can make it just as difficult to locate the right part of the passage to find answers.

Ideally, a passage should feature 8–10 paragraphs, with each paragraph made up of 5–15 lines.

Questions

The questions on the Reading test don't follow a chronological order of the passage, and not every question comes with a line reference. Line references and paragraph references, or questions with highlighted text, are maps, pointing to the precise part of the passage to find the answer. You waste no time getting lost, hunting through the passage to find where to read. Therefore, a passage with only 1 or 2 questions with line and paragraph references or highlighted text will be more challenging than one that features 4, 5, 6, or more (8 is the most we've ever seen).

Answers

Compare the two "questions" and their answer choices below.

13. Blah blah blah blah:

    A. are caused primarily by humanity's overriding concern with acceptance and peace.

    B. are due in part to a faulty understanding of history.

    C. should make historians question the role of the individual in human affairs.

    D. should provoke historical inquiry into humanity's willingness to tolerate adversity.

14. Blah blah blah blah:

    F. more traditional.

    G. more formal.

    H. less rigid.

    J. less informative.

Which do you think is the easier question? Question 14, of course! Long answers usually answer harder questions, and short answers usually answer easier questions. A passage with lots of questions with short answers is a good sign. Remember that if you are taking the Online ACT, it may be harder to catch this since the questions appear one at a time, so rely instead on your interest in the topic, the number and size of the paragraphs, and the instances of highlighted text.

Use Your Eye, Not Your Brain

Look at the passages to evaluate the paragraphs, line references or passage highlights, and answer choices. Don't thoughtfully ponder and consider each element, and don't read through the questions. Quickly check the blurb to see if you recognize the subject or author.

Use your eye to scan the paragraphs, look for numbers amidst the questions, and the length of answer choices. If you see lots of warning signs on what is typically your first passage, leave it for Later. If you see great paragraphs, line references, and lots of short answers on the passage you typically do third, consider bumping it up to second, maybe first. This should take no more than a few seconds per passage.

Exercise: Pick Your Order

Put these passages in your own order: 1st, 2nd, 3rd, and 4th. We listed the number of paragraphs and questions with line references and short answers for the purpose of the exercise. This is not a hint that you need to be overly precise on a real test. You're looking for warning signs, a quick visual task. If you're taking the Online Test, ignore the number of short versus long answers in your ranking, and treat all line and paragraph references as instances of the phrase "highlighted text."

Exercise I

Literary Narrative: ___
>
> Unknown author and title, a ton of dialogue, over 20 paragraphs, many of them only one line, 2 line/paragraph references, and lots of long answers.

Social Science: _____
>
> The title sounds technical, 6 paragraphs, 3 line/paragraph references, and 4 questions with short answers.

Humanities: _____
>
> The title sounds deep, 9 paragraphs, 6 line/paragraph references, 1 question with short answers, and a dual passage.

Natural Science: _____
>
> The title sounds kind of cool, 9 paragraphs, 4 line/paragraph references, and 4 questions with short answers.

Exercise II

Literary Narrative: ___
>
> Familiar author, 7 paragraphs, 8 line/paragraph references, and 4 questions with short answers.

Social Science: _____
>
> The title sounds sort of interesting, 6 paragraphs, 2 line/paragraph references, 2 questions with short answers, and a dual passage.

Humanities: _____
>
> The title sounds sort of interesting, 11 paragraphs, 5 line/paragraph references, and 4 questions with short answers.

Natural Science: _____
>
> The title sounds kind of dull, 9 paragraphs, 4 line/paragraph references, and 6 questions with short answers.

ORDER THE QUESTIONS

In Chapter 22, we'll teach you the Basic Approach of how to attack the passage and the questions, and in that chapter, we'll go into more depth about how you determine the order in which you should do the questions.

The only order you need to know now is the one to avoid: ACT's. The questions aren't in chronological order, nor are they in any order of difficulty from easiest to hardest. You shouldn't work the questions in the order given *just because ACT numbered them in order.*

Now Questions

Work the questions in an order that makes sense for you.

> Now questions are questions for which it is easy to *find* the answer. Calling a question a Now question does not mean it's easy, but as you will see later on, finding the correct part of the passage to answer the question is a huge part of the battle.

What Makes an Answer "Easy to Find?"

First, if a question has line/paragraph references or highlighted text, you know where to look. As discussed before, all of these work like a map, showing you where in the passage to find the answer. On the ACT Online Test, the passage will actually "jump" to the highlighted text, making it even easier to find the answer.

Second, if a question comes with a great lead word, it will be easy to find. Lead words are the nouns, phrases, and sometimes verbs that are specific to the passage. Lead words are not the standard boilerplate language you see on some questions like "What is the main idea of the passage?" or "Which of the following is NOT answered by the passage?" Lead words are likely to stand out and, even better, will probably only occur once or twice in the passage, directing you to where the answer is located.

Look at the following questions from a Social Science and a Natural Science passage. All the lead words have been circled.

11. Jeremy Bentham probably would have said that lawyers:

12. The author states that common law differs from civil law in that:

13. According to the passage the integrative movement produced:

31. The main purpose of the passage is to:

35. Which of the following statements most accurately summarizes how the passage characterizes edema and hypoproteinemia?

Lead words are specific words and phrases that can be found in the passage and are likely to appear only once or twice in the passage.

Great lead words are proper nouns, unusual words, and dates. The more often a word or name appears in the question stems (such as the name of the passage author), the less likely it functions as a great lead word.

Later Questions

Later questions have answers that are difficult to find and are usually also difficult to answer without reading a decent portion of the passage, like question 31 in the last set of examples. Most questions that are difficult to answer require reasoning skills to "show your understanding of statements with implied meaning."

If a question asks about the entire passage and lacks both line/paragraph references (or highlighting) *and* lead words, it's best to come back to that question later.

BASIC QUESTION TYPES

Though your main job is to determine whether a question is Now or Later, it's worth knowing that ACT groups its questions into three categories based on what aspect of reading comprehension that question is testing. ACT uses big, fancy names for these categories, but we've provided some simpler ways to think about them below.

Information Questions

ACT calls these "Key Ideas and Details" questions. The possible tasks for Information questions include the following:

- determining main ideas
- describing the content of the passage accurately
- demonstrating an understanding of relationships between ideas and characters
- drawing logical inferences and conclusions

These questions often simply ask what the passage says, or as ACT puts it, what is directly stated. Information questions don't require much reasoning; the answer will be waiting in black and white, and the correct answer will be a slightly paraphrased version of what the passage said. Even when a question asks for the main idea of the passage and is therefore a Later question, the answer is still going to be very direct—it will just be based on multiple paragraphs rather than just one or part of one.

It's also worth noting that many of these answers will be relatively short. That's why, on the Paper ACT, you look for plenty of questions with short answers in picking your order of passages—lots of short answers probably means lots of Information questions, which means that passage is, at least, less annoying than the others.

Reasoning Questions

ACT calls these "Craft and Structure" questions. The possible tasks for Reasoning questions include the following:

- determining the meanings of words and phrases
- understanding the impact of the language used in the passage
- noting the overall structure of the passage
- understanding the author's purpose and perspective
- describing characters' points of view
- differentiating between various perspectives and sources of information

These questions can feel more involved than Information questions, as authors typically don't interrupt their passages to yell out, "Here's why I included this!" But do not panic—the author's purpose and intent will still be revealed in lines and sentences you can physically point to. For example, if the author of a Social Science passage wants to establish a contrast between two pieces of legislation, it's very hard to do so without using a word like "however." This, in turn, makes the purpose of that portion of the passage more clear. So, the key difference between Information and Reasoning questions is that answers to Information questions are paraphrased versions of the information in the passage, while answers to Reasoning questions are not directly stated in the passage but supported by the information in the passage.

Answers to Reasoning questions are usually longer than answers to Information questions, but not always—the answer to Vocabulary questions, a type of Reasoning question, are only going to be a word or two long. That's one reason it's important to focus first on questions for which you can locate the answer more than on specific question types.

Analysis Questions

ACT calls these "Integration of Knowledge and Ideas" questions. The possible tasks for Analysis questions include the following:

- understanding what claims the author is making
- differentiating between facts and opinions
- using evidence to make connections between different texts that are related by topic
- using evidence to make connections between information presented in passages and information presented in charts and graphs

These questions are perhaps the oddest, but thankfully, they are also the rarest. The most common place you will see these is on the dual passage—any question that asks about both passages is automatically an Analysis question in ACT's eyes. As long as you've done all of the individual question for each passage, you'll often be able to determine what main points the passages agree on or what one of them discussed but the other did not.

The answers to Analysis questions are frequently longer and contain multiple parts to them. It's important to remember that whether you are asked to determine what claim is being supported, whether something should be taken as fact or opinion, or whether something should be read literally or figuratively, the answer must be consistent with the passage. Furthermore, you can often eliminate two answers for the exact same reason, due to many of these answers having multiple parts.

Pace Yourself

To earn your best possible Reading score, you need to invest your time where it will do the most good. What complicates knowing which passages will be most "worth it" is that one of the four passages will be unscored, meaning that it will not count towards your Reading test score. Therefore, you must balance attempting all four passages without allowing any one question or passage to take too much of your time.

> Restrict yourself to a 10-minute maximum per passage, especially for the first two passages you attempt. Focus on answering as many questions as possible and using Letter of the Day for any "Never" questions.

While ranking passages using POOD will help you generate momentum and earn the points that you absolutely should earn, the fact that you do not know which passage will be unscored means you must attempt all four passages. That means, mathematically, you have a maximum of 10 minutes to spend on each passage. However, this is yet another way in which reordering the passages will help you. The passage you rank as first will likely be on a topic you enjoy, have an ideal number of paragraphs, and have a good number of line references and lead words. With practice, you may be able to do your first and even your second passages in less time than the 10-minute maximum. This, in turn, will bank some extra time for the later, harder passages.

Additionally, many students discover that they have an issue not with a type of passage but instead with a certain type of question. The more quickly you identify a question type that eats up a lot of your clock, the more quickly you may use LOTD on that question type each time it comes up, preserving your time for all of the other Reading questions more suited to your strengths.

That's what timed practice tests will help you discover.

> **Letter of the Day (LOTD)** With only 10 minutes per passage, you may need to skip a question here and there. But that doesn't mean you don't choose an answer. Never leave any questions blank on the ACT. Choose your Letter of the Day for all questions that you don't have time to work.

Be Flexible

Flexibility is key to your ACT success, particularly on the Reading test. Picking the order of the passages rests on your willingness to flip your order when you see that day's test. The passages, after all, are new on each test you see, and you have to look at what you've been given and adapt.

Similarly, you have to be flexible in your pacing. Don't drown in one particular passage or get stuck on one tough question. Move on from a passage on which you've already spent too much time. Force yourself to guess on the question you've been rereading for minutes, use LOTD on any questions still left, and move on.

We're not saying this is easy. In fact, changing your own instinctual behavior is the hardest part of cracking the Reading test. Everyone has made the mistake of ignoring that voice that's screaming inside your head to move on, and we've all answered back, "But I know I'm almost there and if I take just a little more time, I know I can get it."

You may, in fact, get that question. But that one right answer likely cost you 2–3 others. And even worse, you had probably already narrowed it down to two answer choices. You were down to a fifty-fifty chance of getting it right, and instead you wasted more time to prove the one right answer.

In these chapters, we'll show you how to use that time more effectively to begin with and what to do when you're down to two. But both skills depend on the Process of Elimination, POE.

POE

POE is a powerful tool on a multiple-choice, standardized test. On the Reading test, you may find several Now questions easy to answer and be able to spot the right answer right away among the four choices. There will be plenty of tough Reasoning questions, however, whose answers aren't obvious, either in your own words or among the four choices. You can easily fall into the trap of rereading and rereading to figure out the answer. Wrong answers, however, can be more obvious to identify. After all, they are there to hide the right answer. In fact, if you can eliminate all the wrong ones, the right answer will be waiting there for you. Even if you eliminate only one or two, the right answer frequently becomes more obvious.

> **Process of Elimination**
> Each time you eliminate a wrong answer, you increase your chance of choosing the correct answer.

We'll spend more time with POE in the following chapters. For now, just remember that we started this lesson with a reminder that the first step in raising your ACT Reading score is to stop treating this test as if it's a reading assignment for school. You don't get extra points for knowing the answer before you look at the answer choices. You get a point for a correct answer, and you need to get to as many questions as possible in order to answer them. Use POE to escape the time sink questions that will hold you back.

CHAPTER QUESTION ANSWERS AND EXPLANATIONS

1. **C** Choice (C) is correct because Allen has been waiting for *30 minutes* and *tried to be tolerant*, indicating he is running out of patience. Choice (A) is wrong because Allen finds the bracelet's colors *vulgar* and therefore does not approve of its *appearance*. Choice (B) is wrong because while Allen doesn't like the bracelet, the passage never states that he *wished his grandmother to look pretty*. Choice (D) is wrong because Allen associates his grandmother's personality with the word *tasteless*, not *bright*.

11. **A** Choice (A) is correct because the text states that *religion is traceable* to *fear* of natural disasters, and humankind *believed it might control* such catastrophes *by obedience and submission*. Choice (B) is wrong because the text never states that humans did anything to *distinguish themselves* from animals. Choice (C) is wrong because the natural disasters themselves don't cause humans to *sacrifice their lives and goods*. Choice (D) is wrong because the natural disasters don't provide a *need* for ritual and tradition; it's humankind that decides it may need these things.

12. **J** Choice (J) is correct because the author takes the time to trace the origins of religion to *primitive peoples* and cites a historical figure that shares a similar belief to that of the author. Choice (F) is wrong because the author does not say the origins of religion are *extremely easy* to figure out or understand. Choice (G) is wrong because the text never claims that *religion is fundamental to civilized life* or that religion's origins *should not be questioned*. Choice (H) is wrong because although the passage mentions humans' *apelike ancestors*, it does not say they were a *subhuman species* that was tied directly to the *origins of religion*.

24. **G** Choice (G) is correct because the author mentions that *memories that had sat for years* came back *into the limelight*, so she is thinking about them for the first time in a while. Choice (F) is wrong because the author never states she has forgotten what *performance that the ticket stub was for*. Choice (H) is wrong because the reference to *backstage* in the text is not a literal backstage but the author's mind. Choice (J) is wrong because there is no reference to *costumes* or *friends* in the text.

31. **B** Choice (B) is correct because the opening sentence states that the *significant muscle of movement are no longer located lateral to the vertical column*, and then provides an example of *This trend* by using a whale. Choice (A) is wrong because it contradicts the text: the *terrestrial vertebrae's principal movements are fore and back, not side to side*. Choice (C) is wrong because it describes a development only connected to the whale and not *a general trend*. Choice (D) is similarly wrong because it only describes the whale and is not a *general trend* for most or all mammals.

Summary

○ There are always 4 passages and 36 questions on the Reading test. One of these will be a "Dual Passage" that includes two shorter passages by different authors or from different works.

○ The passages are usually in the same order: Literary Narrative, Social Science, Humanities, Natural Science. The later three will likely just be called "Informational," but the order of topics should be as described.

○ Each passage has 9 questions and will be roughly 800–1,000 words.

○ Follow your POOD to pick your own order of the passages.

○ Look for passages to do Now: the best indicators of a Now passage are categories and topics you like best or find easiest, passages with 8–10 paragraphs of 5–15 lines, and passages with lots of line references (or highlighted text on the ACT Online Test).

○ On the Paper ACT, you can also look for passages with lots of questions with short answers.

○ Pace yourself and be flexible. Aim for a maximum of 10 minutes per passage and make use of your Letter of the Day to avoid one question on one passage affecting your ability to finish the section.

○ Use Process of Elimination to get rid of wrong answers and save time.

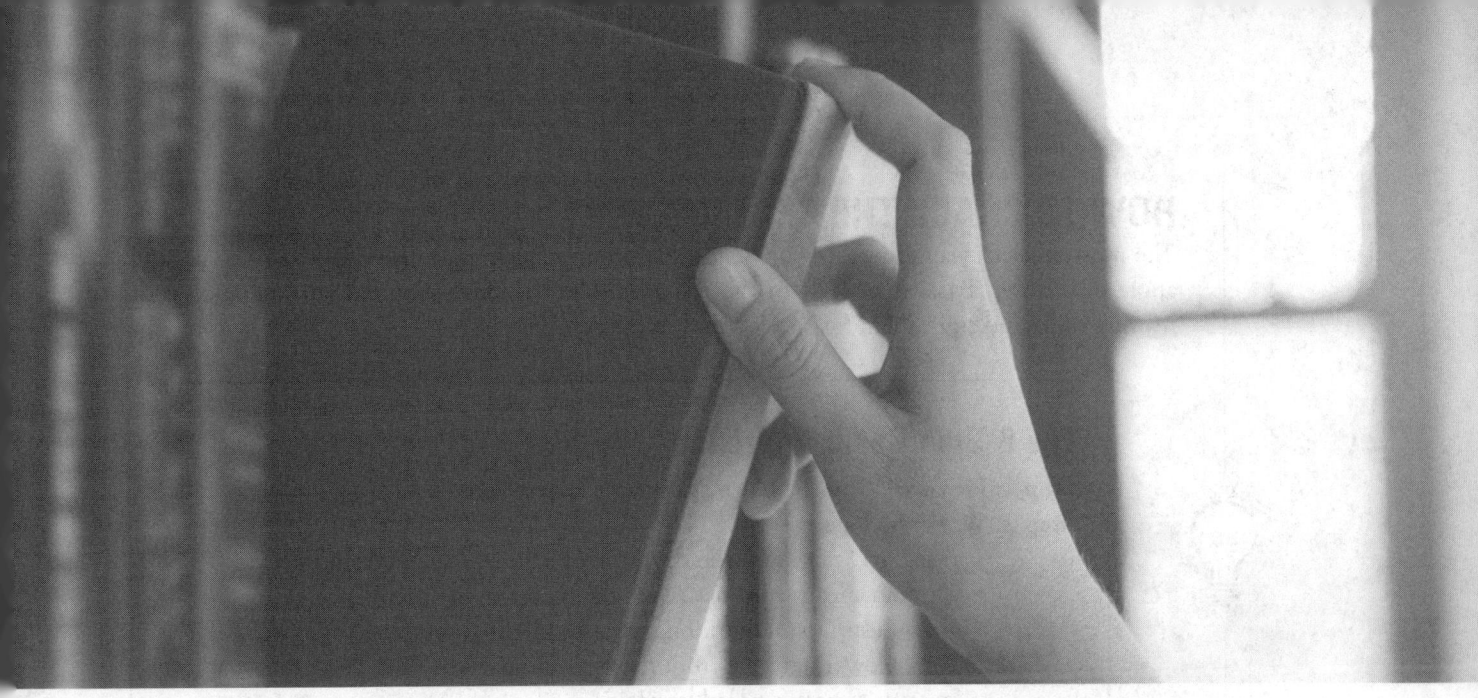

Chapter 22
The 6-Step Basic Approach

To earn your highest possible score on the Reading test, you need an efficient and strategic approach to working the passages. In this chapter, we'll teach you how to work the passages, questions, and answers.

HOW TO CRACK THE READING TEST

The most efficient way to boost your Reading score is to pick your order for the passages and apply our 6-Step Basic Approach to the passages. Use the Basic Approach to enhance your reading skills and train them for specific use on the ACT.

The 6-Step Basic Approach

Step 1: Preview. Read the blurb and map the questions.

Step 2: Work the Passage.

> Paper Test: Start from the beginning of the passage and stop when you find a lead word or arrive at a line/paragraph reference.

> Online Test: Do all questions with highlighted text first using steps 3–6 below, then start from the beginning of the passage and search for your remaining lead words.

Step 3: Select and Understand a Question. Use POOD to choose a question and determine what the question is asking.

Step 4: Read What You Need. Most questions require 5–10 lines.

Step 5: Mark the Answer in the Passage. Use your pencil or highlighting tool to flag phrases or sentences in the passage that answer, or help answer, the question.

Step 6: Use POE.

Before we train you on each step in cracking the test the right way, let's talk about the temptations to attack the passages in the wrong way.

This Isn't School

In the previous chapter, we discussed the reading skills you've spent your whole school career developing. You have been rewarded for your ability to develop a thorough, thoughtful grasp of the meaning and significance of the text. But in school, you have the benefit of time, not to mention the aid of your teachers' lectures, class discussions, and various tools to help you not only understand but also remember what you've read. You have none of those tools on the Reading test, but you walk into it with the instinct to approach the Reading test as if you do.

Where does that leave you on the ACT Reading test? You spend several minutes reading the passage, trying to understand the details and follow the author's main point. You furiously underline or highlight what you think may be important points that will be tested later in the questions. And when you hit a particularly confusing chunk of detailed text, what do you do? You read it again. And again. You worry you can't move on until you have solved this one detail. All the while, time is slipping by....

Now, on to the questions. Your first mistake is to do them in order. But as we told you in the previous chapter, they are not written in order of difficulty or in chronological order. You confront main-idea questions before specific questions. You try to answer the questions all from memory. After all, you've spent so much time reading the passage, you don't have the time to go back to find or even confirm an answer. And when you do occasionally go back to read a specific part of the passage, you still don't see the answer. So you read the chunk of the passage again and again.

If you approach the Reading test this way, you will likely not earn the points you need to hit your goal score.

The Passage

You don't earn points from reading the passage. You earn points from answering the questions correctly. And you have no idea what the questions will ask. You're searching desperately through the passage, looking for conclusions and main points. You stumble on the details, rereading several times to master them. But how do you even know what details are important if you haven't seen the questions?

The Questions

When you answer the questions from memory, you will either face answer choices that all seem right, or you will fall right into ACT's trap, choosing an answer choice that sounds right with some familiar words, but which, in reality, doesn't match what the passage said.

The test-writers at ACT know everyone is inclined to attack the Reading test this way. They write deceptive answer choices that will tempt you because that's what wrong answers have to do. If the right answer were surrounded by three ridiculous, obviously wrong answers, everyone would get a 36. Wrong answers have to sound temptingly right, and the easiest way to do that is to use noticeable terms out of the passage. You gratefully latch onto them the way a drowning person clutches a life preserver.

THE 6-STEP BASIC APPROACH

The best way to beat the ACT system is to use a different one. The 6-Step Basic Approach will help you direct the bulk of your time to where you earn points, on the questions and answers. When you read the passage, you'll read knowing exactly what you're looking for.

Step 1: Preview

The first step, which involves two parts, is the same for both the Paper Test and the Online Test: read the blurb at the beginning of the passage to see if it offers any additional information. Most of the time, all it will offer will be the title, author, copyright date, and publisher. There is even no guarantee that the title will convey the topic. But occasionally, the blurb will define an unfamiliar term, place a setting, or identify a character.

Passage III

> **INFORMATIONAL:** This passage is adapted from the article "The Sculpture Revolution" by Michael Michalski (©1998 Geer Publishing).

True to form, this offers only the basic information.

> **Potholes**
> If you're out driving and you hit a pothole, do you back up and drive over it again? Rereading text you didn't understand is the literary equivalent of driving over the same pothole again and again.

> In this chapter, we've formatted the passage as if it were on the pencil-and-paper ACT. If you're taking the ACT Online Test, remember that the passage won't have line references, and that questions with line references would instead have the relevant parts of the passage highlighted.

> **Second Time Around**
> You'll check the blurb twice. Once when you're confirming your order and now as part of Step 1.

Map the Questions

The goal of mapping the questions is to learn the location of as many answers to questions as possible, or at least, to know what topics to look for as you work the passage. This process should take no more than a minute (and less time with practice). On the Paper ACT, you will:

- Star any question with line or paragraph references, then write that question number near the relevant moment in the passage (such as "Q17" around line 20 if there's a reference to lines 22–28 in question 17)
- Circle any lead words (if a passage has a lead word and a line/paragraph reference, you do not need to circle—the star is enough to know where to go!)
- Put an "L" for Later next to any question that has no line/paragraph references and no lead words

On the Online Test, you will:

- Write the question numbers for the passage on scratch paper vertically, leaving space to the right of each one
- Access all nine question stems at once using the Index tool
- Write an "H" next to any question number whose question refers to highlighted text
- Write the lead words for any question that has lead words next to that question number
- Write an "L" next to any question number that does not reference highlighted text and has no lead words

Lead Words

We introduced lead words in Chapter 21. These are the specific words and phrases that you will find in the passage. They are not the boilerplate language of Reading test questions like "main idea" or "author's purpose." They are usually nouns, phrases, or verbs.

Map the questions for Passage III (a Humanities passage) following the above instructions for the Paper Test.

19. The author expresses the idea that:

20. The information in lines 75–81 suggests that Quentin Bell believes that historians and critics:

21. Which of the following most accurately summarizes how the passage characterizes subjectivism's effect on Rodin?

22. According to the passage, academicism and mannerism:

23. Information in the fourth paragraph (lines 33–41) makes clear that the author believes that:

24. According to the passage, Renoir differs from Daleur in that:

25. Based on information in the sixth paragraph (lines 49–57), the author implies that:

26. In line 65, when the author uses the phrase "modern," he most nearly means sculpture that:

27. Which of the following statements would the author most likely agree with?

Your mapped questions should look like this:

L **19.** The author expresses the idea that:

☆ **20.** The information in lines 75–81 suggests that Quentin Bell believes that historians and critics:

21. Which of the <u>following most accurately</u> summarizes how the passage characterizes (subjectivism's effect on Rodin)?

22. According to the passage, (academicism and mannerism:)

☆ **23.** Information in the fourth paragraph (lines 33–41) makes clear that the author believes that:

24. According to the passage, (Renoir differs from Daleur) in that:

☆ **25.** Based on information in the sixth paragraph (lines 49–57), the author implies that:

☆ **26.** In line 65, when the author uses the phrase "modern," he most nearly means sculpture that:

L **27.** Which of the following statements would the author most likely agree with?

Keep in mind that you would also write "Q20" around line 75, "Q23" around line 33, "Q25" around line 49, and "Q26" around line 65 as part of this process, marking where your line references are in the passage.

Two Birds, One Stone

Mapping the questions provides two key benefits. First, you've just identified (with stars) four questions that have easy-to-find answers. With all those great lead words, you have two more questions whose answers will be easy to find. Second, you have the main idea of the passage *before* you've read it. When you read the passage knowing what to look for, you *read actively*.

Look again at all the words you've circled. They tell you what the passage will be about: modern sculpture, Renoir, Daleur, Rodin, and a bunch of "-isms" that you could safely guess concern art. There is also someone named Quentin Bell, historians, critics, and art. You're ready to move on to Step 2.

Step 2: Work the Passage

Your next step is to work the passage.

For the Paper Test, start skimming the passage from the beginning. You're only looking to understand broadly what is in each paragraph and to find information that will help you answer the questions. You're not reading to understand every word and detail. If you find one of your lead words, circle it. As soon as you either circle one of your lead words or get to a spot where you wrote a question number during Step 1, it's time to pause Step 2 and work Steps 3–6 (described later in this chapter) for that question. In other words, Step 2 isn't something you do once: it's a process that continues until you've answered all of the questions that have either lead words or line/paragraph references.

For the Online Test, you should instead start answering the questions with highlighted text (those you marked with an "H" in Step 1). Again, the passage will automatically jump to these questions, allowing you to use Steps 3–6 to answer 2 or 3 questions right away without even having to deal with the passage as a whole yet. Even so, you are still working the passage: as you read the highlighted excerpts, keep an eye out for your lead words as ACT will very commonly ask about the same chunks of text multiple times, and you may often get a 2-for-1 with your highlighted text also containing a lead word that you need for a different question (which you should do immediately after the highlighted text question, in that case). Once all highlighted text questions are answered, do the exact same process as you would on the Paper ACT, but you will only have lead words to find, since the Online Test's version of "line reference" questions have been handled already.

> When working the passage, as soon as you find information that will help you answer a question, stop and answer that question immediately.

You may correctly ask, "But isn't it awkward to stop and start reading the passage?" However, understand that your job on ACT Reading is not to understand the passage. It is to find the answers to the questions asked, and nothing more. By prioritizing answering each question soon as you are able to, you ensure that your focus is on earning points and not reading and rereading the passage until you fully comprehend it, which is a tall order on a standardized test and not something you have the time for.

Below is what the passage should look like on the Paper Test after Step 1. Using the completed question map from pages 424–425, find and circle each lead word. Then, fill out the order the questions would be answered in on the lines following the passage.

Passage III

INFORMATIONAL: This passage is adapted from the article "The Sculpture Revolution" by Michael Michalski (©1998 Geer Publishing).

If we were to start fresh in the study of sculpture or any art, we might observe that the record is largely filled by works of relatively few great contributors. Next to the influences of these great geniuses, time periods
5 themselves are of little significance. The study of art and art history are properly directed to the achievements of outstanding individual artists, not the particular decades or centuries in which any may have worked.

Nonetheless, when we study art in historical
10 perspective we select a convenient frame of reference through which diverse styles and talents are to be compared. Hence we write of "movements" and attempt to understand each artist in terms of the one to which he "belongs." Movements have limited use, but we should
15 not talk of realism, impressionism, cubism, or surrealism as though they genuinely had lives of their own to which the artist was answerable. We regard the movement as the governing force and the artist as its servant. Yet it is well to remember that the movements do not necessarily
20 present themselves in orderly chronological series, and the individual artist frequently weaves her way into one and out of another over the course of a single career.

Great artists are not normally confined by the "movements" that others may name for them. Rather, they
25 transcend the conventional structure working now in one style, then in another, and later in a third. Picasso's work, for example, echoes many of the artistic movements, and other artists too, moving from one style through another. Indeed, artists are people, and any may decide
30 to alter her style for no more complex a reason than that which makes most people want to "try something new" once in a while.

Q23   In studying modern sculpture one is tempted to begin a history with Auguste Rodin (1840–1917), who
35 was a contemporary of Paul Cézanne (1839–1906). Yet the two artists did not, in artistic terms, belong to the same period. Their strategies and objectives differed. Although Rodin was surely a great artist, he did not do for sculpture what Cézanne did for painting. In fact,

40 although Cézanne was a painter, he had a more lasting effect on sculpture than did Rodin.

Cézanne's work constitutes a reaction against impressionism and the confusion he thought it created. He searched persistently for the "motif." Cézanne strived
45 for clarity of form and was able to convert his personal perceptions into concrete, recognizable substance. He is justly considered to have offered the first glimmer of a new art—a new classicism.

Q25   Rodin was surely a great artist, but he was not an
50 innovator as was Cézanne; prevailing tides of subjectivism came over him. Rodin's mission was to reinvest sculpture with the integrity it lost when Michelangelo died. Rodin succeeded in this mission. His first true work, *The Age of Bronze* (1877), marked the beginning
55 of the end of academicism, mannerism, and decadence that had prevailed since Michelangelo's last sculpture, the *Rondanini Pietà*.

Yet it is largely Cézanne, not Rodin, who was artistic ancestor to Picasso, Gonzalez, Brancusi, Archipenko,
60 Lipchitz, and Laurens, and they are unquestionably the first lights in the "new art" of sculpture. This "new art," of course, is the sculpture we call "modern." It is modern because it breaks with tradition and draws little on that which preceded it.

Q26
65   When I speak of "modern" sculpture, I do not refer to every sculptor nor even to every highly talented sculptor of our age. I do not exclude, necessarily, the sculptors of an earlier time. Modern sculpture, as far as I am concerned, is any that consciously casts tradition
70 aside and seeks forms more suitable to the senses and values of its time. Renoir and Daumier are, in this light, modern sculptors notwithstanding the earlier time at which they worked. Daleur and Carpeaux are not modern, although they belong chronologically to the recent era.

Q20
75   Professor Quentin Bell argues that historians and critics name as "modern" those sculptors in whom they happen to be interested and that the term when abused in that way has no historical or artistic significance. That, I think, is not right. The problem is that Profes-
80 sor Bell thinks "modern" means "now," when in fact it means "new."

Fill in the order that questions 20, 21, 22, 23, 24, 25, and 26 should be done in if you were working the passage from its beginning to its end. (Remember that questions 19 and 27 are Later questions, so they get done once the Work the Passage step is completed.)

1st: _____   4th: _____   7th: _____
2nd: _____   5th: _____
3rd: _____   6th: _____

Your passage should look like this. If you couldn't find all the lead words to circle, don't worry. You can do those questions Later. But did you notice that the first, second, third, and fifth, paragraphs have neither lead words circled nor line references noted by the student? If you hadn't mapped the questions first, you would have likely wasted a lot of time on details that ACT doesn't seem to care about.

Passage III

INFORMATIONAL: This passage is adapted from the article "The Sculpture Revolution" by Michael Michalski (©1998 Geer Publishing).

If we were to start fresh in the study of sculpture or any art, we might observe that the record is largely filled by works of relatively few great contributors. Next to the influences of these great geniuses, time periods
5 themselves are of little significance. The study of art and art history are properly directed to the achievements of outstanding individual artists, not the particular decades or centuries in which any may have worked.

Nonetheless, when we study art in historical
10 perspective we select a convenient frame of reference through which diverse styles and talents are to be compared. Hence we write of "movements" and attempt to understand each artist in terms of the one to which he "belongs." Movements have limited use, but we should
15 not talk of realism, impressionism, cubism, or surrealism as though they genuinely had lives of their own to which the artist was answerable. We regard the movement as the governing force and the artist as its servant. Yet it is well to remember that the movements do not necessarily
20 present themselves in orderly chronological series, and the individual artist frequently weaves her way into one and out of another over the course of a single career.

Great artists are not normally confined by the "movements" that others may name for them. Rather, they
25 transcend the conventional structure working now in one style, then in another, and later in a third. Picasso's work, for example, echoes many of the artistic movements, and other artists too, moving from one style through another. Indeed, artists are people, and any may decide
30 to alter her style for no more complex a reason than that which makes most people want to "try something new" once in a while.

Q23   In studying modern sculpture one is tempted to begin a history with Auguste Rodin (1840–1917), who
35 was a contemporary of Paul Cézanne (1839–1906). Yet the two artists did not, in artistic terms, belong to the same period. Their strategies and objectives differed. Although Rodin was surely a great artist, he did not do for sculpture what Cézanne did for painting. In fact,

40 although Cézanne was a painter, he had a more lasting effect on sculpture than did Rodin.

Cézanne's work constitutes a reaction against impressionism and the confusion he thought it created. He searched persistently for the "motif." Cézanne strived
45 for clarity of form and was able to convert his personal perceptions into concrete, recognizable substance. He is justly considered to have offered the first glimmer of a new art—a new classicism.

Q25   Rodin was surely a great artist, but he was not an
50 innovator as was Cézanne; prevailing tides of subjectivism came over him. Rodin's mission was to reinvest sculpture with the integrity it lost when Michelangelo died. Rodin succeeded in this mission. His first true work, *The Age of Bronze* (1877), marked the beginning
55 of the end of academicism, mannerism and decadence that had prevailed since Michelangelo's last sculpture, the *Rondanini Pietà*.

Yet it is largely Cézanne, not Rodin, who was artistic ancestor to Picasso, Gonzalez, Brancusi, Archipenko,
60 Lipchitz, and Laurens, and they are unquestionably the first lights in the "new art" of sculpture. This "new art," of course, is the sculpture we call "modern." It is modern because it breaks with tradition and draws little on that which preceded it.

Q26
65   When I speak of "modern" sculpture, I do not refer to every sculptor nor even to every highly talented sculptor of our age. I do not exclude, necessarily, the sculptors of an earlier time. Modern sculpture, as far as I am concerned, is any that consciously casts tradition
70 aside and seeks forms more suitable to the senses and values of its time. Renoir and Daumier are, in this light, modern sculptors notwithstanding the earlier time at which they worked. Daleur and Carpeaux are not modern, although they belong chronologically to the recent era.

Q20
75   Professor Quentin Bell argues that historians and critics name as "modern" those sculptors in whom they happen to be interested and that the term when abused in that way has no historical or artistic significance. That, I think, is not right. The problem is that Profes-
80 sor Bell thinks "modern" means "now," when in fact it means "new."

If you found all of the lead words, your order may look something like this:

1st:	Q23
2nd:	Q21
3rd:	Q22
4th:	Q25
5th:	Q26
6th:	Q24
7th:	Q20

Notice that questions 21, 22, and 25 were all part of the same paragraph—all the more reason to spend that precious few moments mapping the questions in Step 1! We have Q25 listed fourth here because it asks about the entire paragraph rather than specific terms from the paragraph, but don't sweat it too much trying to determine a perfect order for questions all asking about the same piece of text—starting to answer questions is more important than spending time perfectly ordering them!

> **Working the Passage, Online Style**
> On the Online Test, Question 25 would show the entirety of the sixth paragraph (lines 49–57) highlighted. You can see why it's critical to look for lead words even as you do those highlighted text questions right away—not one, but two lead words you needed for other questions were in this short excerpt. That's three questions for the price of one, so to speak!

Step 3: Select and Understand the Question

As we mentioned before, you shouldn't do the questions in the order ACT gives you. Although Question 19 is the first question you'd see on the page or on screen, it was marked as a Later question because it has no lead words or line references and asks about the passage as a whole. Question 23, on the other hand, is a more specific Information question with a clear line reference that you would want to do as you as you go to that part of the passage. Remember, all questions with clear line references or lead words are Now questions, unless you feel the task is complicated and want to save them for Later.

On the Online Test, you would do this question even earlier as the line reference would instead be presented as highlighted text.

☆ **23.** Information in the fourth paragraph (lines 33–41) makes clear that the author believes that:

Here's How to Crack It
Make sure you understand what the question is asking. Try rephrasing it as an actual question:

What does the author believe, based on lines 33–41?

Step 4: Read What You Need

> You can use the Line Mask tool on the ACT Online Test to help you focus on your window. Don't feel obligated to use this tool, however—not everyone finds it helpful.

Read what you need in the passage to find your prediction. The line reference points you to lines 33–41, which, conveniently, is both an entire paragraph and a window of 5–10 lines. Read the fourth paragraph and look for a belief of the author's or some claim that he makes.

Step 5: Mark the Answer in the Passage

> On the ACT Online Test, you can highlight portions of the text that are already highlighted. The color will change to "your" highlighter color.

Underline the phrases or sentences in the passage that answer the question. Lines 38–41 feature the author making a very clear comparison, stating that *Although Rodin was surely a great artist, he did not do for sculpture what Cézanne did for painting. In fact, although Cézanne was a painter, he had a more lasting effect on sculpture than did Rodin.* Do you see the importance of making sure you understand the question? We care about what the author actually believes, not the background information he offers at the start of the paragraph.

Step 6: Use POE

If you can dearly identify the answer in the passage, look for its match among the answers. Eliminate any choice that talks about something not found in your window. If you aren't sure if an answer is right or wrong, leave it. You'll either find one better or three worse. If you're down to two, choose key words in the answer choices. See if you can locate them back in the passage, and determine whether the answer choice matches what the passage says.

> **Common Traps Answers**
> Eliminate answers that fit any of the following categories: Out of the Window Words Out of Context Right Answer, Wrong Question.

Here's How to Crack It

A. Rodin was more innovative than Cézanne.

This is the direct opposite of who the author stated had more of an impact. Eliminate it.

B. Cézanne was more innovative than Rodin.

This answer is a good paraphrase of the comparison made in the passage. The author does not directly use the word *innovative* in the passage, but the phrases *what Cézanne did for painting* and that Cézanne had *a more lasting effect on sculpture* indicate that he contributed more to these art forms than Rodin did, so keep it.

C. modem art is more important than classical art.

The author is comparing artists, not art periods, in the window. Eliminate it.

D. Cézanne tried to emulate impressionism.

There is no mention of *impressionism* or any mention of Cezanne trying to emulate certain art forms, so eliminate this answer. Choice (B) is correct.

Before we go any further, let's talk a bit more about POE and common ACT trap answers. When looking for answers to eliminate, focus on a few main reasons that answers may be wrong. If the answer mentions something **Out of the Window**, meaning that it either was not stated in that part of the text or not stated at all, eliminate it. Other trap answers may be tempting because they use **Words Out of Context**. Key words or phrases from the answer may have appeared in the passage, but the answer uses them to say something that isn't true based on the passage. The final common trap is **Right Answer, Wrong Question**, which can be especially sneaky. These answers say something that is true given the passage, but that fact does not answer the actual question being asked.

Steps 3–6: Repeat

For each question where you find the relevant lead word or arrive at another of your line references markings, you'll do these questions Now by repeating Steps 3–6. Make sure you understand what each question is asking. Read what you need to find your answer, usually a window of 5–10 lines. Underline the phrases or sentences in the passage that answer the question. Work the answers using POE until you identify the best match for the answer that's in the passage. For the sake of convenience, we've reproduced the window needed for each question throughout the remainder of this section.

Information Questions

Most of the questions in this passage (and indeed, more than half of the questions you will see overall) are Information questions—those that are looking for key ideas and details from the passage. Read these questions carefully to identify what they're asking. Once you find your window to read, read to find the answer. The correct answers to Information questions can range from slightly paraphrased to heavily paraphrased, but all of them will be directly consistent with a phrase, sentence, or sentences in the passage. Underlining (or highlighting) these parts of the passage is the key to being able to use POE effectively.

> **How to Spot Information Questions**
> - Questions that begin with *According to the passage* or *Based on the passage*
> - Questions that ask what the passage or author *states* or *believes*
> - Questions that use *infer, suggests*, or *implies*
> - Questions that ask what the author or a person written about in the passage would agree or disagree with
> - Questions that ask you to characterize or describe all or part of the passage

21. Which of the following most accurately summarizes how the passage characterizes subjectivism's effect on Rodin?

   A. It ended his affiliation with mannerism.
   B. It caused him to lose his artistic integrity.
   C. It limited his ability to innovate.
   D. It caused him to become decadent.

Rodin was surely a great artist, but he was not an
50 innovator as was Cezanne: prevailing tides of subjectivism came over him. Rodin's mission was to reinvest
sculpture with the integrity it lost when Michelangelo
died. Rodin succeeded in this mission. His first true
work, *The Age of Bronze* (1877), marked the beginning
55 of the end of academicism, mannerism, and decadence
that had prevailed since Michelangelo's last sculpture,
the *Rondanini Pietà*.

Here's How to Crack It

Lines 49–51 state that *subjectivism* coming over, or affecting, Rodin is why *he was not an inno-vator*. The passage states that *mannerism* was one of the things ended by Rodin's *The Age of Bronze*—it was something he was trying to get rid of, not something he is affiliated with, so get rid of (A). Choice (B) and (D) are Words Out of Context traps for *integrity* and *decadence* from the passage, so eliminate them. Choice (C) matches what we found in the passage as the connection between subjectivism and Rodin not being an innovator, so it's the correct answer.

Try another Information question with great lead words.

22. According to the passage, academicism and mannerism:

   F. were readily visible in The Age of Bronze.
   G. were partially manifest in the Rondanini Pieta.
   H. were styles that Rodin believed lacked integrity.
   J. were styles that Rodin wanted to restore into fashion.

Rodin was surely a great artist, but he was not an
50 innovator as was Cezanne: prevailing tides of subjectivism came over him. Rodin's mission was to reinvest
sculpture with the integrity it lost when Michelangelo
died. Rodin succeeded in this mission. His first true
work, *The Age of Bronze* (1877), marked the beginning
55 of the end of academicism, mannerism, and decadence
that had prevailed since Michelangelo's last sculpture,
the *Rondanini Pietà*.

Here's How to Crack It

According to the passage means that this is an Information question and should be easier to answer. Note that even if you missed *academicism* and *mannerism* initially, you would have another chance to catch them when you did question 21, the previous question, as well as when you do question 25, the next question we will do.

Reread and underline the sentence that refers to those ideas: Rodin's *first true work, The Age of Bronze (1877), marked the beginning of the end of academicism, mannerism, and decadence.* Then, use POE. Choices (F), (G), and (J) all contradict both the passage and the sentence you underlined as the answer for this question. Choice (H) matches, and it is the correct answer.

———————○———————

Work the Answers

Some Information questions are more general in scope, failing to provide a single term to focus on or find in the passage. If you ever do struggle to underline or highlight evidence for a question, instead go straight to the answers and use POE: if an answer is inconsistent with the passage if any way, eliminate it, especially if it falls into one of the common trap answer categories we discussed earlier!

———————○———————

☆ **25.** Based on information in the sixth paragraph (lines 49–57), the author implies that:

    A. mannerism reflects a lack of integrity.
    B. Rodin disliked the work of Michelangelo.
    C. Rodin embraced the notion of decadence.
    D. Rodin's work represented a shift in style different from the works of artists who preceded him.

       Rodin was surely a great artist, but he was not an
50 innovator as was Cezanne: prevailing tides of subjec-
    tivism came over him. Rodin's mission was to reinvest
    sculpture with the integrity it lost when Michelangelo
    died. Rodin succeeded in this mission. His first true
    work, *The Age of Bronze* (1877), marked the beginning
55 of the end of academicism, mannerism, and decadence
    that had prevailed since Michelangelo's last sculpture,
    the *Rondanini Pietà.*

Here's How to Crack It

This time, the question is somewhat general, so it may be difficult to mark the answer in the passage while you read. Instead, use POE to eliminate answers that don't match the text. Choices (A) and (C) use terms from the paragraph but change the meaning, making them Words Out of Context trap answers. Rodin wanted to restore elements of sculpture that had changed since the death of Michelangelo, which means he respected Michelangelo's work, so (B) is not supported. The last sentence states that Rodin's work marked the beginning of the end and therefore represented something new, as is stated in (D), which is the correct answer.

———————○———————

Information, Not Interpretation

Many Information questions use language like *implies*, *suggests*, or *most nearly means*. This choice of wording sounds like ACT wants you to interpret the author's meaning, but in reality, the correct answer still needs to be supported directly by evidence in the passage. The only difference is that Information questions with this language may feature more heavily paraphrased answers that ones that say *According to the passage* or *states*.

☆ **26.** In line 65, when the author uses the word "modern," he most nearly means sculpture that:

    F. postdates the *Rondanini Pietà*.
    G. is not significantly tied to work that comes before it.
    H. shows no artistic merit.
    J. genuinely interests contemporary critics.

65   When I speak of "modern" sculpture, I do not refer to every sculptor nor even to every highly talented sculptor of our age. I do not exclude, necessarily, the sculptors of an earlier time. Modern sculpture, as far as I am concerned, is any that consciously casts tradition
70 aside and seeks forms more suitable to the senses and values of its time. Renoir and Daumier are, in this light, modern sculptors notwithstanding the earlier time at which they worked. Daleur and Carpeaux are not modern, although they belong chronologically to the recent era.

Here's How to Crack It

Read the text and underline the answer in the passage, which comes in the statement *Modern art...is any that consciously casts tradition aside and seeks forms more suitable to the senses and values of its time.* Now use POE. The *Rondanini Pieta* is in the wrong window, so eliminate (F). Choice (G) is a good paraphrase of the text you underlined, and it is the correct answer. Choice (H) can't be proven by the passage; the author doesn't state that they have no worth at all. Choice (J) tempts with *contemporary* as a possible match for *modern* or *its time*, but *critics* are not in this window.

Structural Clues

When authors write virtually anything, they usually want their readers to understand their viewpoint and follow the logical flow of their story or article. This is accomplished by using structural clues such as transition words, comparisons and contrasts, attitude words, and even pronouns. When you spot one of these clues, it may help you understand that you need to read more of the window, help you find the most appropriate evidence to answer the question, or both. Structural clues are most helpful on Rhetoric questions, but even Information questions such as the one below become easier when you find and make use of these clue words!

24. According to the passage, Renoir differs from Daleur in that:

F. Daleur had no inspiration, while Renoir was tremendously inspired.

G. Renoir's work was highly innovative, while Daleur's was not.

H. Daleur was a sculptor, while Renoir was not.

J. Renoir revered tradition, while Daleur did not.

65 When I speak of "modern" sculpture, I do not refer to every sculptor nor even to every highly talented
sculptor of our age. I do not exclude, necessarily, the
sculptors of an earlier time. Modern sculpture, as far as
I am concerned, is any that consciously casts tradition
70 aside and seeks forms more suitable to the senses and
values of its time. Renoir and Daumier are, in this light,
modern sculptors notwithstanding the earlier time at
which they worked. Daleur and Carpeaux are not modern,
although they belong chronologically to the recent era.

> On the ACT Online Test, you would likely do question 24 Later—no part of the text would be highlighted. Instead, write down the question number and lead words on your whiteboard (abbreviations and shorthand are fine— "24: Ren. differs from Dal."). Then, when you work the passage after doing all the questions with high-lighted text, you can go directly to question 24 when you come across the lead words.

Here's How to Crack It

Lines 71–73 state that *Renoir was a modern sculptor* and *Daleur* is not. But that same sentence mentions four artists *in this light*. What light? Any time you see pronouns such as *this, that,* or *such* in front of a noun, back up to read the first mention of that topic. *This light* is the author's definition of modern, given in lines 68–71. Underline lines 68–73, beginning with "Modern sculpture."

Now work the answers. Eliminate answers that don't state that Renoir is modern and Daleur is not. *Innovative* in (G) is a good match for modern and is the correct answer. *Inspiration* in (F) doesn't match modern. Choice (H) is disproven by the passage. Choice (J) tempts with *tradition,* but compare it to the text, and the author states modern sculpture *consciously casts tradition aside.*

Hard Work (the Passage) Pays off

While you Work the Passage, there will be several paragraphs that you only skim—after all, the principal reason you are even working the passage is to find answers to questions, and you are only stopping to read the passage carefully as part of Step 4 once you select and understand a question to attempt. However, you'll still wind up reading more than half of the passage, and that's going to be enough for most Later questions. Try one last Now question using all of the skills you've learned so far, before you tackle the Later questions on the next few pages.

☆ **20.** The information in lines 75–81 suggests that Quentin Bell believes that historians and critics:

    F. have no appreciation for the value of modem art.
    G. abuse art and its history.
    H. should evaluate works of art on the basis of their merit without regard to the artist's fame.
    J. attach the phrase "modem art" to those sculptors that intrigue them.

75   Professor Quentin Bell argues that historians and critics name as "modern" those sculptors in whom they happen to be interested and that the term when abused in that way has no historical or artistic significance. That, I think, is not right. The problem is that Profes-

80 sor Bell thinks "modern" means "now," when in fact it means "new."

Here's How to Crack It

The question is asking for Bell's belief regarding historians and critics, which, according to lines 75–78, is that historians and critics use "modern" to describe *sculptors in whom they happen to be interested*. Choice (F) is extreme in saying that these historians and critics have *no* appreciation for the value of modern art, and neither Bell nor the author makes this claim, so eliminate it. The passage states that the term "modern" is abused, not art and its history. So, (G) is a Words Out of Context trap, and it's wrong. Eliminate it. There was nothing in the window about *fame*, so eliminate (H). *Attach the phrase* is a good match for *name* as modem art and *sculptors that intrigue them* is a good match for *in whom they happen to be interested*. This answer is a good paraphrase of the evidence we underlined, so keep it. Choice (J) is correct.

On the Paper Test, Later questions should have been marked with an "L" during the Preview step. On the Online Test, they should have been marked with an "L" next to their question number on your scratch paper. Regardless of the test format, questions without lead words are much easier when answered after you've done as many Now questions as you can possibly find.

Later (or Never) Questions

Once you have worked all the questions with line or paragraph references and great lead words, move to the Later questions. The answers to questions without a line or paragraph reference or any great lead words can be difficult to find, which is why you should do them Later. But the later you do them, the easier they become because you've read enough of the passage to have a general idea of what types of answers will be consistent with all of the information you have so far. Additionally, if you had missed any lead words during the Preview step and didn't find them while working other Now questions, then those lead words must be in the few paragraphs you didn't really read while working the passage.

Do remember that because you want to attempt all four passages, Later questions may become Never questions if you've spent too much time on the current passage and need to move to the next passage. Also, Later questions aren't just questions without great lead words or line references: don't hesitate to make Later any Now question that has a confusing or time-consuming task, and make a mental note to return to it if time allows.

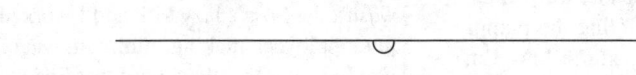

19. The author expresses the idea that:

    A. art should never be studied in terms of movements.
    B. art can be labeled as modem when it introduces a style that is different from those found in works that came earlier.
    C. lesser artists do not usually vary their styles.
    D. great artists are always nonconformists.

Here's How to Crack It

Question 26 helps the most with this question, but several questions echoed the theme of art making a break from the past, which supports (B). Choice (A) is extreme for its use of the word *never*. Lastly, while the passage does compare and contrast artists a few times, none of the windows you've seen made such broad, sweeping statements about what *lesser artists* or *great artists* do, which eliminates (C) and (D). The correct answer is (B).

27. Which of the following statements would the author most likely agree with?

    A. Cezanne had greater influence on modem sculpture than did Rodin.
    B. Rodin made no significant contribution to modem sculpture.
    C. Daumier should not be considered a modem sculptor.
    D. Carpeaux should be considered a modem sculptor.

Here's How to Crack It

Questions 21, 22, 23, 24, and 25 all help eliminate the wrong answers (B), (C), and (D), making (A) the correct answer, which is saying the exact same thing as the correct answer to question 23.

THE 6-STEP BASIC APPROACH

Try a passage on your own. Give yourself up to 12 minutes, but don't worry if you go a little over. Use the passage on the next page to help you master the Basic Approach and worry less about your speed. Later in the chapter and in the next, we'll discuss other strategies to help with time. The answers are given on the page following the questions.

The Basic Approach
1. Preview
2. Work the Passage
3. Select and Understand a Question
4. Read What You Need
5. Mark the Answer in the Passage
6. Use POE

Passage I

LITERARY NARRATIVE: This passage is adapted from the novel *Skyward* by Prakriti Basrai (©2012 by Prakriti Basrai).

Ever since I graduated from high school, I've worked at the company my father started, Singer Stations and Service, a gas station and car maintenance center that was the fulfillment of my father's American dream shortly after he arrived here in
5 the late 1960s and that, if all goes according to plan, will pass to my grandsons and their grandsons in perpetuity, and which is already making its way into the twenty-first century with a Facebook page and a sophisticated iPhone app.

Our family name is still Singh, but in our small town,
10 my father thought it would put a safer face on the business to change the name to Singer, a name which we've all unofficially adopted now that we're in the United States, as I suppose many of our more-established neighbors' ancestors must've done a few generations ago.

15 Also, Singer is just a nice name for a business: it's got a nice, musical ring to it, and the alliterative name of our gas station chain seems to churn up memories of great American businesses and the non-threatening pose that has been necessary to immigrant assimilation from the beginning. When drivers
20 pull up to our pumps, they do so with the sense that we'll smile back at them, whistling while we work, operating the pumps like expert musicians, and it'll cost them a song (a line, I'm sure you can imagine, that is emblazoned proudly on all of our public signage). All of the credit for this name has always gone
25 to my father, and I can believe that he was the one behind this smart change: he was always a good businessman, and he had that added penchant, almost a poetic sense for a clever, musical turn of phrase. My father has always loved his business, and although that love has been diluted as it has come through my
30 generation and my son's, it's nothing that the standard narrative of Americanization and the decline of hard work can't explain, and which I have no interest in rehashing here. We've all had our challenges, regardless of age, so who says one generation has it tougher than the next, and frankly, who cares?

35 When I really think about it, though, I think my son, Ravneet, whom everyone calls Richie, might have it hardest. Even for our relatively small business, Richie's public-relations responsibilities are those of any of the international stations. He's always
40 posting something new to the Internet or monitoring the price of gas all over the world at once. It doesn't hurt that the kid knows how to make a buck—my father marvels every day at what his grandson has been able to do with the family business. You'd think with all that's gone wrong with the economy in the last few years, Richie would've sold his Italian sports car, but the
45 kid actually just bought another one.

Richie's success is undeniable, but sometimes I worry that he works too hard for all that he's got. It's nearly impossible to get him on the phone; he must work 80 hours a week, and he's spent more than one Thanksgiving Day stuck at the office balanc-
50 ing the books. My father at the very least had a family to come home to, and the saving grace of his religious observance forced him to take at least a day off every week. I was pulled neither to overwork nor underwork; I was always focused on maintaining what had been given to me. In later years, my mother told me
55 secretly that she thought I actually had it worst of all—I had no burning desire to enter this business, but I didn't really have any other choice. I did well enough, and if I might've been brilliant at something else, I guess we'll never know.

Even so, I was Raman (The Gas Man) Singer's son, but I
60 never quite shared his pioneer spirit at breaking new ground, nor his enviable belief that he did what he did because it had to be done. I did perfectly well at Singer Stations and Service. I wasn't the boss's lazy kid, and I worked just as hard as any of my employees making minimum wage. I stuck with it. When
65 you look at it this way, I did just fine.

When I fully handed the business over to Richie five years ago, I knew right away that my life couldn't simply be over at the age of 50. As a result, at the urging of my college-aged daughter Geeta, I decided to try something I always wished
70 that I had done. I enrolled in the business program at the State University, and before long, I realized that Geeta knew me better than I knew myself. I had fun like I never had before, and looking back, I came to see that the part of the business that always drew me in was learning: whether it was the stories of
75 my co-workers or the inner workings of a small business that is trying to grow. Now that I'm done with school, I'm starting my own business. In fact, Geeta and I are starting one, and while I've left to her what exactly it is we're selling, I'm brimming with excitement to find out.

1. The passage can be best described as primarily:

   A. one business owner's questioning of the direction his business has taken after he handed the management over to his son.

   B. a son's elegant praise of his father's skill and determination in creating a family business.

   C. a personal narrative that describes one man's role within a business started by his father and passed down through generations.

   D. a story of the changes in American immigrant businesses in the twentieth century.

2. Which of the following actions affecting the family business does the narrator **not** attribute to his father?

   F. A sophisticated iPhone app

   G. The founding of Singer Stations and Service

   H. A change in the family's last name

   J. An alliterative name for the business

3. The narrator explicitly declines to take a firm stand on which of the following issues?

   A. The personal preferences he had that enabled him to succeed in business

   B. The quality of the name Singer Stations and Service

   C. Which generation has had the most difficult time in the world of business

   D. Whether the family should have kept the name Singh rather than Singer

4. According to the passage, what is the narrator's father's attitude toward words?

   F. He treats them like a poet would.

   G. He believes business names should be alliterative.

   H. A man should keep his mouth closed and his ears open.

   J. He believes that advertisers work in the business of deception.

5. As it is used in line 40, the word *hurt* most nearly means:

   A. impede success.

   B. injure.

   C. sting.

   D. cause a bruise.

6. What does the narrator state is his mother's view of his role in Singer Stations and Service?

   F. In actuality, the credit for the business's name should go to him because he was the real artist.

   G. He had the worst time of any of his family members because he ran a business in which he did not have a passionate interest.

   H. His hard work, though less public than his son's, was crucial to the company's success at the time.

   J. He should be more grateful for his inheritance and not insist on changing professions.

7. According to the passage, who or what is "Raman (The Gas Man)"?

   A. Singer's main gas supplier

   B. The business's main competitor

   C. The narrator's son

   D. The narrator's father

8. According to the passage, the narrator's daughter knows the narrator better than he knows himself because:

   F. the company's new Internet presence emerged after he retired.

   G. she suggested that he go back to school, and he enjoyed doing so.

   H. Richie bought a second Italian sports car.

   J. the history of Singer Stations and Service is a history of the immigrant experience.

9. As it is used in line 73, the phrase "came to see" most nearly means:

   A. arrived at.

   B. realized.

   C. attended.

   D. visited.

Score and Analyze Your Performance

The correct answers are (C), (F), (C), (F), (A), (G), (D), (G), and (B). How did you do? Were you able to finish in 12 minutes or less? If you struggled with time, identify what step took up the most time. Identify any questions that slowed you down. Did you make good choices of Now and Later questions? Did you use *enough* time? If you finished in less than 12 minutes but missed several questions, next time plan to slow down to give yourself enough time to evaluate the answers carefully. In Chapter 23, we'll work on skills to help you work the questions and answers with more speed and greater accuracy. But first, we'll finish this chapter with strategies to help you increase your speed working the passage.

> Explanations for these questions start on page 446, but make sure to think about the pacing questions posed here before flipping to those explanations.

BEAT THE CLOCK

When you struggle with time, there are several places within the Basic Approach that are eating up the minutes.

Step 1: Preview

To move at the fastest speed when you preview, you can't read the questions. Let your eye *look* for lead words and numbers. Don't let your brain *read*.

Time yourself to see if you can preview the following questions and blurb in less than a minute.

Passage IV

INFORMATIONAL: This passage is adapted from the article "What Giotto Saw" by James Herndon (©2001 by Galaxy Press).

28. The author characterizes the comparison of the work of Sagdeev to that of Peale as:

29. The main point of the last paragraph (lines 43–48) is to show that Zdenek Sekanina:

30. In terms of their role in studying the rotational period, the 1920 photographs are described by the author as:

31. According to the passage, the nuclear surface of Halley's comet is believed to be:

32. As described in the passage, Giotto's camera was specifically programmed to:

33. As used in the passage, the word *resolution* (line 11) means:

34. The passage indicates that H. Use Keler:

35. Lines 25–28 are best summarized as describing a problem that:

36. According to the passage, the volume of Halley's comet is:

Step 2: **Work the Passage**

If you're struggling to work the passage, you may be doing too much *reading*, which sounds odd considering the name of the section. Remember that your only goal is to find lead words or reach your next line/paragraph reference, stop, answer the question, and keep going. Let's examine how you should actually be interacting with the passage until it's time to answer a question.

Skimming, Scanning, and Reading

If we told you to skim the passage, would you know what that means? If you do, great. If you don't, don't worry. *Skimming* is something many readers feel they're supposed to do on a timed test, but they don't know what it means and therefore can't do it.

Reading needs your brain on full power. You're reading words, and your brain is processing what they mean and drawing conclusions. Reading is watching the road, searching for directional signs, and glancing at the scenery, all for the purpose of trying to figure out where the road is leading.

Skimming means reading only a few words. When you work the passage, your brain can try to process key parts that build to the main idea, but you don't necessarily need to identify the main idea just yet. Working the questions and answers tells you the main idea and all the important details. Skimming is reading only the directional signs and ignoring the scenery.

Scanning needs very little of your brain. Use your eyes. Look, don't think, and don't try to process for understanding. Scanning is looking for Volkswagen Beetles in a game of Slug Bug.

> Depending on where you're from, Slug Bug might be known as Punch Buggy.

When you're working the passage, you can skim or scan, but you shouldn't be reading. Read windows of text when you work the questions.

If you feel you can't turn your brain off when you work the passage, or you even skim and scan too slowly, then focus only on the first sentence of each paragraph. You may find fewer lead words, but you will give yourself more time to spend on working the questions and answers and can find the lead words then.

Time yourself to work the following passage, focusing only on the first sentence of each paragraph. We've actually made it impossible to do otherwise. Look for the lead words you circled in Step 1 and circle any that you see.

Such relatively reliable insights as we have into the nature of Halley's comet's nucleus derive largely from the work done by the Giotto imaging team. Blah blah blah blah blah blah blah blah. Blah blah. Blah blah blah blah blah blah blah blah blah.
5 Blah blah blah. Blah blah blah blah blah blah blah blah blah. Blah blah blah blah blah blah blah blah blah. Blah blah blah blah blah blah blah blah.

Discernibility of detail varies at different points in the photograph. Blah blah blah blah blah blah blah blah. Blah blah. Blah
10 blah blah blah blah blah blah blah. Blah blah blah. Blah blah blah blah blah blah blah blah blah. Blah blah blah blah blah blah blah blah blah. Blah blah blah blah blah blah blah blah blah. Blah blah blah blah blah blah blah blah. Blah blah blah blah blah blah blah blah. Blah blah blah blah blah blah blah blah blah.

15 The Giotto photographs have allowed investigators to conclude that the surface of the nucleus is rough. Blah blah blah blah blah blah blah blah. Blah blah. Blah blah blah blah blah blah blah blah blah. Blah blah. Blah blah blah blah blah blah blah blah. Blah blah blah blah blah blah blah blah blah.
20 Blah blah blah blah blah blah blah blah blah. Blah blah blah blah blah blah blah blah blah.

On the other hand, the Giotto photographs reveal virtually nothing on the interior of the comet's nucleus or its rotational period. Blah blah blah blah blah blah blah blah. Blah blah. Blah
25 blah blah blah blah blah blah blah blah. Blah blah blah. Blah blah blah blah blah blah blah blah blah. Blah blah blah blah blah blah blah blah. Blah blah blah blah blah blah blah blah blah. Blah blah blah blah blah blah blah blah.

Moreover, the comet's overall dimensions were already
30 known to an approximation, and on this basis Rickman took the volume as 500–550 cubic centimeters. Blah blah blah blah blah blah blah blah. Blah blah. Blah blah blah blah blah blah blah blah blah. Blah blah blah. Blah blah blah blah blah blah blah blah blah. Blah blah blah blah blah blah blah blah. Blah blah blah blah
35 blah blah blah blah blah.

Using an analogous technique, R. Z. Sagdeev and colleagues arrived at a value of 0.2 to 1.5 grams per cubic centimeter. Blah blah blah blah blah blah blah blah. Blah blah. Blah blah blah blah blah blah blah blah. Blah blah blah. Blah blah blah blah blah
40 blah blah blah blah. Blah blah blah blah blah blah blah blah blah. Blah blah blah blah blah blah blah blah. Blah blah blah blah blah blah blah blah blah.

Finally, Zdenek Sekanina and Stephen M. Larson studied the rotational period by first processing images of 1920 photographs
45 in an attempt to improve the image of spiral dust features. Blah blah blah blah blah blah blah blah. Blah blah. Blah blah blah blah blah blah blah blah. Blah blah blah. Blah blah blah blah blah blah blah blah blah. Blah blah blah blah blah blah blah blah blah.

Let's see what you learned in less than three minutes.

Now Questions

You should have several Now questions.

- Questions 29, 33, and 35 all have line references.
- Questions 28, 30, 31, 32, 34, and 36 all have lead words, great lead words in some.
- The lead words in 28 can be found in the first sentence of the sixth paragraph.
- The lead words in 30 can be found in the first sentence of the last paragraph.
- The lead words in 31 and 32 can be found in the first sentence of the first paragraph.
- The lead words in 36 can be found in the first sentence of the fifth paragraph.
- Eight of the nine questions have been located, and the great lead word in 34 should be easy to find when you're given the whole passage and not a lot of "blahs."

The Passage

You also have a great outline of the passage. The topic sentences have drawn a map of the passage organization, and the transition words tell you how the paragraphs connect.

> **The Pencil Trick**
>
> When you have to look harder for a lead word, use your pencil or cursor to sweep each and every line from beginning to end. This will keep your brain from reading and let your eye look for the word.

- What is the first paragraph about? The nucleus of Halley's Comet and the Giotto camera.
- The second paragraph? The details that the photographs show.
- The third? What scientists have learned from the photographs.
- How does the fourth paragraph relate to the third? *On the other hand* tells you that it is different from the third.
- How does the fifth paragraph relate to the fourth? *Moreover* tells you that they are similar.
- What is the sixth paragraph about? It's still on *volume*, which came up in the fifth paragraph.
- What is the last paragraph? It's the conclusion, which the transition word *Finally* makes clear.

Topic Sentences and Transition Words

Think of your own papers that you write for school. What does a good topic sentence do? It provides, at worst, an introduction to the paragraph and, at best, a summary of the paragraph's main idea. What follows are the details that clarify or prove the main idea. And do you care about the details at Step 2? No, you'll focus on the details if and when there is a question on them.

Transition words are like great road signs. They show you the route, direct you to a detour, and get you back on the path of the main idea. When you *skim*, you're focusing on topic sentences and transition words.

In the next chapter, we'll cover more strategies for steps 3 through 6. But now it's time to try another passage.

> **Look for Transition Words**
>
> Here are 15 transition words and/or phrases.
>
> - *Despite*
> - *However*
> - *In spite of*
> - *Nonetheless*
> - *On the other hand*
> - *But*
> - *Rather*
> - *Yet*
> - *Ironically*
> - *Notwithstanding*
> - *Unfortunately*
> - *On the contrary*
> - *Therefore*
> - *Hence*
> - *Consequently*

Reading Drill 1

Use the Basic Approach on the following passage.

Passage III

INFORMATIONAL: This passage is adapted from the article "The Buzz in Our Pockets" by Danielle Panizzi (©2013 by Telephony Biquarterly).

To the extent that it has a creator at all, the text message, or SMS (short message service), was created in the early 1980s by Friedhelm Hillebrand and Bernard Ghillebaert, who wanted to find a way to send data over the parts of phone lines that were
5 not being used in normal telephony. The first text messages were 160 characters long. Hillebrand suggested that "160 characters was sufficient to express most messages succinctly," citing typical postcard and Telex lengths.

Although this form might seem to limit the way we commu-
10 nicate, the text message is the most widely used data application in the world, with about 80% of all cellphone users (3.5 billion people) using the medium. Text messages are already a part of the cultural landscape: they are mentioned in rap and rock songs; they show up in billboards and advertisements selling just
15 about anything; and they've even cropped up in serious novels like Jonathan Franzen's *Freedom* and David Foster Wallace's *The Pale King*. Text messages, in fact, move the whole plot of Martin Scorsese's 2006 film *The Departed,* a critical success and eventual Oscar winner for Best Picture.

20 But the text message is more than a cultural fad. It's part of a broader shift in the way we connect with one another. Speaking on an actual telephone is basically defunct in 2013, not only for the economic reason that "time is money" and a text is quicker than a call, but also for a much older desire in all of us for
25 permanence. With a text message, we've got a record of all our communications, and although we may cast them off quickly, even the shortest text message requires more pre-thought than a verbalized remark: we can't go back to our recorded calls, but our texts live on our phones for as long as we choose to keep
30 them there. The text message has made even our most fleeting conversations permanent—and in this way, the text harkens back to one of the earliest modes of communication, even before the telephone: the letter.

Although America was a sprawling, disparate place even
35 before the War for Independence in the 1770s, its residents always felt the need to communicate with those farther and farther away. Ships carried people back and forth across the Atlantic Ocean, but they also carried correspondence, and we could even say that our very nation was founded in these writ-
40 ten communiqués: much of what we know about that era comes from these letters. One day, text messages may provide a similar record of our own moment.

But it would be naïve to say that these quick notes are anything like the voluminous correspondence of ages past. In
45 her recent monograph *Write Me a Letter,* Kari Fields wonders if the sophisticated concentration of that historical correspondence is even available to us anymore. Fields warns not only that we may have been "dumbed down" by our technologies but also that we may have lost one of the essential elements of the human
50 experience. "The content of our communication with each other ('I'll be late to work today'; 'I'll be home at 10'; or even, 'I love you') may be ultimately the same," Fields concedes, "but the real communication lives in the form—the tone, the unsteady hand on a particular word, the hasty erasures." Perhaps Fields herself
55 is missing the point: naysayers have said that everything from the printing press, to the radio, to the movie screen, to Google, has compromised the way we think and understand. It makes no difference whether a letter takes a month by boat, two weeks by Pony Express, a few days by post, or a few seconds by email.
60 The medium, it seems safe to say, is not the message.

However, Fields is aware of all these earlier changes. She is as sophisticated a historian of these media as anyone working in the field today. We cannot deny that text messages and the Internet have isolated us from one another like never before. In
65 addition to placing us alone at our computers or on our phones, these new technologies also force us to spread our limited attention spans thinner and thinner. We may have to think about the text messages we send, but we typically do so while looking at something else on the web, listening to music or podcasts,
70 or seconds before or after sending messages to someone else. It's not merely that our communications are getting shorter and shorter; it's that the time we have for real interactions has shrunk. All of these new devices are supposed to be time-savers, but what they've really given us is more time to use the devices,
75 to the point that a year without seeing a dear friend seems less daunting than a few hours without the phone.

Still, text messages may be our last, best surrogate for the intimacy of "real" communication. As Herberth Chacon observes in *I Like You…on Facebook,* "Whatever the limitations
80 of this new medium of communication, people are interacting on a day-to-day basis with more people than their ancestors might have met in a lifetime." Text messages have gained such currency because, for all their flaws, they do bring us together. After all, even if the words "I love you" are flashing up impersonally on
85 a screen—stripped of all tone and affection—the words are nice to hear nonetheless, and even if our new definition of "friends" may not square with the old definition, it's nice to know there's a world out there that's paying attention to us.

19. The main idea of the passage is that:

A. telephone conversations are defunct because they are so impermanent.

B. telephones took the place of serious long-letter writing.

C. text messages do not provide real interactions for the people who send them.

D. text messaging is a popular medium whose social effects are debatable.

20. Based on the passage, with which of the following statements would Fields most likely agree?

F. The frequent use of text messaging can limit people's other human experiences.

G. Internet users lost their capacity for human experience when they started using Google.

H. Text messages provide a quick, intimate way for people to communicate.

J. Text messages force people to write more thoughtfully to one another.

21. How does the passage's author directly support her claim that the text message is more than a simple message?

A. By citing examples from American culture in which text messaging plays a role

B. By describing famous novels about the cultural role of texting in American society

C. By listing the accomplishments of the two German men who created the medium of text messaging

D. By showing that text messaging was initially limited to 160 characters

22. The passage's author most likely discusses the era before the War of Independence to:

F. demonstrate how historical figures refused to use text-messaging technology.

G. prompt the reader to do more research into the history of communication.

H. give a fun digression in an otherwise dry discussion of communication media.

J. show that forms of communication can provide historical records.

23. Which of the following people think or act in a way that is most similar to that of the naysayers described in the fifth paragraph (lines 43–60)?

A. Scientists who see improvements in medicine as an improvement in the quality of life

B. Sports journalists who say that a change in rules will destroy the integrity of a sport

C. Novelists who prefer to write on computers rather than with pen and paper

D. Historians who would prefer to read official documents rather than letters

24. According to the passage, of the following, who were the earliest contributors to the development of the medium of the text message?

F. Fields and Chacon

G. Scorsese and Franzen

H. Franzen and Wallace

J. Hillebrand and Ghillebaert

25. A character in a short story published in 1994 had this to say about text messages:

> Say what you will about the "decline of real interaction"—I've had plenty of them that would've felt a lot more real if they'd happened in a sentence or two rather than a two-hour phone conversation.

Based on the passage, would Hillebrand agree or disagree with this statement?

A. Disagree, because 160 characters proved to be an inadequate number of characters.

B. Disagree, because he ultimately believed that most communication should occur by letter.

C. Agree, because he felt that the telephone was no longer an effective communicator.

D. Agree, because he thought that 160 characters was adequate to express most messages concisely.

26. Based on the passage, why might *The Departed* have been considered a film interested in contemporary issues?

F. It made a recent communication medium, text messaging, central to its story.

G. Its actors spoke in favor of text messaging, and the medium exploded in popularity after the film's release.

H. It won an important award in honor of the quality of the filmmaking.

J. It showed that letter writing was no longer a sufficient way to communicate.

27. Based on the passage, when the author cites the saying "time is money" (line 23), she most likely means that a text message:

A. is an inexpensive way to send a message.

B. keeps a long-lasting record of people's conversations.

C. is a quick way for people to communicate.

D. allows an intimacy that can otherwise take a long time to develop.

PASSAGE I: LITERARY NARRATIVE ANSWERS AND EXPLANATIONS

1. **C** This Information question asks how the *passage can be best described*. Because this is a general question, it should be done after the specific questions. Look for the Golden Thread (more on this in Chapter 23). The passage is about the narrator's father's business and both the narrator's and narrator's son's experience working there. Eliminate answers that don't match this answer from the passage. Eliminate (A) because no one is *questioning* the *direction of the business*. Although the narrator does *praise* his father, that is not what the passage is *primarily* about, so eliminate (B). Keep (C) because it matches the answer from the passage. Eliminate (D) because the passage is about the experiences of a specific family, not *American immigrant businesses* in general. The correct answer is (C).

2. **F** This Information question asks which action *affecting the family business* the narrator does *NOT attribute to his father*. Work backward and use lead words from the answers to find the window for this question. Lines 1–8 introduce *Singer Stations and Service* and state that it *is already making its way into the twenty-first century with a Facebook page and a sophisticated iPhone app*. The *iPhone app* is not attributed to the narrator's father, so keep (F). Line 2 says, *the company my father started, Singer Stations and Service*, so eliminate (G). Lines 9–11 say, *Our family name is still Singh, but in our small town, my father thought it would put a safer face on the business to change the name to Singer*, so eliminate (H). Lines 24–26 say, *All of the credit for this name has always gone to my father, and I can believe that he was the one behind this smart change*, so eliminate (J). The correct answer is (F).

3. **C** This Information question asks which issue *the narrator explicitly declines to take a firm stand on*. Work backward and use lead words from the answers to find the window for this question. Lines 73–76 say, *I came to see that the part of the business that always drew me in was learning: whether it was the stories of my co-workers or the inner workings of a small business that is trying to grow*. This is a stance on his *personal preferences* when it came to *business*, so eliminate (A). Line 15 says, *Also, Singer is just a nice name for a business*, so the narrator takes a stance on the name. Eliminate (B). Lines 32–34 say, *We've all had our challenges, regardless of age, so who says one generation has it tougher than the next, and frankly, who cares?* The narrator explicitly declines to take a firm stance on *which generation has had the most difficult time in the world of business*, so keep (C). Lines 9–12 say, *but in our small town, my father thought it would put a safer face on the business to change the name to Singer, a name which we've all unofficially adopted now that we're in the United States.* Although the narrator does not give his position on the name change, he does not *explicitly decline* to take a position. Eliminate (D). The correct answer is (C).

4. **F** This Information question asks what *the narrator's father's attitude toward words* is. The question is Hard to Find, so work the question later and use the previous questions to help find the window. The third paragraph, starting at line 15, discusses the name of the business and how it sounds. Lines 26–28 say, *he was always a good businessman, and he had that added penchant, almost a poetic sense for a clever, musical turn of phrase*. Therefore, the narrator's father has a *poetic sense* for words. Eliminate answers that don't match this answer from the passage. Keep (F) because it matches the answer from the passage. Eliminate (G) because, although the narrator's father chose an *alliterative*

name for his business, the passage doesn't indicate that he believes that *business names* in general *should be alliterative.* Eliminate (H) because it is not mentioned in the passage. Eliminate (J) because there is no indication that the narrator's father believes that *advertisers work in the business of deception.* The correct answer is (F).

5. **A**   This Vocabulary in Context question, a type of Rhetoric question, asks what the word *hurt* means in line 40. Go back to the text, find the word *hurt,* and cross it out. Carefully read the surrounding text to determine another word that would fit in the blank based on the context. Lines 40–42 say, *It doesn't hurt that the kid knows how to make a buck—my father marvels every day at what his grandson has been able to do with the family business.* Therefore, *hurt* could be replaced with "detract." Eliminate answers that don't match this answer from the passage. *Impede success* matches "detract," so keep (A). Eliminate (B), (C), and (D) because they do not match "detract." Note that (B), (C), and (D) are trap answers based on other meanings of *hurt* that don't fit the given context. The correct answer is (A).

6. **G**   This Information question asks what the narrator states about *his mother's view of his role in Singer Stations and Service.* Look for the lead word *mother* to find the window for the question. Lines 54–57 say, *my mother told me secretly that she thought I actually had it worst of all—I had no burning desire to enter this business, but I didn't really have any other choice.* Eliminate answers that don't match this answer from the passage. Eliminate (F) because the narrator states that his father named the business, and there is no indication that his mother thinks otherwise. Keep (G) because it matches the answer from the passage. Eliminate (H) because the narrator's mother doesn't comment on how *crucial* his work was to *the company's success.* Eliminate (J) because the mother does not say that the narrator *should be grateful for his inheritance,* nor does she comment on his career change. The correct answer is (G).

7. **D**   This Information question asks who *Raman (The Gas Man)* is. Look for the lead words *Raman (The Gas Man)* to find the window for the question. Line 59 says, *I was Raman (The Gas Man) Singer's son.* Therefore, *Raman (The Gas Man)* is the narrator's father. Eliminate answers that don't match this answer from the passage. Eliminate (A), (B), and (C). The correct answer is (D).

8. **G**   This Information question asks why *the narrator's daughter knows the narrator better than he knows himself.* Look for the lead word *daughter* to find the window for the question. Lines 68–72 say, *at the urging of my college-aged daughter Geeta, I decided to try something I always wished that I had done. I enrolled in the business program at the State University, and before long, I realized that Geeta knew me better than I knew myself. I had fun like I never had before.* Eliminate answers that don't match this answer from the passage. Eliminate (F) because the *company's Internet presence* is not mentioned in relationship to the narrator's daughter. Keep (G) because it matches the answer from the passage. Eliminate (H) because *Richie* buying a *second Italian car* is not mentioned in relationship to the *narrator's daughter.* Eliminate (J) because the lines about the *narrator's daughter* do not mention *Singer Stations and Service.* The correct answer is (G).

9. **B** This Vocabulary in Context question asks what the phrase *came to see* means in line 73. Go back to the text, find the phrase *came to see,* and cross it out. Carefully read the surrounding text to determine another word or phrase that would fit in the blank based on the context. Lines 72–74 say, *I had fun like I never had before, and looking back, I came to see that the part of the business that always drew me in was learning.* Therefore, *came to see* could be replaced with "understood." Eliminate answers that don't match this answer from the passage. *Arrived at* means "got to a location," which doesn't match "understood." Eliminate (A). *Realized* matches "understood," so keep (B). *Attended* means "was present at," which doesn't match "understood." Eliminate (C). *Visited* means "stayed with," which doesn't match "understood." Eliminate (D). Note that (A), (C), and (D) are trap answers based on other meanings of *came to see* that don't fit the given context. The correct answer is (B).

READING DRILL 1 ANSWERS AND EXPLANATIONS

19. **D** This Information question asks for the *main idea of the passage.* Because this is a general question, it should be done after the specific questions. Look for the Golden Thread (more on this in Chapter 23). The passage is about the rise of texting and how it is part of a broader shift in the way we connect with one another. Eliminate answers that don't match this answer from the passage. Eliminate (A) and (B), as *telephones* and *telephone conversations* are not the primary focus of the passage. Choice (C) is too negative about texting to match the answer from the passage, as the final paragraph does indicate that texting has benefits: *for all [text messages'] flaws, they do bring us together.* Eliminate (C). Choice (D), a qualified statement on *text messages,* matches the answer from the passage, so keep it. The correct answer is (D).

20. **F** This Information question asks which statement *Fields* would *most likely agree* with. Look for the lead word *Fields* to find the window for the question. Lines 47–50 state, *Fields warns not only that we may have been "dumbed down" by our technologies but also that we may have lost one of the essential elements of the human experience.* Eliminate answers that don't match this answer from the passage. Choice (F) essentially restates these lines, so it is reasonable to infer that Fields would agree with this choice; keep (F). Eliminate (G) because while *Google* is mentioned in the passage, Fields does not express any views about it. Choice (H) states that texting is an *intimate way for people to communicate,* which contradicts the answer from the passage. Eliminate (H). Eliminate (J) because it is not a view expressed by *Fields.* The correct answer is (F).

21. **A** This Rhetoric question asks how the author supports *her claim that the text message is more than a simple message.* There is not a good lead word in this question, so work the question later. In lines 12–13 the author claims, *Text messages are already a part of the cultural landscape.* She then lists popular culture references to texting such as *rap and rock songs* and *serious novels.* Eliminate answers that don't match this answer from the passage. Keep (A) because it matches the answer from the passage. Although the author does mention *two novels* that include texting, she does not say that

these novels are *about the cultural role of texting*. Eliminate (B). While two people are credited with inventing texting in the first paragraph, the author doesn't list their *accomplishments* to support the claim that *the text message is more than just a simple message*. Eliminate (C) because it doesn't answer the question that was asked. Like (C), (D) includes information that is mentioned in the passage, but it does not answer the question that was asked. Eliminate (D). The correct answer is (A).

22. **J**   This Rhetoric question asks why the author *discusses the era before the War of Independence*. Look for the lead words *War of Independence* to find the window for the question. Lines 34–42 discuss the letters that were exchanged during the time *before the War of Independence*, stating, *we could even say that our very nation was founded in these written communiqués: much of what we know about that era comes from these letters. One day, text messages may provide a similar record of our own moment*. The author discusses the era before the War of Independence to make the point that correspondence can provide a historical record. Eliminate answer choices that don't match this answer from the passage. The passage indicates that *text-messaging* was not around until the early 1980s, long after such *historical figures* from the War of Independence, so eliminate (F). The author does not mention doing *more research*, so eliminate (G). There is no *digression* (which means "a change in topic") from the topic of *communication media*, so eliminate (H). Keep (J) because it matches the answer from the passage. The correct answer is (J).

23. **B**   This Analysis question asks which *people think or act in a way that is most similar to that of the naysayers described in the fifth paragraph*. Read the fifth paragraph as the window. Lines 55–57 state, *naysayers have said that everything from the printing press, to the radio, to the movie screen, to Google, has compromised the way we think and understand*. In other words, these *naysayers* predict that changes in technology will impair our ability to think. Eliminate answers that don't match this answer from the passage. Eliminate (A) because the *scientists* make a positive judgment, rather than a negative one. Keep (B) because the sports journalists *say that a change in rules will destroy the integrity of a sport*, which is a prediction that a change will have a negative outcome. Eliminate (C) because a personal preference is not a prediction about a negative outcome. Similarly, eliminate (D) because the historians' preference is not a prediction of a negative outcome. The correct answer is (B).

24. **J**   This Information question asks for *the earliest contributors to the development of the medium of the text message*. Work backward and use lead words from the answers to find the window for this question. Eliminate (F) because *Fields and Chacon* are described as authors who write about text messaging, not as early developers of the technology. Eliminate (G) because *Scorsese* is described as a filmmaker and *Franzen* as an author; neither helped develop text messaging. Similarly, eliminate (H) because *Wallace and Franzen* are described as authors. Keep (J) because lines 1–3 describe *Hillebrand* and *Ghillebaert* as creators of *the text message*. The correct answer is (J).

25. **D**   This Analysis question asks whether *Hillebrand* would *agree or disagree* with a given statement. Look for the lead word *Hillebrand* to find the window for the question. Lines 6–7 state, *Hillebrand suggested that "160 characters was sufficient to express most messages succinctly."* The given statement expresses a preference for a message of *a sentence or two rather than a two-hour phone conversation*.

Therefore, Hillebrand would likely agree with the statement. Eliminate answers that don't match this answer from the passage. Eliminate (A) and (B) because *Hildebrand* would *agree*. Eliminate (C) because *Hillebrand* does not discuss *the telephone*. Keep (D) because it matches the answer from the passage. The correct answer is (D).

26. **F** This Information question asks why *The Departed* might have been *considered a film interested in contemporary issues*. Look for the lead words *The Departed* to find the window for the question. Lines 12–13 state, *Text messages are already a part of the cultural landscape*, and lines 17–19 state, *Text messages, in fact, move the whole plot of Martin Scorsese's 2006 film* The Departed, *a critical success and eventual Oscar winner for Best Picture*. Eliminate answers that don't match this answer from the passage. Keep (F) as it matches the answer from the passage. Eliminate (G) because there is no support for the idea that text messaging *exploded in popularity after the film's release*. Eliminate (H) because, although it is true that the film won an *award*, (H) does not provide a reason the film might be considered *interested in contemporary issues*. Eliminate (J) since the passage does not mention *letter writing* in relationship to *The Departed*. The correct answer is (F).

27. **C** This Information question asks why the author mentions the phrase *time is money* in line 23. Read a window around the given line reference. Lines 21–24 read, *Speaking on an actual telephone is basically defunct in 2013* in part *for the economic reason that "time is money" and a text is quicker than a call*. Eliminate answers that don't match this answer from the passage. Eliminate (A) since the phrase refers to the value of time, rather than the literal cost of a text message. Eliminate (B) because, while the passage also mentions that a text creates a *long-lasting record*, (B) does not provide the reason the author mentions the phrase *time is money*. Keep (C) because it matches the answer from the passage. Eliminate (D) because there is no indication that text messaging has any positive effects on *intimacy*. The correct answer is (C).

Summary

o   Use the 6-Step Basic Approach.

o   *Step 1:* Preview. Read the blurb and map the questions. Star line and paragraph references and circle lead words.

o   *Step 2:* Work the Passage. Start from the beginning of the passage. As soon as you find a lead word or arrive at a line/paragraph reference you marked in Step 1, stop and proceed to Steps 3–6.
   •   On the Online Test, do all of the questions with highlighted text first, then begin to Work the Passage to scan for your lead words only.

o   *Step 3:* Select and Understand a Question. Do Now questions whose answers are easy to find. Save for Later questions that are hard to find, hard to answer, or both. Make sure that you understand what each question is asking.

o   *Step 4:* Read What You Need. Read a window of 5–10 lines to find your answer.

o   *Step 5:* Mark the Answer in the Passage. Underline the phrases or sentences that answer the question.

o   *Step 6:* Use POE. Eliminate answers that don't match the prediction.

o   *Skim* and *scan* when you work the passage.

o   *Read* windows of text when you work the questions.

o   Look for topic sentences and transition words.

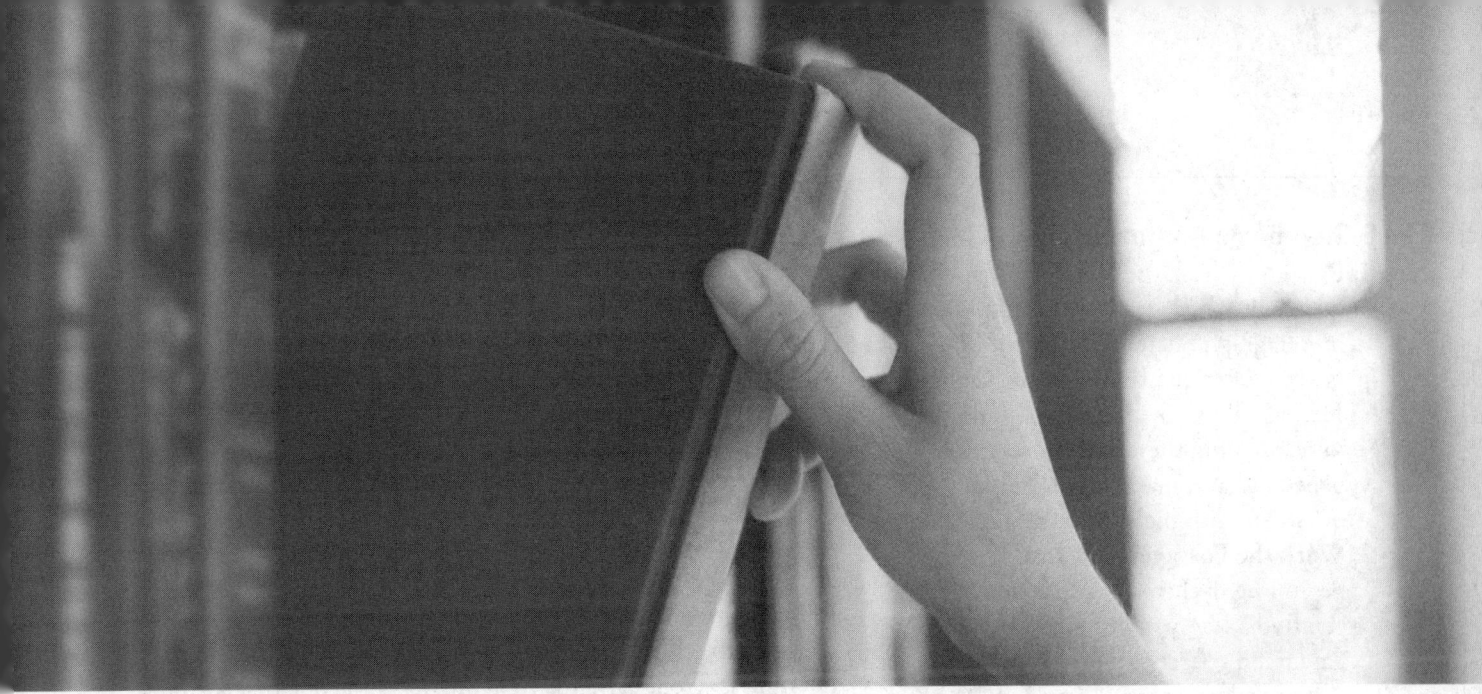

Chapter 23
Advanced Reading Skills

In this lesson, we'll help you hone your skills to crack specific question types and the most challenging and difficult texts. We'll also build on your mastery of the 6-Step Basic Approach by teaching you advanced POE (Process of Elimination) strategies.

The 6-Step Basic Approach

Step 1: **Preview.** Check the blurb and map the questions. Circle lead words, star line or paragraph references, and put an "L" next to Later questions. On the Online Test, you'll use the Index tool to do the same, making these marks on scratch paper and also marking an "H" for questions with highlighted text.

Step 2: **Work the Passage.** Start from the beginning of the passage. As soon as you find a lead word or arrive at a line/paragraph reference you marked in Step 1, stop and proceed to Steps 3–6.
  • On the Online Test, do all of the questions with highlighted text first, then begin to Work the Passage to scan for your lead words only.

Step 3: **Select and Understand a Question.** Use your POOD to find Now, Later, and Never questions. Make sure you understand what each question is asking.

Step 4: **Read What You Need.** Read 5–10 lines from the passage.

Step 5: **Mark the Answer in the Passage.** Underline the phrases and sentences that answer the question.

Step 6: **Use POE.**

LATER QUESTIONS

On the Reading test, some questions appear in unique formats that make them stand out from the regular question types. These questions still require you to show your understanding of what is directly stated or what is implied. However, it's useful to have specific strategies to crack these.

Negatives

The test-writers can throw a curveball at you when they ask a question in the negative using **except**, **least**, or **not** to twist the task. These questions are inherently tricky. What's right is wrong, and the right answer is the one that's wrong. Clear as a bell, isn't it?

No wonder it's so easy for your brain to trip all over itself. You may even start off trying to find the one choice that is false. But you somehow lose sight of the trap, and when you come across one of the answers in the passage, you think, "Eureka! This answer is true. I found it right here." Of course it's "right" in the passage: two other answer choices are somewhere in the passage as well. It's the choice that isn't in the passage that is the "right" answer.

Here's a better approach. Let's take a look at a question after it has been previewed in Step 1.

30. The passage mentions transportation of bees by river in all of the following countries except:
  F. Scotland.
  G. France.
  H. Poland.
  J. Egypt.

When you map the questions, circle *transportation of bees by river* and *countries,* but don't circle or mark *except.* Wait until you work the question to deal with the trick.

This is an Information question. If the negative weren't there, it would be easy to answer. What country transports bees by river? Still, it wouldn't be easy to find the answer since there is no line or paragraph reference, and none of these lead words qualify as great.

Occasionally, an **except** question will come with a line or paragraph reference to help narrow down your search, but most times they don't. The answers can be scattered throughout the passage or grouped together in one paragraph.

That's why you should always do a negative question Later. By the time you get to it, you should be able to identify where in the passage you'll find at least some of the answers, or you will have narrowed down where to look.

When you do work this question, mark the **except** so your eye can help your brain. You can double underline it. You can circle it and jot down two double exclamation points. You can cross it out altogether and write "True/False" or "T/F." On the ACT Online Test, use your whiteboard, write down ABCD, and mark the answers T/F. Do whatever you need to keep yourself focused on the goal: identify the one answer that is not like the others.

> **28.** The passage mentions transportation of bees by river in all of the following countries **except**:
>
> **F.** Scotland.
> **G.** France.
> **H.** Poland.
> **J.** Egypt.

For question 28, the answers happen to be grouped into the same paragraph, something you would have found easier to spot by using the great lead words in the answers. Always let the answers help in an **except** question.

Now use POE. Locate the countries in the window of text, and read to find out which use rivers. When you find one, eliminate it in the answers.

> In Scotland, after the best of the Lowland bloom is past, the bees are carried in carts to the Highlands and set free on the heather hills. In France, too, and in Poland, they are carried from pasture to pasture among orchards and fields in the same way and
> 5 along the rivers in barges to collect the honey of the delightful vegetation of the banks. In Egypt they are taken far up the Nile and floated slowly home again, gathering the honey-harvest of the various fields on the way, timing their movements in accord with the seasons. Were similar methods pursued in California,
> 10 the productive season would last nearly all the year.

The correct answer is (F). All four countries are listed, but only Scotland doesn't involve *rivers*.

Particularly difficult are questions that ask what is **not** answered by the passage. These essentially require four times the amount of work, since you have to look for four answers instead of just one. Sometimes, the question is asked but not answered, and other times, the topic may not arise at all, both of which can frustrate you and make you waste a lot of time scouring the passage over and over. That's why Negative questions can be good candidates for Never. If you do work a Negative question, always use POE. Eliminate the ones that you know are true. If you're stuck between two, or even among three, don't waste that much more time before forcing yourself to guess and move on.

> **Answer Choice Lead Words**
> In any type of question, lead words may be found in the answers instead of the question.

These next two questions would both be the last questions you do, and you would have gained a good grasp of the passage, even the details, by reading small windows as you worked the rest of the questions.

For the purposes of this exercise, don't worry about time. Read the excerpt of the passage and use POE.

---

33. Which of the following questions is **not** answered by information given in the passage?

A. How many bee ranches might be successfully established in the Sierra Mountains?

B. What types of flowers attract bees?

C. Where did the honeybees in the Sierra Mountains come from?

D. How much honey is produced by bee-trees in the Sierra Mountains?

35. Which of the following statements is **least** supported by the passage?

A. The Sierra Mountains have the appropriate requirements to support bee ranching activities.

B. Bees flourish in the Sierra Mountains in part because the area is not hospitable to traditional cattle ranching.

C. The presence of bees in the Sierra Mountains prevents sheep from grazing in certain areas.

D. Bee-ranching is an economically viable and environmentally sound enterprise.

The Sierra region is the largest of the three main divisions of the bee-lands of the State, and the most regularly varied in its subdivisions, owing to its gradual rise from the level of the Central Plain to the alpine summits. Up through the forest region, to a height of about 9,000 feet above sea-level, there are ragged patches of manzanita and five or six species of ceanothus, called deer-brush or California lilac. These are the most important of all the honey-bearing bushes of the Sierra.

From swarms that escaped their owners in the lowlands, the honey-bee is now generally distributed throughout the whole length of the Sierra, up to an elevation of 8,000 feet above sea-level. At this height they flourish without care, though the snow every winter is deep. Even higher than this, several bee-trees have been cut, which contained over 200 pounds of honey. Wild bees and butterflies have been seen feeding at a height of 13,000 feet above the sea.

The destructive action of sheep has not been so general on the mountain pastures as on those of the great plain. Fortunately, neither sheep nor cattle care to feed on the manzanita, spiraea, or adenostoma; these fine honey-bushes are too stiff and tall or grow in places too rough and inaccessible to be trodden under foot. Also the canyon walls and gorges, which form so considerable a part of the area of the range, while inaccessible to domestic sheep, are well fringed with honey-shrubs and contain thousands of lovely bee-gardens, lying hidden in narrow side-canyons and recesses fenced with avalanche taluses, and on the top of flat, projecting headlands, where only bees would think to look for them.

The plow has not yet invaded the forest region to any appreciable extent, nor has it accomplished much in the foot-hills. Thousands of bee-ranches might be established along the margin of the plain and up to a height of 4,000 feet, wherever water could be obtained. The climate at this elevation admits of the making of permanent homes, and by moving the hives to higher pastures as the lower pass out of bloom, the annual yield of honey would be nearly doubled. The foot-hill pastures, as we have seen, fail about the end of May; those of the chaparral belt and lower forests are in full bloom in June, those of the upper and alpine region in July, August, and September.

Of all the upper flower fields of the Sierra, Shasta is the most honeyful, and may yet surpass in fame the celebrated honey hills of Hybla and hearthy Hymettus. In this flowery wilderness the bees rove and revel, rejoicing in the bounty of the sun, clambering eagerly through bramble and hucklebloom, ringing the myriad bells of the manzanita, now humming aloft among polleny willows and firs, now down on the ashy ground among gilias and buttercups, and anon plunging deep into snowy banks of cherry and buckthorn....

Here's How to Crack Them

Work questions 33 and 35 as your last questions. For 33, double underline, highlight, circle, or cross off the **not** when you work it. As you find the answers to the answer choices—that is, the answers to the questions in the answer choices—cross off those choices or mark them on your whiteboard. Choice (A) is answered in lines 30–32. Choice (B) is answered in lines 6–8 and again in 18–21. Choice (C) is answered in lines 9–11. Choice (D) is never answered, and it is therefore the correct answer.

Question 35 is less specific and less dependent on detail than is question 33. Remember, the answers to your questions should all agree with each other, at least in terms of reinforcing the main points. Double underline, highlight, circle, or cross off the **least**, and use POE for any answer that doesn't reinforce the theme in the rest of the questions. Choice (C) is not supported by the passage and is therefore the correct answer. Choices (A) and (D) describe positive benefits of bees to the Sierra Mountains, and they would likely be the easiest choices to eliminate right away. Choice (B) is supported by lines 18–28.

Vocabulary in Context

For this special type of Rhetoric question, you'll have to determine the meaning of a word or phrase as it's used in context. The level of the vocabulary can vary, and many of these questions test secondary meanings of relatively common words.

You don't need to read a full window of 5–10 lines for Vocabulary in Context questions, but you do need to read at least the full sentence to determine the meaning in its context. Cross off the phrase (or simply ignore the word on the ACT Online Test), and try to substitute your own word. Then move to the answers, and use POE to eliminate choices that don't match your word. Beware the most common definition! Vocabulary in Context questions often test a secondary meaning.

Don't Know the Word?

If the Vocabulary in Context question tests a more difficult word that you're not familiar with, you can still try to read the context to see if you can come up with your own word that fits the meaning, and then use POE among the answers. But if you can't eliminate three choices, guess from what's left and move on. Similarly, if you are pressed for time and need to get to the next passage, mark this a Never. Choose your LOTD and move on.

Let's try an example.

The plow has not yet invaded the forest region to any appreciable extent, nor has it accomplished much in the foot-hills.
30 Thousands of bee-ranches might be established along the margin
of the plain and up to a height of 4000 feet, wherever water could
be obtained. The climate at this elevation admits of the making
of permanent homes, and by moving the hives to higher pastures
as the lower pass out of bloom, the annual yield of honey would
35 be nearly doubled. The foot-hill pastures, as we have seen, fail
about the end of May; those of the chaparral belt and lower forests
are in full bloom in June, those of the upper and alpine region in
July, August, and September.

34. As it is used in line 32, the phrase *admits of* most nearly means:

   F. makes possible.
   G. grants permission.
   H. confesses guilt.
   J. leaves out.

Here's How to Crack It

Admits is a common word, but it has different definitions depending on the context. The phrase *admits of* may be a less common phrase, but if you cross it out and read the sentence, you may come up with a word like "allows." Choice (F) works the same way "allows" does, and it's the correct answer. Choice (G) is close, but a climate can't literally "permit" something. Choice (H) is tempting if you don't use the context of the sentence, since *confesses guilt* is a correct definition of *admits* in another context. Choice (J), *leaves out*, does not match the meaning of "allows."

Roman Numerals

Roman numeral questions show up on the Reading test very rarely. They may come with line references or great lead words, or they may not. Use those factors to determine when to work the question, but in general, Roman numeral questions are good choices for Later when you know the passage better.

When you do work a Roman numeral question, be efficient. Choose the easiest of the Roman numerals to look up in the passage. Once you know yes or no, go to the answer choices and use POE. Look up only the Roman numerals that are still in the running among the answers.

Let's try an example.

They consider the lilies and roll into them, and, like lilies, they toil not for they are impelled by sun-power, as water-wheels by water-power; and when the one has plenty of high-pressure water, the other plenty of sunshine, they hum and quiver alike.
5 Sauntering in the Shasta bee-lands in the sun-days of summer, one may readily infer the time of day from the comparative energy of bee-movements alone—drowsy and moderate in the cool of the morning, increasing in energy with the ascending sun, and, at high noon, thrilling and quivering in wild ecstasy, then gradually
10 declining again to the stillness of night.

36. The passage describes the movement of the bees during the day as which of the following?

   I.   Drowsy and moderate
   II. Thrilling and quivering
   III. Cool and still

   F. I only
   G. III only
   H. II and III only
   J. I and II only

Here's How to Crack It

Work efficiently. Use the lead words in the Roman numerals to find them in the passage, beginning with I. *Drowsy* and *moderate* are used in line 7 to describe the bees in the morning. Eliminate (G) and (H) because neither includes the Roman numeral I. That leaves you with just II to review. *Thrilling* and *quivering* are used in line 9 to describe the bees at high noon. Choice (J) is correct.

Visual and Quantitative Questions

One passage in the Reading test may be accompanied by one or more tables, graphs, or other figures that contain information related to the passage. In the question sets associated with these, some of the questions will ask you to use information from the figures or to put together information from the passage and the figure.

These "Visual and Quantitative Questions" are a type of Analysis question. If you see any of these questions in the Reading test, follow the Science Basic Approach Steps from Chapter 26:

   1.   Work the Figure
   2.   Work the Question
   3.   Work the Answers

For questions that ask you to put together information from the figure and passage, follow Steps 1 and 2 above. Then, underline information in the passage that helps answer the question before doing Step 3.

Dual Reading Passages

Both the Reading and the Science tests include a "Dual Passage" in which you have two separate passages with questions about each passage individually and then questions about both together.

The Basic Approach still applies, but work the passages one at a time.

A NOTE ON THE GOLDEN THREAD

As you may have noticed, correct answers seem to repeat in a lot of ACT passages. It almost seems like sometimes if you get one answer, you can get three more with the same information. We call this phenomenon "The Golden Thread": some main idea or topic that threads through many of the answer choices.

On Dual Passages, it's more important than ever to find the Golden Thread. If you think about it, the questions that ask about both passages are really just variations on the theme, "What do these two passages have to do with each other?"

As you read through the two passages separately, try to answer this question even if only in a vague way. "What's the link between these two passages?" "Why are these passages on the same page together?" Any kinds of answers you can generate to these Golden Thread-type questions will help you down the line.

Here is what one of the passages will look like. Note how ACT has kindly separated the questions for you; on the ACT Online Test, the questions will be grouped together, but instead of a box above the first question for each passage, all the questions will have a label indicating if they ask about Passage A, Passage B, or both.

Here's the strategy we'll be using in this section:

1. **Preview.** Read the Blurb and decide which passage to do first. Map the questions for that passage.

2. **Work the Passage.**

3. **Select and Understand a Question.** As always, work the easier questions first.

4. **Read What You Need.** It can be easier to find the correct answer because the passages are short.

5. **Mark the Answer in the Passage.**

6. **Use POE.**

7. **Repeat.** Map the Questions for the second passage; then repeat steps 2–6. Answer the questions about both passages last.

INFORMATIONAL: Passage A is adapted from the 2015 *Time* article "What We Can Learn From Coca-Cola's Biggest Blunder" by James C. Cobb (© 2015 TIME USA LLC). Passage B is adapted from the 2007 *Washington Post* article "The Flop Heard Round the World" by Peter Carlson (© 2007 The Washington Post).

Passage A by James C. Cobb

Network executives had been understandably hesitant to interrupt the nation's most popular daytime soap opera. Yet viewers raised few complaints after ABC's Peter Jennings broke into General Hospital, on July 10, 1985, to tell them that, bow-
5   ing to public outrage and stunned by the anemic sales figures of its replacement, Coca-Cola was moving to put its original soft-drink formula back on the market.

This decidedly welcome news came just 79 days after the traditional version had been pulled abruptly to make way
10 for "New Coke." The almost palpable chagrin enveloping the company's official press briefing on the about-face was a far cry from the unrestrained bravado that had marked CEO Roberto Goizueta's announcement back on April 23 that Coca-Cola was scrapping its jealously guarded secret formula, which had
15 gone unchanged for almost a century, in favor of a new mixture that he promised would be a "bolder," "rounder" and more "harmonious" flavor. He failed to mention that it would also be markedly sweeter—doing so would have meant admitting that the more sugary appeal of Pepsi was steadily encroaching
20 on Coke's market share. The radical change struck consumer-marketing experts as more than a little risky, though Goizueta insisted at the time that he and his colleagues considered it "the surest move ever made."

Not for long, for company switchboards were soon drown-
25 ing in a torrent of as many as 8,000 calls a day from irate consumers suddenly deprived of the dependable drink that had always suited them just fine. Like the otherwise matronly lady interviewed by *Newsweek* at an Atlanta supermarket who needed but a single sip of New Coke to declare "it sucks," most who
30 rallied to pop-up protest groups like "Old Coca-Cola Drinkers of America" may have simply been taking their cue from their palates. Yet others appeared to be speaking more from their hearts as they likened Coke's switcheroo to a blasphemous assault on their most cherished icons and precepts. Some
35 compared it to burning the flag or rewriting the Constitution. "God and Coca Cola" had been "the only two things in my life," one complained in a letter, "now you have taken one of those things away from me."

Stunned by this fierce and unrelenting backlash, not to
40 mention New Coke's disappointing sales, Coke's spin-meisters scrambled to put the best possible face on the fiasco. Company President Donald Keough observed that, despite the extensive and expensive taste-testing that seemed to confirm New Coke's surefire appeal, there had simply been no way to gauge the
45 "deep and abiding emotional attachment to original Coca-Cola felt by so many people"....

Passage B by Peter Carlson

Fifty years ago today, Don Mazzella skipped out of school to see the hot new car that everybody was talking about, the hot new car that almost nobody had actually seen.

50 Ford Motor Co. had proclaimed it "E-Day." Mazzella and two buddies sneaked out of East Side High School in Newark, N.J., and hiked 13 blocks to Foley Ford so they could cast their gaze upon the much-ballyhooed new car that had been kept secret from the American public until its release that day.

55 It was called the Edsel.

"The line was around the block," recalls Mazzella, now 66 and an executive in a New Jersey consulting firm. "People were coming from all over to see this car. You couldn't see it from the street. The only way you could see it was to walk into
60 the showroom and look behind a curtain."

Mazzella and his truant friends waited their turn, thrilled to be there. "Back then for teenagers, cars were the be-all and end-all," he explains. They'd read countless articles about the Edsel and seen countless ads that touted it as the car of the future. But
65 they hadn't seen the car. Ford kept it secret, building excitement by coyly withholding it from sight, like a strip-tease dancer.

Finally, Mazzella and his friends reached the showroom. Finally, they were permitted to peek behind the curtain. They saw a cream-colored car with a strange oval grille that looked
70 like a big chrome O.

"We looked at it and said, 'What?'" Mazzella recalls. "It was just a blah car. I remember my friend Joe Grandi, who later became a Newark cop—he had a gruff voice, and he said, 'This is what we waited all this time for?' We all felt betrayed."

75 They weren't alone. The rest of America was equally dis-appointed. The Edsel fizzled. It flopped. It tanked. It became a national joke, the car that launched a million punch lines. By November 1959, when Ford finally mercy-killed the Edsel, it had lost an estimated $250 million—nearly $2 billion in
80 today's dollars.

Forget New Coke or the Susan B. Anthony dollar or the over-hyped Segway scooter or those pathetic dot-coms that went belly up in the late '90s. The Edsel was the most colossal, stupendous, and legendary blunder in the history of American
85 marketing....

10. Which of the following explains how Passage A characterizes the failure of New Coke?

    F. It happened gradually and was initially unnoticed by Coca-Cola executives.

    G. It happened quickly and dramatically.

    H. It was spearheaded by underground consumer protest groups.

    J. It occurred only after the renewed success of the classic formula.

11. Passage A quotes Roberto Goizueta at the end of the second paragraph in order to:

    A. support the idea that the launch of New Coke was inherently risky.

    B. suggest that consumers and executives rarely agree on matters of product innovation.

    C. emphasize the misguided sentiments of the promoters of New Coke.

    D. provide further evidence that Pepsi would continue to dominate the soft drink market.

12. Which of the following events referenced in Passage A occurred first chronologically?

    F. Peter Jennings's announcement to soap opera audiences

    G. The launch of New Coke

    H. New Coke's disappointing sales

    J. Increased market share by Pepsi

13. As used in lines 33–34, the "blasphemous assault" is most nearly similar to:

    A. "a torrent of as many as 8,000 calls a day" (line 25).

    B. "pop-up protest groups" (line 30).

    C. "burning the flag" (line 35).

    D. "unrelenting backlash" (line 39).

14. Which of the following statements in Passage B is used to convey irony?

    F. "hot new car" (lines 48–49)

    G. "much-ballyhooed" (line 53)

    H. "strip-tease dancer" (line 66)

    J. "legendary blunder" (line 84)

15. Much of Passage B focuses on Don Mazzella because:

    A. he was typical of the type of customer for whom the Edsel was created.

    B. he waited in line to buy the Edsel on the day of its unveiling.

    C. he was too young to properly appreciate the Edsel.

    D. his reaction to the Edsel was typical of that of many Americans in the 1950s.

16. A similarity between the two passages is that they both:

    F. examine their topics in an objective manner.

    G. describe the reactions of ordinary people to new products.

    H. assert that product innovations are generally unwise ventures.

    J. incorporate advice to corporations about how to avoid product failure.

17. An element in Passage B that is not present in Passage A is a reference to:

    A. specific information regarding product market share.

    B. public opinion.

    C. other failed products.

    D. quotations from experts.

18. If advertisers for New Coke had used tactics similar to those used to promote the Edsel, they would most likely have:

    F. run ads promoting a new secret formula but not allowed anyone to taste it until the day it was launched.

    G. kept the launch day of New Coke a secret until its unveiling.

    H. limited the number of ads promoting New Coke.

    J. promised that it would improve upon an old formula.

How to Work Through a Dual-Passage Reading Section

Step 1: Preview

As the blurb indicates, these passages are adapted from a couple of essays. It doesn't tell much more than that. A quick count will show that there are more questions about Passage A than there are about Passage B. Let's do Passage A first!

Map the questions for Passage A. Lead words include *New Coke, failure,* and *Roberto Goizueta.* On the Paper Test, you may notice that question 14 has lots of lead words in its answer choices. If your timing has been going well up to this point, you can also look for these lead words now to save yourself some searching later on. Otherwise, you'll search for these terms when you attempt question 14 later on, working backwards from the answers.

Step 2: Work the Passage

Work Passage A. Depending on the order you find the lead words as you work the passage, you'll probably do question 10, then 11, then 13. Question 12 will likely be last unless you had time to both catch the lead words in its answers during the Preview step and find those lead words in the passage. If you're taking the ACT Online Test, do question 13 first, and then go back to the other questions. As always, as soon as you find a lead word or arrive at a line reference you flagged, move on to Step 3.

Step 3: Select and Understand a Question

Start with question 10 (or 13 on the Online Test) and make sure you understand what it is asking. Work the specific questions roughly in chronological order, but remember POOD!

Step 4: Read What You Need

On the Paper ACT, for question 10, work the passage through the beginning of the second paragraph, where New Coke and its failure are mentioned. After you finish Steps 5 and 6 for question 10, resume skimming the passage and scanning for lead words, stopping when you find another lead word or arrive at a line reference.

On the Online ACT, you'll complete the steps needed for question 13. Since that's the only highlighted question, you'll then begin working the passage just as you would on the Paper Test, following the same advice above. The only real difference is you're starting the Work the Passage step with one question answered already and do not need to look for any line references.

Step 5: **Mark the Answer in the Passage**

After you read the window for the question, underline the phrases or sentences that answer the question.

Step 6: **Use POE**

Eliminate answers that don't match the answer that's in the passage.

Step 7: **Repeat**

After you've worked the general questions for Passage A, repeat Steps 2–6 for Passage B, working questions 14 and 15.

By this point, you have hopefully noticed what unites these passages. Passage A describes the introduction of—and negative reaction to—New Coke. Passage B describes the introduction of—and negative reaction to—the Edsel. Use your POOD to answer questions 16–18, which ask about both passages. Once you've finished working the questions on this Dual Passage, you can check your answers on page 474.

CRITICAL READING

Your use of the 6-Step Basic Approach and your personal order of difficulty (POOD) of both passages and questions should by now make you feel more confident on the Reading test. But you also may still be struggling with time and feel that you just can't work fast enough to get to enough questions.

In Chapter 22, we discussed ways to use your time better when you preview and work the passage. But you may also be wasting time when you work the questions, reading and rereading the window of text, trying to figure out what it's saying. You may have eliminated two answers, but when you're still not sure what the correct answer is, what do you do? You read the window yet again, desperate to figure out the meaning and answer the question in your own words.

We've all been there. Part of what makes standardized tests so evil is how they encourage us to listen to our worst instincts. You can't treat the Reading test as you would a school assignment, and you can't fall prey to your own panicked responses. You have to develop both strategies and skills specific to *this* test.

Critical Thinking

The key to better reading skills is to *think* better, which means to think critically. Getting lost in even a small window of text that makes no sense is like getting lost on unfamiliar roads. You don't stare down at the yellow line. You look around, looking for landmarks and road signs, trying to figure out where you are and where the road is going.

When you're lost in a tough section of text, use topic sentences and transitions as your landmarks and road signs. Don't try to understand every single word. Use the topic sentences to identify what the main point of the paragraph is. Look for transitions to see if points are on the same side or different sides from each other.

Topic Sentences and Main Points

Think of how you write papers for school. A good topic sentence makes clear the main subject of the paragraph, and it may even provide the author's main point on the subject. The rest of the paragraph will be details or examples that explain that point, and it may also include a more explicit conclusion of the main point. If you don't understand the details, read the main point to know what they mean. Examples and details usually come right before or right after the main point. If you don't understand the details, read the sentence before or after to see if it gives you the main point. If you don't understand the main point, read the sentence before or after to see if the details explain it for you.

Let's see how this works. Read the following topic sentence.

> Studies of American middle and high school students have shown that there is considerable uncertainty among students about what behaviors count as cheating.

What's going to come next in the paragraph? It could be examples of the behaviors. It could be an explanation of why students are uncertain. It could even be a statement of a different study that contradicts this one. You would be safe anticipating any of those outcomes, but the anticipation is the key. Don't sit back and wait to see where the road is going. Lean forward and look for the fork in the road or the detour sign telling you to turn around. In other words, look for transitions.

Transitions

The first word or phrase after the topic sentence can tell you what direction you're heading.

Let's look at some choices for our cheating sentence.

If the next words were *In particular*, what does that tell you is coming next? Examples of the behavior.

If the next word were *However*, what does that tell you is coming next? A contradiction to this study.

Transitions play a key role in critical thinking. Look for transitions to announce additional points, contradictory points, cause-and-effect relationships, examples, or conclusions. Here are just a few common transitions.

Additional Points	Cause and Effect Relationships
And	Because
Also	Since
As well	So
In addition	
Furthermore	
Moreover	**Examples**
	For example
	In particular
	Such as
Contradictory Points	
Although	
But	**Conclusions**
Even though	Consequently
However	In other words
Nevertheless	That is
On the other hand	Therefore
Rather	Thus
Yet	

Modifiers

Nouns and verbs reliably give you the facts in a statement, but they don't necessarily provide the author's point. Look at the two adverbs in the prior sentence and see how they helped shape the point. *Reliably* means you can infer that nouns and verbs *almost always* give facts. *Necessarily* modifies the verb phrase *don't provide*. Without it, you could infer that nouns and verbs never give you the point. Adjectives and adverbs are just as useful as transitions, conveying the author's opinion on what would otherwise be a statement of fact.

Consider this sentence.

> Surprisingly, students do not consider sharing notes to be cheating.

The point of this sentence is that *sharing notes* is a form of *cheating*, and the author believes students should know this. If you removed *surprisingly* from the sentence, it's just a factual statement of what students think. On the Reading test, most Reasoning questions involve the author's opinion or main point, or as ACT puts it, "the implied meaning."

Try another.

> Students offered a refreshingly candid explanation for their behavior.

Refreshingly means that the author judged the admission as unexpected but welcome. *Candid* means the students were honest and open.

Translation

When you're struggling to make sense of a window of confusing text, look for transitions and modifiers to help you determine the main point. You may be in the thick of a body paragraph with the topic sentence in the rearview mirror. Instead of focusing on every single word, use the transitions and modifiers to get the general direction of points and the connections between them.

Let's look at a tough window to see how this works.

The strikingly tolerant attitudes demonstrated by the students toward cheating cannot be explained by mere immorality and laziness, but may rather point to a sobering conclusion that high-stakes tests have created a ruthless atmosphere in which
5 students are desperate to succeed at any cost.

Here's How to Crack It

Focus on the transitions and modifiers. *Strikingly* tells you that the author finds the students' tolerance of cheating noteworthy and unusual. The key verb phrase *cannot be explained* directs you away from what <u>is not</u> the cause, and the transitions *but* and *rather* direct you to what <u>is</u> the cause. Even if you didn't understand all the vocabulary words, the transitions act as huge road signs that identify the most important part of the sentence. Students don't cheat because of *immorality* and *laziness* but because *high-stakes tests* have made things *ruthless* and *desperate*. Even just knowing which sentence, or which part of the sentence, to focus on will help, along with POE, to find the right answer.

ADVANCED POE SKILLS

When you're stuck on a confusing window of text, the best use of your time is spent working the answers. Reread your window, even to spot transitions and modifiers, in conjunction with working the answers.

In an ideal situation, you read a question, read the window of text looking for your answer, answer the question in your own words, and then work through the answer choices looking for the best match, using POE to get rid of those that don't.

But situations are seldom ideal on the Reading test. When you don't quite understand the window and therefore have no clue about the answer, go straight to working the answers.

The Art of Wrong Answers

If you worked for ACT, you'd have to sit in a cubicle all day writing test questions. The easy part of the job is writing the correct answer. You may even know that before you write the question. The harder part is coming up with three wrong answers. If you didn't write great wrong answers, everyone would get a 36. So you have to come up with temptingly wrong answers.

Let's take a look at some ways to make wrong answers.

Read the following question, correct answer, and text. We don't care about the right answer in this exercise, so you can read it before you read the window.

> **13.** The main point of the fifth paragraph (lines 40–48) is that:
>
> **A.** cultural norms affect how students judge cheating behaviors.

40   The authors of one such study contend that differences between German students and the other students in the study regarding what constitutes cheating can be explained by differences in social norms. In particular, German students viewed passive cheating more as "helping others" or "cooperation" rather than
45   as unethical or immoral behavior. Costa Rican students also were more liberal than Americans in their views of passive cheating, also due to a cultural tendency toward cooperation rather than competition.

Our goal here is to examine *why* the three wrong answers are wrong.

> **B.** German students consider passive cheating to be unethical and immoral.

Look carefully at lines 43–45. Choice (B) took tempting words out of the passage and garbled them. The passage disproves this answer.

> **C.** American students have a less liberal view of passive cheating than do Costa Rican students.

Since lines 45–46 say Costa Rican students are *more liberal than Americans*, (C) is true. But it's not the correct answer because it's not the main point of the paragraph.

> **D.** Russian students do not consider passive cheating to be unethical.

Russian students are not mentioned in this window and have instead been taken from a different window.

Answers can be wrong because they don't match what the passage says, because they answer the wrong question, or because they're not even found in the right window. But no matter how tempting or obvious wrong answers are, they are all easier to understand than 5–10 lines of text, simply because they're shorter. So when you're stuck on tough questions on tough windows, work backwards with the answers.

Work Backwards

Instead of rereading the window to try to determine the meaning, read the answer choices for their meaning. Then see if you can match each back into the passage.

> Read to understand the meaning of the answer choices instead of rereading the window.
>
> - Look for lead words or phrases in the answer choices.
> - Determine if the words match those found in the window.
> - Use POE to eliminate choices that don't match the window.

Let's see how this works. Read the following question and window.

> The dictionary defines cheating as unfairly gaining advantage in a given situation by deliberately violating established rules. Cheating behaviors may include plagiarism, copying exam answers, using crib notes, obtaining test questions beforehand (all
> 5 active behaviors), as well as allowing others to copy from you, taking advantage of teacher scoring errors, and failing to report cheating (more passive behaviors). The definition of cheating is not under debate, but the way that students define their behavior, in relation to this definition, and how morally acceptable they
> 10 deem such behavior, is. In other words, there is a large variance regarding which behaviors students consider to be cheating.

13. It can reasonably be inferred that the author provides the dictionary definition of cheating (lines 1–2) in order to:

Take the answer choices one at a time. In each choice, we've put in bold a lead word or phrase in the answer. Can you match these words, or a paraphrased meaning of them, in the window of text?

A. argue that passive behaviors **are more morally acceptable** than active behaviors.

Morally acceptable appears in line 9, but the phrase isn't used to compare *passive* and *active behaviors*. Tempting, but wrong.

B. illustrate what behaviors will get students **expelled or suspended**.

Expelled and *suspended*, or any paraphrases of those words, don't appear anywhere in the window, so (B) can't be the right answer.

C. prove that students **deliberately violate established rules**.

Deliberately violating established rules appears in line 2, but it's used as part of the definition of cheating, not as proof of students' conduct. We've eliminated three answers, so (D) must be right. But always check all four answers to be sure the one you choose is better than the three you've eliminated.

D. show that students may not consider their own **behavior to be cheating**.

Students' *own behavior* is in the last sentence, and (D) matches well the point of that sentence.

Try another example. Choose your own words or phrases out of each answer to work backwards with. Does the passage match the answer?

     Patterns of individual cheating behavior in different societies typically reflect their respective normative climates. Students recognize certain activities as cheating and may be able to provide
60 justifications for their unethical behavior in some way. Yet cheating, when identified as such, is overall felt to be wrong. However, an eye-opening study of Russian university students' cheating behaviors by Yulia Poltorak reveals a different type of normative climate that is a unique part of the Communist legacy. According
65 to this study, cheating behavior in Soviet Russia was not only very widespread, but also widely accepted as an appropriate response to social conditions.

12. It can reasonably be inferred by information in the seventh paragraph (lines 57–67) that:

  F. cheating in Soviet Russia was widely rejected as an acceptable response.

  G. the cold climate in Russian classrooms motivated students to cheat.

  H. the normative climate that produced cheating in Soviet Russia may be explained by the role of the Communist legacy.

  J. students in Soviet Russia failed to provide justifications for their unethical behavior.

Here's How to Crack It

In (F), you could choose *widely rejected* and try to place it in line 66. The passage disproves this, stating that cheating is *widely accepted*, so eliminate (F). Choice (G) misuses the word *climate*, but it also discusses *classrooms*, which are nowhere to be found in the passage. Eliminate it. Choice (H) offers *Communist legacy*, an easy lead word phrase to locate in the passage. Choice (H) could match lines 62–64, so keep it. Choice (J) offers *justifications for their unethical behavior*, words right out of the passage. But the passage doesn't state that Russian students *failed to provide* them. The correct answer is (H).

Reading Drill 2

Use the 6-Step Basic Approach on the following passage, and apply your advanced reading skills. Time yourself to complete in 10–11 minutes.

Passage III

INFORMATIONAL: The following passage is adapted from the article "Conquering Jazz" by Patrick Tyrrell (© 2006 by Patrick Tyrrell).

From the time I started playing instruments, I have been intrigued and slightly mystified by the world of jazz. I'm not talking about adventurous, atonal, confusing jazz that normal music listeners have a hard time following. I'm talking about the lively,
5   accessible, beautiful jazz that came of age in the swinging 1920s and 1930s: the simultaneously hip and regal symphonic swing of Duke Ellington and Count Basie; the carnival of contrapuntal melodies that inexplicably harmonize with each other in New Orleans' jazz; the buoyant, atmosphere-touching saxophone solos
10   of Charlie Parker and the young John Coltrane.

The one thing I had always heard about jazz but could never accept was that jazz was an improvised form of music. How could this be?

The trademark of beautiful jazz is the complexity of the
15   music. All the instrumentalists are capable of dizzying arrays of notes and rhythms. The soloists find seemingly impossible transitions from one phrase to the next that are so perfect one would think they had spent weeks trying to devise *just* the right route to conduct safe passage. To think they spontaneously craft
20   these ideas seems preposterous.

My first nervous jabs into the world of jazz came during college. I was in a rock band, but my fellow guitarist and bandmate, Victor, also played in a jazz ensemble. At our practices, I would sometimes show off a new chord I had just "invented" only to
25   have him calmly and confidently name it, "Oh, you mean C-sharp diminished?" Often, in between our band's simplistic rock songs, I would look over and see him playing chord shapes on his guitar I had never seen before. Were we playing the same instrument?

Of course, rock music, as well as most early classical mu-
30   sic, operates within a much simpler harmonic world than does jazz. There are 12 tones in Western music: A-flat, A, B-flat, B, C, D-flat, D, E-flat, E, F, G-flat, and G. There are major chords, which sound happy, and minor chords, which sound sad. Essentially, rock music requires only that you learn the major and
35   minor chord for each of the 12 tones. If you do, you can play 99 percent of all the popular radio songs from the 1950s onward.

Jazz uses the same twelve tones as do rock and classical, but it employs a much more robust variety of chords. Major sevenths, augmented fifths, flat ninths, and diminished chords all add to
40   the depth and detail of the music. These often bizarre-sounding chords toss in subtle hints of chaos and imbalance, adding a worldly imperfection to otherwise standard chord values. Jazz starts sounding better the older you get, just as candy starts tasting too sweet and a bit of bitterness makes for a more appealing flavor.

45   For the most part, Victor's elliptical personality prevented him from ever giving me straightforward explanations when I asked him to divulge the "magician's secrets" of jazz. But I did learn that jazz is only *partly* improvised. The musicians aren't inventing the structure of songs spontaneously, just the specific
50   details and embellishments. A sheet of jazz music doesn't look like a sheet of classical music. There aren't notes all over the page dictating the "ideas." There are just chord names spaced out over time, dictating the "topic of conversation."

There's a legendary book in the jazz world known as *The
55   Real Book*. It's a collection of a few hundred classic songs. Open it up in any room full of jazz musicians, and they could play in synchrony for a week. For years, I wanted my own copy, but I had always been too afraid to buy it, afraid that I wouldn't know how to use the book once I had it. Then, at age 30, more than a
60   decade since Victor and I had gone our separate ways, I bought myself a copy. I resolved to learn how to play all the chords on guitar and piano. For the next few months, I quietly plucked away at these strange, new combinations. F-sharp minor-7 flat-5? Each chord was a cryptic message I had to decode and then
65   understand. It felt like being dropped off alone in a country where I didn't speak the language.

But I made progress. Chords that initially took me twenty seconds to figure out started to take only a few. My left hand was becoming comfortable in its role of supplying my right hand
70   with a steady bass line. Meanwhile, to my amazement, my right hand began to improvise melodies that sounded undeniably *jazzy*.

It seemed like the hard work of figuring out the exotic jazz chords had sent new melodic understanding straight to my hand, bypassing my brain entirely. I felt like a witness to performances
75   by detached hands; I couldn't believe that I was the one creating these sounds. I'm sure this feeling will not last, but for now I'm enjoying the rare and miraculous feeling of improvising music that I still consider beyond my abilities.

19. Which chord, if any, does the author eventually conclude is the most confusing jazz chord to play?

 A. The passage does not indicate any such chord.
 B. C-sharp diminished
 C. Major sevenths
 D. F-sharp minor-7 flat-5

20. As it is used in line 47, "magician's secrets" most nearly means:

 F. information on how to play jazz.
 G. forbidden bits of knowledge.
 H. instances of harmless trickery.
 J. the true nature of a private person.

21. As portrayed by the author, Victor responds to the author's *invented* chord with what is best described as:

 A. amazement.
 B. jealousy.
 C. confusion.
 D. nonchalance.

22. The author states that *The Real Book* was something he explored for a few:

 F. years.
 G. months.
 H. weeks.
 J. days.

23. The details in lines 40–44 primarily serve to suggest the:

 A. aspects of jazz's complexity that more mature listeners enjoy.
 B. lack of depth and detail found in rock and classical music.
 C. confusion and awkwardness of standard jazz chord values.
 D. unpleasantly bitter taste of candy that develops with age.

24. In the context of the passage, the author's statement in lines 72–74 most nearly means that:

 F. he was so overworked that his hands could still move, but his thoughts were turned off.
 G. he had accidentally trained his hands to resist being controlled by his brain.
 H. it was easier to decode the exotic jazz chords by pointing at them with his hands.
 J. he was capable of playing music without consciously choosing what to play.

25. The author implies that F-sharp minor-7 flat-5 is an example of a chord that he:

 A. had little trouble decoding now that he had *The Real Book*.
 B. had previously only seen during his travels abroad.
 C. knew how to play on guitar but not on a piano.
 D. initially found confusing and struggled to understand.

26. The passage supports which one of the following conclusions about Victor?

 F. He played music with the author until the author turned 30 years old.
 G. He gave his copy of *The Real Book* to the author as a gift.
 H. He was at one time a member of multiple musical groups.
 J. He invented a chord and named it C-sharp diminished.

27. The passage is best described as being told from the point of view of someone who is:

 A. reviewing the chain of events that led to his career in jazz.
 B. discussing reasons why jazz is less complicated than it seems.
 C. relating his impressions of jazz music and his attempts to play it.
 D. highlighting an important friendship that he had in college.

INFORMATIONAL DUAL PASSAGE ANSWERS AND EXPLANATIONS

10. **G** This Information question asks which statement *explains how Passage A characterizes the failure of New Coke*. Because this is a general question, it should be done after all the specific questions for Passage A. Look for the Golden Thread. The passage is about the rapid negative public response to the release of New Coke and how the response surprised Coca-Cola company executives. Eliminate answers that don't match this answer from the passage. Eliminate (F) because the failure did not happen *gradually*; it happened after just *79 days*. Keep (G) because it matches the answer from the passage. Eliminate (H) because there is no mention in the text of *underground consumer protest groups*. Eliminate (J) because it's inconsistent with the passage—the classic formula's return was the end of New Coke. The correct answer is (G).

11. **C** This Rhetoric question asks why *Passage A quotes Roberto Goizueta at the end of the second paragraph*. Read the second paragraph as the window. Lines 21–23 state that *Goizueta insisted at the time that he and his colleagues considered* New Coke *"the surest move ever made,"* but the rest of the paragraph indicates that other people thought New Coke would perform poorly and that it did indeed perform poorly. The author discusses Goizueta's quote to make it clear that Goizueta's confidence in New Coke was unwarranted. Eliminate answers that don't match this answer from the passage. Eliminate (A) because while the author would likely agree with the statement, it does not address the confidence from Goizueta at the end of the paragraph. Eliminate (B) because the passage does not discuss whether *consumers and executives* often agree or disagree on products. Keep (C) because it matches the answer from the passage. Eliminate (D) because the focus of Goizueta's quote is on New Coke, not its competitor, *Pepsi*. The correct answer is (C).

12. **J** This Information question asks which event from Passage A *occurred first chronologically*. Work backward and use lead words from the answers to find the window for the question. Eliminate (F) and (H) because, in lines 2–7, both the announcement by Peter Jennings regarding the return of Coca-Cola's *original soft-drink formula* and New Coke's *anemic sales* must happen after the release of New Coke in (G). Eliminate (G) because lines 10–20 indicate that New Coke was launched in response to Pepsi *steadily encroaching on Coke's market share*. Keep (J) because lines 17–20 support that the reason for the development of New Coke was the loss of *market share*, which precedes all of the other events described in the answer choices. The correct answer is (J).

13. **C** This Information question asks which idea from the text *is most nearly similar to* the *blasphemous assault*. Read lines 32–38, where the text states that the *blasphemous assault* of *Coke's switcheroo* to New Coke was compared to *burning the flag or rewriting the Constitution*. Eliminate answers that don't match this answer from the passage. Eliminate (A) because lines 24–27 demonstrate the public resentment toward the change but don't offer a situation similar to *burning the flag or rewriting the Constitution*. Eliminate (B) because lines 27–32 discuss groups who dislike the flavor of New Coke but do not offer any situation synonymous to those from lines 32–38. Keep (C) because it matches the answer from the passage. Eliminate (D) because lines 39–41 only discuss what the Coca-Cola executives did in response to the backlash rather than any situation comparable to those in lines 32–38. The correct answer is (C).

14. **F**   This Rhetoric question asks which statement from Passage B *is used to convey irony*. Word backward and use the line references from the answers to find the window for the question. Keep (F) because lines 47–49 state that there is a *hot new card that everybody was talking about*, but one *that almost nobody had actually seen*. This contrast is an example of irony. Eliminate (G) because lines 50–54 only discuss an attempt by *Mazzella and two buddies* to see the car but do not show any unexpected contrast. Eliminate (H) because lines 61–66 only discuss how the Ford Motor Company had built anticipation for the car and *kept it secret* but do not show any contrast. Eliminate (J) because lines 81–85 only discuss how the Edsel was a failure but do not show any contrast. The correct answer is (F).

15. **D**   This Rhetoric question asks why *Much of Passage B focuses on Don Mazzella*. Because this is a general question, it should be done after all the specific questions. Look for the Golden Thread. The first six paragraphs discuss the anticipation and excitement of Mazzella, his friend, and the general public regarding the Edsel. The last three paragraphs describe the disappointment of all of those groups upon finally seeing the car. Eliminate answers that don't match this answer from the passage. Eliminate (A) and (B) because the text never indicates that Mazzella represents a *typical customer* or that he is looking to buy the car at all; he just wants to see it. Eliminate (C) because the passage never claims that Mazzella is *too young* to appreciate the Edsel. Keep (D) because it matches the answer from the passage. The correct answer is (D).

16. **G**   This Analysis question asks for *a similarity between the two passages*. Eliminate any answer choices that misrepresent either passage. Both passages discuss the negative public reaction to a new product. Eliminate (F) because neither passage discusses this reaction in an *objective manner*. Passage A notes in the second paragraph that the end of New Coke was *decidedly welcome news*, and the last paragraph of Passage B calls The Edsel a *colossal, stupendous, and legendary blunder*. Keep (G) because it matches the answer from the passages. Eliminate (H) because each passage discusses one specific product and neither makes a general claim regarding *product innovations*. Eliminate (J) because neither passage offers any *advice to corporations* that would help avoid product failure. The correct answer is (G).

17. **C**   This Analysis question asks for an *element in Passage B that is not present in Passage A*. Eliminate answers that do not appear in Passage B or do appear in Passage A. Eliminate (A) because only Passage A mentions *market share*, which appears in its second paragraph. Eliminate (B) because both passages mention *public opinion*. Keep (C) because Passage B mentions *other failed products* in the last paragraph, while Passage A only discusses New Coke. Eliminate (D) because only Passage A includes quotations from *experts*; the only quotations in Passage B are from Mazzella and his friends, who are students. The correct answer is (C).

18. **F**   This Analysis question asks what advertisers for New Coke *would most likely have done* if they *had used tactics similar to those used to promote the Edsel*. Eliminate answers that misrepresent how the Edsel is promoted in Passage B. Keep (F) because the Ford Motor Company kept the Edsel *a secret* and built anticipation for the reveal. Eliminate (G) because the *launch day* of the Edsel was not the secret—it was the physical product itself that was the secret. Eliminate (H) because it contradicts Passage B—lines 64 describes the number of ads for the Edsel as *countless*. Eliminate (J) because

the Ford Motor Company does not promise that the Edsel *would improve upon an old formula*—if anything, this is more consistent with Passage A, which is not the focus of this question. The correct answer is (F).

READING DRILL 2 ANSWERS AND EXPLANATIONS

19. **A** This Information question asks which chord the author concludes is *the most confusing to play*. Work backwards and use lead words from the answers to find the window for this question. Start with (B). Lines 23–26 say, *At our practices, I would sometimes show off a new chord I had just "invented" only to have him calmly and confidently name it, "Oh, you mean C-sharp diminished?"* The text does not say that this chord is the *most confusing*, so eliminate (B). *Major sevenths* are mentioned in line 38; lines 37–40 say, *Jazz uses the same twelve tones as do rock and classical, but it employs a much more robust variety of chords. Major sevenths, augmented fifths, flat ninths, and diminished chords all add to the depth and detail of the music. Major sevenths* are not described as confusing, so eliminate (C). *F-sharp minor-7 flat-5* is mentioned in lines 63–64; lines 62–64 say, *For the next few months, I quietly plucked away at these strange, new combinations. F-sharp minor-7 flat-5? Each chord was a cryptic message.* Although the chord is described as *strange, new,* and *a cryptic message*, the window does not say the chord is the *most confusing*, so eliminate (D). The correct answer is (A).

20. **F** This Vocabulary in Context question asks what the phrase *magician's secrets* most nearly means as it is used in line 47. Go back to the text, find the phrase *magician's secrets*, and cross it out. Carefully read the surrounding text to determine another word or phrase that would fit in the blank based on the context. Lines 45–47 say, *For the most part, Victor's elliptical personality prevented him from ever giving me straightforward explanations when I asked him to divulge the "magician's secrets" of jazz.* Therefore, *magician's secrets* could be replaced with "special knowledge." Eliminate answers that don't match this answer from the passage. Keep (F) because *information* matches "special knowledge." Eliminate (G) because there is no indication that the "special knowledge" is *forbidden*. Eliminate (H) because *trickery* does not match "special knowledge." Eliminate (J) because the phrase is about *jazz*, not about *Victor's* personality. The correct answer is (F).

21. **D** This Information question asks how *Victor responds to the author's invented chord*. Look for the lead words *Victor* and *invented* to find the window for the question. *Victor* is introduced in line 23; lines 23–26 say, *I would sometimes show off a new chord I had just "invented" only to have him calmly and confidently name it, "Oh, you mean C-sharp diminished?* Eliminate answers that don't match this answer from the passage. Eliminate (A), (B), and (C) because *amazement, jealousy,* and *confusion* do not match *calmly and confidently*. Keep (D) because *nonchalance* matches *calmly and confidently*. The correct answer is (D).

22. **G** This Information question asks *how long the author explored The Real Book*. Look for the lead words *The Real Book* to find the window for the question. *The Real Book* is mentioned in lines 54–55. Later in the paragraph, lines 62–63 state that the author *plucked away* at the chords *for the next few months*. Eliminate answers that don't match this answer from the passage. Eliminate (F) because, although the word *years* appears in the passage, it describes how long the author wanted a copy of *The Real Book*, not how long the author explored *The Real Book*. Keep (G) because it matches the answer from the passage. Eliminate (H) because, although the word *week* appears in the passage, it describes how long jazz musicians could play together using *The Real Book*, not how long the author explored it. Eliminate (J) because there is no reference to *days* in the text. The correct answer is (G).

23. **A** This Rhetoric question asks what the *details in lines 40–44 primarily serve to suggest*. Read a window around the given line reference. Lines 38–44 say, *Major sevenths, augmented fifths, flat ninths, and diminished chords all add to the depth and detail of the music. These often bizarre-sounding chords toss in subtle hints of chaos and imbalance, adding a worldly imperfection to otherwise standard chord values. Jazz starts sounding better the older you get, just as candy starts tasting too sweet and a bit of bitterness makes for a more appealing flavor.* Therefore, the lines suggest that older listeners may enjoy jazz more because of the way the chords add to the *depth and detail of the music*. Eliminate answers that don't match this answer from the passage. Keep (A) because *depth and detail of the music* matches with *jazz's complexity*. Eliminate (B) because these lines are about *jazz*, not about *rock and classical music*. Eliminate (C) because *confusion and awkwardness* are negative, but the author describes the *bizarre-sounding chords* in positive terms. Additionally, the description *bizarre-sounding* applies to the *Major sevenths, augmented fifths, flat ninths, and diminished chords*, rather than to the *standard chord values*. Eliminate (D) because these lines are *primarily* focused on jazz rather than *candy*, and the author does not say that *candy* starts to taste bitter. The correct answer is (A).

24. **J** This Information question asks what *the author's statement in lines 72–74 most nearly means*. Read a window around the given line reference. Lines 72–74 say, *It seemed like the hard work of figuring out the exotic jazz chords had sent new melodic understanding straight to my hand, bypassing my brain entirely.* The paragraph goes on to say, *I felt like a witness to performances by detached hands; I couldn't believe that I was the one creating these sounds…I'm enjoying the rare and miraculous feeling of improvising music that I still consider beyond my abilities.* Therefore, the author was able to play music without fully thinking about what he was playing. Eliminate answers that do not match this answer from the passage. Eliminate (F) because although the author mentions that figuring out the chords was *hard work*, he doesn't indicate that he was *overworked*. Eliminate (G) because the author does not indicate that his hands *resist being controlled by his brain*. Eliminate (H) because the author is playing the chords, not *pointing at them*. Keep (J) because it matches the answer from the passage. The correct answer is (J).

25. **D** This Information question asks what the author implies about the chord *F-sharp minor-7 flat-5*. Look for the lead words *F-sharp minor-7 flat-5* to find the window for the question. Lines 62–65 say, *For the next few months, I quietly plucked away at these strange, new combinations. F-sharp minor-7 flat-5? Each chord was a cryptic message I had to decode and then understand.* Therefore, the chord is an example of one of the *strange, new combinations* the author was learning. Eliminate answers that don't match this answer from the passage. Eliminate (A) because *had little trouble decoding* does not match the description of the chord as a *cryptic message*. Eliminate (B) because there is no mention of literal *travels abroad*; the author compares learning the chords to *being dropped off alone in a country where I didn't speak the language*, but this statement is figurative. Eliminate (C) because the author says that he *resolved to learn how to play all the chords on guitar and piano*, not that he knew how to play the chord on *guitar but not on a piano*. Keep (D) because it matches the answer from the passage. The correct answer is (D).

26. **H** This Information question asks for a conclusion about *Victor* that is supported by the passage. The question is Hard to Find because *Victor* is mentioned in multiple places throughout the passage, so work the question Later. Look for the lead word *Victor* to find the possible windows for the question, and use Process of Elimination with each statement about *Victor*. Lines 22–23 say, *I was in a rock band, but my fellow guitarist and bandmate, Victor, also played in a jazz ensemble.* These lines support (H) because *Victor* was in both a rock band and a jazz ensemble. Keep (H). Eliminate (F) because according to the author, *Victor and I had gone our separate ways* over a decade before the author was 30. Eliminate (G) because the author *bought* himself a copy of *The Real Book*. Eliminate (J) because the author thought that he had *"invented"* a chord; the passage does not indicate that Victor invented the chord. The correct answer is (H).

27. **C** This Rhetoric question asks for the author's *point of view*. Because this is a general question, it should be done after the specific questions. Look for the Golden Thread. The passage is about the author learning about jazz music and then learning to play it. Eliminate answers that don't match this answer from the passage. Eliminate (A) because there is no indication that the author has *a career in jazz*. Eliminate (B) because the author does not argue that *jazz is less complicated than it seems*; instead, he frequently mentions how complex it is. Keep (C) because it matches the answer from the passage. Eliminate (D) because the author's *friendship* with Victor is not the main focus of the passage. The correct answer is (C).

Summary

- o   Work special question types Later. They require more work than a typical question, and they will become easier to do the later you do them.

- o   Double underline, highlight, circle, or cross out negative words **except**, **least**, or **not**. Use POE to eliminate answers that are found in the passage, or use your whiteboard to mark each answer choice "T/F."

- o   For Vocabulary in Context questions, read the entire sentence. Cross off the word or phrase and come up with your own word. Use POE to eliminate answers that don't match your word.

- o   Work Roman numeral questions efficiently, using POE.

- o   Don't waste time on special question types if you can't eliminate three answers. Guess from the choices that are remaining and move on.

- o   Use topic sentences, transitions, and modifiers to help translate confusing windows of text.

- o   Work backwards with answer choices. Try to match the answer to the passage instead of the passage to the answer.

Part V
How to Crack the ACT Science Test

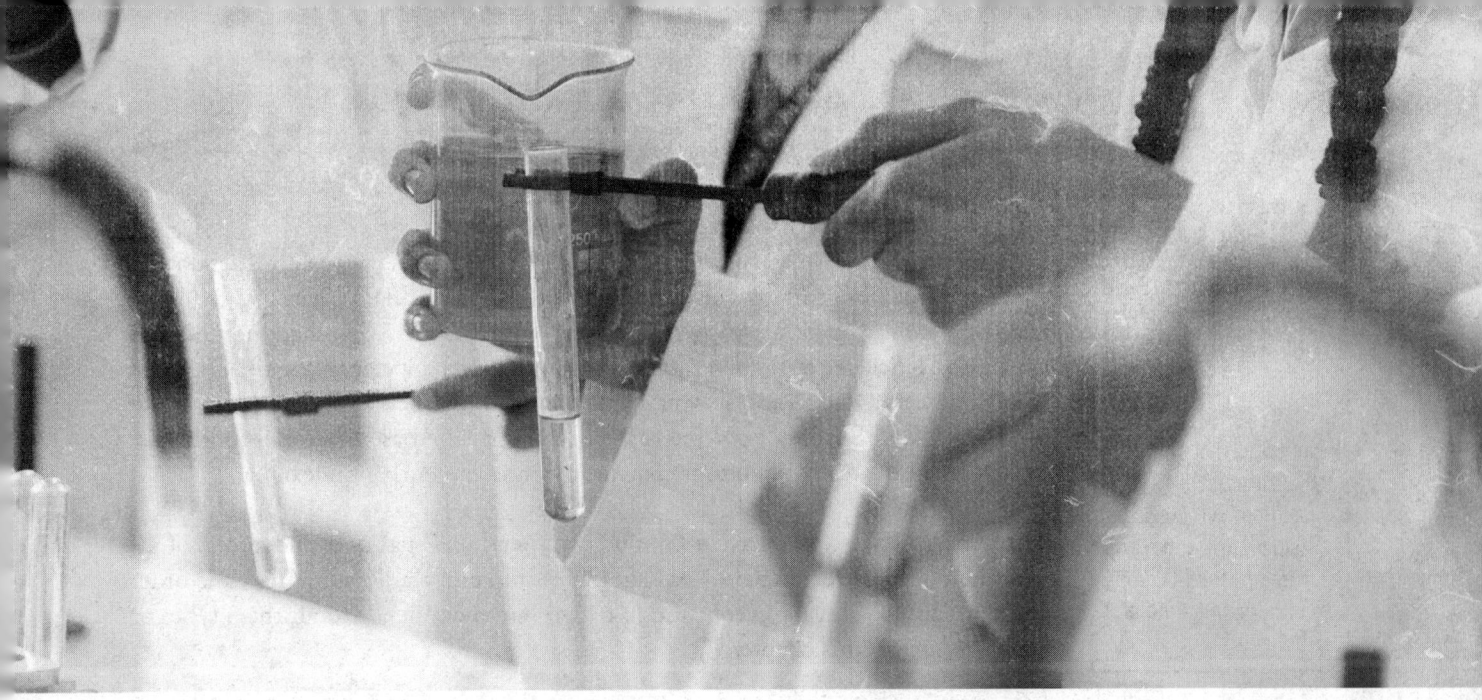

Chapter 24
Introduction to the ACT Science Test

As of September 2025, all ACT test-takers will be able to choose whether they take the optional Science section. When students register for the optional ACT Science test, it will come fourth, after the Reading test and before the optional Writing test. Fatigue can negatively affect even the founding president of the I Heart Science Club. Even if the Science test were first, many students would find it the most intimidating and feel that they need to crack open their first-year bio textbooks. But this is not a test of science facts: it is instead a test of how well you look up and synthesize information from tables, graphs, illustrations, and passages.

To maximize your score on the Science test, you need to work the passages in a personal order of difficulty. We'll teach you how to order the passages, and we'll teach you how to employ a strategic and efficient approach that will earn you your highest possible score.

WHAT'S ON THE SCIENCE TEST

Enhanced ACT Stats

As of the printing of this book, ACT has said that the Enhanced ACT test will have 40 Science questions in 40 minutes. Additionally, more questions will focus on outside knowledge, and one passage will be about engineering and design.

Remember when you had to study for that tough biology exam, memorizing dozens of facts about things like meiosis, mitosis, and mitochondria? When you sat down to take the test, you either knew the answers or you didn't. Well, that's not the case on the ACT Science test. Even though the word *science* appears in the title, this test doesn't look much like the tests you've taken in your high school science classes. Like the English and Reading tests, the Science test is passage-based, but most of the passages present the really important content in figures rather than in text.

On the Science test, you have 40 minutes to spend on 7 passages and a total of 40 questions. There are 3 types of passages, but unlike in the Reading test, the order of the passages will vary every time. We'll go into more detail about the 3 types of passages later in this chapter.

What Do You Need to Know?

For the topics of the passages, ACT pulls content from biology, chemistry, physics, and Earth/space sciences such as astronomy, geology, and meteorology. While you won't be quizzed on obscure facts (and the facts you will be quizzed on are relatively basic—see pages 515–516),), background familiarity with the topics certainly helps. If the passage is on genetics, you'll undoubtedly do better if you've recently finished that unit in school and know it cold. But the information you need in order to answer most of the questions is offered in the passage itself, most frequently presented in a table, graph, or illustration of some kind. The ACT Science test is an open-book test, and you do not need advanced knowledge of any science topic.

Outside Knowledge

Most of the questions can be answered from the information presented in the passages or figures, but be prepared for 4 to 6 questions that require outside knowledge. We will discuss the outside knowledge questions more at the end of Chapter 26, but rest assured that they are nothing to stress over as they are such a small portion of the Science test and are often familiar concepts from introductory science classes.

You may not need an encyclopedic knowledge of science facts. You *do* need good scientific reasoning skills, a personalized pacing strategy, and a smart, effective approach to working the passages. You also need to be flexible, ready to adapt your strategy or abandon a question you've already spent way too much time on: guess and move on. Of all the tests on the ACT, Science is the most time-sensitive. Even the biggest science fans find themselves barely finishing.

On ACT.org, ACT identifies the skills you need for this test: "interpretation, analysis, evaluation, reasoning, and problem solving." We can boil this down to a more concise list.

You need to be able to:

- look up data and trends
- make predictions
- synthesize information

But before you learn how to work the passages, you need to learn how to order them. To understand the reasoning behind the method, it's helpful to know the three categories of passages.

The Passages

All of the passages fall within three categories. The order of the passages will vary on each test, but the distribution of types of passages is typically the same. To pick your order, it's less important what the passage is called than what it looks like. But it is important to know that there are three categories of passages and to know their similarities and differences. ACT has very formal-sounding names for the categories, so we made up our own. The distribution below represents the typical format of the Science test.

Charts and Graphs (aka Data Representation)

2 Passages with 5 Questions Each   These passages will *always* come with figures: it's their purpose in life. You'll see one or more charts, tables, graphs, or illustrations. Charts and Graphs passages are intended to test your ability to understand and interpret the information that's presented. There is a total of 10 questions.

Experiments (aka Research Summaries)

4 Passages with 6 Questions Each   These passages will *usually* come with figures. They're intended to describe several experiments, and they include more text than do the Charts and Graphs passages. But the results of the experiments are frequently presented in tables or in graphs, and you may have trouble distinguishing the Experiments passages from Charts and Graphs passages. That doesn't matter, however, because in Chapter 26 we'll teach you the basic approach that applies to both types of passages. You'll never need to identify one over the other when you're taking the test. For the record, however, Experiments passages come with more questions: a grand total of 24.

Multiple Viewpoints Passages

1 passage with 6 questions   This passage *sometimes* comes with figures. Even when there are figures, however, the passage is fundamentally different from the Charts and Graphs passages and the Experiments passages. That means it also requires a different way to crack it, and we'll teach you how to do just that in Chapter 27. The Multiple Viewpoints Science Passages involve much more reading than you'll need to do for the other two types. In fact, most of the Multiple Viewpoints Science Passages will feel more like the passages on the Reading test, and you'll be able to use some of the skills you learned to crack the Reading test as you compare, contrast, and synthesize the different viewpoints.

When it comes to the topics, ACT may use arguments already resolved by the scientific community as well as more cutting-edge issues that are still contested. In either case, remind yourself again that the Science test is an open-book test, providing you the information you need to answer almost all the questions.

HOW TO CRACK THE SCIENCE TEST

Order the Passages

As always on the ACT, time is your enemy. With only 40 minutes to review 7 passages and answer 40 questions, you can't afford to spend too much time on the most difficult ones only to run out of time for the easiest. ACT doesn't present the passages in order of difficulty, but on every exam, some are easier than others, while some are truly tough. What would happen if on your ACT, the most difficult came first and the easiest last? If you did them in order, you could likely run out of time without a chance to correctly answer all the questions on the easiest passage.

That's why you can't do the passages in the order ACT picks—unless that happens to match your Personal Order of Difficulty (POOD). If time is going to run out, you want it to run out on the hardest passage, not the easiest.

Now, Later, Last

We're using the term "easier" only because we're grading the passages on a curve. "Easy" is a loaded term.

Therefore, it's more useful to think of the passages as those you'd do *Now*, those you'd do *Later*, and those you'd do *Last*.

Now Passages

Your goal with all the passages is to crack the main point. You don't necessarily need to know the topic, but you do need to spot the conclusions the content offers: trends, patterns, and relationships. You will spot these trends faster when those conclusions are presented in figures rather than in text. The easier the figures are to "read," the faster you'll crack the passage.

> **Patterns**
> Look for trends *within* a figure. Look for relationships *between* figures and viewpoints.

As we explained earlier, this is not a test of science knowledge. Instead, it's a test of your scientific reasoning skills. That means spotting the trends and patterns of variables and the relationships between figures and viewpoints.

The best passages to do Now have the most obvious patterns as well as a few other common characteristics.

Look for:

- **Small graphs and tables:** A good Now passage can have only tables, only graphs, or both. Tables should be no more than 3–4 rows and columns, and graphs should have no more than 3–4 lines or curves.
- **Easy-to-spot consistent trends:** Look for graphs with all lines/curves heading in the same direction: all up, all down, or all flat.
- **Numbers in the figures:** To show a consistent trend, the figure has to feature numbers, not words or symbols.
- **Short answers:** Look for as many questions as possible with short answers, specifically answers with numbers and short relationship words like *increase* or *decrease*.

In Chapter 25, we'll discuss trends and patterns in greater detail.

Personal Order of Difficulty (POOD)

There is one additional important characteristic you need to look for: topics you know. Even if the figures are really ugly and confusing, if a passage is on a topic you just finished in school and know cold, you'll pick up on the relationships in the passage quickly, and that's the goal of choosing a Now passage.

Pace Yourself

Unless you're aiming for a 32 or higher on the Science test, you're better off choosing at least some questions as Never. Take 40 minutes, and do fewer questions. You'll give yourself more time per passage and increase your accuracy. As you steadily increase your scoring goals in practice, target the number of questions you need to reach your goal. The more aggressively you can move through the passages finding all the Now questions you can answer—no matter how difficult the passage may be—the better you'll score.

Goal Score

Use the pacing strategies and score grid on pages 115–118 to find your goal score for each practice test and, eventually, the ACT.

Be Flexible

As we've mentioned before, to earn your best score on the ACT, you have to be flexible, and nowhere is this more true than on the Science test. The Science test shows the greatest change in level of difficulty from one administration to the next. There is no way to predict how difficult the Science test will be, nor what the particular topics will be. Certainly, if you know more about the topic, you'll find even an ugly-looking passage more understandable. But that doesn't mean you're relying on luck. The Princeton Review's Basic Approach works regardless of what the topics are. The goal is to practice using the Basic Approach so that the particulars of the passage are irrelevant.

> **Letter of the Day (LOTD)**
> Just because you don't work on a passage doesn't mean you don't answer the questions. Never leave any questions blank on the ACT. Choose your Letter of the Day for all the questions on your Never passages.

However, you have to fight your own instincts, or at least retrain them into those of a great test-taker. Always be prepared to adapt your order based on what you see, both in practice and on a real test. If you choose a passage that looks good and then find yourself struggling, leave it and find another. Ignore the voice in your head that says, "Well, I've put so much time into this incredibly hard passage already, all that time would be a waste if I didn't finish the passage." Nothing could be further from the truth. You're throwing away perfectly good time if you stick with a passage that you're just not grasping.

You have to be just as strict with a tough question. When you're stumped, your first instinct may be to go back and read the passage or stare at the figure *again*, waiting for a flash of inspirational genius to suddenly make everything clear. Instead, focus on using POE to get rid of answers that can't

> **Hard Test = Generous Curve**
> Don't be scared of a hard Science test on any particular administration. Each test is curved against only the students who took that particular exam. If the Science test is hard, *everyone* will struggle with the hardest questions, and the curve will be more generous.

be right. Even if you can eliminate only one answer, guess from what's left and move on. If you stick with one tough question too long, you may be robbing yourself of the time you need for 2–3 questions.

Process of Elimination (POE)

Just as in the other tests, POE is a powerful tool on the Science test. Particularly on tougher questions, use POE to eliminate wrong answers that are clearly contradicted by what you're looking at.

Let's see how POE works on the Science test.

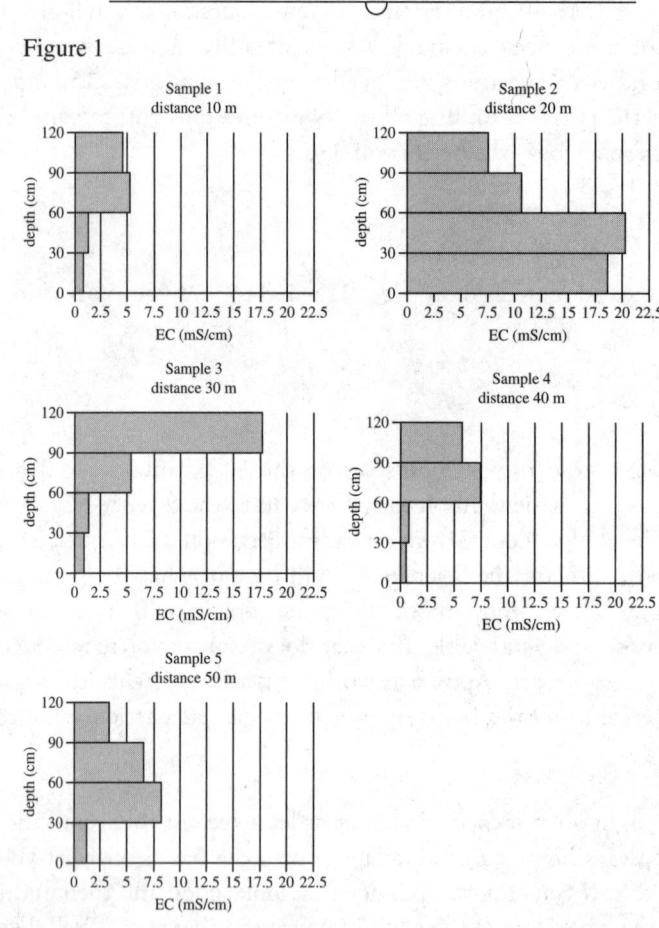

Figure 1

Figure 2

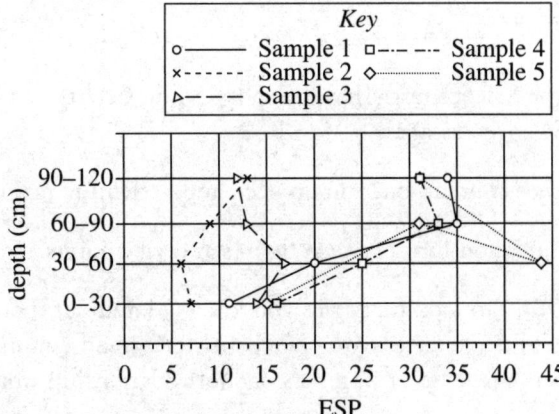

1. A student claimed that as soil moves away from a major water source, such as a river, the salinity of the soil increases. Is this claim supported by Figures 1 and 2?

   A. No; the electrical conductivity and exchangeable sodium percentage both decreased from Sample 1 to Sample 5.

   B. No; there was no consistent trend for electrical conductivity and exchangeable sodium percentage.

   C. Yes; the electrical conductivity and exchangeable sodium percentage both increased from Sample 1 to Sample 5.

   D. Yes; the electrical conductivity increased and exchangeable sodium percentage decreased from Sample 1 to Sample 5.

POE
Each time you eliminate a wrong answer, you increase your chance of choosing the correct answer.

Here's How to Crack It

Don't waste time staring at the figure trying to look up the answer. Look at how descriptive the answer choices are: POE will be much faster. Ignore the "Yes" and "No," and focus on the reasons given. Do they accurately describe the figure? Eliminate any answer choices that do not accurately describe both figures. Neither Figure 1 nor Figure 2 shows a consistent decrease from Sample 1 to Sample 5, so eliminate (A) and (D). Neither figure shows a consistent increase either, so eliminate (C). Choice (B) is consistent with the data because there is no consistent trend from Sample 1 to Sample 5 in either figure. The correct answer is (B).

Maybe you read the question and a quick glance at the figure was all you needed to know the answer was "No." Great, eliminate (C) and (D), and then compare what's different between (A) and (B). The point is to save time by looking at the answers and then the figure rather than staring at the figure and then the answers. The harder the figure, the more important POE is to your success.

Summary

o   There are always 40 questions on the Science test. They are split up into Charts and Graphs, Experiments, and Multiple Viewpoints Science Passages.

o   You don't need to know much science content, but you do need good scientific reasoning skills.

o   Look for trends within figures and relationships between figures and viewpoints.

o   Order your passages. Use your POOD to look for topics you know a lot about. Look for Now passages, which feature small graphs and tables, easy-to-spot consistent trends, numbers instead of words or symbols, and short answers made up of numbers or short relationship words like *increase* or *lower*.

o   Pace yourself. Slow down and do fewer questions, but work up to your goal score by focusing on the number of points you need to earn your goal score.

o   Be flexible. Be ready to adapt your order, leave a tough passage, or guess on a tough question.

o   Use Process of Elimination to cross off wrong answers and save time.

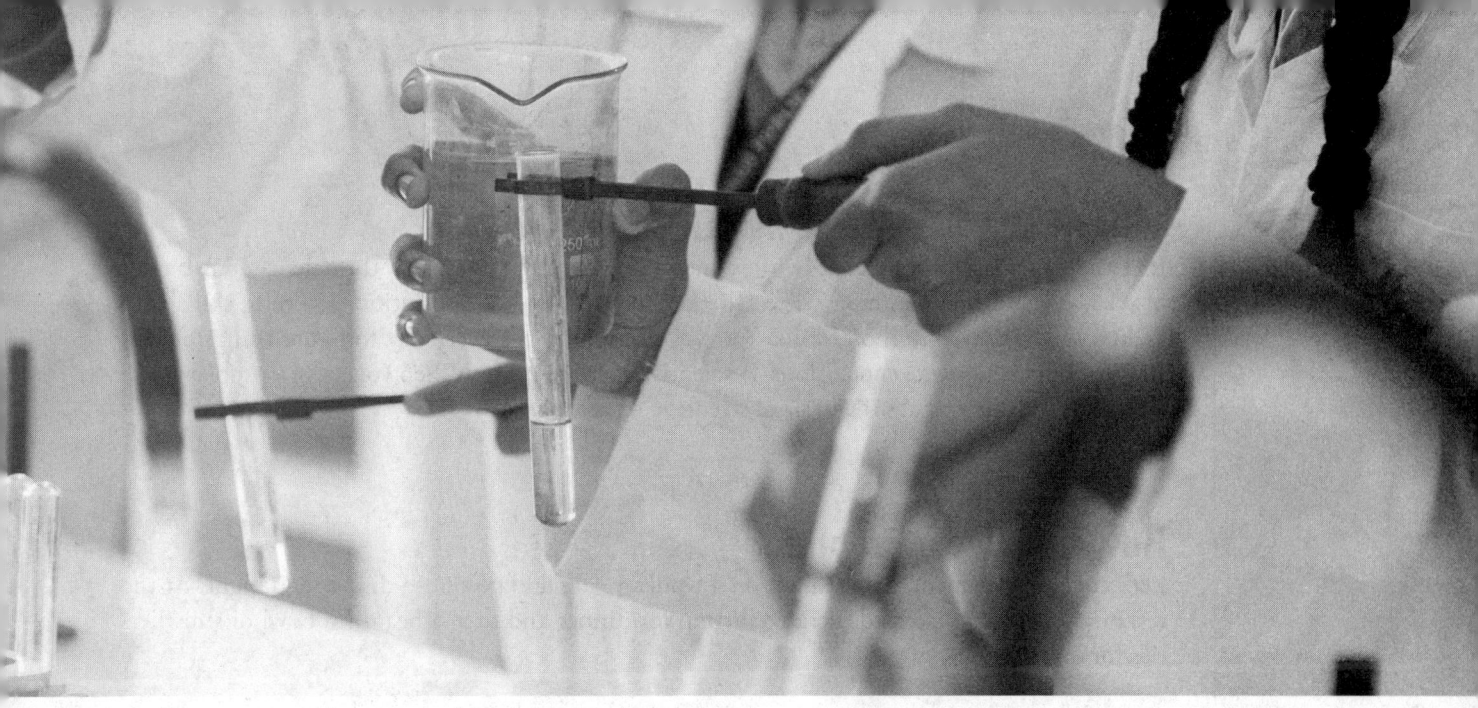

Chapter 25
Scientific Reasoning Skills

You don't need to know science facts for the ACT. For the most part, the Science test is an open-book test, with the passages offering the content you need to answer nearly all the questions. According to ACT, you do need scientific reasoning skills. But all this really means is that you need some common sense. Science may seem intimidating, but it's based on a lot more common sense than you may think.

YOU KNOW MORE THAN YOU THINK

It's easy to feel very intimidated by the content and even the figures on the Science test. But all of science is built on common sense. The key to building good scientific reasoning skills is to realize you *already have* those skills. You use common sense every day to figure things out, to solve problems, to make conclusions. A scientist does the same. When you solve a problem, you think critically, and that's the basis of scientific reasoning.

How to Solve a Problem

Let's try an experiment. Say you put on a wool sweater and go out to dinner one night. At the restaurant you order some delectable shrimp for dinner and then a beautiful bowl of strawberries for dessert.

The next morning, you wake up covered in red, itchy hives. What caused them? Do you jump to the conclusion it was the sweater? What about the shrimp? A lot of people have allergies to shellfish. But so, too, do a lot of people have allergies to strawberries. How are you supposed to know which one caused your hives? How do you know any of these options are the only possible culprits?

You don't. That's the first rule of scientific reasoning: make no assumptions. You can't assume it was the sweater, the shrimp, or the strawberries. But you have to prove it was one and only one of these, if any. So how do you set about finding out which one?

Assumption = Guess

An assumption is nothing more than a guess, and a lazy one at that if you are willing to believe the riddle has been solved. A guess doesn't cut it in the scientific world: only proof does.

You design an experiment. You first need to narrow the list of suspects down to the sweater, shrimp, and strawberries. Begin with a baseline. You need to see what happens on a day with none of the possible causes in play to compare to the days with them. Wear a cotton T-shirt and eat cauliflower and cantaloupe. Do you still have hives? If so, then the three suspects have all been vindicated. But if your hives have cleared up, you've confirmed your first hypothesis that it was indeed the sweater, the shrimp, or the strawberries.

Hypothesis

A hypothesis is a theory. An assumption is a guess with no proof. A hypothesis is more advanced than that. It's a theory that tries to explain what happened, but it requires proof.

Now you have to figure out which one of the three caused your hives. We need a day with one, and one only, of the possibilities, or *variables*, in play. That's the second rule of scientific reasoning: change one variable at a time. One day, wear the sweater, but skip the shrimp and strawberries. On another, lose the sweater, and eat the shrimp but not the strawberries. On yet another, replace the shrimp with the strawberries. On each day, check for hives. The itchy red bumps *depend* on whatever *independent* variable is causing them.

Independent and Dependent Variables

The independent variable affects or creates the dependent variable. Does x create or affect y? Some examples of independent variables include time, temperature, and depth. Dependent variables are the events possibly created or affected by an independent variable, and they can be whatever the scientist is studying. Some examples of dependent variables include volume, solubility, and pressure.

That's all well and good. But what about everything else in your life? Notice we said you couldn't wear the sweater on the days you ate either the shrimp or the strawberries. But other than the sweater, *you have to wear the exact same clothes on the day you eat shrimp and on the day you eat strawberries.* It's not just what you wear. Everything else in your life has to be exactly the same. If on the day you wore the sweater, you worked out at the gym, but on the day you ate shrimp, you lay on your sofa all day watching television, how much would you know? Not much. Certainly not much of anything with proof, and proof is what it's all about in science. The third rule of scientific reasoning is that you have to keep all the other variables in the experiment the same as you vary one and only one independent variable. In the hives experiment, this means that in order to conclusively prove the cause, you have to keep everything else the same on each day that you change one and only one independent variable. Do the same things. Wear the same clothes (except the sweater). Eat the same things (except the shrimp and strawberries).

And that's it. If you follow these three rules, you'll know what causes your hives.

Trends

In our first example, we looked at a dependent variable, hives, that was present only when an independent variable was present. You've undoubtedly faced other situations in which different amounts of a variable seem to have an effect on another variable. The more you study, the better your grades. The more you practice your free throws, the more you make on game day.

Let's look at another situation. You sleep only 5 hours a night, staying up late and getting up early to study, but you're consistently scoring in the high 70s on your daily math quizzes no matter how many hours you study. Suppose you had a hypothesis that if you slept more, your scores would improve. How would you design an experiment to test this? You already have a baseline of 5 hours and consistent scores in the high 70s. So beginning with the first night, you sleep longer, and then see how you score the next day.

The Three Rules of Scientific Reasoning

1. **Make no assumptions.** You need a standard of comparison to measure against your results. How does your dependent variable react without the presence of any of your independent variables?

2. **Change one variable at a time.** Vary each independent variable to see its effect on your dependent variable.

3. **Keep all other variables the same.** Your other independent variables *and everything else* have to be the same as you vary one and only one independent variable.

The next night, you sleep even longer, and check your quiz score the next day. Can you do anything else differently? No, you have to keep all the other variables in your life the same. Each day you eat the same things and study the same number of hours. You even track quiz scores in the same unit to eliminate any possibility that there is any other reason why your quiz scores improve.

To be organized, you record all your data in a simple table.

Table 1	
Hours of sleep	Quiz scores
5	78
6	83
7	88
8	93

Direct Relationship
As *x* increases,
y increases.
As *x* decreases,
y decreases.

As the number of hours of sleep increases, your quiz score increases. In this experiment, the number of hours of sleep is the independent variable, and the quiz score is the dependent variable. You've established that your quiz score is ***directly*** related to the number of hours you sleep.

Let's look at another experiment. Suppose your hypothesis this time is that the more cups of coffee you drink, the fewer hours you sleep. How would you design the experiment? Same rules as always. First, you need a baseline. You need to get all the caffeine out of your system and cut your consumption down to 0 cups each day. You establish a consistent routine of the same diet, exercise, studying, sports practice, and so on. Then, without changing any of those variables, you begin drinking coffee again—same size cup each day—increasing the number of cups and measuring the number of hours you sleep the following night.

Once again, you record your findings in a table.

Table 2	
Cups of coffee	Hours of sleep
0	8
1	7
2	6
3	5

Inverse Relationship
As *x* increases,
y decreases.
As *x* decreases,
y increases.

As the cups of coffee increase, the hours of sleep decrease. This time, the number of hours of sleep is the dependent variable, and the number of cups of coffee is the independent variable. You've established that the amount you sleep is ***inversely*** related to the amount of coffee you drink.

Many passages on the Science test feature passages whose main point is either a direct or inverse trend of the variables. In Chapter 24, we outlined characteristics of Now passages, such as small tables and graphs with easy-to-spot consistent trends.

When you look at the two tables above, the trend is pretty obvious from just a quick glance. You've already cracked the main relationship, and you will find all the questions that much easier to tackle as a result.

Graphs

Both tables and graphs show the trends of variables. Graphs are more visual, making the trends easier to spot.

If you graphed your data from Table 1, what would it look like?

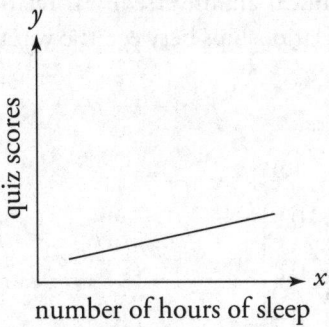

Remember that in math, the horizontal axis is x: it's the independent variable. The vertical axis is y: it's the dependent variable. Science typically follows the same rules. This graph shows you that as x increases, y increases. They have a direct linear relationship with a positive slope.

Let's graph Table 2.

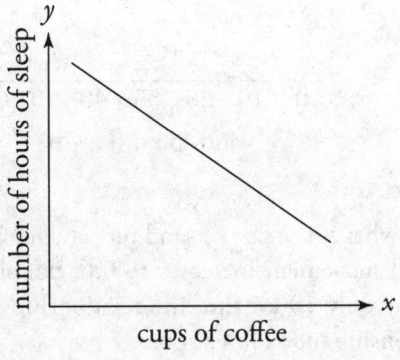

This graph shows you that as x increases, y decreases. They have an inverse relationship, and the slope is negative. Inverse relationships have negative slopes.

There are a few occasions in science in which the independent variable may be displayed on the vertical axis. Variables such as depth, height, or altitude are often depicted on the vertical axis regardless of whether they are the independent or dependent variables. The idea of direct and inverse relationships still apply, and these questions can be worked with the same methods.

TRENDS ON THE SCIENCE TEST

The key to cracking the Science test is to look for trends and patterns. Figures with consistent trends point to a Now passage because the figure has provided the main point of the passage—the relationship between the variables.

In the next chapter, we'll teach you a Basic Approach to cracking each passage, including passages that *don't* feature small tables and graphs with consistent trends. But we hope that this chapter has convinced you to look for passages featuring figures with consistent trends to do Now. You'll find even the hardest questions are easier to tackle when the figure tells you everything you need to know.

We've already seen examples of direct linear and inverse linear relationships. Let's look at a few figures and try to identify additional relationships between the variables. What sort of relationship does this one show?

Curves = Exponential Change

When the dependent variable changes by an increasing or decreasing amount every time the independent variable changes, the result will be a curved line.

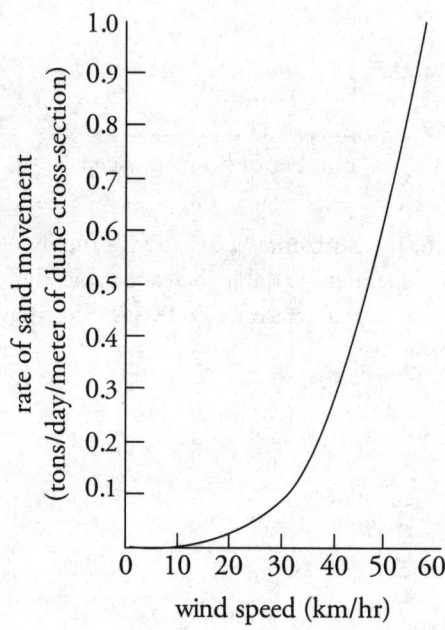

When the wind speed is 40 km/hr, what is the rate of sand movement? It's 0.3. When the wind speed is 50 km/hr, the rate of sand movement increases to 0.6, double the last reading even though the wind speed increased by only 10 km/hr. The relationship is direct, but the curve shows you it's an exponential relationship, not a linear one.

Try the next one.

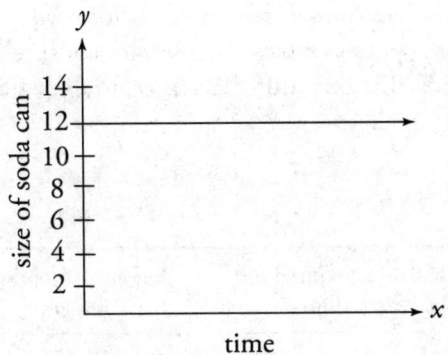

Does time actually affect the size of a soda can? Of course not. As a result, we get a flat line.

Try one more.

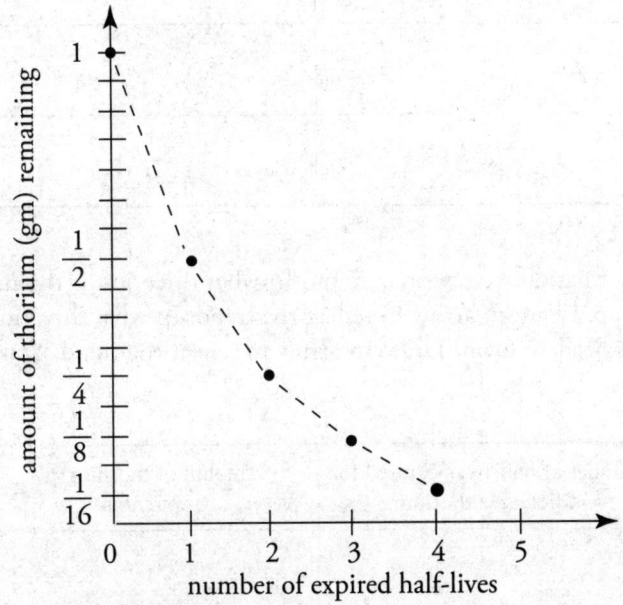

As the number of expired half-lives increases, the amount of thorium remaining decreases, so the two have an inverse relationship.

Do you need to know what "expired half-lives" and "thorium" are? No, you don't need to (but it's always helpful when you're familiar with the content). To answer the questions for this passage, everything you need to know comes from the relationships between the variables. The main point of the passage is just a summary of these relationships.

Tables

When we began this chapter, we showed you tables before switching to graphs. Everything we've discussed about graphs applies to tables. A table with consistent trends is just as helpful as a graph with consistent trends. The only difference is that tables are not as visual as graphs, so it's up to you to make them visual.

Look at the table below.

Number of half-lives expired for radioactive thorium	Amount of thorium (g) remaining
0	1
1	$\frac{1}{2}$
2	$\frac{1}{4}$
3	$\frac{1}{8}$
4	$\frac{1}{16}$

This is the same information we saw in a graph. In what direction is the number of half-lives headed? It's headed up. Draw an arrow to reflect the trend. In what direction is the amount of thorium headed? It's headed down. Draw an arrow to reflect the trend. Your table should now look like this:

Number of half-lives expired for radioactive thorium	Amount of thorium (g) remaining
0	1
1	$\frac{1}{2}$
2	$\frac{1}{4}$
3	$\frac{1}{8}$
4	$\frac{1}{16}$

If you're taking the ACT Online Test, you can't mark the trends on the screen, but you can on your whiteboard. Use abbreviations and mark the trends:

1/2 lives expired ↑ thorium remaining ↓

You've just gotten a preview of the next chapter. Marking the trends in a figure is the first step in the Basic Approach to cracking Science passages.

Inconsistent Trends and No Relationships

Wouldn't it be great if you saw only tables and graphs with consistent trends on the ACT? Yes, it would, but there will be uglier figures as well. Now that you know how powerful consistent trends are, you can actually use that knowledge even when there is no consistency. The absence of consistency tells its own story.

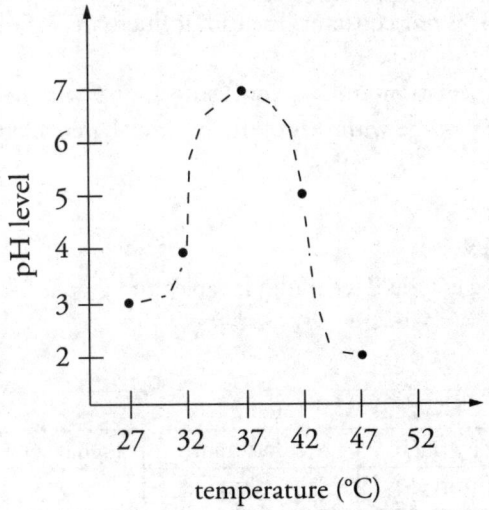

As temperature increases, what does pH do? It barely increases at first and then makes a sharp jump before an equally sharp fall to a point that is lower than where it began. You may have immediately identified this as a **bell curve**. Is a bell curve consistent?

A bell curve is certainly not as consistent as a straight line or even a curve that moves in a positive or negative direction. There is some consistency, however. It increases and then decreases. The problem is that we can't make a prediction of what it will do next. That's the real beauty of consistent lines and curves: we can predict what will happen outside the figure. But with a bell curve, we can't determine whether it will repeat its trend or if it will steadily decrease.

What about the next graph? What story does it tell?

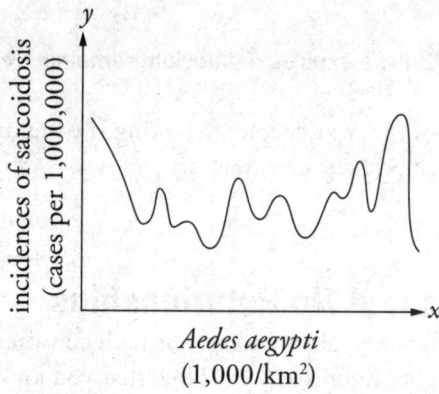

Aedes aegypti
(1,000/km²)

There is no relationship at all between *Aedes aegypti* and sarcoidosis. The incidence of sarcoidosis is *independent* of the *Aedes aegypti*, not *dependent*. And unlike the relationship in a flat line, the incidence of sarcoidosis is not constant. Instead, it fluctuates wildly.

That's a good deal of information from a confusing figure with two strange variables. But would you want to do the passage with this figure Now or Later? Definitely Later.

Multiple Variables

In many Experiments passages, you'll see multiple tables and graphs. Take a look at the following tables (Tables 1 and 2).

Table 1		
Velocity (m/s)	Radius (mm)	Frequency (rev/s)
1,000	5.7	27,952
1,500	8.5	27,952
2,000	11.4	27,952
2,500	14.2	27,952

Table 2		
Magnetic field strength (microTeslas)	Radius (mm)	Frequency (rev/s)
0.25	22.7	6,988
0.5	11.4	13,986
1	5.7	27,952
2	2.8	55,900
4	1.4	111,800

First, mark the trends within each figure. In Table 1, as velocity increases, radius increases and frequency is constant. Velocity is the independent variable, radius is a dependent variable, and the two have a direct relationship. Frequency is another dependent variable, and velocity and frequency have a constant relationship. In Table 2, as magnetic field strength increases, radius decreases, and the frequency increases. Magnetic field strength is the independent variable, and it has an inverse relationship with radius and a direct relationship with frequency. What's the relationship between the figures? Look at the variables they have in common: radius and frequency.

In Experiments passages—as well as in scientific studies in real life—it's common to test different independent variables to measure their effect on the same dependent variable. But recall our second and third rules of scientific reasoning skills:

- **Change one variable at a time.** Vary each independent variable to see its effect on your dependent variable.
- **Keep all other variables the same.** Your other independent variables *and everything else* have to be the same as you vary one and only one independent variable.

When velocity is varied, can magnetic field strength vary at the same time? No, it has to stay the same, that is, constant. And when magnetic field strength is varied, velocity has to stay constant.

On the Science test, you are likely to see a question that tests your ability to spot the constants.

---

1. Based on the results shown in Tables 1 and 2, the magnetic field strength used in the first experiment (resulting in Table 1) was most likely:

   A. 0.25 microTesla.
   B. 0.5 microTesla.
   C. 1.0 microTesla.
   D. 2.0 microTesla.

Here's How to Crack It

Find the link between the two tables by looking at the variables they have in common, radius and frequency. Look for an entry in Table 2 in which the radius and frequency are the same values as one of the entries in Table 1. Since frequency is constant in Table 1, look for the value in Table 2 that matches the value for frequency shown in Table 1. In Table 2, when the magnetic field strength is 1 microTesla, the radius is 5.7 mm and the frequency is 27,952 rev/s. Note that 5.7 mm for radius is also the only value for radius that is in common between the two tables. Therefore, the magnetic field strength used in the first experiment must have been 1 microTesla. The correct answer is (C).

Graphs can also have multiple variables. Take a look at the following graph.

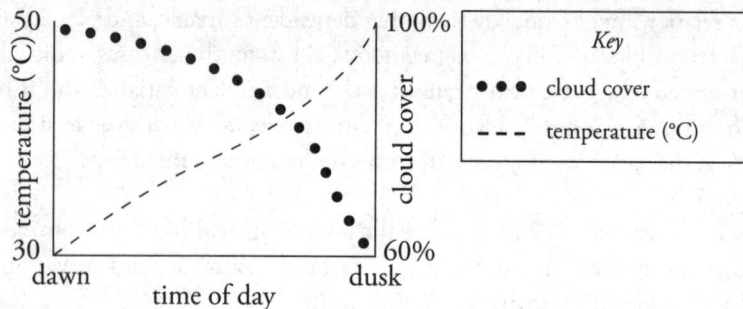

When there are multiple variables on a graph, you always need to be careful to look at the correct line and the correct axis. As time increases, temperature increases. As time increases, cloud cover decreases. Does this data mean that temperature and cloud cover have a direct relationship? Not necessarily. What's the variable they have in common? Time.

Try another question.

2. According to the figure above, what was the temperature, in degrees Celsius, when cloud cover was at its highest?

   F. 20°
   G. 30°
   H. 40°
   J. 50°

Here's How to Crack It

Find the link between the two axes by looking at the variable they have in common, time. Be sure to look at the correct curve on the correct axis. Cloud cover is the bubbled line, and when it's at its highest, the time of day on the *x*-axis is dawn. When the time of day is dawn, look at the dashed line for the temperature. When it's early, the temperature is 30°.

The correct answer is (G).

In the next lesson, we'll teach you how to use your scientific reasoning skills on ACT Science passages, which will feature plenty of tables and graphs with various trends and relationships.

Summary

○ Scientific reasoning is based on common sense.

○ The three rules of scientific reasoning skills are:
- Make no assumptions.
- Change one variable at a time.
- Keep all other variables the same.

○ A hypothesis is a theory that needs proof to become a conclusion.

○ An independent variable creates or causes an effect on a dependent variable.

○ In a direct relationship, as x increases, y increases.

○ Direct linear relationships on a graph have positive slopes.

○ In an inverse relationship, as x increases, y decreases.

○ Inverse linear relationships on a graph have negative slopes.

○ A flat line means the dependent variable is constant, and the independent variable has no effect. Keep in mind that "no effect" is still a consistent trend. Two variables with no consistent trends are said to have "no relationship."

○ When the dependent variable changes by an increasing or decreasing amount each time the independent variable changes, the result is a curved line and the relationship is exponential.

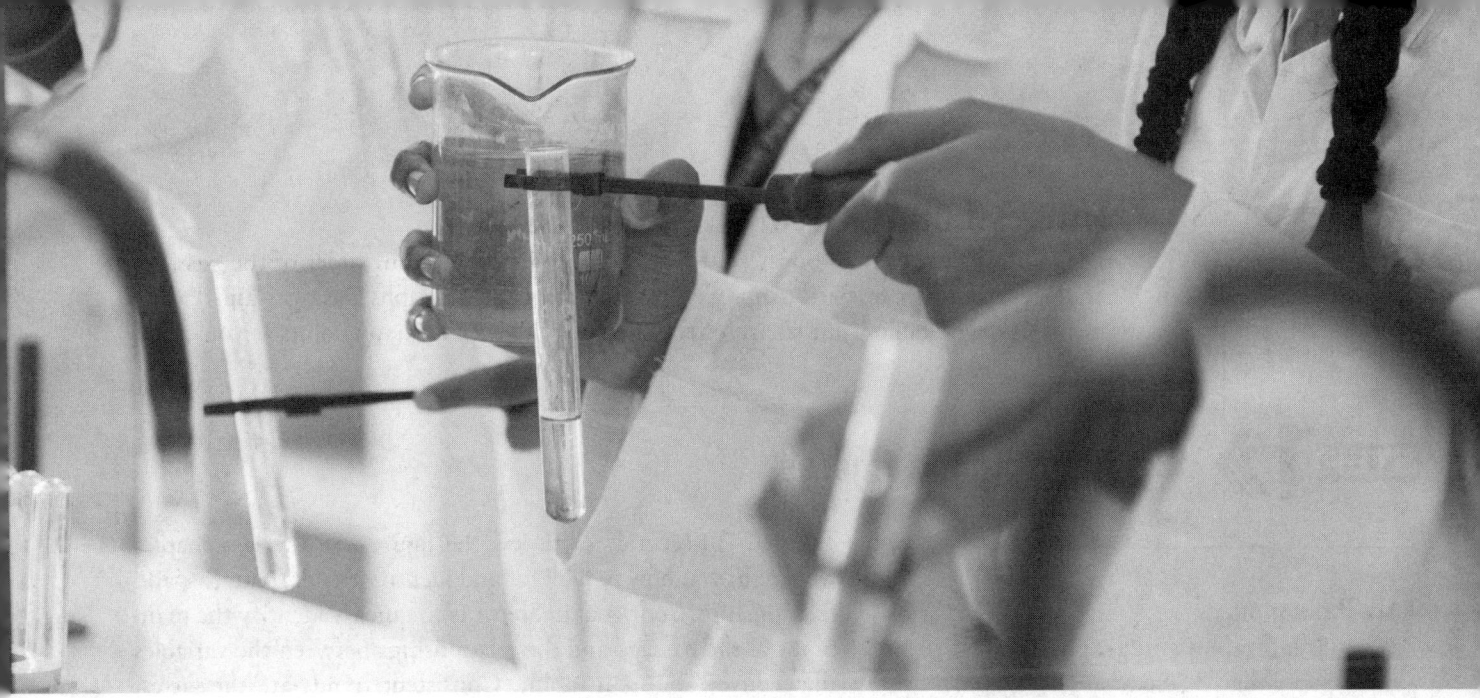

Chapter 26
The Basic Approach

To earn your highest possible score on the Science test, you need an efficient and strategic approach to working the passages. In this chapter, we'll teach you how to apply your scientific reasoning skills to quickly assess the content of the passage and figures and make your way methodically through the questions.

HOW TO CRACK THE SCIENCE TEST

The most efficient way to boost your Science score is to pick your order of the passages and apply our 3-Step Basic Approach to the Charts and Graphs passages and Experiments passages. Follow our smart, effective strategy to earn as many points as you can.

STEP 1 » Step 1: Work the Figures

Now Passages

1. **Small tables and graphs:** No more than 3–4 curves on a graph, no more than 3–4 rows and columns on a table.
2. **Easy-to-spot consistent trends:** All lines headed in same direction, numbers in a table in easy-to-spot order.
3. **Numbers, not words or symbols:** Look for tables and graphs with more numbers and fewer words and symbols.
4. **Short answers:** Numbers or trend words like *increase* and *decrease* or *higher* and *lower*.

Take 10–30 seconds to review the figures. In the last chapter, we taught you how to look for and identify trends, patterns, and relationships. Your goal in Step 1 is to quickly identify the main point of the passage and the relationships between the variables that convey the main point. Consistent trends are the fastest to assess, but all trends and patterns tell a story. In Chapter 24, we gave you a way to spot the Now passages, which are chiefly characterized by consistent trends.

Graphs

Graphs visually represent the relationship between the variables. When you work a graph, identify the relationship, and take note of the variables and their units.

Take a look at the graph below.

Figure 1

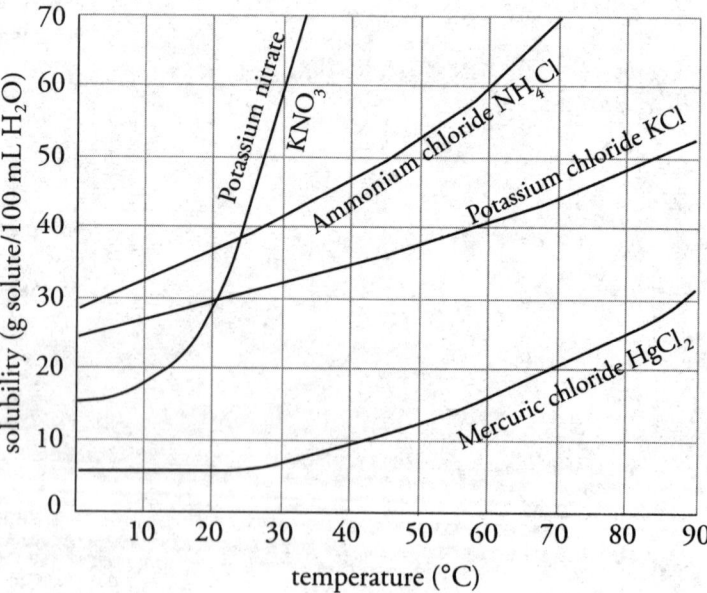

- Look at the direction of the curves: they are all headed up.
- Take note of the variables and their units. Temperature, in °C, is on the *x*-axis; solubility, in g solute/100 mL H_2O, is on the *y*-axis.
- Identify the relationship. A positive slope means it's a direct relationship. As temperature increases, solubility increases.

Tables

For tables, you need to make the trends visual. Take a look at the table below.

Table 1	
Length (m)	Resistance (Ω)
0.9	7.5
1.8	15.0
3.6	30.0

- What is length doing? It's increasing. Mark it with an arrow.
- What is resistance doing? It's increasing. Mark it with an arrow.
- What are the units of the variables? m and Ω.
- Identify the relationship. Both variables move in the same direction, so it's a direct relationship.

Here's what your table should look like.

Table 1	
Length (m)	Resistance (Ω)
0.9	7.5
1.8	15.0
3.6	30.0

⬆ ⬆

If you're taking the ACT Online Test, make notes on your whiteboard instead:

Table 1: Length (m) ↑ , Resist (Ω) ↑

Try another table from the same passage.

Table 2	
Cross-sectional area (mm^2)	Resistance (Ω)
0.8	30.0
1.6	15.0
3.2	7.5

- What is the cross-sectional area doing? It's increasing. Mark it with an arrow.
- What is resistance doing? It's decreasing. Mark it with an arrow.
- What are the units of the variables? mm^2 and Ω.
- Identify the relationship. As the cross-sectional area increases, resistance decreases. It's an inverse relationship.

Here's what your table should look like.

Table 2	
Cross-sectional area (mm^2)	Resistance (Ω)
0.8	30.0
1.6	15.0
3.2	7.5

↑   ↓

Make notes on your whiteboard if you're taking the test on a computer:

Table 2: Cross-sec area (mm^2) ↑ , Resist (Ω)↓

Last, identify the relationship between the tables. Each table has the variable **resistance** in common.

Step 2: Work the Questions

Once you've marked the figures, go straight to the questions.

Now, Later, Never

There is no set order of difficulty of these questions. Follow your Personal Order of Difficulty (POOD): if a question is fairly straightforward, do it Now. Most of the questions you consider straightforward will likely ask you to identify a trend, look up a value, or make a prediction. Now questions will have values or trend words like *increase* or *lower* in the answers. If a question strikes you as confusing or time-consuming, come back to it Later. Occasionally, you'll judge a question tough enough you may Never want to do it. Select your Letter of the Day (LOTD), and move on to the next passage. In Step 3, we'll address how smart use of Process of Elimination (POE) may eliminate the need for any Never questions on a Now passage. But for now, let's look at a sample Now question.

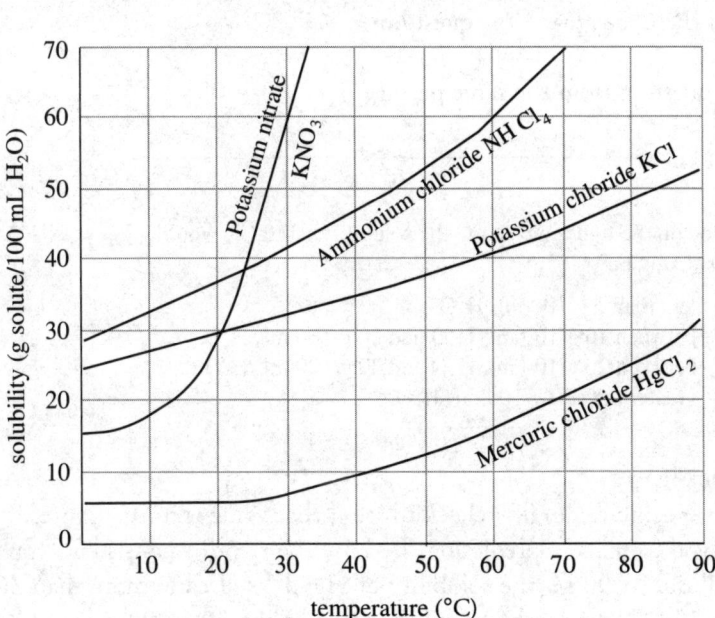

1. Based on the figure, as temperature increases, the solubility of $HgCl_2$:

   A. increases.
   B. decreases.
   C. increases, then decreases.
   D. decreases, then increases.

Here's How to Crack It

This question is asking you to identify a trend. You already cracked this question in Step 1, when you worked the figures and identified the trends. All the curves are headed up, so as temperature increases, the solubility of $HgCl_2$ increases. The correct answer is (A).

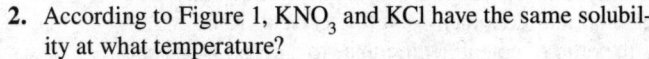

Try another.

2. According to Figure 1, KNO_3 and KCl have the same solubility at what temperature?

   F. Between 0° and 10°
   G. Between 10° and 20°
   H. Between 20° and 30°
   J. Between 30° and 40°

Here's How to Crack It

This question is asking you to look up a value in the figure. Find where KNO_3 and KCl have the same solubility. They have the same solubility when the lines intersect, at a solubility of 30 g/100 mL H_2O. Draw a line or carefully trace your finger down to the x-axis to see what the temperature is when solubility is 30; it's just over 20°, so the correct answer is (H).

Many questions on Science passages will entail nothing more than looking up a trend or value in a figure. Both of these are great Now questions.

Let's try one more question from the same passage.

———————○———————

3. Based on the figure, at 100°C the solubility of $HgCl_2$ would most likely be:

   A. less than 5 g/100 mL H_2O.
   B. between 10 g/100 mL H_2O and 20 g/100 mL H_2O.
   C. between 20 g/100 mL H_2O and 30 g/100 mL H_2O.
   D. greater than 30 g/100 mL H_2O.

Here's How to Crack It

If a question cites a specific value, first check to see if that value is in the figure. If it's not, the question is asking you to make a prediction. Because the trend is consistent, you can predict what the curve will do. At 90°C, the solubility of $HgCl_2$ is already more than 30 g/100 mL H_2O. Therefore, at 100°C, the solubility will be greater than 30 g/100 mL H_2O. The correct answer is (D).

———————○———————

Read If and Only When You Need To

On most of the questions, particularly on Now passages, you will be able to answer the questions based on the figures. Whether it's a Charts and Graphs passage or an Experiments passage, waste no time reading any of the introduction, or in the case of the Experiments passages, the descriptions of each experiment/study. It's only when you can't answer a question from the figures that you should read.

Let's take a look at some questions from an Experiments passage. We've already marked the tables from this passage.

———————○———————

Passage III

The *resistance* of a material that obeys Ohm's Law can be calculated by setting up a potential difference at the ends of a wire made of that material and then measuring the current in the wire; the resistance is the ratio of potential difference to current. Because resistance is dependent on length and cross-sectional area, scientists created a standard measure, *resistivity*, which is the measure of how strongly a material opposes the flow of current. In the experiments below, scientists examined the factors affecting resistance in an Ohmic material that they invented.

Experiment 1

In their first experiment, scientists examined the relationship between the length of a wire and its resistance. The resistivity of the wires used in this experiment was 27.5 ρ, and the cross-sectional area of the wires was 3.2 mm^2.

Table 1	
Length (m)	Resistance (Ω)
0.9	7.5
1.8	15.0
3.6	30.0

↑   ↑

Experiment 2

In their second experiment, scientists examined the relationship between the cross-sectional area of a wire and its resistance. The resistivity of the wires used in this experiment was 27.5 ρ, and the length of the wires was 0.9 m. The results are shown in Table 2.

Table 2	
Cross-sectional area (mm^2)	Resistance (Ω)
0.8	30.0
1.6	15.0
3.2	7.5

↑   ↓

4. *Conductivity* measures a material's ability to conduct an electric current, and it is defined as the reciprocal of a material's ability to oppose the flow of electric current. If the scientists wanted to increase the conductivity of the material they invented, they would:

   F. increase the length.
   G. decrease the cross-sectional area.
   H. increase the resistivity.
   J. decrease the resistivity.

Opposites
Whenever there is only one pair of answers that are exact opposites, the correct answer is frequently one of the two opposites.

Here's How to Crack It

The question defines a new term, **conductivity,** and asks how the scientists would increase the conductivity of their specific material. As part of the definition, the question states that conductivity is the reciprocal of a material's ability to oppose the flow of current. The tables do not feature an obvious variable for this quality, so you have to read the introduction and studies.

When to Read

Read if and only when you can't answer a question from the figures. If a question introduces a new term that you can't identify as one of the variables on the figures, look for information about that term in the introduction and/or experiments.

In the introduction, the term **resistivity** is defined as a material's ability to oppose the flow of electric current. The question adds the information that conductivity is the reciprocal of resistivity. Therefore, to increase the conductivity, the scientists would decrease the resistivity. The correct answer is (J). Notice that (H) and (J) are exact opposites. Whenever there is only one pair of exact opposites, the correct answer is frequently one of the pair.

Step 3: Work the Answers

On more difficult questions, POE will be much faster and more effective than scouring the text or figures to find an answer. If the answers are wordy—that is, anything but a simple value or trend word like *increase* or *lower*—use POE. Read each answer choice, and eliminate any that are contradicted by the figures.

Let's try a question from a different passage.

Passage I

This passage refers to the graph on page 506.

The term *solubility* refers to the amount of a substance (solute) that will dissolve in a given amount of a liquid substance (solvent). The solubility of solids in water varies with temperature. The graph below displays the water solubility curves for four crystalline solids.

6. A solution is *saturated* when the concentration of a solute is equal to the solubility at that temperature. If a saturated solution of potassium chloride (KCl) at 10°C were heated to 80°C, would the solution remain saturated?

   F. Yes, because solubility decreases with increasing temperature.
   G. Yes, because the solubility of potassium chloride is greater than that of potassium nitrate.
   H. No, because solubility is unaffected by increasing temperature.
   J. No, because concentration is unaffected by increasing temperature.

Here's How to Crack It

The question defines a new term, *saturated*, identifies KCl as saturated at a given temperature, and asks if KCl will remain saturated at a new temperature. If you're familiar with the topic of saturation, you may already know whether it's yes or no. If so, eliminate the two answers you know to be wrong and examine the reasons given in the two remaining answers.

But if you didn't understand the new information and can't process what will happen at a new temperature, use POE on all four answers. Ignore the yes/no, and focus on the reasons given in each answer.

Choice (F) says that solubility will decrease with increasing temperature, but the figure disproves this. No matter what the new information in the question is, this cannot be the correct answer. Eliminate it. Choice (G) brings in a new solute, potassium nitrate. Check the figure to see whether what it says about the relationship of the two solutes is correct. At 10°C, the solubility of potassium nitrate is lower than that of KCl, but at 80°C, it is much higher—it is off the chart! Since the reason in (G) is not true, there is no need to worry about whether this answer is correct. However, it is unlikely in any case that the solubility of a different solute tells you something about the saturation of KCl.

Choice (H) is also disproven by the figure, which shows a clear relationship between solubility and temperature. Eliminate (H) as well and you are left with (J), which must be correct. In general, avoid picking an answer in Science that makes an assumption about a trend in an unknown variable if you have no proof of how that variable will behave. Concentration is the number of grams of the substance per unit volume, so that will not change with temperature. Choice (J) is correct.

POE and Pacing

POE is so powerful on Science, you should be able to eliminate at least one, sometimes two, wrong answers even on questions that look like Never questions. This is particularly true on a Now passage.

Depending on your pacing, you may try to reason between the remaining answers, or you may just guess and move on. Don't spend more than another minute. Even if you get the question right eventually, spending too much time on one question will likely cost 2–3 questions later on.

THE 3-STEP BASIC APPROACH AND LATER PASSAGES

The 3-Step Basic Approach works on all passages with figures, not just the Now passages featuring consistent trends in tables and graphs.

Take a look using the 3-Step Basic Approach at a Later passage in the following section.

Step 1: Work the Figures

Some ACT passages will feature an illustration, a diagram, or tables and graphs with no consistent trends. Take 10–15 seconds to review the figure. When there are no consistent trends, a figure doesn't reveal the main point as readily. You'll learn the main point as you work the questions and answers. Spend the limited time devoted to Step 1 looking for any patterns or terms.

Try this figure.

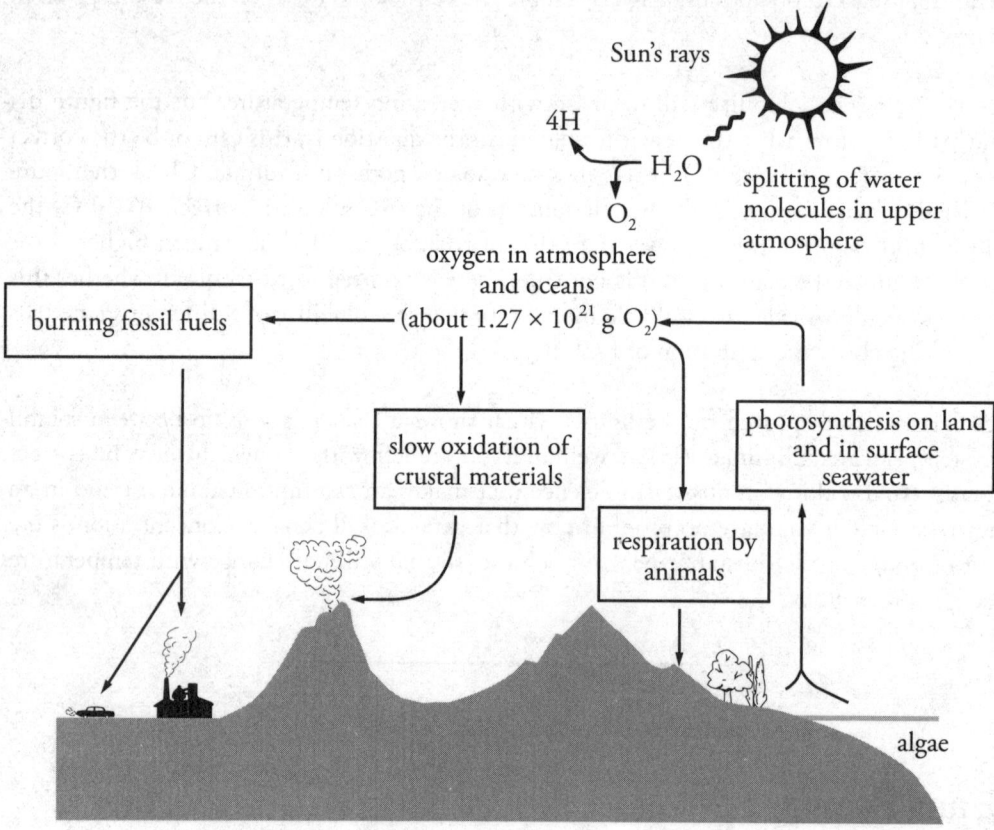

The terms **oxygen**, **fossil fuels**, **oxidation**, **respiration**, and **photosynthesis** all appear.

 **Step 2: Work the Questions**

Even on Later passages, several questions will ask you to look something up in the figure. The more confusing the figure, however, the more likely you are to waste valuable time trying to figure everything out from staring at the figure, waiting for a flash of inspiration to hit. As we mentioned before, spend no more than 10–15 seconds looking for any patterns or terms. Your time is better spent moving to Steps 2 and 3. Working the questions and answers will help you crack the main point of the passage.

Try a question.

13. Based on the information provided, which one of the following statements concerning the oxygen cycle is true?

   A. Photosynthesis on land and in surface seawater uses up oxygen.
   B. Photosynthesis on land and in surface seawater produces oxygen.
   C. Respiration by animals produces oxygen.
   D. Slow oxidation of crustal materials produces oxygen.

Step 3: **Work the Answers**

The wordier the answers, the more you should use POE. Read each answer, and then review the figure: does the answer choice accurately describe the figure?

Here's How to Crack It

Pay attention to arrows. They provide a pattern that tells the story. Choice (A) says that photosynthesis uses oxygen, but the arrows lead toward oxygen, not away. Eliminate (A). Choice (B) is the exact opposite and matches the direction of the arrows. Keep it. Whenever there is only one pair of exact opposites, the correct answer is frequently one of the two opposites. Choices (C) and (D) both describe producing oxygen, but the arrows move away from oxygen, not toward it. Both descriptions are contradicted by the arrows. The correct answer is (B).

OUTSIDE KNOWLEDGE

Now that you know how to work both Now and Later passages, let's talk about one type of Later question: one that requires outside knowledge. While most of the questions can be answered from the information presented in the passages or figures, 4 to 6 questions may require some additional information you should have learned in school. The outside-knowledge questions tend to ask about fairly basic facts, commonly addressed in intro-level high school science courses. For example, you may need to know that a honey badger is a mammal, or you may need to know where acid falls on the pH scale.

There is no way to predict what the outside-knowledge questions will be on the next ACT, but over time, we've seen some topics come up repeatedly. If you are concerned about the outside knowledge questions, review the following short list of commonly tested facts, and then use your Basic Approach for anything else that comes up. Remember, the vast majority of the questions can be answered using only the text that is directly in the passage, so don't worry about these too much.

Atoms contain *subatomic particles* called electrons, protons, and neutrons:
- *electrons* have a negative charge
- *protons* have a positive charge
- *neutrons* have a neutral charge

Atoms or molecules with a positive or negative charge are called **ions**:
- opposite charges attract, while ions with the same charge repel each other

Autotrophs are organisms that produce their own food. Plants are autotrophs that use energy from sunlight to convert carbon dioxide into glucose during *photosynthesis*. *Chlorophyll* is a pigment used during photosynthesis. Autotrophs are all *primary producers*.

Heterotrophs are called *consumers* because they consume other organisms for nutrition. *Herbivores* consume plants, *omnivores* consume both plants and animals, and *carnivores* consume animals.

Plant cells have a **cell wall**, while animal cells have only a cell membrane.

Cellular respiration is a process in which organisms convert sugars into energy. Most cellular respiration is *aerobic respiration*, which means it requires oxygen.

Prokaryotes are single-celled organisms that do not contain a nucleus or organelles while **eukaryotes** have cells with a defined nucleus. All living things are eukaryotes except for bacteria and archaebacteria.

Density is mass divided by volume. Density increases as mass increases and decreases as volume increases.

A liquid mixture is a **solution** only if all solutes are fully dissolved and the solution is *homogenous* (meaning "consistent throughout"). Any mixture that contains undissolved particles is not a solution.

A substance is:
- a **solid** if it is below the freezing point
- a **liquid** if it is between the freezing point and boiling point
- a **gas** if it is above the boiling point

pH measures the acidity or alkalinity of a substance. A solution with a pH below 7 is *acidic*. A solution with a pH above 7 is *basic* or *alkaline*.

In a **chemical reaction**, the *reactants* are on the left side of the equation, and the *products* are on the right side of the equation. In the reaction below, carbon (C) and oxygen (O_2) are the reactants and carbon dioxide (CO_2) is the product.

$$C + O_2 \rightarrow CO_2$$

The following relationships exist for **gases** when all other variables are held constant:
- **Volume** and **pressure** are inversely related: if volume increases, pressure decreases.
- **Temperature** is directly related to pressure and volume. If pressure or volume increases, temperature increases.
- As the amount of gas increases, the pressure increases.

Kinetic energy is a form of energy that an object possesses due to its motion. The temperature of a substance is directly proportional to the average kinetic energy of its particles, so as kinetic energy increases, temperature increases.

Basic Approach Drill 1

Use the Basic Approach on the passage below.

When introduced into H_2O, many solid substances are able to dissolve, or disperse evenly throughout the solvent. Salts have been found to dissolve easily when introduced into H_2O, since they readily dissociate to yield ions that may interact directly with H_2O. Molecular compounds, on the other hand, do not dissolve as easily. Two experiments were conducted to better understand the solubility of salts and molecular compounds in water at various temperatures. The solubility, S, was measured as follows:

$$S = (m_{sub}) / (m_{H_2O})$$

where m_{sub} was the mass of the substance dissolved in water, and m_{H_2O} was the mass of the water itself. ΔS, or the change in solubility (from 0° C), was calculated in the experiments for three salts and three molecular compounds with increasing temperature. The mass of water was held constant at 100 g for each of these experiments.

Figures 1 and 2 show the changes in solubility at different temperatures for three salts and three molecular compounds, respectively. Molecular masses (MM) are shown for each substance.

Figure 1

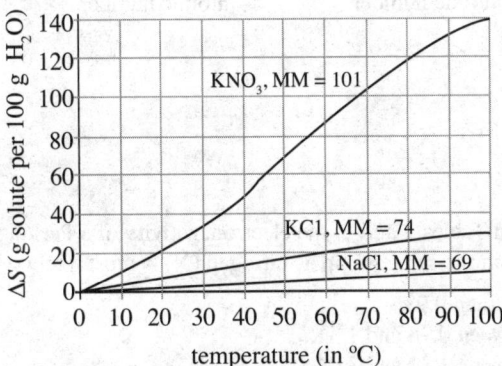

Figure 2

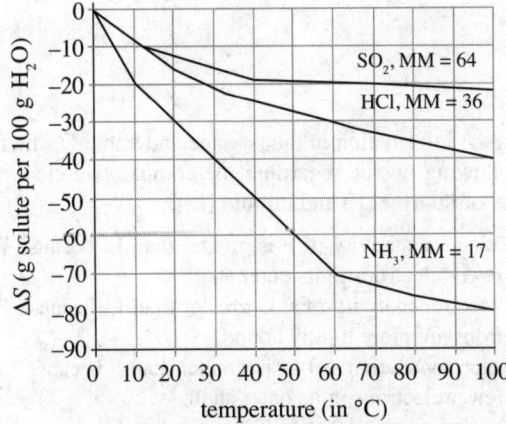

1. Based on Figure 1, at 40°C, as the molecular masses of the salts increase, the ΔS:

   A. decreases, because a greater mass of substance dissolves in the same mass of water.
   B. decreases, because a smaller mass of substance dissolves in the same mass of water.
   C. increases, because a greater mass of substance dissolves in the same mass of water.
   D. increases, because a smaller mass of substance dissolves in the same mass of water.

2. If an additional trial had been done in which a salt with an MM of 80 dissolved in H_2O at 50°C, the ΔS, in g solute per 100 g H_2O, most likely would have been:

   F. less than 10.
   G. between 10 and 20.
   H. between 20 and 60.
   J. greater than 60.

3. According to Figure 2, when a solution of NH_3 in water is heated from 0°C to 20°C, the solubility of the NH_3:

   A. increased, because ΔS was positive.
   B. increased, because ΔS was negative.
   C. decreased, because ΔS was positive.
   D. decreased, because ΔS was negative.

4. Based on Figures 1 and 2, which of the following combinations of solute and temperature at a known m_{H_2O} would produce the greatest increase in solubility?

   F. CH_4 (molecular compound, MM = 16) at 40°C
   G. CH_4 (molecular compound, MM = 16) at 80°C
   H. NaF (salt, MM = 42) at 40°C
   J. NaF (salt, MM = 42) at 80°C

5. The solubility of Substance X is 26.9 g per 100 g H_2O at 0°C and 37.1 g per 100 g H_2O at 25°C. Based on the information in the passage and figures, is Substance X most likely a salt or a molecular compound?

   A. Salt, because the solubility increases with increasing temperature.
   B. Salt, because the solubility decreases with increasing temperature.
   C. Molecular compound, because the solubility increases with increasing temperature.
   D. Molecular compound, because the solubility decreases with increasing temperature.

Basic Approach Drill 2

Use the Basic Approach on the passage below.

Each element is arranged in the periodic table according to its atomic number, which represents the number of protons in the nucleus. In every neutrally charged atom, the number of electrons equals the number of protons. *Electronegativity* is a measure of the relative strength with which the atoms attract outer electrons. Elements with higher electronegativity have tighter bonding between protons and electrons than elements with lower electronegativity.

The different rows of the periodic table are called periods, and all elements in a period have the same number of electron shells. Table 1 shows the characteristics of the elements in Period 2.

Table 1				
Element	Atomic number	Atomic radius (pm)	Electro-negativity	Type
Li	3	167	0.98	metal
Be	4	112	1.57	metal
B	5	87	2.04	metalloid
C	6	67	2.55	nonmetal
N	7	56	3.04	nonmetal
O	8	48	3.44	nonmetal
F	9	42	3.98	nonmetal

The different columns of the periodic table are called groups. Elements in the same group share similar chemical behaviors. Table 2 shows some characteristics of several Group 2 elements.

Table 2				
Element	Period	Atomic radius (pm)	Electro-negativity	Type
Be	2	112	1.57	metal
Mg	3	145	1.31	metal
Ca	4	194	1.00	metal
Sr	5	219	0.95	metal
Ba	6	253	0.89	metal

1. Which of the following graphs best represents the relationship between atomic number and atomic radius for Period 2 elements?

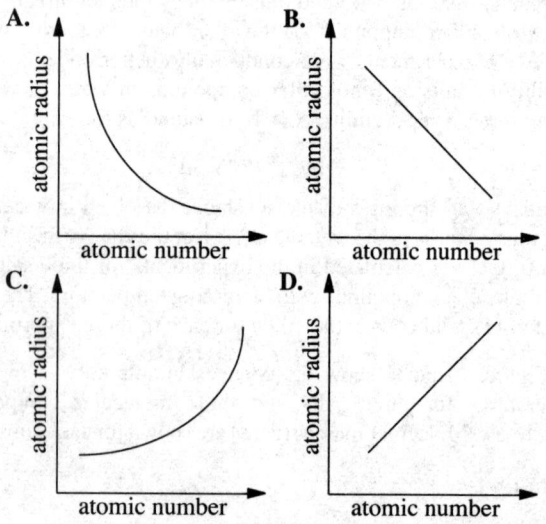

2. Based on Tables 1 and 2, the electronegativity of a Period 3 element in the same group as nitrogen (N) is most likely:

   F. less than 0.98.
   G. between 0.98 and 1.31.
   H. between 1.31 and 3.04.
   J. greater than 3.04.

3. Based on the information in the passage and Table 1, which of the following is true regarding the comparative electronegativity of fluorine (F) and lithium (Li)?

   A. The electronegativity of F is greater than Li because F has fewer electrons in its outer shell.
   B. The electronegativity of F is greater than Li because F electrons are more tightly bound.
   C. The electronegativity of Li is greater than F because Li has fewer electrons in its outer shell.
   D. The electronegativity of Li is greater than F because Li electrons are more tightly bound.

4. Generally speaking, elements with a high electronegativity also have a high ionization energy. Based on Table 1, which of the following is a correct order of elements with *increasing* ionization energies?

F. Be, O, Li

G. F, N, Li

H. B, N, Be

J. Li, N, F

5. Potassium (K) is a Period 4 element with an electronegativity of 0.82. Based on the information in Tables 1 and 2, is K more likely to be a metal or a nonmetal?

A. Metal, because K has a lower electronegativity than Ca.

B. Metal, because K has a higher electronegativity than B.

C. Nonmetal, because K has a higher electronegativity than Ca.

D. Nonmetal, because K has a lower electronegativity than B.

Basic Approach Drill 3

Use the Basic Approach on the passage below.

Amphibians are unique organisms that undergo drastic physical changes during the transformation from an immature organism into an adult form during a process called *metamorphosis*. The process begins with cell determination in the embryo stage. Figure 1 shows the stages of development in frogs.

Figure 1

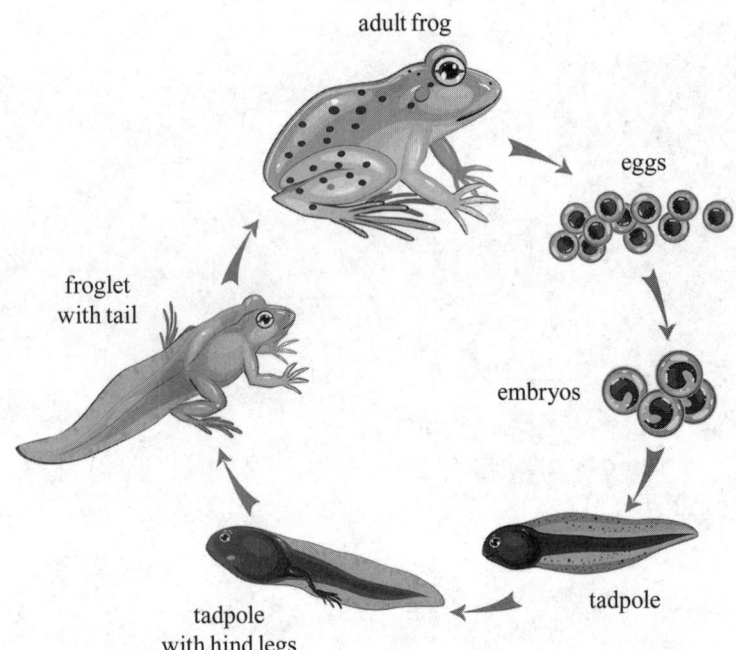

Experiment

An experiment was conducted using tadpoles to determine the influence of thyroxine (a hormone) on metamorphosis. The researchers predicted that increased levels of thyroxine would lead to an earlier appearance of adult characteristics such as lungs and hind legs and tail reabsorption. Twenty recently emerged tadpoles were divided into four treatment groups. Five tadpoles were placed into each of 3 aqueous solutions containing various concentrations of thyroxine. The remaining five tadpoles were placed in pure distilled water. The researchers measured the tail width of each tadpole every 12 hours and calculated the average percent decrease in tail width over the course of the study for each group (see Figure 2).

Figure 2

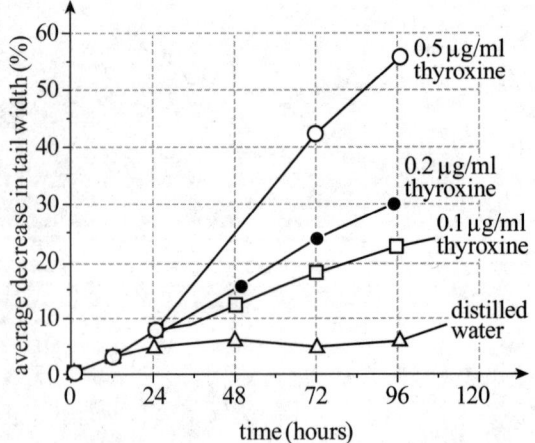

1. Suppose that an additional group of recently emerged tadpoles were immersed in a 0.3 μg/ml thyroxine solution for 72 hours. Based on Figure 2, the approximate average decrease in tail width would most likely have been closest to:

   A. 22%.
   B. 30%.
   C. 41%.
   D. 50%.

2. Which of the following assertions about tadpoles is supported by the results of the experiment?

   F. They will not undergo metamorphosis if they are not exposed to thyroxine.
   G. Metamorphosis in a tadpole not given thyroxine takes at least five days.
   H. The most rapid disappearance of the tail is associated with the immersion of tadpoles in the most dilute thyroxine solution.
   J. Temperature plays a major role in metamorphosis.

3. After four days of immersion, the tadpoles are checked for other signs of development. In all tadpoles exposed to thyroxine, at which of the following concentrations of thyroxine would the tadpoles be likely to show the **least** development?

   A. 0.1 μg/ml
   B. 0.2 μg/ml
   C. 0.5 μg/ml
   D. All of the tadpoles would show the same development.

4. Based on the information in the passage and Figure 1, which of the following would be a correct order of the stages of frog development?

   F. Tadpole → hind leg development → reabsorption of tail → cell determination
   G. Tadpole → cell determination → reabsorption of tail → hind leg development
   H. Cell determination → reabsorption of tail → tadpole→ hind leg development
   J. Cell determination → tadpole → hind leg development → reabsorption of tail

5. According to Figure 2, after approximately how many hours of immersion does exposure to thyroxine first show a measurable effect on the rate of tadpole metamorphosis?

   A. 0 hours after immersion; the thyroxine affects the rate of metamorphosis immediately.
   B. 0–12 hours after immersion
   C. 12–24 hours after immersion
   D. 24–36 hours after immersion

6. Suppose a recently emerged tadpole is immersed in a 0.15 μg/ml thyroxine solution. Based on Figure 2, if after *t* hours, the tadpole has undergone a 23% decrease in tail width, which of the following is likely closest to the value of *t*?

   F. 60
   G. 72
   H. 84
   J. 96

BASIC APPROACH DRILL 1 ANSWERS AND EXPLANATIONS

1. **C**   The question asks, *based on Figure 1*, what ΔS does at 40°C *as the molecular masses of the salts increase*. Look at Figure 1. Since ΔS is on the vertical axis, a rising line indicates an increase, and a falling line indicates a decrease. Since all three lines are rising at 40°C, ΔS must be increasing, so eliminate (A) and (B). Additionally, Figure 1 indicates that the units for ΔS are g solute per 100 g H_2O. This means that, if ΔS is increasing, then the g solute per 100 g H_2O is also increasing, which means there is a greater mass of the substance dissolved in the same mass of water. Eliminate (D). The correct answer is (C).

2. **H**   The question asks what the ΔS would most likely have been *if an additional trial had been done in which a salt with an MM of 80 was dissolved in H_2O at 50°C*. According to the passage, Figure 1 shows *three salts*, so look at Figure 1. Since the figure contains no salt with an MM of 80, look at the surrounding salts to determine whether there is a pattern or trend. At 50°C, each salt with a higher MM has a higher ΔS. According to the figure, KNO_3 has an MM of 101 and a ΔS of approximately 68 g solute per 100 g H_2O at 50°C, and KCl has an MM of 74 and a ΔS of approximately 18 g solute per 100 g H_2O at 50°C. Therefore, *a salt with an MM of 80 dissolved in H_2O at 50°C* would be expected to have a ΔS between approximately 18 g and 68 g solute per 100 g H_2O at 50°C. Eliminate (F) because it is too low. Because an MM of 80 is much closer to 74 than it is to 101, the ΔS should be closer to 18 than to 68. Eliminate (J) because 60 is too high. Notice that as the MM increases from 69 for NaCl to 74 for KCl, the ΔS at 50°C increases by approximately 15 g solute per 100 g H_2O. Therefore, increasing the MM from 74 to 80 will likely increase the ΔS to above 20. Eliminate (G) because it is too low. The correct answer is (H).

3. **D**   The question asks, *according to Figure 2*, what happens to *the solubility of the NH_3...when a solution of NH_3 in water is heated from 0°C to 20°C*. Look at Figure 2 to see what happens to the solubility of NH_3 when the temperature increases. When the temperature increases from 0°C to 20°C on the line representing NH_3, the solubility of the NH_3 (represented by ΔS) decreases from 0 to –30 g solute per 100 g H_2O. Since solubility decreases, eliminate (A) and (B), which state that it increases. Next, look at the vertical axis to see the values of ΔS at the temperatures indicated. The value of ΔS is negative, so eliminate (C). The correct answer is (D).

4. **J**   The question asks *which of the following combinations of solute and temperature at a known m_{H_2O} would produce the greatest increase in solubility...based on Figures 1 and 2*. Look at Figures 1 and 2. According to the passage, Figure 1 represents *three salts* and Figure 2 represents *three molecular compounds*. Notice that in Figure 2, as temperature increases, solubility (ΔS) decreases, which means that a molecular compound at any temperature above 0°C will yield a decrease in solubility. Eliminate (F) and (G) since they both incorrectly indicate that a molecular compound at temperatures above 0°C will produce an *increase in solubility*. Since (H) and (J) deal with NaF, which is a salt, refer to Figure 1. In Figure 1, for all of the salts listed, as temperature increases, solubility increases. Therefore, *the greatest increase in solubility* will occur at the highest temperature. Eliminate (H) because it contains a lower temperature. The correct answer is (J).

5. **D** The question asks whether a substance with a solubility of *26.9 g per 100 g H₂O at 0°C and 37.1 g per 100 g H₂O at 25°C* is *most likely a salt or a molecular compound*. Look at Figures 1 and 2. According to the passage, Figure 1 represents *three salts* and Figure 2 represents *three molecular compounds*. The question says that the solubility of Substance X changes from *26.9 g per 100 g H₂O at 0°C* to *37.1 g per 100 g H₂O at 25°C*, which means that the solubility of the substance increases as temperature increases. According to Figure 2, the solubility of a molecular substance decreases as temperature increases. Eliminate (C) and (D). Since Figure 1 indicates that the solubility of a salt increases as temperature increases, the correct answer should reflect this relationship. Eliminate (B), which says that solubility decreases with increasing temperature. The correct answer is (A).

BASIC APPROACH DRILL 2 ANSWERS AND EXPLANATIONS

1. **A** The question asks which graph *best represents the relationship between atomic number and atomic radius for Period 2 elements*. Table 1 shows the atomic numbers and atomic radii of the elements in Period 2, so look at Table 1. According to Table 1, as the atomic number increases for Period 2 elements, the atomic radius decreases. Eliminate (C) and (D), which incorrectly indicate that atomic radius increases as the atomic number increases. While the atomic radius decreases in Table 1, it does not decrease at a steady rate—the change in atomic radius between atomic numbers 3 and 4 is much larger than the change in atomic radius between atomic numbers 8 and 9, for example. Eliminate (B), which indicates that the atomic radius decreases at a linear rate as the atomic number increases. The correct answer is (A).

2. **H** The question asks what is *most likely…the electronegativity of a Period 3 element in the same group as nitrogen (N)…based on Tables 1 and 2*. Look at Table 1, which shows characteristics of several Period 2 elements, including N. According to Table 1, N is a nonmetal with an electronegativity of 3.04. Now look at Table 2. According to Table 2, electronegativity decreases as period increases. Since the element in the question is in the same group as N, but the period is increased by one (from Period 2 to Period 3), the electronegativity of the element should be lower than 3.04. Eliminate (J) since this is too high. Also notice in Table 2 that Mg is a Period 3 metal with an electronegativity of 1.31. Table 1 shows that, for a given period, nonmetals have higher electronegativity values than metals. Since N is a nonmetal, then the Period 3 element in the same group as N must also be a nonmetal and would therefore have an electronegativity higher than the 1.31 value of Mg, a Period 3 metal. Eliminate (F) and (G), which are too low. The correct answer is (H).

3. **B** The question asks which statement *is true regarding the comparative electronegativity of fluorine (F) and lithium (Li)…based on the information in the passage and Table 1*. The electronegativity values for fluorine (F) and lithium (Li) are given in Table 1, so look at Table 1. According to the table, fluorine (F) has a higher electronegativity than lithium (Li). Eliminate (C) and (D), which both say that lithium (Li) has the higher electronegativity. Now look at the passage for an explanation of elements with higher electronegativity. According to the first paragraph of the passage, *elements with higher electronegativity have tighter bonding between protons and electrons than elements with lower electronegativity*. Eliminate (A) because it does not match this definition. The correct answer is (B).

4. **J** The question asks *which of the following is a correct order of elements with increasing ionization energies…based on Table 1* and the statement that *elements with a high electronegativity also have a high ionization energy*. Table 1 lists the electronegativity of the given elements, so look at Table 1. If a high electronegativity accompanies a high ionization energy, then as electronegativity increases, ionization energy also increases. Place the elements in order from lowest electronegativity to the highest. Of the elements listed, Li has the lowest electronegativity, so Li should be listed first. Eliminate (F), (G), and (H) because they do not list element Li first. The correct answer is (J).

5. **A** The question asks whether *Potassium (K)*, which has *an electronegativity of 0.82*, is *more likely to be a metal or a nonmetal…based on the information in Tables 1 and 2*. The answer choices compare the electronegativity of K to that of Ca and B, so look at Tables 1 and 2 to find these elements. Table 1 shows that K has a lower electronegativity than B. Eliminate (B). Table 2 shows that K has a lower electronegativity than Ca. Eliminate (C). Now, look back at Table 1, which shows the electronegativity for both metals and nonmetals in Period 2. Lower electronegativity values tend to accompany metals, while higher values tend to accompany nonmetals. Since the electronegativity of K is 0.82, a lower value, K is most likely a metal. Eliminate (D). The correct answer is (A).

BASIC APPROACH DRILL 3 ANSWERS AND EXPLANATIONS

1. **B** The question asks for the *most likely…approximate average decrease in tail width…based on Figure 2…* if *an additional group of recently emerged tadpoles were immersed in a 0.3 μg/ml thyroxine solution for 72 hours*. Look at Figure 2, which shows the average decrease in tail width for tadpoles in four different thyroxine solutions at different elapsed times. Look for the average decreases in tail width at 72 hours. The 0.2 μg/ml thyroxine solution has an average decrease in tail width of approximately 24% at 72 hours, while the 0.5 μg/ml thyroxine solution has an average decrease in tail width of approximately 42% at 72 hours. The average tail width decrease for a solution of 0.3 μg/ml thyroxine would fall between the values for the solutions of 0.2 μg/ml thyroxine and 0.5 μg/ml thyroxine on the figure. Eliminate (A) and (D) because they fall outside of this range. Since 0.3 μg/ml is closer to 0.2 μg/ml than to 0.5 μg/ml, the average tail width decrease for a 0.3 μg/ml solution will be closer to 24% than to 42%. Eliminate (C). The correct answer is (B).

2. **G** The question asks which of the *assertions about tadpoles is supported by the results of the experiment*. The results of the experiment are shown in Figure 2, so look at Figure 2 and use POE. The tadpoles exposed only to distilled water did see a decrease in tail width, just at a slower rate than the other groups, which means that they did undergo metamorphosis, even without exposure to thyroxine. Eliminate (F). The data in Figure 2 ends just before 120 hours, which is 5 days. At this point, the average tail width of the tadpoles in distilled water has increased by approximately 10%, which means that these tadpoles have not completed metamorphosis. Therefore, metamorphosis for tadpoles not exposed to thyroxine must take longer than 5 days. Keep (G). The largest rate of average tail decrease at every interval past 24 hours is associated with the tadpoles immersed in the 0.5 μg/ml thyroxine solution, which is the most concentrated solution, not the most diluted one. Eliminate (H). The experiment measured the decrease in average tail width based on variations in thyroxine concentration and time,

but temperature played no role in the experiment. This does not support the assertion that temperature plays a major role in metamorphosis. Eliminate (J). The correct answer is (G).

3. **A** The question asks *at which of the following concentrations of thyroxine would the tadpoles be likely to show the LEAST development* if they *are checked for other signs of development…after four days of immersion*. Look at Figure 2, which shows development by thyroxine concentration. At 96 hours, which is four days, the thyroxine concentration with the lowest average decrease in tail width, and thus the lowest development, is the 0.1 µg/ml thyroxine solution. It is logical to conclude that the least development in other areas would also occur in the same solution concentration after the same amount of time. Eliminate (B), (C), and (D). The correct answer is (A).

4. **J** The question asks which of the answer choices *would be a correct order of the stages of frog development…based on the information in the passage and Figure 1*. Look at the passage. The second-to-last sentence of the first paragraph of the passage states that *the process begins with cell determination in the embryo stage*, so you know cell determination is the first stage of frog development. Eliminate (F) and (G) because they do not place cell determination first. Now look at Figure 1. Reabsorption of the tail comes after the tadpole stage. Eliminate (H), which places reabsorption of the tail before the tadpole stage. The correct answer is (J).

5. **C** The question asks *after approximately how many hours of immersion does exposure to thyroxine first show a measurable effect on the rate of tadpole metamorphosis…according to Figure 2*. Look at Figure 2. According to the figure, after 12 hours, the values for the average decrease in tail width show no difference; the earliest time on the figure at which there is a discernible gap between the average decrease in tail width for tadpoles in the thyroxine solutions compared to tadpoles in distilled water only is 24 hours. Therefore, the divergence in the effect of thyroxine on metamorphosis occurs sometime between 12 hours and 24 hours of immersion. Eliminate (A), (B), and (D). The correct answer is (C).

6. **H** The question asks which answer choice *is likely closest to the value of t* if *a recently emerged tadpole… has undergone a 23% decrease in tail width* after being *immersed in a 0.15 µg/ml thyroxine solution for t hours…based on Figure 2*. Look at Figure 2. A thyroxine solution with a concentration of 0.15 µg/ml will produce results somewhere between the results of the 0.1 µg/ml thyroxine solution and those of the 0.2 µg/ml solution. Look at 60 hours, which is the hashmark halfway between 48 and 72 hours. Both the 0.1 and 0.2 solutions have a percent decrease in tail width of 20% or less at this point, so a 0.15 solution, which is between them, would also be less than 20%. Eliminate (F). At 72 hours, the 0.1 µg/ml thyroxine solution is at about 18% and the 0.2 µg/ml thyroxine solution is at about 24%, so a 0.15 µg/ml thyroxine solution would likely produce results around 20%, which is too small. Eliminate (G). At 84 hours, which is the hashmark halfway between 72 and 96 hours, the 0.1 µg/ml thyroxine solution is at about 21% and the 0.2 µg/ml thyroxine solution is at about 26%, so a 0.15 µg/ml thyroxine solution would likely produce results around 23%. Keep (H), but check (J) just in case. At 96 hours, the 0.1 µg/ml thyroxine solution is just over 20% and the 0.2 µg/ml thyroxine solution is almost 30%, so a 0.15 µg/ml thyroxine solution would likely produce results around 25%, which is too large. Eliminate (J). The correct answer is (H).

Summary

o   All Charts and Graphs passages and most Experiments passages come with figures.

o   Use the 3-Step Basic Approach on passages with figures.

- **Step 1. Work the Figures.** Look at the trends and patterns in the figure(s) to identify the relationship between the variables. Mark trends in tables with arrows.
- **Step 2. Work the Questions.** Do Now the straightforward questions that involve looking up a trend or value on the figure or making a prediction of what a variable will do. Read if and only when you can't answer a question from the figures. Do Later any question that strikes you as more difficult or time-consuming.
- **Step 3. Work the Answers.** For tougher questions, POE should help you eliminate at least one wrong answer, if not three.

o   Pace yourself. If you've eliminated at least one wrong answer on a tough question, guess and move on.

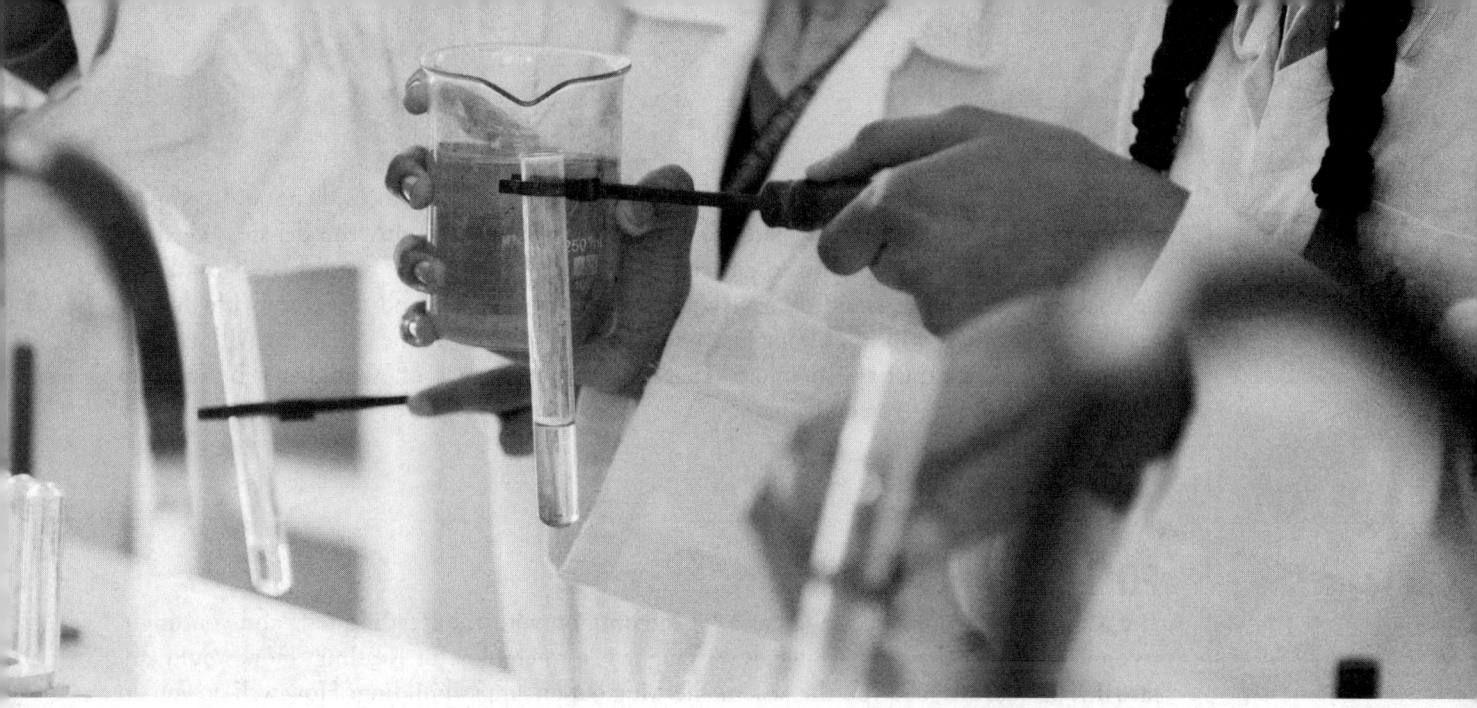

Chapter 27
Multiple Viewpoints
Science Passages

The third type of passage on the Science test is based on more than one passage. Two, three, or possibly more conflicting views on a scientific phenomenon will be presented. Make a plan of the order in which you will read the scientists, and work one theory at a time before tackling the questions that require comparing and contrasting all of the theories.

Think of it as a debate. Each debater proposes a hypothesis and then supports that hypothesis with facts, opinions, and assumptions. The ACT test-writers want you to evaluate and compare the arguments made by each debater, but they don't care who wins the debate. We don't care either, but we do want you to correctly answer questions about the debate. In order to do that, you must understand each viewpoint and how it agrees and disagrees with the others. Some questions will ask about just one theory, but most of the questions will ask you to compare and contrast two or more. That's a lot to keep track of. Wouldn't it be easier to navigate this passage if you had a plan?

FOLLOW A PLAN

The Multiple Viewpoints passage has a lot in common with the Reading test, and you might recognize some of the same strategies we taught you to employ for Reading. How would you fare if your boss assigned you the task of checking out an empty building? How well do you do when you don't know what you're looking for? Not very well. How well would you fare if you dived right into a passage on the Reading test if you didn't know what you're looking for? Right. So how can you succeed on the Multiple Viewpoints passage if you don't know what you're looking for?

Step 1: Preview

Your first task is to read the introduction to identify the disagreement.

> Approximately 65 million years ago (at the boundary between the Cretaceous and Tertiary periods, known as the K-T boundary), the dinosaurs became extinct.
>
> Here are two of the hypotheses that have been presented to explain their disappearance.

What will the hypotheses debate? They will debate what caused the extinction of the dinosaurs.

Your next task is to map the order in which you will read the scientists. Just as on the Reading test, you should look at the questions first. On the Multiple Viewpoints passage, the questions help you determine which hypothesis to read and which questions to answer first.

Let's try this with the questions below. Read each question, and mark it with a "1" if it asks about Hypothesis 1, a "2" if it asks about Hypothesis 2, and a "1 & 2" if it asks about both hypotheses. On the ACT Online Test, use your whiteboard instead: write the question number, then "1," "2," or "1 & 2" next to the number.

1. Hypotheses 1 and 2 agree that the dinosaurs:

2. The basis of Hypothesis 1 is that a meteorite striking Earth was the primary cause of the dinosaurs' demise. Which of the following discoveries would best support this theory?

3. Suppose a geologist discovered that the fossilized bones of dinosaurs contained traces of radioactive iridium. How would this evidence influence the two hypotheses?

4. If current climatic changes turn out to be as dramatic as those described by the author of Hypothesis 2, which of the following would he say is most likely to occur?

5. Recent studies have shown that climatic conditions at the K-T boundary were interdependent. As conditions became less favorable for life in one locale, they improved in another. Do the results of these recent studies strengthen or weaken Hypothesis 2 ?

6. Both Hypothesis 1 and 2 would be supported by evidence showing that:

You should have a "1 & 2" next to questions 1, 3, and 6. Question 2 should have a "1" next to it, and questions 4 and 5 should have a "2" next to them. What does this tell us? We should read Hypothesis 2 first.

Step 2: One Side at a Time

In order to compare and contrast multiple hypotheses, you need to understand each viewpoint and how it agrees and disagrees with the others. Reading and working the questions for one scientist at a time will give you the firm grasp of each theory you need.

Start by reading Hypothesis 2. You don't need to comprehend everything in the passage or remember every point of fact or argumentation, and until you read the other hypothesis, you have no basis for comparison. You do need to grasp the argument each is making, so as you read Hypothesis 2, find and underline or highlight the scientist's answer to the question—that is, what caused the extinction of the dinosaurs.

Hypothesis 2

   This event at the K-T boundary was neither sudden nor isolated. It was a consequence of minor shifts in Earth's weather that spanned the K-T boundary. Furthermore, its effect was not as sweeping as some have suggested. While the majority of dinosaurs disappeared, some were able to adapt to the changing world. We see their descendants every day—the birds.

   Alterations in Earth's *jet stream* (a steady, powerful wind that blows from west to east, circling the globe) shifted rains away from the great shallow seas that extended across much of what is now North America. As these late-Cretaceous seas began to dry

What Are They Fighting About?

Some of the scientific theories you'll read about in a Multiple Viewpoints Science passage were settled a long time ago. In reading a passage arguing that Earth is the center of the solar system, you may think, "Wait, Earth is NOT the center of the solar system—why in the world are they arguing about this?" For the ACT, the arguments presented are what count. Even though an argument may have been disproved a long time ago, it's still possible to evaluate it scientifically, and that's all you're being asked to do on this test.

up, a chain reaction of extinctions was set into motion. First affected was plant life. Next, animals that fed on plants began dying off. Ultimately, the lack of prey caused the demise of the majority of the dinosaurs. It was the mobility of the winged dinosaurs that saved them, allowing them to move to more favorable locations as conditions in their ancestral homes deteriorated.

What is the main point of Hypothesis 2?

According to Hypothesis 2, the extinction of dinosaurs was caused by a chain reaction prompted by changes in the weather.

Your Underlined Version Should Look Like This

Hypothesis 2

This event at the K-T boundary was neither sudden nor isolated. It was a consequence of minor shifts in Earth's weather that spanned the K-T boundary. Furthermore, its effect was not as sweeping as some have suggested. While the majority of dinosaurs disappeared, some were able to adapt to the changing world. We see their descendants every day—the birds.

Alterations in Earth's *jet stream* (a steady, powerful wind that blows from west to east, circling the globe) shifted rains away from the great shallow seas that extended across much of what is now North America. As these late-Cretaceous seas began to dry up, a chain reaction of extinctions was set into motion. First affected was plant life. Next, animals that fed on plants began dying off. Ultimately, the lack of prey caused the demise of the dinosaurs. It was the mobility of the winged dinosaurs that saved them, allowing them to move to more favorable locations as conditions in their ancestral homes deteriorated.

Did you notice that we didn't underline the details of the theory in the second paragraph? It's not that they are unimportant, but until we dive into the questions, we don't know what to pay attention to other than the main point. As we work the questions for Hypothesis 2, we'll gain a deeper understanding of the details of the theory.

Without further ado, let's go to the questions about Hypothesis 2.

———————○———————

4. If current climatic changes turn out to be as dramatic as those described by the author of Hypothesis 2, which of the following would he say is most likely to occur?

   F. A rapid extinction of most of Earth's life, beginning with sea dwellers such as krill (a microscopic crustacean) and progressing through the food chain

   G. A gradual and complete extinction of Earth's life forms that moves through the food chain from the bottom up

   H. An extinction of most life forms on Earth that is gradual and simultaneous, affecting predators as well as prey at roughly the same rates

   J. A progressive extinction that begins with vegetation and eventually reaches to the top of the food chain, affecting most dramatically those life forms least suited to relocation

Here's How to Crack It

The main point of Hypothesis 2 is that changes in the weather prompted a chain reaction of extinctions through the food chain until the dinosaurs were affected. We need to look for an answer that would predict a similar result from today's climatic changes. Use POE as you make your way through the answer choices.

Choice (F) is tempting because it mentions a progression *through the food chain*, but the word *rapid* contradicts the first sentence of Hypothesis 2: *The event at the K-T boundary was neither sudden nor isolated.* Choice (G) looks good until we go back to the passage to confirm it and see that some dinosaurs survived: those that evolved into birds. Because of the word *complete*, we have to eliminate it. Choice (H) is out because of the word *simultaneous*, which we know from evaluating (F) is contradicted by the passage. The answer must be (J) since it paraphrases nicely what Hypothesis 2 proposes.

———————○———————

5. Recent studies have shown that climatic conditions at the K-T boundary were interdependent. As conditions became less favorable for life in one locale, they improved in another. Do the results of these recent studies strengthen or weaken Hypothesis 2?

    A. Strengthen, because they support the assumption that there were some locations with more favorable conditions to which the winged dinosaurs could migrate.

    B. Strengthen, because they support the assumption that worsening climatic conditions led to the extinction of dinosaurs before the Tertiary period.

    C. Weaken, because they refute the assumption that there were some locations with more favorable conditions to which the winged dinosaurs could migrate.

    D. Weaken, because the area of improving climatic conditions should have provided a means for the survival of the dinosaurs well into the Tertiary period.

Here's How to Crack It

We've learned a lot about Hypothesis 2. We read it and underlined the main point, and then we evaluated some of the nuances of the argument to eliminate wrong answers for question 4. When you consider the import of these new studies, you should draw upon the deeper understanding you've gained. The correct answer to question 4 reminded us that those *least* suited to relocation are more impacted by the changes in weather. Hypothesis 2 stated explicitly that some winged dinosaurs survived and evolved into birds because their mobility allowed *them to move to more favorable locations.* Eliminate (B) and (D) because both imply that Hypothesis 2 states that no dinosaurs survived into the Tertiary period. Eliminate (C) because the recent studies support rather than refute the idea that there were some locations in which conditions improved. The correct answer is (A).

Step 3: The Other Side

Now it's time to read Hypothesis 1, but we know more than we did before reading Hypothesis 2 and thus should read more proactively. When you read the second theory, you should look for and underline or highlight the following:

> - the main idea
>
> - how this hypothesis disagrees with the first
>
> - how this hypothesis agrees with the first

Differentiate Between Theories

Questions on the Dual Science passages often ask about the areas of agreement as well as disagreement between the scientists' theories. Make sure you know what both the similarities and differences are.

Hypothesis 1

For many years, scientists have speculated about the cause of the extinction of the dinosaurs. Fossil records confirm that dinosaurs as well as other life forms were suddenly wiped out. The natural cause of extinction is the inability of an organism to adapt to environmental changes, yet the extinction of all life forms is unlikely. Chemical analysis of clay found from this era attributes the sweeping extinction of dinosaurs to the collision of a huge meteorite with Earth. These fossil records confirm the presence of a high concentration of iridium, a rare heavy metal that is abundant in meteorites. It is believed that a meteorite hit Earth and created a huge crater, which threw up a dust cloud that blocked the sun for several months. This event led first to the destruction of much plant life and eventually all other life forms that consumed plants and/or herbivores, including the dinosaurs.

> **Write, Write, Write**
> Underlining or highlighting and taking notes in the margins or on your whiteboard can help you keep track of the differences between the scientists.

What is the main point? Hypothesis 1 believes a meteorite struck Earth and wiped out the dinosaurs.

How do the two hypotheses differ? Hypothesis 2 believes the extinction was gradual; Hypothesis 1 believes it was sudden.

How do they agree? Both hypotheses mention the food chain.

If you didn't come up with those points, look at the underlined portions of the passage below.

Hypothesis 1

For many years, scientists have speculated about the cause of the extinction of the dinosaurs. <u>Fossil records confirm that dinosaurs as well as other life forms were suddenly wiped out.</u> The natural cause of extinction is the inability of an organism to adapt to environmental changes, yet the extinction of all life forms is unlikely. <u>Chemical analysis of clay found from this era attributes the sweeping extinction of dinosaurs to the collision of a huge meteorite with Earth.</u> These fossil records confirm the presence of a high concentration of iridium, a rare heavy metal that is abundant in meteorites. It is believed that a meteorite hit Earth and created a huge crater, which threw up a dust cloud that blocked the sun for several months. <u>This event led first to the destruction of much plant life and eventually all other life forms that consumed plants and/or herbivores, including the dinosaurs.</u>

> **Multiple Viewpoints (A Science Duel?)**
> In a Multiple Viewpoints passage, you're given two or more opinions about a scientific phenomenon. Your job is to identify the differences between or among the viewpoints and the information the scientists use to support their points of view.

Now let's do the one question on Hypothesis 1 before we tackle the questions on both.

2. The basis of Hypothesis 1 is that a meteorite striking Earth was the primary cause of the dinosaurs' demise. Which of the following discoveries would best support this theory?

    F. The existence of radioactive substances in the soil

    G. The presence of other rare metals common to meteorites in the clay beds of the ocean from that period

    H. Fossil records of land-dwelling reptiles that roamed Earth for an additional 10 million years

    J. Evidence of dramatic changes in sea levels 65 million years ago

Here's How to Crack It

What type of evidence would support Hypothesis 1? Any evidence that shows that dinosaurs were wiped out as a result of the impact of a meteorite. Would the presence of radioactive substances in the soil support Hypothesis 1? It could support the passage only if the radioactive elements were from meteorites (like iridium). Choice (F) did not specify that. Would the fact that some land-dwelling reptiles survived past this period support Hypothesis 1? No, so (H) is out. We can also get rid of (J) because it supports Hypothesis 2. What about (G)? What if other rare metals that are known to be found in meteorites were discovered? Would this support Hypothesis 1? Yes. The correct answer is (G).

Step 4: Compare and Contrast

We are now armed with a clear understanding of the main point of each hypothesis, how the two differ, and how they agree.

1. Hypotheses 1 and 2 agree that the dinosaurs:

    I. vanished because of a meteorite impact with Earth.

    II. became extinct due to disruptions in their food chain.

    III. became extinct due to some external force other than predation.

    A. I only

    B. I and II only

    C. II and III only

    D. III only

Here's How to Crack It

We've already identified the area in which the two agree: the impact on the food chain. Look for a statement that reflects that—it's Statement II. Eliminate the answers that do not include Statement II, which are (A) and (D). Now check either Statement I or III to decide between the remaining answer choices. Statement I is true only for Hypothesis 1, not both, so eliminate (B). The only answer that remains contains Statements II and III, so III must be true. Do both hypotheses state that dinosaurs became extinct because of some external force? Yes, so the correct answer is (C).

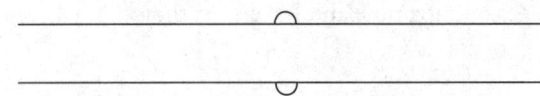

3. Suppose a geologist discovered that the fossilized bones of dinosaurs contained traces of radioactive iridium. How would this evidence influence the two hypotheses?

   A. It would support both hypotheses.
   B. It would support Hypothesis 1 and weaken Hypothesis 2.
   C. It would support Hypothesis 2 and weaken Hypothesis 1.
   D. It would not support Hypothesis 1 or Hypothesis 2.

Here's How to Crack It

Which of the hypotheses would be supported if a geologist found fossil bones that contained traces of radioactive iridium? Hypothesis 1, of course! The passage states that radioactive iridium is abundant in meteorites. If dinosaurs were exposed to the dust of meteorites, their bones would contain this metal. Hypothesis 2 didn't mention anything about iridium, so (B) is the correct answer.

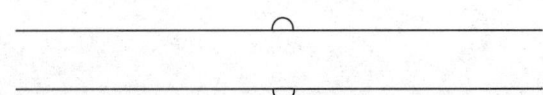

6. Both Hypotheses 1 and 2 would be supported by evidence showing that:

   F. pterodactyls (winged dinosaurs) survived well into the Tertiary period, adapted to changes in Earth's environment, and eventually evolved into a non-dinosaur life form.
   G. blockage of the sun's rays by particles measurable only on the microscopic scale can still have a significant effect on rates of photosynthesis.
   H. even apparently minor degradation of the plant population in a given ecosystem can have far-reaching effects on the animal population within that ecosystem.
   J. iridium is extremely likely to remain trapped in an ocean's bed when that ocean dries up.

Study Break!
You're almost finished with Science! Tackle the Dual Science Drills, and then give yourself some downtime before diving into Part VI.

Here's How to Crack It

On what point do the hypotheses agree? Look for an answer choice that provides evidence about the food chain. Eliminate any answer choice that supports only one hypothesis. Choice (F) is out because Hypothesis 1 never mentioned relocation or winged dinosaurs. Choice (G) looks good because it mentions photosynthesis, a necessary step in the food chain, so keep it. Choice (H) looks much better because it explicitly mentions the effects of plants on animals. Choice (J) is incorrect because Hypothesis 2 never mentioned iridium, and Hypothesis 1 never mentioned the ocean drying up. The test-writers are trying to distract you with a switch, but you won't fall for it when you take the passages one at a time and learn each thoroughly before working the questions on both. The correct answer is (H).

Multiple Viewpoints Passage Drill 1

Natural gas (a variable combination of methane and other heavier hydrocarbons) is extracted and brought to the surface from reservoirs located between 0 and 0.5 miles beneath Earth's surface. Two scientists discuss the origin of natural gas in a particular undersea reservoir.

Scientist 1

All of the natural gas present in the reservoir was formed within the last 500 million years from the decay of organic matter. Natural gas formation began when the remains of marine organisms and terrestrial plants piled up on land and on the seafloor over a long period. Mud and other sediments then buried the accumulated plants and organisms. Deep beneath the surface, at depths greater than 10 miles, high temperatures and pressure converted the buried organic matter into natural gas over millions of years.

After its formation, the natural gas rises toward the surface. Some is dissipated into the air, but a significant amount is trapped under the specific geological formation overlaying the reservoir. Fossils from the plants and marine organisms that provided the organic matter can be found in rocks brought to the surface from locations in Earth's crust where natural gas forms.

Because of the unique geological conditions and time required for formation of such reservoirs, Earth's crust contains only a small amount of natural gas formed in this manner.

Scientist 2

All of the natural gas present in the reservoir was formed by the action of microorganisms at depths from 2 to 10 miles beneath the surface of Earth. The supply of natural gas has been in constant production since soon after the reservoir's formation. The production begins as various microorganisms digest buried organic material to produce simple, inorganic carbon compounds. Other microorganisms convert the carbon compounds and water into the hydrocarbons of natural gas.

After its formation, the natural gas rises and subsequently amasses in significant quantities in the reservoir. Many natural gas deposits can be found in deep rock layers, where the gas can be released by procedures such as *hydraulic fracturing*, the fracturing of rock by a pressurized liquid. A carbon-13 isotope, commonly linked to natural gas produced from microorganism involvement, is contained in the natural gas brought up to the reservoir.

Since natural gas is always forming and rising toward reservoirs such as this one, there is an infinite amount obtainable.

1. A natural gas deposit has been found at a depth of 20 miles below Earth's surface. Is this information consistent with the position expressed by Scientist 1?

    A. No, because Scientist 1 indicates that natural gas forms at depths greater than 10 miles below Earth's surface.

    B. No, because Scientist 1 indicates that natural gas forms at depths between 2 and 10 miles beneath Earth's surface.

    C. Yes, because Scientist 1 indicates that natural gas forms at depths greater than 10 miles beneath Earth's surface.

    D. Yes, because Scientist 1 indicates that natural gas forms at depths between 2 and 10 miles beneath Earth's surface.

2. Which scientist indicates that the natural gas found in the reservoir formed in the lower pressure environment?

    F. Scientist 1, because that scientist states that the natural gas formed at depths of more than 10 miles beneath Earth's surface.

    G. Scientist 1, because that scientist states that the natural gas formed at depths between 2 and 10 miles beneath Earth's surface.

    H. Scientist 2, because that scientist states that the natural gas formed at depths of more than 10 miles beneath Earth's surface.

    J. Scientist 2, because that scientist states that the natural gas formed at depths between 2 and 10 miles beneath Earth's surface.

3. Which of the following diagrams is most consistent with Scientist 2's description of the formation and migration of natural gas?

(Note: Diagrams are not to scale.)

A.
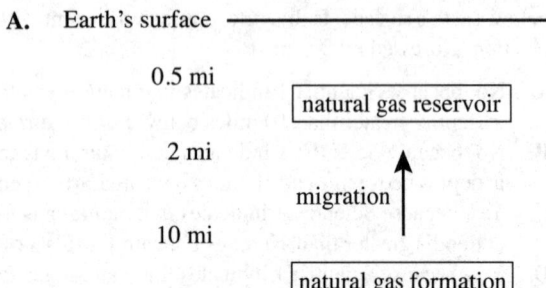

B.
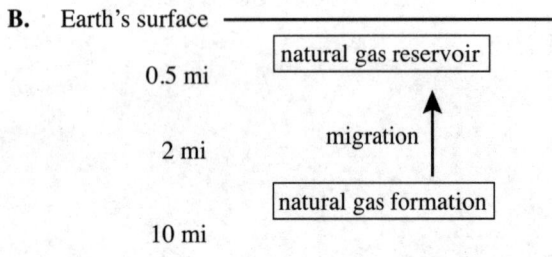

C.
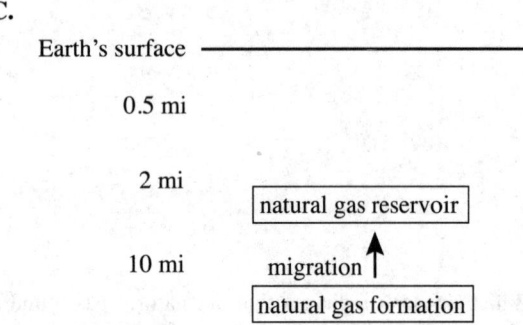

D.
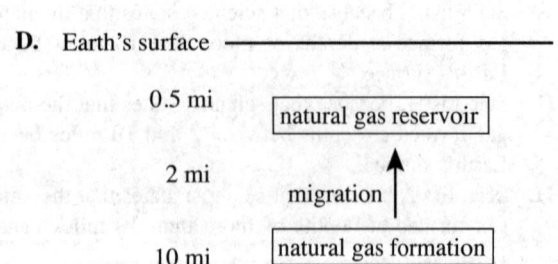

4. An experiment showed that natural gas can be formed through a reaction of carbon dioxide and water. Which scientist would most likely use this result to support his/her viewpoint?

F. Scientist 1, because it would demonstrate how, under high temperature and pressure, organic material can be converted into natural gas.
G. Scientist 1, because it would demonstrate a chemical reaction that microorganisms might carry out to convert organic material into natural gas.
H. Scientist 2, because it would demonstrate how, under high temperature and pressure, organic material can be converted into natural gas.
J. Scientist 2, because it would demonstrate a chemical reaction that microorganisms might carry out to convert organic material into natural gas.

5. Based on Scientist 2's discussion, which of the following statements describes two properties of natural gas that migrated to the reservoir in which it accumulated? The natural gas:

A. does not contain carbon-13 and is less dense than the material through which it migrates.
B. does not contain carbon-13 and is more dense than the material through which it migrates.
C. contains carbon-13 and is less dense than the material through which it migrates.
D. contains carbon-13 and is more dense than the material through which it migrates.

6. Based on Scientist 2's discussion, which of the following compounds is involved in the formation of natural gas?

  I. F_2
 II. KCl
III. CO_2

F. I only
G. III only
H. I and II only
J. II and III only

Multiple Viewpoints Passage Drill 2

A professor placed 100 mL of Gas A at 25°C into a syringe. The syringe was then inserted into a rubber stopper placed in the top of an empty flask (see Figure 1). The escape of gas molecules from the syringe into the evacuated flask is known as *effusion*.

Figure 1

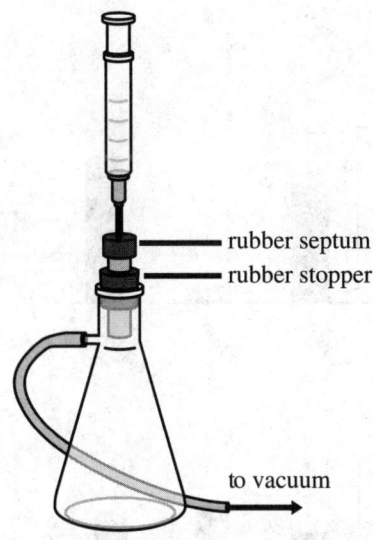

rubber septum
rubber stopper

to vacuum

After insertion of the syringe into the flask, the *total effusion time*, the time required for all 100 mL of the gas to effuse from the syringe into the flask, was measured and found to be 4 sec. The procedure was repeated with Gas B, which had a total effusion time of 16 sec.

Three students proposed explanations for why the total effusion time for the two gasses differed.

Student 1

Gas B effused more slowly than Gas A because it has greater *molecular mass* (the mass of each molecule) than Gas A. The temperature of a gas is a measure of the average kinetic energy of the molecules of that gas. If the temperature of each gas is the same, then the average kinetic energy of the molecules of both gasses is also equal. Since average kinetic energy depends on both the mass and the velocity of gas particles, gases with greater molecular masses travel with a smaller average velocity. Therefore, if two gases are at the same temperature, the gas with the greater molecular mass will effuse more slowly.

Student 2

Gas B effused more slowly than Gas A because it has greater *molecular volume* (the volume occupied by each molecule) than Gas A. Because of their greater molecular volume, fewer larger molecules are able to pass through the opening between the syringe and flask in a given period of time when compared to the number of smaller molecules that are able to pass through the opening in the same period of time. Therefore, if two gases are at the same temperature, the gas with the greater molecular volume will effuse more slowly.

Student 3

Gas B effused more slowly than Gas A because it has greater density than Gas A. Because Gas B has a greater density, its molecules are nearer one another than are the molecules of Gas A. The close proximity of the molecules of Gas B increases the likelihood of collisions, which slow the speed of the molecules. Therefore, if two gases are at the same temperature, the gas with the greater density will effuse more slowly.

Table 1 gives the molecular mass (in atomic mass units, amu), molecular volume (in cubic Angstroms ($Å^3$), where 10 billion $Å$ = 1 m), and density for several gases at 25°C.

Table 1			
Gas	Molecular mass (amu)	Molecular volume ($Å^3$)	Density (kg/L)
Oxygen	32.00	52.86	1.429
Hydrogen	2.016	37.54	0.089
Xenon	131.3	42.12	5.894
Krypton	83.80	34.45	3.749
Helium	4.003	11.46	0.179
Fluorine	38.00	21.17	1.696

1. Based on Student 1's explanation, which of the gases listed in Table 1 would effuse most quickly at 25°C?

   A. Hydrogen
   B. Xenon
   C. Helium
   D. Fluorine

2. Suppose that the professor had also tested nitrogen gas and found that it had an effusion time of 9 seconds. Student 1 would claim that nitrogen:

F. has a smaller molecular mass than Gas A but a greater molecular mass than Gas B.
G. has a greater molecular mass than Gas A but a smaller molecular mass than Gas B.
H. has a smaller molecular volume than Gas A but a greater molecular volume than Gas B.
J. has a greater molecular volume than Gas A but a smaller molecular volume than Gas B.

3. Is the claim "At 25°C, xenon effuses more quickly than krypton" consistent with Student 2's explanation?

A. No, because xenon has a larger molecular volume than krypton.
B. No, because xenon has a greater density than krypton.
C. Yes, because xenon has a larger molecular volume than krypton.
D. Yes, because xenon has a greater density than krypton.

4. Which of the following graphs of the relative effusion rates of oxygen, xenon, and krypton at 25°C is most consistent with Student 3's explanation?

F.

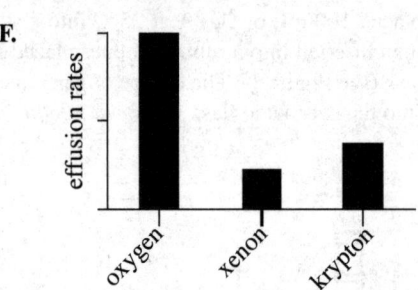

G.

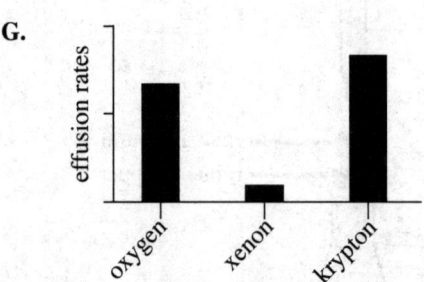

H.

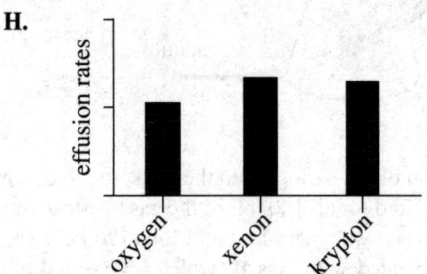

J.

5. Suppose that Gas A had been hydrogen and Gas B had been helium. The results of the professor's experiment would have supported the explanation(s) provided by which student(s)?

A. Student 1 only
B. Student 2 only
C. Students 1 and 2 only
D. Students 1 and 3 only

6. Consider the data for carbon dioxide (a gas) at 25°C shown in the table below:

Molecular mass (amu)	Molecular volume (Å³)	Density (kg/L)
44.01	34.87	1.77

Which student(s) would predict that carbon dioxide would have a shorter effusion time than krypton?

F. Student 1 only
G. Students 1 and 2 only
H. Students 1 and 3 only
J. Students 1, 2, and 3

MULTIPLE VIEWPOINTS PASSAGE DRILL 1 ANSWERS AND EXPLANATIONS

1. **C** The question asks whether a *natural gas deposit* having *been found at a depth of 20 miles below Earth's surface* is *consistent with the position expressed by Scientist 1*. The passage asks about Scientist 1's discussion, so look at the first passage. The passage states that natural gas was created *beneath the surface, at depths greater than 10 miles*. This is consistent with a *natural gas deposit* having *been found at a depth of 20 miles below Earth's surface*. Eliminate (A) and (B), which say that the new deposit is not consistent with the first passage. The passage says that natural gas forms *at depths greater than 10 miles*, which is not consistent with gas forming *at depths between 2 and 10 miles beneath Earth's surface*. Eliminate (D). The correct answer is (C).

2. **J** The question asks *which scientist indicates that the natural gas found in the reservoir formed in the lower pressure environment*. The question asks for a choice between Scientist 1 and Scientist 2, so refer to both passages. In the first passage, Scientist 1 states that *high temperatures and pressure converted the buried organic matter into natural gas over millions of years*. This is the opposite of a *lower pressure environment*. Eliminate (F) and (G). Now look at the second passage. Scientist 2 states that natural gas was formed *at depths from 2 to 10 miles beneath the surface of Earth*. Choice (H) states that natural gas was formed *at depths of more than 10 miles beneath Earth's surface*. Eliminate (H). If natural gas forms closer to the surface, it will form in a lower-pressure environment. Keep (J). The correct answer is (J).

3. **B** The question asks which of the given diagrams *is most consistent with Scientist 2's description of the formation and migration of natural gas*. Look at the second passage and use POE. Scientist 2 states that natural gas was formed *at depths from 2 to 10 miles beneath the surface of Earth*. Eliminate (A) and (C), which indicate that natural gas formed at depths greater than 10 miles below the Earth's surface. Now look at the introduction before the two passages. This introduction states that natural gas reservoirs are *located between 0 and 0.5 miles beneath Earth's surface*. Eliminate (D), which indicates that natural gas reservoirs are greater than 0.5 miles below the Earth's surface. Choice (B) indicates that natural gas reservoirs are located less than 0.5 miles below the Earth's surface, which is consistent with the text. Keep (B). The correct answer is (B).

4. **J** The question asks *which scientist would most likely use* the *result* of an experiment showing *that natural gas can be formed through a reaction of carbon dioxide and water…to support his/her viewpoint*. Look at the first passage. Scientist 1 states that *all of the natural gas…was formed within the last 500 million years from the decay of organic matter*. A chemical reaction between carbon dioxide and water does not support Scientist 1's assertion. Eliminate (F) and (G). Now look at the second passage. Scientist 2 makes no reference to *high temperature and pressure*. Eliminate (H). Scientist 2 does state that formation occurs when *microorganisms convert the carbon compounds and water into the hydrocarbons of natural gas*. This is consistent with natural gas being *formed through a reaction of carbon dioxide and water*. Keep (J). The correct answer is (J).

5. **C**   The question asks *which of the following statements describes two properties of natural gas that migrated to the reservoir in which it accumulated…based on Scientist 2's discussion*. All the answer choices discuss carbon-13, so locate a reference to this in the second passage. Scientist 2 states that *a carbon-13 isotope, commonly linked to natural gas produced from microorganism involvement, is contained in the natural gas brought up to the reservoir*. Eliminate (A) and (B), which incorrectly state that natural gas does not contain carbon-13. The remaining answer choices discuss relative density, so locate a reference to this in the passage. Scientist 2 states that *after its formation, the natural gas rises and subsequently amasses in significant quantities in the reservoir*. Natural gas will rise only if it is less dense than the material through which it is migrating. Eliminate (D), which incorrectly states that the natural gas is *more dense* than the surrounding material. Keep (C), which correctly states that the natural gas is *less dense* than the surrounding material. The correct answer is (C).

6. **G**   The question asks *which* of the *compounds is involved in the formation of natural gas…based on Scientist 2's discussion*. Look at the second passage. This is a Roman numeral question, so eliminate answer choices as statements are eliminated. Scientist 2 states that *microorganisms convert the carbon compounds and water into the hydrocarbons of natural gas*. Neither F_2 nor KCl is a carbon compound of water, so neither is involved in natural gas formation. Therefore, Statements I and II are incorrect, so eliminate (F), (H), and (J), which each contain either Statement I, Statement II, or both. The compound CO_2 is a carbon compound, so it is involved in the formation of natural gas. Therefore, Statement III works. Keep (G), which contains only Statement III. The correct answer is (G).

MULTIPLE VIEWPOINTS PASSAGE DRILL 2 ANSWERS AND EXPLANATIONS

1. **A**   The question asks, *based on Student 1's explanation…which of the gases listed in Table 1 would effuse most quickly at 25°C*. Look at Student 1's explanation. Student 1 states that *if two gases are at the same temperature, the gas with the greater molecular mass will effuse more slowly*. This means that the gas with the smaller molecular mass will effuse more quickly. Look at Table 1, which lists the molecular masses of several gases. Based on Student 1's explanation, hydrogen should effuse the fastest because it has the smallest molecular mass. Keep (A). Eliminate (B), (C), and (D), all of which contain gases with higher molecular masses than that of hydrogen. The correct answer is (A).

2. **G**   The question asks what *Student 1 would claim* if *the professor had also tested nitrogen gas and found that it had an effusion time of 9 seconds*. Look at the experiment description. The *total effusion time of Gas A was measured and found to be 4 sec*, while *Gas B* was found to have *a total effusion time of 16 sec*. Now look at Student 1's explanation, which states that *if two gases are at the same temperature, the gas with the greater molecular mass will effuse more slowly*. Eliminate (H) and (J) since both refer to molecular volume, which Student 1 does not mention. If nitrogen were found to have an effusion time of 9 seconds, which is more than the 4-second effusion time of Gas A, then Student 1's explanation would indicate that nitrogen must have a greater molecular mass than that of Gas A.

Eliminate (F), which incorrectly states that nitrogen *has a smaller molecular mass than Gas A*. Since (G) correctly places the molecular mass of nitrogen relative to the molecular masses of Gas A and Gas B according to Student 1's explanation, keep (G). The correct answer is (G).

3. **A** The question asks whether *the claim "At 25°C, xenon effuses more quickly than krypton" is consistent with Student 2's explanation*. Look at Student 2's explanation. Student 2 states that *if two gases are at the same temperature, the gas with the greater molecular volume will effuse more slowly*. Look at Table 1. According to Table 1, xenon (42.12 Å^3) has a greater molecular volume than krypton (34.45 Å^3). Therefore, according to Student 2's explanation, xenon should effuse more slowly than krypton, so the statement that *xenon effuses more quickly than krypton* is not consistent with Student 2's explanation. Eliminate (C) and (D), which say that the result is consistent. Choice (B) refers to density, which Student 2 does not discuss. Eliminate (B). The statement that *xenon effuses more quickly than krypton* means that xenon has a lower molecular volume than krypton. This is not consistent with Table 1, which shows that xenon has a greater molecular volume than krypton. Keep (A). The correct answer is (A).

4. **F** The question asks which of the given *graphs of the relative effusion rates of oxygen, xenon, and krypton at 25°C is most consistent with Student 3's explanation*. Look at Student 3's explanation. Student 3 states that *if two gases are at the same temperature, the gas with the greater density will effuse more slowly*. The densities of the gases are provided in Table 1, so look at Table 1. Of the three gases, oxygen (1.429 kg/L) has the lowest density, so according to Student 3's explanation, oxygen should have the highest effusion rate. Eliminate (G), (H), and (J), all of which show krypton with a higher effusion rate than oxygen. Only (F) correctly shows oxygen with the greatest effusion rate, so keep (F). The correct answer is (F).

5. **D** The question asks which student's explanation would be supported by *the results of the professor's experiment* if *Gas A had been hydrogen and Gas B had been helium*. Look at the passage introduction to see the experiment results. The experiment found that Gas A had a total effusion time of 4 seconds and Gas B had a total effusion time of 16 seconds. If Gas A were hydrogen and Gas B were helium, then hydrogen would have a lower effusion time and therefore a higher effusion rate. Student 1's explanation involves an inverse relationship between *molecular mass* and *effusion rate*. Table 1 lists the various characteristics for hydrogen and helium, so look at Table 1. According to the table, hydrogen has a lower molecular mass than helium, so according to Student 1's explanation, hydrogen should have a higher effusion rate. This is consistent with the results of the experiment, so the correct answer should contain Student 1. Eliminate (B), which does not contain Student 1. Student 2's explanation involves an inverse relationship between *molecular volume* and *effusion rate*. According to Table 1, hydrogen has a higher molecular volume than helium, so according to Student 2's explanation, hydrogen should have a lower effusion rate. This is not consistent with the results of the experiment, so the correct answer should not contain Student 2. Eliminate (C), which does contain Student 2. Student 3's explanation involves an inverse relationship between *molecular density* and *effusion rate*. According to Table 1, hydrogen has a lower molecular density than helium, so according to Student 3's explanation, hydrogen should have a higher effusion rate.

This is consistent with the results of the experiment, so the correct answer should contain Student 3. Eliminate (A), which does not contain Student 3. Choice (D) does contain Student 3, so keep (D). The correct answer is (D).

6. **H** The question asks *which student(s) would predict that carbon dioxide would have a shorter effusion time than krypton*. Note that *effusion time* is inversely related to effusion rate. Look at the table provided in the question for information on carbon dioxide and at Table 1 for information on krypton. Table 1 says that krypton has a molecular mass of 83.80 amu, while the new table says that carbon dioxide has a molecular mass of 44.01 amu. Now look at the answer choices. All the answer choices contain Student 1, so there is no need to evaluate this student's prediction. Start with Student 2. According to Student 2's explanation, carbon dioxide, with a slightly higher molecular volume (34.87 Å^3) than the molecular volume of krypton (34.45 Å^3), should have a slightly lower effusion rate and therefore a longer effusion time. Student 2's prediction does not match the prediction in the question, so the correct answer should not contain Student 2. Eliminate (G) and (J), which do contain Student 2. Now look at Student 3. According to Student 3's explanation, carbon dioxide, with a lower density (1.77 kg/L) than the density of krypton (3.749 kg/L), should have a higher effusion rate and therefore a shorter effusion time. Student 3's prediction does match the prediction in the question, so the correct answer should contain Student 3. Eliminate (F), which does not contain Student 3. Keep (H), which does contain Student 3. The correct answer is (H).

Summary

- In Multiple Viewpoints passages, two, three, or more scientists present their differing views on a scientific subject.

- Don't pick a side. The ACT test-writers want you to evaluate and compare the arguments presented, not decide which one is correct. Even if you know something about the topic, answer the questions using only what is presented in the passage.

- Follow the Multiple Viewpoints Basic Approach:
  1. Preview: Read the introduction to determine what the theories disagree upon, and then map the questions and determine which passage to read first.
  2. One Side at a Time: Read the theory and work the questions for one scientist at a time.
  3. The Other Side: When reading the next theory, look for the main idea and the ways in which this theory agrees with and disagrees with the first.
  4. Compare and Contrast: Always save the questions that compare or contrast multiple theories for last when you are already familiar with all of the different theories.

- Leave the questions on more than one theory for last.

- Don't forget to use your Letter of the Day if there are questions that you don't know how to do.

Part VI
The Princeton Review ACT Practice Exams

*Practice Exams 3 and 4 can be found online via your Student Tools. Follow the directions on page viii to access your additional practice tests.

Chapter 28
Practice Exam 2

*Make sure to download a bubble sheet for this test via your online Student Tools.

ENGLISH TEST

35 Minutes—50 Questions

DIRECTIONS: In the passages that follow, certain words and phrases are underlined and numbered. In the right-hand column, you will find alternatives for the underlined part. You are to choose the best answer to each question. If you think the original version is best, choose "**No Change**."

You will also find questions about a section of the passage or about the passage as a whole. These questions do not refer to an underlined portion of the passage, but rather are identified by a number or numbers in a box.

For each question, choose the alternative you consider best, and fill in the corresponding oval on your answer document. Read each passage through once before you begin to answer the questions that accompany it. For many of the questions, you must read several sentences beyond the question to determine the answer. Be sure that you have read far enough ahead each time you choose an alternative.

PASSAGE I

Crocheting Makes a Good Hobby

Crocheting is the art of making fabric by twisting yarn or thread with a hook. Although many associate it by older people,
$\overline{1}$

crocheting can be a fun hobby for people of all ages. Once you
$\overline{2}$
start crocheting, you won't be able to put down the hook;

1. Which choice makes the sentence most grammatically acceptable?

   A. **No Change**
   B. to
   C. on
   D. with

2. Which choice is least redundant in context?

   F. **No Change**
   G. people of all ages, young and old.
   H. young and old people of all ages.
   J. people of all ages, both young and old people alike.

GO ON TO THE NEXT PAGE.

you'll have a hobby for life. ☐3

Crocheting is an easy hobby to pick up. Instructional books are readily available, and once you've learned a few basic stitches. Picking up the more advanced ones is a snap. Once you ___4___ learn how to crochet, you can buy pattern books that tell you exactly how to make the projects that interest you. All you need are a crochet hook, yarn, and a pair of scissors.

You can crochet while watching television, listening to music, or visiting with other people. It is fun and relaxing and allows you to express your creative side in an easy way. Also, you have finished a project, you have a cherished keepsake. ___5___ Whether you have made a throw blanket to keep you warm on cold winter nights or a lace tablecloth to add a touch of elegance to your dining room, your creation is sure to be cherished for a long time to come.

3. At this point, the author is considering adding the following true statement:

> Irish nuns helped save lives with crocheting when they used it as a way to make a living during the Great Irish Potato Famine of 1846.

Should the writer add this sentence here?

A. Yes, because it is essential to know when crocheting became internationally prominent and how it did so.

B. Yes, because the reference to the Great Irish Potato Famine demonstrates that the author is conscious of historical events.

C. No, because the reference to the Great Irish Potato Famine is not relevant to the main topic of this essay.

D. No, because many people who left Ireland in 1846 brought crocheting with them to the United States and Australia.

4. Which choice makes the sentence or sentences most grammatically acceptable?

F. **No Change**
G. stitches; picking
H. stitches, picking
J. stitches since picking

5. Which choice makes the sentence most grammatically acceptable?

A. **No Change**
B. finally you
C. despite the fact that you
D. once you

GO ON TO THE NEXT PAGE.

PASSAGE II

Seurat's Masterpiece

[1] How can I describe the wonder I felt the first time I saw my favorite painting, Georges Seurat's *A Sunday on La Grande Jatte*? [2] I had admired the work for years in art books, but I never thought I would see the actual painting, which was housed in Chicago, many miles from where I lived. [3] I finally got my chance when I met someone else who loved the painting as much as I did. [4] We both had three days off at the same time, so we decided to make a road trip to Chicago so we could see the painting in all <u>it's</u> grandeur.
₆

[5] We packed our bags, <u>jumped into the car, and headed on our</u>
₇

way toward Chicago. 8

6. Which choice makes the sentence most grammatically acceptable?

   F. **No Change**
   G. our
   H. its
   J. its'

7. Which choice makes the sentence most grammatically acceptable?

   A. **No Change**
   B. jumped into the car, and had headed
   C. jumped into the car, and head
   D. had jumped into the car, and headed

8. Upon reviewing this paragraph and noticing that some information has been left out, the writer composes the following sentence, incorporating the information:

> Her name was Lisa; she lived in my dorm, and a mutual friend had introduced us to each other, knowing how much both of us loved art.

For the sake of the logic of this paragraph, this sentence should be placed:

   F. after Sentence 2.
   G. after Sentence 3.
   H. after Sentence 4.
   J. after Sentence 5.

GO ON TO THE NEXT PAGE.

[1] The first thing that struck me as we entered the room where the painting was displayed; was the size of the painting. [2] A common size for canvases is 24 by 36 inches. [3] It was enormous! [4] It covered a large part of an even larger wall. [5] The painting's size amazed me since it was painted with dots, a technique called pointillism. [6] To create a painting of such magnitude using this technique seemed an almost impossible task.

[7] Seurat had done it, though, and had made it look easy! [11]

Even more impressive, however, was the beauty of the painting. Viewed from a distance, the colors looked muted, capturing the idyllic mood of a summer day in the park.

When I approached the painting, though, its colors exploded into myriad hues, illustrating the artist's skill in combining colors to create a mood. Even the parts of the painting that appeared white from a

distance were vibrantly multicolored when viewed up close. [14] The effect was incredible; we sat and stared at the painting in wonder for a good portion of the afternoon.

9. Which choice makes the sentence most grammatically acceptable?
   A. **No Change**
   B. displayed:
   C. displayed,
   D. displayed

10. Which choice is least redundant in context?
    F. **No Change**
    G. task and difficult to complete.
    H. task, difficult to complete.
    J. task, overwhelming in its difficulty.

11. Which of the following sentences is **least** relevant to the development of this paragraph and therefore could be deleted?
    A. Sentence 2
    B. Sentence 4
    C. Sentence 5
    D. Sentence 6

12. Given that all of the choices are accurate, which provides the most effective and logical transition from the preceding paragraph to this one?
    F. **No Change**
    G. One thing that struck me was
    H. Many art critics have written about
    J. The debate rages on over

13. Which of the following alternatives to the underlined portion would **not** be acceptable?
    A. As I approached the painting, though,
    B. However, as I approached the painting,
    C. I approached the painting, though,
    D. However, when I approached the painting,

14. If the writer were to delete the phrase "from a distance" from the preceding sentence, the paragraph would primarily lose:
    F. an essential point explaining the author's love of the painting.
    G. the first part of the contrast in this sentence, which the author uses to describe viewing the painting.
    H. a further indication of the length of the road trip taken by the author and the friend.
    J. nothing, because the information provided by this phrase is stated more clearly elsewhere in the paragraph.

GO ON TO THE NEXT PAGE.

My friend and I saw many other sights on our trip to Chicago, but the best part by far was being able to see our favorite work of art. The image is forever imprinted in my mind at the museum gift shop, even when I'm not looking at the souvenir print I bought.

15. The best placement for the underlined portion would be:

A. where it is now.
B. after the word *image*.
C. after the word *looking*.
D. after the word *bought* (ending the sentence with a period).

PASSAGE III

The Language of Cats

Many people believe that language is the domain of human beings. However, cats have developed an intricate language, not for each other, but for the human beings who have adopted them as pets.

When communicating with each other, cats "talk" with a complex system of nonverbal signals. In particular, their tails and physical contact are used to express their feelings. With other cats, cats use their voices only to express pain. ⬚17

However, cats use a wide range of vocal expressions when they communicate with people, from affectionate meows to menacing hisses. Since cats verbal expressions are not used to communicate with other cats, it is

logical and reasonable to conclude that cats developed this "language" specifically to communicate with their human owners.

16. Which choice would most clearly and effectively express the ownership relationship between humans and cats?

F. **No Change**
G. like to have cats around.
H. often have dogs as well.
J. are naturally inclined to like cats.

17. If the preceding sentence were deleted, the essay would primarily lose:

A. a redundant point made elsewhere in the essay.
B. another description of the ways in which cats communicate nonverbally.
C. an exception to the general trend described in this paragraph.
D. a brief summary of the information contained in the essay up to this point.

18. Which choice makes the sentence most grammatically acceptable?

F. **No Change**
G. cat's verbal expressions
H. cats' verbal expressions
J. cats verbal expressions,

19. Which choice best avoids wordiness and redundancy in context?

A. **No Change**
B. logical and well-reasoned
C. logical to a startling degree
D. logical

GO ON TO THE NEXT PAGE.

Since cats learned to meow for the sole purpose of communicating with humans, owners should learn what different meows mean. If an owner knows which meow means the cat is hungry, which means the cat wants to be petted, and which means the cat wants to have a little "conversation," the bond between cat and owner will grow deeper. After all, your cat isn't just meowing for the sake of making noise; however, cats are less communicative than many other animals.
                        20

20. Which choice would best summarize the main point the essay makes about cats' communication with their human owners?

   F. **No Change**
   G. rather, there's a good chance your cat is trying to tell you something.
   H. instead, your cat is probably trying to communicate with other cats by meowing.
   J. on the other hand, it is better to have more than one cat so they can undergo a natural development.

PASSAGE IV

Visiting Mackinac Island

Visiting Mackinac (pronounced "Mackinaw") Island is like taking a step back to the past in time. Victorian houses and a fort
                        21
dating back to the War of 1812 surround the historic downtown, where horses and buggies still pull passengers down the road.

21. Which choice best avoids wordiness and redundancy in context?

   A. **No Change**
   B. moving in a past-related direction
   C. going back to the past, not the future,
   D. stepping back

The only ways to get to Mackinac Island are by boat or
                        22
private plane, and you may not bring your car. Automobiles are

22. Which choice most effectively maintains the essay's tone?

   F. **No Change**
   G. your sweet self over to
   H. yourself on down to
   J. over to

outlawed on the little, isolated, Michigan, island, so visitors can
                        23
see the sights only by horse, carriage, or

23. Which choice makes the sentence most grammatically acceptable?

   A. **No Change**
   B. isolated Michigan island
   C. isolated Michigan island,
   D. isolated, Michigan, island

GO ON TO THE NEXT PAGE.

by riding a bicycle—or on foot. Luckily, the island is small
_____
     24
enough that cars are not

necessary, Mackinac measures only a mile and a half in
_____
     25
diameter.

     There are many things to see while visiting Mackinac Island.
The majestic Grand Hotel is a popular tourist spot, as are the
governor's mansion and Arch Rock, a towering limestone arch
formed naturally by water erosion. 26 Fort Mackinac, where
cannons are still set off every hour, is also a popular place to
visit. Visible from parts of the island are Mackinac Bridge—the
longest suspension bridge ever built—and a picturesque old
lighthouse.

     Shopping is also a favorite pastime on Mackinac Island.
The island's biggest industry is tourism, so there are many
                                                     27
souvenir stores, T-shirt shops, and candy and ice cream parlors.
                                            27
For the island's many tourists, the most popular item for sale on
Mackinac Island is fudge. The downtown streets are lined with
fudge shops, where tourists can watch fudge of all different
flavors being made before buying some for themselves. These

fudge shops are so numerous and abundant that the local
                                  28
residents call the tourists "fudgies."

     Apart from sightseeing and shopping, Mackinac Island is a
great place to just sit back and relax. In the summer, the gentle
lake breeze creates a beautiful, temperate climate. It is peaceful
to sit in the park and watch the boats float into the harbor. The

24. Which choice makes the sentence most grammatically
    acceptable?

    F. **No Change**
    G. by bicycle
    H. riding on a bicycle
    J. bicycle

25. Which choice makes the sentence or sentences most
    grammatically acceptable?

    A. **No Change**
    B. necessary, furthermore, Mackinac
    C. necessary. Mackinac
    D. necessary Mackinac

26. If the writer were to delete the phrase "formed naturally by
    water erosion" (placing a period after the word *arch*), this
    sentence would primarily lose:

    F. a detail describing the particular formation of the Arch
    Rock.
    G. factual information concerning the geological formations
    of the tourist attractions on Mackinac Island.
    H. a contrast to the governor's mansion, which was con-
    structed by human hands.
    J. nothing; this information is detailed elsewhere in this
    paragraph.

27. Given that all the following are true, which one provides the
    most effective transition to the topic discussed in the sentence
    that follows?

    A. **No Change**
    B. so Mackinac Island has not been negatively affected by
    outsourcing.
    C. which is a big change from the island's eighteenth-century
    use in the fur trade.
    D. but it's not a tourist attraction like many others with theme
    parks and chain restaurants.

28. Which choice is least redundant in context?

    F. **No Change**
    G. abundantly numerous
    H. numerous
    J. of an abundance truly numerous

GO ON TO THE NEXT PAGE.

privacy of the island's environs certainly <u>don't give</u> it the
                                              29
hustle-bustle quality of a city, but the relaxing atmosphere makes

Mackinac Island the perfect place to get away from the hectic

pace of everyday life.

29. Which choice makes the sentence most grammatically acceptable?

   A. **No Change**
   B. aren't giving
   C. weren't giving
   D. doesn't give

Question 30 asks about the preceding passage as a whole.

---

30. Suppose the writer had intended to write an essay on the difficulty the residents of Mackinac Island have had prohibiting automobile traffic from the historic island. Would this essay have successfully fulfilled that goal?

   F. Yes, because the automobile has become such an essential part of American tourist travel that the residents are clearly threatened.
   G. Yes, because this essay discusses the fact that automobiles are outlawed and goes on to detail many of the reasons this was possible.
   H. No, because the essay focuses instead on other aspects of Mackinac Island, mentioning automobiles in only one part of the passage.
   J. No, because this essay describes the ways the residents of Mackinac Island have sought to bring automobiles back to the island, not to outlaw them.

PASSAGE V

Fun with Karaoke

[1]

[1] Karaoke is one of the most popular forms of

entertainment in the world. [2] What defies understanding,

though, is why so many people insist on getting up on stage in

public, humiliating themselves in front of both their <u>friends; and</u>
                                                          31
peers. [3] Whether practiced at home, in a restaurant, or at a

party, karaoke is a form of

31. Which choice makes the sentence most grammatically acceptable?

   A. **No Change**
   B. friends and
   C. friends, and
   D. friends and,

GO ON TO THE NEXT PAGE.

entertainment that provides people with a great time. [4] It is understandable that people would enjoy singing in the privacy of their homes. [5] There are many

different ways to respond to this question. ☐33

[2]

Look more closely, and you'll see that a main reason for karaoke's success is its glamor. Karaoke lets people be more than just everyday folks—they are stars. Even though their performances may be heard only in dimly lit bars or busy restaurants, but karaoke singers are still performing with such concert-hall staples as microphones, lights, and applause. Although the singers' voices are not spectacular, the

audience has known that it's all for fun and responds anyway.

Karaoke is as close as many people will get to fame and stardom, but this is not the only reason for its enduring popularity.

32. Which of the following alternatives to the underlined portion would not be acceptable?

F. entertainment that can provide
G. entertainment, providing
H. entertainment, one which provides
J. entertainment that having provided

33. For the sake of logic and coherence, Sentence 2 should be placed:

A. where it is now.
B. after Sentence 3.
C. after Sentence 4.
D. after Sentence 5.

34. Which choice makes the sentence most grammatically acceptable?

F. **No Change**
G. restaurants which
H. restaurants,
J. restaurants but

35. Which choice makes the sentence most grammatically acceptable?

A. **No Change**
B. is knowing
C. knew
D. knows

36. Given that all the choices are true, which one would most effectively conclude this paragraph while leading into the main focus of the next paragraph?

F. **No Change**
G. This is why AudioSynTrac and Numark Electronics were so successful in debuting the first sing-along tapes and equipment back in the 1970s.
H. Japan's lasting influence on karaoke is obvious all the way down to its name—the Japanese word karaoke translates roughly to "empty orchestra."
J. Singing in front of an audience is, for many people, more fun than singing in the shower or in the car.

GO ON TO THE NEXT PAGE.

[3]

There is another reason singing in public is such fun. The average person's singing is heard only in the shower or in the car. Karaoke, by contrast, allows the average person the opportunity to share that ordinarily solitary experience with other people. Regardless of how good or bad their voices are,

people can experience the joy of music with others, whose singing is mostly a private affair as well, through karaoke.

[4]

The effect karaoke has on people may also provide an explanation for its popularity: it helps bring people who are ordinarily shy out of their shells. 39 Karaoke helps them build their self-confidence and conquer their fears. The singers may feel nervous or silly at first, but when the audience breaks out into applause, singers feel rewarded.

[5]

Whatever the reason, karaoke continues to grow in popularity. Many dismiss it as a fad, but as long as karaoke is fun and leaves people feeling good, it will not disappear.

37. Which transition word or phrase is most logical in context?

A. **No Change**
B. furthermore,
C. moreover,
D. as a result,

38. Which choice makes the sentence most grammatically acceptable?

F. **No Change**
G. who
H. whom
J. who's

39. If the writer were to delete the clause "who are ordinarily shy" from the preceding sentence, the essay would primarily lose:

A. a detail that demonstrates why karaoke is so popular in the international community.
B. a detail meant to explain why karaoke is popular among those not normally inclined to sing in public.
C. information that emphasizes the possible psychological benefits of karaoke for the chronically shy.
D. an indication that karaoke may be used at some future time to help singers overcome stage fright.

Question 40 asks about the preceding passage as a whole.

---

40. Upon reviewing notes for this essay, the writer comes across some information and composes the following sentence incorporating that information:

While different regions of the United States prefer different artists, the most popular karaoke requests are invariably for country artists, from the modern Luke Combs to the classic Dolly Parton.

For the sake of the logic and coherence of this essay, this sentence should be:

F. placed at the end of Paragraph 3.
G. placed at the end of Paragraph 4.
H. placed at the end of Paragraph 5.
J. not added to the essay at all.

GO ON TO THE NEXT PAGE.

PASSAGE VI

Do Blue Bags Make a Green City?

In 1995, Chicago implemented its Blue Bag recycling program. Residents would place their recycling in blue garbage bags. These bags would be picked up by the normal garbage collectors, and the blue bags would be rerouted to recycling facilities. This program was still going strong when I moved to Chicago, but a study showed that <u>as few as</u> 9% of the city's
41
waste was being recycled.

[1] What was wrong <u>for</u> this program? [2] Chicago is not
42
overwhelmed by landfill issues, so many people didn't think diverting waste was important. [3] Then there were the actual

mechanics of <u>running</u> the program. [4] The biggest problem was
43
probably residents' lack of interest. [5] These turned out to be much more complicated than expected. [6] Imagine, for example, the magnitude of labor power and financial investment that was required to pull these bags out of tons of garbage! [7] What happens to all the bags that rip in transit, with recyclables then mixed in with other garbage? [44]

In May 2008, the city decided to discontinue its Blue Bag program and replace it with a new <u>one the</u> Blue *Bin* program.
45
Many of us hoped that this program could right the wrongs of the last program and make Chicago the truly green city we knew it could be.

41. Which choice makes the sentence most grammatically acceptable?

A. **No Change**
B. as little as
C. no less then
D fewer than

42. Which choice is clearest and most grammatically acceptable in context?

F. **No Change**
G. to
H. with
J. from

43. Which choice is clearest and most precise in context?

A. **No Change**
B. chasing
C. hiring
D. performing

44. For the sake of the logic and coherence of this paragraph, Sentence 4 should be placed:

F. where it is now.
G. after Sentence 1.
H. after Sentence 5.
J. after Sentence 7.

45. Which choice makes the sentence most grammatically acceptable?

A. **No Change**
B. one:
C. one;
D. one, and

GO ON TO THE NEXT PAGE.

PASSAGE VII

Thrill Seekers Wanted

My father is a businessman by day and a thrill-seeking adrenaline fanatic by night. I have been lucky to be his sidekick on many an adventure. We started out small by conquering America's fastest roller coasters. Most recently, we attempted "canyoning," <u>because of which</u> was our most exhilarating

46

adventure yet! It began with a 90-foot rappel down a canyon wall into a rushing, ice-cold river. Intrepidly, we traversed the bone-chilling water toward the mouth of the river, to a panoramic view of the basin.

We had to navigate both the flowing river and the canyon <u>walls we became amphibious</u>, moving seamlessly between land

47

and water. We slid over slick rocks at one moment, leapt from waterfalls and swam through underwater tunnels the next.

Certainly, danger from possible <u>miscalculations were lurking in</u>

48

each of these activities, but that very danger provided the rush.

Canyoning was one thrill after another, <u>from beginning to end.</u>

49

While canyoning is possible only in certain locales, adventure can be found anywhere. We continue to seek the big thrills, but we have learned to enjoy lesser forms of excitement in daily life as well. After all, we can't go canyoning every day, <u>and small thrills are better than none for us thrill seekers.</u>

50

46. Which choice makes the sentence most grammatically acceptable?

- **F.** **No Change**
- **G.** and which
- **H.** which
- **J.** in which

47. Which choice makes the sentence most grammatically acceptable?

- **A.** **No Change**
- **B.** walls,
- **C.** walls so
- **D.** walls, so

48. Which choice makes the sentence most grammatically acceptable?

- **F.** **No Change**
- **G.** miscalculations will be
- **H.** miscalculations was
- **D.** miscalculations

49. Given that all the choices are true, which one best clarifies the distinction between the two types of activities mentioned in this paragraph?

- **A.** **No Change**
- **B.** both on rocky surfaces and in the chilly water.
- **C.** adventure after adventure.
- **D.** long after the waterfalls.

50. Given that all the choices are true, which one concludes the paragraph with a phrase that relates to the main topic of the essay?

- **F.** **No Change**
- **G.** and that's a shame.
- **H.** because we don't live near any canyons.
- **J.** but it's the last thrill I'll ever need!

END OF TEST 1
STOP! DO NOT TURN THE PAGE UNTIL TOLD TO DO SO.

MATHEMATICS TEST

50 Minutes—45 Questions

DIRECTIONS: Solve each problem, choose the correct answer, and then fill in the corresponding oval on your answer sheet.

Do not linger over problems that take too much time. Solve as many as you can; then return to the others in the time you have left for this test.

You are permitted to use a calculator on this test. You may use your calculator for any problems you choose,

but some of the problems may best be done without using a calculator.

Note: Unless otherwise stated, all of the following should be assumed:

1. Illustrative figures are **not** necessarily drawn to scale.
2. Geometric figures lie in a plane.
3. The word "line" indicates a straight line.
4. The word "average" indicates arithmetic mean.

DO YOUR FIGURING HERE.

1. If $\dfrac{5y-1}{3} = -6$, then which of the following must be true?

   A. $y = -18$

   B. $y = -\dfrac{19}{5}$

   C. $y = -\dfrac{17}{5}$

   D. $y = -1$

2. The expression $\dfrac{12z^{10}}{4z^{2}}$ is equivalent to:

   F. $3z^{5}$
   G. $8z^{5}$
   H. $3z^{8}$
   J. $8z^{12}$

3. If $f(x) = \dfrac{x^{2}-18}{x+2}$, then $f(12) = ?$

   A. -4
   B. 3
   C. 9
   D. 126

GO ON TO THE NEXT PAGE.

4. In one month, Rebecca, an entertainment journalist, recorded how many movies she watched and how many articles she wrote. She plotted this data in the graphs shown: Graph 1 shows the relationship between the time elapsed and the number of movies watched; Graph 2 shows the relationship between the number of movies watched and the number of articles written. According to this data, how many articles did she write in the first 3 weeks of this month?

DO YOUR FIGURING HERE.

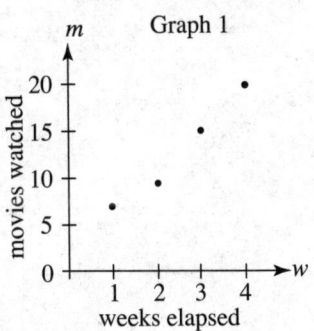
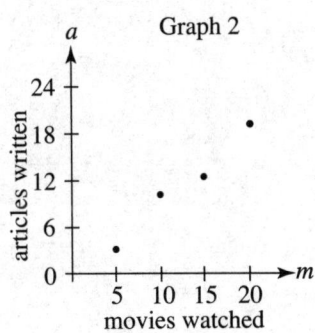

F. 5
G. 8
H. 12
J. 15

5. A restaurant has 4 napkins at each table, plus 20 extra napkins held in reserve. If the restaurant has a total of 100 napkins, how many tables are in the restaurant?

A. 15
B. 20
C. 25
D. 30

6. Six points (U, V, W, X, Y, Z) appear on a number line in that order, as shown in the figure. Which of the following rays does **not** contain WX?

U V W X Y Z

F. $\overrightarrow{UY}$
G. $\overrightarrow{VZ}$
H. $\overrightarrow{YV}$
J. $\overrightarrow{YZ}$

GO ON TO THE NEXT PAGE.

7. If $ab = 32$, $bc = 40$, and $c = 5$, then which of the following is the value of a?

   A. 4
   B. 6
   C. 8
   D. 10

DO YOUR FIGURING HERE.

8. Yunyun swam 4 laps, and her coach recorded her time for each as 43.4 seconds, 44.1 seconds, 42.9 seconds, and 45.4 seconds, for a total of 175.8 seconds. If Yunyun must swim her 5th lap in x seconds in order to make her average time for all 5 laps 43 seconds, then which of the following equations could be solved for the correct value of x?

   F. $\dfrac{175.8 + x}{5} = \dfrac{43}{60}$

   G. $\dfrac{175.8 + x}{5} = 43$

   H. $\dfrac{175.8 + x}{4} = 43$

   J. $\dfrac{175.8}{5} + x = 43$

9. For how many integers from 123 through 132 is the tens digit greater than the ones digit?

   A. 2
   B. 3
   C. 9
   D. 10

10. The number of points Julie scores in a basketball game is proportional to the amount of time she practiced that week. Last week, Julie scored 20 points after practicing for 12 hours. How many hours should Julie practice this week if she wants to score 35 points?

   F. 7
   G. 14
   H. 16
   J. 21

GO ON TO THE NEXT PAGE

11. Rectangle *ABCD* is graphed in the (*x*,*y*) coordinate plane shown. What fraction of rectangle *ABCD* lies in Quadrant IV?

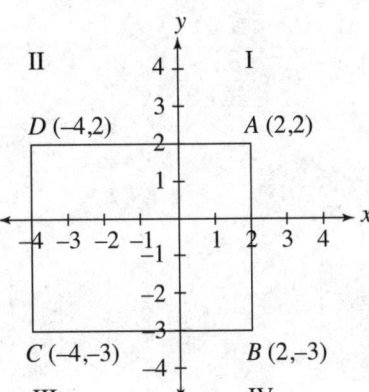

DO YOUR FIGURING HERE.

A. $\dfrac{2}{15}$

B. $\dfrac{1}{5}$

C. $\dfrac{4}{15}$

D. $\dfrac{2}{5}$

12. Which of the following is equivalent to the expression $\dfrac{2(z+3)-9}{5+4(z+3)}$?

F. $-\dfrac{9}{10}$

G. $-\dfrac{7}{9}$

H. $\dfrac{-7z-21}{9z+15}$

J. $\dfrac{2z-3}{4z+17}$

13. A circle with the equation $x^2 + y^2 = 49$ is graphed in the standard (*x*,*y*) coordinate plane. At which 2 points does this circle intersect the *x*-axis?

A. (–1,0) and (1,0)

B. (–7,0) and (7,0)

C. (–14,0) and (14,0)

D. (–49,0) and (49,0)

GO ON TO THE NEXT PAGE.

14. For a decorating project, Beatrice found the area and perimeter of a drawing she made of a beach scene. She found that the area of her rectangular drawing was 144 square inches and that the perimeter was 80 inches. When she arrived at the craft store to purchase a frame for her drawing, she discovered that she had forgotten to write down the dimensions of her drawing. What are the dimensions of Beatrice's drawing in inches?

F. 4 by 36
G. 6 by 24
H. 8 by 18
J. 9 by 16

DO YOUR FIGURING HERE.

15. Which of the following is equivalent to $\dfrac{6.0 \times 10^5}{1.5 \times 10^7}$?

A. 4.0×10^2
B. 4.0×10^{-2}
C. 4.5×10^{12}
D. 4.5×10^{-2}

16. All 7-digit phone numbers at a university start with the same 3-digit prefix. How many phone numbers can be generated for the university before a new prefix must be used?

F. 10^7
G. 7^{10}
H. 9^4
J. 10^4

17. The degree measures of the 4 angles of quadrilateral *LMNO*, not shown, form a geometric sequence with a common ratio of 2. What is the last term of the sequence?

A. $96°$
B. $160°$
C. $192°$
D. $216°$

GO ON TO THE NEXT PAGE.

18. If $6x + 10y = 14$ and $3x + 4y = 2$, then what is the value of $5x + 7y$?

    F. 5
    G. 2
    H. −7
    J. −12

19. Which of the following correctly solves the equation $\dfrac{a-b}{2} = 6$ for any b?

    A. $b = 12 - a$
    B. $b = 13 - a$
    C. $b = a - 3$
    D. $b = a - 12$

20. The product of which of the following results in a negative odd number?

    F. A positive even number and a negative even number
    G. Two negative odd numbers
    H. A positive even number and a negative odd number
    J. A positive odd number and a negative odd number

21. A bag contains 11 purple marbles, 11 yellow marbles, 11 red marbles, and 11 black marbles. John begins removing marbles at random from the bag, and the first 4 marbles removed are all purple. What is the probability that the fifth marble removed will also be purple?

    A. $\dfrac{7}{44}$

    B. $\dfrac{7}{40}$

    C. $\dfrac{5}{11}$

    D. $\dfrac{7}{11}$

DO YOUR FIGURING HERE.

GO ON TO THE NEXT PAGE.

22. A student in Miss Ruane's class must repeat a test if that student earns less than 70% of the points available on that test. There were 30 points available on the first test of this semester. If Oliver scored p points on this test and therefore must repeat it, then which of the following must be true?

F. $p < 20$
G. $p > 20$
H. $p < 21$
J. $p > 21$

DO YOUR FIGURING HERE.

23. The owners of the Movie Palace use the *Illuminator 100* light bulb in their projectors, but are now considering switching to the *Illuminator 100 Plus*, a more powerful light bulb that projects movies onto larger screens farther away. The *Illuminator 100 Plus* projects movies onto screens 108 feet wide and 180 feet from the projector, while the *Illuminator 100* projects movies onto screens only 81 feet wide, as shown in the figure. How much farther from the projector, in feet, is the screen for the *Illuminator 100 Plus* than the screen for the *Illuminator 100*?

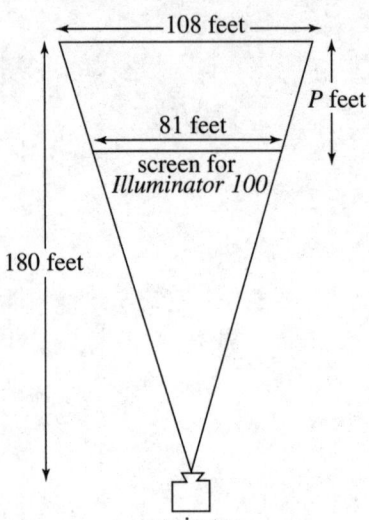

A. 27
B. 40
C. 45
D. 50

24. What is the distance, in coordinate units, between points $J(-5,4)$ and $K(6,-2)$ in the standard (x,y) coordinate plane?

F. $\sqrt{15}$
G. $\sqrt{17}$
H. $\sqrt{157}$
J. 17

GO ON TO THE NEXT PAGE

DO YOUR FIGURING HERE.

25. Cynthia decorates the ceiling of her bedroom with stars that glow in the dark. She puts 1 star on the ceiling on the 1st day of decorating, 2 stars on the ceiling on the 2nd day of decorating, 3 stars on the 3rd day, and so on. If she puts stars on the ceiling in this pattern for 30 days (so she puts 30 stars on the ceiling on the 30th day), then what will be the total number of stars on the ceiling at the end of the 30 days?

    A. 435
    B. 450
    C. 465
    D. 480

26. In $\triangle PQR$, side $\overline{PQ}$ is 12 inches long and side $\overline{QR}$ is 41 inches long. Which of the following **cannot** be the length, in inches, of side $\overline{PR}$?

    F. 17
    G. 30
    H. 38
    J. 52

27. Points G and H lie on circle F as shown. If the measure of $\angle FGH$ is 40°, then what is the measure of central angle $\angle GFH$?

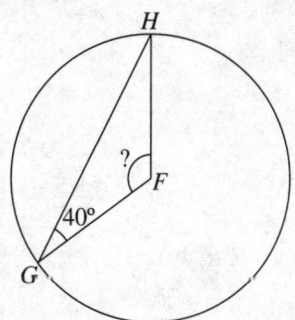

    A. 60°
    B. 80°
    C. 100°
    D. 120°

GO ON TO THE NEXT PAGE.

28. The pie chart shown shows the operating expenses of Stephanie's office for the month of July, during which time the expenses totaled $10,000.

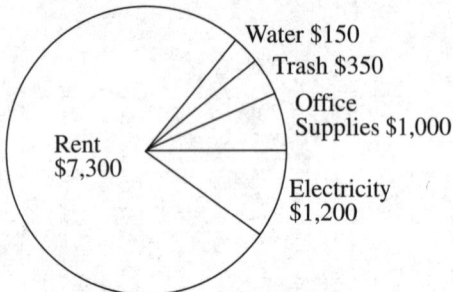

Water $150
Trash $350
Office Supplies $1,000
Rent $7,300
Electricity $1,200

Stephanie tries to reduce her operating expenses for August by making her office more energy efficient and asking her landlord to lower her rent. She hopes to reduce her electricity expenses by $700 and her rent by $1,300. If she is successful in both of these goals and the rest of her expenses are unchanged, then what percent of her August expenses will be for office supplies?

F. 5.0%
G. 7.5%
H. 12.5%
J. 15.0%

29. Assuming q is a positive integer, then the difference between $14q$ and $5q$ is always divisible by:

A. 5
B. 9
C. 14
D. 70

30. Ron earns $1,800 for a 6-week assignment. While working a 6-week assignment, Ron works a minimum of 20 hours each week. Ron's hourly rate of pay, therefore, depends upon how many hours he works. If r is Ron's average hourly pay, in dollars, for a 6-week assignment, then which of the following best describes r?

F. $r \le$ $15.00
G. $r \ge$ $15.00
H. $r \le$ $90.00
J. $r \ge$ $90.00

GO ON TO THE NEXT PAGE

31. P and Q both represent complex numbers. If $P = 2 + i$ and $Q = 6 + 4i$, what is the distance in coordinate units between P and Q in the complex plane?

A. $\sqrt{5}$
B. $\sqrt{7}$
C. 4
D. 5

DO YOUR FIGURING HERE.

32. Two wires connect the top of a flagpole to the ground, as shown. Each wire has a length of 23 feet and attaches to the ground at a point 8 feet from the flagpole. Which of the following expressions gives the angle measure, in degrees, of the angle that the wire makes with the ground?

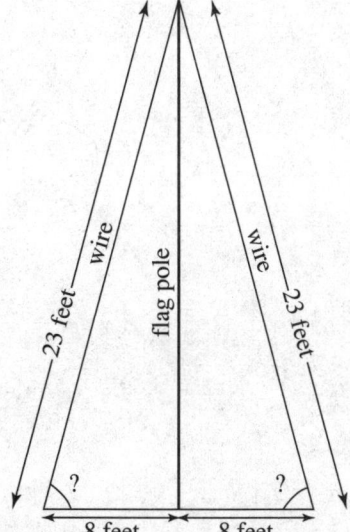

F. $\tan^{-1}\left(\dfrac{23}{8}\right)$

G. $\tan^{-1}\left(\dfrac{8}{23}\right)$

H. $\cos^{-1}\left(\dfrac{8}{23}\right)$

J. $\cos^{-1}\left(\dfrac{23}{8}\right)$

GO ON TO THE NEXT PAGE.

As shown in the figure, ΔXYZ is a right triangle with legs of length x units and y units and hypotenuse of z units, such that $0 < x < y$. Quadrilaterals $ABYX$, $CDZY$, and $EFXZ$ are squares.

DO YOUR FIGURING HERE.

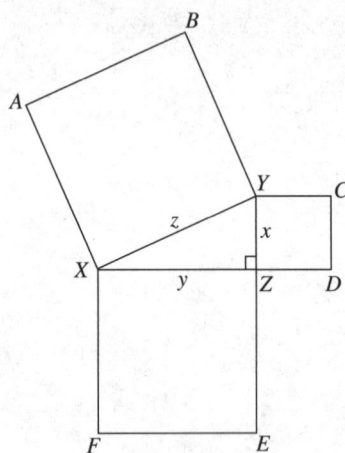

33. What is the perimeter, in units, of polygon $CDZXY$?

   A. $3x + y + z$
   B. $3x + 2y + z$
   C. $4x + y + z$
   D. $4x + 4y + 4z$

34. The sum of 4 consecutive even integers is t. What is the sum, in terms of t, of the 2 largest of these integers?

   F. $\dfrac{t}{2} - 4$

   G. $\dfrac{t}{2} + 4$

   H. $t + 2$

   J. $t + 4$

GO ON TO THE NEXT PAGE.

35. Figure 1 shows the graph of $y = x^2$ in the standard (x,y) coordinate plane. Which of the following is the equation for the graph in Figure 2?

DO YOUR FIGURING HERE.

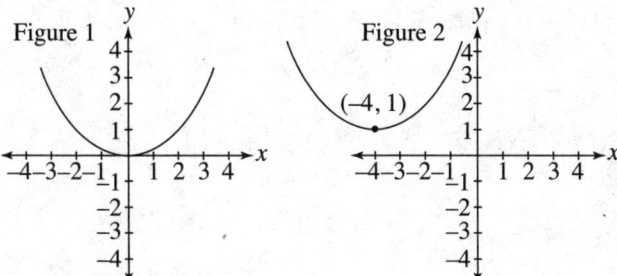

A. $y = (x - 4)^2 - 1$

B. $y = (x - 4)^2 + 1$

C. $y = (x + 4)^2 - 1$

D. $y = (x + 4)^2 + 1$

36. In a piggy bank, there are pennies, nickels, dimes, and quarters that total $5.29 in value. If there are 3 times as many dimes as there are pennies, 1 more dime than nickels, and 2 more quarters than dimes, then how many nickels are in the piggy bank?

F. 11

G. 13

H. 17

J. 21

37. The mean of 5 numbers is 87. The smallest of the 5 numbers is 75. What is the mean of the other 4 numbers?

A. 72

B. $88\dfrac{2}{5}$

C. 90

D. $108\dfrac{3}{4}$

38. "If Jenny is home, then her car is in the driveway." If the previous statement is true, then which of the following must also be true?

F. "If Jenny's car is in the driveway, then she is home."

G. "If Jenny is not home, then her car is not in the driveway."

H. "If Jenny's car is not in the driveway, then she is home."

J. "If Jenny's car is not in the driveway, then she is not home."

GO ON TO THE NEXT PAGE.

DO YOUR FIGURING HERE.

39. If $g(x) = \csc x \tan x$, then which of the following trigonometric functions is equivalent to $g(x)$?

(Note: $\csc x = \dfrac{1}{\sin x}$, $\sec x = \dfrac{1}{\cos x}$, and $\cot x = \dfrac{1}{\tan x}$)

  A. $g(x) = \sin x$

  B. $g(x) = \cos x$

  C. $g(x) = \csc x$

  D. $g(x) = \sec x$

40. Evan and Ron play a game of Rock, Paper, Scissors. Each round has three equally likely outcomes for Evan: win, lose, or tie. Evan earns 2 points for a win, but he earns nothing for a loss or a tie. Let the random variable N represent the total number of points he has after 5 rounds. What is the expected value of N?

  F. $\dfrac{5}{3}$

  G. 3

  H. $\dfrac{10}{3}$

  J. 5

41. If the volume of a sphere is 288π cubic inches, then which of the following is the surface area, in square inches, of the same sphere?

(Note: For a sphere with radius r, the volume is $\dfrac{4}{3}\pi r^3$ and the surface area is $4\pi r^2$.)

  A. 6π

  B. 24π

  C. 36π

  D. 144π

42. When $x > 1$, $3\log_x x^{-2} = ?$

  F. -6

  G. $-\dfrac{2}{3}$

  H. 1

  J. $\dfrac{3}{2}$

GO ON TO THE NEXT PAGE

43. An angle with vertex at the origin and measure θ is shown in the standard (*x*,*y*) coordinate plane. If one side of the angle includes the positive *x*-axis and the other side passes through (−12,−5), then what is the sine of θ?

DO YOUR FIGURING HERE.

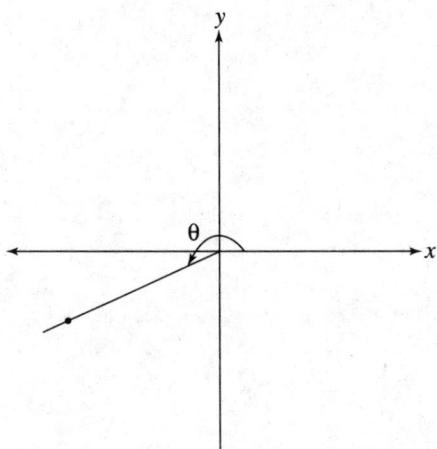

A. $-\dfrac{12}{13}$

B. $-\dfrac{5}{13}$

C. $\dfrac{5}{12}$

D. $\dfrac{13}{12}$

44. Side $\overline{AB}$ of parallelogram *ABCD* is shown in the figure. If the coordinates of *A* are (7,6) and those of *B* are (5,1), then $\overline{CD}$ could lie on which of the following lines?

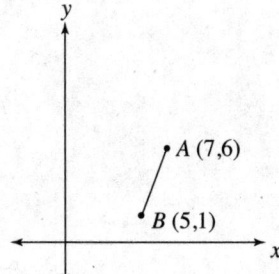

F. $y = \dfrac{5}{2}x + 9$

G. $y = \dfrac{2}{5}x - 4$

H. $y = -\dfrac{2}{5}x + 4$

J. $y = -\dfrac{5}{2}x - 9$

GO ON TO THE NEXT PAGE.

45. If the function $f(x,y)$ is defined as $f(x,y) = (x - y)^2 + (x + y)^2$, then, for all values of c and d, $f(c^2, d^2) = ?$

    A. $4c^2d^2$

    B. $2c^4 + 2d^4$

    C. $2c^4 - 2d^4$
    D. $-4c^2d^2$

DO YOUR FIGURING HERE.

END OF TEST 2

STOP! DO NOT TURN THE PAGE UNTIL TOLD TO DO SO.

DO NOT RETURN TO A PREVIOUS TEST.

THIS PAGE INTENTIONALLY LEFT BLANK

READING TEST

40 Minutes—36 Questions

DIRECTIONS: There are several passages in this test. Each passage is accompanied by several questions. After reading a passage, choose the best answer to each question and fill in the corresponding oval on your answer document. You may refer to the passages as often as necessary.

Passage I

LITERARY NARRATIVE: Passage A is adapted from the essay "What Baseball Taught Us" by Richard Brown (©2007 by Richard Brown). Passage B is adapted from the essay "The Major Leagues" by Jack Bryant (©1998 by Jack Bryant).

Passage A by Richard Brown

April 15, 1947: I happen to be home sick from school, and my grandfather is delighted to have someone to share his anticipation with. He's been pacing the house all morning, occasionally sitting down but quickly hopping back up, adjusting the TV
5 antennas, cleaning his glasses, flicking an imaginary piece of lint off the television screen. Amidst my mother's protestations, I am brought out of my stuffy, dark bedroom where I have been confined to fight my fever and propped up on the sofa with four quilts over me, at least three more than I really need. Fever or
10 no, my grandfather wants me to witness history.

Jackie Robinson is making his major league debut for the Brooklyn Dodgers, the first African American player in the Major League Baseball. I'm not sure what's more stifling, the quilts, or my grandfather's tense excitement that has us all on edge. I'm
15 proud that Robinson is playing—there's been a long build-up to this day, and he has taken people's prejudice and abuse like a gentleman, never losing his cool. I know he'll do the same today. I wonder, through my fever and quilts, just what my grandfather thinks will happen.

20 We were not Dodgers fans before Jackie Robinson. Our team was the Memphis Red Sox, in the Negro League. But now we are watching the small, jerky figures take the field hundreds of miles away in Brooklyn. At first base, number 42, is a black man. My grandfather has finally settled down, staring at the tele-
25 vision in disbelief. My mother has tears in her eyes. The Braves are at bat, and Robinson gets the first man out, on a ground ball thrown from third. The crowd cheers. In the bottom of the first inning, he grounds out. I let out a loud groan. My grandfather turns to look at me, his eyes ablaze. He quietly tells my mother
30 to take me back to bed.

Later, I try to apologize to my grandfather, and I blame my outburst on the fever. It's partly true—I needed to break the tension, which I probably felt more keenly because of my illness, but he doesn't buy it. *He needs our support, son. Take a cue from*
35 *the way he's stood up to his critics, and stand up for him. What matters is how he plays the whole game, not an occasional out.* I realize then that I had been nervous, too. I had expected the impossible—I had wanted him to bat a thousand.

Passage B by Jack Bryant

Opening Day, 1947—some friends and I cut school and in-
40 stead made our way to Ebbets Field to see Jackie Robinson make his major league debut. We hadn't expected to get in; everyone thought the game would be sold out, with crowds overflowing into the streets near the stadium. We just wanted to be part of that crowd. We had been saving up money, just in case, and it paid
45 off. The game was not sold out, and we got in. I hadn't been to a major league game before, and inside the stadium I felt I was in some utopian society that existed without segregation and racism. The crowd, which was more than half black, cheered as Jackie made the first out of the game at first base. Though
50 he didn't get a hit in the game, he scored a run after drawing a walk, and got eleven put-outs at first base.

My friends and I were flying high as we left the stadium. If a black man was now playing for the Brooklyn Dodgers, we felt there was nothing we couldn't do. Later that same season,
55 Larry Doby signed with the Cleveland Indians to become the first African American player in the American league. Change, we thought, was rapidly coming. To a certain extent that was true, but racism and injustice also persisted. Other teams treated Jackie badly, calling him names, threatening to strike if he played, and
60 handling him roughly. When the Dodgers were on the road, he often was not allowed to stay at the hotels where the rest of the team stayed. These injustices weren't new, but somehow I had thought they would go away when he took the field, that when Branch Rickey had offered him a contract, he was extending
65 an olive branch to all African Americans on behalf of white Americans.

GO ON TO THE NEXT PAGE.

Twenty-one years later, I remembered that day as I grieved the death of Dr. Martin Luther King, Jr., a victim of the struggle for racial equality that was ongoing. I had been so young, and so hopeful, and so hopelessly naïve. At times it felt like nothing
70 had been accomplished in those 21 years. But that isn't entirely true. In baseball, getting a hit three out of every ten at bats is considered a good record. While I wish the struggle for equality were more like golf, in which the professionals hit the ball every
75 time, we have come a long way since that day in 1947. But the season is 162 games long, and we are only part way through it.

1. The last paragraph of Passage A (lines 31–38) marks a shift in the passage from:

A. the time when baseball was segregated to after African Americans started playing in the major leagues.

B. the narrator seeing things through a fever-induced delirium to his understanding of how he had misinterpreted events.

C. a description of the experience of a historical moment to a lesson learned from that moment.

D. the narrator's grandfather's happy anticipation of an event to his anger at how the event unfolded.

2. In Passage A, the narrator's descriptions of Jackie Robinson suggest that he sees him as ultimately:

F. a gentleman and a hero.

G. capable of doing the impossible.

H. a disappointing player.

J. overly excited and tense.

3. The narrator's statement "inside the stadium I felt I was in some utopian society that existed without segregation and racism" (lines 46–48) is most nearly meant to:

A. describe the way people interact with each other inside a baseball stadium.

B. express the narrator's feelings of the momentousness of the occasion.

C. illustrate the way that Jackie Robinson changed society by playing in the major leagues.

D. foreshadow the way the narrator would feel 21 years later.

4. Passage B indicates that compared to the narrator's expectation about how Jackie Robinson's appearance in Major League Baseball would affect segregation, its actual effect was:

F. different; the narrator had thought the crowd at the game would be bigger than it was.

G. different; the narrator had thought segregation would quickly disappear.

H. similar; the narrator had thought Robinson was a good choice for the Dodgers.

J. similar; the narrator had thought racism and injustice would last for a long time.

5. Based on the passage, the information about Dr. Martin Luther King, Jr. provided in lines 67–69 is most likely included to:

A. show that not all of the narrator's role models were baseball players.

B. provide historical context for the importance of Jackie Robinson's role in baseball.

C. illustrate how little progress the narrator felt had been made in the struggle for racial equality.

D. convey the idea that Jackie Robinson's influence was felt far beyond the world of sports.

6. The narrator of Passage B makes a comparison between:

F. the struggle for racial equality and the baseball season.

G. professional golf and major league baseball.

H. tense excitement and bed covers.

J. striking out in baseball and experiencing injustice.

7. Which of the following statements provides the most accurate comparison of the tone of each passage?

A. Passage A is hopeful and cheery, while Passage B is dreary and pessimistic.

B. Passage A is objectively factual, while Passage B is descriptive and detailed.

C. Both passages maintain a sense of disappointment throughout.

D. Both passages begin with a sense of optimism and end with a sense that expectations had been too high.

8. Compared to the narrator of Passage A, the narrator of Passage B provides more information about:

F. the play-by-play analysis of Jackie Robinson's first major league game.

G. the long-term effects of Jackie Robinson's appearance in the major leagues.

H. Jackie Robinson's baseball career before signing with the Dodgers.

J. the role of Negro League baseball in the early 20th century.

9. It can reasonably be inferred that after seeing Jackie Robinson play, compared to the narrator of Passage B, the narrator of Passage A felt:

A. less optimistic about how race relations would change.

B. less interested in continuing to follow the Dodgers.

C. more disappointed that he hadn't played better.

D. more excited about the future for African American baseball players.

GO ON TO THE NEXT PAGE.

Passage II

INFORMATIONAL: This passage is adapted from T. H. Watkins' *The Great Depression* (©1993, Little, Brown and Co.; Blackside Inc.).

One of the most durable and well regarded of all the New Deal's programs came from President Roosevelt himself, who had his own share of inventiveness. If the president cared about the fate of people, he also cared about the fate of trees, having
5 practiced the art of silviculture on his Hyde Park estate with such enthusiasm that on various official forms he was fond of listing his occupation as "tree farmer." It was in early March, 1933, that he proceeded to bring the two concerns together—enlisting young unemployed men in a kind of volunteer "army" to be put to
10 work in the national forests, national parks, and on other federal public lands. When he went to Congress for authorization of the program, he called the new agency the Civilian Corps Reforesta-tion Youth Rehabilitation Movement, but before sinking under the weight of an acronym like CCRYRM, it was soon changed
15 to the Civilian Conservation Corps (known forever after as the CCC). Congress chose not to handle the details itself. It simply authorized the president to create the program and structure it as he saw fit by executive order; it was to last two years. Responsi-bility was divided up among the Labor Department, which was
20 to screen and select the enrollees, the War Department, which would house and feed them in their nonworking hours, and the Departments of Agriculture and Interior, which would design and supervise projects in regional and national forests, national parks, and other public lands. The men would be paid $30 a
25 month, anywhere from $23 to $25 of it to be sent to their families.

The CCC officially began on April 5, 1933, calling for an enrollment of 250,000 to be housed in 1,468 camps around the country. The cost for the first year was estimated at $500 million. The men had to be US citizens between the ages of seventeen
30 and twenty-seven (later, twenty-four), out of school, out of work, capable of physical labor, over 60 inches but under 78 inches in height, more than 107 pounds in weight, and had to possess no fewer than "three serviceable natural masticating teeth above and below." They would serve terms of no more than nine months
35 so that as many as possible could be accommodated over the course of time.

Among the earliest enrollees were some veterans who had returned to Washington, setting up camp and demanding pay-ment of their bonuses for service during the war. While making
40 it clear that he opposed the payments on economic grounds, FDR provided tents, showers, mess halls, and latrines, and, waiving the age restriction for them, invited the members of this new Bonus Army to join his new agency. What was more, Eleanor Roosevelt dropped by one rainy day for a visit, slogging through
45 ankle-deep mud to meet and talk with the men. "Hoover sent the army," said one veteran of the previous summer's BEF disaster, "Roosevelt sent his wife." When it became clear that no bonus would be forthcoming, about twenty-five hundred of the men took Roosevelt up on his offer and joined the CCC.

50 In the summer of 1934, Roosevelt expanded the size of the CCC to 350,000 and would raise it to 500,000 in 1935. Congress continued to reauthorize it faithfully over the next seven years, and by the time it was closed out in 1942, the CCC had put more than three million young "soil soldiers" to work. In the national
55 forests alone they built 3,470 fire towers, installed 65,100 miles of telephone lines, scraped and graded thousands of fire breaks, roads, and trails, and built 97,000 miles of truck trails and roads, spent 4.1 million man-hours fighting fires, and cut down and hauled out millions of diseased trees and planted more than 1.3
60 billion young trees in the first major reforestation campaign in the country's history. For the National Park Service, they built roads, campgrounds, bridges, and recreation and administration facilities; for the Biological Survey (a predecessor of today's Fish and Wildlife Service), they conducted wildlife surveys
65 and improved wildlife refuge lands; and for the Army Corps of Engineers, they built flood control projects in West Virginia, Vermont, and New York State.

In return, the CCC, at its best, took at least some young men out of the urban tangle of hopelessness where so many resided,
70 introduced them to the intricacies and healing joy of the outdoors, and clothed and fed them better than many had been for years. Moreover, the program taught more than a hundred thousand to read and write, passed out twenty-five thousand eighth-grade di-plomas and five thousand high-school diplomas, gave structure and
75 discipline to lives that had experienced little of either, strengthened bodies and minds, and for many provided a dose of self-esteem they had never known.

GO ON TO THE NEXT PAGE.

10. The main idea of the passage is that:

    F. the CCC forced unemployed young men to work in the national forests, national parks, and on other federal public lands for no payment or bonus.
    G. it was only after President Roosevelt created the CCC that veterans had suitable employment during the Great Depression.
    H. research into the history of the New Deal shows that the idea for the CCC came from Congress.
    J. among the programs of the New Deal, the CCC employed young men to build public works projects on public lands in return for modest wages, food, clothing, and some education.

11. The main idea of the third paragraph (lines 37–49) is that:

    A. President Hoover had dispatched the army to meet with disgruntled veterans, but President Roosevelt sent his wife, Eleanor, to meet with the Bonus Army.
    B. when they realized President Roosevelt would not pay the bonus, many veterans abandoned the Bonus Army and accepted his invitation to join the CCC.
    C. President Roosevelt supplied shelter and food to the veterans before paying the bonus the veterans demanded.
    D. many of the veterans were above the age requirement of the CCC.

12. As it is used in line 7 to describe President Roosevelt, the term *tree farmer* most nearly means that Roosevelt:

    F. had supported his family by growing trees before he entered politics.
    G. believed in an agrarian economy over urban industrialization.
    H. continued his successful business selling trees while in office.
    J. had a great interest in trees and knew a good deal about them.

13. According to the passage, which of the following was a project the CCC performed for the National Park Service?

    A. Building fire towers
    B. Building campground facilities
    C. Installing telephone lines
    D. Conducting wildlife surveys

14. According to the passage, which of the following statements is true about the CCC?

    F. The agency provided enrollees with academic instruction.
    G. The agency provided enrollees with urban job training.
    H. The agency accepted only men with six teeth.
    J. The agency offered courses in nutrition and self-esteem.

15. Information in the fourth paragraph (lines 50–67) makes it clear that the CCC:

    A. was voluntary and therefore did not pay members anything.
    B. ran for more years and employed more men than was originally intended.
    C. employed 4.1 million men.
    D. battled fires in West Virginia, Vermont, and New York.

16. The passage most strongly suggests that before the 1930s, the national forests:

    F. received no federal support or aid for projects to clear diseased trees.
    G. included land reserved for wildlife refuges.
    H. had never undergone a major reforestation campaign.
    J. experienced more floods than forest fires.

17. According to the passage, when did the CCC change its name?

    A. After President Roosevelt received authorization from Congress
    B. After Congress protested that CCRYRM was too difficult to say
    C. In the same year the size expanded to 500,000 men
    D. After the Bonus Army disbanded

18. The passage states that the same year the CCC was authorized enrollees had to be:

    F. over 78 inches in height.
    G. in school.
    H. between the ages of seventeen and twenty-seven.
    J. between the ages of seventeen and twenty-four.

GO ON TO THE NEXT PAGE.

Passage III

INFORMATIONAL: This passage is adapted from John Gattuso, ed., *Insight Guides: Native America* (©1993, Houghton Mifflin Co., APA Publications).

Northwest natives are carvers by tradition, but it was the natives of the far north, in what is now British Columbia and Alaska, who first carved totem poles. The history of these fascinating works is surprisingly brief, for it wasn't until the mid-18th
5 century, when European explorers first encountered these remote tribes, that the unique sculptures began to appear. Although the natives were already expert carvers of canoes, tools, longhouses, and furniture, they lacked the iron tools necessary to fell a massive tree in one piece and carve its entire length.

10 With the iron axes they got in trade for their baskets, boxes, and pelts, the coastal tribes of the far north could take advantage of the trees that grew so tall and straight in their wet climate. Initially, the poles were made to stand against the front of a house, with figures facing out and a door cut through the base, so all
15 would enter the house through the pole. In this case, the totem pole functioned as a family crest, recounting genealogies, stories, or legends that in some way identified the owner. Towards the end of the 19th century, the poles stood free on the beach or in the village outside the carvers' homes. Some villages were virtual
20 forests of dozens, sometimes hundreds, of poles.

The family that carved the pole gave a potlatch with feasting, games, and much gift-giving. The guests, in return, raised the pole. These gatherings were costly and required a great deal of preparation and participation. The custom frustrated whites
25 trying to "civilize" the Indians, especially missionaries who solved the problem by knocking the poles down. Employers, too, complained that their Indian workers were unreliable when a pole was being carved or a potlatch planned. Eventually, both the Canadian and United States governments banned potlatches,
30 and pole carving nearly died out. The ban was lifted in the 1950s.

The Tlingit, on the southeastern coast of Alaska, and the Haidas and Tsimshian of western Canada are known for their pole carving. On a tour in 1899, a group of Seattle businessmen visited the Tlingit village of Tongas and, finding no one there, took
35 one of the poles. They erected it in Seattle where, at a towering 50 ft., it became one of the city's most distinctive monuments. In 1938, Tlingit carvers copied the pole after the original was destroyed by fire, and it remains in Pioneer Square today.

Poles serve the important purpose of recording the lore of
40 a clan, much as a book would. The top figure on the pole identifies the owner's clan, and succeeding characters (read from top to bottom) tell their stories. Raven, the trickster, might tell the story of how he fooled the Creator into giving him the sun, or Frog might tell how he wooed a human woman. With slight
45 variations between villages, everyone knew these stories, and potlatch guests dramatized them at the pole-raising with masks,

drumming, and songs. And so the legends were preserved from one generation to the next.

There is a story behind almost every image on the pole. For
50 example, if an animal had the power to transform itself into other beings, the carver would portray it in all its forms. If Raven were sometimes bird, sometimes human, he would be carved with both wings and limbs, or have a human face with a raven's beak. Other images are used to describe the spirits' special abilities.
55 Eyes are frequently used to suggest acuteness or skill. So, for example, if an eye appears in an animal's ear, it might indicate that that animal has a sharp sense of hearing. And human figures in unexpected places, like an ear or nose, might mean that the animal has great powers.

60 Learning to read totem poles is like learning to read a language. They speak of history, mythology, social structure, and spirituality. They serve many purposes and continue to be carved by the descendants of the original carvers.

Today, Haida, Tlingit, Tsimshian, Kwakiutl and other na-
65 tive craftsmen carve, predominantly for the tourist trade, small "souvenir" totem poles in wood and black slate (or argillite). They also carve extraordinarily beautiful masks, effigies, boxes, house posts, and fixtures….

19. Which of the following statements best expresses the main idea of the passage?

A. Many Native American tribes created totem poles with meaningful symbols, but these poles were less important than the canoes carved before the mid-18th century.

B. Although the Tlingit village was deserted, the Seattle businessmen who took the totem pole were not right to take it without permission.

C. The history of totem pole carving dates back to only the mid-18th century, but these poles have played an important role in Native American culture since that time.

D. The ban issued by the Canadian and United States governments against potlatches was lifted in the 1950s, but interest in totem-pole carving had diminished by that time.

GO ON TO THE NEXT PAGE.

20. Which of the following questions is NOT answered in the passage?

   F. In terms of geographical region, which were the first groups to carve totem poles?

   G. What is the tallest totem pole in North America?

   H. What is the predominant use of the small totem poles carved today?

   J. What prevented Native American tribes from carving totem poles before the 18th century?

21. The passage suggests that one of the main purposes of totem poles is the way in which they:

   A. demonstrate the artistic skill of the carvers.

   B. function as landmarks in major North American cities.

   C. document the history and mythology of various clans.

   D. complement the festivities of the potlatch.

22. The main function of the sixth paragraph (lines 49–59) is to:

   F. identify the origins of the stories behind every image on a totem pole.

   G. describe and explain some of the images that might appear on a totem pole.

   H. contrast the images on the totem poles of the Northwest natives with those of British Columbia and Alaska.

   J. explain the role of the Raven in Native American mythology.

23. The second paragraph (lines 10–20) establishes all of the following about the totem poles carved by the coastal tribes of the far north EXCEPT that they were:

   A. initially used as the entryways of houses.

   B. fashioned from tall, straight trees.

   C. used to identify the owners of the poles.

   D. produced only by clans with family crests.

24. One of the main points of the fifth paragraph (lines 39–48) is that the various characters on a totem pole are meant to represent:

   F. the owner of the totem pole.

   G. the lore of the owner's clan.

   H. Raven, the trickster, fooling the Creator.

   J. Frog wooing a human woman.

25. According to the passage, which of the following places is home to the Tlingit?

   A. Seattle

   B. Western Canada

   C. Pioneer Square

   D. Alaska

26. The author most likely includes the information in lines 60–63 to suggest that:

   F. totem poles are notable for reasons beyond physical beauty.

   G. totem poles have replaced books for Native American tribes.

   H. Native American tribes have no spoken or written language.

   J. the descendants of the original carvers of totem poles carve copies of older poles.

27. Which of the following words best describes the attitude of the employers referred to in the third paragraph (lines 21–30) in reaction to potlatches?

   A. Patient

   B. Accepting

   C. Irritated

   D. Civilized

GO ON TO THE NEXT PAGE.

Passage IV

INFORMATIONAL: This passage is adapted from the article "The Pioneer Mission to Venus" by Janet G. Luhmann, James B. Pollack, and Lawrence Colin (©1994, Scientific American).

Venus is sometimes referred to as the Earth's "twin" because it resembles the Earth in size and in distance from the sun. Over its 14 years of operation, the National Aeronautics and Space Administration's *Pioneer Venus* mission revealed that the relation
5 between the two worlds is more analogous to Dr. Jekyll and Mr. Hyde. The surface of Venus bakes under a dense carbon dioxide atmosphere, the overlying clouds consist of noxious sulfuric acid, and the planet's lack of a magnetic field exposes the upper atmosphere to the continuous hail of charged particles from the
10 sun. Our opportunity to explore the hostile Venusian environment came to an abrupt close in October 1992, when the *Pioneer Venus Orbiter* burned up like a meteor in the thick Venusian atmosphere. The craft's demise marked the end of an era for the U.S. space program; in the present climate of fiscal austerity, there is no
15 telling when humans will next get a good look at Earth's nearest planetary neighbor.

The information gleaned by *Pioneer Venus* complements the well-publicized radar images recently sent back by the *Magellan* spacecraft. *Magellan* concentrated on studies of Venus's surface
20 geology and interior structure. *Pioneer Venus*, in comparison, gathered data on the composition and dynamics of the planet's atmosphere and interplanetary surroundings. These findings illustrate how seemingly small differences in physical conditions have sent Venus and the Earth hurtling down very different evo-
25 lutionary paths. Such knowledge will help scientists intelligently evaluate how human activity may be changing the environment on the Earth.

Well before the arrival of *Pioneer Venus*, astronomers had learned that Venus does not live up to its image as Earth's near-
30 twin. Whereas Earth maintains conditions ideal for liquid water and life, Venus's surface temperature of 450 degrees Celsius is hotter than the melting point of lead. Atmospheric pressure at the ground is some 93 times that at sea level on Earth.

Even aside from the heat and the pressure, the air on Venus
35 would be utterly unbreathable to humans. The Earth's atmosphere is about 78 percent nitrogen and 21 percent oxygen. Venus's much thicker atmosphere, in contrast, is composed almost entirely of carbon dioxide. Nitrogen, the next most abundant gas, makes up only about 3.5 percent of the gas molecules. Both planets
40 possess about the same amount of gaseous nitrogen, but Venus's atmosphere contains some 30,000 times as much carbon dioxide as does Earth's. In fact, Earth does hold a quantity of carbon dioxide comparable to that in the Venusian atmosphere. On Earth, however, the carbon dioxide is locked away in carbonate
45 rocks, not in gaseous form in the air. The crucial distinction is responsible for many of the drastic environmental differences that exist between the two planets.

The large *Pioneer Venus* atmospheric probe carried a mass spectrometer and gas chromatograph, devices that measured the
50 exact composition of the atmosphere of Venus. One of the most stunning aspects of the Venusian atmosphere is that it is extremely dry. It possesses only a hundred thousandth as much water as Earth has in its oceans. If all of Venus's water could somehow be condensed onto the surface, it would make a global puddle
55 only a couple of centimeters deep.

Unlike Earth, Venus harbors little if any molecular oxygen in its lower atmosphere. The abundant oxygen in Earth's atmosphere is a by-product of photosynthesis by plants; if not for the activity of living things, Earth's atmosphere also would be
60 oxygen poor. The atmosphere of Venus is far richer than Earth's in sulfur-containing gases, primarily sulfur dioxide. On Earth, rain efficiently removes similar sulfur gases from the atmosphere.

Pioneer Venus revealed other ways in which Venus is more primordial than Earth. Venus's atmosphere contains higher con-
65 centrations of inert, or noble, gases—especially neon and isotopes of argon—that have been present since the time the planets were born. This difference suggests that Venus has held on to a far greater fraction of its earliest atmosphere. Much of Earth's primitive atmosphere may have been stripped away and lost into space
70 when our world was struck by a Mars-size body. Many planetary scientists now think the moon formed out of the cloud of debris that resulted from such a gigantic impact.

28. With regard to the possibility of returning to the planet Venus, information presented in the passage makes it clear that the authors are:

   F. cheerful and optimistic.
   G. sarcastic and contentious.
   H. doubtful and pragmatic.
   J. uncertain and withdrawn.

GO ON TO THE NEXT PAGE.

29. Which of the following statements most accurately summarizes how the passage characterizes the state of scientific knowledge about Venus before the *Pioneer* mission?

A. The scientific community was hesitant to return to Venus after an earlier mission had ended in disaster.
B. Scientists saw Earth and Venus as near polar opposites in atmospheric conditions.
C. The common belief that Earth and Venus were "twins" had been eroding under the weight of scientific evidence.
D. Scientists knew little about the planet Venus because they were more interested in other planets.

30. Based on the passage, Earth may have retained less of its early atmosphere than Venus did due to:

F. the impact that occurred when Earth was struck by Mars.
G. a cloud of debris that stripped the atmosphere away.
H. rain that removes sulfur gases from the atmosphere.
J. a collision between Earth and another massive object.

31. The main point of the second paragraph (lines 17–27) is to:

A. account for the failure of the *Magellan* mission and to show the superiority of the *Pioneer* mission.
B. suggest that information from both the *Magellan* and *Pioneer* missions can bring the scientific community to a deeper understanding of Venus.
C. show that the *Magellan* had sent back information regarding physical characteristics while the *Pioneer* had not.
D. hypothesize that the findings of the *Pioneer* mission will help scientists to approach problems more intelligently.

32. The passage indicates that if humans were to attempt to live on the planet Venus, survival would not be possible because:

F. of the mistaken belief that Venus and Earth are "twin" planets.
G. carbon dioxide is locked away in bicarbonate rocks, not in gaseous form.
H. the atmospheric pressure, heat, and air are not suitable for human life.
J. all of the water on Venus is condensed onto the surface.

33. According to the passage, some evidence gained before the *Pioneer Venus* mission suggesting that Earth and Venus are not near-twins stated that:

A. Venus produces no lead on or underneath its surface.
B. Earth was found to be much farther from the sun than was previously thought.
C. the atmosphere of Venus contains 78 percent nitrogen and 21 percent oxygen.
D. the surface temperature of Venus is 450 degrees Celsius and thus unlivable for humans.

34. As it is used in line 56, the word *harbors* most nearly means:

F. shelters.
G. hides.
H. holds.
J. cherishes.

35. According to the passage, "primordial" most nearly refers to planets that:

A. are oxygen-poor due to a lack of activity by living things.
B. are not hospitable to humans because they have thick atmospheres and high surface temperatures.
C. have preserved many of the characteristics present when the planets were formed.
D. have been struck by large bodies which have altered the planets' atmospheres.

36. According to the passage, the *Pioneer Venus* mission to Venus involved investigating details relating to the planet's:

F. surface geology and interior structure.
G. atmosphere as it has been changed by the influence of photosynthesis.
H. similarities to the planet Earth.
J. atmospheric contents.

END OF TEST 3
STOP! DO NOT TURN THE PAGE UNTIL TOLD TO DO SO.
DO NOT RETURN TO A PREVIOUS TEST.

SCIENCE TEST

40 Minutes–40 Questions

DIRECTIONS: There are several passages in this test. Each passage is followed by several questions. After reading a passage, choose the correct answer to each question and fill in the corresponding oval on your answer document. You may refer to the passages as often as necessary.

You are **not** permitted to use a calculator on this test.

Passage I

The sea snail *Littorina littorea* eats algae as one of its primary food sources. An experiment investigated whether the consumption of algae by *L. littorea* varies with the species of algae or the amount of sunlight exposure of the algae population. Isolated populations of 5 species of algae were introduced to glass tanks containing 1 liter of water and allowed to grow for 30 days. During this time, the populations were exposed to direct sunlight for either 3, 6, or 9 hours each day. The water was filtered out, and the resulting algae samples were allowed to dry completely. Then, 30 grams of each species of algae exposed to 3 hours of sunlight per day were placed in an empty fish tank, 30 grams of each species of algae exposed to 6 hours of sunlight per day were placed into a second tank, and 30 grams of each species of algae exposed to 9 hours of sunlight per day were placed into a third tank. Next, 3 *L. littorea* of similar size, age, and mass were added to each tank. After 2 weeks, the mass of algae consumed, in grams (g), was determined for each species of algae at each length of daily exposure to direct sunlight (see figure).

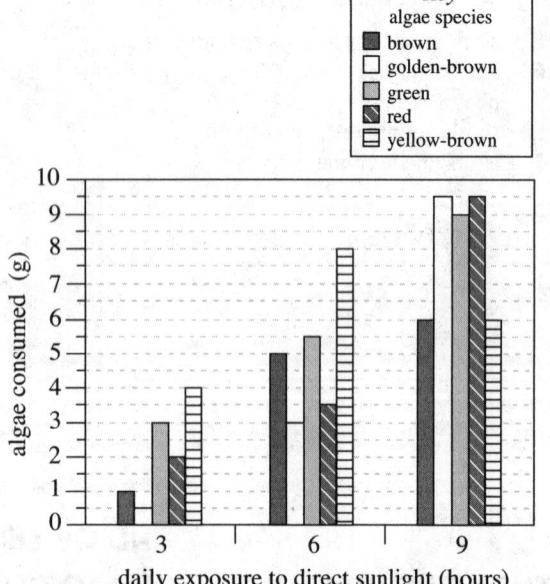

1. Of the following combinations of species of algae and length of daily direct sunlight exposure, which combination resulted in the greatest mass of algae consumed by *L. littorea*?

A. Algae species: green
   Daily sunlight exposure: 6 hours

B. Algae species: green
   Daily sunlight exposure: 9 hours

C. Algae species: yellow-brown
   Daily sunlight exposure: 6 hours

D. Algae species: yellow-brown
   Daily sunlight exposure: 9 hours

2. Which of the following statements about the effect of sunlight exposure of the algae population on the consumption of algae by *L. littorea* is consistent with the figure? As amount of sunlight exposure increased from 3 hours through 9 hours, the mass of algae consumed by *L. littorea*:

F. increased for all 5 species of algae.
G. decreased for all 5 species of algae.
H. initially increased for all 5 species of algae, but then decreased for at least 1 of the 5 species of algae.
J. initially decreased for all 5 species of algae, but then increased for at least 1 of the 5 species of algae.

GO ON TO THE NEXT PAGE.

3. Based on the passage, would *L. littorea* be classified as an autotroph or a heterotroph?

   A. Heterotroph, because *L. littorea* consumes another organism to obtain its energy.
   B. Heterotroph, because *L. littorea* produces its own energy from sunlight.
   C. Autotroph, because *L. littorea* consumes another organism to obtain its energy.
   D. Autotroph, because *L. littorea* produces its own energy from sunlight.

4. Based on the passage, does the primary food source of *L. littorea* likely contain chlorophyll or hemoglobin?

   F. Hemoglobin; *L. littorea* consumes algae, and algae species use hemoglobin to undergo cellular respiration.
   G. Hemoglobin; *L. littorea* consumes algae, and algae species use hemoglobin to undergo photosynthesis.
   H. Chlorophyll; *L. littorea* consumes algae, and algae species use chlorophyll to undergo cellular respiration.
   J. Chlorophyll; *L. littorea* consumes algae, and algae species use chlorophyll to undergo photosynthesis.

5. What mass, in *milligrams* (NOT grams), of the brown algae exposed to 6 hours of sunlight per day was consumed by *L. littorea*?

   A. 5,000 mg
   B. 6,500 mg
   C. 50,000 mg
   D. 65,000 mg

GO ON TO THE NEXT PAGE.

Passage II

The replication and infectivity of viruses is dependent on their environmental conditions. Viruses can be made harmless by varying these conditions, such as temperature and pH. Acidic solutions have been investigated as surface disinfectants and medications for viral diseases.

Researchers investigated the *acid-mediated inactivation* (the process of being made non-infective through exposure to low pH) of two types of HSV virus, HSV-1 and HSV-2.

Experiment 1

The researchers prepared eight petri dishes of a cell culture at a temperature of 25°C and added 10 μL of a solution containing active HSV-1 virions by pipette. The *virion* is the form of HSV-1 that can persist outside of the host body and infect cells. Then, 200 μL of four different buffer solutions, each at a specific pH, was added to each of the petri dishes. After the addition of the buffer solution, 2 of the petri dishes had a pH of 3.5, 2 had a pH of 4, 2 had a pH of 4.5, and 2 had a pH of 5.

For each pH, one of the petri dishes was left to stand for 1 day and one was left to stand for 1 hour. At the end of the assigned time period, each of the virus samples was added to a fresh cell culture and tested for its *relative infectivity* (the number of cells infected by the sampled virus divided by the number of cells infected by an HSV-1 virus that has not been exposed to acid). The results are shown in Table 1.

Table 1			
		Relative infectivity	
Virus type	pH	1 hour	1 day
HSV-1	3.5	0.00	0.00
	4.0	0.45	0.33
	4.5	0.82	0.81
	5.0	0.97	0.94

Experiment 2

The researchers repeated the procedure of Experiment 1 with a related type of virus, HSV-2, instead of HSV-1. The results are shown in Table 2.

Table 2			
		Relative infectivity	
Virus type	pH	1 hour	1 day
HSV-2	3.5	0.00	0.00
	4.0	0.18	0.07
	4.5	0.64	0.42
	5.0	0.88	0.88

6. Which of the following statements describes a difference between Experiments 1 and 2?

   F. A different type of HSV virus was tested in Experiment 1 than in Experiment 2.
   G. A different value of pH was used in Experiment 1 than in Experiment 2.
   H. Viruses in Experiment 1 were inactivated with an acid, while viruses in Experiment 2 were inactivated with a base.
   J. Viruses in Experiment 1 were left to stand for 1 hour before being added to a fresh culture, while viruses in Experiment 2 were left to stand for 1 day before being added to a fresh culture.

7. Suppose the researchers had determined the relative infectivity of a virus sample exposed to a pH of 4.3 for 1 hour in Experiment 2. The relative infectivity of the HSV-2 virions in the sample would most likely have been:

   A. 0.00.
   B. between 0.00 and 0.18.
   C. between 0.18 and 0.64.
   D. between 0.64 and 0.88.

GO ON TO THE NEXT PAGE.

8. At which 2 pH values was the relative infectivity of HSV-2 virions less for the longer exposure time than for the shorter exposure time?

   F. 3.5 and 4.0
   G. 3.5 and 4.5
   H. 4.0 and 4.5
   J. 4.5 and 5.0

9. Which of the following questions was **not** addressed by either experiment?

   A. Does pH affect the relative infectivity of HSV-1 and HSV-2 virions after acid-mediated inactivation?
   B. Does time of exposure to acid affect the relative infectivity of HSV-1 and HSV-2 virions after acid-mediated inactivation?
   C. Do HSV-1 virions have a greater relative infectivity than HSV-2 virions after acid-mediated inactivation?
   D. Does the concentration of HSV-1 and HSV-2 virions in solution affect their relative infectivity after acid-mediated inactivation?

10. After one day of exposure to an acidic solution, which of the 4 samples of HSV-2 virions would have been the **least** likely to infect chicken egg cells in a cell culture after being added to a petri dish containing the cell culture by pipette?

   F. The sample exposed to a pH of 3.5
   G. The sample exposed to a pH of 4.0
   H. The sample exposed to a pH of 4.5
   J. The sample exposed to a pH of 5.0

11. Suppose that a researcher wants to weaken a sample of HSV-1 virions without completely inactivating them. Based on the results of Experiment 1, which of the following combinations of pH and exposure time would most likely ensure the lowest relative infectivity of the virions?

   A. pH 4.0 and 1 hour
   B. pH 4.0 and 1 day
   C. pH 4.5 and 1 hour
   D. pH 4.5 and 1 day

GO ON TO THE NEXT PAGE.

Passage III

When an object is hung vertically from the end of a spring, the spring stretches to a point of equilibrium where the upward *spring force* is exactly equal to the downward gravitational force. When a spring is stretched beyond the point of equilibrium, the upward force is greater than the downward force, and the spring bounces back to the equilibrium point.

A group of scientists conducted 2 experiments on spring forces using 3 springs of equal length, diameter, and number of coils made of different combinations of metals—steel, Alloy X, and Alloy Y—having spring constants of 2.5 N/m, 3.0 N/m, and 3.5 N/m, respectively.

Experiment 1

The scientists attached a mass onto the end of the spring made of steel and determined the distance the spring stretched from its initial position to reach the point of equilibrium. They then repeated this procedure with identical masses for springs made of Alloy X and Alloy Y (see Figure 1).

Figure 1

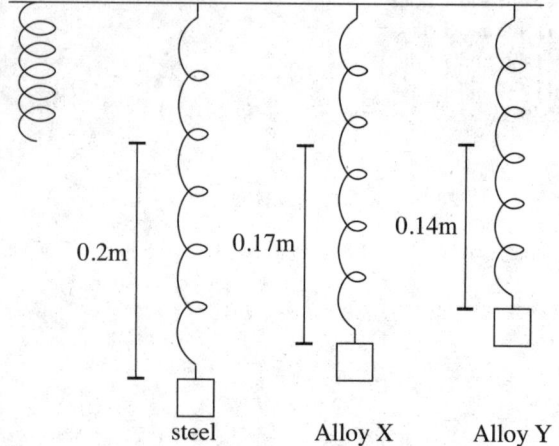

steel   Alloy X   Alloy Y

0.2m   0.17m   0.14m

Experiment 2

The scientists positioned a cubic mass—either Mass 1, Mass 2, or Mass 3—on top of each spring and allowed the spring to compress to equilibrium. They measured the distance the spring compressed and recorded it as displacement, D. They then removed the mass and allowed the spring to return to its neutral position (see Figure 2).

Figure 2

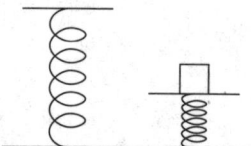

The scientists calculated the spring force exerted by each spring as D multiplied by the spring constant for that spring. They repeated this procedure to test all 3 masses on all 3 springs. Table 1 lists each mass's length, and D, in meters (m), as well as the spring force, in N, exerted by each spring.

Table 1					
Mass	Length (cm)	D (m)	Spring force (N)		
			steel	Alloy X	Alloy Y
1	5.0	0.15	0.38	0.45	0.53
2	10.0	0.15	0.38	0.45	0.53
3	10.0	0.25	0.63	0.75	0.88

12. Based on the results of Experiment 2, as the spring constant of the spring on which Mass 2 was placed decreases, the spring force on Mass 2:

   F. decreases only.
   G. increases only.
   H. increases and then decreases.
   J. varied with no general trend.

GO ON TO THE NEXT PAGE.

13. In Experiment 1, did the spring made of Alloy X or the spring made of Alloy Y experience more strain on its coils?

   A. Alloy X, because the distance the spring stretched was greater for Alloy X than for Alloy Y.
   B. Alloy X, because the distance the spring stretched was greater for Alloy Y than for Alloy X.
   C. Alloy Y, because the distance the spring stretched was greater for Alloy X than for Alloy Y.
   D. Alloy Y, because the distance the spring stretched was greater for Alloy Y than for Alloy X.

14. Suppose the scientists decide to study whether a mass's shape determines the distance the spring of a certain composition stretches. Which of the following procedural changes should the scientists make to Experiment 1? The scientists should test:

   F. a single mass with multiple springs; the springs should each have the same spring constant.
   G. multiple masses with a single spring; the masses should have different shapes but the same mass.
   H. a single mass with multiple springs; the springs should have different spring constants.
   J. multiple masses with a single spring; the masses should have different masses but the same shape.

15. Based on the results of Experiment 2, for Mass 3, what was the difference between the spring force exerted by the spring made of Alloy X and the spring force exerted by the spring made of Alloy Y?

   A. 0.08 N
   B. 0.13 N
   C. 0.25 N
   D. 0.35 N

16. Suppose that in Experiment 1 the scientists had attached the mass onto the end of a spring with a spring constant of 2.0 N/m. The distance of the stretch would most likely have been:

   F. less than 0.14 m.
   G. between 0.14 m and 0.17 m.
   H. between 0.17 m and 0.20 m.
   J. greater than 0.20 m.

17. Assume that an exercise machine contains two spring hangers to hold counterweights. The first spring on the machine has a spring constant of 15.2 N/m, and the second spring on the machine has a spring constant of 13.1 N/m. Based on the results of Experiment 1, which spring hanger would most likely have the greater distance stretched when a 25 kg mass is hung from it?

   A. The first spring, because the results of Experiment 1 indicate that distance stretched increases as spring constant increases.
   B. The first spring, because the results of Experiment 1 indicate that distance stretched increases as spring constant decreases.
   C. The second spring, because the results of Experiment 1 indicate that distance stretched increases as spring constant increases.
   D. The second spring, because the results of Experiment 1 indicate that distance stretched increases as spring constant decreases.

GO ON TO THE NEXT PAGE.

Passage IV

Chemical compounds that are *hydrophilic* can dissolve in water. When a hydrophilic liquid is mixed with water, the freezing point of the mixture is different from that of each component.

Ethylene glycol is a hydrophilic liquid that is used in anti-freeze. To determine the effectiveness of different formulations of antifreeze, a product scientist mixed ethylene glycol and water in different proportions and studied the freezing points of the mixtures.

Experiment

For each of 7 batches numbered 1–7, the scientist followed the procedure in Steps 1–5:

1. Known volumes of distilled water, pure ethylene glycol, or both, were combined in a glass flask at 70°F until the total volume of the liquid in the flask equaled 200 mL.

2. The top of the flask was sealed with a cork through which a thermometer was inserted until the thermometer bulb came into contact with the liquid in the flask.

3. The flask was placed into a cold bath containing dry ice and acetone.

4. When solid appeared in the flask and the temperature stopped changing, the thermometer reading, in degrees Fahrenheit, was recorded as the freezing point (*fp*) of the liquid.

5. The *freezing point depression* (Δfp) was determined using the following formula:

$$\Delta fp = fp - 32$$

The results for each batch are shown in Table 1.

Table 1				
Batch number	Water added (% by volume)	Ethylene glycol added (% by volume)	fp (°F)	Δfp (°F)
1	100	0	32	0
2	80	20	19.4	−12.6
3	60	40	−14.8	−46.8
4	50	50	−36.4	−68.4
5	35	65	−61.6	−93.6
6	25	75	−56.2	−88.2
7	0	100	8.6	−23.4

The scientist made a graph of Δfp versus percent by volume of ethylene glycol for each batch and connected the data points with a trendline (see Figure 1).

Figure 1

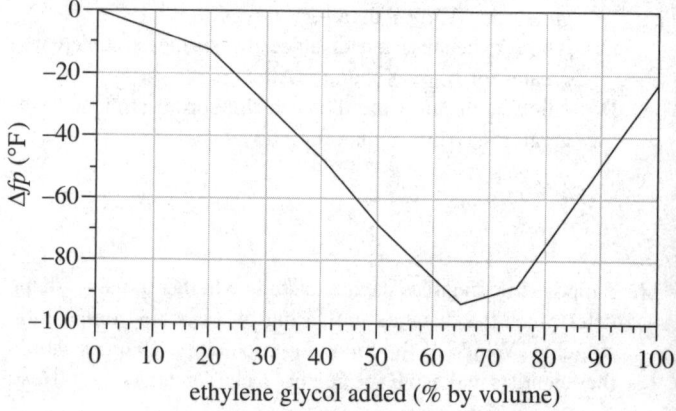

The scientist then identified which batch had the most negative value of Δfp. This batch was identified as the *eutectic mixture*.

18. If a batch had been mixed with 55% water by volume and 45% ethylene glycol by volume, *fp* would most likely have been:

F. less than −36.4°F.
G. between −36.4°F and −14.8°F.
H. between −14.8°F and 19.4°F.
J. greater than 19.4°F.

19. Before the experiment, the scientist predicted that *fp* for Batch 7 would be greater than the *fp* for Batch 2. Do the results shown in Table 1 support this prediction?

A. Yes; *fp* for Batch 7 was 8.6°F greater than *fp* for Batch 2.
B. Yes; *fp* for Batch 7 was 10.8°F greater than *fp* for Batch 2.
C. No; *fp* for Batch 7 was 8.6°F less than *fp* for Batch 2.
D. No; *fp* for Batch 7 was 10.8°F less than *fp* for Batch 2.

GO ON TO THE NEXT PAGE.

20. For each batch, the *difference* between *fp and Δfp* was:

    F. 16.0°F.
    G. 32.0°F.
    H. 48.0°F.
    J. 64.0°F.

21. Consider the batch for which the volume of ethylene glycol was 3 times as great as the volume of water. For this batch, *fp* was:

    A. −61.6°F.
    B. −56.2°F.
    C. 8.6°F.
    D. 19.4°F.

22. Suppose a batch had been prepared with 65% water by volume and 35% ethylene glycol by volume. Based on Figure 1, *Δfp* for this new batch would most likely have been closest to which of the following?

    F. −80°F
    G. −60°F
    H. −40°F
    J. −20°F

23. Suppose the compound added to the water had been *hydrophobic*. As the hydrophobic compound was added to the water, would the freezing point of the water most likely have decreased or stayed the same?

    A. Decreased, because the compound would have dissolved in water.
    B. Decreased, because the compound would not have been able to mix with water.
    C. Stayed the same, because the compound would have dissolved in water.
    D. Stayed the same, because the compound would not have been able to mix with water.

GO ON TO THE NEXT PAGE.

Passage V

The Earth's oceans contain a mixture of dissolved salts. The *salinity* (concentration of total dissolved salts) of seawater varies by location and affects its physical properties. Figure 1 shows how salt concentration (in percent by mass) affects density, in g/cm³, at 20°C for seawater and 3 aqueous solutions of pure salts (NaCl, LiCl, and NH₄Cl).

Figure 1

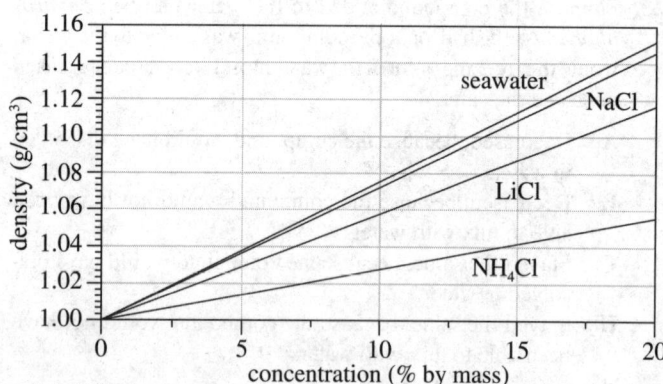

Figure 2 shows how the density of seawater at 0°C varies with ocean depth at 3 different concentrations of dissolved salt.

Figure 2

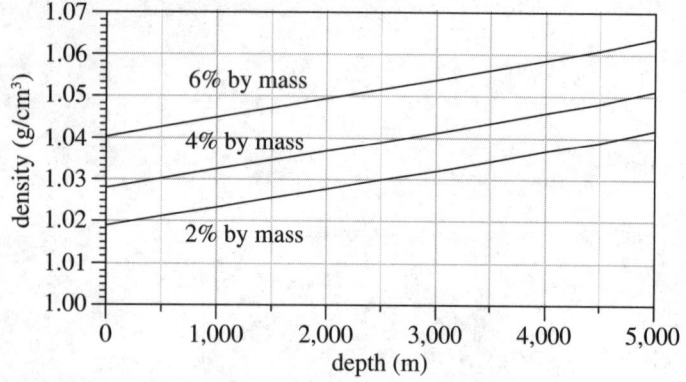

Figure 3 shows how the density of seawater at the surface varies with temperature at 4 different concentrations.

Figure 3

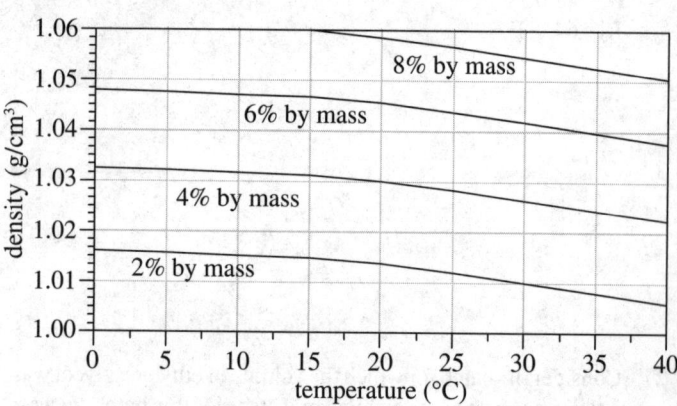

24. According to Figure 2, at 2% by mass of salt, the density of seawater is closest to 1.03 g/cm³ at which of the following depths?

   F. 2,000 m
   G. 2,500 m
   H. 3,000 m
   J. 3,500 m

GO ON TO THE NEXT PAGE.

25. Based on Figure 3, at the surface and at 7% by mass of salt, seawater having a density of 1.045 g/cm^3 would most likely have a temperature that is:

   A. less than 15°C.
   B. between 15°C and 20°C.
   C. between 20°C and 25°C.
   D. greater than 25°C.

26. According to Figure 1, at 20°C, the density of NaCl solution and the density of LiCl solution are closest in value at which of the following pairs of concentrations?

   F. NaCl: 2.5% by mass
   LiCl: 10% by mass

   G. NaCl: 2.5% by mass
   LiCl: 15% by mass

   H. NaCl: 7.5% by mass
   LiCl: 10% by mass

   J. NaCl: 7.5% by mass
   LiCl: 15% by mass

27. According to Figure 1, increasing concentration from 5% by mass to 20% by mass has a *lesser* effect on the density of which solution, LiCl or NH$_4$Cl?

   A. LiCl; the density increases by about 0.04 g/cm^3.
   B. LiCl; the density increases by about 0.09 g/cm^3.
   C. NH$_4$Cl; the density increases by about 0.04 g/cm^3.
   D. NH$_4$Cl; the density increases by about 0.09 g/cm^3

28. Consider the density of seawater at a depth of 0 m and a salt concentration of 6% by mass, as shown in Figure 2. According to Figure 3, this seawater would have a temperature closest to which of the following?

   F. 5°C
   G. 15°C
   H. 25°C
   J. 35°C

GO ON TO THE NEXT PAGE.

Passage VI

A solar eclipse occurs when the Sun, Earth, and Moon are all aligned, and the Moon casts a shadow on the Earth. In a *total eclipse*, the Moon completely covers the Sun's disc, whereas in an *annular eclipse* the Moon obscures all but the outer ring of the Sun. For example, Figure 1 shows how all of the solar eclipses occurring between January 2001 and January 2004 appeared when observed from Earth.

Figure 1

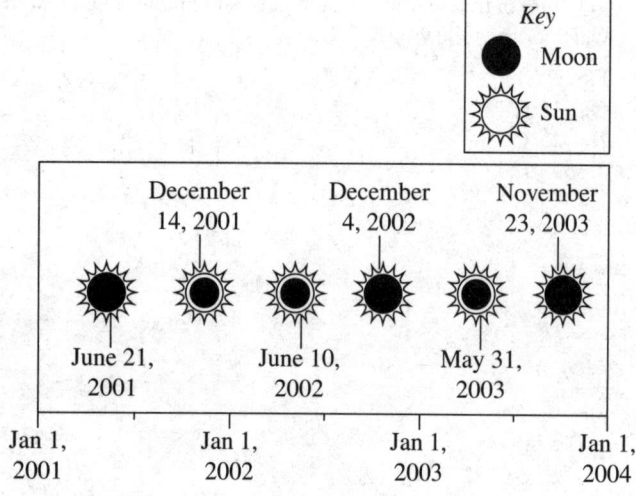

Two theories were presented to explain why solar eclipses sometimes appear as annular rather than total.

Theory 1

The Moon orbits the Earth in a circular path in which the Earth is the center. When the Moon passes between the Sun and Earth, it creates a shadow called an *umbra*, in which the entire Sun is obscured from view. Whether the umbra reaches the Earth or not depends on the size of the Sun, which varies over time due to expansion and contraction. In Figure 2, the top image shows an eclipse when the Sun is in a period of contraction, and the bottom image shows an eclipse when the Sun is in a period of expansion.

Figure 2

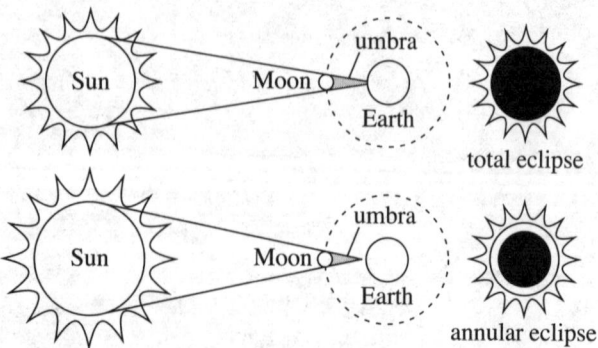

When the Sun is in a period of contraction, the umbra reaches the Earth and a total eclipse is observed. When the Sun is in a period of expansion, the umbra does not quite reach the Earth and an annular eclipse is observed.

Theory 2

The Moon orbits the Earth in an elliptical path in which the Earth is the center. In an elliptical path, the Moon is sometimes located closer to or further away from the Earth depending on where it is in its orbit. As a result, the amount of the Sun obscured by the Moon varies depending on how far the Moon is from the Earth. Figure 3 shows where the Moon was located in its orbit around the Earth during two of the solar eclipses labeled in Figure 1. For each eclipse, the reach of the umbra, the shadow in which the Sun is completely obscured, relative to Earth is shown.

There are 2 rules for when a solar eclipse will be annular:

- An eclipse will be total when the Moon is located in the region of its orbit that is a *smaller* distance from the Earth. The umbra will reach all the way to the Earth's surface, leading to a complete obstruction of light from the Sun.

- An eclipse will be annular when the Moon is located in the region of its orbit that is a *greater* distance from Earth. The umbra will not reach all the way to Earth's surface and the outer ring of the Sun will still be visible from the Earth.

Figure 3

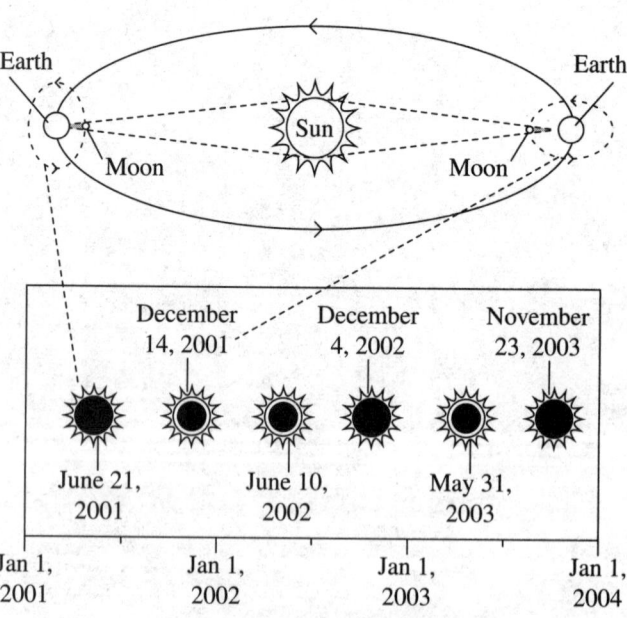

GO ON TO THE NEXT PAGE.

29. Which of the following statements best explains a primary difference between the two theories? Theory 1 states that the Moon follows:

    A. an elliptical orbit around the Earth, whereas Theory 2 states that the Moon follows a circular orbit around the Earth.
    B. an elliptical orbit around the Earth, whereas Theory 2 states that the Moon follows a circular orbit around the Sun.
    C. a circular orbit around the Earth, whereas Theory 2 states that the Moon follows an elliptical orbit around the Earth.
    D. a circular orbit around the Earth, whereas Theory 2 states that the Moon follows an elliptical orbit around the Sun.

30. Assuming that Figures 2 and 3 are drawn to scale, which of the figures, if either, implies that the distance between the Moon and Earth is constant over time?

    F. Figure 2 only
    G. Figure 3 only
    H. Both Figure 2 and Figure 3
    J. Neither Figure 2 nor Figure 3

31. Consider the eclipses in 2001 represented in Figures 1 and 3 and also the reason that, according to Theory 2, the amount of the Sun obscured by the Moon varies depending on how far the Moon is from Earth. Is the top portion of Figure 3 consistent with that reason?

    A. No; the Moon is shown as having a circular orbit and as being located closer to the Earth during some points of its orbit and farther from the Earth during other points of its orbit.
    B. No; the Moon is shown as having an elliptical orbit and as being located closer to the Earth during some points of its orbit and farther from the Earth during other points of its orbit.
    C. Yes; the Moon is shown as having a circular orbit and as being located closer to the Earth during some points of its orbit and farther from the Earth during other points of its orbit.
    D. Yes; the Moon is shown as having an elliptical orbit and as being located closer to the Earth during some points of its orbit and farther from the Earth during other points of its orbit.

32. A proponent of Theory 1 and a proponent of Theory 2 would both be likely to agree with which of the following statements? When an annular eclipse is observed from the Earth, the umbra:

    F. is as long as the distance between the Earth and Moon.
    G. is not as long as the distance between the Earth and Moon.
    H. is longer than the umbra during a total eclipse.
    J. is the same size as the umbra during a total eclipse.

33. Based on Figures 1 and 3, if Theory 2 is correct, which of the following figures could represent the positions of the Sun, Moon, and Earth on May 31, 2003?

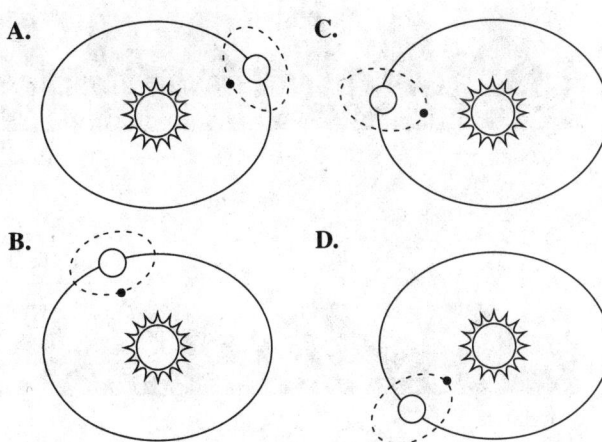

34. Can Theory 2 be used to explain why some ocean tides are stronger than others?

    F. Yes, Theory 2 accounts for the varying distance between the Earth and the Sun, whose gravitational field is the primary driver of tides.
    G. Yes, Theory 2 accounts for the varying distance between the Earth and the Moon, whose gravitational field is the primary driver of tides.
    H. No, Theory 2 does not account for the varying distance between the Earth and the Sun, whose gravitational field is the primary driver of tides.
    J. No, Theory 2 does not account for the varying distance between the Earth and the Moon, whose gravitational field is the primary driver of tides.

GO ON TO THE NEXT PAGE.

Passage V

Earthquakes disrupt the infrastructure of buildings and dwellings by displacing the ground beneath them as a result of surface waves. The origin of an earthquake is known as the *epicenter*. Surface waves propagate from the epicenter outward and are directly affected by the density of the ground through which they propagate. As seen in Figure 1, the strength of the wave may be characterized into three distinct types: strong, moderate, and weak.

Figure 1

Strong

Moderate

Weak

In order to study the effect of ground density on wave propagation, a seismologist has assembled circular small-scale models with varying densities. Propagation duration was held constant in the experiment. In each study, the procedure was repeated at various densities of earth and clay from 1,000 to 2,000 kg/m³. Seismometers were positioned to detect the type of waves propagating at specific locations. A large speaker was placed 2 m below the surface of the epicenter to mimic an earthquake and each study was conducted over a period of 2 min with a fixed frequency of 10 Hz.

Study 1

The sound source was adjusted to 60 dB to mimic the impact of a magnitude 5 earthquake. The resulting *waveform plot* (exhibits wave type as a result of varying densities and distances from the epicenter) is shown in Figure 2.

Figure 2

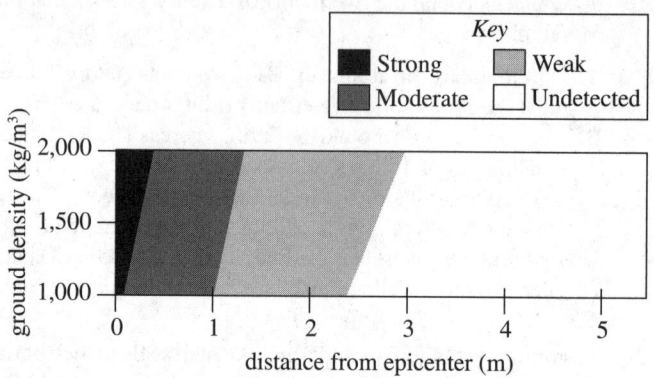

Study 2

Study 1 was repeated with the sound source adjusted to 80 dB to mimic the impact of a magnitude 7 earthquake. The resulting waveform plot is shown in Figure 3.

Figure 3

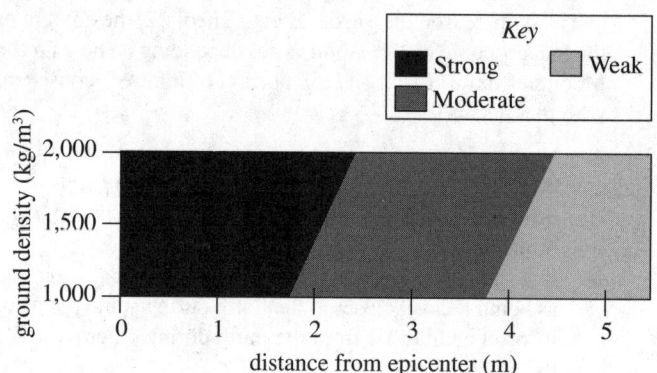

Study 3

The study was repeated with the sound source adjusted to 100 dB to mimic the impact of a magnitude 9 earthquake. The resulting waveform plot is shown in Figure 4.

Figure 4

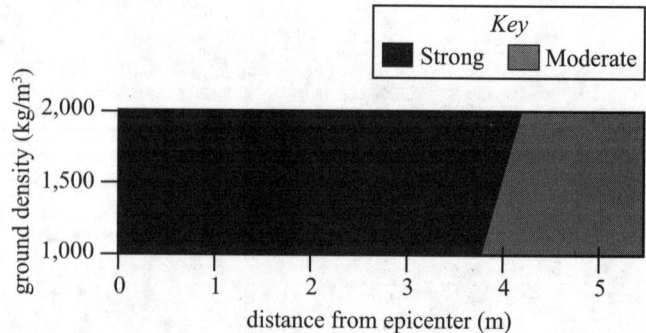

GO ON TO THE NEXT PAGE.

35. What was the independent (manipulated) variable across the 3 studies, and what was the independent variable within each study?

    A. Across the studies: distance from epicenter
        Within each study: wave type
    B. Across the studies: sound intensity
        Within each study: ground density
    C. Across the studies: ground density
        Within each study: distance from epicenter
    D. Across the studies: sound intensity
        Within each study: wave type

36. According to the results of Study 2, for all ground densities between 1,000 and 2,000 kg/m^3, as the distance from the epicenter increases from 0 to 3 m, the type of wave observed:

    F. remained strong.
    G. changed from strong to moderate.
    H. changed from moderate to strong.
    J. remained moderate.

37. According to the results of Studies 2 and 3, which of the following statements comparing the maximum distance from the epicenter for strong wave propagation and maximum distance for moderate wave propagation is true?

    A. At all ground densities studied, the maximum distance from the epicenter at which strong waves may propagate was greater than the corresponding maximum distance from the epicenter at which moderate waves propagated.
    B. At all ground densities studied, the maximum distance from the epicenter at which strong waves may propagate was less than the corresponding maximum distance from the epicenter at which moderate waves propagated.
    C. For some of the ground densities studied, the maximum distance from the epicenter at which strong waves may propagate was greater than the corresponding maximum distance from the epicenter at which moderate waves propagated.
    D. For some of the ground densities studied, the maximum distance from the epicenter at which strong waves may propagate was less than the corresponding maximum distance from the epicenter at which moderate waves propagated.

38. Which of the following factors in the seismologist's studies was **not** directly controlled?

    F. Sound intensity (in dB)
    G. Ground density
    H. Propagation duration
    J. Wave type

39. Suppose Study 1 were repeated using a sound intensity of 70 dB. The resulting waveform plot would include which of the wave types referred to in the passage?

    A. Strong waves only
    B. Strong and weak waves only
    C. Strong and moderate waves only
    D. Strong, moderate, and weak waves

40. A study was conducted using a sound intensity between 75 dB and 85 dB. The minimum ground density where strong waves began propagating ranged from 1,000 kg/m^3 to 2,000 kg/m^3. Based on the information presented, the distance from the epicenter was most likely:

    F. less than 2.5 m.
    G. between 2.5 and 3.5 m.
    H. between 3.5 and 4.5 m.
    J. greater than 4.5 m.

END OF TEST 4

STOP! DO NOT RETURN TO A PREVIOUS TEST.

DIRECTIONS

This is a test of your writing skills. You will have forty (40) minutes to write an essay. Before you begin planning and writing your essay, read the writing prompt carefully to understand exactly what you are being asked to do. Your essay will be evaluated on the evidence it provides of your ability to express judgments by taking a position on the issue in the writing prompt; to maintain a focus on the topic throughout your essay; to develop a position by using logical reasoning and by supporting your ideas; to organize ideas in a logical way; and to use language clearly and effectively according to the conventions of standard written English.

You may use the unlined pages in this test booklet to plan your essay. These pages will not be scored. *You must write your essay on the lined pages in the answer folder.* Your writing on those lined pages will be scored. You may not need all the lined pages, but to ensure you have enough room to finish, do NOT skip lines. You may write corrections or additions neatly between the lines of your essay, but do NOT write in the margins of the lined pages. *Illegible essays cannot be scored, so you must write (or print) clearly.*

If you finish before time is called, you may review your work. Lay your pencil down immediately when time is called.

DO NOT OPEN THIS BOOK UNTIL YOU ARE TOLD TO DO SO.

ACT Assessment Writing Test Prompt

Population Growth

Since the Industrial Revolution, the growth rate of Earth's human population has increased dramatically. It took mankind until the 1800s to reach one billion, but only 120 years after that to reach two billion, and less than 40 years after that to reach three billion. We continue to increase our numbers, measuring in at 8.2 billion in 2025. Some express a great deal of concern about this trend, arguing that the increasing population uses more resources than the planet can provide and encourages harmful practices such as deforestation and industrial pollution. Others say that while our population is at higher numbers than ever before and the subsequent problems are very real, the issues are caused less by the actual number of people and more by the unequal distribution of resources.

Read and carefully consider these perspectives. Each suggests a particular way of thinking about human population growth.

Perspective One	**Perspective Two**	**Perspective Three**
Overpopulation is one of the most serious environmental issues humans face. Our increasing numbers are causing myriad problems from loss of fresh water to extinction of species to lowered life expectancy in developing countries.	The number of people on Earth is not a problem. We have less than 9 billion people, while scientists predict our planet can support up to 10 billion. The real problem is the unequal distribution of resources. A more equitable use of water, land, food, and fuel would eliminate many of the problems we currently face.	Though our population numbers are higher than they've ever been, this is not a cause for alarm. Our growth rate is already beginning to slow. As we approach critical mass, that decrease in rate will continue until we're at "replacement" levels of reproduction, allowing the human race to continue without drastically increasing the overall numbers.

Essay Task

Write a unified, coherent essay in which you evaluate multiple perspectives on the issues connected with population growth. In your essay, be sure to:

- clearly state your own perspective and analyze the relationship between your perspective and at least one other perspective
- develop and support your ideas with reasoning and examples
- organize your ideas clearly and logically
- communicate your ideas effectively in standard written English

Your perspective may be in full agreement with any of those given, in partial agreement, or completely different.

Chapter 29
Practice Exam 2:
Answers
and Explanations

*Note on scoring: please refer to the Scoring Conversion Worksheet and Score Conversion Chart on pages 76 and 77.

To grade your essay, see the Essay Checklist and an example of a top scoring essay online on your Student Tools.

English		Math		Reading		Science	
1. D	26. F	1. C	24. H	1. C	19. C	1. B	21. B
2. F	27. A	2. H	25. C	2. F	20. G	2. H	22. H
3. C	28. H	3. C	26. F	3. B	21. C	3. A	23. D
4. H	29. D	4. H	27. C	4. G	22. G	4. J	24. G
5. D	30. H	5. B	28. H	5. C	23. D	5. A	25. D
6. H	31. B	6. J	29. B	6. F	24. G	6. F	26. H
7. A	32. J	7. A	30. F	7. D	25. D	7. C	27. C
8. G	33. C	8. G	31. D	8. G	26. F	8. H	28. J
9. D	34. H	9. B	32. H	9. C	27. C	9. D	29. C
10. F	35. D	10. J	33. A	10. J	28. H	10. F	30. F
11. A	36. F	11. B	34. G	11. B	29. C	11. B	31. D
12. F	37. A	12. J	35. D	12. J	30. J	12. F	32. G
13. C	38. F	13. B	36. F	13. B	31. B	13. A	33. C
14. G	39. B	14. F	37. C	14. F	32. H	14. G	34. G
15. D	40. J	15. B	38. J	15. B	33. D	15. B	35. B
16. F	41. B	16. J	39. D	16. H	34. H	16. J	36. G
17. C	42. H	17. C	40. H	17. A	35. C	17. D	37. B
18. H	43. A	18. F	41. D	18. H	36. J	18. G	38. J
19. D	44. G	19. D	42. F			19. D	39. D
20. G	45. B	20. J	43. B			20. G	40. F
21. D	46. H	21. B	44. F				
22. F	47. D	22. H	45. B				
23. C	48. H	23. C					
24. J	49. B						
25. C	50. F						

ACT TEST 2 ENGLISH ANSWERS AND EXPLANATIONS

1. **D** This is a Grammar question, so look to see what's changing in the answers: prepositions. Look for an idiom. Here, the word that goes with the preposition is *associate*. The correct idiom is "associate with."

   - (A), (B), and (C) are wrong because *associate by, associate to,* and *associate on* aren't correct phrasings.
   - (D) is correct because the idiom is "associate with."

2. **F** This Content question is asking for the *least redundant* answer, so underline this phrase and start with the shortest option. Then, consider the other options and look for words that are redundant with this sentence or the one(s) before.

   - (F) is correct because it doesn't contain any redundancies.
   - (G), (H), and (J) are wrong because *of all ages* is redundant with *young and old*.

3. **C** This Content question is asking whether the sentence should be added, so underline this question. Consider the content of the new sentence and that of the surrounding sentences. The paragraph introduces the hobby of *crocheting*. The new sentence is about a historical event related to crocheting. Although the new sentence is about crocheting, it wouldn't be logical to add a single sentence about the historical event if nothing else is going to elaborate on it. Therefore, the sentence shouldn't be added. Eliminate any answer that is inconsistent with this.

   - (A) and (B) are wrong because the sentence is not consistent enough with the content of the paragraph to be added.
   - (C) is correct because it's accurate to say that the new sentence *is not relevant to the main topic*.
   - (D) is wrong because it doesn't provide a valid reason not to add the sentence.

4. **H** This is a Grammar question, so look to see what's changing in the answers: punctuation. The answer choices contain STOP punctuation, so use the Vertical Line Test between stitches and *Picking*. The part before the line says *Instructional books are readily available, and once you've learned a few basic stitches*, which is an incomplete idea. The part after the line says *Picking up the more advanced ones is a snap*, which is a complete idea. Eliminate any answer that doesn't properly connect the incomplete idea and the complete idea.

   - (F) and (G) are wrong because both a period and a semicolon can only be used if both parts of the sentence are complete.
   - (H) is correct because a comma can connect the incomplete idea to the complete idea.
   - (J) is wrong because there is no reason to use the word *since* here.

5. **D** This is a Grammar question, so look to see what's changing in the answers: wording before the word *you*. Since the answers contain connecting words, consider complete sentences. The original sentence as written contains two complete ideas (*you have finished a project* and *you have a cherished keepsake*) with only a comma in between, which isn't allowed, so try the other options to see which one produces a complete and correct sentence.

   - (A) and (B) are wrong because each contains two complete ideas with only a comma in between.

- (C) is wrong because a contrast isn't appropriate in this sentence.
- (D) is correct because it makes the first idea incomplete, allowing the use of a comma, and creates a logical connection between the ideas.

6. **H** This is a Grammar question, so look to see what's changing in the answers: pronouns. Identify and underline the word the pronoun refers back to, which in this case is *the painting*. This noun is singular, so a singular pronoun should be used. Eliminate any answer that isn't singular or has incorrect punctuation.

- (F) is wrong because *it's* means "it is," which isn't correct in this context.
- (G) is wrong because *our* is plural.
- (H) is correct because *its* is the correct spelling for a possessive pronoun.
- (J) is wrong because *its'* isn't a word at all.

7. **A** This is a Grammar question, so look to see what's changing in the answers: verbs. The sentence involves a list, which needs to be parallel. The other complete item in the list is *packed our bags*, so the other verbs should be consistent with *packed*. Eliminate any answer that's not consistent with *packed*.

- (A) is correct because *jumped* and *headed* are consistent with *packed*.
- (B) is wrong because *had headed* isn't consistent with *packed*.
- (C) is wrong because *head* isn't consistent with *packed*.
- (D) is wrong because *had jumped* isn't consistent with *packed*.

8. **G** This Content question is asking where a new sentence should be placed, so underline the goal and identify any clues in the new sentence. The new sentence refers to *Her*, so it must be placed after some mention of a person. Use Process of Elimination.

- (F) is wrong because Sentence 2 doesn't mention any person.
- (G) is correct because Sentence 3 refers to *someone else*, which is a person whom *Her* could refer back to.
- (H) and (J) are wrong because the new sentence introduces the person by giving her name, but Sentences 4 and 5 refer to *We*, suggesting that Lisa should have already been introduced.

9. **D** This is a Grammar question, so look to see what's changing in the answers: punctuation. The answer choices contain STOP punctuation, so use the Vertical Line Test between *displayed* and *was*. The part before the line says *The first thing that struck me as we entered the room where the painting was displayed*, which is an incomplete idea. The part after the line says *was the size of the painting*, which is also an incomplete idea. Eliminate any answer that doesn't properly connect the incomplete ideas to form a complete sentence.

- (A) and (B) are wrong because both a semicolon and a colon require the first part of the sentence to be complete.
- (C) is wrong because there is no reason to use a comma here.
- (D) is correct because no punctuation is needed.

10. **F** This Content question is asking for the *least redundant* answer, so underline this phrase and start with the shortest option. Then, consider the other options and look for words that are redundant with this sentence or the one(s) before.

- (F) is correct because it doesn't contain anything redundant.
- (G), (H), and (J) are wrong because *difficult* and *overwhelming in its difficulty* are redundant with *almost impossible.*

11. **A** This Content question is asking for the sentence that is least *relevant to the development of this paragraph and therefore could be deleted*, so underline this phrase. Consider the content of the four sentences in the answer choices and their relevance to the focus of the paragraph, which is the *size and impressiveness* of the painting, given its technique.

- (A) is correct because this sentence is about paintings in general, whereas the paragraph is focused on a specific painting, so this sentence is not *relevant and could be deleted.*
- (B), (C), and (D) are wrong because they are all specific to the painting that the paragraph is focused on, so they are relevant and shouldn't be deleted.

12. **F** This Content question is asking for an answer that *provides the most effective and logical transition from the preceding paragraph to this one*, so underline this phrase. Ignore the underlined sentence and identify the subject of the preceding paragraph and that of this one. The preceding paragraph is about the *enormous* size of the painting and how surprised and impressed the narrator was, given the seemingly *impossible* technique. This paragraph is about the *beauty* and *colors* of the painting. Eliminate any answer inconsistent with these ideas.

- (F) is correct because *Even more impressive* transitions from one impressive aspect of the painting, its *size*, to another, its *beauty* and *colors.*
- (G) is wrong because, although it effectively introduces the new paragraph, it doesn't tie back to anything from the *preceding paragraph*, as stated in the question.
- (H) and (J) are wrong because nothing in either paragraph relates to *art critics* or any *debate.*

13. **C** This Content question is asking for an alternative that *would not be acceptable*, so underline this phrase. Try each answer choice and mark it with a checkmark or an "X," then choose the odd one out.

- (A), (B), and (D) are wrong because they are all acceptable alternatives, since each produces a complete sentence.
- (C) is correct because it produces a sentence with two complete ideas connected with only a comma, since it doesn't contain a word such as *When* that would make the first idea incomplete.

14. **G** This Content question is asking what the paragraph *would primarily lose* if the phrase were deleted, so read the sentence with and without the phrase to determine the difference. With the phrase *from a distance*, the sentence creates a contrast between how *parts of the painting* look *from a distance (white)* compared with *up close (multicolored)*. Without this phrase, the contrast isn't clear. Eliminate any answer inconsistent with this difference.

- (F) is wrong because the phrase doesn't explain *the author's love of the painting* in and of itself.
- (G) is correct because *from a distance* contrasts with *up close.*

- (H) is wrong because the *distance* in this phrase isn't about the *road trip*.
- (J) is wrong because the information is needed and isn't *stated more clearly elsewhere*.

15. **D** This Content question is asking for the *best placement for the underlined portion*, so underline this phrase. Try the underlined portion in each spot and eliminate any that doesn't provide a clear and correct meaning.

- (A) is wrong because it's not logical that the narrator's *mind* was *at the museum gift shop*.
- (B) is wrong because the *image* refers back to seeing our *favorite work of art* from the previous sentence, not something from the *gift shop*.
- (C) is wrong because the sentence is referring to a time when the narrator has left the museum but is still thinking about it, so *looking at the souvenir print* would happen in the narrator's home, not at the *gift shop*.
- (D) is correct because the idea that the narrator bought a *souvenir print* at the *museum gift shop* is logical.

16. **F** This Content question is asking for an answer that *would most clearly and effectively express the ownership relationship between humans and cats*, so underline this phrase. Read the context of the sentence and eliminate any answer that doesn't fulfill this goal.

- (F) is correct because *adopted them as pets* matches with *ownership relationship*.
- (G) and (J) are wrong because having cats *around* or liking cats does not necessarily imply an *ownership relationship*.
- (H) is wrong because it's not about *cats*.

17. **C** This Content question is asking what the essay *would primarily lose* if the sentence were deleted, so read the paragraph with and without the sentence to determine the difference. The sentence describes the *only* way that cats *use their voices* among each other, in contrast to the *nonverbal signals* mentioned previously in the paragraph. So, without the sentence, the paragraph doesn't indicate any use for vocal communication between cats. Eliminate any answer inconsistent with this difference.

- (A) is wrong because the sentence isn't *redundant* and doesn't provide information that appears *elsewhere*.
- (B) is wrong because the sentence is about vocal communication, not nonverbal communication.
- (C) is correct because the other sentences in the paragraph are about *nonverbal signals*, so this sentence on cats' voices is an *exception*.
- (D) is wrong because this sentence provides new information, not a *summary* of previous information.

18. **H** This is a Grammar question, so look to see what's changing in the answers: apostrophes on nouns as well as a comma. Consider whether any apostrophes or commas are needed. The *verbal expressions* belong to the cats, so there should be an apostrophe on *cats*. There is not a reason to use a comma after expressions, as it would separate the subject (*expressions*) from its verb (*are*). Eliminate any answer that misuses apostrophes or commas.

- (F) and (J) are wrong because *cats* should be possessive and have an apostrophe.

- (G) is wrong because the paragraph is about *cats*, not one cat.
- (H) is correct because it correctly makes *cats* possessive.

19. **D** This Content question is asking for the choice that *best avoids wordiness and redundancy*, so underline this phrase and start with the shortest option. Then, consider the other options and look for words that are redundant with this sentence or the one(s) before.

- (A) and (B) are wrong because *reasonable* and *well-reasoned* mean the same thing as *logical*, so these answers are redundant.
- (C) is wrong because there is no need to say to a *startling degree*; this answer is overly wordy.
- (D) is correct because it's concise and clear.

20. **G** This Content question is asking for an answer *that would best summarize the main point the essay makes about cats' communication with their human owners*, so underline this phrase. Read the context of the sentence and eliminate any answer that doesn't fulfill this goal. The essay's *main point* about *cats' communication with their human owners* is that cats use a *wide range of vocal expressions* and that *different meows* have different meanings, allowing owners to increase the *bond* they have with their cats.

- (F) is wrong because *other animals* don't relate to the *main point* of the essay.
- (G) is correct because it emphasizes the point that cats' noises are meant to communicate their needs or emotions.
- (H) is wrong because the essay indicates that meowing is *not used to communicate with other cats*.
- (J) is wrong because *have more than one cat* and *undergo a natural development* don't relate to the *main point* of the essay.

21. **D** This Content question is asking for the choice that *best avoids wordiness and redundancy*, so underline this phrase and start with the shortest option. Then, consider the other options and look for words that are redundant with this sentence or the one(s) before.

- (A) and (C) are wrong because *back...in time* and *to the past* are redundant.
- (B) is wrong because it's overly wordy compared to (D).
- (D) is correct because it's concise and clear.

22. **F** This Content question is asking for the choice that *most effectively maintains the essay's tone*, so underline this phrase. Consider the tone of the essay, which is friendly but not overly casual. Eliminate any answer that is inconsistent with this tone.

- (F) is correct because there is nothing inconsistent with the essay's *tone*.
- (G) is wrong because *your sweet* self is overly casual compared to the tone of the essay.
- (H) and (J) are wrong because they are overly wordy and informal compared with (F).

23. **C** This is a Grammar question, so look to see what's changing in the answers: commas. Consider whether there is a reason for each comma. A comma should not be used between *Michigan* and *island* because Mackinac is being described as a *Michigan island*. There should be a comma after *island* because the sentence contains two complete ideas, so the comma with the FANBOYS word (so) properly connects these ideas. It may not be clear whether a comma should be used between

isolated and *Michigan*, but luckily, the other spots are enough to get the correct answer. Eliminate any answer that uses commas incorrectly.

- (A) and (D) are wrong because there shouldn't be a comma between *Michigan* and *island*.
- (B) is wrong because a comma must be used after *island*, before the FANBOYS word, to properly connect the complete ideas.
- (C) is correct because it doesn't make any comma errors.

24.   **J**   This is a Grammar question, so look to see what's changing in the answers: phrasing. The sentence involves a list, which needs to be parallel. The other items in the list are *horse* and *carriage*, which are nouns, so this list item should also be a noun. Eliminate any answer that's not consistent with the other list items.

- (F) and (G) are wrong because the word *by* shouldn't be repeated since it doesn't appear in the second list item (*carriage*).
- (H) is wrong because the list items are nouns and don't contain *-ing* verbs.
- (J) is correct because bicycle is consistent with the other list items, *horse* and *carriage*.

25.   **C**   This is a Grammar question, so look to see what's changing in the answers: punctuation. The answer choices contain STOP punctuation, so use the Vertical Line Test between *necessary* and *Mackinac*. The part before the line says *Luckily, the island is small enough that cars are not necessary*, which is a complete idea. The part after the line says *Mackinac measures only a mile and a half in diameter*, which is also a complete idea. Eliminate any answer that doesn't properly connect the two complete ideas.

- (A) and (B) are wrong because commas alone can't connect two complete ideas.
- (C) is correct because it makes each complete idea its own sentence.
- (D) is wrong because two complete ideas need some type of punctuation between them.

26.   **F**   This Content question is asking what the sentence *would primarily lose* if the phrase were deleted, so read the paragraph with and without the phrase to determine the difference. The phrase gives a brief explanation of how the arch formed. Without the phrase, the sentence doesn't contain details on how it formed. Eliminate any answer inconsistent with this difference.

- (F) is correct because the phrase does describe how the Arch Rock formed.
- (G) is wrong because the phrase is only about one tourist attraction.
- (H) is wrong because there is no indication in the text about how the *governor's mansion* was *constructed*.
- (J) is wrong because the information is not *detailed elsewhere*.

27.   **A**   This Content question is asking for an answer that *provides the most effective transition to the topic discussed in the sentence that follows*, so underline this phrase. Ignore the underlined sentence and identify the subject of the following sentence. It discusses the *most popular item for sale* among *tourists*, which is *fudge*. Eliminate any answer inconsistent with these ideas.

- (A) is correct because *souvenir stores, T-shirt shops, and candy and ice cream parlors* is consistent with items *for sale* to tourists and *fudge*.
- (B), (C), and (D) are wrong because *outsourcing*, the *fur trade*, and other *tourist attractions* aren't consistent with the content of the following sentence.

28. **H** This Content question is asking for the *least redundant* answer, so underline this phrase and start with the shortest option. Then, consider the other options and look for words that are redundant with this sentence or the one(s) before.

   - (F), (G), and (J) are wrong because *numerous* and *abundant* are synonyms, so only one should be used.
   - (H) is correct because it doesn't contain any redundancies.

29. **D** This is a Grammar question, so look to see what's changing in the answers: verbs. Identify the subject of the verb, which is *privacy*. This subject is singular, so eliminate any answer that is plural or makes another error.

   - (A), (B), and (C) are wrong because *don't*, *aren't*, and *weren't* are all plural.
   - (D) is correct because *doesn't* is singular.

30. **H** This Content question is asking whether the essay is about the *difficulty the residents of Mackinac Island have had prohibiting automobile traffic from the historic island*, so underline this phrase and consider the overall point of the essay. The essay mentions that *you may not bring your car* because *Automobiles are outlawed*, but there is no additional information about *prohibiting automobile* traffic or any *difficulty* associated with it. Thus, the essay does not accomplish this goal. Eliminate any answer that doesn't match with this.

   - (F) and (G) are wrong because the essay doesn't accomplish the stated goal.
   - (H) is correct because it accurately represents the focuses of the essay.
   - (J) is wrong because the essay doesn't mention residents seeking *to bring automobiles back to the island*.

31. **B** This is a Grammar question, so look to see what's changing in the answers: a semicolon or a comma before or after the word *and*. Consider whether any punctuation is needed. Here, there is a list of two things: *friends and peers*. A list of only two items doesn't need punctuation, so eliminate any option with punctuation.

   - (A) is wrong because a semicolon can only link two complete ideas, which isn't the case here.
   - (B) is correct because no punctuation is needed in a list of two items.
   - (C) is wrong because a comma before the word *and* can only be used in a list of three or more things or if there are two complete ideas.
   - (D) is wrong because there is no reason to put a comma after *and*.

32. **J** This Content question is asking for an alternative that *would not be acceptable*, so underline this phrase. Try each answer choice and mark it with a checkmark or an "X," then choose the odd one out.

   - (F), (G), and (H) are wrong because they all create a complete sentence, so they all are acceptable alternatives.
   - (J) is correct because the phrase *that having provided* makes the sentence incomplete, so this alternative *would not be acceptable*

33. **C** This Content question is asking where a sentence should be placed, so underline the goal and identify any clues in the sentence. Sentence 2 uses the contrast word *though* to refer to the fact that it *defies understanding* for people to do karaoke *in public*, so this sentence must come after a mention of something that doesn't defy understanding. Use Process of Elimination.

- (A) is wrong because Sentences 1 and 3 should be paired together, since Sentence 3 elaborates on why karaoke is popular.
- (B) is wrong because there is nothing in Sentence 3 that provides a clear idea for Sentence 2 to contrast with.
- (C) is correct because Sentence 4 refers to the *understandable* idea of people doing karaoke at home, so Sentence 2 then follows it with the contrasting idea that public karaoke *defies understanding*.
- (D) is wrong because the *question* in Sentence 5 refers back to the idea in Sentence 2 that *defies understanding*.

34. **H** This is a Grammar question, so look to see what's changing in the answers: punctuation and connecting words. The original sentence has a comma + FANBOYS, so use the Vertical Line Test, drawing lines before and after *but*. The first part of the sentence, *Even though their performances may be heard only in dimly lit bars or busy restaurants*, is an incomplete idea. The second part, *karaoke singers are still performing with such concert-hall staples…*, is a complete idea. Eliminate any answer that doesn't properly connect the incomplete idea to the complete idea.

- (F) is wrong because a comma + FANBOYS can only be used with two complete ideas.
- (G) is wrong because the word *which* has no clear purpose in this context.
- (H) is correct because it uses a comma between the incomplete idea and the complete idea.
- (J) is wrong because the first part of the sentence says *Even though*, so a second contrast word (but) isn't needed.

35. **D** This is a Grammar question, so look to see what's changing in the answers: verbs. Identify the subject of the verb, which is *audience*. This subject is singular, but all of the answers work with a singular subject, so consider tense. The first part of the sentence uses the verb *are*, so this verb should also be in present tense. Eliminate any answer that's not consistent with *are*.

- (A) and (B) are wrong because *has known* and *is knowing* aren't consistent with *are*.
- (C) is wrong because *knew* is in past tense.
- (D) is correct because *knows* is in present tense and is consistent with *are*.

36. **F** This Content question is asking for an answer that *would most effectively conclude this paragraph while leading into the main focus of the next paragraph*, so underline this phrase. Ignore the underlined sentence and identify the subject of this paragraph and that of the next one. This paragraph is about how karaoke lets *everyday folks* perform like stars at a real concert. The next paragraph is about *another reason* people enjoy karaoke, which is that *people can experience the joy of music with others* instead of alone. Eliminate any answer inconsistent with these ideas.

- (F) is correct because *as close as many people will get to fame and stardom* is consistent with the focus of this paragraph, and *not the only reason for its…popularity* is consistent with the second reason that appears in the next paragraph.

- (G) and (H) are wrong because the *first sing-along tapes* and *equipment* and *Japan's lasting influence* aren't consistent with the focus of either paragraph.
- (J) is wrong because it relates to the topic of the next paragraph but doesn't effectively *conclude this paragraph*.

37.   **A**   This Content question is asking for a *logical transition word*, so underline these words and consider the relationship between this sentence and the one before. The preceding sentence describes how singing typically isn't heard by others, and this sentence describes how karaoke lets people *share that ordinarily solitary experience* with others. These ideas disagree, so eliminate any answer that doesn't match this relationship.

- (A) is correct because *by contrast* is an opposite-direction transition.
- (B), (C), and (D) are wrong because they're all same-direction transitions.

38.   **F**   This is a Grammar question, so look to see what's changing in the answers: pronouns. Identify and underline the word the pronoun refers back to, which in this case is the *people*. The pronoun refers to their singing, so a possessive pronoun is needed. Eliminate any answer that isn't possessive or isn't consistent with *people*.

- (F) is correct because *whose* is a possessive pronoun to refer back to *people*.
- (G) and (H) are wrong because they're not possessive pronouns.
- (J) is wrong because *who's* means "who is," which is not possessive.

39.   **B**   This Content question is asking what the essay *would primarily lose* if the clause were deleted, so read the sentence with and without the clause to determine the difference. With the clause *who are ordinarily shy*, the sentence identifies the type of people who can be brought *out of their shells* by doing karaoke. Without this phrase, the sentence doesn't specify a personality trait of people who might enjoy karaoke. Eliminate any answer inconsistent with this difference.

- (A) is wrong because the phrase doesn't mention *the international community*.
- (B) is correct because the focus of the sentence is on how karaoke can make *shy* people feel more confident.
- (C) is wrong because the phrase isn't specifically about *psychological benefits*, nor does it necessarily refer to those who are *chronically shy*.
- (D) is wrong because nothing about overcoming *stage fright* is implied by the phrase.

40.   **J**   This Content question is asking where a new sentence should be placed, if at all, so underline the goal and identify any clues in the new sentence. It relates to *popular karaoke requests* in *the United States* and *country artists* specifically. Use Process of Elimination.

- (F), (G), and (H) are wrong because none of these spots relates to *country artists or* any specific types of songs that are popular; each paragraph is about reasons for karaoke's popularity.
- (J) is correct because this sentence isn't consistent with the subjects of any of the paragraphs offered.

41. **B** This is a Grammar question, so look to see what's changing in the answers: grammatical phrasing. The answer choices involve the similar words *few*, *little*, *less*, and *fewer* as well as frequently confused words *then* and *than*. The words *few* and *fewer* are used for countable nouns, and a percentage is not a countable noun. Eliminate any answer that uses incorrect words.

- (A) and (D) are wrong because *few* and *fewer* can't be used with a percentage.
- (B) is correct because it doesn't make any grammatical errors.
- (C) is wrong because although *less* works with *9%*, the word "than" should be used to make a comparison instead of the word *then*.

42. **H** This Content question asks for the *clearest and most grammatically acceptable answer*, so underline this phrase. The answers contain prepositions, so look for an idiom. Here, the word that goes with the preposition is *wrong*. The correct idiom is "wrong with" something.

- (F) is wrong because although *wrong for* can be a correct phrase, it isn't appropriate in this sentence.
- (G) is wrong because although *wrong to* could work if it were followed by a verb, there isn't a verb here.
- (H) is correct because *What was wrong with this program?* is a correct phrasing.
- (J) is wrong because *wrong from* isn't a correct phrasing.

43. **A** This Content question asks for the *clearest and most precise* answer, so underline this phrase. The answer choices are vocabulary words, so try each one and eliminate any that isn't clear and precise.

- (A) is correct because *running the program* provides a clear and correct meaning.
- (B) is wrong because one wouldn't chase a *program*.
- (C) is wrong because a *program* can't be hired.
- (D) is wrong because *performing the program* isn't as clear and precise as *running the program* in (A).

44. **G** This Content question is asking where a sentence should be placed, so underline the goal and identify any clues in the sentence. Sentence 4 mentions the *biggest problem* with the program, the *residents' lack of interest*, so the sentence that follows it will likely expand on this idea. Use Process of Elimination.

- (F) is wrong because Sentences 3 and 5 should be put together since *These* in Sentence 5 refers back to the mechanics in Sentence 3.
- (G) is correct because in this spot the sentence answers the question in Sentence 1, and then Sentence 2 elaborates on why people weren't interested in recycling.
- (H) and (J) are wrong because the last few sentences go together to explain the issues with the *mechanics* of the program and shouldn't be interrupted with a different idea about people's *lack of interest*.

45. **B** This is a Grammar question, so look to see what's changing in the answers: punctuation. The answer choices contain STOP punctuation, so use the Vertical Line Test between *one* and *the*. The part before the line says *In May 2008, the city decided to discontinue its…program and replace it with a new one*, which is a complete idea. The part after the line says *the Blue Bin program*, which is an incomplete idea. Eliminate any answer that doesn't properly connect the complete idea and the incomplete idea.

- (A) is wrong because some type of punctuation should separate the complete idea from the name of the new program.
- (B) is correct because a colon is used when the second part elaborates on the first, such as by giving the name of the program.
- (C) and (D) are wrong because both a semicolon and a comma + FANBOYS (*and*) require two complete ideas.

46. **H** This is a Grammar question, so look to see what's changing in the answers: connecting words. Eliminate any answer that doesn't produce a complete sentence.

- (F) is wrong because there is no reason to use the phrase *because of* here.
- (G) is wrong because it uses a comma + FANBOYS, which isn't acceptable because the second part of the sentence isn't a complete idea.
- (H) is correct because it creates a complete sentence.
- (J) is wrong because the word *in* shouldn't be used before *which* in this sentence.

47. **D** This is a Grammar question, so look to see what's changing in the answers: punctuation. The answer choices contain STOP punctuation, so use the Vertical Line Test between *walls* and *we*. The part before the line says *We had to navigate both the flowing river and the canyon walls*, which is a complete idea. The part after the line says *we became amphibious…*, which is also a complete idea. Eliminate any answer that doesn't properly connect the two complete ideas.

- (A) is wrong because some type of punctuation is needed between two complete ideas.
- (B) is wrong because a comma alone can't connect two complete ideas.
- (C) is wrong because a FANBOYS word (*so*) alone can't connect two complete ideas.
- (D) is correct because a comma + FANBOYS can connect two complete ideas.

48. **H** This is a Grammar question, so look to see what's changing in the answers: subjects and verbs. Look for a complete sentence. Outside of the underlined portion, the sentence contains a subject (*danger*) but not a verb, so the answer needs to provide the verb. Eliminate any option that doesn't produce a complete sentence or makes another error.

- (F) is wrong because although it has a verb, the plural verb *were* doesn't agree with the singular subject *danger*.
- (G) is wrong because the verb is in future tense, which isn't consistent with the rest of the sentence.
- (H) is correct because it contains a verb, *was*, that is consistent with the subject, *danger*.
- (J) is wrong because it doesn't contain a verb, which means the sentence is incomplete.

49. **B** This Content question is asking for an answer that *best clarifies the distinction between the two types of activities mentioned in this paragraph*, so underline this phrase. Read the context of the sentence and eliminate any answer that doesn't fulfill this goal. The two types of activities relate to *the flowing river* and the *canyon walls*.

- (A) and (C) are wrong because they don't relate to either activity.
- (B) is correct because *rocky surfaces* matches with *canyon walls* and *chilly water* matches with *flowing river*.
- (D) is wrong because it relates to only one type of activity.

50. **F** This Content question is asking for an answer that *concludes the paragraph with a phrase that relates to the main topic of the essay*, so underline this phrase. Ignore the underlined sentence and identify the *main topic* of the essay. The essay focuses on how the narrator enjoys seeking thrills and describes a particular experience. Eliminate any answer inconsistent with these ideas.

- (F) is correct because the passage is focused on thrill-seeking.
- (G) and (H) are wrong because they don't relate to the *main topic* of the essay.
- (J) is wrong because the last paragraph says *We continue to seek the big thrills*, so this isn't *the last thrill* the narrator will ever need.

ACT TEST 2 MATH ANSWERS AND EXPLANATIONS

1. **C** The question asks for the value of y in the equation. Since the question asks for a specific value and the answers contain numbers in increasing order, Plugging In the Answers is an option. The equation is not too complicated, though, so it may be faster to solve for y. Begin by multiplying both sides of the equation by 3 to get $5y - 1 = -18$. Add 1 to both sides to get $5y = -17$. Divide both sides by 5 to get $y = -\frac{17}{5}$. The correct answer is (C).

2. **H** The question asks for an equivalent expression. Use Bite-Sized Pieces and Process of Elimination. The result of dividing the coefficients is $\frac{12}{4} = 3$. Eliminate (G) and (J) because they have a different coefficient. When dealing with questions about exponents, remember the MADSPM rules. The DS part of the acronym indicates that Dividing matching bases means to Subtract the exponents. The result of subtracting the exponents of the z terms is $z^{10-2} = z^8$. Eliminate (F). The correct answer is (H).

3. **C** The question asks for the value of a function. In function notation, the number inside the parentheses is the x-value that goes into the function, and the value that comes out of the function is the y-value. Plug $x = 12$ into the function to get $f(12) = \frac{12^2 - 18}{12 + 2} = \frac{144 - 18}{14} = \frac{126}{14} = 9$. The correct answer is (C).

4. **H** The question asks for the number of articles Rebecca writes in the first 3 weeks of the month. Read carefully and use Bite-Sized Pieces to tackle this question. Graph 2 relates number of articles written to movies watched, so first determine how many movies she watched. Graph 1 indicates that at week 3, Rebecca had watched 15 movies. Graph 2 then indicates that when Rebecca had watched 15 movies, she had written 12 articles. The correct answer is (H).

5. **B** The question asks for the number of tables in a restaurant given information about napkins and tables. Since the question asks for a specific value and the answers contain numbers in increasing order, plug in the answers. Begin by labeling the answers as "tables" and start with (C), 25. The question states there are 4 napkins at each table, so with 25 tables the restaurant would have $4(25) = 100$ napkins at tables. The restaurant also has 20 napkins in reserve, so the total number of napkins would be $100 + 20 = 120$ napkins. Since the question says the restaurant has 100 napkins total, this is too many, and the restaurant must have fewer tables. Eliminate (C) and (D). Try (B), 20. With 20 tables the restaurant would have $4(20) = 80$ napkins at tables. With the 20 napkins in reserve, that means the restaurant would have $80 + 20 = 100$ napkins total. This matches the information in the question, so stop here. The correct answer is (B).

6. **J** The question asks which ray does **not** contain $\overline{WX}$. A ray is part of a line which has an endpoint and extends infinitely from that endpoint in only one direction. The first letter in the name of a ray is the endpoint. For each choice, start at the first letter listed and travel toward the second letter to see if the ray passes over $\overline{WX}$. The ray will pass over $\overline{WX}$ for every choice except (J), $\overrightarrow{YZ}$. The correct answer is (J).

7. **A** The question asks for the value of a in a set of equations. Since the question asks for a specific value and the answers contain numbers in increasing order, Plugging In the Answers is an option. The equations are not too complicated, though, so it may be faster to solve for a. The third equation specifies that $c = 5$. Plug this value into the second equation to get $b(5) = 40$. Divide both sides of the equation by 5 to get $b = 8$. Plug this value into the first equation to get $a(8) = 32$. Divide both sides by 8 to get $a = 4$. The correct answer is (A).

8. **G** The question asks for an equation that models a specific situation. Translate the information in bite-sized pieces and eliminate after each piece. The question asks about Yunyun's average time. For averages, use the formula $T = AN$, in which T is the total, A is the average, and N is the number of things. Calculate the total of the original set of numbers, using x for the missing 5th number. In this situation, the total time is the sum of the first four laps plus the time of the fifth lap, which is $175.8 + x$. Choice (J) does not contain this expression, so eliminate it. In this situation, the number of things is the number of laps being averaged, which is 5. This does not appear in (H), so eliminate it. The last part of the equation for average is A, which is 43. Eliminate (F), which divides 43 by another number. The correct answer is (G).

9. **B** The question asks how many integers in a certain range of numbers have a tens digit that is greater than the ones digit. There are not too many numbers in the range, so list them all out. They are 123, 124, 125, 126, 127, 128, 129, 130, 131, and 132. Circle the numbers that have a tens digit greater than the ones digit. There are only three: 130, 131, and 132. The correct answer is (B).

10. **J** The question asks how many hours Julie must practice in order to score 35 points. Use Ballparking to eliminate incorrect answers. Since it takes 12 hours of practice for Julie to score 20 points, she will have to practice longer than that to score 35 points. Eliminate (F), which is less than 12 hours. Set up a proportion, being sure to match up units. The proportion is $\frac{20 \text{ points}}{12 \text{ hours}} = \frac{35 \text{ points}}{x \text{ hours}}$. Cross-multiply to get $20x = 420$. Divide both sides of the equation by 20 to get $x = 21$. The correct answer is (J).

11. **B** The question asks for the fraction of a rectangle drawn on the coordinate plane that is in Quadrant IV. Begin by writing out the formula for the area of a rectangle, which is $A = lw$. Since the lines forming left and right sides of the rectangle are parallel to the y-axis, the length of the large rectangle can be found by subtracting the y-coordinates of the end points of those sides. This is $(2) - (-3) = 5$. The lines forming the top and bottom sides of the rectangle are parallel to the x-axis, so the width of the large rectangle can be found by subtracting the x-coordinates of the end points of those sides. This is $(2) - (-4) = 6$. Plug these into the formula for area to get $A = (5)(6) = 30$. The portion of the rectangle in Quadrant IV is also a rectangle; its area can be found by the same method. The length of this portion is $(0) - (-3) = 3$, and the width is $2 - 0 = 2$. Plug this into the formula for area to get $A = (3)(2) = 6$. The fraction this area is of the large rectangle is then $\frac{6}{30}$, which reduces to $\frac{1}{5}$. The correct answer is (B).

12. **J** The question asks for an equivalent form of an expression. There is a variable in the answer choices, so plug in. Make $z = 2$. The expression in the question becomes $\frac{2(2+3)-9}{5+4(2+3)}$. This simplifies to $\frac{2(5)-9}{5+4(5)} = \frac{10-9}{5+20} = \frac{1}{25}$. This is the target value; circle it. Now plug $z = 2$ into the answer choices to see which one matches the target value. Choices (F) and (G) do not contain a variable and do not match the target value, so eliminate them. Choice (H) becomes $\frac{-7(2)-21}{9(2)+15} = \frac{-14-21}{18+15} = \frac{-35}{33}$. Eliminate (H). Choice (J) becomes $\frac{2(2)-3}{4(2)+17} = \frac{4-3}{8+17} = \frac{1}{25}$. The correct answer is (J).

13. **B** The question asks at what two points a circle crosses the x-axis. A point on the x-axis must have a y-coordinate of 0, so set $y = 0$ in the circle's equation. This becomes $x^2 - (0)^2 = 49$, or $x^2 = 49$. Take the square root of both sides of the equation, remembering to consider both the positive and negative roots. This gives $x = 7$ or $x = -7$. Therefore, the two points at which the circle crosses the x-axis are $(7, 0)$ and $(-7, 0)$. The correct answer is (B).

14. **F** The question asks for the dimensions of a drawing given information about its area and perimeter. Use the Geometry Basic Approach. Start by drawing a figure and labeling it with the given information like this:

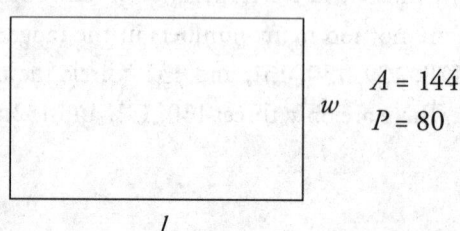

$A = 144$
$P = 80$

Write down the formula for the area of a rectangle, which is $A = lw$, and for the perimeter of a rectangle, which is $P = 2l + 2w$. Since the question asks for specific values and the answers contain numbers, plug in the answers. Begin by labeling the answers as "dimensions." Since the first dimension is increasing but the second is decreasing, just start with (F). Plug these numbers into the formula for area to get $A = (4)(36) = 144$. This matches the area given in the question, but the perimeter has to be checked as well. Plug the values into the formula for perimeter to get $P = 2(4) + 2(36) = 8 + 72 = 80$. Since all the information matches, these are the correct dimensions. Checking other choices would show that they either do not give the proper area or do not give the proper perimeter. The correct answer is (F).

15. **B** The question asks for a number equivalent to a fraction with numbers in scientific notation. Begin by dividing the digits before the multiplication sign to get $\frac{6.0}{1.5} = 4.0$. Eliminate (C) and (D) since they do not start with the correct digits. When dealing with exponents, remember the MADSPM rules. The DS part of the acronym indicates that Dividing matching bases means to Subtract the exponents. The result of subtracting the exponents on the 10's is $10^{(5-7)} = 10^{-2}$. Eliminate (A), which has the wrong exponent. The correct answer is (B).

16. **J** The question asks for the number of 7-digit phone numbers that can be generated which all have the same 3-digit prefix. Since digits can be any number from 0 to 9, there are 10 possibilities for each digit. Because digits can be selected independently of each other, simply multiply the number of possibilities for each digit together. The three digits in the prefix cannot change, so there are $10 - 7 = 4$ digits that can be selected. The number of possible combinations for these digits is $10 \times 10 \times 10 \times 10$, or 10^4. The correct answer is (J).

17. **C** The question asks for the last term in a geometric sequence consisting of the measure of the angles in a quadrilateral. Any quadrilateral, or four-sided figure, will have 4 angles that add up to $360°$. Since the question asks for a specific value and the answers are in increasing order, plug in the answers. Begin by labeling the answers as "last term" and start with (B), $160°$. If the last term is 160, and the common ratio between the degree measures is 2, then the degree measure of the third angle is $160 \div 2 = 80°$. The measure of the second angle is then $80 \div 2 = 40°$, and the measure of the first angle in the sequence is $40 \div 2 = 20°$. The sum of these angles would be $160 + 80 + 40 + 20 = 300°$. This doesn't match the sum of the angles in a quadrilateral, so eliminate (B). Since the sum was not large enough, the largest angle must be even larger, so eliminate (A) as well. Try (C), $192°$. The other three angles would be $96°$, $48°$, and $24°$. Add these angles to get $192 + 96 + 48 + 24 = 360°$, which is the correct sum. The correct answer is (C).

18. **F** The question asks for the value of an expression with two variables given two equations containing the variables. First solve the system of equations to get the values of x and y. One way to do this is to stack and add the equations to eliminate a variable. To eliminate x, multiply the second equation by -2 so that the equations have the same x coefficient with opposite signs. The second equation becomes $-2(3x + 4y) = -2(2)$ or $-6x - 8y = -4$. Then stack the equations and add:

$$6x + 10y = 14$$
$$\underline{-6x\; -8y = -4}$$
$$2y = 10$$

Divide both sides of the result by 2 to get $y = 5$. Plug this into one of the equations and solve for x. The original version of the second equation becomes $3x + 4(5) = 2$. This simplifies to $3x + 20 = 2$. Subtract 20 from both sides to get $3x = -18$. Divide both sides by 3 to get $x = -6$. Plug the values for x and y into the expression $5x + 7y$ in the question to get $5(-6) + 7(5) = -30 + 35 = 5$. The correct answer is (F).

19. **D** The equation asks for the form of an equation solved for b. There are variables in the answer choices, so Plugging In on this question is an option. It would be tricky to find numbers that make the equation true, though, so it may be faster to solve for b. Start by multiplying both sides of the equation by 2 to get $a - b = 12$. Subtract a from both sides to get $-b = 12 - a$. Multiply both sides by -1 to get $b = -12 + a$, or $b = a - 12$. The correct answer is (D).

20. **J** The question asks for a product that results in a negative odd number. A product is the result of multiplying two values together. Plug in some values to determine what kind of numbers work. Select numbers that satisfy the conditions in the answer choices and multiply them together to see if the result is a negative odd number. Choice (F) specifies a positive even number and a negative even number. Try 2 and -4. The product of these is $(2)(-4) = -8$. This is not an odd number, so eliminate (F). Choice (G) specifies two negative odd numbers. Choose -3 and -5. The product of these is $(-3)(-5) = 15$. This is not a negative number, so eliminate (G). Choice (H) specifies a positive even number and a negative odd number. Choose 2 and -3. The product of these is $(2)(-3) = -6$. This is not an odd number, so eliminate (H). Choice (J) specifies a positive odd number and a negative odd number. Choose 3 and -3. The product of these is $(3)(-3) = -9$. This is a negative odd number. The correct answer is (J).

21. **B** The question asks for the probability that the fifth marble removed from a bag will be purple. Probability is defined as $\dfrac{part}{whole}$. The *part*, or the number of outcomes that fit the requirements, is the number of purple marbles available when the fifth marble is removed. The bag initially contained 11 purple marbles, but 4 are removed, so the number of purple marbles currently in the bag is $11 - 4 = 7$. The *whole* is the total number of marbles that can be selected. The bag started out with $11 + 11 + 11 + 11 = 44$ marbles, but 4 are removed. Therefore, before the fifth marble is removed, there are $44 - 4 = 40$ marbles available. Plug these numbers into the expression for probability to get $\dfrac{7}{40}$. The correct answer is (B).

22. **H** The question asks for an inequality describing the number of points Oliver got if he must repeat a test. Use Ballparking to eliminate answers that do not make sense. Since a high score would mean that a test doesn't have to be repeated, choices that allow the score to be as high as possible cannot be correct. Eliminate (G) and (J), which allow p to be as high as possible. There is a variable in the answer

choices, so plug in. Examine the remaining answer choices to determine what number to plug in. Try $p = 20$. If Oliver scores 20 points on a test with 30 available points, the percentage of points he earned is $\frac{20}{30} \times 100 = 66.\overline{6}\%$. This is less than 70%, so it means that Oliver would have to repeat the test. Eliminate (F) since it is not necessarily true that $p < 20$. The correct answer is (H).

23. **C** The question asks for the distance in feet between two different screens and the projectors used for each one. Whenever dealing with relationships between parts of triangles, look for similar triangles and then set up proportions between corresponding sides. The figure contains two triangles sharing a common angle at the projector. Since the screens are parallel, the angles formed by the left sides of the triangles and the two screens are equal. Also, the angles formed by each of the right sides of the two triangles and the two screens are equal. Since all the angles between the two triangles are equal, the two triangles are similar. Set up proportions involving corresponding lengths of the two triangles. The widths of the screens represent corresponding sides on the triangles, so one proportion that can be formed, putting the value for the smaller triangle on top, would be $\frac{81}{108}$. The other value in the question, 180, represents the distance to the screen for the *Illuminator 100 Plus* and is also the height of the larger triangle. The height of the smaller triangle, which represents the distance from the projector to the screen for the *Illuminator 100*, is unknown, so call it x. Another proportion that can be set up, again putting the value for the smaller triangle on top, is $\frac{x}{180}$. Set these proportions equal to get $\frac{81}{108} = \frac{x}{180}$. Cross-multiply to get $(81)(180) = 108x$. This simplifies to $14{,}580 = 108x$. Divide both sides by 108 to get $x = 135$. This is the distance from the *Illuminator 100* to the screen. To get the distance between the screens, subtract this from the distance between the projector and the *Illuminator 100 Plus*. This is $180 - 135 = 45$. The correct answer is (C).

24. **H** The question asks for the distance between two points in the standard coordinate plane. Draw the points on the coordinate plane. Add two lines to form a right triangle with $\overline{JK}$ as the hypotenuse. Then use the Pythagorean Theorem, $a^2 + b^2 = c^2$, to calculate the length of the hypotenuse:

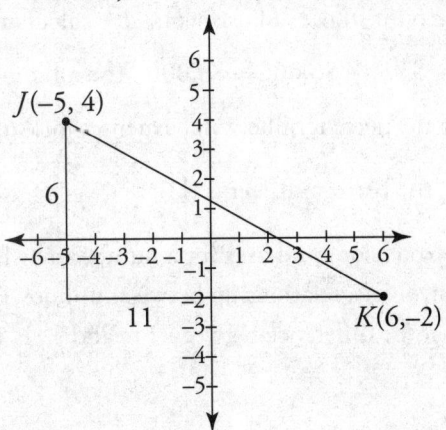

The height of the triangle is 4 − (−2) = 6 units. The base of the triangle is 6 − (−5) = 11 units. Put these into the Pythagorean Theorem to get $6^2 + 11^2 = c^2$. This simplifies to $c^2 = 36 + 121$, or $c^2 = 157$. Take the square root of both sides to get $c = \sqrt{157}$. The correct answer is (H).

25. **C** The question asks for the total number of stars Cynthia places on her bedroom ceiling after 30 days. This total is just the sum of the number of stars Cynthia places each day, or 1 + 2 + 3 + ... + 30. Because there are only 30 numbers to be added, just carefully add them up on a calculator. The total is 465. The correct answer is (C).

26. **F** The question asks which number **cannot** be the length of a side of a triangle given the lengths of the other two sides. The sum of the lengths of any two sides of a triangle must be greater than the third side. In particular, the sum of the lengths of the two smaller sides of a triangle must be greater than the largest side. Add $\overline{PQ}$ and $\overline{QR}$ to get 12 + 41 = 53. Since this is larger than the largest choice, none of the answers is too large. To see if any are too small, plug in the answers. Start with the smallest choice which is (F), 17. If $\overline{PR}$ is 17, the three sides of the triangle are 12, 41, and 17. Verify that the sum of the two smaller numbers is greater than the third: 12 + 17 = 29. This is not greater than 41, so these three sides cannot be the lengths of the sides of a triangle. The correct answer is (F).

27. **C** The question asks for the measure of a central angle of a circle. Start with Process of Elimination. The angle is a large angle—larger than a right angle, which is 90°. Eliminate (A) and (B) because they are less than 90°. Note that the figure includes a triangle. Two of the sides of that triangle are radii of the circle and must be the same length. That means the angles opposite those sides are also equal. Therefore, the triangle has two 40° angles. Use the fact that the three angles of a triangle always add up to 180° to determine the measure of the third. Let x be the measure of the third angle, so 40 + 40 + x = 180. This becomes 80 + x = 180, so the central angle, x, is 100°. The correct answer is (C).

28. **H** The question asks what percent of Stephanie's August expenses will be for office supplies. Translate the English into math in bite-size pieces. The question states Stephanie will *reduce her electricity expenses by $700* in August. The pie chart indicates that she spent $1,200 on electricity in July so she will spend $1,200 − $700 = $500 on electricity in August. The question states she will reduce her rent *by $1,300* in August, and it was $7,300 in July, so she will spend $7,300 − $1,300 = $6,000 on rent. The question states that *the rest of her expenses are unchanged*. Add all her expenses for August, taking into account those adjustments, to calculate her total expenses for August: $150 + $350 + $1,000 + $500 + $6,000 = $8,000. The amount she will spend on office supplies will still be $1,000. Find the percent of her total expenses for August that will be for office supplies: $\frac{\$1,000}{\$8,000} \times 100 = 12.5\%$. The correct answer is (H).

29. **B** The question gives two expressions and asks for a number by which their difference will always be divisible. The question involves a relationship between unknown numbers, so plug in. Make $q = 2$. Plug 2 in for q to find that the difference between $14q$ and $5q$ is 14(2) − 5(2) = 28 − 10 = 18. Of the

answer choices, 18 is only divisible by (B), 9, so that is the answer. Alternatively, use algebra to find that the difference between 14*q* and 5*q* is 14*q* – 5*q* = 9*q*, which is always divisible by 9. Either way, the correct answer is (B).

30. **F** The question asks for an inequality representing a specific situation. Translate the English into math in bite-size pieces. There is a variable in the answer choices, so plug in. As the question states, Ron's hourly rate of pay, *r*, is dependent on how many hours Ron works, so select a number of hours Ron could have worked. The question says he works for a minimum of 20 hours per week, so for 6 weeks he works at least 6(20) = 120 hours. If Ron works for 120 hours, his hourly rate of pay will be *r* = $1,800 ÷ 120 = $15 per hour. Eliminate (H) and (J) as they do not have $15 as an extreme. To determine whether (F) or (G) is correct, select another number of work hours. Try 30. If Ron works for 30 hours per week, he works for 6(30) = 180 hours total, and his hourly rate of pay will be *r* = $1,800 ÷ 180 = $10 per hour. Eliminate (G). The correct answer is (F).

31. **D** The question asks for the distance between two points in the complex plane. The complex number *a* + *bi* is plotted in the complex plane as (*a*, *b*) with *a* representing the real part of the complex number and *b* representing the imaginary part. This means that *P* = 2 + *i* would be plotted as the point (2, 1), and *Q* = 6 + 4*i* would be plotted as the point (6, 4). Draw these points on a coordinate plane. Add two lines to form a right triangle with $\overline{PQ}$ as the hypotenuse. Then use the Pythagorean Theorem, $a^2 + b^2 = c^2$, to calculate the length of the hypotenuse:

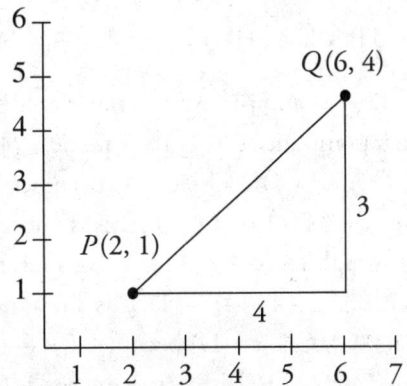

The height of the triangle is 4 – 1 = 3 units. The base of the triangle is 6 – 2 = 4 units. Plug these values into the Pythagorean Theorem, $a^2 + b^2 = c^2$, and solve for *c* to get the hypotenuse, or simply note that the triangle is a 3-4-5 right triangle with a hypotenuse of 5. Either way, the distance between the points is 5. The correct answer is (D).

32. **H** The question asks for the inverse trigonometric expression that represents an angle on the figure. Write out SOHCAHTOA to remember the trig functions. Let θ represent the angle. The 8 in the figure corresponds to the length of the side adjacent to θ, and the 23 in the figure corresponds to the hypotenuse. The CAH part of SOHCAHTOA defines the cosine as $\dfrac{adjacent}{hypotenuse}$, so $\cos\theta = \dfrac{8}{23}$. The answer choices contain inverse trig functions, which are simply the functions that take a ratio of the sides of a triangle and return the appropriate angle. Therefore, $\cos\theta = \dfrac{8}{23}$ means $\cos^{-1}\left(\dfrac{8}{23}\right) = \theta$. The correct answer is (H).

33. **A** The question asks for the perimeter of a polygon. The perimeter of a shape is simply the measure of the line around the shape. The perimeter of polygon *CDZXY* is the sum of the lengths of all the individual sides. Since *CDZY* is a square, all of its sides are equal. This means that $\overline{CD} = x$. Another side of the square is $\overline{DZ}$, so it also has a length of *x*. The length of $\overline{ZX}$ is given as *y*. The length of $\overline{XY}$ is given as *z*. Continuing around the polygon, $\overline{YC}$ is another side of the square, so its length is again *x*. Add these all together to get the perimeter of *CDZXY* as *x* + *x* + *y* + *z* + *x*, which simplifies to $3x + y + z$. The correct answer is (A).

34. **G** The question asks for the sum of the two largest integers in a series of four consecutive even numbers. There is a variable in the answer choices, so plug in. Since *t* must be the sum of four consecutive, even integers, select four such integers and add them together. Use the numbers 2, 4, 6, and 8. This means $t = 2 + 4 + 6 + 8 = 20$. Take care to identify what the question asks for. The question asks for the sum of the 2 larger integers, which is $6 + 8 = 14$. This is the target value; circle it. Now plug $t = 20$ into the answer choices to see which one matches the target value. Choice (F) becomes $\frac{20}{2} - 4 = 10 - 4 = 6$. This does not match the target value, so eliminate (F). Choice (G) becomes $\frac{20}{2} + 4 = 10 + 4 = 14$. This matches the target, so keep (G), but check the remaining answers just in case. Choice (H) becomes $20 + 2 = 22$. Eliminate (H). Choice (J) becomes $20 + 4 = 24$. Eliminate (J). The correct answer is (G).

35. **D** The question asks for the equation shown in the graph in Figure 2. The graph in Figure 2 has a labeled point. Since that point must satisfy the equation, plug its coordinates into the answer choices. For point (–4, 1), $x = -4$, and $y = 1$. Choice (A) becomes $1 = (-4 - 4)^2 - 1$, which simplifies to $1 = (-8)^2 - 1$. This becomes $1 = 64 - 1$ or $1 = 63$. This is not true, so eliminate (A). Choice (B) becomes $1 = (-4 - 4)^2 + 1$. This simplifies to $1 = (-8)^2 + 1$, which becomes $1 = 64 + 1$ or $1 = 65$. Eliminate (B). Choice (C) becomes $1 = (-4 + 4)^2 - 1$. This simplifies to $1 = (0)^2 - 1$, which becomes $1 = 0 - 1$ or $1 = -1$. Eliminate (C). Choice (D) becomes $1 = (-4 + 4)^2 + 1$. This simplifies to $1 = (0)^2 + 1$, which becomes $1 = 0 + 1$, or $1 = 1$. The correct answer is (D).

36. **F** The question asks the number of nickels in a piggy bank. Since the question asks for a specific value and the answers contain numbers in increasing order, plug in the answers. Begin by labeling the answers as "nickels" and start with (H), 17. The question states that there is one more dime than there are nickels, so there are $17 + 1 = 18$ dimes. The question states that there three times as many dimes as pennies, so there are $18 \div 3 = 6$ pennies. The question says there are two more quarters than dimes, so there are $18 + 2 = 20$ quarters. Multiply the number of each type of coin by its value to get the total amount of money in the piggy bank as $17(0.05) + 18(0.10) + 6(0.01) + 20(0.25) = \$7.71$. This doesn't match the amount in the question, \$5.29, so eliminate (H). Since more nickels would only increase the amount of money in the bank, there must be fewer nickels. Eliminate (J). Try (G). If there are 13 nickels, then there are 14 dimes. There are supposed to be three times as many dimes as pennies, but since 14 is not divisible by 3, this is impossible. Eliminate (G). Try (F). If there are 11 nickels, then there are 12 dimes, 4 pennies, and 14 quarters. The total in the piggy

bank is then 11(0.05) + 12(0.10) + 4(0.01) + 14(0.25) = $5.29. This matches the information in the question. The correct answer is (F).

37. **C** The question asks for the mean of a set of numbers given information about how the set relates to another set. For averages, use the formula $T = AN$, in which T is the total, A is the average, and N is the number of things. The average is 87, and the number of things is 5, so $T = (87)(5) = 435$. The new set removes the number 75, so the new total is $435 - 75 = 360$. To find the new average, plug $T = 360$ and $N = 4$ into the formula to get $360 = A(4)$. Divide both sides of the equation by 4 to get $A = 90$. The correct answer is (C).

38. **J** The question asks which statement is true given another true statement. For any true if-then statement, the statement's contrapositive is also true. The original statement is *"If Jenny is home, then her car is in the driveway."* Determine the contrapositive of this by flipping the two parts of the statement and reversing those parts. This means that the contrapositive is *"If Jenny's car is not in the driveway, then she is not home."* The correct answer is (J).

39. **D** The question asks for an equivalent equation involving trig functions. When dealing with trigonometric expressions, write out SOHCAHTOA to remember the trig functions. The question includes functions that are not defined in SOHCAHTOA, but it also includes some definitions to relate those functions to SOHCAHTOA functions. Use those definitions to convert the equation to SOHCAHTOA functions. The function $g(x) = \csc x \tan x$ becomes $g(x) = \left(\dfrac{1}{\sin x} \right)(\tan x)$. The SOH part of SOHCAHTOA defines the sine as $\dfrac{opposite}{hypotenuse}$. The TOA part of SOHCATOA defines the tangent as $\dfrac{opposite}{adjacent}$. The function includes the reciprocal of sine, so take the reciprocal of the expression to get $\dfrac{1}{\sin x} = \dfrac{hypotenuse}{opposite}$. Substitute these definitions into the equation to get $g(x) = \left(\dfrac{hypotenuse}{opposite} \right) \left(\dfrac{opposite}{adjacent} \right)$. The *opposite* sides cancel to give $g(x) = \dfrac{hypotenuse}{adjacent}$. Use SOHCAHTOA one more time to turn this back into a trig function. The CAH part of SOHCAHTOA defines the cosine as $\dfrac{adjacent}{hypotenuse}$. Since the equation now contains the reciprocal of this, the equation can be rewritten as $g(x) = \dfrac{1}{\cos x}$. Per the definitions in the question, this is the same as sec x. The correct answer is (D).

40. **H** The question asks for the expected value of a random variable representing the total number of points in five rounds of a game. Expected value is calculated by multiplying each possible outcome by the probability of its occurrence and then adding the products. As stated in the question, each round of the game has three possible outcomes: win, lose, or tie. Since the question says that the

outcomes are all equally likely, they each have a probability of $\frac{1}{3}$. Multiply the probability of each one by the point value each one earns and add the results. The result is $2\left(\frac{1}{3}\right) + 0\left(\frac{1}{3}\right) + 0\left(\frac{1}{3}\right) = \frac{2}{3}$. This is the expected result of one round. To get the expected result of five rounds, multiply by 5 to get $5\left(\frac{2}{3}\right) = \frac{10}{3}$. The correct answer is (H).

41. **D** The question asks for the surface area of a sphere given the volume. The question gives the equations for the surface area and volume of a sphere. Both involve radius, so find the radius of the sphere. Set the volume given for the sphere equal to the expression for volume to get $\frac{4}{3}\pi r^3 = 288\pi$. Multiply both sides by 3 to get $4\pi r^3 = 864\pi$. Divide both sides by 4π to get $r^3 = 216$. Take the cube root of both sides to get $r = 6$. Plug this value for the radius into the expression for surface area to get $4\pi(6)^2 = 4\pi(36) = 144\pi$. The correct answer is (D).

42. **F** The question asks for the value of x in an equation involving a logarithm. Logarithms are another way of expressing exponents such that $\log_b = x$ can be written as $b^x = n$. Set the expression equal to a variable, such as y. Therefore $3\log_x x^{-2} = y$. Divide both sides by 3 to get $\log_x x^{-2} = \frac{y}{3}$. Using the identity for logs, this becomes $x^{\frac{y}{3}} = x^{-2}$. Since the bases are the same, the exponents are equal, so $\frac{y}{3} = -2$. Multiply both sides by 3 to get $y = -6$. The correct answer is (F).

43. **B** The question asks for the sine of an angle depicted in the coordinate plane. Start with Process of Elimination. Using the mnemonic device All Students Take Calculus, determine the sign of the trig functions in Quadrant III, where θ terminates. This indicates that only the tangent is positive in Quadrant III, so the sine must be negative. Eliminate (C) and (D). When dealing with trigonometric expressions, write out SOHCAHTOA to remember the trig functions. The SOH part defines the sine as $\frac{opposite}{hypotenuse}$. Trigonometric functions relate to right triangles, so draw a line from the point $(-12, -5)$ to the x-axis to create a right triangle like this:

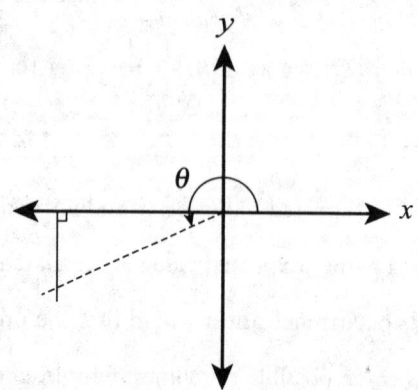

Even though θ includes the angle measure from the positive x-axis to the negative x-axis, sin θ will have the same value but the opposite sign as the angle that is formed with the negative x-axis. The side opposite that angle is represented by the distance between the point and the x-axis, which is 5. To find the hypotenuse, use the Pythagorean Theorem or realize this is a 5-12-13 triangle, so the hypotenuse is 13. The sine of this angle is $\frac{5}{13}$, but it must be negative. The correct answer is (B).

44.　**F**　The question asks which line could contain the side of a parallelogram with one side given. Since the given side, $\overline{AB}$, and the side in question, $\overline{CD}$, have no points in common, they are opposite sides of the parallelogram and so are parallel to each other. Two lines containing the two line segments would also be parallel. Lines that are parallel have the same slope. Calculate the slope of the line through $\overline{AB}$. The formula for slope is $\frac{y_2 - y_1}{x_2 - x_1}$. Plug in the values from the two endpoints of $\overline{AB}$ to get $\frac{6-1}{7-5} = \frac{5}{2}$. The answer choices are already in slope-intercept form, $y = mx + b$, where m represents the slope. The only one with a slope of $\frac{5}{2}$ is (F). The correct answer is (F).

45.　**B**　The question asks for the evaluation of a function with two variables. Since there are variables in the answers, plug in. Make $c = 2$ and $d = 3$, so $c^2 = 4$ and $d^2 = 9$. Plug these into the function for x and y to get $(4 - 9)^2 + (4 + 9)^2 = (-5)^2 + (13)^2 = 25 + 169 = 194$. This is the target value; circle it. Now plug $c = 2$ and $d = 3$ into the answer choices to see which matches the target value. Choice (A) becomes $4(2)^2(3)^2 = 4(4)(9) = 144$. This doesn't match the target value, so eliminate (A). Choice (B) becomes $2(2)^4 + 2(3)^4 = 32 + 162 = 194$. This matches the target, so keep (B), but check the remaining answers just in case. Choice (C) becomes $2(2)^4 - 2(3)^4 = 32 - 162 = -130$. Eliminate (C). Choice (D) becomes $-4(2)^2(3)^2 = -4(4)(9) = -144$. Eliminate (D). The correct answer is (B).

ACT TEST 2 READING ANSWERS AND EXPLANATIONS

1.　**C**　This reasoning question asks about the *shift in the passage* found in the last paragraph of Passage A. Because this is a general question, it should be done after all the specific questions. Look for the Golden Thread. Once you identify the Golden Thread, read the last paragraph. While the majority of the passage describes watching Jackie Robinson *making his major league debut* as the first African American to play in Major League Baseball, the last paragraph finds the narrator apologizing for his actions and starting to understand that his expectations had been unrealistic. Eliminate answers that don't match this answer from the passage. Eliminate (A), as the passage begins with the end of segregation in baseball. Eliminate (B), as while the narrator does blame his outburst on his fever, he admits it's only *partly true*. Choice (C) matches the answer from the passage, so keep it. While the narrator's grandfather's *anticipation* is mentioned early in the passage, *anger* doesn't fit the grandfather's tone in the last paragraph, so eliminate (D). The correct answer is (C).

2. **F** This reasoning question asks what the narrator's ultimate opinion was of *Jackie Robinson*. Look for the lead words *Jackie Robinson* to find the window for the question in Passage A. In the second paragraph, the narrator describes Robinson as a *gentleman, never losing his cool*. Additionally, he mentions that he is *proud that Robinson is playing*. Eliminate answers that don't match this answer from the passage. Choice (F) matches the answer from the passage, so keep it. Choice (G) is mentioned in the passage, but it answers the wrong question: while the narrator initially thinks Robinson is *capable of doing the impossible*, the question asks how he *ultimately* sees Robinson; eliminate (G). While the narrator is at one point disappointed in a play by Robinson, he learns that *what matters is how he plays the whole game*, so eliminate (H). Eliminate (J) because the passage describes the narrator and his grandfather as *excited and tense*, but the question asks about *Robinson*. The correct answer is (F).

3. **B** This reasoning question asks for the purpose of the *narrator's statement* in lines 46–48. Although this question includes a line reference, it asks about the purpose of the statement in relationship to the passage as a whole; it is a general question and should be done after all of the specific questions about Passage B. Look for the Golden Thread. In Passage B, the narrator notes a change in how he felt about progress toward racial equality: he felt excited and hopeful at the game but disappointed by the slow pace of change outside the stadium. This question asks about the narrator's description of how he felt *inside the stadium*. He says, *I felt I was in some utopian society that existed without segregation and racism*. Eliminate answers that don't match this answer from the passage. Eliminate (A) because the narrator is describing the feelings he has about the significance of the event; it is not a literal description of how people were interacting in the stadium. Choice (B) matches the answer from the passage, so keep it. Choice (C) uses words from the passage but doesn't match what the passage says; while the narrator believed that Jackie Robinson playing in the major leagues would change the world, the rest of the passage shows that society was not free from *segregation and racism*. Eliminate (C). Eliminate (D) as the statement in the window is largely positive and does not reflect the negative feelings of the narrator 21 years later. The correct answer is (B).

4. **G** This referral question asks how the *narrator's expectations about how Jackie Robinson's appearance in Major League Baseball would affect segregation* compared to its *actual effect*, based on Passage B. Because this is a general question, it should be done after all the specific questions. Look for the Golden Thread. In lines 52–58, the narrator recounts, *My friends and I were flying high as we left the stadium. If a black man was now playing for the Brooklyn Dodgers, we felt there was nothing we couldn't do...Change, we thought, was rapidly coming. To some extent that was true, but racism and injustice also persisted.* In lines 67–70, as he recounts the death of Martin Luther King, Jr., the narrator describes his earlier sentiments as *hopelessly naïve*. This indicates that the effect of Robinson's playing in the Major Leagues was different than anticipated, so eliminate (H) and (J). Eliminate (F) as the size of the *crowd* is not related to the effect on segregation. Choice (G) aligns closely with the narrator's statement: *Change, we thought, was rapidly coming*. The correct answer is (G).

5. **C** This reasoning question asks why *the information about Dr. Martin Luther King, Jr.* in lines 67–69 was included. Read a window around the given line reference. As the narrator contrasts the death of Martin Luther King, Jr. with Jackie Robinson's first major league game, he says *at times it felt like nothing had been accomplished* regarding the struggle for racial equality in the 21 years since the baseball game. Eliminate answers that don't match this answer from the passage. Nothing is said about

role models, so eliminate (A). Eliminate (B) as the mention of King does not point to Robinson's importance *in baseball*. Choice (C) matches the answer from the passage about the narrator's feeling that *nothing had been accomplished* with regard to racial equality; keep (C). Eliminate (D) because the lines referenced in the question do not touch on *Robinson's influence*. Eliminate (D). The correct answer is (C).

6. **F**   This reasoning question asks what the *narrator of Passage B makes a comparison between*. There is not a good lead word in this question, so work the question later. Choice (F) mentions comparing *the struggle for racial equality* and *the baseball season*. In the final paragraph, the narrator states that *the season is 162 games long, and we are only part of the way through it* and compares that to the slow pace of change in equality issues. Keep (F). Choice (G) uses words from the passage but does not match what the passage says: the passage brings up both *baseball* and *golf*, but there is no direct comparison between the two. Eliminate (G). The references to *tense excitement* and *bed covers* are made only in Passage A, so eliminate (H). Eliminate (J) as Passage B never mentions *striking out*. The correct answer is (F).

7. **D**   This reasoning question asks for a *comparison of the tone of each passage*. Because this question asks about both passages, it should be done after the questions that ask about each passage individually. Consider the Golden Thread of both passages. Passage A starts with a tone of excitement but finishes with a more somber tone, which is similar to the positivity in the first half of Passage B, followed by disappointment in the latter half. Eliminate answers that don't match this answer from the passage. Eliminate (A), as *hopeful and cheery* doesn't describe the full progression of Passage A, nor does *dreary and pessimistic* reflect the tone of Passage B. Eliminate (B) because Passage A is not objectively factual; it is a story that includes subjective descriptions such as, *I realize then that I had been nervous, too. I had expected the impossible—I had wanted him to bat a thousand*. Eliminate (C) as it disregards the positive aspects of both passages. Choice (D) matches the answer from the passage, so keep (D). The correct answer is (D).

8. **G**   This referral question asks what *the narrator of Passage B provides more information about* than *the narrator of Passage A* does. Because this question asks about both passages, it should be done after the questions that ask about each passage individually. Eliminate any answer choices that misrepresent either passage. While Passage A describes the events of only one day, Passage B relays the events of that day along with future events. Eliminate (F), as a *play-by-play* is not included in either passage. Keep (G), as the narrator of Passage B relates Jackie Robinson's actions to the long-term *struggle for racial equality*. Eliminate (H) since Passage B does not discuss Robinson's career prior to that day's events. Eliminate (J) as only Passage A mentions the *Negro League*. The correct answer is (G).

9. **C**   This reasoning question asks how the narrator of Passage A felt *after seeing Jackie Robinson play*, compared to the way the narrator of Passage B felt. Because this question asks about both passages, it should be done after the questions that ask about each passage individually. The narrator of Passage A says that he *let out a loud groan* when another player got Robinson out and realizes that he had wanted Robinson *to bat a thousand*. The narrator of Passage B describes himself as *flying high* after seeing Robinson play. In other words, the narrator of Passage B was excited, and the narrator of Passage A was disappointed. Eliminate any answer choices that misrepresent either passage. Eliminate (A), as the narrator for Passage B focuses more on race relations than the narrator for

Passage A does. Eliminate (B) as there is no indication that the narrator of Passage A is likely to stop following the Dodgers. Keep (C) because it matches the answer from the passage. Eliminate (D) as the narrator of Passage A does not mention excitement about *the future for African American baseball players*. The correct answer is (C).

10. **J** This reasoning question asks about the *main idea of the passage*. Because this is a general question, it should be done after all the specific questions. Look for the Golden Thread. The passage focuses on the CCC, a program that arose from the New Deal that put many young men to work in forests, parks, and other public lands in return for pay, housing, education, food, and clothing. Eliminate answers that don't match this answer from the passage. Eliminate (F) because the CCC never *forced unemployed young men to work*. Eliminate (G) because the passage does not suggest that there was no *suitable employment* for *veterans* before the CCC. Eliminate (H) because the passage states that the *idea for the CCC* came from *President Roosevelt*, not from *Congress*. Keep (J) because it is consistent with the main idea of the text. The correct answer is (J).

11. **B** This reasoning question asks about the main idea of the third paragraph. Read the third paragraph. The paragraph states that the *earliest enrollees were some veterans who returned to Washington…demanding pay….When it became clear that no bonus would be forthcoming, about twenty-five hundred of the men took Roosevelt up on his offer and joined the CCC*. Eliminate answers that don't match this answer from the passage. Choice (A) includes a statement that is mentioned in the passage, but it answers the wrong question: while the paragraph mentions that *Eleanor Roosevelt* met with the Bonus Army, this is not the main idea of the paragraph. (Also, *Hoover* was not President, but ACT doesn't expect you to know information that is not included in the passage.) Keep (B) because it matches the answer from the passage. Eliminate (C) because the fact that *Roosevelt* provided *food* and *shelter* is not the main idea of the paragraph. Additionally, the passage doesn't indicate that Roosevelt paid the veterans a *bonus*. Eliminate (D) because the paragraph does not mention the *age requirement*. The correct answer is (B).

12. **J** This reasoning question asks why President Roosevelt described himself as a *tree farmer* in line 7. Read a window around the line reference. The passage states that the president *cared about the fate of the trees* and *was fond of listing his occupation as "tree farmer."* The phrase *"tree farmer"* means he enjoyed caring for the trees on his estate. Eliminate answers that don't match this answer from the passage. Eliminate (F) because the passage never mentions Roosevelt growing trees to support his *family*. Eliminate (G) because the passage never states that he *believed in agrarian economy over urban industrialization*. Eliminate (H) because the passage does not mention a *successful business selling trees*. Note that (F) and (H) take the description *tree farmer* literally, which is not supported by the text. Keep (J), which is consistent with the passage. The correct answer is (J).

13. **B** This referral question asks for a project *the CCC performed for the National Park Service*. Look for the lead words *National Park Service* to find the window for the question. In lines 61–63 the passage states, *For the National Park Service, they built roads, campgrounds, bridges, and recreation and administration facilities*. Choices (A), (C), and (D) all include details that are mentioned in the passage but that answer the wrong question: they describe projects that were done in the *national forests* or for the *Biological Survey*, instead of for the *National Park Service*. Keep (B), which is consistent with the passage. The correct answer is (B).

14. **F** This referral question asks for a true statement *about the CCC*. There is not a good lead word in this question, so work the question later. Eliminate answers that are not consistent with the passage. Keep (F) since lines 72–74 state that the program *taught more than a hundred thousand to read and write* and passed out eighth grade and high school diplomas. Eliminate (G) because the CCC did not focus on *urban job training*. Eliminate (H), which uses words from the passage but doesn't match what the passage says: lines 32–34 indicate that the CCC required enrollees to have at least six teeth; it does not say that the CCC accepted *only men with six teeth*. Eliminate (J) because the passage never mentions *courses in nutrition and self-esteem*. The correct answer is (F).

15. **B** This referral question asks what the fourth paragraph *makes clear* about the CCC. Read the fourth paragraph. Lines 51–54 state that *Congress continued to reauthorize [the CCC program] faithfully over the next seven years* and that *the CCC had put more than three million young "soil soldiers" to work*. Eliminate answers that don't match this answer from the passage. Eliminate (A), which is only partially true; the organization was *voluntary*, but workers were compensated. Keep (B) because Congress kept reinstating the program year after year, and line 18 states that the CCC was originally *to last two years*. Eliminate (C) because the number *4.1 million* refers to the *man-hours fighting fires*, not the number of men *employed*; this answer uses words from the passage but doesn't match what the passage says. Eliminate (D), which also uses words from the passage but doesn't match what the passage says: the passage mentions *flood controls* in West Virginia, Vermont, and New York, rather than fighting *fires* in these states. The correct answer is (B).

16. **H** This reasoning question asks what the passage suggests about *national forests before the 1930s*. Look for the lead words *national forests* to find the window for the question. Lines 54–61 describe the work the CCC did in the *national forests*. According to the passage, the CCC existed from *1933 to 1942*, but this question asks about the period *before the 1930s*. Lines 59–61 say that the CCC *planted more than 1.3 billion young trees in the first major reforestation campaign in the country's history*. This implies that before the 1930s, there had not been a major reforestation campaign. Eliminate answers that don't match this answer from the passage. Choices (F) and (G) use words from the passage, but neither matches what the passage says: the passage doesn't give any information about *diseased trees* or *wildlife refuges* in the national parks before the 1930s. Eliminate (F) and (G). Keep (H) because it matches the answer from the passage. Eliminate (J), which uses words from the passage but doesn't match what the passage says: the passage does not indicate that there were *floods* in the national forests before the 1930s. The correct answer is (H).

17. **A** This referral question asks *when the CCC changed its name*. Work backwards and use lead words from the answers to find the window for this question. The lead words *CCRYRM* and *Congress* appear in the first paragraph. Lines 11–15 state that when President Roosevelt *went to Congress for authorization of the program, he called the new agency the Civilian Corps Reforestation Youth Rehabilitation Movement, but before sinking under the weight of an acronym like CCRYRM, it was soon changed to the Civilian Conservation Corps*. Eliminate any answers that do not match this answer from the passage. Keep (A), as the name was *soon changed* after the program was approved by Congress. Eliminate (B) because Congress never *protested that CCRYRM was too difficult to say*. This answer uses words from the passage but doesn't match what the passage says. Eliminate (C) because lines 7–16 imply that *the CCC changed its name* in 1933, soon after Roosevelt *went to Congress for authorization of the program*, and lines 50–51 state that Roosevelt *expanded the size*

of the CCC…to 500,000 in 1935. Eliminate (D), which uses words from the passage but doesn't match what the passage says: the passage never states that the *Bonus Army disbanded,* and lines 47–49 state that men from the Bonus Army *joined the CCC,* suggesting that the name had already been changed when they joined. The correct answer is (A).

18. **H**   This referral question asks what requirements enrollees had to meet *the same year the CCC was authorized.* Work backwards and use lead words from the answers to find the window for the question. Lines 29–34 state, *The men had to be US citizens between the ages of seventeen and twenty-seven…out of school, out of work, capable of physical labor, over 60 inches but under 78 inches in height, more than 107 pounds in weight, and had to possess no fewer than "three serviceable natural masticating teeth above and below."* Eliminate answers that don't match this answer from the passage. Eliminate (F) because the passage states that the men should be *over 60 inches but under 78 inches,* not *over 78 inches.* Eliminate (G) because the passage states that the men needed to be *out of school,* not *in school.* Keep (H) because it matches the answer from the passage. Eliminate (J) because, according to line 30, the age limit changed *later,* not in *the same year the CCC was authorized.* Choices (F), (G), and (J) each use words from the passage but don't match what the passage says. The correct answer is (H).

19. **C**   This reasoning question asks for the *main idea of the passage.* Because this is a general question, it should be done after all the specific questions. Look for the Golden Thread. This passage deals with the importance of the totem pole and the role the totem pole plays in Native American culture. Eliminate answers that don't match this answer from the passage. Choice (A) stresses the importance of *canoes* over *totem poles.* Eliminate (A). Choice (B) focuses too narrowly on the history of a single totem pole, so eliminate (B). Choice (C) matches the answer from the passage, so keep it. Like (B), (D) focuses too narrowly on one detail (specifically on the potlatch ban) and can be eliminated. The correct answer is (C).

20. **G**   This referral question asks for a question that is *NOT answered in the passage.* When a question asks what is **not** mentioned in the text, eliminate answers that are mentioned. Work backwards and use lead words from the answers to find the window for this question. Lines 1–3 state that *it was the natives of the far north, in what is now British Columbia and Alaska, who first carved totem poles,* so eliminate (F). Lines 64–66 state, *Today, Haida, Tlingit, Tsimshian, Kwakiutl and other native craftsmen carve, predominantly for the tourist trade, small "souvenir" totem poles,* so eliminate (H). Lines 3–9 indicate that totem poles were not carved before *the mid-18th century* because the Native Americans *lacked the iron tools necessary to fell a massive tree in one piece and carve its entire length.* Eliminate (J). Only the question posed in (G) goes unanswered in the passage. The correct answer is (G).

21. **C**   This referral question asks for *one of the main purposes of totem poles.* Look for the lead words *poles* and *purpose* to find the window for this question. Lines 39–40 state that *poles serve the important purpose of recording the lore of a clan, much as a book would.* Eliminate answers that don't match this answer from the passage. Choice (A) is stated in the passage but answers the wrong question; the idea that the totem poles display the carvers' *artistic skill* is stated in the passage, but the passage doesn't indicate that this is a main purpose of totem poles. Eliminate (A). While (B) is mentioned in the passage, it similarly answers the wrong question: the passage does not state that serving as a landmark is a main purpose of totem poles. Eliminate (B). Choice (C) matches the answer from

the passage, so keep it. Choice (D) is stated in the passage but answers the wrong question: totem poles are associated with potlatches, but only lines 39–40 identify an *important purpose* of totem poles. Eliminate (D). The correct answer is (C).

22. **G** This reasoning question asks how the sixth paragraph functions in the context of the passage. Read the sixth paragraph. Lines 49–59 describe the meanings of some of the symbols used on totem poles. Eliminate answers that don't match this answer from the passage. Choice (F) uses words from the passage but doesn't match what the passage says: the passage indicates that there is a story behind *almost every*, not *every*, image. Eliminate (F). Choice (G) matches the answer from the passage, so keep it. There are no comparisons of regional totem poles in the paragraph, so eliminate (H). Eliminate (J), as the paragraph describes how Raven is depicted, but not Raven's *role* in *mythology*; this answer comes from the wrong window since Raven's role in mythology is mentioned in the fifth paragraph. The correct answer is (G).

23. **D** This referral question asks which fact about the *totem poles carved by coastal tribes of the far north* is NOT included in the second paragraph. Read the second paragraph. When a question asks what is **not** mentioned in the text, eliminate answers that are mentioned. Choice (A) is addressed in lines 13–15, which state that *initially, the poles were made to stand against the front of a house…so all would enter the house through the pole*. Eliminate (A). Choice (B) is addressed in lines 11–12, which state that the coastal tribes of the far north *used trees that grew so tall and straight in their wet climate*. Eliminate (B). Choice (C) is addressed in lines 15–17, which state that the totem poles in *some way identified the owner*. Eliminate (C). Choice (D) uses words from the passage but doesn't match what the passage says; the *family crest* is mentioned in line 16, but there is no evidence in the passage that the poles were constructed *only* by clans who had family crests. The correct answer is (D).

24. **G** This referral question asks what *the various characters on a totem pole* represent according to the fifth paragraph. Read the fifth paragraph. Lines 40–42 indicate that the *top figure on the pole identifies the owner's clan, and succeeding characters…tell their stories*. Eliminate answers that don't match this answer from the passage. Choice (F) uses words from the passage but doesn't match what the passage says, as the *owner's clan* is identified only by the top figure on the totem pole, not by the *various characters* underneath it. Eliminate (F). Choice (G) matches the answer from the passage, so keep it. Eliminate (H) and (J), which are stated in the passage but answer the wrong question. *Raven* and *Frog* are specific examples (lines 42–44) of the *various characters*; neither answers the question about what the *various characters* represent. The correct answer is (G).

25. **D** This referral question asks for the *home* of the *Tlingit*. Look for the lead word *Tlingit* to find the window for the question. Line 31 indicates that the Tlingit are from *the southeastern coast of Alaska*. Eliminate (A), (B), and (C) because they do not match the answer from the passage. The correct answer is (D).

26. **F** This reasoning question asks why the author includes the information in lines 60–63. Read a window around the given line reference. This paragraph suggests that the broad importance of totem poles is related to the poles' *history, mythology, social structure, and spirituality*. Eliminate answers that don't match this answer from the passage. Choice (F) matches the answer from the passage, so keep it. Choice (G) uses words from the passage but doesn't match what the passage says: while

totem poles can function *as* books do, there is no evidence in the passage that the poles have *replaced* books. Eliminate (G). Choices (H) and (J) also use words from the passage but don't match what the passage says. Lines 60–61 say, *Learning to read totem poles is like learning to read a language.* The passage does not say that *Native American tribes have no spoken or written language.* Eliminate (H). Lines 62–63 state that *totem poles continue to be carved by the descendants of the original carvers*, but there is no indication in the passage that these *descendants* carve *copies*. Eliminate (J). The correct answer is (F).

27. **C** This reasoning question asks for a word to describe the employers' attitude toward *potlatches* in the third paragraph. Read the third paragraph. Lines 26–28 state, *Employers, too, complained that their Indian workers were unreliable when a pole was being carved or a potlatch planned.* Eliminate answers that don't match this answer from the passage. Eliminate (A) and (B), as there is no evidence that the employers were *patient* or *accepting* regarding the potlatches. Choice (C) matches the answer from the passage, so keep it. Eliminate (D) because the mention of the employers' complaints offers no evidence of civility. The correct answer is (C).

28. **H** This reasoning question asks for the authors' attitude about the *possibility of returning to the planet Venus*. There is not a good lead word in this question (the word *Venus* appears throughout the passage), so work the question later. Lines 14–16 say, *in the present climate of fiscal austerity, there is no telling when humans will next get a good look at Earth's nearest planetary neighbor.* Based on those lines, the authors are unsure about the possibility of returning to Venus for financial reasons. Eliminate answers that don't match this answer from the passage. Eliminate (F) because there is no indication that the authors are *cheerful and optimistic* about the possibility of returning to Venus. Eliminate (G) because *sarcastic and contentious* are not supported by the passage. Choice (H) matches the answer from the passage; *doubtful* is supported by the phrase *there is no telling when* and *pragmatic* (which means "practical") is supported by the mention of *fiscal austerity*. Although *uncertain* matches the answer from the passage, *withdrawn* is not supported, so eliminate (J). The correct answer is (H).

29. **C** This reasoning question asks how the passage describes the *state of scientific knowledge about Venus before the Pioneer mission*. Look for the lead words *before the Pioneer mission* to find the window for the question. Lines 28–30 say, *Well before the arrival of Pioneer Venus, astronomers had learned that Venus does not live up to its image as Earth's near-twin.* Eliminate answers that don't match this answer from the passage. Eliminate (A) because it doesn't mention any *scientific knowledge*. Additionally, the passage does not mention an *earlier mission* that *ended in disaster*, nor does it support the idea that the scientific community was *hesitant to return to Venus* before the Pioneer mission. Eliminate (B) because it goes beyond what is stated in the passage: although the answer from the passage does support the idea that Earth and Venus are not twins, it doesn't indicate that the planets are *polar opposites in atmospheric conditions*. Keep (C) because it matches the answer from the passage; in addition, lines 30–33 give *scientific evidence* of how Earth and Venus are different. Eliminate (D) because there is no mention of scientists' interest in *other planets* in the window for the question. The correct answer is (C).

30. **J** This referral question asks why *Earth may have retained less of its early atmosphere than Venus did*. Look for the lead words *early atmosphere* to find the window for this question. Lines 67–70 state that *Venus has held on to a far greater fraction of its earliest atmosphere. Much of Earth's primitive atmosphere may have been stripped away and lost into space when our world was struck by a Mars-size body*. Eliminate answers that do not match this answer from the passage. Eliminate (F), which uses words from the passage but doesn't match what the passage says: the passage states that Earth was *struck by a Mars-size body*, not by Mars itself. Eliminate (G), which also uses words from the passage but doesn't match what the passage says: the passage mentions a *cloud of debris* that resulted from the impact but does not say that the cloud of debris stripped the atmosphere away. Eliminate (H) because *rain* that removes *sulfur gases* is not mentioned in the window for the question, nor does the passage indicate that rain removed Earth's early atmosphere. Keep (J), which matches the answer from the passage. The correct answer is (J).

31. **B** This reasoning question asks about the *main point* of the second paragraph. Read the second paragraph. The paragraph discusses what *Magellan* and *Pioneer Venus* studied on Venus. Lines 22–25 state, *These findings illustrate how seemingly small differences in physical conditions have sent Venus and the Earth hurtling down very different evolutionary paths*. Eliminate answers that don't match this answer from the passage. Choice (A) uses words from the passage but doesn't match what the passage says; although the paragraph discusses both *Magellan* and *Pioneer Venus*, there is no indication that one mission was better than the other. Eliminate (A). Keep (B) because it matches the answer from the passage; it says that information from both *Magellan* and *Pioneer Venus* contributed to a *deeper understanding of Venus*. Eliminate (C) because both missions, not just the *Magellan*, studied *physical characteristics*. Choice (D) uses words from the passage but doesn't match what the passage says; the paragraph says that the *knowledge will help scientists intelligently evaluate how human activity may be changing the environment on the Earth*; it does not say that the knowledge will help them *approach problems*, in general, more intelligently. Additionally, this sentence is a detail, rather than the main point of the paragraph. Eliminate (D). The correct answer is (B).

32. **H** This referral question asks what makes it impossible for *humans to live on the planet Venus*. Work backwards and use lead words from the answers to find the window for this question. For (A), look for the lead words *"twin" planets* in the passage. Lines 1–2 say, *Venus is sometimes referred to as the Earth's "twin" because it resembles the Earth in size and in distance from the sun*, and lines 28–30 say, *astronomers had learned that Venus does not live up to its image as Earth's near-twin*. Although these lines support (F), (F) answers the wrong question; the fact that Venus and Earth are not twin planets does not answer the question about why humans cannot live on Venus. Eliminate (F). For (G), look for the lead words *carbon dioxide* and *bicarbonate rocks*. Lines 43–45 say, *On Earth, however, the carbon dioxide is locked away in carbonate rocks, not in gaseous form in the air*. Choice (G) uses words from the passage but doesn't match what the passage says; the lines are about Earth, but the question is about Venus. The passage also says *carbonate rocks*, rather than *bicarbonate rocks*. Eliminate (G). For (H), look for the lead words *heat, pressure*, and *atmosphere*. Lines 34–35 say, *Even aside from the heat and the pressure, the air on Venus would be utterly unbreathable to humans*. These lines support (H) and answer the question, so keep (H). For (J), look for the lead words *water* and *condensed*. Lines 53–55 say, *If all of Venus's water could somehow be condensed onto the surface, it would make a global puddle only a couple of centimeters deep*. Choice (J) uses words from the passage

but doesn't match what the passage says; the passage discusses the water on Venus being condensed on the surface as a hypothetical situation, not the actual condition on Venus. Eliminate (J). The correct answer is (H).

33. **D** This referral question asks for evidence gathered before *Pioneer Venus* that supports the idea that *Earth* and *Venus* are *not near-twins*. Look for the lead words *near-twins* to find the window for the question. Lines 28–30 say, *Well before the arrival of Pioneer Venus, astronomers had learned that Venus does not live up to its image as Earth's near-twin.* Lines 30–33 contrast conditions on Earth, which *maintains conditions ideal for liquid water and life*, with the high *surface temperature* and *atmospheric pressure* of Venus. Eliminate answers that don't match this answer from the passage. Choice (A) uses words from the passage but doesn't match what the passage says; although the paragraph mentions *lead*, it says that Venus's surface temperature is *hotter than the melting point of lead*, not that Venus does not produce *lead*. Eliminate (A). Eliminate (B) because it doesn't mention evidence gathered about Venus and Earth that shows they are different. Furthermore, the passage never mentions a new discovery about Earth's distance from the *sun*. Choice (C) uses words from the passage but doesn't match what the passage says; *78 percent nitrogen and 21 percent oxygen* describe Earth's atmosphere, not Venus's. Eliminate (C). Keep (D) because it matches the answer from the passage; the paragraph says, *Venus's surface temperature is 450 degrees Celsius.* The correct answer is (D).

34. **H** This Vocabulary in Context question asks what the word *harbors* most nearly means as it is used in line 56. Go back to the text, find the word *harbors*, and cross it out. Carefully read the surrounding text to determine another word that would fit in the blank based on the context. Lines 56–57 say, *Unlike Earth, Venus harbors little if any molecular oxygen in its lower atmosphere.* In the context of the sentence, *harbors* means something like "contains." *Shelters* does not match "contains," so eliminate (F). *Hides* does not match "contains," so eliminate (G). *Holds* matches "contains," so keep (H). *Cherishes* does not match "contains," so eliminate (J). Note that (F), (G), and (J) are other meanings of *harbors*, but they answer the wrong question because they do not match the way the word *is used in line 56*. The correct answer is (H).

35. **C** This referral question asks what kinds of planets the word *primordial* refers to. Look for the lead word *primordial* to find the window for the question. Lines 63–64 state, *Pioneer Venus revealed other ways in which Venus is more primordial than Earth.* The paragraph goes on to say that *Venus's atmosphere* contains gases *that have been present since the time the planets were born* and that this *difference suggests that Venus has held on to a far greater fraction of its earliest atmosphere.* Therefore, *primordial* describes a planet where current conditions are similar to conditions that existed near the time the planet was formed. Eliminate answers that don't match this answer from the passage. Choices (A) and (B) are true statements about Venus, but they answer the wrong question. The passage does indicate that Venus's atmosphere is *oxygen-poor* and that *activity by living things* generates oxygen; however, this is not the meaning of *primordial*. Eliminate (A). The passage indicates that Venus has a thick atmosphere and high surface temperature and that it is not hospitable to humans, but this is not the meaning of *primordial*. Eliminate (B). Keep (C) because it matches the answer from the passage. Eliminate (D) because it describes a characteristic of *Earth*, which the passage does not characterize as a *primordial* planet. The correct answer is (C).

36. **J** This referral question asks what details the *Pioneer Venus* studied. There is not a good lead word in this question (*Pioneer Venus* appears throughout the passage), so work the question later. Lines 20–22 say, *Pioneer Venus...gathered data on the composition and dynamics of the planet's atmosphere and interplanetary surroundings.* Eliminate answers that don't match this answer from the passage. Choice (F) includes details that are mentioned in the passage, but it answers the wrong question; *surface geology and interior structure* were studied by *Magellan*, not *Pioneer Venus*. Eliminate (F). Eliminate (G) because the passage does not indicate that *photosynthesis* was studied on Venus. Eliminate (H) because the window mentions *differences*, not *similarities*, between Earth and Venus. Keep (J) because it matches the answer from the passage. The correct answer is (J).

ACT TEST 2 SCIENCE ANSWERS AND EXPLANATIONS

1. **B** The question asks for the combination of *species of algae and length of daily direct sunlight exposure* that *resulted in the greatest mass of algae consumed*. Look at the figure to determine the *mass of algae consumed* for each combination. Look at green first. The amount of green algae consumed increases from 6 to 9 hours, so eliminate (A) because it says the mass consumed is greatest at 6 hours of sunlight exposure. At 9 hours, the amount of green algae consumed is 9 grams. Now, look at yellow-brown algae. Yellow-brown algae have 8 grams consumed at 6 hours of exposure to sunlight and 6 grams consumed at 9 hours of exposure to sunlight. Eliminate (C) and (D) as both of these values are less than the mass of green algae consumed at 9 hours of sunlight exposure. The correct answer is (B).

2. **H** The question asks how the *mass of algae consumed* varies as *sunlight exposure* is increased, based on the figure. Look at the figure to find the relationship between the values of *sunlight exposure* and the *mass of algae consumed*. For all 5 species of algae, the *mass of algae consumed* increases as the *sunlight exposure* increases from 3 to 6 hours. Eliminate (G) and (J) because they indicate that the *mass of algae consumed* decreases as the *sunlight exposure* increases from 3 to 6 hours. For most of the 5 species of algae, the *mass of algae consumed* also increases as the daily *sunlight exposure* increases from 6 to 9 hours. The masses of *brown* and *yellow-brown* algae consumed, shown by the dark gray bar and the white bar with black stripes, decrease as the daily *sunlight exposure* increases from 6 to 9 hours. Eliminate (F) as it indicates that the *mass of algae consumed* increases only as *sunlight exposure* is increased. The correct answer is (H).

3. **A** The question asks whether *L. littorea* would be *classified as an autotroph or a heterotroph*. Use the information in the passage and POE. The first paragraph states that *Littorina littorea eats algae and barnacle larvae*. Eliminate (B) and (D) because they indicate that the sea snail produces its own energy without consuming another organism. To choose between the remaining choices, outside knowledge is necessary. Heterotrophs consume other organisms to obtain their energy, while autotrophs produce their own energy from sunlight. Eliminate (C) as it states that an *autotroph... consumes another organism to obtain its energy*. The correct answer is (A).

4. **J**   The question asks whether the *primary food source* of the sea snail contains *chlorophyll or hemoglobin*. The passage states that one of the primary food sources of *L. Littorea* is *algae* but does not mention *chlorophyll* or *hemoglobin*. Therefore, this question requires outside knowledge. Algae are *autotrophic*, meaning they are a species that produces its own energy from sunlight utilizing the process of *photosynthesis*. Eliminate (F) and (H) because these answer choices state that algae undergo cellular respiration. *Photosynthesis* relies on the color pigment *chlorophyll*. Eliminate (G) because it states that algae use hemoglobin. The correct answer is (J).

5. **A**   The question asks for the mass consumed, *in milligrams…of the brown algae exposed to 6 hours of sunlight per day*. Look at the figure to determine the *mass of algae consumed* for *brown algae*, represented by the dark gray bar. At 6 hours of *daily sunlight exposure*, the *mass of algae consumed* is 5 grams for *brown algae*. Eliminate (B) and (D) because both start with numbers other than 5. To decide between the remaining choices, outside knowledge is necessary. There are 1,000 *milligrams* in 1 gram. Therefore, to convert grams into milligrams, multiply the value in grams by 1,000, or 5 × 1,000 = 5,000 mg. Eliminate (C) as it multiplies the value by a factor larger than 1,000. The correct answer is (A).

6. **F**   The question asks for *a difference between Experiments 1 and 2*. The results of the experiments are shown in Table 1 and Table 2, so look there to find a difference. According to Table 1, the virus type used in Experiment 1 was HSV-1, while in Table 2, the virus type used in Experiment 2 was HSV-2. Since the virus types are different, keep (F). The pH values listed in the two tables are the same for both experiments, 3.5, 4.0, 4.5, and 5.0. Eliminate (G) since it states that the pH values differed between the two experiments. Neither Table 2 nor the description of Experiment 2 mentions use of a *base*, so eliminate (H), which states a base was used in Experiment 2. Both Table 1 and Table 2 show results for 1 hour and 1 day of exposure. Eliminate (J) since it claims that only the viruses in Experiment 1 were left to stand for 1 hour. The correct answer is (F).

7. **C**   The question asks for the *relative infectivity of a virus sample* at a pH of 4.3 after 1 hour of exposure in Experiment 2. The results of Experiment 2 are shown in Table 2. A pH of 4.3 is not shown in Table 2, so look for nearby values. After 1 hour of exposure, the relative infectivity at a pH of 4.0 is 0.18, and the relative infectivity at a pH of 4.5 is 0.64. Since relative infectivity increases as pH increases, the relative infectivity at a pH of 4.3 is likely between 0.18 and 0.64. The correct answer is (C).

8. **H**   The question asks for the *pH values* at which *the relative infectivity of HSV-2 virions* was lower after a *longer exposure time*. The results for HSV-2 are shown in Table 2. In Table 2, at a pH of 3.5, the relative infectivity was 0.00 after both 1 hour and 1 day of exposure. Eliminate (F) and (G) since both state that the relative infectivity would be different at different exposure times at a pH of 3.5. The relative infectivity is also the same, 0.88, at both exposure times at a pH of 5.0. Eliminate (J), which includes 5.0. Only (H) does not include 3.5 or 5.0. The correct answer is (H).

9. **D**   The question asks which question was *NOT addressed by either experiment*. The results of the experiments are shown in Table 1 and Table 2. Look for changes corresponding to each answer choice in Table 1 and Table 2. In both Table 1 and Table 2, pH was varied, and this resulted in different *relative infectivity* for the viruses. Eliminate (A) since it states that the relationship between pH and *relative infectivity* was not explored. The tables also show different exposure times, 1 day and 1 hour, with different *relative infectivity* at each time. Eliminate (B) since exposure time was

varied. Table 1 shows results for HSV-1, and Table 2 shows results for HSV-2. Eliminate (C) since it claims that the experiment did not compare the two types of viruses. Neither table contains data about different concentrations of virions. The correct answer is (D).

10. **F** The question asks which sample of HSV-2 would be *LEAST likely to infect chicken egg cells* after *one day of exposure* to acid. Table 2 contains the results for HSV-2, so look at Table 2. The virus sample *LEAST* likely to infect cells is the one with the lowest relative infectivity. According to Table 2, at 1 day of exposure, relative infectivity increases as pH increases. The lowest relative infectivity, 0.00, corresponds to the lowest pH, 3.5. The correct answer is (F).

11. **B** The question asks which of the given conditions would give the *lowest relative infectivity* in Experiment 1. The results of Experiment 1 are shown in Table 1, so look at Table 1. In Table 1, relative infectivity increases as pH increases. Eliminate (C) and (D) since the two virus samples at a pH of 4.5 have a higher relative infectivity than those at a pH of 4.0. At this pH, samples left for 1 hour have a higher relative infectivity than those left for 1 day. Eliminate (A) since it corresponds to a relative infectivity of 0.45, which is higher than the corresponding value for the virus left for 1 day, or 0.33. The correct answer is (B).

12. **F** The question asks how the *spring force on Mass 2* varies as the *spring constant of the spring* is decreased, *based on the results of Experiment 2*. The results of Experiment 2 are shown in Table 1. Use Table 1 and look for the values of *spring force* for each type of spring. For *Mass 2*, the spring force is 0.38 N for the spring made of steel, 0.45 for the spring made of Alloy X, and 0.53 for the spring made from Alloy Y. Look for information in the passage about the *spring constant* of each spring. The second paragraph states that the spring constant of the spring made of steel is 2.5 N/m, the spring constant of the spring made of Alloy X is 3.0 N/m, and the spring constant of the spring made of Alloy Y is 3.5 N/m. For the three types of spring, as the *spring constant* decreases from Alloy Y to Alloy X to steel, the *spring force* also decreases. The correct answer is (F).

13. **A** The question asks whether *the spring made of Alloy X or the spring made of Alloy Y* experiences *more strain on its coils* in Experiment 1. Since the reasons in the answer choices discuss the distances the springs stretched, refer first to Figure 1, which shows how the three springs stretched when a mass was attached to them in Experiment 1. Based on Figure 1, the spring made of Alloy X stretched a greater distance than the spring made of Alloy Y. Eliminate (B) and (D) because they incorrectly state that the spring made of Alloy Y stretched a greater distance. To choose between the remaining choices, outside knowledge is necessary. When a spring stretches, it experiences *strain on its coils*. A spring stretched to a greater distance will experience more strain on its coils than one stretched a shorter distance. Eliminate (C) as it incorrectly states that the spring with a smaller distance of stretch will experience more *strain on its coils*. The correct answer is (A).

14. **G** The question asks for a procedural change that will allow the scientists to *study whether a mass's shape determines the distance the spring of a certain composition stretched*. When testing one variable, a scientist must change only that variable and keep all other variables constant across trials. To test how the *mass's shape* affects the *distance the spring…stretched,* the scientists must use multiple masses and vary the shape of the masses while keeping all other factors the same. Eliminate (F) and (H) because they incorrectly state that only one mass should be used. Eliminate (J) as it indicates that the masses should have the *same shape*. The correct answer is (G).

15. **B**   The question asks for the *difference between the spring force exerted by the spring made of Alloy X and the spring force exerted by the spring made of Alloy Y…for Mass 3*, according to *Experiment 2*. The results of Experiment 2 are shown in Table 1. Use Table 1 and look for the spring force for Mass 3 for springs made of Alloy X and Alloy Y. The spring force of the spring made of Alloy X on Mass 3 is 0.75 N, and the spring force of the spring made of Alloy Y on Mass 3 is 0.88 N. Subtract the two values to find the difference: 0.88 N – 0.75 N = 0.13 N. The correct answer is (B).

16. **J**   The question asks what the *distance of the stretch* would be for a mass attached to a spring with a *spring constant of 2.0 N/m*, according to *Experiment 1*. The results of Experiment 1 are shown in Figure 1. Look at Figure 1 to determine how different springs stretched when a mass was attached to them. The spring made of steel stretched 0.2 m, while the spring made of Alloy X stretched 0.17 m, and the spring made of Alloy Y stretched 0.14 m. Look for information in the passage about the *spring constant* of each spring. The second paragraph states that the spring constant of the spring made of steel is 2.5 N/m, the spring constant of the spring made of Alloy X is 3.0 N/m, and the spring constant of the spring made of Alloy Y is 3.5 N/m. As the spring constant decreases, the distance of the stretch increases. Thus, the distance of the stretch for a spring with a spring constant of 2.0 N/m will be greater than the distance of the stretch of the steel spring, or greater than 0.2 m. The correct answer is (J).

17. **D**   The question asks for the spring hanger that would have the *greater distance stretched when a 25 kg mass is hung from it.* Since the reasons in the answer choices discuss the distances the springs stretched, refer first to Figure 1, which shows how three springs stretched when a mass was attached to them. Based on Figure 1, the spring made of steel stretched a greater distance than the spring made of Alloy X. Look for information in the passage about the *spring constant* of each spring. The second paragraph states that the spring constant of the spring made of steel is 2.5 N/m and the spring constant of the spring made of Alloy X is 3.0 N/m. As the spring constant decreases, the distance of the stretch increases. Eliminate (A) and (C) because they incorrectly state that *distance stretched increases as spring constant increases.* The question states that *the first spring on the machine has a spring constant of 15.2 N/m, and the second spring on the machine has a spring constant of 13.1 N/m.* Thus, the second spring will have the *greater distance stretched* because it has the smaller spring constant. The correct answer is (D).

18. **G**   The question asks for the *fp* of a batch with 55% water and 45% ethylene glycol. Look at Table 1 to find the *fp* for the different batches. According to Table 1, a batch with 40% ethylene glycol has an *fp* of –14.8°F and a batch with 50% ethylene glycol has an *fp* of –36.4°F. Therefore, the *fp* for a batch with 45% ethylene glycol is likely between –36.4°F and –14.8°F. The correct answer is (G).

19. **D**   The question asks whether the experimental results support the scientist's prediction that the *fp* for Batch 7 would be greater than the fp for Batch 2. Table 1 shows the *fp* for the different batches. According to Table 1, for Batch 2 the *fp* is equal to 19.4°F, while for Batch 7 the *fp* is equal to 8.6°F. Eliminate (A) and (B) because the value of *fp* was greater for Batch 2, and the scientist's prediction was incorrect. Next, eliminate (C) since 8.6°F is the value of *fp* for Batch 7 rather than the difference between the 2 values of *fp*, which is 19.4°F – 8.6°F = 10.8°F. The correct answer is (D).

20. **G**   The question asks for the *difference between fp and Δfp* for each batch. Look at Table 1 to find *fp* and Δ*fp* for the batches. In Batch 1, the *fp* is equal to 32°F, while the Δ*fp* is equal to 0°. Subtract these values from each other to obtain a difference of 32°F. The question indicates that the difference will be the same for the other batches. Alternatively, scan the passage for the relationship between *fp* and Δ*fp*. According to the equation given in the passage, Δ*fp = fp – 32*, indicating a difference of 32°F between the two variables. The correct answer is (G).

21. **B**   The question asks for the *fp* of *the batch for which the volume of ethylene glycol was 3 times as great as the volume of water*. The compositions of the batches are shown in Table 1. In Table 1, the batch with three times as much ethylene glycol as water is Batch 6, which contains 25% water and 75% ethylene glycol. For Batch 6, the *fp* is equal to –56.2°F. The correct answer is (B).

22. **H**   The question asks for the Δ*fp* of a batch with 65% water and 35% ethylene glycol based on Figure 1. Figure 1 contains marks for 30% and 40% ethylene glycol, so look between those to estimate the Δ*fp* for 35%. At 35% ethylene glycol, Δ*fp* is approximately –40°F. The correct answer is (H).

23. **D**   The question asks how the *freezing point of the water* would change if a *hydrophobic compound was added*. Outside knowledge is helpful but not required to answer this question. The passage states that *compounds that are hydrophilic dissolve in water*. Hydrophobic is the opposite of hydrophilic. Thus, a hydrophobic compound would not dissolve in water, so eliminate (A) and (C). According to the passage, *when a hydrophilic compound dissolves in water, the freezing point of the mixture is different from that of each component*. However, a hydrophobic compound would not dissolve or form a mixture with water, so the freezing point of the water would be unchanged, which is consistent with (D). Eliminate (B), which claims that the hydrophobic compound would lower the freezing point of water. The correct answer is (D).

24. **G**   The question asks for the depth at which the *density of seawater* with *2% by mass of salt…is closest to 1.03 g/cm³* based on Figure 2. In Figure 2, the bottom-most line represents *2% by mass of salt*. For this line, at a density of 1.03 g/cm³, the depth is halfway between 2,000 m and 3,000 m, corresponding to a depth of 2,500 m. The correct answer is (G).

25. **D**   The question asks for the temperature at which the density of seawater with *7% by mass of salt* is equal to 1.045 g/cm³ based on Figure 3. Figure 3 does not show seawater with *7% by mass of salt*. However, as percent by mass of salt increases, the density at a given temperature increases as well. Therefore, the density for 7% by mass of salt should be between those for 6% and 8% by mass of salt. The line corresponding to a concentration of 6% by mass shows a density of 1.045 g/cm³ at a temperature of about 20°C. The density of *7% by mass of salt* seawater should be higher than 1.045 g/cm³ at this temperature, as well as all lower temperatures since there is an inverse relationship between temperature and density. Eliminate (A) and (B) because they state that the density will be equal to 1.045 g/cm³ at a temperature equal to or less than 20°C. Both (C) and (D) contain a temperature of 25°C. At 25°C, the density of 6% by mass seawater is about 1.043 g/cm³, and the density of 8% by mass seawater is about 1.057 g/cm³. The *7% by mass of salt* density would be between the two, or approximately 1.05 g/cm³. Eliminate (C) since at temperatures below 25°C the density would be even higher than this value and above 1.045 g/cm³. The correct answer is (D).

26. **H** The question asks for the concentrations at which *the density of NaCl solution and the density of LiCl solution are closest in value* based on Figure 1. Begin by looking at Figure 1 to find density values for the listed concentrations. For NaCl, when the concentration is equal to *2.5% by mass*, the density is approximately 1.02 g/cm³. For LiCl, when the concentration is equal to *10% by mass*, the density is approximately 1.06 g/cm³. Eliminate (F) since the LiCl density is significantly larger. Choice (G) can be eliminated since there is a direct relationship between concentration and density, so at a LiCl concentration of *15% by mass*, the density would be even larger than 1.06 g/cm³. At a NaCl concentration of *7.5% by mass* the density is approximately 1.06 g/cm³. This matches the density obtained for *10% by mass* LiCl, so keep (H). Eliminate (J) since at an LiCl concentration of *15% by mass*, the density would be larger than 1.06 g/cm³. The correct answer is (H).

27. **C** The question asks whether the LiCl or the NH_4Cl solution would be less affected by *increasing concentration from 5% by mass to 20% by mass*. Figure 1 shows that the line corresponding to NH_4Cl has a smaller slope than the line corresponding to LiCl. Since slope represents rate of change, this means that the density of the NH_4Cl solution would change less in response to increasing concentration. Eliminate (A) and (B) since both claim that the density of the LiCl solution would be less affected by increasing concentration. In Figure 1, at a concentration of 5% by mass, the NH_4Cl solution density is about 1.01 g/cm³, and at 20% by mass, its density is about 1.05 g/cm³. Subtract these values to obtain a difference of 0.04 g/cm³. The correct answer is (C).

28. **J** The question asks for the temperature of seawater at *a depth of 0 m and a salt concentration of 6% by mass*. Depth and concentration are shown in Figure 2. According to Figure 2, at a depth of 0 m, seawater with a concentration of *6% by mass* has a density of about 1.04 g/cm³. To find the temperature of this water, look at Figure 3, which shows the relationship between temperature and density at different concentrations. According to the passage, Figure 3 shows *seawater at the surface*, or at a depth of 0 m, which matches the water with a density of 1.04 g/cm³ from Figure 2. In Figure 3, seawater with a concentration of *6% by mass* and a density of 1.04 g/cm³ has a temperature of 35°C. The correct answer is (J).

29. **C** The question asks for *a primary difference between the two theories.* Look at each theory to find what they say about the Moon's *orbit around the Earth.* Theory 1 states that *the Moon orbits the Earth in a circular path.* Eliminate (A) and (B) because both incorrectly say that Theory 1 states that the Moon follows *an elliptical orbit.* Theory 2 states that *the Moon orbits the Earth in an elliptical path.* Eliminate (D) because it says that Theory 2 states that the Moon orbits *around the Sun.* The correct answer is (C).

30. **F** The question asks *which of the figures…implies that the distance between the Moon and Earth is constant over time.* Look at Figures 2 and 3, and check to see which one shows a constant distance between the Moon and Earth. Figure 2 shows a circular orbit for the Moon, which implies that *the distance between the Moon and Earth is constant.* Eliminate (G) and (J) because they don't include Figure 2. Figure 3 shows an elliptical orbit for the Moon. The Moon looks closer to the Earth on the left side of the figure and farther from the Earth on the right side of the figure. This implies that *the distance between the Moon and Earth* is not constant. Eliminate (H) because it includes Figure 3. The correct answer is (F).

31. **D** The question asks whether the *top portion of Figure 3* is consistent with the reason provided by Theory 2 that *the amount of the Sun obscured by the Moon varies depending on how far the Moon is from Earth*. Begin by examining Theory 2 to find the reason why *the amount of the Sun obscured by the Moon varies*. Theory 2 states that *the Moon is sometimes located closer to or further away from the Earth depending on where it is in its orbit*. Now look at Figure 3 to see if it is consistent with this reason. Figure 3 shows an elliptical orbit for the Moon. The Moon looks closer to the Earth on the left side of the figure and farther from the Earth on the right side of the figure. This implies that the distance between the Moon and Earth is not constant, which is consistent with the reason. Eliminate (A) and (B), which both state that the figure is not consistent. Eliminate (C) since it says *the Moon is shown as having a circular orbit*. The correct answer is (D).

32. **G** The question asks for a statement that *a proponent of Theory 1 and a proponent of Theory 2 would both be likely to agree with*. Begin by examining Theory 1 to find what it says about the umbra during an annular eclipse. Theory 1 states that the umbra doesn't reach Earth during an annular eclipse, but it does during a total eclipse. Eliminate (F), (H), and (J) because all of these statements indicate that the umbra is either longer or the same size as the *distance between the Earth and Moon* and the *umbra during a total eclipse*. The correct answer is (G).

33. **C** The question asks for the figure that could *represent the positions of the Sun, Moon, and Earth on May 31, 2003*, according to Figures 1 and 3. Look at Figure 1 to determine what kind of eclipse occurred on *May 31, 2003*. Figure 1 shows that the Moon is blocking only some of the light from the Sun, so the eclipse was an annular eclipse. Look at Theory 2 to determine where the Moon will be located in its orbit during an annular eclipse. Theory 2 states that *an eclipse will be annular when the Moon is located in the region of its orbit that is a greater distance from Earth*. Eliminate (A) and (B) because they incorrectly place the Moon at a closer location in its orbit to the Earth. Look at Figure 3 to determine where this date falls in terms of the locations pictured. The date May 31 will occur between December 14 and June 21. Based on Figure 3, the Moon and Earth are on the right side of the orbit in December and on the left side of the orbit in June. The arrows indicate that the Earth will travel counterclockwise around the Sun. Therefore, the Earth should fall somewhere in between the locations for December and June in the top half of the orbit. Eliminate (D) because it shows the Earth in the bottom half of the orbit. The correct answer is (C).

34. **G** The question asks whether Theory 2 can *be used to explain why some ocean tides are stronger than others*. The information in Theory 2 is summarized in Figure 3, so look at Figure 3. Figure 3 shows that the distances between the Earth and the Moon and the Sun and the Moon vary throughout the Moon's orbit. Eliminate (H) and (J) because both state that the theory *does not account for the varying* distances between these bodies. To choose between the remaining choices, outside knowledge is necessary. The *gravitational field* of the Moon is the *primary driver of tides*. Eliminate (F) because it incorrectly states that the *gravitational field* of the Sun drives tides. The correct answer is (G).

35. **B** The question asks for the *independent (manipulated) variable* across all 3 studies and within each individual study. Read the descriptions of each study to determine what was changed, or manipulated, *across all 3 studies*. Study 1 used a sound source of 60 dB, Study 2 used a sound source of 80 dB, and Study 3 used a sound source of 100 dB. Therefore, *sound intensity* was varied across all 3 studies; eliminate (A) and (C). *Within each study,* the type of wave that was produced was measured by

the experimental conditions. This is the result of the experiment and not a manipulated variable, so eliminate (D). Each study varied the density of the ground from 1,000–2,000 g/km³, so this is the independent variable within each study. The correct answer is (B).

36. **G** The question asks what happens to *the type of wave observed* as the *distance from the epicenter increases from 0 to 3 m* in Study 2. The *y*-axis in Figure 3 shows ground densities between 1,000 to 2,000 kg/m³, so look at the entire graph. As the distance from the epicenter increases from 0 m to 3 m, the wave type changes from strong (black) to moderate (dark grey). The correct answer is (G).

37. **B** The question asks which statement is true regarding *the maximum distance from the epicenter for strong wave propagation and maximum distance for moderate wave propagation,* according to the results of Studies 2 and 3. Check each answer choice against the information found in Figures 3 and 4. Eliminate (A), (C), and (D) because *the maximum distance from the epicenter for strong wave propagation* is always less than the *maximum distance for moderate wave propagation*. Keep (B) because it states this relationship. The correct answer is (B).

38. **J** The question asks which *factors in the seismologist's studies* were *NOT directly controlled.* Since the question asks for the factors that were *NOT* controlled, eliminate factors that **were** controlled. Because there is no information in the figures about which factors were controlled, look for the word *controlled* in the text. Paragraph 2 states that *propagation duration was held constant in the experiment;* eliminate (H). Additionally, the paragraph states that *the procedure was repeated at various densities of earth and clay,* which means that the seismologist controlled the density within each trial. Eliminate (G). It also states that *seismometers were positioned to detect the type of waves,* which means *wave type* was not being controlled; keep (J). Paragraph 3 states that *the sound source was adjusted to 60 dB,* meaning the seismologist was controlling the sound intensity; eliminate (F). The correct answer is (J).

39. **D** The question asks which wave types would be included in the *waveform plot* if Study 1 *were repeated using a sound intensity of 70 dB,* according to the passage. There is no information about *dB* in the figures, so look for *dB* in the text of the passage. The description of each study indicates the dB level at which each was performed. Study 1 was done at *60 dB,* and Study 2 was done at *80 dB.* Since all three wave types were present in both Study 1 and Study 2, all three would also be present at 70 dB, which falls between the levels in those studies. The correct answer is (D).

40. **F** The question asks for the likely distance from the epicenter when *a study was conducted using a sound intensity between 75 dB and 85 dB,* based on information in the passage. There is no information about *dB* in the figures, so look for *dB* in the text of the passage. The description of each study indicates the dB level at which each was performed. Study 2 was done at *80 dB,* so look at Figure 3 and use the data as a comparison. Strong waves begin between 1.8 and 2.3 m from the epicenter depending upon the ground density, so the distance should be less than 2.5 cm. The correct answer is (F).